Everyone Loves a Parade!

A Guide to New York City's Ticker Tape Parades

By John Walter and Mark Walter

Everyone Loves a Parade!
A Guide to New York City's Ticker Tape Parades
Published by Subscription Marketing Services
358 Mohonk Road, High Falls, NY 12440

Copyright © 2021 Mark Walter
ISBN #978-1-7376959-1-2

Library of Congress Control Number: 2021919746

Cover by Sue Kenner
Maps by Jon Rosenthal

DEDICATION

To my father, John Walter,
who taught me that knowledge of the Past provides insight to the Present

and

To my partner, Aaron Lee,
who helped me enjoy the Present before the parades pass by
and march into the Future

Downtown New York
Pre-1960

A	Pier A	**T**	Woolworth Building
B	Battery Park	**U**	Park Row Building
C	City Hall	**V**	NY Times Building
D	Brooklyn Bridge	**W**	Tribune Building
E	One Broadway	**X**	Fraunces Tavern
F	Bowling Green	**Y**	One Wall Street
G	Produce Exchange	**Z**	City Hall Plaza
H	Cunard Building	**1**	Beekman Hospital
J	Standard Oil Building	**2**	NY World Building
K	Exchange Court	**3**	Former Slave Market
L	American Express Building	**4**	American Stock Exchange
M	NY Stock Exchange	**5**	Castle Clinton
N	Trinity Church	**6**	Whitehall Building
P	Federal Hall	**7**	US Customs Building
Q	Singer Building	**8**	Evening Post Building
R	Equitable Life Building	**9**	American Exchange Bank
S	St. Paul's Chapel		

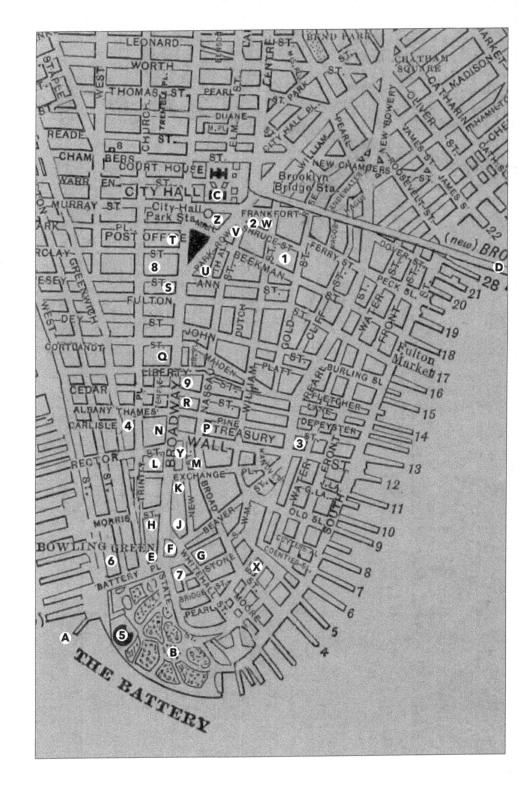

Downtown New York
Post-1960

A	Pier A		**T**	Woolworth Building
B	Battery Park		**U**	Park Row Building
C	City Hall		**V**	NY Times Building
D	Brooklyn Bridge		**W**	One Pace Plaza
E	One Broadway		**X**	Fraunces Tavern
F	Bowling Green		**Y**	One Wall Street
G	Two Broadway		**Z**	City Hall Plaza
H	Cunard Building		**1**	One World Trade Center
J	Standard Oil Building		**2**	Two World Trade Center
K	Staten Island Ferry Terminal		**3**	South Street Seaport
L	American Express Building		**4**	American Stock Exchange
M	NY Stock Exchange		**5**	Castle Clinton
N	Trinity Church		**6**	Whitehall Building
P	Federal Hall		**7**	US Customs Building
Q	Zuccotti Park & One Liberty		**8**	World Financial Center
R	Equitable Life Building		**9**	American Exchange Bank
S	St. Paul's Chapel			

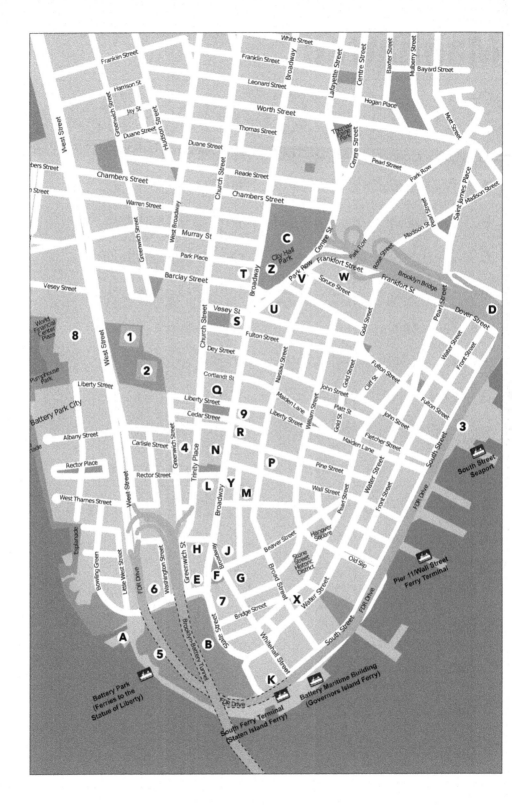

Manhattan

South of Central Park

A	Brooklyn Bridge		**N**	Madison Square
B	Battery Park		**P**	NY Public Library
C	City Hall		**Q**	The United Nations
D	Times Square		**R**	Empire State Building
E	Penn Station		**S**	St Patrick's Cathedral
F	Wanamaker's Store		**T**	Plaza Hotel
G	Grand Central Terminal		**V**	Lincoln Center
H	Waldorf Astoria Hotel		**W**	Brooklyn Navy Yard
J	Madison Square Garden		**X**	Washington Square
K	Metropolitan Opera		**Y**	Pier 99
L	Advertising Club of NY		**Z**	NY Yacht Club Landing
M	Union Square		**1**	Columbus Circle

New York City
Metropolitan Area

A	Brooklyn Bridge	**P**	Ebbets Field
B	Battery Park	**Q**	Queens Midtown Tunnel
C	City Hall	**R**	Roosevelt Field
D	Grant's Tomb	**S**	Lake Success
E	Polo Grounds	**T**	World's Fair Ground
F	Columbia University	**U**	Brooklyn Navy Yard
G	Gracie Mansion	**V**	Quarantine Islands
H	Triborough Bridge	**W**	Governors Island
J	LaGuardia Airport	**X**	Statue of Liberty
K	Idlewile/JFK Airport	**Y**	Verrazano Bridge
L	Newark Airport	**Z**	Jersey City
M	Floyd Bennett Field	**1**	Coney Island
N	Yankee Stadium	**2**	Sandy Hook

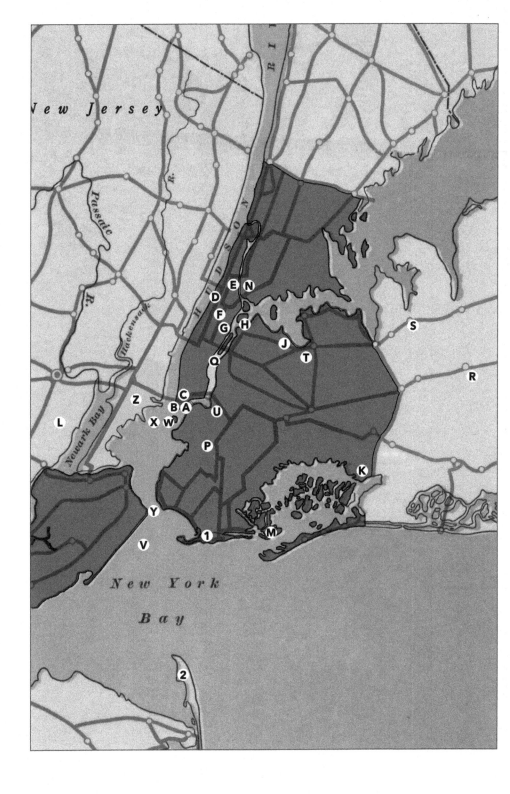

TABLE OF CONTENTS

CHAPTER 5 V for Victory! (1940-1946) 145

CHAPTER 6 Capital of the World (1947-1953)...............................173

John Walter and Mark Walter

PREFACE

What do Queen Elizabeth II, Howard Hughes and David Ben-Gurion have in common?

That question, which my father emailed me in 2004, began a journey of discovery into a fascinating part of New York City history that we both had witnessed but never given much thought to. It led us to City Hall and the New York Archives, to old copies of *Life* magazine still hiding in the attic and to the online archives of the *New York Times* and other publications. For a day it even turned me into a New York Giants fan (dad had always been one). This book is the result of that journey, and though my father was one of the early victims of the Covid pandemic, it was his hard work researching and writing most of the contents that made it possible.

I both love and hate being stumped by him with a question like that, and he knew it. I did not have any idea what those three people had in common, but I was hesitant to dive into an online search that would lead me into a wiki-hole. What could the Queen of England, an eccentric millionaire and the first Prime Minister of Israel have in common? Two were wealthy, two were political figures, two were dead, but I could not think of anything that fit them all. Reluctantly, I gave up and waited for his reply, which surprised me.

They all had been honored with a ticker tape parade.

Really? It certainly seemed likely that Queen Elizabeth had received one, though I couldn't guess when. It was a little harder, but not impossible, to imagine one for David Ben-Gurion. But Howard Hughes -- what had he done to get a ticker tape parade? Dad's reply to that question was priceless. "I don't know yet, but I want to find out." Attached was a list of almost 200 parades, many for people I had never even heard of. "I think it would make a great idea for a book," his email continued, "want to help me write it?"

My father, John Walter, was a historian. Not a tweed jacket attired professor who drills dates of battles into the heads of befuddled students, nor an academician in an ivory-tower studying the causes and effects of the rise and fall of empires. He certainly knew a lot of dates, and his knowledge (especially of the American Civil War) was prodigious, but what dad loved most was the "story" part of history: how large events affect everyday individuals (and vice versa). Dad was also in love with New York City. Except for a short period in 1962, when he received basic training in the National Guard, he lived his entire life in Middle Village, Queens. He helped organize our neighborhood's Bicentennial events in 1976, ran a local after-school teen program for over 25 years, and appeared on camera in the 2015 documentary *Middle Village* by David Lee Madison. He loved exploring the city, giving more than his fair share of tours to friends and first-time visitors.

The backstory behind his question was more than enough to get me excited. Walking in downtown Manhattan one day, dad noticed plaques with a name and date embedded in the sidewalk of Broadway. His curiosity piqued, he learned that the plaques had been installed to commemorate the city's ticker tape parades. He was amazed to learn that there had been over 200 such parades, but there was no explanation for many of them, and no book about them. Dad had already published one book about an often-forgotten part of New York City history, *The Confederate Dead in Brooklyn*, and this new idea excited him since it was less obscure and had more potential interest.

We quickly noticed that the type of person honored with a parade changed over time, offering a lens through which to view the city's history and culture. I had always heard about the celebrations after Lindbergh's historic transatlantic flight but reading the stories about the other aviators feted during the late 1920s and early 1930s gave me a deeper appreciation for life before commercial aviation. For somebody who thinks nothing of attaching a document to an email, it was fascinating to read that Commander Byrd's flight to Paris in 1927 was financed to prove the economic viability of flying mail to its destination.

Already a frequent visitor of the NY Public Library and the New York Archives, dad plunged into the list of parades, gathering facts and details about each event, while I began gathering notes for the chapter openings and the introduction. One name previously unknown to us soon began appearing repeatedly in dad's notes about the early parades, and we were excited to learn that Grover Whalen had written an autobiography which was still in publication. I found myself learning more about the city that I have always loved and lived in and, in some ways had taken for granted. As I read about the early skyscrapers that used to line Broadway before they were torn down, I found myself looking at old photographs and movies with New York's skyline, getting excited when I began to recognize the tops of the Singer or New York World Buildings, both of which were demolished before I was born.

One decision we made early in the writing process was to include a paragraph or two at the end of each parade description about what happened to the honoree after their big day. These codas, as I call them, were important for the famous as well as the less-famous parade recipients, and they show that some people went on to bigger and better things while others soon faded from public view. These codas are also valuable reminders to the reader to view people and events in the context of their times, while also being aware of larger historic narratives and people's latter actions. The exuberant reception that Marshal Pétain received in 1931, for example, predates the stain of his collaboration with the Nazis during World War II, while the prejudice faced by people like Jim Thorpe, Albert Einstein and Jesse Owens should remind us that racism and nativism have a long history in this country, and not just in southern states or the distant past.

Once the complete archives of the *New York Times* became available online, the research became easier. For parades with a known date, we could easily pull the next day's edition and read the paper's coverage from the comfort of home. For older parades, we learned that it was just as important to search the papers a few days before the parade as afterward. In the days before television, newspapers were a major source of disseminating information about upcoming events, and those announcements were just as informative as coverage after the fact. Dad failed to learn why the Maquis de Dampierre received a parade in 1930, and it was only when I stumbled on a small notice about the maiden voyage of the *Lafayette* in the *Times* three weeks prior to his parade that the mystery began to unravel.

More challenging, but also more rewarding, was the research into parades that were not on the semi-official lists, especially those listed only with just a month and year on Wikipedia. We almost gave up looking for a parade in December 1950 for Ralph Bunche before attempting a desperate but fruitful search of articles from 1949 containing both his name and Mr. Whalen's. Sometimes, the most important piece of information is found in unexpected places; while reading an article one day about parades for NASA's astronauts, I gasped when the author mentioned "Jonas Salk famously turned down a ticker tape parade for the creation of the Polio vaccine," which opened whole new doors for research. How does one find information about events that didn't happen? Attempts to grapple with that conundrum led not just to Dr. Salk's story, but also the story about Joe Namath and the 1969 Jets. Has every "might have been" parade been included? There's no way to guarantee that, as exemplified by the story of the parade for Alan Shepard in 1961 that NASA aborted, which was discovered and quickly added during the final stages of proof-reading.

Online databases of historic photographs were also fertile grounds for clues, and as the family photographer, my mother also became involved with the project by searching for photographs of the smaller parades. I share my dad's love of history and enjoyed seeing the photos mom discovered, so the project gave me a chance to work with both my parents on something we all enjoyed. It also gave us a chance to reminisce about the parades we had each witnessed in the past, and to create some new memories together.

As luck would have it, the New York Giants won the Super Bowl in 2008, and were honored with a parade. It was the first ticker tape parade in almost 8 years, so of course the three of us attended. The crowds were so thick we never made it all the way to Broadway itself, but we found a good vantage point on Wall Street, and mom took photos of us with Trinity Church in the background (see back cover). The air around us was alive with confetti drifting in the wind. Ticker tape no longer exists, but the excitement and thrill of a ticker tape parade still does.

I thought of that day when I attended the most recent parade, honoring the essential workers who helped New York through the darkest days of the Covid pandemic. The speed with which our world changed in March 2020 was a shock to all. Non-essential businesses were ordered to close, and residents were told to shelter at home. The once-vibrant "city that never sleeps" soon seemed like a ghost town, the quiet often broken by the sirens of ambulances taking patients to hospitals. One of those ambulances took my father to Mt. Sinai Hospital, and for several weeks we waited anxiously, unable to visit him when he needed his family most. His story ended on May 10, but the history of the pandemic continued, killing many thousands of New Yorkers, and millions worldwide.

As the initial phase of the city's shut down stretched into the autumn and winter, I kept myself occupied by completing this project. I visited the downtown area several times that year, walking the eerily empty length of Broadway, appreciating the architecture of the buildings in the area, and reading each of the sidewalk plaques that had piqued my father's interest in this topic. Without the usual hustle and bustle of pedestrians and the noise of city traffic, I tried to imagine what life was like for the people who stood where I was standing, cheering as John Kennedy or General MacArthur or Charles Lindbergh or Admiral Dewey had passed. Like them, I stood in the shade along Bowling Green, cheering and waving for the recipients of the latest ticker tape parade, the Hometown Heroes. As the doctors and nurses of Mt. Sinai passed, blue and orange confetti burst from an air cannon into the sky. The colors of New York City filled the air, and my cheers was mixed with tears, knowing I was watching a parade was not on dad's list.

This is history. Each of us gets to witness and participate in it in our own way, for however long or short a time we get. Dad so loved sharing the history he knew, hoping to breathe new life into people and stories from the past. If reading these pages makes you feel the energy and excitement of ticker tape parades, he and I will have succeeded.

INTRODUCTION

Visitors to New York City's Financial District in lower Manhattan often gaze up at the skyscrapers towering overhead, staring in amazement at the engineering marvels of the sleek new One World Trade Center building, or at the ornate façade of the Woolworth Building. A dominant feature of the city's skyline for well over a century, the earliest skyscrapers would seem like dwarfs next to their modern descendants, but the pedestrians of 1890 likely gazed upward at the new 20-story New York World Building with the same amazement experienced by today's tourists.

How many people, though, look down at the pavement and notice the long black granite plaques embedded in the sidewalk of Broadway, engraved with a name and a date?

If one starts at the correct spot (in front of One Broadway, across from Battery Park), the first plaque explains their purpose. For the remaining mile between there and City Hall, the plaques appear every several feet, showing in chronological order (on alternating sides of Broadway) the recipients of New York's ticker tape parades. The pedestrian who glances down at the sidewalk in front of 150 Broadway and sees "Captain Alan J. Villiers and Crew of the Replica Ship *Mayflower II*" can be forgiven if he just shrugs and moves on.

Installed by the Alliance for Downtown New York in 2003, the plaques recall the city's ticker tape parades. Since 1886, over 200 ticker tape parades have marched along Broadway's "Canyon of Heroes" celebrating warriors and athletes, retiring generals and admirals, aviators and astronauts, politicians and world leaders, victorious sports teams and Olympic champions, and sometimes just ordinary people who achieved momentary fame. A ticker tape parade is a uniquely New York experience. The narrow streets of downtown Manhattan, surrounded by towering buildings that reflect the city's importance, provide the perfect venue for a celebration enjoyed by thousands of viewers, both at street level and from above, leaning from windows and perched on building ledges. Long swirls of ticker tape mingle with confetti to cascade through the air, dancing in the breeze and covering the marchers below as they make their way toward City Hall. Cheered by thousands of spectators, many honorees have said that a ticker tape parade was one of the highest honors they have ever received.

This book explores the history and details of these parades and the people being honored. Who were the honorees, and why did they get parades? How did this uniquely New York tradition begin, and how has it evolved? What is ticker tape, and what makes a ticker tape parade? Who organizes them, and who decides who gets honored? Has anybody turned down the honor, and what happens if it rains?

In the process, the history of the City itself is explored. As New York evolved from the country's most important harbor into the multi-cultural financial capital it is today, our culture and the types of heroes and celebrations we enjoy have changed. The city has seen both prosperity and hardship, from Depression to war, from economic collapse to terrorist attack, and these experiences are reflected in the history of its ticker tape parades. The answer to "why" somebody receives a parade has varied over the generations. The historical march of these parades reveals something about our heroes. and in doing so, also reveals something about who we were, and who we are today.

Parades are certainly not unique to New York City, nor is every parade in New York a ticker tape parade. The city has often been called a "melting pot" and owes much of its vibrancy to the impact of over 400 years of migration to its shores. As each wave of immigrants arrived and passed through it, bringing with them a little of their native culture, the city has absorbed pieces of that culture (sometimes imperfectly). From St. Patrick's Day to West Indian Day, Von Steuben Day to Nigerian Independence Day, it seems as if every ethnicity and demographic, no matter how small, has a festival or parade somewhere in New York.

These annual parades, though important to both the participants and the city, are not the subject of this book.

Other parades are held to mark the time of year, civic holidays or other cultural events. Labor Day and Memorial Day both have parades, though many New Yorkers might ignore them and just enjoy the day off from work. Some traditional parades and holidays have faded over time, like Evacuation Day, while others have grown from small neighborhood events into large-scale celebrations attracting national media coverage, such as the Coney Island Mermaid Parade. Some New Yorkers parade up Fifth Avenue "in their Easter bonnet, with all the frills upon it" while others create fantastic costumes for the annual Halloween Parade. It wouldn't be November in New York without the Macy's Thanksgiving Day parade with its enormous hot-air balloons, and the city's LGBTQ community celebrates throughout the entire month of June, with not one but five parades, culminating in one of the city's largest events, the Pride March down Fifth Avenue to the Stonewall bar.

As important as these parades are, they too are not the subject of this book.

What this book is about are those parades that the city holds to honor somebody special. The biggest and most famous of these, and the first one that comes to mind, will vary depending on the reader's generation: for the pre-war generation, nothing will surpass the excitement and crowds that cheered Charles Lindbergh after his famous flight across the Atlantic in 1927. New Yorkers who struggled and survived through the Depression and WWII will never forget the enormous crowds that rejoiced at the parade for General Douglas MacArthur in 1951. Baby boomers will recall the enormous celebration in 1981 for the men and women released from hostage in Iran, while younger generations may remember the excitement of the 2015 parade for the US Women's Soccer Team, the first ever for a female sports team.

Many cities honor great moments in their history and celebrate their heroes. Ever since the Middle Ages, VIPs have been given the "keys to the city" and victorious generals and their armies have marched through countless city streets to the adoration of citizens, like Julius Caesar's triumphal entry into Rome. Other cities have even incorporated ticker tape into their parades, though it has never been associated with Chicago or Los Angeles as much as it has with New York.

What makes New York's ticker tape parades so special? One factor is the city's size and importance, to the country and to the world. For most of the period covered by this book, New York was the largest city in the United States, and one of the largest in the world. With the exception of London, no city could rival New York's importance in banking and finance, and New York was the country's major port of entry for hundreds of thousands of visitors and immigrants. After the advent of jet planes, which dramatically changed the city's relationship with its harbor, the city's three major airports (JFK, LaGuardia and Newark) form the largest transportation network in the country, with over 143 million passengers annually as of 2019, second only to London worldwide.

2

Another factor that makes New York's ticker tape parades so special is that New York is one of the world's most influential media centers. For almost the entire period covered by this book, New York City was both the largest media market in the United States (with a population often larger than the next two cities combined) as well the largest producer of news content. The spectacle of a ticker tape parade created newsworthy images that were disseminated around the world by each new media platform introduced over the years. The excitement of each parade comes alive in newspapers, radio broadcasts, movie newsreels, photo-magazines, television and the internet.

A third factor is the parade route itself. Many major cities have a favorite boulevard or thoroughfare used for celebrations. The Mall in London, running from Buckingham Palace to Admiralty Arch and Trafalgar Square, is famous for its coronations, royal weddings and state funerals. Since the days of Napoleon Bonaparte, Paris' Champs Élysées, passing from the Place de la Concorde to the Arc de Triomphe, has witnessed many military parades, including conquering German troops during the Fall of France in 1940 and the triumphant liberation by Free French and Allied troops in 1944. Rome has its Via della Conciliazione, Moscow's Soviet-era May Day celebrations marched through Red Square, and Carnivale is celebrated in Venice's enormous Piazza San Marco, with partiers arriving via gondola from the Grand Canal.

By comparison to those thoroughfares, New York's Broadway may not seem like an ideal place for a parade, especially in the Financial District. Passing through the oldest and busiest part of the city, Broadway is barely wide enough for two lanes of traffic. On weekdays, its narrow sidewalks are crowded with workers rushing to get to their offices or to the many transportation hubs that serve the area, and for most of the time period covered, the area was largely empty on weekends. Skyscrapers soar above the sidewalk, reducing the amount of sunlight reaching the street. The overall effect is that of a canyon, through which cold winds howl in the winter, and stifling heat will radiate from the steel and cement in the summer. In fact, most of the city's "regular parades" are held in midtown Manhattan, usually on Fifth Avenue.

The Canyon of Heroes

Far from being a disadvantage, however, Broadway's narrowness makes it ideal for a parade to welcome a dignitary or hero to the city. The southern tip of Manhattan Island was the first area settled by Europeans in the 1600s, and the city's population remained centered in that area for the next 100 years. By 1800, the city had expanded north to about present-day Houston Street, though most of its 60,000 residents lived below Chambers Street. As the city's population grew during the 1800s, pushing further northward along Manhattan Island, the area now known as the Financial District remained the busy heart of the city, and Broadway its most important street.

The city's first parade to welcome a distinguished foreign visitor was held on April 16, 1824, long before the creation of ticker tape. The last surviving general of the Revolutionary War, the Marquis de Lafayette, was visiting the city as the first stop on a "grand tour" of the country he helped create. A 13-gun salute was fired as his ship sailed in the harbor, and a military escort waited for him at Castle Clinton in the Battery. According to the *New York Mirror*, church bells rang while a huge crowd watched as the Marquis was driven in a horse-drawn coach up Broadway to City Hall, where he was greeted by the mayor and given the Key to the City.

The original Dutch settlers built their "Breede Wegh" (Broad Way) along a path the native Indians had used to travel northward up the length of Manhattan Island.

3

During the British Colonial era, the portion of the road below Wall Street was called "Great George Street," but north of that the Dutch name stuck, translated into English. As the city grew, the "Broadway Street" grew with it, running from the Battery past City Hall to Union Square, where it turns diagonally toward Columbus Circle, designed in 1857 as one of several grand entrances to the city's new Central Park. During the 1870s, as the street was extended further north into the then undeveloped Upper West Side, Broadway was widened to resemble a European boulevard, complete with a median.

Downtown, however, the street could not be widened, though its 80-foot width still made it wider than the other streets in that part of town. In need of more space for their growing businesses, banks and other corporations began to expand in the only way possible: skyward. The first tall office building with an elevator, the Equitable Life Assurance Building at 120 Broadway opposite Trinity Church, was erected in 1870 thanks to technological changes allowing building construction using steel frames instead of stone or brick. Considered by many to be the first skyscraper, the Equitable Building had 10 floors and stood 155 feet tall, yet that was still lower than the spire of Trinity Church, which was the tallest structure in Manhattan.

Without the help of aerial photography, it can be challenging for the modern reader to fully appreciate what the city looked like in the 1880s. Maps can show how the city had expanded, but unless one has a very good three-dimensional imagination, it is hard to see downtown Manhattan without all the skyscrapers it has today. A rare 1876 photograph taken from a balloon shows the construction of the Brooklyn Bridge: the bridge's tower on the Manhattan side rises over the rest of downtown, and you can easily spot Trinity Church in the center of the photograph.

Over the next two decades, taller buildings were erected along Broadway, but those on neighboring streets were lower, and long warehouses lined the street opposite the wharves on both sides of the island. Viewed from a ship in the harbor, the island must have looked like a stegosaurus, with a spiky spine of tall buildings running up its main artery of Broadway.

Picture all the sunlight streaming down onto Broadway, which today sits in the shadows of its buildings for almost the entire day. Imagine the awe inspired in a visitor, parading along the bottom of this man-made canyon of steel and concrete, as ribbons of ticker tape fall down from the windows above. Nobody knows when the phrase "Canyon of Heroes" originated, though it was already in use by the late 1920s, when more and more heroes were carried up Broadway to City Hall.

By 1927 when Charles Lindbergh's transatlantic flight was celebrated, most of the tall buildings lining Broadway between the Battery and City Hall had been erected. Broadway was lined with skyscrapers, many the headquarters of America's largest corporations at the time: Standard Oil, American Express, Singer, Equitable Life, Western Union, US Realty, AT&T, and Woolworth. Even so, the adjacent streets had fewer tall buildings until the mid-1950s, when the real estate around the island's edge became more valuable for tall buildings than the wharves and warehouses lining the suddenly obsolete harbor. As the buildings along the waterfront were dismantled to make room for new skyscrapers, some of the earlier skyscrapers along Broadway, such as the Produce Exchange and the Singer Building, would be torn down and replaced with taller ones. The canyon became deeper, and towering edifices were no longer just along Broadway but throughout the Financial District. By the 1970s, the street was shadowed

4

even further by the new World Trade Center. Rising more than 1,300 feet, the twin towers cast their shadows across all of Lower Manhattan.

Sidebars

A complete tour of the architecture and buildings along Broadway from the Battery to City Hall is beyond the scope of this book, though some of the more notable ones are highlighted in sidebars like this throughout the text. Sidebars also provide information about other important locations in New York City and people appearing in the descriptions of multiple parades. The table of contents has a list of all the sidebars so you can easily find them.

If you are having trouble envisioning downtown Manhattan without all the tall buildings that exist today, search online for photographs or videos on YouTube of "Downtown New York over time" or "Construction of Brooklyn Bridge." The quality and accuracy of the time lapse videos vary, but the better ones which use photographs and drawings from different time periods can be very helpful.

What is Ticker Tape?

The image of a blizzard of snow has often been used to describe a ticker tape parade, and looking at photographs of these events, especially older black and white photos, one can easily see why: the sky is filled with paper drifting downward, the pavement is covered in white, and the parade's participants often brushed it off their shoulders and hats.

That effect can be achieved by tossing any type of paper out of a window, and confetti has the advantage of being colorful and able to sparkle in the sunlight. Invented in Italy in the 1870s, confetti had been thrown at New Year's Eve events in Paris as early as 1885. Its use at ticker tape parades was mentioned as early as 1919 during the parade for General Joffre, when "showers of confetti, long trailing paper streamers, and clouds of paper snow helped the gayety" of the celebration.

In fact, confetti is a primary component of the "precipitation" falling down on parades now, since actual ticker tape disappeared during the 1970s. Despite this, the term "ticker tape parade" is still used to describe the events, not just because of its long association with New York's parades through the Canyon of Heroes, but also because of its connection with the city's history as a financial powerhouse.

Today, anybody with a smart phone can open an app and instantly see the price of any stock, not just those traded at the local exchange but in any market around the globe. But before technology made this possible, the information had to be relayed in other ways, and for a long time, the fastest method was via ticker tape. When the New York Stock Exchange was first started in 1792, messengers would run from the exchange to neighboring banks with the results of the latest trades, and newspapers would print the day's closing prices. That changed in 1867, when Edward Calahan reconfigured a telegraph machine to print financial numbers faster than it took for a messenger to run several city blocks.

A few years later, Thomas Edison patented his own version of Calahan's invention and called it the Universal Stock Printer. Connected to telegraph wires, it transmitted abbreviations for each company's stock and the corresponding prices, printing them onto a long strip of paper about an inch wide. The clock-like noise as the machine typed out each letter and number led to the device being called a "ticker" and the strips of paper printed upon were soon known as "ticker tape." An immediate success, the new invention revolutionized Wall Street. Over 5,000 were sold within a year, and the profits helped fund Edison's lab in Menlo Park, NJ. By the mid 1880s, there were several thousand ticker machines in downtown Manhattan alone, and hundreds of miles of paper would be tossed into trash bins every day.

In their heyday, ticker tape machines filled the offices of banks, stock exchanges, and brokerage houses around the world. Many hotels had at least one installed so business guests could stay on top of the market, as did the headquarters of many corporations. In a virtuous circle, by providing faster information about market trades, the tickers also increased the speed and volume of trading itself, fueling the growth of stock markets and the need for faster tickers.

As with all technology, though, newer inventions caused older ones to become obsolete, and by the 1960s, computers were beginning to take over the role of information dissemination. The last new version of a stock ticker machine was introduced in the 1960s, and though capable of printing 900 characters per minute, it could not keep up with the versatility as well as speed of computers, and by the time that PCs were landing on office desktops in the mid 1970s, the ticker tape machine was already obsolete.

As early as 1959, many businesses along Broadway no longer produced or kept an abundant supply of wastepaper," the *New York Times* reported, so the Alliance for Downtown New York bought cartons of paper streams and other paper waste to supply businesses so they could "produce a proper display of enthusiasm" during parades.

But the ticker lives on today in two forms: the narrow strip at the bottom of television screens during news shows displaying stock quotes scrolling across the screen, and the electronic "news zipper" running around the base of One Times Square (the former home of the *New York Times*, which introduced the electric news display in 1928).

How Did This Tradition Begin?

History happened on October 28, 1886, as New York celebrated the dedication of the new Statue of Liberty with a five-mile-long parade down Fifth Avenue and Broadway to the Battery. Few of the financial companies in the area had given their staff the day off, and office windows were filled with bank clerks and other office workers cheering and waving in excitement as the parade passed below them.

Nobody knows who did it first. It may have been an exuberant clerk, caught up in the excitement of the moment, or perhaps a cleaning person who thought of a clever way to empty an overflowing waste basket. Whatever happened; somebody dumped a basket full of discarded ticker tape out the window onto the parade passing below.

The tape gently floated in the air, unfurling into long white ribbons as it spiraled downward. The wind caught the strands, and they seemed to dance on their way to the ground below. Some ribbons were caught on flagpoles and lampposts, while others were snagged by cornices and ornamentations on building facades, until gravity and the wind pulled them down. Other streamers of ticker tape became tangled with the spires of Trinity and St Paul's Churches, remaining there as they flapped and waved in the breeze. Seeing the effect, workers from other buildings started emptying their own wastebaskets, and soon the narrow canyon above Broadway was snowing with ribbons of ticker tape. A New York tradition had been born.

This then, is what makes New York's parades so unique and special, and why Broadway is ideal for such celebrations. The street's very narrowness amplifies the effect of the falling ticker tape. On a wider street, the cascading ribbons of paper would fall mostly on the spectators at ground level. Because the buildings around Broadway are so tall and the street so narrow, the swirling tape falls on honoree and spectator alike, and everybody becomes part of the event.

Grover Whalen

Spontaneity created the effect, but it took some foresight and organization to turn it into the spectacle and tradition that it became. The man most responsible for ticker tape parades becoming iconic is Grover Whalen.

Born to immigrant parents in New York in 1886, Grover Whalen worked in advertising at Wanamaker's Department store on Broadway and Ninth Street. Like his boss and mentor, Rodman Wanamaker, Grover was interested in local politics, and volunteered with the 1918 mayoral campaign of John Hylan. After Hylan won the election, Wanamaker gave Whalen the equivalent of a sabbatical from the department store to work as the Mayor's secretary. In that role, he helped run the newly formed Mayor's Committee for the Reception of Distinguished Guests, which Rodman chaired when it was formed in 1919.

In his dual capacity working in City Hall and on the Reception Committee, Whalen helped organize the logistics for the parades after the end of World War I. Within a span of 10 weeks in autumn 1919, New York would be visited by General Pershing, the King and Queen of Belgium, and the Prince of Wales. As heir to the British throne, the last name on that list posed a potential challenge in a city with many Irish immigrants and for the mayor himself, who was proud of his Irish ancestry. After helping convince the Mayor that the City had to hold a reception to welcome the Prince, Whalen realized the event needed to be spectacular. As Whalen described in his autobiography, he began contacting many offices along Broadway, asking them to save their wastepaper for the day of the event, then encourage their workers to "throw it in great volume from tens of thousands of windows." The Prince of Wales was delighted by the blizzard during his parade, and "since that day, no New York welcome has ever been complete" without a snowstorm of paper.

After Hylan left City Hall, Whalen returned to Wanamaker's, becoming General Manager of the New York store. In 1928, Mayor Jimmy Walker convinced Rodman to give Whalen another leave of absence to become New York's Police Commissioner, a role he held until 1930. Despite his many innovations and reforms within the Police Department, his attempts to enforce Prohibition laws caused friction with the Mayor, and his vigorous opposition to "socialists" during the early months of the Depression led to Whalen's resignation after police violently ended a demonstration on International Unemployment Day in March 1930.

Throughout this time, though, Whalen continued to serve on the Mayor's Reception Committee, and Mayor LaGuardia named him its chair after the death of Major William Deegan, the Tenement and Housing Commissioner who chaired it from 1930 to 1932. Whalen served in that role until 1953, organizing and attending more than 70 ticker tape parades, as well as countless other welcome ceremonies that did not involve a parade.

A tireless civil servant, Grover Whalen was also the man largely responsible for the 1939 World's Fair, serving as president of the organization that coordinated that event.

He also served on the board of the Advertising Club of New York, using the dining facility in the organization's building to host luncheons for many dignitaries after a ticker tape parade. In 1953, Mayor-elect Robert Wagner announced that Whalen would be replaced as the chair of the Reception Committee by Richard Patterson. According to the *New York Times*, Whalen "was surprised and hurt when he lost the unpaid post." He retired soon afterward, wrote his autobiography while consulting on preparations for the 1964 World's Fair, and died in 1962.

Though he never received a ticker tape parade, he attended more of them than any other person. In 1950, he was given the city's Gold Medal by Mayor O'Dwyer, who cited Whalen's "30 years of extraordinary public service to various Mayors as a volunteer creator of goodwill towards the city." In its front-page obituary, the *Times* noted that "in addition to establishing the ticker tape blizzard as a symbol of New York's welcome to the great and near-great, Whalen gained a reputation as a persuasive salesman."

Parade Basics

Every ticker tape parade is different, but most share a common structure, starting with the arrival of the parade honoree at the start of Broadway near Battery Park. In the earlier part of the 20th century, most arrivals were by ship, and the guest of honor was met either at Pier A or on their incoming ship by the Mayor's Reception Committee. After World War II, planes became the dominant mode of transportation and the greetings moved to the city's airports, after which a caravan escorted the honored guest to the Battery.

From the Battery, the honoree is paraded up Broadway to City Hall, usually sitting in an open limousine or on top of a large vehicle, to see and be seen by the crowd of spectators lining the streets and leaning out of windows above. The weather and security concerns will sometimes dictate a closed-top vehicle, though some parade recipients have chosen to walk all or part of the almost mile to City Hall.

Many guests of honor travel with an entourage riding behind them in other limos, although sometimes the VIP is joined by just a spouse or other family members. The parade often starts with a police motorcade, and usually includes at least one marching band. If the guest of honor is from the military or is a foreign dignitary, the parade also often includes a military honor guard or band.

Spectators watch and cheer from the crowded sidewalks, and the windows of the office buildings lining Broadway are filled with workers tossing ticker tape, confetti, and other types of paper out of the windows, so that the parade is snowed upon in a blizzard of paper.

Upon reaching City Hall, the honored guest usually meets the Mayor of New York, and is sometimes given a Key to the City or a medal, and often is presented with a citation. Depending on the weather, the expected size of the crowd and other factors, including security, this ceremony is sometimes held inside City Hall's large council chamber room.

Most parades end at City Hall Park, though some have continued further uptown, and a few have travelled different routes. While the official ceremony is taking place, the city's sanitation workers are busy cleaning the streets, and the Department of Sanitation's report about the amount of trash cleaned is often as newsworthy as the Police Department's estimate of the number of spectators.

This is the end of the festivities for the crowd of spectators, but for the honored guest, the day's event usually continues after the City Hall ceremony with a luncheon, reception or dinner, held at one of the city's famous hotels or private clubs. Many foreign guests spend the night at the Waldorf Astoria Hotel, although sometimes the celebrations are held at the Plaza Hotel, or one of New York's many other fine hotels or restaurants.

The Committee to Welcome Distinguished Guests

As one can imagine, a lot of planning is needed to organize these events. Coordination is needed between numerous parts of the city government, especially the police and sanitation departments. Marching bands must be contacted and given instructions if certain songs are needed, the correct number of limousines must be determined based on the size of the VIPs entourage, and businesses along Broadway notified. Ceremonies held outdoors in City Hall Park will need bandstands and daises erected, while indoor ceremonies will need coordination with the city's legislative body, as the only room in City Hall large enough for a ceremony is their chamber. The council would also need to vote to approve any other honors bestowed, such as a Key to the City. If there is to be a reception or luncheon after the ceremony at City Hall, a venue must be booked, the menu planned, guests and speakers invited, and seating assignments made. Extra security may be needed for foreign guests, who may also need overnight hotel accommodations as well as coordination with US Customs and the State Department, and additional logistical details will be needed if military units or bands are involved. The number of details could be quite daunting, especially if more than one parade is being planned at the same time, as was often the case.

The Mayor, who is the one making the final decision about who receives a ticker tape parade, has many other responsibilities. Faced with needing to plan for three important visits within 10 weeks of each other in 1919, Mayor Hylan established the Mayor's Committee for the Reception of Distinguished Guests. The *New York Times* reported that the committee's function would be "to provide proper welcome and reception to foreign dignitaries....and other distinguished visitors" to the city, and then went on to list the members, which included luminaries such as William Randolph Hearst, Solomon Guggenheim, Conde Nast, Adolph Ochs, and Alfred E. Smith, as well as many others, including Grover Whalen. Rodman Wanamaker was named the chair, a role he would fill until 1926, when Jimmy Walker became Mayor.

Mayor Walker's approach to the committee was slightly different than that of his predecessor. Grover Whalen became the committee's Executive Vice President, and honorary Chairs were named for different parades, such as Public Works Commission Joseph Johnson (a native of Georgia who chaired the events for fellow-Georgian Bobby Jones) and Dudley Malone (who financed Gertrude Ederle's swim across the English Channel). This arrangement worked until Grover Whalen resigned from his position as Police Commissioner in 1930, when Mayor Walker named retired US Major William Deegan to chair the Reception Committee. Deegan served in that role until his unexpected death in 1932, after which Bronx businessman George Mand took over. Mand had been the committee's treasurer under Major Deegan and served as its Chair until Mayor Walker left City Hall.

Throughout this time, though, Grover Whalen continued serving on the committee, and in 1936 Mayor LaGuardia made him its Chair. He would continue in that role until 1953, when incoming Mayor Wagner named a replacement. Perhaps in recognition of the fact that Whalen had been the driving force on the committee, the *New York Times'* coverage in 1953 says that he had been the city's "official greeter" for 35 years, and that "no returning hero, no prince, no foreign potentate was officially inside the city gates until he had shaken hands with Mr. Whalen."

As a replacement for Mr. Whalen, Mayor Wagner selected his friend Richard Patterson, a business executive who had been New York City's Commissioner of Corrections during Mayor Walker's administration before serving as ambassador to Yugoslavia, Guatemala and Switzerland. Patterson, whose title changed to Commissioner of Public Events, served until 1966, during which time he oversaw almost as many parades as had Mr. Whalen.

Parade Costs

Large-scale events come with large-scale price tags, and even in the most prosperous times, defraying those costs was an important consideration for the organizing committee. The two most obvious, and frequently reported, costs are overtime for the Police Department and the clean-up by the Sanitation Department.

As early as 1928, the *New York Times* reported that the city "has made a move to eliminate indiscriminate paper snowstorms." The article reports that the "welcomes to the distinguished have cost $200,000 since January 1926, including the $71,850 spent" for Lindbergh's parade (the equivalent of almost $3 million in total in today's dollars). Mr. Whalen's approach to controlling those costs involved not giving a parade to every visiting guest, and by selling tickets to the post-ceremony luncheons and receptions for the guests who did receive a parade.

After World War II, as more parades were held to welcome foreign politicians visiting the United Nations and meeting with the President, the US State Department helped fund the growing cost of these events, as NASA would during the 1960s for at least some of the parades held for its astronauts. How much of the total cost was covered by the Federal government became a growing source of contention between City Hall and Washington, and was cited as one reason behind Mayor Wagner's opposition to parades for some visitors; in 1957, City Councilman and Democratic Majority Leader Joseph Sharkey supported the mayor's decision not to hold a parade for King Saud *(see: January 29, 1957)* in part because "when we entertain half of [these foreign dignitaries]....it's on orders of the State Department."

Even so, the impact to the city's budget was significant, and candidate John Lindsay made curtailment of those costs a campaign issue in the mayoral election of 1968. When he entered City Hall, Mayor Lindsay re-organized several city departments, including the Public Events Commission. He named former basketball player John "Bud" Palmer to replace Richard Patterson, saying that the 44-year-old former NY Knicks player's "youthfulness, vitality and innovation" would "help visitors from all countries enjoy and benefit from New York's many cultural, historic, educational business and civic assets."

Since the cost of each parade was escalating, Bud Palmer shifted away from ticker tape parades to less costly forms of entertainment. When Sir Gilbert Ingelfield visited New York in 1968, Palmer escorted the Lord Mayor of London on a tour of the city that included the Empire State Building, Lever House and the Seagram's Tower, lunch at Bethesda Restaurant in Central Park, and a boat ride around Manhattan. Though the *New York Times* did not report the cost of this day's activities, it was doubtless significantly less than the ticker tape parade accorded to Ingelfield's predecessor, Sir Denys Lowson, during his 1951 visit to the city *(see: September 17, 1951)*.

Palmer resigned in April 1973 and was replaced by investment banker Walter Curley, who served until the end of that year, when incoming Mayor Abe Beame selected former Ambassador Angier Biddle Duke to replace him. Duke had been the US Chief of Protocol under Presidents Kennedy and Johnson and would oversee New York's renamed Department of Civic Affairs and Public Events until July 1976.

Mayor Beame was facing the city's deepest financial crisis, so Mr. Duke's resignation in 1976 provided an opportunity to save over $100,000 annually by cutting 7 of the department's 15 staff members. The Mayor named Francis Plimpton, partner of the law firm Debevoise & Plimpton and chairman of the city's Board of Ethics, to head the renamed Commission for Distinguished Guests. Conscious of the city's budgetary concerns, Mayor Beame stressed that Mr. Plimpton's new role was an unpaid position, noting in a 1976 interview with the *New York Times* that Mr. Plimpton "has given so much of himself without the question of recompense, everything he does is for nothing." Like his predecessors, Plimpton received only $1 per year for his work as the city's "official greeter."

The Commission shrank even further over the next few years in the city's efforts to reduce its budget. By 1979, when Mayor Ed Koch named Barbara Margolis as Vice Chair, it had only one paid position and 24 volunteer commissioners. Known as Bobbie, Ms. Margolis noted in a *New York Times* interview that "we will never again see the days when Grover Whalen used to bring buckets of champagne and long-stemmed roses to the ocean liners…but I'll try to do an exciting job." She stayed in that role for the rest of Koch's administration, serving as the city's official welcomer for a decade.

In 1990, incoming Mayor Dinkins did not replace Ms. Margolis, instead asking his Chief of Staff, Mae Ngai, to coordinate efforts between the various city departments for the first parade of his administration. Since then, the staff responsible for coordinating inter-agency parade logistics has reported to the Mayor's Chief of Staff. In 2007, Mayor Bloomberg formed the Mayor's Office for Citywide Events Coordination Management. As of 2020, this team is responsible for oversight of all "public events, including outdoor concerts, large-scale citywide events, gatherings in city parks, parades, plaza events, sporting events, street events, street festivals and water events."

Although the committee's name and membership have changed over time, its general responsibilities remained the same. Not all distinguished guests visiting New York receive a ticker tape parade, of course, but some logistical coordination is needed even for those simply meeting the Mayor at City Hall.

How Many Ticker Tape Parades Have There Been?

This question might seem surprising, but there is no official list of ticker tape parades, and the several lists that are available provide different answers based on their definition of which events to include or exclude.

The list which would seem to be definitive is the one maintained by the Alliance for Downtown New York, the organization responsible for the plaques embedded in the sidewalk along Broadway. Their original list, published in brochure format in 2003, contained 200 parades. When it was updated a decade later, the list had grown, and not just because four parades had occurred in the intervening years. The updated list added two parades missing from their earlier brochure, bringing their new total to 206. Their definition seems to include parades that travelled the route from Battery to City Hall, excluding ones in other parts of the city like the 1946 parade for the 82nd Airborne celebrating the end of World War II or the 1971 parade for Alan Shepard.

Another list considered somewhat definitive is the one provided in *The Encyclopedia of New York* by Kenneth Jackson. First published in 1988 with updated revisions in 1991 and 1995, the list includes 166 parades. A number of the events on the list have incorrect dates, however, and the list also includes planned events that were cancelled (like the 1964 parade for Antonio Segni). Compiled in a time before online databases, this list is also missing many of the less-well known parades, such as the 1930 parade for Henry Stimson or the 1950 parade for Mayor O'Dwyer.

The most easily accessed list is, of course, online at Wikipedia.com, though by its very nature, Wikipedia can be updated at any time by anybody who wants to add or remove parades from the list. Though its editors rely on the two lists mentioned above, errors have appeared on Wikipedia's list and can easily spread to other websites in a vicious cycle of circular reporting. For example, when the work on this book began, Wikipedia included the 1921 parade for Albert Einstein, though that has subsequently been removed, and the site's Talk page provides a fascinating look under the hood into Wikipedia's editorial process. The reverse is true for the 1957 parade for King Mohammed V of Morocco, which is listed on Wikipedia currently but was not there in 2004. It also includes a 1950 event for Ralph Bunche, included on neither of the other two lists, and it took much research to unearth the truth; Mr. Bunche was honored in 1949, but not with a parade *(see: May 17, 1949)*.

For the purposes of this book, the authors decided to research and describe the events on all of these lists, and also discovered a few not on any of them. Do all the events qualify as ticker tape parades? Most do, depending on your definition, but certainly not all of them. Some events included no parades at all, either because the event was cancelled (like the 1928 parade for the US Olympic team) or because no parade was included in the plans to welcome a visitor to the city (such as the 1957 visit by King Saud). Other events involved a parade that did not go along the traditional route (like the 1946 Victory Parade celebrating the homecoming of the 82nd Airborne Division) or because no ticker tape was showered onto the honoree (like the 1921 arrival of Albert Einstein). We have also included the only known example of a person declining the honor of a ticker tape parade *(see: April 21, 1955)* and a few other "nonevents" that have appeared on the Wikipedia page (like the 1962 event for astronaut Scott Carpenter). The Appendix at the back of this book should help the reader make sense of the differences between the various lists of ticker tape parades.

Regardless of how many parades meet your definition, the following chapters explore how New York evolved over time, followed by the details of the more than 200 ticker tape parades. Many went off without a hitch, with military-like precision. Others did not. Some parades are remembered to this day as famous and spectacular events. Most have been long forgotten, and a few never even happened. Yet each event provides a fascinating slice of New York history.

About the Maps

Four maps have been included on the following pages to assist readers unfamiliar with the geography of New York City, especially the downtown area where many of the events described in this book took place. Even current residents of New York City may find these maps helpful since that area has changed several times in the past century. Landmarks mentioned often in the text have been indicated on these maps.

The first map depicts downtown Manhattan prior to the 1960s and is based on a 1911 map of the southern part of the borough of Manhattan of the City of New York, prepared expressly for the Trow Directory, Printing and Bookbinding Co, and now part of the New York Public Library Digital Collection. Some extraneous items were removed from the original, which can be seen in its entirety at https://digitalcollections.nypl.org/items/5bb5d220-f78e-0130-1868-58d385a7b928. Readers should note Manhattan's original shoreline along the Hudson River, as well as the wharves and piers extending from the foot of almost every street, and the absence of the Brooklyn-Battery Tunnel and highway exit ramps off the Brooklyn Bridge (symbol "D" on the map).

Prior to the 1950s, most parade recipients arrived in New York via ship and were ferried to Pier A ("A"). After a brief welcome from the Mayor's Committee for the Reception of Distinguished Guests, the parade would form along Battery Place in front of Pier A or along State Street in front of the US Customs Building (symbol "7"). Passing One Broadway ("E") and Bowling Green ("F"), the parade would proceed up Broadway past Trinity Church ("N") to City Hall ("C"). Ticker tape descended from the many tall buildings lining Broadway, including the headquarters of Cunard ("H"), Standard Oil ("J"), American Express ("L"), Equitable Life Insurance ("R"), and Singer Sewing Machines ("Q"). After crossing Fulton and Ann Streets, most parades passed the Woolworth Building ("T") to enter City Hall Plaza ("Z") from Broadway, though a few turned onto Park Row, passing the offices of the New York Times ("V"), the Tribune ("W") and the New York World ("2").

The second map shows the same area of downtown Manhattan after 1960 and the construction of the World Trade Center, when 1.2 million cubic yards of soil and rock were used as landfill to extend the island's shoreline, and dozens of city blocks west of Greenwich Street were demolished in order to create Battery Park City. It is based on a map that has been released into the public domain by its creator, user PerryPlanet on Wikimedia Commons, and found at https://commons.wikimedia.org/ wiki/ File:Lower_manhattan_map.png.

During this period, jet planes became the dominant means of transportation for both passengers and cargo, and the enormous decline in shipping led to the dismantling of most of the wharves which had previously lined the island's waterfront; one of the few remaining in this part of the city later became the South Street Seaport Museum ("3" on this map). The cycle of construction and demolition can be seen by comparing this map with the first one; for example, the Produce Exchange was replaced in 1957 by Two Broadway ("G" on both maps), and in 1968 the Singer Building was demolished and replaced in 1972 by Zuccotti Park and One Liberty ("Q" on both maps). The impact of Robert Moses' highway construction can be seen with the extension of the FDR Drive through tunnels built under Battery Park, the Brooklyn-Battery Tunnel (opened in 1950) and new exit ramps from the Brooklyn Bridge (1956), which required the demolition of the New York World Building and altered the streets around Park Row. The most dominant feature of New York's skyline during this era were the twin towers of the World Trade Center ("1" and "2"), which towered over all the other skyscrapers in the area.

After the terrorist attack of September 11, 2001, downtown Manhattan saw more changes. The original World Trade Center towers collapsed and have been replaced by the 9/11 Memorial Pools and a new One World Trade Center tower, and a new transportation hub called the Oculus was built west of Church Street. Few of these changes factor into the stories about ticker tape parades in this era, however, so no map showing the current geography of downtown Manhattan was included in this book; curious readers can find updated maps online.

Not all the events described in this book happened in Manhattan's financial district, however, so two other maps have been included. The third map shows Manhattan Island south of 64th Street and is based on the same 1911 map that was the basis of map #1.

This map identifies midtown locations mentioned in the text, though many were erected after this map was created in 1911. Many parade recipients stayed at the Waldorf Astoria Hotel ("H"), shown at its current location which it has occupied since 1930; the original hotel was demolished to make way for the Empire State Building ("Q"). The city's two major train terminals, Penn Station ("E") and Grand Central Terminal ("G") were often used by parade recipients travelling elsewhere in the country. When not performing duties as the city's official greeter, Grover Whalen worked at Wanamaker's Department Store ("F"), and he hosted many post-parade luncheons at the Advertising Club of New York ("L"). Many of the landmarks identified on this map still exist today, such as the United Nations Headquarters ("Q") and St. Patrick's Cathedral ("S"), though some have moved to different places. For example, Madison Square Garden ("N") is shown in the location it occupied from 1925 until 1968; it currently sits atop Penn Station, ("E"). Likewise, the original Metropolitan Opera House ("K") was demolished in 1967 after the company's move to Lincoln Center ("T") in 1966.

The fourth and final map shows the greater New York City metropolitan area and is based on the Wanamaker Diary Automobile Road Map, which was included in the 1917 edition of the annual desk diary book published annually by Wanamaker's beginning in 1910. A digitized copy of this map was retrieved from the Library of Congress and can be found at https://www.loc.gov/item/76695282/ in its original form. The map shows the entire City of New York, and the dark lines are major roads connecting the city to towns (indicated by circles) on Long Island to the east, Westchester to the north, and New Jersey in the west.

Although the original map was created in 1917, locations outside of Manhattan mentioned frequently in the text from all eras have been identified. As with map #3, the Battery ("B") and City Hall ("C") are included to help orient readers unfamiliar with the location of downtown. Several landmarks shown on this map no longer exist, including the Polo Grounds ("E", demolished in 1964) and Ebbetts Field ("P", demolished in 1960). Many parade honorees arrived in New York via plane, arriving at Floyd Bennett Field ("M"), LaGuardia Airport ("J"), Newark International ("L") or JFK Airport, originally named Idlewild ("K"). The United Nations held meetings at the site of the 1939 World's Fair ("T") and in Lake Success ("S") in Nassau County before its new headquarters on the East River were built. This map also shows New York Bay, divided into the Upper and Lower Bay by the Narrows now crossed by the Verrazano Bridge ("Y"). Fort Jay on Governor's Island ("W") and the Statue of Liberty ("X") are well-known landmarks in the Upper Bay, but the two small islands in the Lower Bay commonly referred to as Quarantine ("V") may be unfamiliar even to native New Yorkers.

CHAPTER 1
Prosperity and Progressivism (1886-1916)

New York City was very different in the 1880s than it is today. The city itself was smaller, consisting of only Manhattan and the Bronx plus several small islands in the Upper Harbor. In the century since the American Revolution, the city's population had grown from 33,000 to just over 1.2 million, making it the largest city in the United States, and more than double that of its neighbor across the East River, the city of Brooklyn. The most important factor contributing to this growth was immigration, and close to a third of the city's residents were foreign-born. Unlike the first wave of migration in the 1840s-1850s, when most new arrivals came from Ireland, more and more of the recent immigrants came from central and eastern Europe and were non-English speaking. Some immigrants continued westward, seeking fortune, or at least farmland, in the vast western territories that were quickly earning statehood. Many others stayed in New York, hoping to create a new life for themselves and earn enough money to buy passage for relatives still in the old country. These new arrivals crowded into tenements and fueled the city's economy.

That economy was dependent on cheap labor and technological advances. In addition to being the country's main port of entry for immigrants, New York was also the country's leading center of commerce, with close to 70% of the nation's imported goods arriving through its harbor. The second phase of the Industrial Revolution brought mechanization to more and more industries, resulting in increased worker productivity while decreasing the need for skilled labor. With the nation's economy increasing at its fastest pace ever, many of the city's newest arrivals found jobs working on the docks, or in factories and sweatshops. Raw materials arriving in the harbor were converted into finished goods, which could then be transported for sale across the growing nation thanks to a burgeoning network of transcontinental railways. Laying iron tracks across the country required money, of course, and the city had funded much of that expansion. The return on those investments catapulted Wall Street's growth to dominate the country's finances.

Technological advances and the prosperity enjoyed by New York and its wealthy citizens was already having a transformative impact, and much of the infrastructure of our modern city started to take shape during the Gilded Age and the Progressive Era, between 1880 and 1915. Electric streetlights were installed along Broadway and Fifth Avenue starting in the 1880s, replacing gas and oil lamps, and the streets themselves, some of which were covered in cobblestone or rectangular bricks, would be paved with asphalt during the 1890s, when the first automobiles started appearing. Construction and engineering advances, especially the invention of the passenger elevator, enabled large corporations to build skyscrapers, but also led to larger apartment buildings where the middle class could afford to live. These buildings increasingly had modern conveniences such as steam-powered heat (reducing the need for wood or coal burning stoves), electric power for lighting and a growing number of home appliances, and indoor plumbing. The Old Croton Aqueduct, which had supplied the city with drinking water since the 1840s, could not keep up with the growing population, and a second Aqueduct was built in 1890, followed in 1915 by the Catskill Aqueduct. Wastewater, which for decades had flowed from outhouses and privies behind saloons into street gutters, was increasingly channeled into a growing network of sewers, while overhead a chaotic cobweb of telephone wires was strung between buildings and across streets.

These advancements, of course, came swiftest for the rich and the middle class, who were increasingly moving out of older neighborhoods, filling in the open areas in Brooklyn and nearby Queens, thanks to a growing network of horse-drawn streetcars and electric trolleys. Neighborhoods like the Lower East and West Side, the Tenderloin and Hell's Kitchen were still filled with over-crowded tenements and squalid living conditions. Jacob Riis' photojournalistic *How the Other Half Lives* helped inspire reforms like the creation of a Tenement House Act and a city department empowered to enforce the new regulations. Progressive leaders like Theodore Roosevelt, William Jennings Bryan and Charles Evans Hughes focused attention on addressing the problems caused by industrialization, enacting child labor laws, improving school and public health systems, and exposing corruption in politics and business.

These reforms were not embraced by all, and during this period the political bosses of Tammany Hall were able to defeat or delay some of the Progressives' most idealistic goals like women's suffrage and prohibition. Jobs with the city's new Street Cleaning Department could be doled out to loyal supporters as easily as those in the Police and Fire Departments. The opportunities for graft and corruption expanded with the 1898 Consolidation, when the merger of Brooklyn and New York increased the city's geography six-fold and tripled its population.

As the 20th century dawned, New York was taking its place alongside other leading cities like Paris and London, with new cultural institutions like the Metropolitan Museum (opened in 1872), the Metropolitan Opera (1883) and Carnegie Hall (1891). The Brooklyn Bridge, which opened in 1883, would be followed soon by the Williamsburg (1903), Manhattan (1909) and Queensborough Bridges (1909) and starting in 1904 commuters could ride in underground trains from City Hall to the newly created Times Square on 42nd Street. By 1915, the new subway system had annual ridership over 800 million, alleviating some of the traffic on the city's busy streets, which were seeing a slow but growing number of automobiles. The subway also had a positive effect aboveground, as overhead telephone lines were torn down and replaced with new ones installed in the new tunnels.

This was the city where a statue celebrating liberty was erected on an island in the harbor *(see: October 28, 1886)*. The gift from France soon became a symbol of America's ideals as the country took its place among the world's mighty empires. The nation had already begun flexing its naval muscles with the Perry expedition to open Japan for trade in the 1850s. In the late 1800s US navy ships, many built in the Brooklyn Navy Yards, led to the defeat of the Kingdom of Hawaii (1893) and the annexation of Samoa (1899). After defeating Spain in 1898 *(see: September 30, 1899)*, Puerto Rico, Guam and the Philippines were added to the growing American Empire, followed soon by the Panama Canal Zone. Though New York was not the political capital of the nation, it was its financial and cultural center. It should come as no surprise, then, that the city celebrated its own importance *(see: April 29, 1889)* as well as its heroes *(see: June 18,*

1910) with massive parades, and that those celebrations would organically incorporate one of the very instruments of finance: ticker tape.

Thursday, October 28, 1886:
Dedication of the Statue of Liberty

On October 23, 1886, the final copper sheet of a statue more than 150 feet tall was riveted into place on New York's Bedloe's Island, completing a tale 21 years in the making. All that remained was a ceremony scheduled for October 28 at which President Grover Cleveland would dedicate the new Statue of Liberty.

Preparations were made. Grand marshals for a parade were named, and the nearly five-mile route from Fifth Avenue and 57th Street to the Battery was decorated and festooned with flags and bunting. The enormous wood frame scaffolding around the Statue was draped in cloth, so the colossal Statue could be revealed during the Dedication ceremony. Boats were hired to transport people from the Battery to the island. Hotels began filling with guests from France and across the US. Newspapers informed the public that the parade could be viewed by all, but access to Bedloe Island for the ceremony was limited to guests, and those guests had all been invited.

Almost all the invited guests were men. The Dedication Committee had decided that the size of the crowd and the excitement of the occasion would be too strenuous for women. The First Lady, Frances Cleveland, was one of the few women allowed on the island.

The irony of the situation was not lost to the members of the New York State Woman's Suffrage Association, who made plans to protest the Dedication. Denouncing the ceremonies as a mockery, they said, "to make the Statue of Liberty a woman is simply setting up a gigantic lie" since women could not vote in America, much less have an equal voice in the administration of the city and the country.

The day of the Dedication dawned to rainy skies, but spectators in the hundreds of thousands stood on sidewalks or rooftops, watched at windows, and even climbed to the tops of lampposts and telegraph poles. At 10 o'clock, a troop of cavalry and a battalion of the Old Guard, the Army's oldest regiment dating from 1783, led the parade as it moved south from Fifth Avenue. President Cleveland rode in a carriage while military bands played and those watching cheered. As the parade continued people attached themselves to it, first in ones and twos and then in groups, and the length of the parade grew as it advanced.

The procession halted at Madison Square, where a reviewing stand had been built on the spot in the park where the statue's arm and torch had been displayed from 1877 to 1882 before being sent back to France. Joining the president on the reviewing stand was Lieutenant General Philip Sheridan, Civil War hero and ranking officer of the Army. A large gathering of other generals and admirals were also there. Civilian representatives on the reviewing stand included diplomats from numerous nations, New York Governor David Hill and New Jersey Governor Leon Abbett; Richard Butler, Secretary of the American Committee for the Statue of Liberty; sculptor Frédéric Bartholdi; and Ferdinand de Lesseps, builder of the Suez Canal and Chairman of the Franco-American Union for the statue.

For more than two hours those on the stand reviewed the parade that marched by as a fine misty drizzle continued through the day. Army regiments, New York and New Jersey National Guard detachments, and sailors from the Brooklyn Navy Yard were followed by crews from warships in the harbor, engineers, batteries of artillery, and cavalry on splendidly matched horses. Civil War veterans paraded too, some wearing their old, faded uniforms, and some who had been prisoners of the Confederacy during the war. There were militia groups from Newark, Brooklyn, and Philadelphia. Throughout the long parade, brass band after brass band played marching music. Schools in New York and Brooklyn were closed for the day and groups of students strolled past the reviewing stand; what they lacked in military precision they made up for in enthusiasm. Even a group of New York University students, chanting "Columbia" and "Bartholdi" passed in review.

Charles Stone, construction manager for the statue's pedestal, led the parade south after the review ended, continuing down Fifth Avenue to Washington Square, then onto Broadway. As the procession approached City Hall, Stone led it down Park Row past the offices of the *New York World*. The newspaper's publisher, Joseph Pulitzer, had organized a subscription campaign that finally provided the necessary funds for the statue's pedestal. Donations large and small flowed in, including many nickels and dimes sent by city school students. The *World* had constructed a temporary arch in front of its building, through which the parade marched as it continued down Broadway, joined now by the original carriage in which George Washington rode to his inauguration.

The American and Produce Exchanges were closed because of the day's festivities but not the New York Stock Exchange. As the parade snaked by on Wall Street, employees of the exchange unraveled large spools of ticker tape which floated down from the upper floors. The result made the parade even more exciting and, unwittingly, gave birth to what would become the hallmark of New York parades: ticker tape.

At the Battery, the steamers *Florence* and *Magenta,* the barge *Republic,* and other ships of all sorts had been hired to transport the larger number of invited guests to Bedloe's Island. On the island, a force of 150 New York City policemen guarded the docks where the steamers discharged statesmen and generals, congressmen and judges, millionaires and reporters, Americans and French alike. An infantry company stood at attention along the edges of the platform. Out of sight behind the pedestal, Gilmore's band played patriotic and popular tunes until all the guests had arrived and were in place. Originally attached to a Massachusetts infantry regiment in the Civil War, Gilmore's band had been providing music for official functions since the end of the war.

The President and First Lady were the last to arrive on the island. A series of speeches was included on the program, starting with Senator William Evarts of New York, former Secretary of War, and Chairman of the American Committee for the Statue. His speech was filled with patriotic statements and praise for France and her friendship with American, and the marvels of the statue behind him. He paused to collect his breath and for a sip of water.

His pause was mistaken for the signal to reveal the Statue, the ropes were pulled, the cloth fell, and before Evarts could say another word, New York harbor was filled with the noise of whistles, bells, gongs, and horns. The flagship of the North Atlantic Squadron and largest warship in the Navy, the screw frigate *Tennessee* unleashed a broadside in salute. Echoes rebounded from the hills of Staten Island. For more than 15 minutes the noise of the salute reverberated. Then, according to the *New York Times* reporter covering the event, whatever Senator Evarts "might have said had he spoken out of the fullness of his heart at the moment will never be known, because he sat down."

18

The ceremony continued without further interruption. President Cleveland spoke, followed by the French Minister to the United States, W. Albert Lefaivre, and then Chauncey Depew, President of the New York Central Railroad. Depew gave a lengthy speech, after which it was decided to skip the reading of a long poem entitled *Liberty* which had been written for the occasion. It was growing late, and the rain began falling harder as New York Episcopal Bishop Horatio Potter gave the Benediction.

As the guests slowly returned to the Battery, they passed the excursion boat *John Lenox*. Chartered by the New York State Woman's Suffrage Association, the ship had sailed around Bedloe's Island during the Dedication Ceremony while its passengers, women who paid $1 to witness the statue's unveiling, listened to speeches deriding the representation of "Liberty as a woman in a nation that denies liberty to women."

Receptions, dinners, and parties were held throughout the city that night, though a fireworks and illumination display was cancelled due to the inclement weather.

The idea for the statue, officially named *Liberty Enlightening the World*, was made in 1865 by the French scholar, Édouard Laboulaye, as an expression of French grief over President Lincoln's assassination and as a gift to celebrate a century of American independence. The statue was designed and constructed by the French sculptor, Frédéric Auguste Bartholdi. During the 20 years since the proposal France had changed from an Empire to a Republic, lost a war against Prussia, and its capital city had been besieged and bombarded. The project had run out of funds. Parts of the incomplete statue were sent to the United States for display at the 1876 Centennial Exhibition in Philadelphia and in Madison Square in New York and then returned to France for completion. Formally presented to the United States on July 4, 1884, the statue was disassembled, shipped from Paris to New York, and reassembled piece by piece on a stone pedestal on Bedloe's Island, New York.

Almost 100 years later, in honor of the statue's centennial, President Ronald Reagan declared July 3-6, 1986 as Liberty Weekend. The statue was given needed repairs and restoration. Speeches were recited, no rain fell, and fireworks lit up the night sky. This time, women were invited.

Monday, April 29, 1889:
Centenary of George Washington's Inauguration

New York City's second ticker tape parade celebrated the 100th anniversary of George Washington's inauguration as President. It was part of a three-day re-enactment, beginning with President Benjamin Harrison and Vice President Levi Morton retracing Washington's journey from Trenton, New Jersey, across the Hudson River to Federal Hall at the corner of Broad and Wall Streets on April 28. President Harrison rode in the same carriage used by the first president for part of the journey, and only one section of the route was not followed, because recent spring rains had made the road impassable near Elizabeth, New Jersey. In addition to re-enacting the events of 1789, the 1889 plans included a huge parade for more than 5,000 participants, followed by a lavish banquet.

When President Harrison and Vice President Morton arrived at Jersey City, many of the groups that would take part in the march to Wall Street were already in place. Numerous boats and small craft ferried them across the Hudson where they landed at piers from the foot of Wall Street to the Battery. Shortly before 11 o'clock, the President and Vice-President stepped into the police boat *Dispatch* that transported them to the Navy steamer *Sirius,* while members of the cabinet were taken to the foot of Wall

Street on the police boat *Meteor*. The President and Vice President then climbed into a large naval gig, similar to the boats used when Washington and his troops crossed the Delaware at the Battle of Trenton. Pulling at the oars was a party of sailors drawn from the navy vessels riding at anchor in the harbor and river. Guns on the ships fired blank charges in salute, the heavy black smoke from the charges almost hiding the naval vessels from view.

The Battery was decorated with countless American flags as well as the flags of all 38 states. Among the American flags were replicas of the flags flown over the years, including the 15 stars and 15 stripes version that had inspired Francis Scott Key to compose *The Star-Spangled Banner*, approved earlier that year to be used for official occasions (it would not be designated the National Anthem until an Act of Congress in 1931). The parade's contingents slowly gathered into position, forming a column divided into seven divisions the first of which was composed of military and naval detachments, and National Guard and Militia units of the original 13 states. Next in the column rode President Harrison and Vice President Morton, now joined by their wives, Caroline Harrison and Anna Morton, in the original carriages used by Washington. Following the chief executive was a carriage carrying the event's co-chairmen, Mr. Hamilton Fish and Mr. Elbridge Gerry.

The second division was composed of members of 36 different Civil War veteran groups, mostly from the Grand Army of the Republic and a handful from the United Confederate Veterans. The division also contained descendants of Revolutionary War soldiers. The third and fourth divisions were composed of members of fraternal organizations: Masons, Knights of Pythias, Ancient Order of Hibernians, and others. Representatives of manufacturing and agricultural organizations marched in the fifth division. The sixth division contained members of Police and Fire departments from New York and other cities, near and far. In the words of the *New York Times*, the seventh and final division was composed of "Colored Citizens." A cavalry detachment followed the final division, completing the marching elements.

Every building on Broadway was decorated with flags and other patriotic symbols or artwork, including many images of the first President. Bands stationed along the route played patriotic music. Neither banks nor brokerage houses had closed for the day but as the parade passed little or no business seemed to be transacted. A cascade of paper, ticker tape, and flowers fell down from the higher floors of many of the buildings along Broadway, and sections of the street appeared carpeted in paper and petals.

As the parade continued past Trinity Church at the corner of Wall Street, the church's bells rang a welcome and announced the time as 1 o'clock. At the Equitable Life Assurance Company Building (120 Broadway) the presidential party descended from the carriage for a luncheon attended by hundreds of the city's wealthiest and most influential citizens. During the luncheon New York Mayor Hugh Grant officially welcomed the president and his party to New York. He proposed a toast to President Harrison and Vice President Morton. The president then raised a toast to George Washington. Additional toasts followed: to the Republic, the mayor, the city of New York, the governor, and dozens of other people, living and dead.

It was 3:30 when the president emerged to be greeted by hundreds of school children. With them as an escort, the presidential party walked to the Federal Hall (also known as the Subtreasury Building) where a re-enactment of Washington's inauguration took place. Temporary seating had been provided for hundreds of guests, including the Justices of the Supreme Court, most members of Congress, the governors of more than two dozen states, and other political figures. Using the bible that George Washington placed his hand on in 1789, President Harrison repeated the oath of office. He then gave a patriotic address lasting more than two hours, extolling the virtues of the Father of the Country, the history of the republic, and the promise of its virtue.

When he finished speaking, the presidential party walked north to City Hall. Hundreds of spectators crowded Broadway and there was barely space to walk. A phalanx of escorts surrounding the presidential party cleared a path, and President Harrison signed a proclamation commemorating the day. Due to the lateness of the hour, plans for the President to enter City Hall were cancelled, and it would be almost 60 years before a sitting president did enter it *(see: October 27, 1945)*.

There was a five-course banquet in the evening, where President Harrison was greeted by more than 2,000 people. In keeping with the custom of a century earlier, hands were not shaken. Instead, guests were greeted with a polite bow, as would have happened in President Washington's day. It was well past midnight when the last guest departed, and the party ended.

The following morning a joint naval review and parade of civilian vessels was held. It began near the five-year-old Brooklyn Bridge and continued into New York Harbor, past the three-year-old Statue of Liberty. Then the naval vessels exited through the Narrows in an orderly flotilla while civilian craft returned to their berths or duties. The final event of the centennial celebration took place that afternoon when President Harrison dedicated a wooden arch in George Washington's honor at Washington Square Park. In 1892, it was replaced by the permanent arch, designed by Stanford White, that now stands in the park.

Within the next few days all the officials and dignitaries left New York City and returned to their homes. The city would not host another event such as this for another ten years when the hero of the Spanish American War, Admiral Dewey, would be honored *(see September 30, 1899)*.

Mayor Hugh Grant (1889-1892)

Born in 1858 on West 27th Street, Hugh Grant studied law at Columbia University, then pursued a career in politics. A Democrat during the Tammany Hall era, he served on the city's Board of Aldermen for two years before becoming Sheriff of New York County. Elected Mayor in 1889, his administration focused on re-organizing the city's bureaucracy and began moving the city's electrical system underground, to prevent damage like happened when 40 inches of snow fell in the Great Blizzard of 1888. He was the city's second Catholic mayor, and to date, the youngest person elected Mayor.

Early in his career, he avoided the financial scandals often associated with Tammany Hall, but in 1890 he became involved in a financial scheme with the Broadway Surface Railroad, which ran streetcars up Broadway from City Hall to Union Square. After deciding not to run for re-election in 1892, he attempted a return in the next election. He retired from politics after being defeated by an opponent who reminded voters of the scandal. →

Hugh married Julia Murphy in 1895, living with her in Washington, DC while her father served in the US Senate, then moved to New Jersey. They maintained a residence on West 72nd Street, where he died of a heart attack in 1910. Several years later, Julia Grant used her inheritances to establish funds for Regis High School, an all-scholarship school for Catholic boys on East 85th Street, and the alma mater of one of the authors.

Saturday, September 30, 1899:
Admiral George Dewey

The cruiser *Olympia* slowly steamed past Fort Jay on Governors Island, revealing the view up the East River. Spanning the river and connecting the former city of Brooklyn to Manhattan was the 16-year-old Brooklyn Bridge. Five silver letters, 15 feet tall, gleaming in the late afternoon sun, were attached to the center of the span, facing seaward for all incoming vessels to view. Even without the aid of binoculars the letters were readable, because of their prominence and size. They spelled out one word, a name: DEWEY.

Admiral George Dewey, the victor of the Battle of Manila Bay where the entire Spanish Pacific fleet had been destroyed almost 18 months earlier, had arrived in New York. What awaited him was a welcome the likes of which no American city had ever seen. Bearing to port, the *Olympia* cruised up the Hudson River. More than 20 naval vessels rode at anchor just north of 60th Street. Flags, pennants, and bunting of every size and style fluttered from the ships, saluting the Admiral. The battleships *New York, Indiana, Massachusetts,* and *Texas* were present, with cruisers *Brooklyn, Lancaster, Chicago,* and a host of other vessels: monitors, gunboats, patrol boats and torpedo boats. Standing on the bridge of *Olympia* was Admiral Dewey, acknowledging the naval welcome. The guns on Fort Jay boomed, salute pieces on the navy vessels barked, navy bands played. Sailors lined up topside of the flotilla, silently saluting while officers unsheathed their swords in tribute. Slowly, carefully, the Admiral's flagship slid into position at the far north of the naval column, south of 110th Street. Two floats, one with the allegorical figure of Victory and the other of Peace, marked the northern end of the column. Made of plaster and wood, the floats were anchored in line with Grant's Tomb at Riverside Drive and 122nd Street.

The following day dignitaries visited the Admiral on board his flagship. Admirals Winfield Schley and William Sampson, and Generals Nelson Miles and Wesley Merritt, who had played a part in the war against Spain paid their respect, as did the recently elected Governor of New York, Theodore Roosevelt. The Admiral was also visited by the Mayor of New York City, Robert Van Wyck and former Mayor George McClellan, Jr., along with the Governor of New Jersey, Foster MacGowan, and many others.

Early the next morning, September 30, Admiral Dewey transferred to the patrol boat *Corsair,* which carried him to the pier at Grant's Tomb where the Admiral placed a wreath in respect for the hero of a previous war. Escorted by companies of sailors and marines he entered the first of a caravan of 44 horse-drawn carriages and broughams for the parade that would travel from 122nd Street along Riverside Drive to 72nd Street, then east to Fifth Avenue, and directly down Fifth Avenue to Washington Square. Riding in the carriages were Army and Navy Officers and the Governors or their representatives of 16 of the 45 states, including New York and the latest addition,

Utah. The final carriage in the procession carried the Co-Chairmen of the Reception Committee, Chauncey Depew, William McAdoo, and Richard Crocker, along with the British yachtsman and president of the tea company that bore his name, Sir Thomas Lipton.

The first of many bands in the parade was the Marine Corps band under the baton of John Philip Sousa. Other bands were from many of the ships moored in the river, army units, the New York and New Jersey State militias. Bands from New York City Police, Fire, and Street Cleaning were also present. The last band in the more than three-mile-long parade was composed of veterans of Colored Troops who had served in the Civil War. Between the carriages and bands were the actual marching units, more than 35,000 strong. These too were drawn from the Army and Navy, the militias of five states, the Civil War Veterans organization (the Grand Army of the Republic), a company of Teddy Roosevelt's Rough Riders, and even war-bonneted Native Americans. The student bodies of both the Military and Naval Academies marched, and among them was a first-year cadet, Douglas MacArthur, who would receive a parade in his honor more than 50 years later *(see April 20, 1951)*.

Portable grandstands had been constructed along the entire route, some offering free seating to those who arrived early enough to find a seat, others by pre-purchased tickets. The Tammany Hall Society sold tickets at 25 cents printed on yellow cardboard. Hundreds of similar tickets had been counterfeited and when there were far more ticker-bearers than seats, it caused an overflow of people near 68th Street that the police had to control. Municipal grandstands held city and state employees. Civic groups had their own reserved grandstands. School and church groups filled others.

Often as the Admiral's carriage approached certain grandstands or groups of people lining the route, the spectators would break into whatever song Sousa's band was playing. The Admiral and Governor Roosevelt were both moved to tears when passing groups of school children singing patriotic songs. When the Admiral passed St. Patrick's Cathedral on 50th Street, he was surprised to hear its bells rung in his honor. He commented later that while in the Philippines, Catholics avoided him after he defeated Spain with its long tradition of Catholicism.

At Madison Square the parade passed through an arch specially constructed for him. Named the Dewey Arch, the archway was 25 feet tall and 20 feet wide. Built of plaster and wood, subscriptions were being collected to replace it with a permanent structure similar to Washington Arch. It proved too narrow to permit all the marching units to pass through it though many tried, causing it to be badly damaged.

Admiral Dewey finally arrived at the parade's destination, Washington Square. Over the next four and half hours, he reviewed the contingents that marched in salute to him and his role in defeating the Spanish, a defeat that cost Spain its possessions of the Philippines and Guam in the Pacific and Cuba and Puerto Rico in the Caribbean.

That evening the admiral dined with the commanders of the naval ships. He saw no other guests and retired early, exhausted by the day's excitement and activity. Less than a week later he met with President William McKinley in Washington and was awarded a special jewel-encrusted sword, designed by Tiffany's, at the cost of $10,000. In 1900 he was considered a candidate for the Presidency by the Democratic Party. After he admitted that he had never voted in any election and that he thought a war was imminent between the United States and Germany, he withdrew his name. In 1903 Congress created a special rank for him, Admiral of the Navy, which no other individual has ever been granted. He died in 1917 in Washington, DC, and his remains were interred in the Bethlehem Chapel of the Washington National Cathedral.

Attempts were made to construct a permanent arch to replace the Dewey Arch but after he withdrew from the race for president subscriptions fell off sharply. The plaster model at Madison Square was rotting and it became a dangerous obstruction in Fifth Avenue. In December 1900, it was broken up and carted off to the city dumping grounds in southern Brooklyn.

Mayor Robert Van Wyck (1898-1901)

In 1898, the independent cities of Brooklyn and Long Island, plus the remaining towns in Queens County and Staten Island, merged with the city of New York, which until then had included just Manhattan and the Bronx. The idea had been discussed since the 1850s, when the State Legislatures voted that combining the area into one city would improve management of the harbor and reduce expense. Consolidation also ensured that the larger city (sometimes referred to as Greater New York) remained the largest city in the nation. The term in office for mayor of the newly enlarged city was increased to four years, and the city's Board of Aldermen was expanded to 73 districts.

The first mayor for the newly enlarged city was Robert van Wyck, born in 1849. He practiced law before entering politics and served as the city's Chief Judge prior to running for mayor in 1897. His focus upon taking office was overseeing and consolidating the bureaucracies of the new city, adjusting the city's budget, and creating some sense of order. He also authorized construction of the city's first underground subway line and began plans for a tunnel under the East River.

A Democrat under the control of Tammany Hall, van Wyck became embroiled in a financial scandal in 1900. Though later cleared of personal involvement, the scandal led to his defeat in the election of 1901 and ended his political career. He moved with his wife to Paris, where he died in 1918.

Saturday, June 18, 1910:
Theodore Roosevelt, Former President

If pre-parade preparations and decorations along with frenzied newspaper reporting are any indication, Theodore Roosevelt may have been the most popular ex-President the country ever had. His accomplishments and activities include, in no particular order: mountain climber, New York City Police Commissioner, Governor of New York State, commander of the Rough Riders in the Spanish American War, winner of the Noble Peace Prize in 1906 for his efforts to end the Russo-Japanese War, historian, author of a naval history of the War of 1812, big game hunter, driving force behind the completion of the Panama Canal, Assistant Secretary of the Navy, Governor of New York, youngest Vice President and, on the death of William McKinley, the youngest President. He served as president from 1901 to 1909 and when he finally left office, he undertook a safari to Africa which provided numerous species of animals and insects to the Museum of Natural History of New York and the Smithsonian Institute. He and his companions on the safari killed or trapped more than 11,000 animals and insects as small as ants and as large as elephants. Although billed as a scientific expedition it had heavy political ramifications which increased when the ex-President extended his trip, left Africa, and visited European countries. He met with royalty and he particularly

24

enthralled Kaiser Wilhelm II of Germany. When Roosevelt announced he was finally returning to America, he sailed on the German liner *Kaiserin Auguste Victoria*. On leaving Europe he compared his time away from the United States as a self-imposed exile and as "a return from Elba."

A group of New York's wealthiest and most influential citizens composed the committee that arranged for his homecoming. He would land at the Battery after a naval review in New York Harbor and a naval parade up the North River (as the Hudson was frequently called at the time). The battleship *South Carolina* and five "torpedo boat destroyers" (*Smith, Flusser, Lamson, Reid* and *Preston*) were provided for the occasion. Passing Fort Jay on Governors Island, the former President would receive a 21-gun salute. Upon landing at Pier A, Roosevelt would be met by Mayor William Gaynor, the committee and other dignitaries. Surrounded by a veritable sea of American flags, he would say a few words and then begin a procession that would move up Broadway to City Hall, and then on to his home at Oyster Bay. The day before the parade the streets were decorated along the route and the *New York Times* printed a special rotogravure supplement featuring Roosevelt and his accomplishments.

June 18 dawned bright and sunny. Roosevelt's arrival ran perfectly according to schedule. The parade began exactly at noon, led by the US Army marching band, followed by 2,000 veterans of the Spanish American War, many in their old uniforms. They were followed by a contingent of 14 carriages, with "Teddy" and his family in the first carriage. The remaining 13 contained members of the President Taft's Cabinet as well as former members of Roosevelt's Cabinet, the governors of more than a dozen states, and mayors of Pittsburgh, Boston, and elsewhere. A group of young men from New Jersey marched next, carrying "the largest American flag ever made" according to newspaper reports that did not give its exact dimensions. They were followed by hundreds of marchers from civic and political organizations.

It was reported that the ex-President passed through the five miles of spectators who lined the route with a smile on his face as he acknowledged what was described as one continuous cheer. At City Hall, Roosevelt expressed delight in the entire event and described it with his characteristic comment "Bully." After leaving City Hall, the band of the Seventh New York National Guard Regiment joined the parade and, at Union Square Park, mounted veterans of the Rough Riders in their distinctive uniforms formed an honor guard around Roosevelt's carriage.

All was running smoothly and according to plan until late afternoon, when nature stepped in to cause serious complications to the proceedings. A violent storm forced the parade to halt shortly after 3 o'clock. Participants scattered or sought shelter, spectators dispersed, and torrential rains poured down driven by gale force winds. The entire storm lasted less than an hour and the rain had become a drizzle in half that time. When the skies cleared, Roosevelt and family returned to Long Island with less fanfare than expected, though the storm had not affected much of his route on Long Island. Later it was learned that the storm had killed 13 New Yorkers, some struck by flying objects, at least one drowned and one blown from a rooftop. The subway system in northern Manhattan was flooded and service would not return to normal for a week. At the Navy Yard in Brooklyn, damage was reported at $50,000 (equivalent to over $1.3 million in 2020 dollars).

Teddy Roosevelt attempted to regain the presidency, running as a third-party candidate with his own Progressive Party in the election of 1912. He came in second behind the Democratic candidate, Woodrow Wilson, and ahead of William Taft on the

Republican ticket. The survivor of an attempted assassination during the campaign, the charismatic Theodore Roosevelt died in early 1919, at the age of 60.

Mayor William Gaynor (1910-1913)

A Roman Catholic born in 1849, William Gaynor initially studied for the priesthood during his youth, but lost faith in organized Christianity before becoming ordained or taking religious vows. He then studied law and entered politics, was appointed a judge and served on the state Supreme Court from 1893-1909, gaining a reputation as a skilled writer of judicial rulings, and as an honest reformer.

Believing they could control him, Tammany Hall nominated Gaynor for mayor in 1909, but soon grew disappointed. As Mayor, he was determined to reform city government, defied Tammany's system of patronage by filling high-level positions with qualified candidates and was a frequent critic of police abuse.

In August 1910, he was shot by a former city employee who had recently lost his job as a dock watchman. Though he recovered, the bullet remained lodged in his throat for the rest of his life. Without Tammany Hall's support for re-election, he decided to run as an independent, but died of a heart attack in September 1913. The three months left in his term were served by Adolph Kline, President of the Board of Aldermen.

Saturday, August 24, 1912:
US Olympians from V Olympic Games

"You are the greatest athlete in the world." So said Sweden's King Gustav V to American athlete Jim Thorpe at the closing ceremony of the fifth Summer Olympics, held in Stockholm, Sweden. Born in 1887 in the territory that later became the state of Oklahoma, Thorpe dominated the track and field events, winning nine of his 15 performances. He also won the decathlon and pentathlon, both first-time events at the 1912 games, which helped the American team win 25 gold medals, more than any other nation, and 63 medals in total, behind only Sweden.

When the athletes returned to the US, sailing into New York City before travelling on to their home states, the city decided to honor them with a celebratory parade. When the announcement was made on August 6, the *New York Times* reported that the event would be "a monster parade" and that President Taft had been invited to attend.

The weather was clear and mild, as the athletes and other marchers gathered just north of 42nd Street on Fifth Avenue. The parade was kicked off at 10 o'clock in the morning by the parade's grand marshal, Brigadier General George Dyer. Behind him came a contingent from the Coast Artillery Corps, followed by veterans of the Spanish-American War, and then a group of 48 Boy Scouts of America, one representing each of the nation's states. Next came an honor guard bearing the American flags that had flown at the Olympic games, followed by the athletes riding in open motor vehicles bearing signs indicating the names of its passengers. Most of the cars held two athletes, but Jim Thorpe rode alone. The athletes were arranged alphabetically, so his car was near the end, but easily recognized by the car ahead of his, which carried the "massive bronze bust of King Gustav Adolphus of Sweden" which he was awarded for winning the first-ever Olympic pentathlon.

Behind the athletes came members of several amateur Athletic Clubs, the Catholic Athletic League, the Young Men's Christian Association, the Bohemian Gymnastic

Association, and the Public Schools Athletic League. Bringing up the rear was the "Swedish delegation," consisting of members of the Stockholm Club of New York, the Swedish American Athletic Club, and about 100 Swedish men and women dressed in national costumes from different periods of Swedish history.

The parade marched down Fifth Avenue from 41st Street to Washington Square. Turning onto Waverly Place, it then continued down Broadway until it reached City Hall. All along the route, "the procession was greeted with greatest enthusiasm" according to the *New York Times*. The *New York Tribune* reported that the 59 athletes "were triumphantly borne through miles of cheering home folk and showered with all the welcome that enthusiastic lungs and waving arms could produce."

A large reviewing stand was set up at City Hall. President Taft had not been able to attend, so Mayor Gaynor reviewed the parade as it arrived in the plaza. The athletes exited their vehicles and formed ranks before the speaker's dais to listen to the Mayor officially welcome them home and praise their performance. After the speech, the plaza was opened to the public to meet the athletes.

That evening, a dinner was held at Terrace Garden for the athletes and 500 guests. Funds raised by the tickets to the dinner were used to pay for the day's events. The next day, members of the team began travelling to their own hometowns.

Like the others, Jim Thorpe returned home, but a year later, a newspaper reported that he had been paid as a minor league baseball player in 1910-1911, and a controversy developed over whether he was a "professional" athlete and therefore not eligible to play at the Olympics. A member of the Sac and Fox Nation, Thorpe wrote a reply saying that he "was simply an Indian schoolboy and did not know" that he had done wrong and that "several other men had done [the same thing], except they did not use their own names." The controversy grew, and newspaper coverage varied from uncharitable to overt racism, reporting how cheating was typical of a "redskin" or "halfbreed." The International Olympic Committee stripped him of his medals, despite his plea that he had been unaware of the rules prohibiting professional athletes from the games.

In 1982, thirty years after his death, the International Olympic Committee agreed to re-investigate the matter. They decided to restore his gold medals, since the complaint about his amateur status was not made within 30 days of the games, as stipulated by the rules, yet he is listed as "co-champion" alongside the runner-up. His children were given commemorative medals, since his original ones had been lost over the years.

By all accounts, the celebratory parade for the 1912 Olympians was a success. The *New York Sun* called it "a pageant worthy to take its place among the greatest of the civic parades ever held in this cosmopolitan city." But was it a ticker tape parade? It is not included on either of the two semi-official lists of ticker tape parades, although the Wikipedia list hs included it for many years, and still does as of 2020. None of the contemporaneous newspaper articles reviewed by the authors mention ticker tape, or anything else falling from the windows of the buildings overlooking the several-mile long parade route along Fifth Avenue, and the photographs included with these articles are too grainy to tell for sure, but do not appear to include ticker tape. It seems likely, therefore, that this event was not a ticker tape parade, however, in an era before such parades became commonplace, paper falling from the sky onto a parade just may not have seemed a newsworthy detail.

John Walter and Mark Walter

CHAPTER 2
The Victors of Versailles (1917-1923)

"War in Europe!" screamed the newspaper headlines in August 1914. Almost 100 years after the battle of Waterloo and the end of the Napoleonic Wars, during which time the major powers in Europe had crafted a balance of power and a complex web of alliances, the assassination of the heir presumptive of the Austro-Hungarian Empire had led to war. The very alliances which were intended to maintain peace dragged first Russia, then Germany, France and Great Britain into what was known then as the Great War, the "war to end all wars." Germany's hope to swiftly defeat France so its armies could turn their attention to Russia ground to a halt in the trenches of northern France and Belgium, and for the next four years, Europeans watched in horror as the scientific and technological advances that had modernized everyday life now ushered in death and destruction. Machine guns, chlorine and mustard gas, barbed wire, shell shock and trench foot, armored cars and tanks, flamethrowers, submarines and even airplanes became the new horrors of war. By the time the war ended in November 1918, over 9 million soldiers and 7 million civilians had died.

The war was immediately followed by the Spanish Flu pandemic, resulting in at least 17 million and possibly as many as 50 million deaths worldwide. Combined with the millions of wounded from the war and non-fatal infections from the flu, the combined toll was so staggering that authors Gertrude Stein and Ernest Hemingway would coin the phrase "the lost generation" to refer to the no-longer innocent youths who came to adulthood during these years. Also lost were several empires, and the map of Europe would never look the same. The Austro-Hungarian Empire was divided into several newly independent countries, while the Russian Empire collapsed and fell into a Civil War that would soon be won by Lenin's Bolshevik Party. The Treaty of Versailles dismantled the German Empire and replaced it with a Republic. Great Britain, France and Belgium took control of Germany's former colonies in Africa and Asia, and the new League of Nations granted the victors mandates to govern areas once part of the Ottoman Empire which disintegrated as the war spread to Palestine, Syria and Mesopotamia.

President Wilson had promised in 1914 to "keep America out of the war," but for New York City, the war was more than just front-page news. The 1910 U.S. Census reported that over 40% of the city's 4.8 million residents were "foreign-born" and 10% more had at least one parent who was born outside the US. As the war began, the city's newspapers serving the immigrant communities began supporting the causes of their former homelands. The German-language *New York Staats-Zeitung* praised the Kaiser, the Slovakian newspaper called for the fall of the Austro-Hungarian Empire, several Yiddish newspapers denounced the anti-Semitism of Tsarist Russia, and the *Gaelic American* newspaper demanded an end to Great Britain's colonial rule over Ireland. The city passed an ordinance banning public demonstrations supporting the warring nations, and in October 1915, Mayor John Mitchel formed a Committee on National Defense, which began monitoring the patriotism of immigrants. The following year, a Preparedness Parade was held after German agents exploded munitions in the harbor, causing damage to many buildings in downtown Manhattan.

The loyalty of New York's immigrant communities came under even more scrutiny after the United States declared war on Germany in April 1917. The city had over 300,000 residents born in Germany and close to as many in Austria-Hungary. The Committee on National Defense began collecting loyalty oaths from "non-citizens," with petitions placed in city offices, hotels and bars, police stations and telegraph offices. Fear of civil disorder increased after rationing led to food riots in Brooklyn. Companies changed their name to demonstrate their loyalty, including the German Savings Bank which became Fulton Savings Bank, the German Life Insurance Company which took the name Guardian Life, and the German Hospital becoming Lenox Hill Hospital.

Many of the 1 million troops that the United States sent to war passed through New York before being shipped to France. "New York has been a garrison town for over a year, and hundreds of thousands of soldiers have filled the streets over the weekends," reported *Vanity Fair* magazine in July 1918, adding "a state of war quickly became habitual to New York." Recruited from all over the country, many of these "doughboys" were seeing big city life for the first time. "How do ya keep 'em down on the farm once they've seen Paree?" asked the lyric of a popular song at the time, but the same question could be posed about New York.

The city was changed by the war, but also by the flu epidemic that followed. One of the earliest cases was an army cook stationed in Camp Funston, Kansas in January 1918. The virus travelled with US troops to Queens, New York, and from there to Europe. It spread rapidly through army camps in France to Italy, Great Britain, Spain and beyond. Spain was neutral during the war, so there was no censorship of news when King Alfonso XIII became gravely ill, leading the first newspaper reports to dub the illness the "Spanish flu." By August, a Norwegian ship docked in New York City with 21 active cases, and though the ship was quarantined, the illness spread. Within a month, the city's first death had been reported, cases were mounting, and hospitals became overrun. Bellevue Hospital had so many patients that cots lined the hallways, and three children were assigned to each bed.

Though initially slow to respond, the city's newly appointed health commissioner, Royal Copeland, was decisive when he finally did react. Businesses were ordered to stagger hours of operation to alleviate congestion in public transportation, and more than 150 temporary neighborhood health centers were set up city-wide. Theaters were allowed to stay open if every show was proceeded with a public health announcement explaining the risk of infection from coughing and sneezing, and city employees were ordered to wear face masks. Most school children at the time lived in crowded tenements, so schools were kept open, both to allow school nurses to watch for early symptoms and also to keep children off the streets where they could infect others. Many apartment buildings installed steam radiators so tenants could keep their windows open and breathe fresh air even in winter, and health inspectors were given authority to close restaurants or food stores with unsanitary storage facilities. By the time the epidemic ended in 1920, more than 33,000 New Yorkers died, though the death rate was lower than in other US cities.

As the 1920s began, New Yorkers were ready for something new. War and the disease were behind them, and prosperity was bound to return. The generals and wartime leaders who had won the "war to make the world safe for democracy" were visiting the United States, sailing through New York harbor *(for example, see: September 8, 1919 and October 3, 1919)*. So too were the leaders trying to prevent future wars *(see: November 18, 1922)*. The city welcomed them with a shower of ticker tape, though the greeting for one person whose work would have an impact on future wars was less enthusiastic *(see: April 2, 1921)*. While it's easy to celebrate victory with a huge parade and tons of ticker tape streaming down upon the conquering heroes, it is harder to recognize and applaud important scientific advances

Wednesday, May 9, 1917: Joseph Joffre, Marshal of France

The United States declared war on the Central Powers of Germany, Austria-Hungary, and Turkey on April 6, 1917. Less than a month later, on May 9, 1917, Joseph Joffre, Marshal of France, accompanied by Rene Viviani, President of the French Council of Ministers and other French military and diplomatic figures arrived in New York City. It was the culmination of a two-week tour through American cities to increase support for the Allied cause against Germany, Austria-Hungary, and the Ottoman Empire.

The visiting French delegation arrived from Philadelphia at the Communipaw Railroad Terminal in Jersey City, where they were by Joseph Choate, the Chairman of the Mayor's Reception Committee. The Marshal wore a dark blue overcoat on the unusually damp and chilly afternoon. Draped over his shoulders was a blue cape, and his red kepi bore the embroidered insignia of Marshal of France. The bright red trousers of the French Army's dress uniform and spotlessly shined black boots completed his attire. Other military members of the delegation were dressed similarly, only their kepi insignia differing from the Marshal's. Mr. Viviani and other members of the French civilian government wore long black coats and top hats. Most were gloved and two carried walking sticks or canes.

Mr. Choate led the group on board the police boat *Patrol* which carried them across the Hudson River to Battery Park. The boat docked at Pier A shortly after 4 o'clock in the afternoon. Thousands of spectators were on hand when the parade began moving up Broadway through the shadows of the approaching sunset. Never before had such a huge crowd of spectators gathered to view a parade. No accurate attendance figures for either the parades for Admiral Dewey *(see: September 30, 1899)* or ex-President Theodore Roosevelt *(see: June 18, 1910)* existed but reporters and city officials were unanimous in calling this the largest gathering to date.

As the parade moved up Broadway, the Marshal pointed with delight to the height of the buildings in downtown Manhattan. When ticker tape began to swirl, he smiled broadly, pointing to the cascading paper. Mr. Viviani, seated next to him, soon had strands of ticker tape falling on his hat and in his lap. He tried, without success, to brush them off his hat. The officers and diplomats in the following vehicles were soon showing their amusement at the tumultuous welcome. A short distance from City Hall, a cold drizzle began to fall but it failed to dampen the enthusiasm of the parade's participants or its viewers.

Waiting at City Hall was Mayor John Mitchel, a group of city officials, and representing the armed forces, Major Generals Leonard Wood and J. Franklin Bell and Rear Admiral Nathaniel Usher. When the car carrying the Marshal braked to a halt at the steps of City Hall, the American military representatives snapped to attention and saluted smartly. Mr. Choate formerly introduced the members of the French party to the mayor and others. With the drizzle suddenly turning into a steady rain, everyone walked up the City Hall steps and entered the Aldermanic Chambers.

Mayor Mitchel spoke of the debt the United States owed to France since the American Revolution when leaders like the Marquis de Lafayette and Françoise de Grasse helped the United States achieve independence through victory. The mayor added that America's entry into the Great War was one small payment for that debt.

Responding to the mayor's remarks in English, Mr. Viviani spoke of the bond of friendship between the two nations and said that he looked forward to the day when American, French, and other Allied forces would fight side by side and bring an end to the scourge of the war then ravishing Europe. The Marshal smiled through the speeches of both men, then stood and acknowledged the cheers of the hundreds gathered in the Chamber by touching the brim on his kepi in salute. As those in attendance began to chant his name, he raised his hand to silence them, stepped to the mayor and in true Gallic fashion, kissed him on both cheeks. Then he turned to face the audience again and said simply, "I thank you."

Darkness had fallen by the time the reception at City Hall concluded. A dinner at the Waldorf Astoria followed. The Marshal was joined there by French Vice Admiral Paul Chocheprat who had arrived in the city the previous day. In attendance were members of the Old Guard Infantry and the Veteran Corps of Artillery, the units of the American military with the longest continuous service, wearing Revolutionary War style uniforms and accouterments.

The following day began for the French party at Prospect Park in Brooklyn, where they laid a wreath at the Soldiers and Sailors Arch at Grand Army Plaza and concluded with a visit to Grant's Tomb where another wreath was laid. Mr. Arthur Balfour, representing the British Commission visiting the United States, joined the French group the following day, and on Saturday, May 12, both the French and British parties sailed back to Europe. The name of their ship and the exact date of their departure were not released to the press to prevent German spies from somehow contacting German submarines and attacking it.

In 1918 the Marshal was named leader of the Supreme War Council to better coordinate the activities of Allied forces. The Great War ended in November 1918. Joffre retired from the Army in 1919 and was made a member of the Académie Française.

The Marshal returned to New York in 1922 at the end of cross-country tour of the United States. Arriving from Washington via train. A large crowd waited at Pennsylvania Station to give him an "enthusiastic, unofficial greeting" and was met there by Major Ulysses Grant III, grandson of the late Civil War general and President. He was driven in a police-escorted motorcade to City Hall, and "although the route had not previously been announced, passers-by halted and applauded or waved as the procession sped by," according to the *New York Times*. Mayor Hylan welcomed the Marshal back to the city, led him into the Aldermanic Chamber, and presented him with Freedom of the City in front of a crowd of 700 guests. After some speeches, the Marshal retired for the evening at the Hotel Plaza, cancelling a scheduled appearance at a reception at the Seventh Regiment Armory. He spent several days in the city before returning to France.

The Marshal died in Paris in 1931 at the age of 78. He was buried on his estate in Louveciennes, now a suburb of Paris.

Mayor John Mitchel (1914-1917)

An Irish Catholic born in 1879, John Mitchel studied at Columbia University and New York Law School, and in 1906 started working at the US Customs Office. An anti-Tammany reformer, he served as counsel during several investigations into government inefficiency and incompetence, earning a reputation for honesty and professionalism. He joined the Republican party and was elected to the Board of Aldermen. In 1909 he became its President, and enacted fiscal reforms to cut waste and improve accounting practices.

In 1910, Mitchel served as Acting Mayor for six weeks while Mayor Gaynor recovered from injuries sustained in an assassination attempt. Running for Mayor In 1913, Mitchel promised to modernize and streamline city government, leading to an easy victory in an era of anti-Tammany sentiment. He was only 34 years old, and the press often referred to him as the "Boy Mayor."

As Mayor, Mitchel continued his focus on reform, especially in the Police Department and the Board of Education. The popularity of his fiscal policies began to wane when he tried cutting teacher salaries and because of his pro-military positions as the war in Europe dragged on. He lost the Republican Primary for Mayor in 1917 but ran for re-election as a pro-war Fusion Party candidate. Despite support from former President Theodore Roosevelt, he lost to the Democratic candidate in a landslide.

After leaving City Hall, Mitchel joined the Army, completed training as a cadet in the new Air Service, and was promoted to Major. During a training flight in Louisiana in July 1918, his plane stalled and began to nosedive, and he fell to his death. The US Army named its new airstrip in Hempstead, Long Island "Mitchel Field" in his memory.

Monday, September 8, 1919:
General John Pershing

The troop ship *Leviathan* made its way slowly through the Verrazano Narrows and into New York Harbor. A flight of Army biplanes suddenly appeared in the east and, in perfect formation, zoomed low over the ship. As they flew overhead, they dropped hundreds of notes that fell like snow onto the deck of the liner. Written by politicians, business leaders, committees, veterans, and average citizens, the notes were letters of welcome and congratulations to the most important passenger of the 1,500 returning American servicemen aboard the liner. That man, General John Pershing, commander of American troops in the Great War, was shocked, surprised, and slightly embarrassed by the welcome and the sight of Doughboys scampering about the deck retrieving the notes as souvenirs.

A 17-gun salute from Fort Wadsworth, Staten Island, boomed and echoed as the *Leviathan* moored at its dock in Hoboken, New Jersey. Army bands played patriotic and military tunes as the 59-year-old general disembarked and was met by Deputy Police Commissioner Rodman Wanamaker, Chairman of the Mayor's Committee on the Reception of Distinguished Guests. The general was escorted to the police boat *Patrol,* which set out immediately and cut its way across the Hudson River into the harbor and towards the Battery. Every ship, boat, tug, freighter, ferry, and yacht in the harbor sounded a welcome with their horns and whistles, and the sound they produced was unlike anything ever heard in the city before. Old-time New Yorkers swore it was louder than the welcome 20 years earlier for Admiral Dewey *(see: September. 30, 1899).*

The *Patrol* docked at Pier A. Newton Baker, Secretary of War, was the first to extend his hand in welcome to the general as another military band played. More than 3,000 soldiers, sailors, and civilians stood, ready to escort the general up Broadway to City Hall. General Pershing's horse, Kidron, was there, nervously shuffling its feet amid the noise and confusion. The general, a skilled and life-long horseman, easily quieted the animal. His first assignment after graduating from West Point in 1886 was in the Sixth Cavalry, stationed at Fort Bayard in the New Mexico Territory, where he took part in the last of the Indian Campaigns against Apaches and in 1890 against the Lakota Sioux. The general grasped the pommel and, with one easy motion, mounted Kidron. With a blare of bugles and ruffling drums, the parade set out.

If the snowfall of notes dropped on the *Leviathan* had surprised the general, the blizzard of ticker tape that descended as he rode up Broadway stunned him. Streamers danced through the air and wrapped around telephone and light poles, ledges, cornices, and marchers alike. A few days earlier the city had gone through a minor panic in fear that there would not be enough flags and bunting to decorate the route perfectly. The countless flags indicated that whatever shortage there might have been had been resolved. General Pershing saluted time after time at flags to his right and left, only occasionally stopping to remove strips of ticker tape from himself or from Kidron.

The number of spectators was beyond count. They lined both sides of Broadway, in places four or five deep. Many waved small flags. Some, discharged veterans, wore their uniforms and saluted their former commanding officer. Other spectators wore the gold-starred black armband indicating the loss of a loved one. Every available space in City Hall Park was filled and people were seen at the windows of the surrounding buildings. Some had even climbed trees in the park for a better view.

After General Pershing dismounted, he joined the Mayor, Secretary of War, and others on the reviewing stand erected in front of City Hall. Secretary Newton read a personal message of welcome from President Wilson and then commissioned the general to the Army's highest rank, General of the Armies. This lifetime rank had been held previously by only four men, Generals Washington, Grant, Sherman, and Sheridan. The mayor expressed the city's welcome and thanked General Pershing for being instrumental in bringing about the end of the War the previous November. In response, the General humbly took no credit for victory and said that the fighting men of his command and those at home who supported them, deserved it all. He remembered those who remained in France, buried in foreign soil, vowing that they will never be forgotten, and challenged all Americans to be mindful of their sacrifices.

Following the City Hall reception, the parade continued to Union Square. The general spoke briefly there as well but refused to answer any questions about the Peace Conference in France and his future plans, especially any political ambitions. That afternoon he met with his family at the Waldorf Astoria, where he remained the rest of the day, dining in his hotel suite.

The next morning an announcement signed by Grover Whalen, Vice Chairman of the Reception Committee, appeared in newspapers. It stated that the reception planned for that evening sponsored by the George Washington Memorial Association at Carnegie Hall was cancelled due to over-subscription, and that all who purchased tickets would be reimbursed. It added that other events planned for the general would however be held as scheduled. At the first of these events, General Pershing spoke in Central Park to a crowd estimated at more than 25,000, aiming his words at the younger members of the assembly. He said that, if war ever again calls for American involvement, they should be prepared to serve proudly. The following day the General led the entire First Division in a military review along Fifth Avenue from Central Park to Washington Square. The *Saturday Evening Post* called it a "parade that breaks all records," and according to the *New York Sun*, "30,000 men and all the panoply of modern war pranced and strode and rumbled and roared, even flew overhead, down Fifth Avenue."

General Pershing retired from active service in 1923 and later formed the Reserve Officers Association. His memoir *My Experience in the World War* was awarded the Pulitzer Prize for history in 1932. In 1940 he spoke out against America's neutrality and urged the country to enter the war to aid Great Britain. In 1944 he was confined to the Walter Reed Military Hospital for coronary problems and remained there until his death in 1948. He is buried in Arlington National Cemetery with only a simple military headstone marking his grave.

Mayor John Hylan (1918-1925)

Born in 1868 in Hunter, New York, John Francis Hylan moved to New York at the age of 19 and got a job with the Brooklyn Union Elevated Railroad. He worked there in various jobs over the next decade, putting himself through night school and then law school, and passed the bar exam in 1897. He then worked at a legal firm in Brooklyn for eight years, making connections at the Court House, joining the Democratic Party and making his way up the party's ranks.

In 1917, the Democratic party nominated Hylan for mayor, and he defeated Republican Mayor Mitchel and two Fusion party candidates. He easily went on to re-election in 1921, campaigning to maintain the five-cent subway fare. His administration helped launch the Independent Subway System, and he often gave speeches against the "special interests" that had unfair influence over the city bureaucracy. In retaliation, Tammany's bosses decided to replace him on the party's ticket in 1925. After leaving City Hall, Hylan was appointed judge of the Queen's Children Court, where he served for 10 years. He died of a heart attack in 1936.

Friday, October 3, 1919:
King Albert and Queen Elisabeth of Belgium

When German troops crossed the borders of Belgium on August 4, 1914 their violation of Belgium's neutrality was one of many steps that escalated the conflict into the four-year Great War that spread through much of the world. Rather than surrender the small nation unfortunate enough to be between the advancing German armies and the northern regions of France, King Albert Leopold Clement Marie Meinhard continued to fight. Much of Belgium's 43,000-man army was quickly destroyed but Albert refused to surrender. He rallied his troops and recruited replacements but was forced to retreat and yield most of his nation to Germany. In the tiny portion that never fell to the Germans some of the fiercest and bloodiest battles of that War were fought at Ypres and Paschendaele. But Albert never gave in, his nation never yielded, and in November 1918, after the fighting ended in Europe, he returned to Brussels, Belgium's capital, and began the extensive task of rebuilding his war-ravaged country.

Not quite a year later King Albert I and his wife, Queen Elisabeth arrived in the United States with their oldest son, Prince Leopold, to meet with President Wilson and tour several American cities. The Royal Couple arrived in New York on board the liner *George Washington* on October 2, 1919 having first visited California, Arizona, and New Mexico and then sailing from New Orleans. They were met by Rodman Wanamaker, Chairman of the Reception Committee, and Mr. Breckenridge Long, Third Assistant Secretary of State. It was Mr. Long's task to inform His Majesty that President Wilson was seriously ill and was forced to cancel many of his appointments (it was not revealed until years later that the president had suffered a series of strokes, one on September 27, 1919 while riding in his special train carriage from Washington to New York in order to meet the King). The King was informed that Mr. Wilson had returned to Washington and was under doctor's orders not to receive visitors. King Albert thanked Mr. Long and advised him that he would modify his plans accordingly.

After disembarking, the Royal Couple were escorted to their suite at the Waldorf Astoria. At 10 o'clock the following morning, Mr. Wanamaker and Mr. Long arrived and, with a motorcycle police escort, brought the Royal Family to the pier on West 46th Street where Mr. Wanamaker's yacht, the *Noma*, was moored. A tour of the harbor had not been scheduled as part of the activities, but the King agreed that it would be a nice way to start the day. The yacht, formerly owned by Vincent Astor, sailed down the Hudson River, passing docked liners, cargo ships, freighters, and circling around tugboats and smaller vessels. The Belgian flag and the King's personal flag flapped from the stern of the *Noma* and every vessel the yacht sailed by raised a salute with horns, bells, whistles, or dipped colors.

At the Battery, the Fire Department band played "Over There" as the *Noma* docked at Pier A. King Albert was observed humming the tune as they stepped ashore and soon Queen Elisabeth could be seen swaying her head in time with the George M. Cohan tune. The King and Mr. Wanamaker entered the first flag-bedecked touring car, Queen Elisabeth and Mr. Long the second. Prince Leopold and a military aide rode in the third car and the fourth was occupied by the Belgian Ambassador to the United States, the Baron Emile de Cartier de Marchienne and his wife. The 22nd US Infantry band from Fort Jay led off the parade exactly at noon. A battalion of the regiment marched along with detachments of Coast Artillery from Forts Hamilton, Totten, and Schuyler, as well as nine companies of sailors and marines. Immediately behind the motorcade came the naval band from the battleship *Arizona*, recently honored as "Best in the Fleet." Bringing up the rear were 30 mounted policemen.

The King and Queen seemed truly moved by the display of emotion shown as they proceeded towards City Hall. They waved, pointed, and clapped in response to cheers, applause, and a constant stream of ticker tape and torn paper. Mayor Hylan greeted the Royal Family at City Hall and led them into the Aldermanic Chambers. The room had never been so crowded, filled with almost 500 people cheering as the King entered. After the Street Cleaning Department band played the American and Belgian National Anthems, Mr. Wanamaker formally introduced the mayor to the king and queen.

Mayor Hylan referred to the king as "the soldier-sovereign" and praised his courage and unselfish devotion to liberty and the independence of his people. The king was presented with a scroll commemorating his visit and extolling his actions. He was then given a silk American flag which the mayor draped over the sovereign's shoulders. The king was informed that the flag had flown at General Pershing's headquarters during the final days of the War. Before making a short speech, the king brought the flag to his lips and kissed it in appreciation of America's role in defeating Germany.

King Albert briefly described the damage to his country and recounted how it had already begun rebuilding. He spoke about a new Belgium "rising from the ashes of war" and hoped that the lesson of the Great War would be the end of all war. His words were met with thunderous applause before the reception ended. A late luncheon at the Waldorf followed.

During the next two days the King and Queen visited a number of sites in the city, traveling incognito to see the Statue of Liberty and Grant's Tomb and on the second day, the grave of Theodore Roosevelt in Oyster Bay, New York. Dressed as wealthy tourists, only a handful of people recognized them or noticed the small group of plain-clothes police guarding them. At the end of the two days King Albert announced that because of the president's illness he was cutting short his visit and would only briefly visit Boston and Buffalo, canceling his plans to visit Washington, Baltimore, and Chicago.

The Royal Family returned to Belgium in early November where the king worked tirelessly to restore his war-ravaged country. He was instrumental in efforts to rebuild many of the country's ruined cities, revitalized the economy, and brought about universal suffrage to his people. He was a life-long hiker, camper, and mountaineer. On February 17, 1934, while climbing the Roche du Vieux Bon Dieu in the Ardennes near Namur, Belgium, he fell, struck his head on a rock, and died. Albert was interred in the Church of Our Lady of Laeken, Brussels. His son, Leopold, assumed the throne as Leopold I. King Albert's wife, Elisabeth, did not pass away until 1965 at the age of 89 and was interred beside her husband.

The Aldermanic Chamber

New York City's legislature has evolved several times over the centuries. Established by a State Act in 1824, it had two chambers, the Board of Aldermen and the Board of Assistants. The latter was dissolved in 1875, and for two decades the city had a unicameral Board of Aldermen, with 27 members elected for one-year terms. They held their sessions in a chamber on the first floor of the east wing of City Hall.

A new city charter was adopted during the Consolidation in 1898, which re-established a bicameral legislature. The Board of Aldermen became the lower chamber, with a newly created City Council as the upper. A revision in 1902 eliminated the City Council, and the once-again unicameral Board of Aldermen had 73 members serving two-year terms, though the number of seats was soon reduced to 65. The President of the Board was elected directly by voters, rather than the other Aldermen, for a four-year term. This structure remained in effect until another new charter was adopted in 1938.

By increasing the size of the legislative body, the city's Consolidation in 1897 created the need for a new chamber for their sessions. Two former court rooms on the second floor of the east wing of City Hall were gutted to create the new Aldermanic Chamber. Mahogany walls with a decorative plaster ceiling were added, as was a horseshoe-shaped spectator's gallery and an ornately carved desk for the presiding officer. The chamber was finished in time for the Board to meet there in 1898, though the ceiling was not finished until 1903. The room can hold upwards of 400 guests and is used for ceremonies when the Council is not in session.

Tuesday, November 18, 1919:
Edward Albert, Prince of Wales

The Prince of Wales, heir apparent to the British throne, Edward Albert George Andrew Patrick David, arrived in Jersey City by train. The handsome 25-year-old Prince made New York City the last stop during his goodwill visit to the United States. With the first anniversary of the armistice that ended the Great War in Western Europe a week past, the Prince was visiting a number of Allied nations in gratitude for assisting in the defeat of Germany, in keeping with the wishes of his father, King George V.

There had been death threats from members of the Irish Republican Army (IRA) and other anti-British groups prior to the prince's arrival. Some were delivered through the mail, crude, barely legible and often unsigned predictions of bombs or bullets. The police took more seriously the rumors of assassination, untraceable tales told in saloons and in tenements. As a precaution extra police were assigned to duty for the prince's protection. Included among the security were members of the Broadway Squad, the Police Department's elite unit composed of burly, muscular men, all at least six feet tall. Mayor Hylan had been against offering an official reception to the Prince, partly out of concern for his security, but also because of the Mayor's personal pro-Irish, anti-English views. He had been persuaded to extend the welcome only days before at a meeting in the office of Grover Whalen, chosen to be the city's host to the Prince. The meeting was attended by State Department officials, and representatives from Buckingham Palace, Scotland Yard, and the New York Police Department.

Grover Whalen and State Department officials greeted the Prince as he exited the train. The party boarded a borrowed Police Department boat and proceeded across the Hudson River to Pier A at the Battery. This boat would be used often, and the city was at a loss as to what its name should be. Finally, Grover Whalen suggested taking the words "Mayor's Committee" and combining them into one word: *Macom*. Under this name the steamer took part in many official welcomes thereafter.

Every ship in the harbor saluted the Prince with a symphony of horns, bells, and whistles. The Prince stood and admired the view, pointing towards the Statue of Liberty and the tall buildings that towered beyond the Battery. Cannon in Fort Jay on Governors Island roared a salute as the Prince stepped ashore and saluted the flags of the United States and United Kingdom flying side by side.

Detachments of the Army, Navy, Marine Corps, and Coast Guard, along with uniformed members of the Police, Fire, and Street Cleaning Departments stood ready to escort the Prince up Broadway. Bands from the Army and the Navy walked in front of and to the rear of the motorcade of vehicles taking part in the parade. The city's plans, formulated and organized by Mr. Whalen, were for the welcome to be on a scale unlike previous parades. Ticker tape had been part of the New York City welcome since its spontaneous use at the dedication of the Statue of Liberty *(see: October 28, 1886)*, and as recently as six weeks earlier when the King and Queen of Belgium visited *(see: October 3, 1919)* ticker tape had fallen during their parade. But Mr. Whalen planned to make the Prince's welcome more memorable. He met with officers of the shipping companies, banks, insurance firms and brokerage houses lining Broadway and suggested that the more ticker tape that rained down on the visitors the better it would be for the prestige of the city and, indirectly, for business.

As the parade started up Broadway it was evident that Mr. Whalen's suggestion worked wonders. Ticker tape in vast streams and bundles flew down. Not only did slender threads of ticker tape descend from the buildings along Broadway, but also torn newspapers and telephone directories. The large black convertible the Prince rode in was decorated with paper, and Prince Edward was delighted by the spectacle. He smiled and laughed, commenting to Mr. Whalen that it was "all great fun." He pointed to handmade signs of welcome, to the clusters of spectators cheering for him, and to the flags fluttering from every flagpole along the route.

At City Hall Plaza the Prince was greeted by Mayor Hylan. Because of the mayor's known pro-Irish sentiments, his remarks had been read and approved by both the State Department and the officials from Buckingham Palace The mayor extended Freedom of the City to the Prince throughout his three-day visit and hoped he would find the city so welcoming that he would return frequently. In the Aldermanic Chambers, the Prince responded that the welcome was "wonderful beyond belief" and that he planned to see as much of the city as possible during his short stay.

Immediately after the City Hall ceremony, the Prince was driven to the Waldorf Astoria guarded by a large police escort. Earlier in the day before the Prince arrived, a few protestors had been observed at City Hall carrying signs and placards advising the Prince to go home (or somewhere considerably hotter) but the Broadway Squad kept them from getting too close to His Highness. Other such groups were encountered on the way uptown, but they too were hustled away, possibly without being noticed by the Prince.

That evening the Prince visited the Metropolitan Opera House for a command performance in his honor. Hours before warnings of a bomb at the Opera House had been received and the entire building had been searched from top to bottom, disrupting rehearsals but finding no explosives. The featured star was Enrico Caruso who led a performance of the first act of *Pagliacci*. The Prince was so moved by the opera and its cast that he requested and received an encore.

The English battle-cruiser *Renown* had arrived at New York two days earlier and the Prince resided on it as it rode at anchor in the Hudson River. During the remainder of his visit, the Prince visited Grant's Tomb, the Statue of Liberty, and Central Park, which he thought superior to Hyde Park in London. The Prince then returned to England on the *Renown*.

King George V died on January 30, 1936, and his eldest son ascended the throne as King Edward VIII. Still unmarried, Edward had previously scandalized his family and the British government with his affairs and liaisons. Shortly before his father died, Edward privately announced his engagement to a twice-divorced American, Wallis Simpson. His plans to marry her caused a constitutional crisis for Great Britain. He was informed by the Archbishop of Canterbury that the Church of England could not sanctify a marriage with Mrs. Simpson. His own cabinet and the Prime Ministers of Canada, Australia, and South Africa, all members of the British Commonwealth, advised him that they were opposed to his planned marriage.

Faced with opposition from both inside and outside of his government, Edward VIII abdicated the throne and his brother Albert ascended to the throne as King George VI, and Edward was given the title Duke of Windsor. He married Wallis Simpson in a private ceremony on June 3, 1937, near Tours, France, but members of his family were forbidden to attend the ceremony by his brother, the King.

When the Second World War began the Duke and Duchess of Windsor were living in France and Edward was commissioned a major-general in the British Army. He had previously met Adolf Hitler and had spoken highly of the German leader and Nazism. When France was occupied by German troops, he and Mrs. Simpson moved first to

Spain and then Portugal, where he publicly expressed doubts about English victory. Finally, threatened with a court-martial at home, he was ordered to the British colony of Bahamas where, according to Winston Churchill, "he can do the least damage to the British war effort."

After the war, the Duke and Duchess of Windsor returned to France. For the remainder of their lives, they shuttled between Paris and New York City, were considered celebrities and were constant guests at parties, receptions, and balls, but never with members of the Royal family. A heavy smoker throughout his life, Edward died of throat cancer in May 1972. He is buried in the Royal Burial Ground at Westminster Cathedral, behind the grave of his grandmother, Queen Victoria. His wife died 14 years later and is buried beside him, her tombstone reading simply, "Wallis, Duchess of Windsor."

SS *Macom*

In 1919, the Mayor's Committee for the Reception of Distinguished Guests decided the city needed an official ship to greet guests sailing into New York harbor. They commandeered a police tugboat named Patrol, which had been built in Maryland in 1894. Berthed at Pier A, the ship was renamed *Macom*, formed from the first syllables of the name of the committee which she served from 1919 until 1934. The ship had an eight-man crew, and her only captain during this period was William Hamilton.

A yacht would have been more suitable for transporting VIP guests, so in 1920 Rodman Wanamaker paid $30,000 to refurbish the tug, adding accoutrements like wicker chairs under an awning on the aft deck, two interior saloons with upholstered furnishings, and a radio room at the top of a curved staircase with a hand-cut balustrade. Wiring and microphones for broadcasting to local radio stations were installed, and in 1930, the Federal Radio Commission granted a license allowing broadcast directly from the ship. Rarely used except by the Mayor's Reception Committee, she was considered the "queen of the harbor" whenever she sailed, and all other craft in the bay would salute her.

In 1934, incoming mayor Fiorello LaGuardia decided the $35,000 annual cost to maintain the *Macom* could not be justified in the Depression, and ordered the ship drydocked and stripped of its furnishings. The silverware and table service were sent to Gracie Mansion. In 1944, *Macom* was bought by tugboat magnate Joseph Moran for $3,150. Renamed the *James J. Walker*, she was put into service around Manhattan for a new company called Circle Line Sightseeing.

Saturday, April 2, 1921:
Albert Einstein and Dr. Chaim Weizmann

"Can you explain, in simple terms, your theory of relativity?"

That question was asked repeatedly by reporters during Albert Einstein's first visit to the United States in the spring of 1921. His journey was announced in late February and was proceeded by excited reporting in the press. Accompanied by his wife Elsa and Dr. Chaim Weizmann, President of the Zionist World Organization, the scientist had three reasons for his visit: academic lectures about his theories, fundraising for a hoped-for Jewish University in Jerusalem, and support of Zionist causes.

Mayor Hylan formed a Reception Committee, chaired by Nathan Straus, co-owner of two of the city's largest department stores, and consisting of prominent New Yorkers, several of them Jewish. The committee "requested that all Jewish sections of the city be decorated in honor of the visitors" and planned an official greeting at City Hall on Tuesday, April 5.

Arriving four hours behind schedule, the *Rotterdam* sailed into New York Harbor on April 2. She was met by the police boat *John F Hylan*, flying "Jewish flags of white with two blue bars" and carrying the members of the Reception Committee. Wearing a faded gray raincoat and carrying his violin, Einstein answered questions from reporters as the boat sailed toward the Battery. A crowd of several hundred had been waiting there for hours, and loud cheers were raised as the police boat approached.

Dozens of automobiles waited at Pier A for the guests and the Reception Committee. According to the book *Albert Meets America*, it was some time before the police could clear the road for the procession, which headed for the Lower East Side before proceeding up Second Avenue to the Commodore Hotel on 42nd Street.

The streets in the Lower East Side and along Second Avenue were packed, and the caravan and its police escort moved uptown slowly. "After a long and noisy procession," the *Jewish Independent* reported, "the delegation arrived at the Hotel Commodore shortly before midnight." The same report goes on to mention that "to land at the Battery and not on the wharves above Greenwich Village is characteristic of grand receptions" and compares Einstein's arrival with that of "celebrities to whom the mayor of New York, in a snowstorm of ticker tape, gave the Freedom of the City." The only difference, it notes, is that "in this case, the snowstorm of ticker tape was replaced by little American and Zionist flags."

Einstein's official reception in New York took place at City Hall on Tuesday, April 5, and Mayor Hylan was set to greet him and bestow Freedom of the City to him and Dr. Weizmann. According to the daily Jewish newspaper the *Yidishes Tageblat*, the Reception Committee escorted Einstein and Dr. Weizmann from their hotel to City Hall. The ceremony would take place in the Aldermanic Chamber, but speeches were made on the steps of City Hall "in view of the wide-spread desire to witness the event." The *Times* estimated that as many as 5,000 spectators filled City Hall Park, while the *New York American* estimated that 10,000 people were there, and that "it took the greatest effort" for the police to "prevent the crowd from surging in around the autos."

The Mayor welcomed the party and made a speech praising the German-Jewish community in New York, especially during the recent war against their former homeland, adding that Einstein was "the greatest scientist since Copernicus." Dr. Weizmann then gave his first public speech in New York, in which he appealed for help in the "material and spiritual rebuilding of the Jewish homeland." Throughout the speeches, Einstein listened and seemed to drift off with a distant bewildered expression.

The party moved into the Aldermanic Chamber, where the plans to bestow the city's Freedom fell apart. As the resolution was being read, Alderman Bruce Falconer raised an objection, claiming he knew nothing about the two men about to receive this honor.

According to the *New York Call*, the chambers erupted with laughter and protests. Other members tried in vain to persuade Falconer to retract his objection. Claims of anti-Semitism were hurled, and the meeting devolved into an argument when the Rules Committee suggested waiving the need for unanimous consent to the resolution. Viewers in the chamber balcony became heated, and at least one fist fight broke out before the police cleared the chamber. At an impasse, the Aldermen adjourned without passing the Resolution.

The next day, the New York State Senate adopted a resolution granting both Einstein and Weizmann "Freedom of the State," and on Friday April 8, the city Board of Aldermen met again. Several members gave impassioned speeches calling Falconer a 'bigot" and a "disgrace to the city." In his response, Falconer said that Einstein was German and therefore "an enemy alien," adding that the Freedom of the City had been bestowed too often on foreign visitors. He said the city had become embroiled in foreign affairs, closing that "America is for Americans. America first."

The resolution passed by 56 to 1, and the city's Freedom was finally bestowed on Einstein. The Aldermen also passed a resolution denouncing Falconer's "bigotry, narrow-mindedness and intolerance" and that he was "a champion of anti-Semitism, which is only a stepchild of anti-Americanism."

Einstein remained in New York for several more days, visiting Columbia University and the City University of New York, and giving a standing-room-only lecture at the Metropolitan Opera House on Sunday April 10, before departing for Chicago.

Einstein returned to New York in December 1930. On December 13, Mayor Walker greeted him at City Hall, and in a ceremony that lasted 30 minutes, presented him with the Keys to the City. In his speech, the Mayor referred to the 1921 visit and the honors that "were never delivered" then. He added that there are no real keys to the city, but that Einstein had won "the keys to our hearts and our imaginations."

Trained as a chemist, Weizmann is sometimes considered the father of industrial fermentation, and his work led to improved explosives used during World War I. He was a major leader in Zionist causes during World War II, meeting with both British Prime Minister Winston Churchill and President Franklin Roosevelt to discuss the Holocaust and the creation of a Jewish state in Palestine. When the state of Israel was created in 1948, he became its first President, serving until his death in 1952.

Albert Einstein revolutionized physics with his theory of relativity, though he is probably best known for his famous equation $E=mC^2$, which explained the potential of atomic energy. He was visiting the United States in 1932 when the Nazi Party took power in Germany; he refused to return to Europe and became a US citizen in 1940. In 1939, he warned President Franklin Roosevelt that the Germans were working on developing a nuclear weapon, leading the President to authorize the Manhattan Project. After the first atomic bomb was dropped on Hiroshima, Einstein denounced the use of nuclear fission as a weapon. He died in Princeton, New Jersey, in 1955.

Einstein never received a ticker tape parade, and to date, no scientist has ever been awarded one, though another scientist declined the honor (see: April 21, 1955). The newspaper reports of the caravan through the Lower East Side mention the absence of ticker tape, and the only known photograph of the caravan supports this. The Reception Committee had planned for the Mayor to greet Einstein at City Hall several days after his arrival in the city, unlike other guests who were paraded up Broadway on the way to City Hall. The debates in the Aldermanic Chambers on both April 5 and April 8 focus on whether to grant Freedom of the City, not whether a parade should be held. Bruce Falconer, a Republican whose district covered east Manhattan near Central Park, served on the city's Board of Aldermen from 1918 to 1925. Over the years, he objected to granting Freedom of the City many times and was involved in several fist fights with his colleagues. He was ousted by Republican leaders in 1925 in favor of Ruth Platt, who was the first woman to serve in the city's legislature.

Wednesday, October 19, 1921:
General Armando Diaz, Chief of Staff of the Italian Army

As the Italian ocean liner *Giuseppe Verdi* arrived at Quarantine, it was met by a flotilla of United States destroyers to honor its most distinguished passenger, General Armando Diaz, commander-in-chief of the Italian Armies in the final year of the Great War. Steaming into the harbor the liner was met by the Army tug *Lexington* and the ferries *Mayor Gaynor* and *Correction*. Crowded on the ferries was the Second Corps band and dozens of dignitaries from the state and city of New York and Italian societies and organizations. The *Giuseppe Verdi* listed noticeably to port as the Reception Committee, chaired by Grover Whalen, was transferred aboard to meet the short, stocky 59-year-old Italian general. He was accompanied by Alton Roberts and William Deegan, representing the American Legion, State Senator Salvatore Cotillo, the Italian Consul-General to New York Themistocles Bernadi, and United States General George Wingate. After the Reception Committee exchanged a few words (translated by his aide, Italian General Kennedy DeLuca, who had resided in New Orleans a number of years before the War), they returned to the Army tug for the final leg of the journey to the waiting reception. A 17-gun salute sounded from Fort Jay and a battalion of tin helmeted soldiers presented arms in salute from the shore of Governors Island.

Disembarking at Pier A, the general was greeted by a loud cheer of "*Viva!*" from the thousands of spectators packed in Battery Park. The Italian and American national anthems were played. The general and Reception Committee passed between two rows of American soldiers also presenting arms. The General touched the brim of his cap in answering salute. As he and members of the Reception Committee stepped into a waiting open convertible, a large number of overly enthusiastic spectators broke through the police line and nearly reached the vehicle before being stopped.

The parade up Broadway began when the crowds were cleared. More than 700,000 people waved, cheered, and shouted along the route. More small Italian flags than American were obvious in the crowd, and surges of people frequently broke through police lines and raced for the General's car. A number of them were almost trampled by the horses of the mounted police escort. An even larger crowd of on-lookers waited at City Hall Plaza and again it took the efforts of mounted police to control them.

Waiting at City Hall was Lieutenant-Governor Jeremiah Wood and Mayor John Hylan. Mr. Wood welcomed the general to the United States and called him the "Hero of the Plave, destroyer of Austria's unholy ambitions, and distinguished soldier of Italy." General Diaz was introduced to the mayor by Rodman Wanamaker from the Reception Committee. The mayor then introduced General Diaz to the crowds, saying it was his honor to offer a "cordial and hearty welcome" to a man who had distinguished himself "not only as a soldier but as a statesman and diplomat."

General Diaz replied in English, his words briefly interrupted by an incident at the rear of the crowd. Police were arresting a 22-year-old veteran of the Italian Army, Pizzuti Coria, who had torn an American flag from a pole and was seen trampling it and shouting oaths against the United States. The swift action by the police saved the life of the young man who was in danger of being torn apart the crowd. Two months later Coria was found guilty of disrespecting the flag and creating a public nuisance, and he was deported to Italy.

The General resumed his speech once order had been restored. He gave his thanks and spoke of his impression of New York. "My reception today reminded me of

Naples, which is the most expansive city in the world. The spirit of the American people is the same spirit of Italy, and if it were not for the difference in language, I would imagine myself back in Naples…I saw the same faith in the eyes of Italians and Italian Americans as I saw in the eyes of Italian soldiers going into battle."

Mayor Hylan presented General Diaz with the City's Medal of Honor and provided him with the Freedom of the City, adding that the city was proud of its vast Italian population.

Police reserves cleared a path through the crowd and the Italian commander entered a sedan for the drive to the Ritz-Carlton Hotel. Sidewalks along the entire route were filled with cheering people. That night he was the guest of honor at a dinner hosted by the American Legion at the Vanderbilt Hotel. The next day the General was driven to Oyster Bay where he laid a wreath on the grave of Theodore Roosevelt. His visit included trips to a number of Civil War battlefields, and he attended the groundbreaking of the Liberty Memorial in Kansas City, Missouri in mid-November.

The general returned to Italy in late November. Unlike other military leaders arriving in the United States at that time, he was not a delegate to the disarmament conference scheduled in Washington. He did not even know of the conference, he confessed, until informed of it after he arrived in New York.

King Victor Emmanuel III of Italy knighted the general later that year, conferring on him the title *Duca della Vittoria* (Duke of Victory). He was promoted to the rank of Marshal by Benito Mussolini in 1922 and named Minister of War. He retired two years later and died in Rome in 1928.

Freedom of the City

Dating from the early Middle Ages, when cities could grant their residents freedom from serfdom to the local lord, a custom gradually evolved of bestowing a visiting dignitary an honorary freedom from paying an entrance toll. The tradition continues today primarily in the United Kingdom and countries in the British Commonwealth, where it is largely symbolic though sometimes accompanied by a gold "freedom box" or a certificate or scroll. The first person awarded Freedom of the City to New York was Viscount Edward Cornbury in 1702, the royal Governor of New York and New Jersey. During the Colonial era, the Freedom of the City was the highest honor the city could bestow.

After the American Revolution, Freedom of the City was granted rarely and only to distinguished guests, including the Marquis de Lafayette, George Washington, Alexander Hamilton and John Jay. Its use declined over the century, and it was bestowed only 23 times between 1860 and 1900. Controversy arose in 1909, when the Council revoked the Freedom it had granted to Dr. Frederick Cook, when his claim to be the first person to reach the North Pole was discredited.

During the early 1920s, Mayor Hylan granted Freedom of the City to many foreign dignitaries visiting after WWI, and the honor again became controversial. In October 1921, the *New York Times* reported that "it has now become so cheap and ordinary." Later mayors have largely discontinued granting it, opting instead to bestow VIPs with a Key to the City.

Friday, October 21, 1921:
Admiral Lord Beatty

When the liner *Aquitania* steamed into New York Harbor, she flew no special flags or pennants to indicate that a passenger on board was more than just an ordinary traveler arriving from Great Britain. The presence of 12 destroyers (six American and six British) escorting her and a flight of military aircraft circling above, however, proved that someone of importance was on board. The "someone" was Admiral David Beatty, commander of the First Battle Cruiser Division at the Battle of Jutland in 1916 and subsequently Admiral of the British Home Fleet and, by war's end, commander of the Allied fleets based at Scapa Flow and aligned against the Germany Navy.

While still sailing through the Narrows, the US Navy tug *Vigilant* sailed out to meet *Aquitania* with the welcoming party on board. Accompanying the tug was New York City Police boat *John F Hylan* which carried newspaper men and the Police Department band. Onboard *Vigilant* the official party consisted of US Admiral Hugh Rodman, Commissioner Grover Whalen, Alton Roberts representing the American Legion, and Adjutant General J. Leslie Kincaid, representing Governor Nathan Miller. Off Governors Island those on the tugboat transferred to the liner as a 19-gun salute from Fort Jay boomed. When *Aquitania* finally docked at Pier A, Admiral Beatty and his wife stepped ashore to the music provided by Army and Navy bands. At the Battery the Admiral and his wife were officially welcomed to the United States by both the State Adjutant General, and New York's Mayor John Hylan.

The Admiral's wife, Lady Ethel Beatty, was the daughter of American entrepreneur and department store founder Marshall Field. Although Lord and Lady Beatty would stay at the Field's residence on Park Avenue, this was not a social visit.

Admiral Beatty arrived in the city prior to attending the Washington Disarmament Conference as Naval Advisor for Great Britain scheduled to begin in Washington the following month. The conference planned to discuss ways to avoid the huge naval construction programs that had indirectly contributed to the start of the Great War.

Not since the visit of the Prince of Wales two years earlier *(see: November 18, 1919)* had security for a visitor been so high. With mounting tensions between Ireland and Great Britain that would soon ignite the Irish Civil War, and the large number of Irish immigrants in the city, no chances were being taken of any possible actions against the Admiral that would mar the day's activities. Three secret service men were assigned to be with the Admiral during his entire visit. Once the welcoming speeches were concluded and the parade up Broadway began, the agents rode on the running boards of the open top limousine carrying Admiral Beatty, Lady Beatty, and Admiral Rodman. The parade followed a detachment of mounted policemen. A cordon of uniformed police kept pace with the slow-moving procession and another mounted police detachment followed. A larger force than usual of policemen was on duty stationed no more than six feet apart, holding back the crowds which lined the route. Plain clothes officers were scattered among the crowd, estimated as larger than the one which had welcomed Italian General Diaz two days earlier *(see: October 19, 1921)*. No incidents occurred although the shout "Hurrah for Ireland" was often heard above the din of the cheering thousands. A number of negative comments referring to Great Britain were also heard. Nevertheless, a blizzard of ticker tape fell from buildings along the way.

Unlike most parades this one did not end at City Hall. After a stop there for additional words of welcome and a few remarks by the Admiral himself, the procession continued north up Lafayette Street and Fifth Avenue to the Wanamaker Mansion on

East 90th Street, a distance of over three miles. Fifth Avenue had been closed to all traffic, so spectators could line the entire route, though the streets were most crowded south of 14th Street and north of 86th Street. For the first time New York midtown and uptown streets were the scene of a New York welcome parade, keeping the city's broom-pushing sanitation workers busier than usual.

Admiral Beatty was an avid horseman. When the parade finally reached its destination, Lord Beatty stepped out of his limousine and inspected the mounted troops that had accompanied him uptown. He spoke to some of the officers and patted and petted a few of the steeds. He then entered the mansion only to reappear an hour later in mufti for his daily walk. He had been much impressed by New York on his previous visit 15 years earlier, and he and his family planned to enjoy the city's many sights on this trip.

The Washington Disarmament Conference was attended by delegates from nine nations. The five nations with the largest navies (United Kingdom, United States, France, Italy, and Japan) agreed to scrap a number of prewar battleships and cancel the construction of others. More battleships were scrapped because of the conference than were lost in any single naval battle in history. Japan, instead of canceling construction of some ships, converted the unfinished hulls into aircraft carriers later in the decade. None of the participating powers were satisfied with the results of the conference and a second conference was held in London in 1930. Instead of ending naval construction the two conferences helped Japan to become a major sea power and to increase the number and type of cruisers, smaller ships, and submarines built prior to the outbreak of World War II.

Admiral Beatty returned home before the end of the Washington Conference. He retired from active service in 1927 and served as First Sea Lord in the British Cabinet until 1935. Early the following year, he served as a pall bearer at the funeral of his superior at the Battle of Jutland, Admiral Jellicoe. Beatty died in London on March 11, 1936 of pneumonia caused by a chill and cold he caught as pallbearer.

Police Department Band

Formed in 1901 by 20 patrolmen who enjoyed playing music, the Police Department Band primarily played in its early years during the annual Police Parade. Its membership and talent increased, and in 1925 it was named the official band of the City of New York, and a Glee Club was also formed around this time. In 1933, it played at the Presidential Inauguration of former NY governor, Franklin Delano Roosevelt. Membership increased and by the early 1950s, the band had over 65 members and had performed in many events. In 1955, facing budget problems and the need for increased police presence on the streets, Commissioner Francis Adams eliminated the band and glee club, saving the city over $500,000 annually.

In 1991, Police Commissioner Raymond Kelly requested that the band be reformed, and two years later, the Police Band once again marched at the head of a parade. Dressed in the dark blue uniforms of the NYPD, the band has performed at every major parade in the city since 1994, including the Thanksgiving Parade and the LGBTQ Pride March, as well as every ticket-tape parade since the 1994 parade for the New York Rangers. →

During the three decades when there was no official NYPD band, Irish American officers of the police and fire department formed the Emerald Society, a fraternal organization for members of the city's uniformed agencies. In 1960, some members of the Emerald Society started the NYPD Pipe and Drum Corps. Separate from the revived NYPD Band, Pipe and Drum Corps members dress in kilts and wear a foot-tall busby festooned with ostrich feathers. They play bagpipes at funerals for police officers and in the city's St. Patrick's Day parade.

Friday, October 28, 1921:
Ferdinand Foch, Marshal of France

"Sirens, foghorns, steam whistles, bands and cannons, hundreds of thousands of voices, a snowstorm of torn paper and ticker tape which piled up in drifts on lower Broadway, the tricolor and the Stars and Stripes fluttering together everywhere, a ceaseless shouting of *Viva le France!* and the highest military and civil honors greeted Marshal Foch." With this exuberant opening sentence, the *New York Times* reported the arrival, parade, and reception given to the French Marshal, the man whom many historians credit as being the co-author of the plans that finally defeated Germany in World War I. The Marshal had sailed from France aboard the liner *Paris* and was transferred to the tug *Vigilant* at Quarantine. As the tug cruised up the bay, it was greeted by a noisy salute of cannons from Fort Jay on Governors Island. Police estimated than no fewer than 100,000 people awaited the Marshal at the Battery and perhaps triple that number lined Broadway from the Custom House to City Hall. The welcome was, again according to the *Times*, "the greatest ever paid to a foreigner."

The New York City fireboat *George Washington* arrived at the Battery minutes before the tug carrying the Marshal. The fireboat carried General John Pershing, commander of the American forces in the Great War. He had raced north from his home in New Jersey, where he had been staying with his ailing wife, but had vowed he would be on hand to welcome his French counterpart (and technically his superior officer during the hostilities) to American soil. Along with General Pershing, Captain Edward Rickenbacker, top American flying ace with 26 confirmed kills, was on hand as the Marshal stepped ashore. They saluted and the Marshal smiled broadly beneath his braided kepi as he returned the salutes.

As the parade made its way up Broadway accompanied by five bands and a full military escort, reporters commented on seeing wastebaskets filled with paper emptied on the marchers. Each band in turn played the French National anthem, "La Marseillaise," followed by the "Star Spangled Banner." It was reported that the mass of people lining Broadway was so dense that those in the parade could only be seen by those in the front row, the tall, those who climbed lamp poles, and those in the windows of the skyscrapers crowning the route. At City Hall, Marshal Foch was welcomed by Mayor John Hylan, who then introduced a young girl whose father had been killed in France in the closing days of the Great War. She presented the Marshal with a bouquet of flowers and requested, in words barely above a whisper, that he place a similar bouquet on her father's grave in France. Translated by the French Ambassador to the United States, Jules Jusserand, the Marshal accepted the flowers and kissed the girl on both cheeks. The mayor then spoke and proclaimed the French commander "a living example of the bond between our two nations," granted him Freedom of the City, and bestowed upon him honorary citizenship of New York. The Marshal responded in

French, again translated by Ambassador Jusserand, and expressed happiness at being made a citizen of "that city which produced so many fine warriors." This comment brought thunderous cheers from the crowd.

While all this was transpiring outside City Hall, panic was ensuing in the Aldermanic Chambers inside. It had been discovered that there were insufficient chairs for all of those invited to the chambers to greet the Marshal and, to compound the matter, the City Hall janitors were outside as part of the crowd welcoming the Marshal. Somehow two janitors were found by city officials and policemen, and they succeeded in locating additional seats and placing them in the chambers as the guests entered.

Later that afternoon, mounted police escorted a caravan of 20 automobiles to Penn Station for the Marshal's meeting with President Warren Harding in Washington. The procession contained more vehicles than had been expected and the police reported that there had been no time to check the credentials of all who followed. Once in Washington, the Marshal was again honored by a vast crowd and was presented with the Distinguished Service Medal to wear along with decorations from the United Kingdom, Belgium, Poland, Italy, and other nations. Before returning to France, he traveled to Kansas City, Missouri, for the dedication of the Liberty Memorial being constructed there.

Marshal Foch retired from the Army in 1923 and died in 1929. His tomb is in Les Invalides in Paris.

Fort Jay

Built on Governors Island, a 172-acre island sitting in New York Harbor just down channel from the East River, Fort Jay has a commanding view of the entire Upper Bay. In April 1776, American troops fortified the island and positioned cannons to prevent British ships from sailing up the East River, which helped General George Washington's army escape across Manhattan after the defeat in the Battle of Brooklyn.

In 1797, the island was sold to the Federal government, and a decade later the Army Corps of Engineers constructed a star-shaped fort. Originally named after Founding Father John Jay, the Army called it Fort Columbus until 1904, when it was officially renamed Fort Jay.

The fort was part of the defense system for New York City's Upper Harbor, but that role became less important when other forts were built on Staten Island and Brooklyn to guard the Narrows in 1820. Well protected for attack from sea, Governors Island was used as a prison for Confederate soldiers during the Civil War. After the War, the fortifications on other islands in the Upper Harbor were repurposed (Bedloe's Island for the Status of Liberty, and for an Immigration Station on Ellis Island) but the military continued using Governors Island. In the early 1900s, the island was expanded with landfill from subway excavations, and the officer's buildings and barracks were replaced with structures still standing on the island today.

During World War II, Fort Jay was headquarters of the First Army. When the Army HQ moved to Fort Meade in 1964, Fort Jay was decommissioned. The island was transferred to the Coast Guard, and in 2001 to the Parks Department. It opened as a recreational area for the general public in 2003.

Saturday, November 18, 1922:
Georges Clemenceau, Former Premier of France

Georges Clemenceau, the octogenarian "Tiger of France" who led his nation through the darkest days of the Great War, arrived in New York Harbor aboard the French liner *Paris*. Retired from active political life, the former Prime Minister announced before his trip to the United States that he was "on a mission" to this country, that he was arriving as a private citizen without instructions from the French government, and that his "mission" was of vital importance to the world.

The city's reception boat, the *Macom,* met the French liner off Quarantine at 10 o'clock in the morning. On board the *Macom* was George Wickersham, Chairman of the Reception Committee, along with Bernard Baruch, and other dignitaries and politicians, photographers, members of the press, and the Police Department band. There was no sign of the French statesman as the city's boat approached the starboard side of the liner. Many of the liner's passengers were visible at every window and porthole and along every foot of railing. Because so many people stood watching the city's boat approach, the *Paris* listed, and it became clear that it would be unsafe for *Macom* to come along the starboard side. As the smaller steamer swung around to the liner's port side, Mr. Baruch, who had spent many days with Mr. Clemenceau at the Peace Conference at Versailles, recognized the French visitor and waved to him. Waving in return, Mr. Clemenceau disappeared for a few minutes, reappearing at the ramp leading down the liner's side. He wore a gray overcoat with a dark fur collar, a cloth hat, white gloves, and supported himself with a cane. To ease his transfer from the liner, the city police boat *Manhattan* came between it and the *Macom,* serving as a "bridge" for him to cross. Once safely aboard the city's boat, the *Macom* turned and sped up the harbor.

Horns, whistles, and bells greeted the former Prime Minister as the city's boat approached Pier A. Mr. Clemenceau put both hands to his ears to partially shut out the din, but an artillery salute from Fort Jay on Governors Island startled him and he stepped away from the railing of the *Macom* and retreated into the boat's cabin.

Five thousand spectators were gathered in the Battery, cheering in welcome. Acting Mayor Murray Hulbert, President of the Board of Aldermen, greeted Mr. Clemenceau as he stepped ashore at Pier A. He welcomed the French visitor and apologized for the absence of Mayor John Hylan. Dozens of photographers gathered, their cameras constantly recording Mr. Clemenceau's every step, their flashbulbs blinding him. Turning to Mr. Baruch, he asked loudly enough for those nearby to hear, "Is there no way in this country to kill photographers?" Obviously annoyed, Mr. Clemenceau entered an open car with the Acting Mayor and Mr. Baruch. A military band began the parade up Broadway, escorted by a large military detachment, along with contingents from the American Legion and the Police, Fire, and Sanitation Departments. Mr. Clemenceau appeared sullen and did not wave back to the mass of spectators; nor did he seem to take notice of the streamers of ticker tape and torn paper that fluttered down on the parade.

As his car passed Wall Street, however, a flock of New York's ubiquitous pigeons rose up suddenly from Trinity churchyard. At the front of the flock was a white pigeon. Finally breaking into a smile, Mr. Clemenceau pointed with his cane and called the bird of "dove of peace." The flight of startled birds seemed to relax him and changed his dour mood, his walrus-like mustache barely revealing his smile. For the rest of the parade route, he smiled and waved his gloved hands at the crowds along the route. At

49

City Hall, the combined Police and Fire Department bands played the French and American National Anthems.

Inside the Aldermanic Chambers, the "Tiger of France" was introduced to the more than 300 invited guests. Acting Mayor Hulbert presented him with the city's Medal of Honor and read him a telegram of welcome from former President Woodrow Wilson. Mr. Clemenceau, who had lived in New York almost 60 years earlier as a physician and writer, addressed the audience in only slightly accented English, giving the first indication of the reason for his visit to America. The United States must become a member of the League of Nations, he stressed. He admitted that, at the age of 81, he would never again take an active part in politics or statesmanship, and that he had seen too much of war. He warned that Germany, though defeated by the Allies and stripped of much of its ability to wage war in the future because of the Treaty of Versailles, still posed a threat to the democracies of the world. "In my lifetime I have seen my country twice invaded by the Germans," he said emotionally, "I don't want to see" a third invasion. He announced that he would visit Washington, Philadelphia, and Boston to rally support for the League in an attempt to persuade Congress that a League of Nations without America would eventually fail.

His words seemed stronger than his audience expected, and he received only muted approval when he finished. Later that afternoon Mr. Clemenceau was feted at a luncheon at the Waldorf Astoria before retiring early due to "the exertions of the day." The next evening, he spoke to a capacity audience at the Metropolitan Opera House and repeated, in more detail, his hopes for American entry into the League and the need for a Germany that would be unable to wage war.

The following day he visited the Museum of Natural History. When told that many of the displays there were the result of the work of the German naturalist, Alexander von Humboldt, he commented, "If all Germans were like him, talking to them would be some use." Later that day he was driven to Oyster Bay, Long Island, to visit the grave of Theodore Roosevelt.

Georges Clemenceau's efforts to have the United States join the League of Nations failed. Despite the fact that the League had first been suggested by President Wilson, isolationism had taken hold of the country after the War ended. America's loss of more than 115,000 men in the brief period it was engaged in the War weighed heavily against future international entanglement and involvement. He returned to France, exhausted from his travels but still vehemently opposed to any softening of relations with Germany. He died in 1929 at the age of 88 and is buried near his home in Mouchamps in western France.

Quarantine

After an outbreak of Yellow Fever in the 1790s, New York passed a Quarantine Law and opened a hospital on the east shore of the mostly uninhabited Staten Island. Called the New York Marine Hospital, it had 1,500 beds. When Irish immigration increased during the 1840s, though, the hospital was over-crowded, treating as many as 8,000 patients annually. The small but growing population on the island resisted the city's attempt to build a second hospital. In September 1858, locals attacked the hospital, killing several guards and patients. The New York militia was called in to restore control, and the patients temporarily moved to Ward Island until a longer-term solution was devised. →

The solution was the creation of two man-made islands, about two miles from South Beach on Staten Island and opposite Coney Island on the Brooklyn side. Called Swinburne and Hoffman Islands, they were created in the 1870s by adding landfill to some natural shoals and were used to quarantine immigrants with severely contagious diseases such as cholera, yellow fever and typhoid. Passengers on ships sailing to New York exposed to or suspected of having such diseases would be taken to the 10-acre Hoffman Island before being allowed to continue to Ellis Island. Individuals with active cases were sent to the hospital on the 3-acre Swinburne Island. Better known simply as "Quarantine," the islands were last used for that purpose during a cholera outbreak in 1910, when over 250 passengers of a liner from Naples, Italy were quarantined there, and at least 8 died. When the Federal government closed the hospital in 1937, the New York Times reported that "thousands were detained" and "hundreds died" on Quarantine during the hospital's 50 years of operation.

Since then, the islands have been used as a stopping point for ocean vessels to meet local pilots and tugboats, and during WWII were used to help anchor anti-submarine nets to protect New York from U-Boat attacks. After the war, most of the buildings on the islands were razed. Plans in the 1980s to create homeless shelters on the island were supported by Staten Island residents but were rejected because of costs. Now managed by the National Park Service as part of Gateway National Recreational Park, the islands have become a haven for wildlife, including egrets and herons. The islands are also home to a growing population of harbor and grey seals.

Friday, October 5, 1923:
David Lloyd George, Former Prime Minister of Great Britain

Although David Lloyd George, the former Prime Minister of Great Britain, arrived in the United States on an unofficial basis, he was accorded all diplomatic privileges. As the liner *Mauritania* steamed slowly past Quarantine, New York City's reception boat *Macom* pulled beside her and the Mayor's Reception Committee boarded the larger ship. In the absence of Chairman Rodman Wanamaker, Vice Chairman Grover Whalen was the first aboard. He was joined by Assistant Secretary of State J. Butler Wright, Secretary of Labor James Davis, President of Bethlehem Steel Charles Schwab, novelist Peter Kyne and others, including reporters and photographers. The entire party proceeded to the ship's library to meet Mr. Lloyd George, only to discover he was still in his stateroom with his wife and daughter. A few minutes later they arrived, and the entire party transferred to the *Macom*.

Mr. Lloyd George stood with Grover Whalen and Butler Wright as the *Macom* drew closer to the Battery. Gazing and pointing at the skyscrapers, he commented to them saying "Amazing" and as they passed the Statue of Liberty, the former Prime Minister stared at it and muttered "Most impressive."

A larger impression waited at Pier A where the Police Department band waited to lead the parade up Broadway. Military detachments from both the Army and Navy stood at attention. A large police presence was obvious due to the numerous reports received indicating that members of various Irish groups would protest Mr. Lloyd George's arrival. A squad of police on horseback joined a squad on motorcycles to provide whatever security might be necessary.

Mr. Lloyd George rode in the first car of the motorcade, sharing it with Mr. Whalen and Mr. Wright. The former Prime Minister's wife, Margaret, and daughter, Gwilym, rode in the second car with Mr. Kyne, who would be acting as the unofficial tour guide while the English family was visiting New York and other cities in the country.

The parade began a few minutes after noon marching under a bright blue sky. Earlier clouds that threatened rain had drifted away, and the sun cast long shadows in the Canyon of Heroes. Mr. Lloyd George stood in his vehicle, wearing the traditional morning suit of a diplomat and carrying a blackthorn walking stick which he used for balance as the car slowed or accelerated. He held his top hat in his left hand, occasionally tipping it to the crowd of spectators in appreciation of the welcome, and smiled at the spectacle of falling ticker tape.

Near City Hall a group of protestors booed the former Prime Minister, while another group carried banners and signs with anti-British sentiments. Members of the Police Department chased the first group and seized the banners and signs of the second, arresting four protestors who resisted the police.

Mayor Hylan was absent, recovering from illness, so Acting Mayor Murray Hulbert, President of the Board of Aldermen, presided over the reception at City Hall Park. He welcomed the Englishman to New York and extended him the Freedom of the City immediately after the combined Police and Fire Departments bands played the British and American national anthems.

Called upon to speak, Mr. Lloyd George stated that he had come to the United States to learn. How was America handling the post war unemployment problem, which was not as severe here as in his country? How did the United States stand on the Versailles Treaty, the League of Nations, and preventing a rebirth of militarism in Germany? On a less serious note, he commented on the large Staten Island ferries he had seen as the *Macom* approached the Battery. He wished to see regular ferry service in London, and hoped to learn how New York managed to provide the ferry service without heavy government subsidies. He stated that this was his first visit to the United States and as a student of its history, he would like to see Civil War battlefields, especially Gettysburg. And, finally, he liked to play golf and was aware that the United States had excellent golf courses.

That afternoon the former Prime Minister and his family were guests at a luncheon at the Hotel Biltmore. He met with reporters after the affair and answered numerous questions about the Irish situation and the Treaty of Versailles. He stated that the Irish question would soon be settled peacefully and that he considered the Treaty to be completely fair and just to all parties. Following the reception, the British family checked into their suite at the Waldorf Astoria Hotel.

Before attending a performance of the *Music Box Revue* later that day, Mr. Lloyd George requested a "typical American meal" from the Waldorf's chef. He subsequently dined on blue point oysters, sorrel soup, mousse of sole with oyster-crab sauce, potatoes *parisienne*, breast of chicken, new lima beans, Waldorf salad, ice cream, cakes, and coffee. At the Music Box Theater, he was introduced to the audience and two other celebrities also in attendance: Charlie Chaplin and Irving Berlin. As Mr. Lloyd George exited the theater, a well-dressed man (who later stated he was an "Irish Republican") threw an egg at him. It missed the former Prime Minister and broke against the brow of an unidentified bystander.

Mr. Lloyd George returned to England in December, coincidentally with Mr. Chaplin. During much of the time in America he played golf and saw various sights, including Gettysburg. He became the leader of the Liberal Party on his return to England but was not reelected to Parliament until 1936. His wife died in 1941 and he married his former secretary in 1943. His diaries, published posthumously, revealed that he had been having an affair with her since 1913. He was 80 years old and serving as an unofficial advisor to the Churchill cabinet when the news of the affair was broken. He died in late March 1945 and is buried near his estate in Llanyumdey Wales.

Pier A

By 1789, New York City was one of the largest seaports in the newly formed United States, and during the next 50 years the port fueled the city's economic and population growth. In 1821, the new Erie Canal opened shipping to the interior of the westward-expanding nation. Factories, warehouses and sweatshops lined the city's waterfront, turning raw materials into products that were shipped and sold around the world, and importing products bound for sale in the rest of the US. By 1870, New York Harbor was the busiest port in the Western Hemisphere, and the city's new Department of Docks began upgrading the piers as part of a massive project to improve the harbor, installing concrete breakfronts along the shore, reinforcing docks and re-numbering the piers, starting on the Hudson with Pier 1 at Battery Place, and progressing up to Pier 99 at 59th Street on the Hudson River.

In 1884, the Department built a new pier next to Pier 1 as its headquarters and for the Police Department's steam-powered tugboat Patrol. Opened two years later, it was named Pier A to differentiate it from the numbered piers, and atop the pier was an attractive brick and terra cotta building heavily insulated to protect it from storms. A third story was added in 1900, and the building was embellished with wrought iron lamps and decorations. In 1919 a ship's clock and bell were installed in the building's tower as a memorial to sailors lost in World War I.

Used exclusively by official city boats, Pier A was the home dock for the Macom and police patrol boats throughout the early 1900s, and in 1959 the Fire Department began using it also. During the next decade though, the harbor's traffic waned as more commercial and passenger travel shifted to jet planes, and by the early 1970s, the Pier was badly in need of repair. Plans to demolish it and build a new marine facility were too expensive given the city's fiscal crisis, so the pier was locked behind a fence, and the building covered with plyboard. In 1975, It was designated a Historical Location, but sat neglected for another 30 years. In 2008, with Federal government funding, a much-needed restoration was begun, and the Pier reopened in 2014. The building now houses a restaurant and bar, with exhibits about the harbor's history.

CHAPTER 3
Soaring through the Roaring Twenties (1924-1929)

The death toll of almost 800,000 from war and flu in the United States was far lower than the estimated 60 million worldwide, but by 1920 the country was ready for change. The new decade would be affected by two Constitutional Amendments adopted just before it began. The 18th Amendment banned the sale, manufacture and transportation of alcoholic beverages, while the 19th Amendment gave women the right to vote in time for the 1920 Presidential election (though in New York State that right had been granted in 1917).

The immediate impact of women's suffrage was less seismic than feared by politicians worried about a "women's voting bloc." Perhaps that was because suffrage was not truly universal (many African American women were still disenfranchised because of racist policies in many states), or because, like men, women voted on issues based on their socio-economic status rather than their gender. In 1921, Congress did pass the first nationwide maternity and childcare laws, and in some states, support for Prohibition succeeded because legislators feared retaliation from women in the next election if the proposed Amendment failed. Social changes were greater than the political ones though.

The many deaths over the past decade gave young men and women a feeling that life was short and should be enjoyed quickly. Having won the right to vote, the era's "new woman" wanted to enjoy the same experiences her male counterparts could, from having careers and being economically independent to driving cars and dancing at night clubs. Young women also wanted sexual freedom, and the decade saw a rise in "petting parties" and the introduction of birth-control for women by Margaret Sanger's American Birth Control League. Social customs were changing quickly, and the iconic image of the era was the flapper. Wearing skirts with hemlines just below the knees, long necklaces and feather boas, and short, boyish hair styles, flappers could be seen smoking cigarettes and drinking cocktails at speakeasies that, despite the new ban on alcohol, sprang up all over the city.

Prohibition had been a goal for temperance groups like the Anti-Saloon League as early as the 1870s but became a national debate when progressives in the late 1800s added it to their agenda. The "drys" argued that banning alcohol would increase worker productivity, improve morality and family life, and reduce crime and corruption, while the "wets" insisted it would impose rural Protestant values on the country's urban and more diverse areas, and decrease tax revenues. The passage of the 16th Amendment in 1913, enabling Congress to create a national income tax, helped win the argument for the drys, and in January 1920, Prohibition went into effect. The law had varying degrees of compliance and effectiveness across the nation, but many in New York City ignored it. With over 9,000 hotels and saloons plus many beer breweries, the city stood to lose $18 million in taxes. The NY Police Department was in charge of enforcing

Prohibition, forming special task forces to conduct raids on bootleggers and breweries, but it also closed one eye to violators. In addition to the thousands of speakeasies opening in the city, the number of pharmacies tripled during Prohibition, since pharmacists could prescribe whiskey as a remedy for anxiety and many illnesses.

Many speakeasies were small establishments serving bad or watered-down booze, but some were glamorous clubs catering to celebrities and the rich and famous, such as the 21 Club and the Players Club. One frequent visitor of these clubs was Jimmy Walker, a wealthy politician with a reputation as a flamboyant "man about town" who was often seen with beautiful chorus girls. After 10 years in the State Senate, Walker successfully ran for Mayor in 1925. He instructed Police Commissioner Joseph Warren to stop the raids, and during the next 4 years at least 30,000 clubs were in operation within the city.

One of the most famous nightclubs in this era was the Cotton Club on 142nd Street and Lenox Avenue in uptown Manhattan. Harlem was one of the major destinations of the Great Migration, when over 6 million African Americans moved to northern cities in search of better opportunities and to escape the discrimination of the Jim Crow Southern states they left. The mid-1920s was the height of the Harlem Renaissance, and as the new sounds of jazz swept across the nation, the elegant and flamboyant fashions of artists like Josephine Baker were setting trends for flappers in Europe as well as the US.

Despite the city's concerns about lost tax revenue and a brief post-war recession, the national economy was soaring by 1924, and technology was the driving force. Mass production, popularized by Henry Ford in the 1910s, made technology more affordable for middle-class households. More Americans could buy products introduced before the war, such as electric irons, toasters and refrigerators, washing machines and vacuum cleaners, and phonographs. Technology was also changing the corporate office, and creating opportunities for (mostly young, unmarried) women as typists, stenographers, and telephone switchboard operators. With employment for both men and women increasing, the standard of living was rising, especially in cities, which meant that middle-class New Yorkers had more disposable income than before. Labor unions had recently succeeded in establishing the 5-day work week, which meant Americans also had more leisure time than in the past.

In addition to changing the way office work and housekeeping were done, science and technology were also providing more sources of enjoyment. Two of the important innovations of this era were radio and motion pictures. Radio had been invented in the 1890s but became practical for home use after the invention of the vacuum tube in 1905. By 1920 when the Federal Government began issuing broadcast licenses, many people had a radio. The new devices could bring both information and entertainment into the home, and broadcasters soon found the perfect blend of both: sports. For the first time, baseball fans could hear the excitement of the 1921 World Series from their own homes, as the New York Giants defeated their crosstown rivals, the New York Yankees. Baseball's slow pace made it perfect for radio announcers, and radio helped baseball become the "national pastime."

Motion pictures were another invention that Americans were increasingly turning to as a way to enjoy their leisure time. Vaudeville theaters across the country began playing movies, and for a city that already had a vibrant theater industry, New York soon also had some of the nation's best movie palaces. For just 25 cents, New Yorkers could enjoy a double feature and a news reel at the Paramount Theater in Times Square, the Astoria Theater in Queens, or one of the five Loew's "wonder theaters" like the Kings Theater in Brooklyn.

The most important new invention, however, was the automobile. Introduced in 1909, the Model T Ford became the symbol of modernization and middle-class ambition. By 1920, Ford Motor was selling more than 1 million cars a year, and the already crowded streets of New York had become dangerous. As early as 1913, the *New York Times* reported that more pedestrians died from collisions with automobiles than streetcars or trolleys. By 1920, traffic was so bad it took 40 minutes to go from 34th to 57th Street, leading the city to install its first traffic lights along Fifth Avenue. The experiment worked, and over the next several years, the city replaced traffic cops with streetlights on every avenue in Manhattan.

Americans were on the go, and if the car was taking them to new places, they were even more fascinated by the daring feats of those who were going places nobody had gone before. The first generation of "aeroplanes" were built with lightweight materials and had canvas-covered wings, and were powered by motors not much more complicated than those in automobiles. Needing just a short dirt runway for lift-off and landing, pilots trained during the war could support themselves by flying at county fairs, transporting sightseers or dusting crops. Over 4,600 airplanes were sold annually by 1928, and several landing fields were created in less developed areas in Queens and Long Island. Aviators were the new pioneers, soaring further and higher every year and capturing the imaginations of this new "anything goes" era. Eager to move past the challenges of the war era and enjoy life while they could, New Yorkers began celebrating women and men making achievements of athletics and aviation *(for example, see: August 27, 1926 and July 6, 1928)*, more than generals and war leaders. It was the Roaring Twenties, and everybody was soaring high.

Wednesday, August 6, 1924:
US Olympians from VIII Olympic Games

In 1924, Paris became the first city to be a repeat host for the Olympic Games, having hosted the games before in 1900. Athletes from 44 nations participated in the VIII Olympics, which were portrayed in the movie *Chariots of Fire*. For the second Olympics in a row, the US team won the most medals: 45 gold, 27 silver, and 27 bronze for a total of 99. France came in second with 38 medals, followed by Finland with 37. New York City decided to hold a ticker tape parade for the victorious US Olympic team, and 120 of the 299 team members were able to attend. Among them was the handsome 22-year-old Johnny Weissmuller, who had won 3 gold medals in swimming, setting Olympic Records in the 100-meter and 400-meter freestyles, and capturing his third gold in the 4 by 200-meter freestyle team event.

New York was sweltering in a heat wave. Multiple deaths from the effects of the heat were recorded daily. Tenement dwellers slept on roof tops and fire escapes, in parks, and even on the beaches in order to escape from the oppressive heat. Despite this, thousands crowded the streets of downtown Manhattan to welcome the Olympians. Scheduled to begin at noon, the parade failed to get under way until 5 o'clock. The liner *America* carrying the athletes was delayed at Quarantine and docked in Hoboken, New Jersey, and the city's welcoming vessel *Macom* ferried them from there to Pier A at the Battery. The delay frustrated many who had waited but once the parade began, the weather cooled slightly with the thermometer dropping under 90 degrees.

A color guard of National Guard officers and detachments of the 14th and 23rd Infantry regiments and the 102nd Medical Corps led the procession. They were followed by five members of the US Olympic Committee and then by the various teams, marching in columns of four. Each group was led by an athlete carrying a banner identifying the team, and the athletes were dressed in their Olympic costumes. "The girls of the triumphant swimming and tennis combinations marched in white costumes with white cloches crowning their bobbed heads," the *New York Times* reported, and "all the men, including the big fellows of the wrestling teams and the smaller athletes of the running track, were arrayed in the conventional blue serge coats, white flannel trousers, white shoes and socks and straw hats, bearing blue hatbands with the insignia of the Olympic teams. All the contestants…bore on their left breast the shield of the United States embroidered in the tricolor." As the parade moved up Broadway another reporter wrote that the falling ticker tape resembled snow squalls, a bit of wishful poetic license perhaps inspired by the heat.

Once the marchers reached City Hall, they were serenaded by the Fire Department Band playing the National Anthem. President Coolidge then addressed those assembled by radio from the White House in Washington. Immediately afterwards, Mayor John Hylan presented a Gold Medal to each athlete and thanked them for their efforts and victories. Then, broadcasting over radio station WNYC, each athlete was introduced and asked to make a brief statement.

Later that evening the Olympic team was officially disbanded at a beefsteak dinner held at the Hotel Astor and arranged by the Mayor's Committee for the Receptions to Distinguished Guests. Addressing the athletes, Colonel Robert Thompson, President of the American Olympic Committee, ended the evening with the following remarks:

> *"The time for parting has come. When you leave this room the American team for the eighth Olympic Games will be dissolved. Some of you will go back again to compete for the American team in the Olympic Games at Amsterdam. Some of you will not, but if the team that goes to Amsterdam is as good as the team which had just returned from Paris, America will win again, for there is not a more formidable athletic team anywhere in the world."*

Johnny Weissmuller was among the American athletes competing in the 1928 Olympics in Amsterdam. He won another two gold medals that year, before signing a contract with MGM Studios in Hollywood, starring in 1932's *Tarzan, the Ape Man*. He went on to play the character created by Edgar Rice Burroughs in a dozen full-length movies. Many actors have played the "Lord of the Jungle" over the years, and many critics agree Weissmuller's portrayal is the best. He retired from acting in the late 1950s, moving first to Chicago and Florida, and finally to Mexico, where he died in 1984 at the age of 79.

Thursday, October 29, 1925:
Captain Paul Grening and Crew of SS *President Harding*

New York City parades have honored kings, queens, generals, admirals, princes, and athletes, but the one on October 29, 1925 honored a group of men for their heroic actions. Paul Grening, captain of the US Lines freighter *President Harding*, and his crew received a ticker tape parade for rescuing 28 officers and crew of the Italian freighter *Ignazio Florio*. Battered by a violent hurricane more than 1,700 miles east of Ambrose

Light on October 23, the Italian ship was in danger of sinking, flashed an SOS message, and Captain Grening raced to the scene.

The first two attempts at rescuing the crew failed as huge waves prevented the ships getting close. A lifeboat was smashed to pieces by the surf, fortunately without loss of life. After keeping vigil with the slowly sinking freighter throughout the night, the crew finally secured a line, and lifeboats carried the crew of the stricken vessel to safety. The *President Harding* was able to keep in constant wireless contact with the US Lines Company headquarters on Broadway and the news of the rescue was relayed around the country.

The morning after Captain Grening returned to New York and brought the rescued seamen ashore, he and his crew were the recipients of a parade. Captain Grening and his first officer, Giles Stedman, sat in an open vehicle beside the chairman of the reception committee, George MacDonald, Honorary Police Commissioner. An honor guard of sea cadets marched with the vehicles of the motorcade. The parade was led by a squad of mounted policemen and the Street Cleaning Band. As the motorcade moved through the Canyon of Heroes, the band played "Hail, the Conquering Hero Comes." Thousands of spectators lined the streets, and the police were forced to restrain some well-wishers from jumping on the running-board of Captain Grening's vehicle to shake his hand.

Mayor Hylan greeted the captain at the steps of City Hall. Mrs. Grening and other members of the captain's family joined the officer as the mayor welcomed home the Brooklyn native. The mayor congratulated the captain and his crew for their bravery. Mr. Thomas Rossbottom, General Manager of US Lines, presented the captain with a Certificate of Excellence from the line. Bonuses were announced for each of the officers and men of the *President Harding*. Present also was a representative of the Italian language newspaper *Il Progresso*, who presented the captain with an inscribed silver trophy and awarded a $500 purse to be divided among the crew of the *President Harding*.

Called upon to say a few words, Captain Grening explained that "we have only done what the dictates of humanity require of all those on the high seas in the presence of an impending disaster." He added that the real heroes were the crew of the Italian vessel who managed to prevent their ship from sinking before help arrived. He especially commended the wireless operator of the *Ignazio Florio* whose work brought about the rescue.

The reception ended with the captain's remarks. He and his crew returned to their ship which was scheduled to sail to England in a day's time. The *President Harding* was renovated in 1930 to carry passengers, and operated under the command of Captain Grening between New York and Bremen, Germany until sold in 1936.

The Street Cleaning Band

Though the Department of Street Cleaning was created in 1881, it wasn't until 1895 that its workers began cleaning streets throughout the city. Dressed in white and pushing carts and brooms, workers were responsible for removing trash, horse manure, household refuse, and even snow in the winter. In what might be an early example of recycling, horse carcasses were collected and sold for glue, and manure was sold for fertilizer. In 1929, it was renamed the Department of Sanitation. →

In 1912, foreman James Cunningham and other musicians who worked for the department formed a marching band, and the Street Cleaners Band began performing at parades and other civic events. During the 1920s, they marched in parades as each avenue in Manhattan was re-opened after the installation of traffic lights, and in 1930 began playing concerts at hospitals and homes for the aged. Cunningham rose through the department's ranks to field superintendent, became the band's musical director, and conducted the band during a series of radio concerts during the 1920s and 1930s.

Briefly disbanded to save money during the Depression, the band was reinstated in 1933 by Commissioner George McAneny, who restricted the number of events the 70-member band would perform at. Two years later, all three of the city's uniform department bands were sued by a group of unemployed professional musicians. The case was dismissed, but the court ruled the city bands could only perform at official functions and that "musical entertainment should be left to private musicians." The city responded by paying its band performers their normal salaries during those official functions.

The Police and Fire Department bands were eliminated in the 1950s, but the Sanitation Department Band continued until 1967, when Mayor Lindsay cut the band's $400,000 budget. Despite efforts by the city council to restore funding, the band played its last performance in July 1967. After the band was dissolved, the Emerald Society started its own DSNY marching band, similar to the ones it had formed for the Police and Fire Departments.

Tuesday, February 16, 1926:
Captain George Fried and Crew of SS *President Roosevelt*

For four days in January 1926, the British freighter *Antinoe* was buffeted by a North Atlantic gale, slowly sinking. An American liner, the SS *President Roosevelt*, had answered her distress signal, and Captain George Fried brought his liner to the stricken freighter's aid. The wind, rain and heavy seas tossed the two ships about, preventing the 25 crew members of the British ship from manning lifeboats and transferring until, on the morning of January 28, two of the *President Roosevelt's* lifeboats were able to come along side as the British ship slowly sank by the stern. As the officers and crew were evacuating, a wave crashed against the lifeboats and two men from the American liner were swept overboard. Although they wore lifebelts, they quickly disappeared in the storm and were never seen again.

Captain Fried sailed his slightly damaged liner to Portsmouth, England, where his steadfast resolve to remain with the British freighter until her crew was saved was rewarded by the British government. King George V presented Captain Fried with a medal, and the captain's heroism was also rewarded with silver service from the French government and an inscribed silver cigarette case from the German government. The SS *President Roosevelt* finally returned to the United States and on February 15 docked at Pier 4, Hoboken, New Jersey for minor repairs in preparation for her next voyage to Europe.

The State of New Jersey accorded the captain and crew a welcome, and Governor A. Harry Moore presented the Captain with the state's Certificate of Valor. There was a reception on the Pier, speeches and tributes, and a dinner aboard the liner.

But a larger welcome followed the next morning when New York's reception steamer, the *Macom*, arrived to transport Captain Fried to the Battery, along with four of his officers and more than 20 crewmembers who had taken an active part in saving the crew of *Antinoe*. Despite the bitter winter cold and a harsh wind blowing across the harbor, Captain Fried and his officers stood at the railing as the city's boat sailed. The Chairman of the Mayor's Reception Committee, Vincent Astor, was unable to attend, so the Committee's Vice-Chairman, Grover Whalen, stood with them and pointed to Fort Jay as a 21-gun salute was fired in their honor. Usually reserved for heads-of-state, the salute was fired to commemorate their bravery. Mortars in the fort fired aerial charges that exploded in mid-air like fireworks. No fewer than six fireboats shot streams of water high in the air. The Battery was filled with more than 3,000 spectators who stood on and around the mounds of the recent heavy snowstorm. As *Macom* approached Pier A, the navy Tug *Iuka's* whistle screeched in greeting. On the shore the Street Cleaning Band played the "Charleston" and other popular tunes.

A detachment of the 16th Infantry from Governors Island and a platoon of sailors from the Brooklyn Navy Yard stood at Bowling Green. After the captain and crew entered six open limousines, they led the motorcade up Broadway. The cold wind whipped remainders of the snowstorm through the Canyon of Heroes. Ticker tape and torn paper of every size and type mixed with it, so it seemed as if the snow from two days earlier was falling once again. Police estimates put the number of shivering spectators at more than 150,000, perhaps as many as 200,000.

Mayor Walker greeted Captain Fried and the others at City Hall. The bands of both the Fire and Police Departments were drawn up in City Hall Park and they joined together to play the National Anthem. Following the anthem, Captain Fried and his crew were brought into the Aldermanic Chambers. More than 200 invited guests filled the room and rose in a standing ovation as the seamen entered.

Mayor Walker introduced Captain Fried and the others to the guests. He presented each with a medal for Bravery. The mayor remarked that the captain was a resident and "true citizen" New York City, living with his wife in an apartment at 193rd Street and St. Nicholas Avenue. He said that when the captain changed course in the middle of a North Atlantic storm and raced almost 100 miles in response to the frantic SOS of the British freighter, "You were doing what New York would do: reach out in any channel, under any circumstances, to lift up those who were in difficulty," he said, adding "I congratulate you and welcome you back to us."

The Captain was then given a scroll with the names of those present and "in a place of honor at the very top the names of Uno Witanen and Ernest Heitman, lost at sea." At the mention of the names of the two deceased members of his crew, Captain Fried turned away from the assembly in the chamber. Overtaken by emotion, he sobbed quietly for a few moments. When he recovered, he asked "How can anyone respond to the tremendous applause and attentions showered upon us? The millions of people on Broadway as we marched up – how can anyone give any response to such a thing?" He singled out those with him as the true heroes of the rescue, pointing out that he had remained on the bridge of the *President Roosevelt* during the four days, but that the real honor belongs to his officers and crew.

Following the City Hall ceremony, the captain and his men were driven to a luncheon at the Advertising Club. As the motorcade passed Public School 106 at Lafayette and Spring Streets, all of the school's pupils stood outside and cheered as the motorcade went by. After the luncheon all those honored were taken to the Hotel Roosevelt where they were guests of the management until the ship's scheduled departure at noon the following Sunday. The Hotel placed a memorial tablet in the lobby containing the names of those who were honored along with the names of the two lost sailors.

Unbelievable as it may seem, Captain Fried took part in another rescue at sea three years later when his ship, the *America,* saved the crew of the Italian freighter *Florida.* He was again honored with a ticker tape parade *(see: January 28, 1929).*

Mayor Jimmy Walker (1926-1932)

Born in New York City in 1881, James Walker did not spend his childhood in poverty, as he later liked to claim. His father, a successful lumber yard owner, was active in Democratic party politics and encouraged his son to enter politics. Jimmy was not a great student, though, dropping out of college and arguing that a career in the growing music industry of Tin Pan Alley would be better. The father won the argument, and Jimmy returned to school, passed the bar exam in 1912 and entered politics, serving in the NY State Assembly from 1910 to 1914 and the State Senate from 1915 to 1925.

Walker developed a reputation as a flamboyant well-dressed man about town who visited speakeasies and had affairs with chorus girls. As a politician, he opposed Prohibition and tolerated corruption, and was suspected of taking bribes. Instead of ending his indiscretions during his 1925 campaign to become mayor, he moved them behind closed doors, using a private bootlegger and penthouse funded by Tammany for his affairs. Keeping scandals out of the press this way proved successful, and after defeating Mayor Hylan in the Democratic primary, he easily won the election.

Walker's first term, during the prosperity of the late 1920s, was successful. He re-organized and re-named the Department of Sanitation, improved the city's public hospitals and parks, and expanded the subway system while maintaining the 5-cent fare. He also discouraged the Police Department from enforcing Prohibition laws, winning favor with working class voters, which led to his successful re-election in 1929.

Coinciding with the Stock Market Crash and the beginning of the Depression, Walker's second term was a disaster. The state's newly elected Governor, Franklin Roosevelt, was determined to do something about corruption in the city and formed an independent committee to investigate Walker as well as Tammany Hall leaders. Turning up evidence that Walker had accepted bribes while mayor and of corruption in the police department, the investigation and resulting scandal led Walker to resign in September 1932, a year and four months before his term was due to expire.

Threatened with criminal prosecution, Walker sailed for Europe with his mistress, Ziegfeld showgirl Betty Compton, announcing he was done with politics. When he finally returned to New York, he pursued his music interests, becoming head of Majestic Records. At the age of 65, he died of a brain hemorrhage in 1946.

Thursday, May 27, 1926: Crown Prince Gustaf Adolph and Crown Princess Louise of Sweden

Even before the Swedish liner *Gripsholm* steamed past Governors Island and received a welcoming 21-gun salute, reporters and photographers had swarmed aboard her to visit Sweden's Crown Prince Gustaf Adolph and his English-born wife, Louise. The royal couple began their nine-week tour of the United States with a brief stay in New York. Their schedule called for them to leave by train for Washington, DC, before 3 o'clock that afternoon, leaving reporters little time for interviews and photographs.

The Crown Prince admitted that he had never seen so many newsmen in one place, but he and his wife answered as many questions as time allowed and they followed the directions of photographers to everyone's satisfaction. Prince Gustaf answered numerous questions on various subjects. Archeology: "They call me an archeologist. I've been digging in Sweden, Turkey, and China." What he wanted to see most in America: "Museums with American art. And your factories." Baseball: "No, I've never seen a baseball game, but my schedule includes one. And, yes, I have heard of Babe Ruth." The princess was also questioned and admitted that the Prince had been very seasick on the voyage, but she had not been. Both spoke in excellent English, his answers in more of an American accent than hers, which was more British

After the Royal Couple received a salute from Fort Jay on Governors Island, they were treated to the tooting and whistling of ferries, tugs, yachts, freighters, and other vessels in the harbor. The final tribute to them before they disembarked at Pier A was the watery salute from the city fireboat *William L. Strong*, which shot huge jets of water into the air in graceful arches. The Prince was informed that this part of a New York welcome was begun under the previous administration of Mayor Hylan and no other port city welcomed visiting dignitaries in a similar fashion.

Once ashore the Prince and Princess were welcomed by Grover Whalen. Streamers of ticker tape and colored papers had already begun swirling from buildings along the Battery and up Broadway. Princess Louise pointed to the Whitehall Building. "It's perfectly lovely," she commented, tugging at the sleeve of the Prince's morning coat. He smiled in agreement as they entered the open car that would carry them up the Canyon of Heroes.

Their 89 pieces of luggage were unloaded before the parade began and placed in Battery Park in front of the statue of John Ericsson, the Swedish-American inventor and designer of the Civil War ironclad *Monitor*. A circle of policeman guarded their luggage, which was to be transferred by truck to Penn Station during the parade. A battalion of the 16th Infantry, stationed on Governors Island, stood in ranks behind the Army band from the island. Detachments of the Police and Fire Departments stood behind the car. Flag bearers carrying the Swedish and American flags were interspaced though the marching ranks. With a blare of trumpets and horns the parade began its slow march towards City Hall and, just as it began to move, a group of 40 musicians wearing faded purple uniforms rushed from behind the police barricades to the front of the parade. Their music almost drowned out the military band. Some of the purple-clad marchers carried placards that read "Subscribe to the Stone Mountain Memorial" revealing that they were not part of the official welcome, but rather an effort to raise funds to complete a memorial in Georgia to Confederate leaders on Stone Mountain. Unaware that they were intruders, the police were slow in removing them from the parade route and, in the words of the *New York Times* article about the parade, "Thousands of yards of ticker tape and acres of paper were wasted" before it was discovered that this band "was not an integral part of the Prince's procession." Much to the chagrin of New York's finest, the group ran and scattered back into the throng of more than 250,000 spectators who lined the parade route. Not until later did the mayor or the Prince and Princess learn of the episode.

When the parade finally reached City Hall, Mr. Whalen introduced the Royal Couple to Mayor Walker, who shook the hand of the tall, bespectacled heir to the Swedish throne. An aide presented the princess with a bouquet of red roses before the mayor escorted the couple into the Aldermanic Chambers, where more than 300 invited guests stood as the Police Department band in the Chambers' balcony played the Swedish and American national anthems.

Mayor Walker spoke, welcoming the Royal Couple in the name of the people of New York. He presented the Prince with the city's Medal of Honor and the Princess with a second bouquet of roses. The mayor gave a brief speech, recalling that Swedish colonists settled in New Jersey and Delaware in 1638 and that a number of the original settlers of New Amsterdam were Swedish. He equated the liberties of New York with those of Sweden and concluded with a reference to the French general, Bernadotte, founder of the royal house of Sweden, whose motto was "the people's love – my reward." Addressing the prince, the mayor said, "That reward for you, sir, is sure in the esteem and admiration of the people of the city of New York."

As it was drawing near the time when the Royal Couple would have to depart for Penn Station, the Prince's response was brief. He explained that they intended to see as much of America as possible, that their schedule was filled with sights to see and people to meet before their trip ended in San Francisco, where they would sail on to Japan and China. He concluded with the words, "We shall always remember the most friendly and most cordial welcome given us on our arrival in the United States by the City of New York."

Hurried photographs were taken and then the Prince and Princess were escorted to their train waiting in Penn Station. They met the next morning with President Coolidge and began an extensive tour of the country.

The Royal Couple returned to Sweden in the fall of 1926. On the death of his father in 1950 the Crown Prince succeeded to the Swedish throne at the age of 67, taking the name King Gustav VI Adolf. At that time, he was the oldest Crown Prince in Europe. He died at the age of 90 in 1973. Princess Louise predeceased him in 1965. During his more than 20-year reign, the Swedish government became more liberal, and the 1809 Constitution was replaced by the more modern Instrument of Government. He was much loved by his people and known for his many life-long interests in sports (he skied and played tennis until he was in his 80's), botany, archeology, criminology, and art.

Wednesday, June 23, 1926:
Lieutenant-Commander Richard Byrd and Floyd Bennett

Early on this mild June morning the mayor's reception committee boat *Macom* sailed out to meet the steamer *Chantier*, flagship of Lieutenant-Commander Richard Byrd. While passing through the Narrows with the steamer in sight, a frantic SOS was received from the freighter *Waukegas*, which had collided with a barge dredging the channel near Buoy 1 in the Ambrose Channel, and was in danger of sinking. On board the *Macom*, Grover Whalen and the other members of the Reception Committee were informed of the message by Captain James Hamilton and told that since their boat was closest to the freighter it was their duty to go to her rescue. The city's boat increased speed and rushed to Buoy 1, all on board ready to assist in a rescue. As they approached the damaged freighter, they observed that she was listing but was under way. Advised that *Waukegas* could make it to her pier in Brooklyn, *Macom* reversed direction and sped back to the *Chantier*. Coming along side of the *Chantier*, Lieutenant-Commander Byrd, the pilot Floyd Bennett, and 16 members of the 50-man team that supported the first flight over the North Pole transferred to *Macom*.

As the mayor's boat entered the harbor, it was greeted by a symphony of horns, bells, and whistles from every ship in sight. Two New York City fireboats shot sprays of water high in the air. The sound of aircraft engines filled the air as a flight of more than a dozen planes flew overhead, including a Fokker VII trimotor, the type of plane piloted by Bennett and navigated by Byrd over the pole. The *Macom* docked at Pier A where her passengers disembarked for the mile-long stroll up Broadway to City Hall.

A detachment from the Seventh Regiment New York National Guard led the way, followed by the regimental band. Behind them walked Byrd, Bennett, and crew. They were followed by the Police Department band. A detachment of sailors from the Brooklyn Navy Yard came next, their lines and ranks dressed in military precision. Following them and constituting the rear of the procession were 300 dignitaries chosen from the almost 1,000 who had asked to have the honor of following in the footsteps of the men who were brave enough to fly above the wind-swept, compass-disorienting North Pole. Represented among the dignitaries were Federal, State, and City politicians, businessmen, reporters, and stage and film entertainers. Hundreds of thousands of noontime spectators lined the route, as miles of ticker tape and tons of confetti and torn paper fell from almost every window along Broadway. The veritable blizzard of paper surely reminded those being honored of the blizzards they had experienced at their base on Spitsbergen Island and over the snowy polar landscape.

The reception at City Hall was tumultuous, as thousands jammed into City Hall Plaza. Both outdoor and indoor receptions were held and radio stations WNYC and WOR had set up microphones for transmission across the surrounding area. More distant radio stations relayed the broadcasts so that much of America could hear it all.

Mayor Walker greeted Commander Byrd and introduced him to the crowd in the Plaza, praising Byrd's courage and skill. Byrd responded briefly and gave credit for the flight to Floyd Bennett and those of his team who had provided all manner of support. Three lusty cheers for the aviators and crew were called for and all of lower Manhattan seemed to echo with the roar.

Led inside to the Aldermanic Chambers, Byrd and the others were welcomed by a serenade from Congressman Clifton Woodrum, representative from Byrd's home district in Virginia. Woodrum, nicknamed the Singing Congressman, sang "Carry Me Back to Old Virginia" for the naval officer and finished his performance with "Dixie" and "The Star-Spangled Banner." Mayor Walker presented both Byrd and Bennett with scrolls commemorating their flight as another jewel in the crown of American aviation history. City Gold Medals were placed around the necks of the aviators and crew.

Commander Byrd responded at length, describing some of their adventures on Spitsbergen and during the flight on May 9th. He praised Floyd Bennett's skill in piloting the plane through the almost impenetrable fog they encountered as they neared the North Pole. He mentioned all of his team and assured one and all that, without them, the flight could not have been successful. Floyd Bennett was asked to speak next, but his reputation for shyness was proven when he declined the honor to speak and only muttered "Thank you" into the microphones.

Later that afternoon Byrd and Bennett attended a luncheon at the Advertising Club, and later that evening they boarded the Colonial Express at Penn Station for a meeting with President Coolidge in Washington. Byrd and Bennett were both members of the US Navy, so were awarded the Medal of Honor, the nations' highest military award. Byrd returned to New York City for a special showing at Carnegie Hall of a filmed record of his expedition. Ahead of him lay more aviation achievements and two more New York City ticker tape parades *(see: July 18, 1927 and June 19, 1930)*.

Floyd Bennett returned to his home in Warrensburg, New York, and in 1927 was asked to join Byrd on a transatlantic flight, but an injury prevented Bennett's participation. In the spring of 1928, he was part of the team who flew supplies to two aviators stranded on Greenly Island, Canada. Bennett became ill in the sub-zero weather, developed pneumonia, and died. He is buried in Arlington National Cemetery. Floyd Bennett Park in Brooklyn (originally Floyd Bennett Airfield) is named for him.

A great deal of controversy exists over the North Pole flight. Byrd's navigation records show changes to the original entries indicating that the flight may have turned back almost 80 miles short of the Pole, and Byrd's diary is missing pages that refer to the flight. Without strong tail winds, their plane could not have made the round-trip flight from Spitsbergen to the Pole in the time recorded, and neither Byrd's diary nor the flight report mentions such winds. Today many geographers and historians believe that Norwegian explorer Roald Amundsen was the first to fly over the North Pole on May 11, 1926, two days after Byrd.

The Advertising Club of New York

The Advertising Club of New York is a non-profit business organization supporting the advertising industry. By the 1860s, over 20 advertising firms had their offices on New York's Madison Avenue, and by the early 20th century, the street's name had become synonymous with the industry.

Originally known as the Sphinx Club when it was founded in 1896, the Advertising Club began when eight executives started meeting for lunch on a regular basis to share ideas. The club's current name was adopted in 1915, and in 1923 it occupied an ornate Italian Renaissance style building at Park Avenue and 35th Street designed by architect Stanford White. The following year, the Club began hosting luncheons and receptions for distinguished guests, some of whom were ticker tape parade honorees. Long-term member Grover Whalen served as its president from 1932-1935. The Club left the Stanford White building in 1977, and still exists today.

Friday, July 2, 1926:
Bobby Jones (Winner of British Open Golf Tournament)

As soon as word was received at Pier A that the ocean liner *Aquitania* was at Quarantine, the City steamer *Macom* cast off to meet its distinguished passenger, Bobby Jones, 24-year-old lawyer, amateur golfer, and winner of the prestigious British Open tournament. He had defeated the top golfers from the US and England at St. Andrews in Scotland. The victory must have pleased him, because just five years earlier, he had quit in frustration after only 11 holes on that same course.

The *Macom* sped across New York Harbor proudly flying the flags of the United States, New York, and Georgia, Jones' home state. Gathered on the steamer was a reception committee, which included his wife and parents, representatives of the golfing community, two US Army Colonels, politicians and dignitaries from New York and Georgia and journalists. Somehow also jammed on board was the Police Department band. As *Macom* approached and circled the liner, the golfer stepped into view, and a boisterous Rebel Yell rang out from the southerners on board the city boat as the band played "Dixie." As the golfers transferred from the liner to the city's boat, it was discovered that Jones had not yet been examined by the medical staff at Quarantine. Forced to return to *Aquitania* he completed his check-up, then re boarded the *Macom* accompanied again by the Rebel Yell and the strains of "Dixie."

Ships and boats of all kinds in the harbor blew their whistles and sounded their horns as the city's boat neared Pier A. Two city fireboats shot fountains of water into the air, which was blown by the warm summer as a fine spray onto the hundreds waiting at the edge of the Battery. Shortly after 1:00 in the afternoon, the steamer docked and among the first to disembark was Jones, the golfing sensation who had captured the imagination of the sports world by defeating second place finisher, Joe Turnesa, by one stroke. Jones was quickly followed by others and the march up Broadway began, led by a city band. Walking with Jones was Major John Cohen, editor of the *Atlanta Journal*, Joseph Johnson, Commissioner of Public Works, who was in charge of the reception, and fellow golfers, Watts Gunn (who had finished third at the Open) and Walter Hagen.

Golfers and non-golfers alike had turned out for the welcome, and the streets were filled with cheering, waving spectators. From windows all along the route came an almost continuous barrage of ticker tape, confetti, and pages torn from telephone directories. Police struggled mightily to keep the stream of well-wishers from surging into the street and joining the march to carry the golfer in triumph to City Hall.

Mayor Walker stood waiting at the steps of City Hall when the procession arrived. He led the golfer and party into his private office for a few minutes of rest and quiet before escorting them into the Aldermanic Chamber. Walking into the Chamber, the party was greeted by the band gathered in the gallery playing "Hail to the Chief," usually reserved for the president but played for Jones as a special honor. Then still another Rebel Yell came from the more than 300 guests, most of whom called Georgia their home. It was as if City Hall had been occupied by a brigade of Confederate veterans. Mayor Walker's words of welcome were almost completely lost in the din of the crowd. Chairman Johnson finally managed to quiet the group and indicated that the mayor was prepared to say a few words into the microphones of radio station WNYC which had been specially placed in the Chamber for the occasion. Confused by the boisterous welcome, Jones stepped up to the microphone before the mayor and started to speak. Reminded by one of the mayor's assistants that the mayor was to speak first, Jones backed away and Mayor Walker, ever the master of the quick line and fast retort, said, "Your very first gesture here, Bobby, explains why you won the championship. You let nothing precede you, not even the Mayor of New York." The embarrassed golfer smiled in response. The mayor went on to describe how proud everyone was of Jones' victory. "You have brought another triumph to American sportsmanship and American sporting skill."

Jones blushed during his introduction. He had been a shy child and remained bashful into adulthood. "This is the most remarkable reception I have ever experienced," he said, with a noticeable southern drawl. "I can't tell you how much I appreciated it. It isn't necessary for me to tell you how I feel about it. You can tell just by looking at me." And once again the room was filled with the Rebel Yell, a sound few thought would ever be heard in the seat of government of New York City.

Following the reception at City Hall, Jones and his party boarded city buses and were driven to the Hotel Vanderbilt, where a dinner dance reception was held in his honor. Georgia Senator Walter George acted as toastmaster and provided anecdotes about the life of the golfer, his college career at Georgia Tech and his law studies at Harvard and Emory Universities. He revealed that Jones almost failed to compete in the Open because of concerns about the amount of time it would take him from the law practice he shared with his father in Atlanta.

When the golfer finally rose to speak, he told the audience that he was undecided about continuing his golf career and would have to spend some time thinking about it, adding, "Today's demonstration has been the greatest thrill of my life. I never expect to have anything like it again."

Bobby Jones could not have been further from the truth in his final words. He was destined to become one of the few people to be honored with a second New York ticker tape parade. Exactly four years later, fresh from his victory in the British Championship Golf Tournament and on his way to winning golf's Big Four events in one year, he would again find himself in the Canyon of Heroes (see: July 2, 1930).

Friday, August 27, 1926: Gertrude Ederle

Not only was Gertrude Ederle the first woman to swim the English Channel, but she was also the first woman to receive a ticker tape parade for her accomplishments. Only five men had accomplished this swimming feat before this daughter of a German immigrant butcher from Amsterdam Avenue in Manhattan succeeded.

A winner of a gold medal and two bronze medals in the 1924 Olympics, Ederle probably marched in the parade in their honor, though she is not mentioned in any news articles about that parade (see: August 6, 1924). A year later, she swam the 21 miles from Manhattan to Sandy Hook, New Jersey, in a little over seven hours. Later that year, her first attempt at swimming the English Channel ended in disappointment when two of her trainers joined her in the water and she was disqualified. But she succeeded in 1926, and the welcome that awaited her was, in many ways, tumultuous and unique.

Miss Ederle arrived on the Cunard liner Berengaria, which was met at Quarantine by the New York City boat Macom. Mayor Jimmy Walker oversaw the transfer of the 21-year-old champion and her parents to Macom. As this smaller craft steamed through the Bay past Ellis Island, Bedloe's Island, and finally Governors Island, the cacophony of the welcome grow louder and louder. The New York Times reporter wrote "the waterfront was a symphony of whistles, sirens, fog horns, and bells."

Once ashore Miss Ederle and her parents joined the mayor and Dudley Field Malone in a large convertible. Mr. Malone, long an advocate of the Women's Suffragette Movement, had been chosen as the chairman of the mayor's Reception Committee. Twenty motorcycle police led the way up Broadway followed by ten mounted policemen. Then came the automobile with the swimmer, her parents, and the mayor and chairman, following by another 20 police marching behind this vehicle. They were followed by 12 vehicles carrying officials of swimming associations, political groups, and other dignitaries. Bands from the Police and Street Cleaning Departments provided marching music. At a number of places along the route the crowd was more than five deep and the Times reported: "At intervals the crowds in the streets broke through the police lines at the curb, and rolled across the street, to delay, but not stop her progress."

Ticker tape fell in continuous streams, twisting and whirling through the warm summer air.

Ten thousand spectators had been allowed into City Hall Plaza, but it had been decided by the Reception Committee to have the Channel swimmer receive her official welcome in the Council Chambers prior to introducing her to those outside. The Committee had decided that only Miss Ederle, the mayor and Mr. Malone could enter the chamber, denying admission to everyone else, including her parents and news reporters. After they entered the Chamber, crowds of onlookers surged forward, shouting and pounding, until the chamber doors were opened to admit her parents and some members of the press.

Mr. Malone introduced Trudy (as she was known by her friends) to the more than 300 guests in the Chamber. He called her the "Queen of the Waves" and presented her with a bouquet of American Beauty roses. Mayor Walker spoke, reading telegrams of congratulations from President Coolidge and Governor Alfred E. Smith. Miss Ederle, whose hearing was damaged by measles when she was a child, leaned forward to hear his words, which were being broadcast on radio station WNYC. More than 50 speakers had been installed outside the Chambers and in the Plaza so that all could hear. The Mayor presented Miss Ederle with a scroll commemorating her deeds and calling her an inspiration to women throughout the city and the country.

Miss Ederle rose to speak. According to the account in the *Times*, "her face was deeply tanned, and her boyish-bobbed hair was bronzed by salt water and sun. She wore a lavender felt hat, a blue serge coat suit, a Paris blue and flowered scarf, gray silk stockings and black pattern leather slippers."

In addition to the dozen roses, she carried her doll mascot, nicknamed "The Channel Sheik." Her first words brought those in the Chambers to their feet and cheers from those listening on WNYC's speakers. "People said women couldn't swim the Channel, but I proved they could." She thanked those who were attending the welcome, as well as the *New York News*, *Baltimore Post* and *Chicago Tribune*. The three newspapers had provided her with financial backing and granted the $20,000 cash reward she had won by her accomplishment. She also related the story that the first person to meet her as she came ashore in England was a British customs official who requested her passport.

When she concluded her statement, Miss Ederle and the mayor proceeded to the steps of City Hall for photographs and the welcome of those gathered in the plaza. As soon as the doors opened the crowd again surged forward, bowling over a number of photographers and their equipment, and endangering the mayor and the swimmer. A New York City policeman, John O'Donovan, pushed his way through the crowd, boldly lifted the swimmer and carried her back into City Hall. Two aides assisted the mayor inside. More than 100 police were called as reinforcements to restore order. When calm finally returned, it was found that six people had been injured in the stampede. The area around City Hall was finally cleared with the assistance of mounted police and police reinforcements.

It was well over two hours before it was considered safe to drive Miss Ederle and her parents to their uptown apartment. Even as the procession drove up Fifth Avenue there were continued problems controlling spectators. The fact that the caravan made a number of stops along the way to receive gifts from Saks & Co., Franklin Simon, and other stores and merchants added to the confusion. Filled with gifts and bouquets, the car carrying the Ederle family finally arrived uptown, to find Amsterdam Avenue between 64th and 65th Streets filled by well-wishers. A police "V" formation protected her and her family as they returned home. Partying in the streets around the Ederle home continued well into the early morning hours.

Among other things received by Miss Ederle were more than $100,000 in contracts to dance and speak on the vaudeville circuit, swim in Billy Rose's Aquacade, and play herself in the motion picture *Swim, Girl, Swim*. By 1929, little of the money remained due to mishandling by her manager and the stock market crash. She fell walking down the stairs of her Amsterdam Avenue apartment, twisted her spine, and was bedridden for several years. She did not swim again in public until the opening of the 1939 World's Fair. She never married. Her childhood hearing loss worsened and by 1945 she was completely deaf. She later taught deaf children how to swim. Gertrude Ederle died in Wyckoff, New Jersey at the age of 93 in 2003. According to *Variety* magazine, her story will be told in a movie titled *Young Woman and the Sea*, based on the book of the same name by Glenn Stout.

Friday, September 10, 1926: Amelia Gade Corson

Two weeks after New York City celebrated Gertrude Ederle for being the first woman to swim the English Channel *(see: August 27, 1926)*, the city turned out to honor the second woman and first mother to accomplish the feat, Danish-born Amelia Gade Corson. Known as "Millie" to her family and friends, she arrived in American waters on the Cunard liner *Aquitania* and was met by the mayor's official boat *Macom* and the Naval Reserve cutter *Eagle 51*. Mrs. Corson taught swimming at the YWCA in Harlem and to the Naval Reserve and Naval Militia, so the cadets on board the cutter loudly cheered when she transferred from the *Aquitania* to the *Macom*. The mayor's boat carried Grover Whalen, Chairman of the Reception Committee, reporters, and the Fire Department band.

Instead of sailing directly from Quarantine to Pier A at the Battery, the *Macom* steamed to Rosebank, Staten Island, where she lived with her husband and children. There the band and Mrs. Corson disembarked. While the band serenaded her, she was reunited with her husband, Clemington Corson, and the population of Rosebank and the surrounding area added their cheers of welcome. Less than 30 minutes later, Mrs. Corson and her husband returned to the *Macom*, members of the band scurrying so as not to be left behind. As the mayor's boat approached Pier A, Mrs. Corson spotted her two children, four-year-old Clemington, Jr., and two-year-old Marjorie. Now it was her turn to wave and cheer, and it was reported that there were tears in her eyes as *Macom* docked and her children ran to her. Her sister and two brothers were also waiting at Pier A with their spouses and children. She was also met by Cal Harris of the Selwyn theatrical agency who told her that 2,000 contract offers had already arrived and that she had been booked to appear at the Loew's State Theatre three days later to speak of her accomplishment.

Mrs. Corson rode in an open car with her husband and children as the parade began. In order to prevent a repeat of the dangerous events that took place during the Ederle parade, extra police were assigned to duty and they stood, almost shoulder to shoulder, along the entire route up Broadway. Wooden barricades stood at cross streets to keep people out of the right of way. Ticker tape and confetti whirled down from skyscrapers, but the Street Cleaning Department spokesman said it was only about half of the amount that greeted Miss Ederle. The crowd's size was estimated at 200,000.

Increased security at City Hall was also apparent. Five hundred members of the Naval Reserve had marched in the parade, then stood in two parallel columns, holding the rifles at "port arms" as the Corson family was welcomed by Mayor Jimmy Walker. The Mayor greeted them, "Mrs. Corson, Mr. Corson, and all the little Corsons. New York City is delighted today to welcome you home." Inside City Hall, in the Aldermanic Chamber, Mayor Walker presented her with a scroll stating that her accomplishment "carried a moral lesson to all mothers." The scroll mentioned that when she stepped from the chilly waters of the channel her first words to those who welcomed her were "I did it for my children." The mayor then pinned the city's Gold Medal on her pink and white dress.

The afternoon's events were far from completed. Mrs. Corson and her family left City Hall along with the mayor and other officials, returning to Pier A with a mounted police escort. There they boarded the *Macom* and *Eagle 51* once more, and the two vessels sailed them to the foot of West 96th Street where the retired battleship USS *Illinois*, which had been turned over to the New York Naval Militia and Naval Reserve as a floating armory, was moored. It was here that Mrs. Corson gave her swimming classes and a reception in her honor was held. Among those attending was the Danish Consul General to New York, George Beck, who presented her with a silver cup. At the reception she also learned that a New York furniture merchant had given her $3,000 worth of new furniture. The reception on the *Illinois* ran late into the evening and a block party in her honor was also held one block north, on West 97th Street.

Prior to swimming the English Channel, Millie Corson swam around Manhattan Island (42 miles). In 1920 she swam from Albany to New York (143 miles in 5 days, 3 hours, and 11.5 minutes), remaining in the water the entire time except for brief periods of sleep each night. She was escorted during the swim by the Assistant Superintendent of the Naval Reserve on the *Illinois*, Clemington Corson, whom she married early the next year.

She never commented about Ederle swimming the Channel close to a tugboat and being helped by the wake from that vessel. As Mrs. Corson swam the Channel her husband was in a small boat following her. Her time across was one hour longer than Miss Ederle. Mrs. Corson's next distance swim was from Santa Catalina Island, California, to the California mainland, to claim the $25,000 prize offered by millionaire William Wrigley, but she was unable to complete the 22-mile distance because of tides.

Having completed the English Channel swim from France to England she planned to swim in the reverse direction, a much more difficult course because of the tides, but there is no record of her having done it. Various promoters attempted to have Miss Ederle and Mrs. Corson compete in a marathon swim but neither woman would agree to the idea. In 1935, she and her family moved from Staten Island to Croton-on-Hudson. She continued as a swimming instructor until the mid-1940's. and died on May 26, 1962.

Monday, October 18, 1926: Queen Marie of Romania

Speaking over the radio for the first time in her life, Her Majesty Queen Marie, Consort of King Ferdinand I of Romania, spoke in English to those listening to radio station WNYC. She said that she had been told of the hospitality extended to those who visited New York but the welcome she received far exceeded her expectations. She had been delighted to see so many smiling faces and Romanian flags along the parade route that seemed to show real love for her and her country. The queen revealed that her "heart had been stolen" by the reception she received.

The parade bestowed on the queen consisted of a mounted escort of New York City police led by a military band that played the Romanian National Anthem before the procession began moving up Broadway. She appeared to be surprised to hear it played. The snowstorm of confetti and ticker tape that cascaded down on her and the other cars in the caravan caused her even more surprise. She waved to the crowd on the warm autumn day as the shadows of New York's skyscrapers occasionally hid the sun.

At City Hall, the Queen received the city's Gold Medal from Mayor Jimmy Walker and a scroll with words of welcome. Seated in the Aldermanic Chambers at City Hall, she spoke of the friendship she and her husband the king had always felt for the United States. One New York newspaper pointed out that the majority of spectators within the Chambers were women. Once she was given the microphone to address the radio audience, she shared her husband's regret at his inability to join her trip to America, noting that "his majesty, the king would have loved to come with me, but he is necessary in his own country."

The queen was interviewed by members of the press after the reception in City Hall and, although she admitted she had never been interviewed before, newspapers reported that she was quite diplomatic in her responses and seemed to enjoy being questioned. None of the reporters asked about the rumors that she and the king, far from being a happy couple, were estranged, or the possibility that at least three of the royal couple's six children were fathered by someone other than Ferdinand. One of the reasons for her trip to America, it was later rumored, might have been their estrangement and a need for separation.

Queen Marie sailed back to Europe on the liner *Leviathan*. King Ferdinand died the following year, and the throne was occupied by their first-born son, Carol II. Marie withdrew from the public eye and spent the rest of her life writing and following the teaching of the Bahai Faith she had converted to. She died in 1939 and was buried next to Ferdinand but at her request, her heart was kept at a Bahai cloister.

Monday, June 13, 1927: Charles Lindbergh

Others had tried to win the Orteig Prize, but none had succeeded. In 1924 New York millionaire Raymond Orteig offered a $25,000 cash prize (equal to more than $375,000 in 2020) to the first person to successfully fly non-stop from North America to Europe or vice versa. The Frenchman Rene Fonck tried in September 1926, only to crash and have two of his three crewmen killed. In late April 1926, Navy Pilots Noel Davis and Stanton Wooster were injured when their plane failed to gain altitude and crashed. Two more Frenchmen, Great War ace Charles Nongesser and François Coli, took off from Paris, headed into a cloud and were never seen again. Richard Byrd and Floyd Bennett, who had already achieved fame for their flight over the North Pole *(see: June 23, 1926)*, had damaged their plane during a test flight in mid-May 1927 *(see: July 18, 1927)*. At 7:52 on the morning of May 20, they were making repairs to their plane at Roosevelt Field on Long Island when a relatively unknown airmail aviator from the Midwest took off. Heavy with extra fuel tanks, the *Spirit of St. Louis* barely cleared telephone wires at the end of the runway before heading east across the Atlantic. Just 33 ½ hours later, Charles Lindbergh taxied his plane to a halt at LeBourget Airfield, Paris. The challenge of flight across the Atlantic had been conquered.

Thousands of cheering Frenchmen welcomed him, hoisting him on their shoulders. He had to be pried away from the crowd by French military police and brought to safety in a hangar. Lindbergh's life would never be the same. There were banquets and receptions in Paris, Brussels, and London. The President of France awarded him the Legion of Honor. He was transported back to the United States on the cruiser *Memphis,* with his dismantled plan stored on board. Arriving on June 11 to meet with President Calvin Coolidge, he was escorted up the Potomac River by the Navy dirigible *Los Angeles,* a fleet of small naval craft, and army planes. On the same day the United States Post Office issued an air-mail stamp with a drawing of the *Spirit of St Louis* and a map of his flight as its design. President Coolidge presented him with the Distinguished Flying Cross Medal. He addressed a joint session of Congress and was the guest at a State banquet in Washington. Early on the morning of June 13 he was driven to Bolling Field, near Washington, for the flight to New York City in his reassembled plane. A valve refused to function, however, and he was given an Army pursuit aircraft which he flew north, landing at Mitchel Field on Long Island. There he transferred to an amphibious aircraft and was flown to New York where the plane splashed to a halt in New York Harbor.

Nearby was the city's official welcoming boat, the *Macom,* carrying Grover Whalen, the Chairman of the City's Reception Committee. The aviator transferred to the boat, and as it sailed toward Pier A, hundreds of craft of all sizes in the harbor sounded their horns and whistles in salute. Mr. Whalen had requested an air armada of 200 military aircraft to fly overhead but his request had been turned down by the military for fear of aerial collisions. Instead, a more modest squadron of only a dozen planes flew overhead.

No fewer than 100,000 people jammed every available space in the Battery. The shy young aviator climbed into an open car with Mr. Whalen. Bands played as mounted police, detachments from the Police, Fire, and Street Cleaning Departments, and more than 15,000 soldiers and sailors escorted the motorcade up the Canyon of Heroes. Police estimated the crowd at 4,000,000. Never before had such a huge crowd turned out to welcome a hero, nor had there been such a blizzard of ticker tape. Neither the number of spectators nor the tonnage of ticker tape would be surpassed until more than a quarter century later when General MacArthur was honored *(see: April 20, 1951).*

Lindbergh smiled and waved to the immense sea of people. The parade frequently halted en route to City Hall as people swarmed through the barricades in attempts to personally welcome the aviator to New York, but outnumbered police succeeded in restoring order each time people burst into Broadway like a human tidal wave. Two temporary grandstands had been erected to seat 3,000 people, but somehow almost double that number filled them. Many thousands more stood trying to see the hero. Mr. Whalen led Lindbergh to the steps of City Hall and introduced him to Mayor Jimmy Walker. The aviator was referred to as "the man who has won the love and admiration of the world." Lindbergh was almost tearful when he accepted a scroll from the mayor as well as the city's Medal of Honor. Waving in appreciation, he told the assembled crowd that he could never have imagined a welcome of this magnitude.

The caravan through the city's streets was far from over, continuing north to the Commodore Hotel on 42nd Street. Along the entire route the crowds never diminished. Police reported 50 injuries in the crowds and one fatality, a 23-year-old woman who suffered a heart attack while watching the parade from the roof of the Hotel Seville. More than 3,200 people attended the dinner at the Hotel Commodore that evening. In his address, Lindbergh predicted that regular flights to Europe were still in the future and might not come about until some sort of "mid-ocean floating airfields" could be constructed. He acknowledged that winning the Orteig Prize was one reason why he made his historic flight but the challenge of the flight itself also figured prominently.

The exhausted aviator cancelled a breakfast scheduled for the next morning and went into temporary seclusion for a brief period, though on June 16 he attended a ceremony at the Brevoort Hotel where Raymond Orteig presented him with the prize money. Over the next few months, he would pilot the repaired *Spirit of St. Louis* throughout the country, visiting 92 cities in all 48 states. He gave 147 speeches about the flight and the future of aviation. Almost two years after he took off on his historic flight, he married Anne Morrow, the daughter of the American Ambassador to Mexico. On March 1, 1932, their first child, 20-month-old Charles Lindbergh, Jr., was kidnapped and murdered. The so-called "Crime of the Century" resulted in the execution of the convicted kidnapper, Bruno Hauptmann. In future years Lindbergh and his wife resided in Europe in semi-seclusion. Having witnessed the progress of German aviation as a guest of Hermann Goering in 1938 he joined forces with the isolationist group America First to avoid a future war, frequently mentioning German military capabilities. When America did enter the war, however, he was made a technical advisor to the Army Air Corps and flew in 50 combat missions against the Japanese as a civilian observer over New Guinea.

After the war he authored a book about his flight that was awarded the Pulitzer Prize in 1954. He was commissioned a Brigadier-General in the Air Corps in 1954 and continued to advise the military. In 1968 he witnessed the launch of Apollo 8, the first manned mission to the moon, and in 1969 he was at Cape Kennedy when Apollo 11 was launched. Lindbergh moved to Hawaii and became involved in environmental issues. He died on the island of Maui in 1974 and is buried in the village of Kipahulu. His wife died in 2001 and is buried with others of the Morrow family in Vermont. The *Spirit of St. Louis* is on permanent display at the Smithsonian Institute's Air and Space Museum, Washington, DC.

Mitchel and Roosevelt Field Airports

In late 1916, the US Army purchased several strips of land in Hempstead, Long Island for its newly created Army Signal Corps and as a landing field for the Army Air Service. Initially called Hazelhurst Field, the two landing strips were renamed in 1918, one after former New York Mayor John Mitchel, the other after former President Theodore Roosevelt's son, Quentin, who was killed in air combat during World War I.

Mitchel Field was used during World War I as an Army pilot training base, and in the 1920s was also used for the US Post Office's new "air-mail" service. During World War II, it was the home base of the Air Defense Command, responsible for defending the eastern coast of the US against air attacks as well as conducting anti-submarine operations. Renamed Mitchel Air Force Base in 1948, it was used as a training field, but the short length of its runways was inadequate to the needs of the air force's newer jet planes. It was decommissioned in 1961 and is now used as a railyard for the Long Island Railroad. →

Roosevelt Field was used by the military during World War I then was turned over to civilian use in 1920. During the 1920s, it was used by many pioneering aviators. Used again by the Navy and Army during World War II, it was sold to real estate developers in 1950. The airfield was closed the following year and converted into a shopping mall which opened in 1956 and is still in operation.

Monday, July 18, 1927:
Transatlantic Flights by Richard Byrd and Clarence Chamberlin

Charles Lindbergh was not the only aviator trying to win the Orteig Prize for flying from New York to Europe in 1927, and within a month of his now-famous flight, two of his rivals accomplished their own successes that would have brought them the fame he achieved, had it not been for twists of fate. Like Lindbergh, the men who flew the second and third transatlantic flights were honored by New York, but they shared the spotlight for New York's only "double" ticker tape parade.

Backed by department store owner Rodman Wanamaker, Commander Richard Byrd planned to take off in early May, but on May 16, 1927 a mishap on a practice take-off at Roosevelt Field delayed him. Not only did his plane, the *America*, need repairs, but both Byrd and his co-pilot Floyd Bennett were injured. Bennett's injuries were severe, so Byrd replaced him with Bernt Balchen. Together with navigator Bert Acosta and engineer George Noville, they took off on the evening of June 29. Onboard was also a bag of US mail, which Wanamaker asked them to carry as a demonstration of the practical and commercial uses of flight. They flew through almost continuous rain, which prevented them from landing in Paris and, after searching for another landing site, *America* crash landed on the Normandy coast on the morning of July 1. None of the crew were injured but the aircraft was destroyed.

Byrd's navigator, Bert Acosta, was originally a part of the third team contending for the Orteig Prize, led by Clarence Chamberlin, a barnstormer who had learned to fly during World War I. His financial backer, millionaire Charles Levine, wanted proof that his monoplane, the *Miss Columbia,* could handle a long-distance flight. So in April 1927, Chamberlin and his co-pilot, Bert Acosta, held an "endurance flight," taking off from Roosevelt Field and flying back and forth over Long Island for 51 hours. The plane endured successfully, but the friendship between the two men did not, and Chamberlin replaced Acosta with Lloyd Bertraud. Everything was set to take off on May 19, the day before Lindbergh, but at the last minute, Levine decided he wanted to be part of history, and ousted Bertraud. Outraged, Bertraud got a court order preventing the flight from taking off, and it was not until June 4 that *Miss Columbia* took to the sky. Foiled from winning the Orteig Prize, Levine changed the flight's mission, promoting it as the first transatlantic flight to carry a passenger (himself), and ordering Chamberlin to fly to Berlin to earn the distinction as the longest transatlantic flight. With one passenger and no co-pilot, they landed 125 miles southwest of Berlin, after a non-stop flight of 3,911 miles in just under 43 hours.

Both Byrd and Chamberlin were celebrated as heroes in Europe, though not as triumphantly as Lindbergh had been. The *New York Times* noted that Lindbergh had "dared the elements first" but Chamberlin "followed and went further" and Byrd succeeded "even when the elements are most unfavorable." Faced with the possibility of celebrations for both flights, plans were simplified when Chamberlin decided to sail back to New York on the *Leviathan*, the same ship Commander Byrd was taking, rather than flying back as Levine wanted to do. A joint ticker tape parade was scheduled to honor both Chamberlin and Byrd when the *Leviathan* sailed into New York on July 18.

The sky was dark with low clouds and rain drizzled throughout the day. Grover Whalen waited on the *Macom* to welcome Chamberlin and Byrd and his crew. Ships of every size and type filled the harbor, their whistles and horns creating a raucous din. A huge American flag draped the Statue of Liberty and *Macom's* whistle sounded as she steamed by it. The whistle had recently been modified and converted to a steam-powered instrument that, according to a contemporary newspaper account, played "a melodious tune, with a rising note of sympathetic inquiry." The police steamer *Riverside*, carrying the Police Department band, drew close to the *Macom* and the band played "Home, Sweet Home" as *Macom* glided into place at Pier A and all on board disembarked.

Just weeks after his own ticker tape parade *(see June 13, 1927)*, Charles Lindbergh was the first to welcome Commander Byrd and Clarence Chamberlin ashore, followed by Floyd Bennett, who had been Byrd's pilot in their flight over the North Pole *(see: June 23, 1926)* and was still using a cane after the injury that kept him from the Transatlantic flight. A fleet of 40 cars filled Battery Park in preparation for the parade to City Hall. The first two cars carried Byrd and Balchen respectively. Colonel Lindbergh declined the offer to join Chamberlin in the third car, saying "I had my day" and departed before the parade began. The first three cars were open limousines, and the riders braved the elements and stood for the duration of the procession. The remaining closed vehicles carried other members of the crew and various notable dignitaries.

Co-Grand Marshals Colonel Peter Traub and Major A. G. Gardner led a platoon of mounted police in the pouring rain. They were followed by two infantry battalions, the Navy Band, 200 sailors and naval cadets from Brooklyn Navy Yard, a company of the 23rd National Guard regiment, another squad of mounted police and the Fire Department band directly in front of the fleet of 40 vehicles. Vast quantities of ticker tape and torn paper, sodden by the rain, fell from every window and littered Broadway. Even embarrassed employees of the Weather Bureau in the Whitehall Building who had predicted a sunny and fair day tossed paper from their observatory. Long streamers of tape twisted and knotted on flagpoles and cornices. Despite the rain a huge crowd lined the thoroughfare. Many of those watching huddled beneath umbrellas or in doorways. At the corner of Courtland Street construction workers stood in a steel steam shovel used to haul cement to the upper floors of the building being built there. It had been raised nearly fifty feet in the air and as Byrd's car passed below, they began a chant of "Byrd...Byrd...Byrd" which was soon taken up by others along the way and echoed through the streets.

Hundreds of portable chairs had been set up in City Hall Plaza but only about 25 were occupied by spectators who wished to be near enough to witness the ceremony as Mayor Walker welcomed the aviators and hung the city's Medal of Valor around their necks. The schedule of speeches and acknowledgements was abbreviated by the rain and those listening to the event on radio station WNYC were given descriptions of the pre-flight plans and the flight.

The motorcade resumed its way up Lafayette Street shortly afterwards, passing the Tombs on Centre Street and the Manhattan Criminal Court on Franklin Street, where a few prisoners joined in the chanting through the barred windows. Further north of

Lafayette Street the motorcade passed through the city's printing district. As the rain suddenly stopped and a faint beam of sunlight emerged from the clouds, young female printer employees opened windows and tossed down colored strips of paper, cards, sheets, and even envelopes. When the motorcade reached Astor Place the sun disappeared once again and rain, accompanied by loud burst of thunder and daggers of lightning, fell anew. On lower Fifth Avenue another ticker tape greeting descended. The caravan finally halted at the Eternal Light in Madison Square, where Byrd and Chamberlin laid a wreath. That was the end of the joint ceremonies. Chamberlin was driven to his hometown of Teterboro, New Jersey, where a small celebration was held that afternoon, while Byrd and his crew headed for the Waldorf Astoria, where they were honored at a dinner that evening.

Clarence Chamberlin continued flying throughout the 1930s, but increasingly turned his attention to designing and selling planes rather than racing. He helped train army pilots during World War II and continued flying small passenger planes until age grounded him. He died in 1976.

A month after this parade, Byrd wrote an article for *Popular Science Monthly*, suggesting that, with certain modifications, an aircraft could cross the Atlantic non-step with 3 or 4 passengers. He predicted that it would be at least 20 years before transatlantic flight would be possible "on a commercial scale." Both Byrd and Balchen made future flights together and in 1930 would receive one more ticker tape parade *(see June 19, 1930)*.

Tuesday, November 11, 1927:
Ruth Elder and George Haldeman

In an attempt to be the first woman to fly across the Atlantic, Ruth Elder took off from Roosevelt Field, Long Island, on Oct. 13, 1927 in a Stinson Detroiter monoplane named *American Girl*. Many called it a foolish stunt on the part of the attractive 28-year-old Alabama woman who had been flying for less than a year. Included among her detractors was Eleanor Roosevelt who considered the flight a publicity stunt. Ruth Elder's comments before the flight added to the controversy, including her statement that one reason for the flight was her hope to buy a new gown in Paris. She had chosen as her flying-mate George Haldeman, an accomplished pilot and navigator.

Whether or not it was an attempt to become "Lady Lindy" by emulating Lindbergh's flight the previous June, the attempt was well-planned and well-financed. Despite choosing a southerly route to avoid the weather encountered by previous transatlantic flights, the *American Girl* encountered a storm, and ice formed on its wings and tail. Ships attempting to follow the plane lost track of it and for hours nothing was seen or heard, until the plane descended from the storm clouds off the island of Horta in the Azores, leveled off a few feet above the ocean and made a watery emergency landing. Within sight and less than two miles away was the Dutch tanker *Barendrecht*. Lifeboats were lowered and as the two aviators exited the plane and stood on its wings, one of the plane's reserve gas tanks burst into flames, probably ignited by one of the flares they carried in the plane. With the flames slowly advancing across the fuselage and towards the wings, a lifeboat reached the two aviators, ropes were thrown to them, and they were pulled to safety, soaking wet.

Huge celebrations, parades, and dinners were held for them after their nearly successful flight. They were feted on the island of Madeira, in Lisbon, Paris, and London before they sailed back to New York on the *Aquitania*. As the liner steamed into New

York Harbor it was met by the city's reception boat, the *Macom*. Aboard was Grover Whalen, Chairman of the Mayor Reception Committee, Mrs. Joseph Dixon, representing the National Woman's Party, Lyle Womack, plus other committee members and newsmen. Mrs. Dixon presented the female flier with a huge bouquet of red roses. Miss Elder and Mr. Haldeman transferred to the smaller vessel, and as it approached the Battery they stood on the top deck while photographers snapped pictures. Miss Elder was married to Lyle Womack, a former football player and prize fighter, but she always used her maiden name. As the *Macom* passed the Statue of Liberty, Mr. Womack lifted her so she could have a better view.

The *Macom* docked at Pier A and the two fliers entered an open car with Grover Whalen for the ride up the Canyon of Heroes. Other vehicles followed, filled with celebrities, dignitaries, and more newsmen. The crowds along the route were large, greater than for the parade awarded Commander Byrd *(see: July 18, 1927)* but not as large as for Lindbergh *(see: June 13, 1927)*. Ticker tape drifted down and swirled around the motorcade. Mr. Haldeman sat for most of the ride and waved to the crowd, but Miss Elder seemed to enjoy it far more than he. She stood and waved and blew kisses to the crowd.

Unlike most parades, the procession did not stop at City Hall. After the cars passed City Hall Park, they increased speed and continued north, driving to the Hotel St. Regis on East 55th Street. Here the fliers were guests of the city at a quick lunch, after which they were driven back downtown to City Hall. The Police Department band provided a musical welcome when they arrived. Grover Whalen introduced them to Mayor Walker, recalling that they had left Long Island a month earlier, had survived a potentially fatal crash, and were experiencing the type of welcome that only New York City could provide.

Mayor Walker kissed Miss Elder and shook Mr. Haldeman's hand. The mayor commented on the modest bravery of Mr. Haldeman, whose piloting skills made the landing in the Atlantic successful. The aviator stood at the mayor's side and smiled in appreciation. Mayor Walker than turned his attention to Miss Elder. With an admiring glance he said, "Pulchritude is no bar to courage," noting that she had taken turns at the controls of the plane during the flight and that "womanhood has a place, even in science, in courage and in self-sacrifice for the world's progress." He concluded by adding that he had just been informed that contracts totaling more than $200,000 from film and vaudeville awaited her signature.

Mr. Haldeman spoke next, very briefly, stating that if he were to make another transatlantic flight, he could think of no one he would prefer sharing the flight with than Miss Elder. When she spoke, she said that the parade was "awesome" and that she had never expected such a "gay welcome." She tried to deliver a prepared speech but apologized, saying that her "heart stuck in her throat" because of the emotional event. Later that day the two dined at the Colony Restaurant at 677 Madison Avenue, then attended a performance of the *Ziegfeld Follies* at the Amsterdam Theater. A crowd of people jammed 42nd Street, waiting for a glimpse of the two after the show, and police had to open a path through the crowd.

Haldeman continued flying and set a number of records for low-level and speed flights. He was a close friend of both Charles Lindbergh and Howard Hughes and worked with Hughes in the construction of his giant flying boat, the *Spruce Goose*. He died in Lakeland, Florida in 1982 at the age of 84.

Ruth Elder turned to acting in 1928 and starred in three silent movies, but the advent of talking films ended her acting career. In 1929 she took part in the Powder Puff Derby, a cross-country airplane race for female pilots. Though she continued to fly, that was her last event. She divorced Lyle Womack in 1929 and eventually married six times, including twice to Hollywood cameraman Ralph King. She died in San Francisco in 1977 at the age of 75.

City Hall Park

When the city government moved out of Federal Hall in 1789 to make room for the new Congress, it decided to build a new home in the greenery known as the Commons. Located a mile north of the Battery on Broadway, the Commons had been a communal pasture for livestock during the 1600s, when it lay just beyond the edge of the city's inhabited areas. By the 1700s, the Commons was a site for rallies, protests and other public gatherings. The city's first Liberty Pole was erected there in 1766, and a decade later, General George Washington read the Declaration of Independence to his troops and a crowd that gathered there.

The new building's cornerstone was laid in 1803, but construction was delayed because the original plans were too expensive. When the building finally opened in 1812, the park became the center of the city's political activity. When slavery was abolished in New York in 1827, a two-day celebration was held there. The Croton Fountain was erected in 1842 to celebrate the opening of the city's new aqueduct system. Many announcements and public speeches were made in the park, and troops were barracked there during the Civil War. In the 1870s the park was re-landscaped, including the installation of a new fountain.

Over the decades, many statues have made the park their home, and the fountain has been replaced several times. The Park was designated a landmark in the 1960s, and in 1991 an African burial ground was uncovered during construction on the park's northern side. Today, the park remains a popular location for both protests against city policies as well as celebrations, including many ticker tape parades.

Friday, January 20, 1928:
William Cosgrave, Prime Minister of the Irish Free State

William Cosgrave, Prime Minister and President of the Executive Council of the Irish Free State, was arriving on the *Homeric*, and Police Commissioner Joseph Warren reported that "numerous letters had been received from officials of Irish Republican sympathizers" warning of demonstrations and violence. Many members of Sinn Féin, Mr. Cosgrave's political party, considered the Anglo-Irish Treaty of 1921 a betrayal because it excluded the seven northern counties of Ireland from independence, and violence between the two political factions was not uncommon. No ticker tape parade to date, other than the one for Charles Lindbergh *(see: June 13, 1927)*, needed so many of New York's Finest on hand to ensure safety; in addition to more than 1,000 uniformed patrolmen guarding the route, 200 plain-clothes officers were assigned to mingle incognito among the crowd.

Mr. Cosgrave's schedule called for him to spend two days in New York before traveling to Chicago but because of winter storms on the North Atlantic, the *Homeric* was 48 hours late. To further complicate the matter, a heavy storm caused the liner to wait for smoother seas. At 8 o'clock in the morning, the city's reception boat, the

Macom, rendezvoused with the *Homeric* anchored neared Quarantine. On board the smaller vessel was Grover Whalen, Chairman of the Reception Committee; Professor T. A. Smiddy, Minister of the Irish Free State to the United States; Lindsay Crawford, Free State Trade Representative; and others. It also carried the Fire Department Band which played the Irish Free State's National Anthem, "The Soldiers' Song" sung by a member of the Police Glee Club. When Mr. Whalen and the others of the party came aboard the *Homeric,* they found the visiting Irish statesman on the upper deck. Greeted by Mr. Whalen, Mr. Cosgrave responded, referring to the band and singer, "I almost thought I was back home. It was like our own Civic Guard band – even the uniforms."

The party transferred to the *Macom* shortly after 9 o'clock. but soon received a radio message that preparations along the parade route were far from ready. *Macom* was advised not to dock at Pier A until preparations were completed, so for more than two hours the city's boat made circles off Staten Island before entering the upper harbor. The *Homeric* passed it on the way to her pier further uptown. The city boat circled the Statue of Liberty and sailed up the river as far as Barclay Street before receiving clearance to dock at 11:15.

Ashore at last, the President was led to a waiting automobile. The crowds in the Battery had been kept back by a strong force of policemen, including 75 mounted officers. The parade began just after noon. The army band from Governors Island led the way, playing marching tunes, followed by a detachment of the 16th Infantry providing a military escort. Close behind the soldiers was a squad of motorcycle police; riding recently purchased Red Indian motorcycles, they hovered around the flanks of the vehicles carrying Mr. Cosgrave and members of his party. Another 30 mounted police followed behind.

It was a bitterly cold day and most of the individuals in open vehicles wore overcoats, mufflers, and gloves. Mr. Cosgrave waved cheerfully as the wind swirled ribbons of ticker tape and torn papers along the route. It was noticed that a window would open in one of the skyscrapers on Broadway, paper of some kind would be thrown out, and just as quickly the window would be closed because of the cold. Facing the crowd rather than the parade, police stood ten feet apart. Police sergeants, with small special details, stood at most intersections. The spectators, who had been standing in the shivering cold for hours, greeted Mr. Cosgrave with both cheers and boos, and some derogatory remarks were shouted at him. "Yes, indeed, I heard them," he laughingly admitted later, adding that he had heard far worse in his own country. But other than the verbal remarks, no acts of violence occurred.

The police had all but emptied City Hall Plaza and when the motorcade arrived there, Mr. Cosgrave and his party were ushered directly to the Aldermanic Chambers. Here he was welcomed by Mayor Walker, the son of an Irish immigrant himself, who said that welcoming the Irish President to New York was one of the proudest moments of his life. As the mayor presented President Cosgrave with a scroll that spoke of the struggle to bring independence to the people of Ireland, he mentioned the huge Irish population of New York and its sympathies to the cause of a free Ireland.

When the President responded, he struggled to hold back tears. "I can't describe my feelings. Your city is so stupendous, and everyone has been so kind," he said. He spoke briefly of his country's unfinished struggle for complete independence and thanked the people of New York for their financial and moral support. Because he was scheduled to leave for Chicago by train later that afternoon, little time was allowed for questions from the press, but two questions brought laughter from the hundreds in the

Chamber. "How about the liquor situation?" he was asked, referring to Prohibition in the United States. "It is fine," he responded, "Ireland makes the best whisky in the world." Another reporter wondered about the number of "Irish cops in New York." The president avoided answering, and later admitted that he did not know the American meaning of the word "cop."

A hurried visit to Cardinal Patrick Hayes at his residence on Madison Avenue followed. Escorted by motorcycle police, Cosgrave was rushed uptown for a 15-minute meeting with the Roman Catholic prelate. The Cardinal told Mr. Cosgrave that he followed the events in Ireland closely and that the Irish people were always in his prayers. From the cardinal's residence it was a short drive to Grand Central Terminal. There the Irish leader and his party boarded the train to Chicago. His schedule called for an additional stop in Philadelphia before returning to New York in a week and a half and then sailing back to Ireland.

Mr. Cosgrave was President of the Executive Committee of the Irish Free State until 1932 and provided the recently independent nation with strong leadership. Animosity towards him lessened over the years. He called for a General Election in 1932 to bring younger leaders into the Irish government (even though he was only 54 at the time). Ireland was also hosting a Eucharist Congress in June 1932, and as a devout Catholic, Cosgrave spent most of his time preparing for the international event and almost none campaigning. As a result, a majority of seats in the Irish Parliament were won by Cosgrave's rival, Eamon de Valera *(see: March 9, 1948)*, forcing Mr. Cosgrave to step down as President.

William Cosgrave remained politically active until 1944 and then retired to his farm near Inchicore, Ireland. He died in The Liberties, Dublin, on November 16, 1965 at the age of 85.

Grand Central Terminal

In 1867, business tycoon Cornelius Vanderbilt bought the Hudson River and North Central Railroads, both of which entered Manhattan from the north and terminated at separate stations near 42nd Street. He decided they should share a terminal in central Manhattan, and created the first Grand Central Depot, which opened in 1871. Train tracks were still at street level, and frequent accidents with pedestrians on Park Avenue led to building underground tunnels starting at 96th Street. Safety improved, even as train traffic increased and quickly outgrew the 12-track station, so a new and larger Grand Central Station was built in 1900. Traffic continued to increase, bringing more soot and smoke from the steam locomotives, which the city banned from Manhattan in 1908 after smoke caused a train collision in the Park Avenue tunnels. Needing to electrify the rail lines leading into the station, the owners of the North Central Railroad demolished the building and built its replacement, which they decided should compete with the newly opened Pennsylvania Station.

Construction began in 1903, working in phases to allow on-going use as a transportation center. Using two architectural teams, one for exterior design and one for interior, the new Grand Central Terminal was completed in 1913. Facing 42nd Street, the building's façade was designed to complement the New York Public Library, with a central window resembling a triumphal arch surmounted by a 13-foot-wide clock and a 42-foot-wide sculpture called the *Glory of Commerce*. Inside, the enormous grand concourse is lit by Beaux-Arts chandeliers, suspended from a massive elliptical barrel vault ceiling. In 1944, a false ceiling was added, painted with an elaborate mural of the constellations with over 2,500 stars painted in gold. →

Facing the same challenges that led to Penn Station's demolition in 1963, the North Central Railroad planned to demolish the Terminal in 1968. During the intervening years, however, the city had created the Landmarks Preservation Committee, which refused to even consider the plans. The building received much needed restoration in 1975 and again in 1998. Over the years, the station has also been expanded to provide connections with the city's subway, and in the mid 2010s, the underground dining area was expanded.

Monday, April 30, 1928: Hermann Koehl, Major James Fitzmaurice, and Baron von Hunefeld

Others had attempted it; none had succeeded. A westward flight flying into the strong winds of the jet-stream posed more difficulties than an eastward flight. Regardless of the problems caused by nature, aviators still attempted it.

In the early morning hours of April 12, 1928, a German-built Junkers W33 named the *Bremen* lifted off from Baldonnel Airdrome, Ireland, heading west to New York. It carried a crew of three: a German pilot, Captain Hermann Koehl; an Irish navigator, Major James Fitzmaurice of the Irish Air Service; and the plane's owner and financial backer, the German Baron Ehrenfried Gunther Freiherr von Hunefeld. Their flight plan called for them to land at Mitchel Field on Long Island, but because of a combination of winds, unexpected storms, a faulty compass, and heavy fog, the first land they sighted 25 hours later was Labrador. Attempting to follow the coast south to New York, they soon ran into more headwinds. Finally, with less than two hours of fuel remaining, they made an emergency landing on Greenly Island in the water separating Labrador and Newfoundland. Their landing was seen by a small dogsled party, and half of the witnesses raced to their aid while the others sped to a village 15 miles away. Using a radio, a message was flashed south that the plane was down, and the aviators were uninjured. It was heard by radio station WCC in Chatham, Massachusetts and within hours it was relayed around the world. A successful westward flight had been accomplished. They had missed their destination by about 1,200 miles, but they had made it over the Atlantic. Within two days they were rescued by Canadian fliers, then flown to Quebec, Montreal, Boston, and finally New York. At each stop the three men were acclaimed but nowhere as great as in New York.

The aviators were given a suite at the Ritz-Carlton Hotel when they arrived from Boston by train on April 29. The following morning the three were met by Grover Whalen, Chairman of Mayor Walker's Reception Committee, and driven to the pier at West 48th Street, where they boarded the city's steamer, the *Macom*. Major Fitzmaurice wore the light brown uniform of the Irish Air Service, his cap at a jaunty angle. The two Germans wore the same dark blue suits they had worn during the flight. The *Macom* sailed down the Hudson River to Pier A, welcomed en route by three liners, the *Leviathan, Thuringia,* and *Deutschland.* Aboard the latter was Koehl's wife and the wife and daughter of Major Fitzmaurice. The deep horns of the three liners did not quite drown out the din of welcome from other vessels in the river.

At Pier A the aviators and their families entered the first two vehicles of a dozen-car motorcade. The parade began shortly after noon with an army band leading the way. It had begun to rain lightly and for some reason this delayed the movement of a large army and navy contingent that was supposed to march directly behind the band. When the troops finally did set out, there was a considerable gap between them and the band. Despite the weather ("We saw much worse over the Atlantic," Major

Fitzmaurice commented later), a blizzard of ticker tape and paper tumbled down, wet from the rain. A huge crowd stood along the route, many standing beneath umbrellas. Once at Wall Street and again near Fulton Street, spectators surged past the police barricade to personally congratulate the aviators but both times the police were able to restrain the well-wishers before they reached the fliers.

Mayor Walker greeted the three at City Hall. The Police Department band played the National Anthems of the Irish Free State, Germany, and the United States. Seven radio stations broadcast the proceedings as the Mayor welcomed them and presented each with the city's Medal of Honor. Major-General William Haskell, commander of the New York National Guard, presented each with the Guard's Medal of Valor. The Irish Major and Captain Koehl thanked the city and its citizens for the welcome. The Baron, who spoke little English, apologized and answered the crowd's cheers only with a wave.

The motorcade continued north following the reception at City Hall. At Union Square, a wreath was placed in honor of America's war dead. Continuing north on Fifth Avenue, the aviators were heartily cheered by thousands of school children who had been gathered in front of the New York Public Library at 42nd Street. The motorcade's final stop was St. Patrick's Cathedral, where they were greeted by Cardinal Patrick Hayes who led them into the cathedral for a brief tour. Two of the aviators, Koehl and Fitzmaurice, were Roman Catholic and had expressed a desire to visit the church. That night the aviators, accompanied by the Mayor and Mr. Whalen, attended the Sharkey-Delaney heavy-weight prize fight at Madison Square Garden. The bout ended suddenly in the first round when Sharkey knocked out his opponent. The fliers admitted that it was a good fight "but too short" the Irish captain reported.

The following day was the baron's 36th birthday. A party, hosted by the mayor, was held at the Ritz-Carlton, before the aviators proceeded to Wall Street, where they placed a wreath at the statue of George Washington at the Sub-Treasury building. The next morning the three men with their families sailed back to Europe on the *Deutschland*.

Baron von Hunefeld died of stomach cancer in Berlin less than a year later. Captain Koehl accepted a position with a German airline but was ousted when the Nazis assumed power in Germany, after which he retired and lived on a farm in Bavaria. He died there in 1939 a few weeks before the start of World War II. Captain Fitzmaurice remained an active flier and commanded the Air Force of neutral Ireland in World War II. He died in Dublin in 1965. The *Bremen* was salvaged and purchased by Henry Ford, and is now at the Henry Ford Museum in Dearborn, Michigan.

Wall Street, Federal Hall and the NY Stock Exchange

Halfway between Bowling Green and City Hall Park, a narrow street runs between Broadway and the East River. Less than half a mile long, it is one of the most famous streets in the world, and its name is synonymous with capitalism and the US system of investment and finances. But Wall Street had humble beginnings, and its name is of uncertain origin. The names most likely source is from the Walloon families that lived there during the Dutch Colonial era, though a wall was built along the street in the 1680s to defend the small city's inhabitants, primarily from pirates. In 1711, the city's first official slave market opened on the corner of Pearl and Wall Streets, operating there until 1762.

In 1789, George Washington was inaugurated as the nation's first President on the steps of Federal Hall at the corner of Wall and Nassau Streets. The building, originally used by the city government, was the meeting place of the first US Congress until the Federal government moved, first to Philadelphia in 1790 and then to Washington DC. The city government then returned there until 1812, when the building was demolished to make way for a new building which still stands on that site today.

Wall Street's fame, however, starts with the Buttonwood Agreement reached in 1792 by a group of security traders. The association they formed grew into the New York Stock Exchange, and the current Exchange Building at 28 Broad Street was constructed in 1903. The American Stock Exchange, formed in 1907 and originally known as the New York Curb Exchange, is located just three blocks away at 86 Trinity Place. The city's third stock exchange, the NASDAQ, was founded in 1971 and is located at One Liberty Plaza on Broadway.

Friday, May 4, 1928:
Prince Ludovico Spado Potenziani, Governor of Rome

A year after Mayor Jimmy Walker visited Rome, Prince Ludovico Spado Potenziani returned the favor. The Fascist Governor of The Eternal City, the Prince arrived accompanied by his daughter Princess Miriam, and an entourage that included a Marquis, a Baron, a Count, a Commander of the Italian Navy, a newspaper editor, and the Prince's private secretary. The Prince and his entourage arrived from Naples on the Italian liner *Conte Biancamano*. Grover Whalen, Chairman of the Reception Committee, met the liner off Quarantine and transported the party to Pier A at the foot of the Battery on board the city's official steamer, *Macom*. As the *Macom* neared the pier the city's fireboat *John Purray Mitchel* shot geysers of water high in the air. The 20-year-old Princess said she had never seen a fireboat before and admitted that she was thrilled by the sight.

At the Battery the Prince and his party stepped into open limousines. They were greeted by more than 2,000 spectators, many of whom gave the Fascist salute in welcome. The Prince sat with his daughter and Mr. Whalen. Police escorts on motorcycles led the parade, which included the First Army band and honor guards drawn from the Army and Navy. To protect against any anti-Fascist demonstrations a larger number of police than usual were stationed along the parade route. Streamers of ticker tape and bits of paper of various color floated down from the skyscrapers. Hundreds stood along the curb at the beginning of the march and the size of the crowd swelled further north.

Mayor Walker awaited the parade at the steps of City Hall and shook the Prince's arm warmly as he exited his vehicle. They exchanged smiles while the Prince gestured to the skyline around him. The mayor escorted the Prince and his party into the Aldermanic Chambers. An assembled crowd of more than 300 stood as soprano Helen Schaefer sang the Italian and American national anthems. Mr. Whalen then formally introduced the Prince to the crowd and the mayor again shook the Prince's hand. Before presenting the Governor of Rome with the city's Gold Medal and a scroll commemorating the visit, the mayor recounted how gracious the Prince had been a year earlier when the mayor had visited Rome. The Mayor reminded the Prince that New York, with more than a million citizens of Italian ancestry, claimed to be the largest Italian city in the world.

At the conclusion of the mayor's remarks, Prince Potenziani thanked all present and suggested that the population of Naples probably exceeded that of New York and the next Italian census would show it. The Prince commented that he had been all over the world, but this was his first visit to the United States. "New York is astounding," he said, "I have saved America for last." Cheers and applause followed his comments about the city. The Prince refused to speak of political matters but only stated that his country and the United States have found different paths to providing for the welfare of their people. He explained that his title of Governor was akin to that of mayor but stated that he had no Board of Estimates, "When we need something, we buy it," he said much to the amusement of some of those present. He also stated that one of the reasons for his visit was to study how New York handled its traffic, admitting that automobile traffic in his city was becoming a nightmare.

An early dinner at the Ritz-Carlton followed. Once more a heavy police presence was obvious, but no demonstrations of any kind took place. Among those at the dinner were financiers, politicians, and a number of Italian Americans from the entertainment field. Following dinner, the Prince, his daughter, and the mayor attended a performance of the George Gershwin musical *Rosalie* at the New Amsterdam Theater. The curtain had already risen when the party arrived, but the performance was halted as the actor Jack Donohue welcomed them and asked the audience to extend a round of applause to them.

A busy schedule lay ahead for the Prince, including receptions and dinners sponsored by Italian American organizations for the next three nights, a visit with President Coolidge, and a sightseeing trip to West Point. The Prince said he most looked forward to seeing a foot race in the city from Cornelia Street in lower Manhattan to Coney Island on the final day of his eight-day visit. The race was sponsored by *Il Progresso*, New York's Italian language newspaper, and the Prince was the official starter.

Following his visit, the Prince returned to Italy on the *Conte Biancamano*. As Fascist power became more entrenched in Italy his position became more symbolic. By the time of his death in 1940 he was a figurehead of the Fascist government with no say in the running of the affairs of the city of Rome.

First Army Band

Military troops have often used musical instruments as a way to communicate over the noise of battle in the years prior to radio and electronic communication. Fife and drum players were so ubiquitous during the American Revolution that they have become symbols of that era, and the US Army began using bugles during the War of 1812. During the American Civil War, each state provided bands with their regiments, and band members were often assigned non-combat duties, including assisting field surgeons and serving as stretcher-bearers. After the war, individual regiments continued having bands if their commanders desired, but Congress provided no funding for bands and their instruments until the First World War. Even then, bands were organized at the regimental level, with varying sets of instruments and levels of musical skill.

During that war, General John Pershing was impressed by the superior playing of European marching bands, so in 1922 he established a band for the US First Army. Relieved of non-musical duties, the First Army Band conducted national tours in the late 1920s, marching in parades on July 4 and other national holidays. During World War II, the band performed in North Africa and Europe, earning a campaign streamer (usually awarded to combat units) for service in the Rhineland.

Often referred to as Pershing's Own, the band was renamed the US Army Band during the 1930s, becoming the premier musical organization of the US military. It has performed in numerous concert halls including Carnegie Hall and Radio City Music Hall, at Presidential Inaugurations and the state funeral for President Kennedy, and at the Pentagon after the attack on September 11, 2001.

Friday, July 6, 1928:
Amelia Earhart, Wilmer Stultz, and Louis Gordon

The liner *President Roosevelt* arrived off Quarantine in the early evening of July 5. Rain and heavy seas prevented the ship from proceeding further into New York Harbor and its three most celebrated passengers, Amelia Earhart, Wilmer Stultz, and Louis Gordon, spent an impatient evening waiting for the arrival of the city's welcoming boat, the *Macom*. Having flown across the Atlantic from Newfoundland to Wales a month earlier, the three reportedly spent a sleepless night waiting for smoother waters and the *Macom*.

As a light rain fell, the city's steamer finally arrived after 9 o'clock the next morning, and whitecaps broke around the larger ship. After attempting to come along side twice, the *Macom* was finally secured to the liner. First down the ramp was Wilmer Stultz, pilot of the Fokker VIIb aircraft named *Friendship* that had crossed the Atlantic in somewhat similar weather. Louis Gordon, co-pilot and mechanic, descended next. Last aboard the *Macom* was Amelia Earhart, female aviator, the first woman to successfully make the transatlantic flight. Greeting them as they came aboard was Grover Whalen, Chairman of the Mayor's Reception Committee. He was joined by other officials from New York, Chicago (pilot Stultz's hometown) and Williamsburg, Pennsylvania, where Miss Earhart had attended school. Members of the Fire Department band and reporters were also crowded aboard, and as the city's boat moved towards the Battery, the band serenaded all on board and reporters interviewed and snapped photographs. Although Mr. Stultz was the pilot, Miss Earhart was the focus of most of the reporters' questions, who asked if she had been afraid during the 20 hours and 40 minutes of the flight.

"Afraid? No, I was too busy. I didn't think of it. I kept my fingers busy," she responded, mentioning to her sole job during the flight was keeping the log of the flight.

A crowd of about 5,000 people waited at Pier A. Although the drizzle had finally ceased, the threat of further inclement weather was given as the reason why the number there, and also along the parade's route up Broadway, was so small. Once ashore, Mr. Whalen presented the aviatrix with a huge bouquet of American Beauty roses. The floral gift was so large that she needed assistance with it as she, Stultz and Gordon entered the back of the waiting white convertible. Before taking hold of the bouquet again, Miss Earhart smoothed her wrinkled blue suit with cream-colored edging and matching white chiffon collar. Her hat was similar to a flying helmet, but it was adorned with a white floral design.

The Fire and Police Department Bands escorted the flyers. A military detachment from Fort Jay served as color bearers and contingents from the Fire, Police, and Street Cleaning Departments marched. A squad of motorcycles cleared the route and rode along each side of the vehicle. Just as the parade was about to begin, Stultz's wife and Gordon's fiancé emerged from the crowd. Long embraces and kisses briefly delayed the start of the parade. There was no such similar greeting for the unwed Miss Earhart, although reporters frequently asked if she was planning to marry a longtime friend from Boston who was a fellow aviator.

The ride to City Hall proceeded smoothly, though the weather conditions were blamed for the small amount of ticker tape that fell. Acting Mayor Joseph McKee greeted the fliers at City Hall. He assisted Miss Earhart out of the automobile and led them to the reviewing stand that had been erected days earlier for the annual Independence Day celebrations in the Park. After the Acting Mayor apologized for the absence of Mayor Walker, he presented the three honorees with the city's Gold Medal and a scroll citing their accomplishment. Miss Earhart's scroll mentioned the courage it took for her to be the first female to make the transoceanic flight. "Your bravery, your indomitable spirit, the feminine modesty which has characterized your victory will, we are sure, be a burning inspiration to the women of America," the Acting Mayor said in tribute to her.

All three were called on to respond, but the two men yielded to Miss Earhart. She praised the piloting abilities of Mr. Stultz and added, "It is always a privilege to come to New York City at any time, but this time seems more glorious than ever." Further festivities were cancelled because rain began to fall as she finished her response.

On the drive uptown from City Hall, Miss Earhart commented on the police motorcycles with side cars and asked if it would be possible for her to ride in one sometime. That afternoon Commander Richard Byrd, a recipient of two ticker tape parades himself (see: June 23, 1926 and July 18, 1927) hosted a reception at the Biltmore Hotel for more than 75 guests. Later the fliers viewed a film of their historic flight at the Paramount Theater, after which they attended a special fund-raising event at the Palace Theater for the 1928 American Olympic team. The silk American flag that Miss Earhart had taken with her on the flight was auctioned, and it was purchased for $650 by actor Charles Winninger, star of the recently opened musical Show Boat.

The following morning the three aviators were taken to Pennsylvania Station for the trip to Washington and a meeting with President Coolidge. The two gentlemen were driven in a city limousine, while Miss Earhart rode in a police sidecar and called the experience one of the most exciting of her life.

Two years later, on July 1, 1929, Wilmer Stultz was killed when he crashed in a test flight near Floyd Bennett Field, Brooklyn. Louis Gordon retired from active flying not long after Stultz died and disappeared from public view.

Amelia Earhart was dissatisfied with her role in the flight and stated that she felt "like a piece of luggage" on the flight. She became determined to attempt a solo flight in the future. She eventually achieved this goal and was honored with a second parade *(see: June 20, 1932)*.

Acting Mayor Joseph McKee (Sept-Dec, 1932)

When Mayor Jimmy Walker abruptly resigned in September 1932, there was a year and four months left in his term. Per the city charter in force at the time, the President of the Board of Aldermen, Joseph McKee became Acting Mayor.

Born in New York City in 1898, McKee started his career as a high school teacher in the Bronx before turning to politics. He served in the State Assembly from 1918 to 1923, then became Municipal Judge from 1925 to 1926. He was elected President of the Board of Aldermen in 1926.

His first priority upon becoming Acting Mayor was to schedule a special election to fill the final year of Mayor Walker's term. When the Democratic party nominated John O'Brien, McKee ran as a write-in candidate, and lost. His four-month term as Acting Mayor ended on December 31, 1932.

McKee ran unsuccessfully for Mayor in 1933 as a third-party candidate, then returned to the Democratic Party, serving as a delegate at the party's National Conventions from 1932 to 1944. He died in 1956.

Wednesday, August 22, 1928:
US Olympians from IX Olympic Games

The United States Olympics team, returning from Amsterdam on the liner *President Roosevelt*, steamed up the harbor from Quarantine in a driving rain. The team brought home a total of 56 medals: 22 gold, 18 silver, and 16 bronze. Two of the gold medals went to Johnny Weissmuller, for the 100-meter freestyle and for the 4 by 200-meter freestyle relay swimming events, adding to the medals he had won four years earlier in Paris. *(see: August 6, 1924)*.

Crowds began lining the area around Pier A and lower Broadway early in the morning, huddling under umbrellas for protection. Those at the Battery saw the ship carrying the Olympians being escorted upriver by a tug, followed by the city boat *Macom*. The *Macom* was carrying Grover Whalen, Chairman of the Mayor's Committee for the Reception of Distinguished Guests, as well as the Fire Department Band and the Street Cleaning Department Band, which played "The Star-Spangled Banner" and "Home Sweet Home" as the ships passed Pier A. Because of the inclement weather, the parade for the day had been cancelled and arrangements for the festivities were changed to be held at pier 84 at West 44th Street. Through some lack of communications, however, this news was not announced until 11 o'clock, when it was broadcast at City Hall Park to a very damp and disappointed crowd.

President Roosevelt's decks were crowded with athletes, the men wearing white flannel trousers and blue blazers, the female athletes all in white. Because of Prohibition the luggage of the arriving athletes was subject to inspection, and a few interesting discoveries were made. One male athlete accidentally dropped his bag and broke several liquor bottles, and inspectors found bottles of champagne, scotch, gin, and whisky in several other bags. The luggage of one male athlete contained 16 bottles of scotch while the bag of a female athlete yielded four jugs of gin. Agents broke all the confiscated bottles and tossed them into the Hudson, but no arrests were made.

Mr. Whalen welcomed the athletes and began to award Gold Medals to each, but also had three apologies for them. First, it was soon discovered that too few medals had been ordered, and a few athletes would have their medals mailed to them. Second, Major General Douglas MacArthur, who was supposed to address them at the luncheon to follow the ceremony, had been ordered to Washington the day before. And third, Mr. Whalen explained that the mayor was absent in Albany.

Nothing seemed to be running smoothly and when it was learned that many of the athletes were scheduled to return to their homes later that day or the next, Mr. Whalen cancelled any other plans for a parade. The luncheon was held at the Hotel McAlpin following the impromptu Pier 84 reception and the 1928 US Olympic team disbanded after the luncheon, ending the day that featured a parade that never kicked off.

Friday, September 21, 1928:
Aimé Félix Tschiffely and Mancha

In the course of performing ceremonial duties, the mayors of New York have provided official greetings to many dignitaries, heads of state, government officials and celebrities visiting the city. One of the more bizarre celebrities welcomed into City Hall was Mancha, a 19-year pinto pony.

The story began in Buenos Aires in 1925, where Swiss-born Aimé Félix Tschiffely was headmaster of the English High School. An outdoorsman at heart, he spent his vacations riding horses in the pampas and befriending ranchers. At the age of 30, he decided to have an adventure, and started a 10,000-mile trek with two Criollo geldings, descendants of the first horses brought to the Americas by the Spanish conquistadors. He rode the horses, named Mancha and Gato, from Argentina to Washington DC.

The journey took three years and was done to prove the hardiness and endurance of Argentine horses. Riding northwest to La Paz in Bolivia, he continued through Lima, Peru and Quito, Ecuador. After passing through Bogotá, he continued into Central America and Mexico, crossing the US border at Laredo, Texas. Then he turned northeast for St. Louis, Missouri, where he stabled Gato because it was no longer possible to travel with two horses on traffic-filled roads. Riding Mancha the rest of the way, he continued to Columbus, Ohio before reaching Washington DC, where President Coolidge hailed him as a hero. He continued onward, reaching New York on September 20, where Mancha was stabled in Fort Jay on Governors Island.

The next day, Tschiffely ferried to Manhattan dressed in the traditional costume of a gaucho, and as reported by the *New York Times* "rode his pet to City Hall" where he "was received by Mayor Walker." In a "simple ceremony" attended by Grover Whalen and the Argentinian Consul General, Alejandro Bollini, the mayor welcomed Tschiffely to the city and presented him with a medal. In return, Tschiffely gave the mayor a bolero, which the *Times* explained is a "string with three metal balls attached which Argentine gauchos employ as our cowboys use a lasso."

As described in the book he later wrote about the journey, after the ceremony "some mounted policemen and a few friends in cars escorted me all the way along Broadway and Fifth Avenue until we reached Central Park, where Mancha was stabled." He felt embarrassed during "this seemingly interminable ride" and "wished that the skyscrapers would fall down and bury me," though it seems the horse felt otherwise, since "Mancha behaved splendidly all the way."

Missing from his own description as well as the coverage from the *New York Times* is any mention of ticker tape, or even confetti, falling from those skyscrapers. While it is clear that the mayor greeted him in City Hall, it is equally clear that there was no parade in his honor. Wikipedia's list of ticker tape parades includes this event, but the authors find no supporting evidence.

Over the next 10 days, the horses were presented at the International Horse Show in Madison Square Garden. Soon afterwards, he journeyed back to Washington, where President Coolidge received him at the White House. He was also the guest of honor at the National Geographic Society. He then sailed back to Buenos Aires on the liner *Pan America*, with both horses travelling for free, courtesy of the Society.

Tschiffely wrote several books about his adventure, starting in 1933 with *Southern Cross to Pole Star*. He and his wife Violet moved to London, where he continued to write, teach, and consult for the National Geographic Society. He returned to South America in 1937 and died in 1953. The Argentine holiday *Día nacional del Caballo* is celebrated annually on September 20, the day Mancha and Gato arrived in New York.

Tuesday, October 16, 1928: Hugo Eckener and Crew of the *Graf Zeppelin* (Transatlantic Flight)

Dr. Hugo Eckener, commander of the huge German airship *Graf Zeppelin*, completed its maiden transatlantic flight despite the need to have its torn tail fin repaired mid-air by his son Knut. After finishing the flight across the ocean, it was moored at the Naval Air Station in Lakehurst, New Jersey. It had carried twenty passengers. The 40-man crew remained at Lakehurst overnight and early on the morning of October 16 they boarded a special Central Railroad of New Jersey train to travel to Jersey City, New Jersey. At Pier 23 there, they boarded New York City's official reception vessel, the *Macom*. Grover Whalen, Chairman of the Reception Committee, was on board to welcome them and be their guide for the day.

The steamer transported them across the Hudson River during a brief shower that hid the tops of skyscrapers in Lower Manhattan. Ships in the harbor welcome them with horns and bells and shrilling whistles coming from ferries, fire boats, freighters, yachts, and tugs. Dr. Eckener was the first to disembark at Pier A, followed by his first officer, Captain Ernst Lehmann. Although all the members of the airship's crew were being celebrated as heroes, most attention was focused on the youngest member, Knut Eckener. The fact that he had volunteered to venture outside the cabin and inside the frame of airship in the midst of an Atlantic storm to manually repair the damaged fin seemed brave beyond comprehension.

A mixed battalion of soldiers and sailors waited to escort the crew up the Canyon of Heroes as soon as they entered the open limousines awaiting them. An Army band from Governors Island waited for the signal to begin the parade, but there was a delay when one car refused to start. Once the malfunctioning auto was replaced, the parade finally began to move up Broadway. Scattered showers continued while the parade moved north. Lieutenant-Colonel Phillipson of the 16th Infantry, Grand Marshal of the parade, rode on horseback, following the flag-bearing members of the Police and Fire Departments. A squad of mounted police completed the parade's complement.

The inclement weather did not dampen the enthusiasm of the spectators, estimated at more than 500,000. Ticker tape fell from the towers along the route, their descent hastened by the weight of the rain. Despite the weather, Dr. Eckener and his fellow airmen rode hatless and waved to acknowledge the cheers of the crowd. The red, black, and yellow striped German flags were displayed along the parade route, a sight rarely seen in New York in the decade since the Great War.

Acting Mayor Joseph McKee met the German fliers at City Hall. He briefly welcomed them on the steps of City Hall and then escorted them into the Aldermanic Chambers for the official welcoming ceremonies. Among the more than 300 guests there were Karl von Lewinski, German Consul-General; Dr. Albert Grazesinki, Prussian Minister of the Interior; Captain Edward Jackson, commander of the Lakehurst Naval Station; Count von Brandenstein-Zeppelin, son-in-law of the late Count Ferdinand Zeppelin, inventor of the rigid airships that bore his name; a number of passengers from the flight, and representatives of the American and Spanish air forces.

Acting Mayor McKee apologized for the absence of Mayor Walker who was in Albany. The ceremonies were broadcast over radio station WEAF and relayed over much of the east coast. McKee congratulated the crew and passengers of the maiden flight. "We were thrilled beyond words at the sight of your beautiful airship floating so majestically over our city yesterday," he said. "May your stay with us be a happy and pleasant one." The Acting Mayor then pinned the city's Gold Medal of Honor on Dr. Eckener's jacket and presented other crew members with the city's Medal of Valor.

Dr. Eckener replied, his words heavily accented. He stated that when the *Graf Zeppelin* left Friedrichshafen, Germany, he had vowed that he would complete the flight regardless of any weather conditions they might encounter. That they had completed the journey proves, he stated, that airships such as his would soon be crossing the oceans regularly, carrying passengers in safety and comfort.

At the conclusion of his speech, the German National Anthem, "Deutschland über Alles," was sung by German-speaking guests, passengers, and crew. This was followed by singing the "Star Spangled Banner." Leaving City Hall, the motorcade then continued uptown to the Warwick Hotel. One of the horses of the mounted police detachment bolted at 14th Street and Fifth Avenue, causing panic in the crowd of spectators until his rider finally reined him in at 23rd Street. Other than frightening on-lookers, no one was injured by the incident.

That night Dr. Eckener and his crew were feted at a dinner at the Ritz Towers. More than 1,000 invited guests attended. Following the dinner and customary speeches, the crew and 40 dignitaries proceeded to the Ziegfeld Theater for a performance of *Show Boat*. From there they continued to the Capitol Theater, where they watched a film of their flight over the city and arrival at Lakehurst.

After the airship was repaired at Lakehurst, the *Graf Zeppelin* departed five days later for its maiden eastward flight to Europe, with Dr. Eckener again at the helm. He later piloted it in its 1929 round-the-world flight. He retired in 1933 when the Nazis assumed power in Germany and nationalized the Zeppelin Company. He never disguised his dislike of the Nazi regime but was not arrested because of his fame and popularity. He died in 1954 at the age of 86 in Friedrichshafen.

The *Graf Zeppelin* made 590 flights, logged over a million miles, and carried more than 34,000 passengers without a single injury during its nine-year career from 1928 to 1937. It remained at Friedrichshafen until March 1940, when it was dismantled by orders of Luftwaffe commander Hermann Goering. Dr. Eckener's prophesy of the future of airship travel was greatly damaged by the disaster of the airship *Hindenburg* in 1937 and the advances in airplane design, construction, speed, and performance.

CHAPTER 4
Dealing with Depression (1929-1939)

On October 29, 1929, the New York Stock Exchange crashed. The Dow Jones Industrial Average fell more than 25% in two days, dropped another 15% during the next month, and by July 1932 bottomed out, having lost 85% of its pre-crash height. Consumer spending dropped, forcing companies to reduce production and lay off workers. Fear led anxious customers to withdraw cash from financial institutions, forcing banks to liquidate, and bank runs caused over 2,000 bank failures by the end of 1930. Compounding the problem was a similar economic crisis in Europe, and dust storms in the Midwest ruined crops, which made it impossible for farmers to pay mortgages. Commodity and food prices plummeted, credit disappeared, and thousands become unemployed and homeless. By 1932, 13 million Americans were unemployed, the GDP had fallen 30%, and New York's Bank of the United States, which had over $200 million in deposits, collapsed in the biggest bank failure in history.

The carefree days of the 1920s were over. The Great Depression had begun.

The early response from Herbert Hoover's Administration, focused on encouraging businesses to maintain wages and reducing the income tax rate, did little to help the many Americans with no jobs or homes. Across the country, the homeless would group together in settlements of make-shift homes built from cardboard boxes, sheets of metal or wooden crates. Known as "Hoovervilles," these shantytowns often squatted on public grounds near soup kitchens. There were several in New York City, including a sites in Riverside Park and Gowanus, and "Slab City" in Red Hook, Brooklyn. The most well-known site was in Central Park, located in the basin recently dug to create the Great Lawn, which at one point had as many as 350 temporary homes until the city forced its closure in 1933.

Unemployment in New York City peaked at about 35%, above the national average of 25%. Throughout the city, breadlines formed around bakeries, restaurants, and churches, and people who could no longer afford food waited for hours on lines that extended for several blocks. Charities and soup kitchen were often overwhelmed, and some people waited in line all day for food for their families. In cities across the country, the situation was the same.

Campaigning on a platform that America needed a "bold experiment," New York Governor Franklin Roosevelt won the White House in the November 1932 election, which also gave Democrats control of both chambers of Congress. With a rapid succession of legislation passed in his first 100 days, the New Deal began, based on the theory that government deficit spending could put people back to work, thereby increasing consumer confidence and spending enough to provide the necessary stimulus to reignite the overall economy. Among other things, the National Recovery

Administration *(see: September 13, 1933)* created standards for minimum wages and maximum work hours, while the Works Progress Administration (WPA) employed millions of Americans to create a vast array of public works, including building bridges and dams, improving public roads and parks, and creating airports and highways. At its peak in 1938, the WPA employed over 3 million people, and a total of over 8 million Americans worked for it at some point between 1935 and 1943.

Fiorello LaGuardia, elected New York mayor in 1933, worked with the Federal government to restore the city's economy and modernize its infrastructure while also helping its neediest residents. He created the NY City Housing Authority, the first agency in the country to provide low- and moderate-income housing by constructing apartment buildings to replace tenements and slums. Many of its new apartment complexes, like the First Avenue Houses on 3rd Street, were built after tenements on the site were condemned and razed. Designed to improve quality of life for residents, they included courtyards to provide more lighting as well as playgrounds and outdoor recreational areas.

New York City also benefited greatly from the New Deal programs thanks to City Parks Commissioner Robert Moses. Moses had already overseen the creation of several highway and parks on Long Island in his prior role as a State Parks Commissioner, but now he launched a huge number of projects that would transform the city's infrastructure. Among the projects he created using WPA funds and employees during the 1930s include the Henry Hudson Parkway and Bridge, the Queens Midtown Tunnel, Jacob Riis Park, the Manhattan Criminal Court and Federal Office building, the Belt and Grand Central Parkways, the Triborough and Whitestone Bridges, and reconstruction of the Brooklyn Navy Yard and Riverside Park, plus numerous parks and swimming pools. After the homeless in "Hoover Valley" were moved out of Central Park, he also completed the Great Lawn and built the Conservatory Garden and North Meadow, Tavern on the Green and the Central Park Zoo. The city's largest WPA project was its first municipal airport, which was later named after Mayor LaGuardia.

Other construction projects were changing the city as well, some of which had started before the market crashed. After the new Grand Central Terminal opened in 1913, the area around it began changing. Park Avenue was rebuilt over the train tracks leading north from the terminal, which had been buried underground. Wider and with landscaped medians, the avenue was soon lined with new apartment towers, and by the mid 1920s, the neighborhood had attracted commercial construction. Two large shopping emporiums, Bergdorf Goodman's and Saks, were built nearby on Fifth Avenue. In 1930-31, the world's largest skyscrapers at the time, the Chrysler Building just opposite Grand Central Terminal and the Empire State Building on Fifth Avenue and 34th Street, opened within 9 months. On nearby Sixth Avenue, Rockefeller Center was being constructed, and by the mid 1930s, the city's skyline was taller and denser in midtown than in downtown.

Not all of the changes were reaching into the skies, of course. As early as 1920, the Port Authority realized that the increasing number of cars and trucks would overwhelm the system of ferries crossing the Hudson, so construction began in 1920 for the Holland Tunnel, which opened in 1927. The Lincoln Tunnel in midtown followed 10 years later, while further uptown, the George Washington Bridge was erected and opened in 1931. And while Robert Moses was building highways, believing the automobile was the preferred mode of transportation for the future, the city's subway system had also expanded into Queens and further into the Bronx and Brooklyn. Plans for a Second

Avenue line in Manhattan and for a tunnel to connect the subway with Staten Island had to be abandoned because of the Depression, but new subway lines were built on Sixth and Eighth Avenues, and the elevated lines on Sixth and Ninth Avenues were torn down.

With all the hardship this decade brought, Americans needed some relief, and not just economic relief. With support from President Roosevelt, who said, "I think this would be a good time for a beer," the 21st Amendment was ratified in 1933, ending Prohibition. Radio continued providing free entertainment, and the 1930s was the golden age of radio shows, with many produced in the new National Broadcasting Company studios in Rockefeller Center.

The movie industry was revolutionized in 1927 with the introduction of sound in *The Jazz Singer*. Within two years, the silent movie era was dead, and Hollywood produced almost nothing except "talkies." New genres of film helped Americans escape and dream: Westerns, comedies, melodramas, monster movies, and the biggest escapist genre of them all, musicals. In addition to a double feature, a typical day at the movies also provided information in the form of news reels, and some live entertainment at larger theaters like New York's new Radio City Music Hall, which opened in December 1932.

With all this development going on, the city was looking toward a future after the Depression. In 1935, a group of businessmen and advertisers led by Grover Whalen convinced Mayor LaGuardia that the city should hold an international exposition, to attract business as well as to excite and entertain residents. With the help of Robert Moses, a site in Flushing, Queens was transformed from a swampy landfill and dump into a 1,200-acre park. Over 44 million people visited the New York World's Fair *(see: June 10, 1939)* to see the "world of tomorrow" as envisioned by the companies and countries that hosted exhibits.

The Depression did not stop New Yorkers from celebrating heroism *(see: July 2, 1931)* or from dreaming about a better tomorrow. In their own ways, the parades of this period offered escape and encouragement *(see: May 14, 1932)*, mixed with a little ticker tape excitement.

Monday, January 28, 1929:
Captain Fried and Crew of the Freighter Florida

Three years after Captain George Fried had been the recipient of a ticker tape parade for the rescue of seamen while in command of the liner *President Roosevelt (see: February 16, 1926)*, he was in command of the cargo ship *America*. Once again, Captain Fried and members of his crew were being honored for saving the lives at sea, this time the officers and crew of the Italian freighter *Florida*.

In many ways the circumstances of this rescue were similar to the prior one. In both cases Captain Fried raced to answer a desperate SOS; both rescues were made during a violent North Atlantic storm; the crew of the *Florida* were taken off their sinking ship by lifeboats as the crew of the *Antinoe* had been three years earlier. On both occasions Captain Fried and his crew were honored by European countries; in 1926 by Great Britain, France, and Germany, and by Italy in 1929. And in both cases Captain Fried's ship docked in Hoboken, New Jersey, before he and his crew received a parade of welcome.

The city's official reception steamer *Macom* arrived at the Hoboken pier on a brisk and windy morning. Captain Fried, was joined by two of the officers who had commanded during the rescue, First-Mate Harry Manning and Radio Officer Nelson Smith. The three officers, plus the eight seamen who had manned those lifeboats, were welcomed by Grover Whalen, Chairman of the Reception Committee. The trip across the Hudson River to Pier A was made to the accompaniment of horns, bells, and whistles from dozens of craft in the harbor. The *Macom* answered the serenade with her own distinctive horn.

Waiting at Pier A when the city's steamer docked were the Italian Consul General, Emanuel Grazzi, other members of the Reception Committee and the wives of Captain Fried and First Mate Manning. Waiting limousines were quickly filled and the motorcade began the slow trip up Broadway, following behind the band of the 16th Infantry, a detachment from that regiment, a naval detachment, and a color guard from the Police and Fire Departments. A squad of mounted police trotted along the flanks of the column. Thousands lined the route or watched from behind skyscraper windows as ticker tape danced and swirled in the wind. At some intersections along the route the wind seemed to play with the ticker tape, blowing it back into open office windows. The eight crewmembers were amused by the cascading paper and they pointed and smiled throughout the journey from Bowling Green to City Hall.

At City Hall Park a musical welcome was provided by the recently organized Municipal Band containing musicians from various city departments. Captain Fried, his officers and sailors waved to the assembled crowd. Mayor Walker welcomed them to the city and added a "welcome back" to Captain Fried before escorting them into the Aldermanic Chambers, where a surprise awaited them. Seated in the first row of invited guests in the Chamber was Giuseppe Favaloro, captain of the *Florida* and the last man to leave during its rescue; the Italian freighter's officers and men were seated in the balcony.

Mayor Walker pinned the city's Medal of Honor to the lapels of Captain Fried, First Mate Manning, and the eight crew members. The embarrassed mayor was forced to explain that the medal for Radio Officer Smith had not arrived with the other medals earlier that morning. The mayor announced that he knew the *America* was due to sail the next day and assured Officer Smith that he would receive the medal before they departed. A scroll commemorating the heroism of those involved in the rescue was then given to Captain Fried. The mayor concluded by saying, "now we have something better than a speech and a scroll for all of you," and called on Paul Block, Borough President of Brooklyn. Mr. Block explained that to reward their heroism a Brooklyn newspaper, the *Standard Union*, had raised money from its employees, advertisers, and readers. He then presented Captain Fried with a check in the amount of $12,000 (equal to about $185,000 in 2020) to be divided among the honorees.

Captain Fried and First Mate Manning both spoke briefly, expressing their gratitude and surprise at the welcome and the financial reward. Captain Favaloro then spoke, his words translated from Italian by Mr. Grazzi, thanking Captain Fried and all concerned in saving him and his crew. The crew of the *Florida* stood and applauded their rescuers. Following the ceremony, a luncheon was held at the Hotel Roosevelt attended by invited dignitaries and politicians. That evening, Captain Fried and the others of the group attended the opening night performance of the Broadway show *Boom Boom*, starring Jeannette MacDonald. They returned to Hoboken after the show where a waiting messenger provided Officer Smith with his medal.

Captain Fried retired from the sea in the mid 1930's and died in Yonkers in 1949. First Mate Manning was later promoted to Commodore of the liner *United States* and

---

Bowling Green

New York's oldest park, Bowling Green is a small, triangular plot sitting in the narrow angle between Broadway and Whitehall Street just opposite Battery Park. Used as a cattle market by the Dutch in the 1640s, the city's first well was dug there after the British took control, and in the 1730s the city created a park around the well for "the delight of the inhabitants." The streets around it were paved in cobblestone, and the park, oval shaped at the time, included an area for bowling, the source of the park's name. In 1770, a massive statue of King George III was erected in the Green, but anti-British protests led the city to pass its first anti-graffiti laws and install a fence around the park. In July 1776, after the Declaration of Independence was read at City Hall to General Washington's troops, the statue was toppled.

As the city grew, more and larger parks were built further uptown, and Bowling Green became a quiet spot of green overshadowed by the city's earliest skyscrapers. Its current dimensions were made when the streets around it were paved for vehicular traffic, and in the 1920s a fountain was installed, used "by local children to cool off in the summer." The park was neglected after the residential areas along the Lower West Side were demolished in the 1960s, and a much-needed renovation was delayed by the city's financial crisis in the 1970s. The Bicentennial revived interest in the green, and tourists re-discovered it after the *Charging Bull* sculpture was installed in 1989. With the addition of the *Fearless Girl* statue in 2017, Bowling Green is now a popular tourist destination.

---

would receive a ticker tape parade after her maiden voyage *(see: July 18, 1952).*

Friday, August 30, 1929: Hugo Eckener and Crew of the Graf Zeppelin (Around the World Flight)

For the second time in less than 12 months, Dr. Hugo Eckener and the crew of the German dirigible *Graf Zeppelin* received a congratulatory parade along Broadway. The first time had been to celebrate the passenger ship's first transatlantic voyage *(see: October 16, 1928)*, the second was for its record-breaking round-the-world voyage. Sponsored by William Randolph Hearst and heavily promoted in his newspapers, the airship had departed from Lakehurst, NJ on August 8, stopping in Friedrichshafen, Germany and then Kasumigaura, Japan. Flying next over the Pacific, it landed in Los Angeles, then made several stops across the US before returning to Lakehurst on Thursday August 29. The journey took 21 days, 5 hours and 31 minutes, beating the previous circumnavigation record. One of the passengers was Hearst newspaper reporter Lady Grace Drummond-Hay, who became the first woman to fly around the globe.

Accompanied by the ship's 33-man crew and its 16 passengers, Dr. Eckener boarded the city's ship *Macom* in Jersey City. Eckener's day had begun extra early, since just the day before he had been congratulated in person by President Hoover at the White House, and flew from Washington to Lakehurst overnight, then joined the rest of the crew on a train to Jersey City that morning.

Ships in the harbor sounded their horns in salute as the *Macom* sailed across the Hudson. Dr. Eckener was introduced to John Henry Meares, who held the previous record for circumnavigation. "I regret that we had to break your record," the Doctor said, though confessed he was uncertain by how many days.

A crowd of about 10,000 spectators waited at Pier A, waving with excitement as the crew disembarked and entered a caravan of vehicles for the drive to City Hall. The sidewalks along Broadway were lined in some places as much as ten deep, and police officers stood arm to arm at intersections to keep control. Ticker tape and confetti rained down on the caravan, and the Department of Street Cleaning estimated about two and half tons of paper were cleaned up before the end of the day.

Another crowd of about 10,000 filled City Hall Plaza, cheering as the caravan arrived. The honorees were escorted into the Aldermanic Chambers, filled with invited guests, many from German and German American societies. Police Commissioner Grover Whalen, chair of the Mayor's Committee for the Reception of Distinguished Guests, introduced the honorees to Mayor Jimmy Walker. Noting that there were more Germans living in New York than any city in Germany except Berlin, the Mayor welcomed Dr. Eckener and his entourage to New York. "We are genuinely proud to receive you as a friend," the mayor said.

A band played "Deutschland über alles" as the mayor presented Dr. Eckener with a gold medal and a scroll, and a bouquet of red roses to Lady Drummond-Hay. He then handed a city medal to each of the crew members and passengers of the history-making flight, while the band played the "Star-Spangled Banner," sung by contralto Helen Schafer.

After the brief ceremony, the entourage caravanned uptown to the Hotel Astor for a luncheon with 2,000 invited guests. Commissioner Whalen began the lunch ceremony saying, "Dr. Eckener has made but one request and that is, before we start our speaking program, the officers of the *Graf Zeppelin* be presented to you." They stood, and the audience applauded as the Police Commissioner read their names.

Several speakers from German American Societies then gave prepared remarks praising the ship's accomplishment as a triumph of German science and engineering, and the pride that German Americans held for their former country. One speaker also noted that the inventor of the dirigible, Count Ferdinand Zeppelin, had aided the US Army during the Civil War. One of the eight speakers, Hearst executive Arthur Brisbane, added a warning to his speech praising the dawn of a new era. Noting that air travel makes the countries of the world closer, he cautioned that "the friend of today may be the enemy of tomorrow" and that the way to prevent trouble is for every American to "demand the greatest air fleet in the world."

Dr. Eckener rose last and spoke of the possibilities that air travel created. It would take some time, he noted, but "regular airship operation on less difficult courses are possible" and it remained for governments to finance the building of airstrips. "We now believe to have done our part" to make commercial air travel possible, he concluded.

William Randolph Hearst had paid almost $200,000 (equivalent to approximately $3 billion in 2020) supporting the round-the-world flight, in exchange for which he gained exclusive coverage of the flight for his newspapers, and the rights to all the photographs taken by the ship's crew, including the first-ever overhead photograph of the Statue of Liberty. He also had a financial interest in several airstrips for zeppelins, including Holmes Airport in New York.

The vision Dr. Eckener had about travel came true, but with planes rather than dirigibles. The *Graf Zeppelin* made 590 flights, logged over a million miles, and carried more than 34,000 passengers without a single injury during its nine-year career from 1928 to 1937. It remained at Friedrichshafen until March 1940, when it was dismantled

---

New York's Early Airports

New York City did not have a municipal airport during the 1920s, so a number of privately held airports began opening, mostly in Queens. One of these was Holmes Airstrip, located just east of St. Michael's Cemetery in Jackson Heights, between 68th and 79th Streets just south of Astoria Boulevard. Opened in 1929 by real estate developer E.H. Holmes, the small landing field hoped to attract dirigible airships as well as airplanes. In 1930, Eastern Air Express operated a 2-day flight to Miami from Holmes Airport, which was soon renamed Grand Central Airport. A year later, Goodyear built a blimp hanger there for sightseeing flights. After losing a legal battle to stop the city from building its own airport less than a mile away, Holmes Airport closed in 1940. The site is now mostly residential.

About a mile east, Flushing Airport had opened in 1927 on a site on the eastern side of Flushing Bay. With 4 runways, Flushing was one of the busiest airstrips in the New York area during the early 1930s, but business suffered once the city opened its own airports. Flushing Airport managed to stay open by catering to short flights crossing Long Island Sound to New England. In the last 1960s and early 1970s, it was used by a skywriting company and the New York Police Department. It closed in 1984 and has mostly reverted to wetlands.

Other small airports along the southern shore of Queens County, including Fort Tilden Blimp Field (1925-1974), Jamaica Sea Airport (1927-1937), and Rockaway Airport (1938-1957), catered to seaplanes, sightseeing flights and helicopters, and were used by the military during World War II. Staten Island also had several early airports, including the short-lived Donovan Hughes (1932-1942), Miller Field (1921-1931) and Bellanca (1927-1928). Staten Island Airport opened in 1942 on the same location as Bellanca. It closed in 1955 and is now a shopping center, while Richmond County Airport operated from 1941 to 1955, and is now the site of a Con Edison power plant.

Not to be left out, the Bronx had an airport where Co-Op City now stands, though no flights ever took off or landed there. In 1928, airplane manufacturer Curtiss-Wright bought land adjacent to the Hutchinson River and began construction of the Bronx Airport, but abandoned it after the stock market crash in 1929. Street maps during the 1940s continued to show the airfield, which was taken over the city in the 1970s to build Co-Op City. Even Manhattan had an airstrip on Governors Island, though its use was restricted to the military, and was in operation between 1909 until 1917.

---

by orders of Luftwaffe commander Hermann Goering. Dr. Eckener's prophesy of the future of airship travel was greatly damaged by the disaster of the airship *Hindenburg* in 1937 and the advances in airplane design, construction, speed, and performance.

Friday, October 4, 1929:
Ramsey MacDonald, Prime Minister of United Kingdom

Shortly before 9 o'clock on the evening before the liner *Berengaria* arrived in New York, the United States cruisers *Trenton* and *Memphis* came into view, their lights reflecting off the choppy Atlantic near the Nantucket Light. They were the first sign of an official welcome being extended to the distinguished passenger aboard the liner, James Ramsey MacDonald, Prime Minister of the United Kingdom. The liner had been delayed for almost a day by a storm and was now in the tail end of a gale. Because of the heavy seas, the *Berengaria* and her two escorting warships anchored off Quarantine until early the next morning.

The city's reception boat, the *Macom*, proved to be late in welcoming the liner as well. Grover Whalen, newly appointed Police Commissioner and the mayor's official representative, delayed *Macom's* sailing for nearly an hour because the British Consul General, Sir Harry Gloster Armstrong and Lady Armstrong had been delayed in traffic. Once they arrived, the steamer sailed and met the liner off the Narrows. Waves were still running high making a transfer difficult and potentially dangerous, but after some difficulty in maneuvering to come along side, the two ships were joined. The British Prime Minister, in a tall silk hat, morning coat, striped trousers, spats and silver-handled walking stick, transferred to the smaller boat accompanied by his attractive daughter, Ishbel MacDonald. Passengers lining the rails of the *Berengaria* cheered and waved as *Macom* pulled away at full steam and the Police Department band on board the steamer began to play "God Save the King." Reporters and photographers were on board and both the Prime Minister and his daughter faced a barrage of questions. Repeatedly he answered questions regarding what he expected from his planned meetings with President Hoover and Congress with his hope for a Pledge of Peace. "If Great Britain and the United States outlaw war, if we stand side by side, who can resist us?" Pressed for details he only suggested that the two nations should create a Council of Peace.

As they entered the harbor the Prime Minister and his daughter stared ahead at the city. When the steamer passed the Statue of Liberty, he climbed to the bridge and watched the skyline come into view. Passing Fort Jay, a 19-gun salute roared. The *Macom* was so close to Governors Island that the concussion was felt on board. Miss MacDonald jumped in fright at the volley, recovered, and laughed when reminded that the saluting guns fired no shells.

The reception boat docked at Pier A at exactly 10 o'clock. Waiting for the Prime Minister was Secretary of State Henry Stimson, and Sir Esme Howard, British Ambassador to the United States. A few words of welcome were spoken, all of which were transmitted by WABC. An airplane hovering overhead relayed this transmission to WMCA and at least four other New York City radio stations. These transmissions were relayed by the short-wave radio stations WGY in Schenectady and KDKA in Pittsburgh, beamed across the Atlantic with an assist from powerful transmitters on ships at sea and received in the United Kingdom by the British Broadcasting Company. For the first time the events of a ticker tape welcome were being broadcast overseas.

A fleet of ten open cars waited. The Prime Minister, Mr. Whalen and Secretary Stimson entered the first; Miss MacDonald and Sir Howard the second. The remaining vehicles contained American and British dignitaries, officials, and reporters. A mounted police company, 100 strong, led the way with the First Army Band and a detachment of the 16th Infantry following. The procession also contained detachments of Marines, sailors from the Brooklyn Navy Yard, and a score of motorcycle police.

Thunderous applause and cheers echoed up Broadway as the parade made its way towards City Hall. Ticker tape, streamers, and torn telephone directories fell, including some directories still intact that fell like small bombs according to a newspaper account. A brisk wind blew through the skyscraper canyon and soon the floors of all the open vehicles were covered in paper. The Prime Minister doffed his hat left and right throughout the route while his daughter waved. Flags of both Great Britain and the United States fluttered from every building.

A detachment of 150 graduates from the Police Academy were lined at attention on the steps of City Hall. They wore white leggings and matching belts across their blue uniforms. Twenty members of the Police Department's pipe and bugle corps skirled a tune as the motorcade drove into City Hall Park. Each piper wore kilts and MacDonald tartan badges. Mayor Walker and William Flynn, representing Governor Franklin Roosevelt, were introduced to the Prime Minister by Mr. Whalen, then the mayor escorted Mr. MacDonald into the Aldermanic Chambers. Because of the delayed arrival the planned ceremonies had been changed and Mr. Walker gave only a brief speech of welcome. He presented the Prime Minister with the city's Medal of Honor and gave his daughter a bouquet of blue and white flowers. The British couple was given Freedom of the City and received a standing ovation from the more than 300 guests.

The Prime Minister announced that he did not have time to deliver his prepared remarks which outlined his appreciation for his welcome and his hopes of an end to war. He announced that a copy of his speech was being left with the mayor and he trusted that he would see that it would be published. Later that day, the speech was read over the elaborate radio hookup and was printed in its entirety in many newspapers the following day.

Shortly after 11 o'clock, a city vehicle with a motorcycle escort rushed the British couple to Penn Station to catch their 11:30 train to Washington. The only unpleasant incident of the day occurred at Penn Station as the Prime Minister and his daughter left their vehicle. A woman burst through the police guards and unrolled a red banner with the words "Down with Imperialists." A known Communist, she was arrested immediately for disorderly conduct.

Later that day, as the sun was setting in Washington, the Prime Minister and his daughter received another welcome in a parade from Washington's Union Station to the White House, met President Hoover, and were his guests for dinner at the White House.

MacDonald was the first Labour Party Prime Minister in British history. His dream of a joint declaration outlawing war never came true. Soon after returning to London he appointed many Liberal and Conservative Members of Parliament to his cabinet,

Penn Station and the Moynihan Train Hall

Prior to 1910, trains headed to New York from west of the Hudson River had to stop in Jersey City, where passengers and freight would board ferries to take them across the river. By the late 1800s, rail companies began exploring alternatives to this costly and time-consuming transfer. Plans for a bridge across the river were rejected as too expensive, and steam locomotives could not use a tunnel because of the excessive smoke in a confined area.

The solution came in the 1900s, when the Pennsylvania Railroad purchased a controlling interest in the small but growing Long Island Railroad Company, which had begun using electric locomotives. Plans were approved to create two tunnels, one under the Hudson and the other under the East River, which would meet and share the same terminal, to be built on land owned by the rail company west of Herald Square. The city condemned many of the tenements already standing between Seventh and Ninth Avenues, and construction began. The tunnels were completed by 1908, and the Pennsylvania Railroad Station opened in August 1910. →

and as a result, his Labour party turned against him. He lost a vote of confidence in Parliament and was replaced as Prime Minister. He died in 1937, age 71, still an MP

The 8-acre building was a masterpiece of Beaux Arts design combined with Classical elements. The exterior featured a colonnade of Doric columns and was covered in pink granite, and the façade was modeled on St. Peter's Basilica in Rome. Grand entrances on each of the building's four sides led into an immense 150-foot-tall concourse with enormous semi-circular windows on the walls, flooding the room with natural light, and a series of steel-and-glass domes in the ceiling.

Penn Station was an enormous success with over 1,000 trains arriving on its tracks every day, and at its height during World War II, over 100 million passengers travelled through it. But the arrival of jet planes and the creation of the Interstate Highway System in the 1950s changed how Americans traveled, and pollution had covered the building's pink granite exterior with soot and grime. As ridership declined, funds for renovation and repair became scarce. By 1954, the Pennsylvania Railroad Company sold the building's air rights to real estate developers, and a decade later agreed to raze the building to make way for a new Madison Square Garden. In exchange, a new underground rail center would be built. Demolition began in 1963, spurring a controversy which led to the creation of the Landmarks Preservation Commission.

The new underground station opened in 1968. Often considered a maze-like catacomb of tunnels connecting a two-level concourse with platforms used by Amtrak, the Long Island Railroad and New Jersey Transit, the station serves over 600,000 commuters every day. It was renovated in the 1990s but was still considered "the ugly stepchild of the city's great rail terminals." In the late 2010s, a massive renovation and expansion of the adjacent Farley Post Office created a new entrance and access to Penn Station's platforms. Opened on January 1, 2021, the Moynihan Train Hall incorporates some Beaux Arts design elements evocative of the original structure, including gigantic skylights in the 92-foot-high ceiling.

(Member of Parliament).

Tuesday, April 29, 1930: Secretary of State Henry Stimson

Secretary of State Henry Stimson arrived in New York on board the liner *Leviathan*. He was accompanied by the other delegates returning from the 1930 Naval Conference held in London: Charles Francis Adams, Secretary of the Navy; Senate Majority Leader Joseph Robinson, Democrat of Arkansas; Dwight Morrow, Ambassador to Mexico; and Admiral William Pratt, Commander of the Battle-Fleet and technical advisor to the delegation. The principal aim of the 1930 Naval Conference was to restrain naval construction, particularly of cruisers, in order to avoid a repeat of the feverish naval construction that preceded the Great War of 1914-1918. Delegates from Great Britain, the United States, France, Italy, and Japan had worked to restructure two previous naval conferences (1921-22 and 1927) to make them agreeable to the five strongest naval powers of the world. It was "a close shave" to reach an agreement according to Stimson, but he was confident that the treaty agreed on in London would be ratified by the Senate and the fear of another destructive war would be eliminated.

At 10 o'clock in the morning, the city's welcome boat *Macom* came alongside the liner and the delegates transferred to it. They were met and welcomed by Police Commissioner Grover Whalen and other federal, state, and city officials. The *Macom* steamed through the harbor and moored at Pier A. Howitzers in Fort Jay on Governors

Island fired a salute as the boat passed, while ships in the harbor sounded horns and whistles. As Secretary Stimson and the other delegates disembarked, a squadron of army airplanes swooped overhead, adding an aerial salute.

The First Army Band and military marching detachments escorted the delegates up Broadway from the Battery to City Hall at noon. Numerous spectators watched the parade pass but there was a subdued restraint in the welcome, no doubt caused by the serious nature of the work the men had been involved in. Flags flew from almost every building, but the volume of ticker tape appeared less than in other parades.

Acting Mayor Joseph McKee greeted Stimson and the other delegates at City Hall in the absence of Mayor Walker. Referring to the group as "emissaries of peace," he introduced them to invited guests in the Aldermanic Chambers. Activities at City Hall, broadcast on most major radio stations, were brief, and by 12:30 all the delegates except Ambassador Morrow were driven to Penn Station, escorted by siren-blaring motorcycles. By 1 o'clock, they were aboard the Washington-bound train to discuss the conference and treaty with President Hoover and Congressional leaders. Ambassador Morrow first went to his home in Englewood, NJ, and joined the others in Washington a day later.

In July 1930, the Senate confirmed the treaty they brought home, which placed proportional limits on the naval strengths of the five great powers, allowing the European and American powers a greater number and tonnage of cruisers than Japan. A clause in the treaty applied only to future new naval construction and not to construction already under way. Japan had already secretly begun construction that exceeded the treaty's limits, and when this was learned another naval conference was called for in 1935, which tried to regain the suggested proportions of the 1930 treaty, but Japanese delegates walked out of the 1935 conference and continued naval construction in open violation of the 1930 Treaty.

Henry Stimson, Chief Delegate, served as Secretary of State until 1933. He had served as Secretary of War from 1911 to 1913 and was reappointed to that post in 1940, serving during the Second World War, the war he and the other delegates had hoped to prevent. He died in 1950 at his estate at Huntington, Long Island, at the age of 83.

Monday, May 26, 1930: Marquis Jacques de Dampierre

"*C'est fantastique!*" The Marquis de Dampierre's younger son Armand said repeatedly as he rode up Broadway with his parents and older brother, Henri, ticker tape falling down on them. The young man probably meant that in the sense of "amazing" but the story of how his father was honored with this parade suggests a better translation would be "unbelievable."

The Thomas Jefferson Memorial Foundation needed to promote awareness of the late President's home in Monticello, which had opened to the public in 1924 but suffered low attendance because of the Depression. When they learned that the Parisian shipping company The French Line was launching a new ship named *Lafayette*, a public relations marketing campaign was born. The Foundation invited descendants of General Lafayette to arrive in America on the new ship's maiden voyage and then visit Monticello.

The only problem with this idea was that the Chambrun family, direct descendants of General Lafayette through his daughter Virginia, were unavailable.

Not wanting to miss out on the opportunity for some free press coverage for his new vessel, French Line President Maurice Tiller mentioned this idea to his friend, the Marquis Jacques de Dampierre, who was the great grand-nephew of the Revolutionary-era General. The Marquis accepted the invitation and booked passage on the ship's maiden voyage, scheduled for May 19, 1930 and bound for New York. His wife Françoise and his sons would accompany him.

Tiller also made plans to ensure the new ship received some free publicity by inviting descendants of the signers of the Declaration of Independence to a gala Revolutionary-era themed costume ball on board the ship when it docked in New York. The *New York Times* reported this on May 12, and within a week, the city announced an official welcome for the famous general's descendant.

The *Lafayette* sailed into New York on May 26 and was met by the *Macom*. The Marquis and his family, along with Maurice Tiller and his wife, boarded the city's yacht and were met by George Ryan, head of the city's Board of Education, who was standing in for Grover Whalen, Chairman of the Reception Committee.

Waiting at the Battery was a motorcade of 20 cars and a detachment of National Guardsmen in dress uniforms. Noontime spectators cheered as the motorcade, escorted by mounted police, made its way up Broadway and ticker tape dropped from windows above.

At City Hall, Mr. Ryan led the de Dampierre family into the Aldermanic Chambers, where he introduced them to Acting Mayor James McKee, who officially welcomed the Marquis to the city. Also invited to the ceremony were 400 school children from Public School 3, which Lafayette had visited when he returned to the United States in 1824. A 13-year-old student presented the Marquis with a bouquet of fleur-de-lis and greeted him in "a sixty-word speech in French of excellent pronunciation and cadence." Replying "in English very difficult to understand," the Marquis spoke of "skyscrapers as symbols of American idealism." The last person to speak was Maurice Tiller, who thanked the mayor for the splendid reception which the city "has seen fit to give our new ship."

After the reception, the Marquis and his family went to the Ritz Hotel, and were the guests of honor at the gala masquerade ball on the ship. The next day they departed for Charlottesville, Virginia, where the Marquis placed a "wreath twined with the Tricolor of France" on the grave of President Jefferson, toured Monticello, and spoke at the University of Virginia.

On May 29, he returned to New York, where Maurice Tiller had one more event planned at Pier 57 where the *Lafayette* was docked. A group of honor students gave farewell speeches in French to the Marquis and then a choir of students sang the "Marseilles." The ship and its "famous" passenger departed for France the next day.

There is no report of the reaction when the Chambruns read the news about the welcome that de Dampierre had received in New York. René de Chambrun was the great-grandson of General Lafayette, so was a closer and more direct relative than the de Dampierre family. He never received his own ticker tape parade but did experience one when he accompanied Marshal Pétain to New York as his translator *(see: October 26, 1931)*.

A minor government official throughout his life, Jacques de Dampierre died in 1947, and the title of Marquis passed to his oldest son Henri. His son Armand died in 1944, a prisoner of war at the Buchenwald concentration camp.

Wednesday, June 11, 1930:
Julio Prestes de Albuquerque, President-Elect of Brazil

The 1930 Presidential election in Brazil was won by the Governor of the São Paulo State, Julio Prestes, with a majority of almost 400,000 votes. Shortly after the election, to revive the flagging Brazilian economy, he began a goodwill trip that took him to the United States, England, France, and other European nations. Sailing on the *Almirante Jaceguay*, Brazil's official presidential ship, and escorted by two Brazilian cruisers, the *Bahia* and the *Rio Grande do Sul*, he arrived off Ambrose Channel in the early evening of June 10, 1930, where they awaited two American cruisers. Because of a heavy fog that had virtually closed the port of New York, the escorts did not arrive until early the following morning, and the fog remained so thick that it was deemed unwise to enter the harbor until weather conditions improved.

Too ill to travel, his wife had remained in Brazil, but his five-year-old son Fernando accompanied him as Prestes transferred to the US cruiser *Macon* (not to be confused with the city's welcome ship, the *Macom*). It was late afternoon when the cruiser steamed into the harbor and was greeted by a 21-gun salute fired from Fort Jay on Governors Island.

Scheduled to arrive at the New York Customs House on lower Broadway before 8 o'clock that morning, it was almost 3:00 that afternoon before Prestes was finally ashore and greeted by Major Jimmy Walker, who joked that his own reputation for arriving late had been exceeded. The parade up Broadway started a short while later and homeward-bound workers in downtown New York were treated to a rare late afternoon parade. Two bands which had been waiting since early morning led the way, playing both the American and Brazilian National Anthems. The parade included a battalion of infantry from Governors Island, a company of Marines, and a naval honor guard from the American cruisers. The *New York Times* reported that only a handful of people still lined the streets as the parade moved uptown but there were still enough office workers to pour enough ticker tape to wreath Trinity Church in streamers. The procession arrived at City Hall after 5 o'clock, and was escorted to the Aldermanic Chambers, where Prestes and his party were officially welcomed to New York in an address broadcast by radio station WNYC. The President-Elect's answering remarks were translated from Portuguese by the Brazilian Ambassador to the United States, Silvino Gurgél do Amaral. Other planned activities were cancelled because of the delay caused by the fog, and Prestes was escorted to Penn Station where he boarded a train for Washington to meet with President Herbert Hoover.

After a reception in Washington and a four-day stay there, Prestes returned to New York, boarded the presidential vessel, and sailed to Europe. The rest of his goodwill mission ran according to schedule and he finally returned to Brazil in early October. But the political situation had turned violent in his absence. A military coup forced both the President-Elect and his predecessor, Washington Luis, to flee to Paris on October 26, 1930, six days before Prestes' scheduled inauguration. His position was usurped by Getúlio Vargas, who ruled Brazil as dictator for more than 15 years. Prestes disappeared from public view until 1942 when, in a statement from Lisbon, Portugal, he praised Brazil's declaration of War against the Axis. Prestes, the "president who never was," returned to Brazil in late 1944 and died in his native São Paulo on February 8, 1945.

105

Alexander Hamilton US Customs Building

Across State Street from the Battery just below Bowling Green stands the Alexander Hamilton US Customs Building, erected in 1902 and named after the first Secretary of the Treasury. Prior to 1913 there was no federal income tax, and import duties generated a significant portion of the federal budget. As the nation's busiest commercial port, the Customs House in New York was responsible for approximately two-thirds of the federal government's revenue during the late 1800s.

Built on the site of Fort Amsterdam, the 7-story Beaux Arts building has a steel frame and mansard roof, and its façade features nautical motifs and sculptures representing the continents and various seafaring nations. The building's architecture and design are distinct from other buildings in the area, and reinforced New York's role as "the leading American metropolis, representative of America's role in the world."

The building was used by the US Customs Service from 1902 until 1973, and also provided office space for other federal agencies, including the Post Office and the Works Projects Administration (WPA). After the Customs Service moved to the World Trade Center, the building sat empty for many years. In 1994, after a $18 million restoration, it became the home of the National Museum of the American Indian and is also used currently by the US Bankruptcy Court and the National Archives.

Wednesday, June 18, 1930: Rear Admiral Richard Byrd

Crowds began forming hours before the scheduled noon start of the parade to honor Rear Admiral Byrd, and all the seats in the temporary grandstand erected in City Hall Plaza were filled before 11 o'clock. Twice before this naval officer, navigator, explorer, and aviator had been the recipient of New York's unique welcome *(see: June 23, 1926 and July 18, 1927)*, and over the years his rank had risen to Commander, and finally to Rear Admiral. The man who had flown over the North Pole and the Atlantic was about to be feted for his explorations in Antarctica and flight over the South Pole.

The parade set off from Bowling Green precisely at noon. Leading the procession was a mounted police escort, followed by a detachment of the 16th Infantry headquartered on Governors Island and the naval band from the Brooklyn Navy Yard. Immediately behind them marched a battalion of the Richmond Light Infantry Blues, representatives of the Admiral's home state of Virginia. In their blue uniforms and white shakos (tall, cylindrical caps similar to those worn by marching bands), this Virginia National Guard unit made a sharp contrast with the khaki-clad 71st New York National Guard battalion, which came next in line. Behind them rode the Admiral, in full dress naval uniform, standing erect in an open vehicle shared with Grover Whalen, Chairman of the Mayor's Reception Committee, and Hector Fuller of Mayor Walker's staff. Behind them followed vehicles which contained other members of the Admiral's expedition.

Almost 50,000 spectators lined the route, showering the procession with ticker tape and torn paper of every size and color. American flags waved in the warm June afternoon. By now a veteran of this type of parade, the Admiral waved to the crowd, doffed his military cap, and pointed to people or sights which seemed to catch his attention.

Once the procession arrived at City Hall, Mr. Whalen introduced Admiral Byrd to Mayor Walker, calling the Admiral the "conqueror of the North Pole, the Atlantic, and now the South Pole." Present at City Hall with the mayor was the Admiral's mother and wife, both of whom held large bouquets, and his son and two daughters. The mayor commented that he knew little about the South Pole and wanted to learn more about the Admiral's exploration, asking about the special attention to planning and detail that the Admiral had used to guarantee all the members of his party returned from the most inhospitable parts of the world. "From the bottom of our hearts," the mayor concluded, "with pride and with love, the people of the city of New York authorize me to say to you, 'Welcome home, welcome home, forever and a day'." The mayor then presented Admiral Byrd with the city's Medal of Merit.

Admiral Byrd spoke next, his words transmitted by radio station WNYC. He commented that the thrill of a "New York welcome" never lessens. He reminded the mayor that before the two-year expedition left for the Antarctic, he had been wished good luck and was promised that the party would be kept in the minds of New Yorkers. He then mentioned the periodic good will messages sent by the Mayor to his expedition via short wave radio, adding that "your cheerful messages" had helped them "endure the monotony" of the long winter nights in Antarctica.

The Admiral ended his remarks by reminding his audience of the two ticker tape parades he had previously received. He praised his crew, pointing out that 12 of them had been members of his North Pole party, and that three men were members of all three of his exploits, including Bernt Balchen who piloted the 1927 transatlantic flight and the South Pole flight of this expedition. Rear Admiral Byrd was then awarded an honorary degree in the Humanities from New York University, presented by the university's president, Dr. George Alexander, and a scroll referring to him as "Admiral of the Icy Seas and of the Viewless Air." Following these ceremonies, Admiral Byrd reviewed the Richmond Light Infantry Blues as they paraded by him in salute, before being driven to the Advertising Club for a luncheon.

Unlike Byrd's North Pole flight, there is no controversy about his flight over the South Pole. Gasoline cans jettisoned from the plane while over the Pole provided physical proof and no errors or changes were found in the expedition's logs or notes. The Admiral undertook four more Antarctic expeditions in 1933-36, 1937-40, 1946-47, and 1955-56, exploring and mapping over 300,000 square miles of the continent. During World War II he held advisory positions concerning national defense. Shortly after returning from his final expedition, he died peacefully in his sleep on March 11, 1957, at his home in Boston, Massachusetts and was buried in Arlington National Cemetery. He was 68 years old. Two naval ships have borne his name, as well as schools in Virginia and Massachusetts, a research center at Ohio State University, a library in Fredericksburg, Virginia, and the Byrd Lunar Crater on the moon. He is the only person to be honored with three of New York's ticker tape parades.

Wednesday, July 2, 1930: Bobby Jones (Winner of British Amateur and British Open Golf Tournament)

Once again Bobby Jones, amateur golf champion, returned from the United Kingdom to a boisterous New York City welcome. Four years to the day after receiving the city's ticker tape welcome, the shy and retiring "Master of the Links" sailed into New York Harbor aboard the *Europa* from England *(see: July 2, 1926)*.

The liner carrying the golfer to New York was delayed by an Atlantic storm and did not enter the lower harbor until well after 2 o'clock in the afternoon. Not wanting to be late when *Europa* arrived, the city's steamer *Macom* had spent more than two hours circling off Coney Island waiting. The steamer met the liner as she cleared customs and the golfer transferred to the smaller craft. On board the *Macom* to welcome him were his parents; Atlanta Mayor Isaac Ragsdale; and Joseph Johnson, former Commissioner of Public Works, serving as the chairman of the welcome reception. Reporters and photographers, along with a contingent from the Sanitation Department band, were also aboard.

It was after 4 o'clock when the party finally disembarked at Pier A. The golfer's wife, Mary, was the first to disembark, carrying a small portable movie camera. Despite the oppressive July heat, large crowds had remained throughout the afternoon awaiting the golfing hero. Many of those present at the Battery were from Jones' home state of Georgia and, as had happened four years earlier, downtown echoed with the sound of the Rebel Yell.

Jones and his wife entered the first car of the caravan, a large open vehicle, accompanied by Mr. Johnson. Led by a detachment of mounted police and the Sanitation Department Band, marchers from the Army and Navy and New York's Police and Fire Departments began the slow procession uptown.

The summer blizzard of ticker tape spiraled down in greeting but something new added to the day's celebration: firecrackers. First a series of individual explosions popped high above the heads of the marchers and vehicles. Just south of the corner of Wall Street, however, an entire package of fireworks was tossed down and exploded like the rattle of a machine gun. A few horses of the mounted police detachment reacted to the rat-a-tat-tat of the fireworks, but their riders were able to control them. Jones, standing in his vehicle, pointed his camera at the crowd and skyscrapers, filming his welcome.

Mayor Jimmy Walker was waiting on the City Hall steps when the lead car of the parade entered City Hall Plaza. Just as the car was braking to a halt, the mayor clapped Jones on the back and helped him from the limousine. The other members of the vehicle followed the mayor and golfer into City Hall for the official welcome in the Aldermanic Chambers.

Mayor Walker began the welcome saying, "Here you are, the greatest golfer in the world being introduced by the worst one." One of the invited guests in the room shouted in response, "Atta boy, Jimmy!" After some laughter from the crowd, the mayor continued to praise Jones for his achievement. "The title you won has been won before and will be won again, but never will it be won be a finer gentleman or better sportsman." Commenting on the heat of the city and the excessive warmth of the council room, Mayor Walker suggested that the golfer might have to return to Georgia to cool off.

"I am overcome by the kind things you have said, and the tremendous welcome accorded me" Jones replied, "I have never been so impressed." When he had finished speaking, the head of the Georgia group of guests shouted, "Three cheers for Jimmy Walker!" Albert Goldman, New York's Commissioner of Plants and Structures, had arranged for more than 150 miles of wires to be strung from the chambers to parks around the city, so that the speeches could be carried by radio station WNYC, and broadcast to the listening audience and golf fans in city parks

After the reception in City Hall, Jones and his wife and parents were driven uptown with the Mayor to the Hotel Vanderbilt for a dinner reception. More than 400 guests attended, including representatives of the major press organizations, municipal officials from New York and Atlanta, and noted amateur and professional golfers. Still shy and reticent, Jones spoke briefly, again expressing how surprised he was by the warmth and magnitude of his welcome. The dinner ended early because Jones was scheduled to board a train the next morning for the long ride to Minneapolis for another tournament.

Bobby Jones retired from competitive golf at the end of that season. He worked briefly with AG Spalding & Co., developing the first set of matched golf clubs, which are still considered among the best-designed sets ever made. In 1931 he purchased a former Civil War-era plantation near Augusta, Georgia, where he designed the Augusta golf course. He designed other golf courses over the following years. His health began to decline in the early 1940's but it was not until 1948 that he was diagnosed with syringomyelia, a fluid-filled cavity in his spinal cord. Paralysis soon restricted him to a wheelchair. Having spent the last few years of his life studying comparative theology, he converted to Catholicism in early December 1971, and died two weeks later in Atlanta, Georgia.

During his playing career, Jones won the US Open seven times, the US Amateur five times, and the British Amateur once. He was admitted to the Golf Hall of Fame in 1974. In 2000 *Golf Digest* magazine ranked him as the fourth greatest golfer of all time, and in 2009 *Golf Magazine* ranked him as the third greatest.

Wednesday, September 3, 1930:
Captain Dieudinné Costes and Maurice Bellonte

French aviators Dieudinné Costes and Maurice Bellonte were determined to win the $25,000 Easterwood prize for the first people to fly from Paris, France to Dallas, Texas via New York, so the original plan for a parade honoring them was to follow a different route than usual. The Mayor's Reception Committee proposed to drive them from their midtown hotel down Fifth Avenue to City Hall before they continued their flight to Dallas. Those plans changed when the public's interest in the flight and the aviators grew, however, and the *New York Times* reported that "these guests of the city must enter its gates at the Battery."

Their Breguet 19 Super Bidon biplane was named *Point d'Interrogation* and had a large white question mark painted on its side because one of the flight's sponsors was anonymous. After landing the plane at Curtiss Field in Valley Stream, New York, on September 2, the two aviators were escorted to the Ritz Hotel in Manhattan.

A pre-parade luncheon was held at the Advertising Club on Park Avenue. Immediately afterwards the French aviators entered an open car. Flanked by police motorcycles, they were driven east on 34th Street, then south on First Avenue to the New York Yacht Club Landing. The route taken by the motorcade had not been announced beforehand but many New Yorkers somehow discovered it. Groups of people waved at the vehicles as they sped by, especially when the motorcade passed Bellevue Hospital.

At the landing, the aviators boarded the yacht *Nenin*, owned by William Woodin, director of the Federal Reserve Bank of New York, which was pressed into service because the city's *Macom* was undergoing repairs. Costes and Bellonte sat on the roof of the yacht along with the French Consul General in New York, Maxime Mongendre, as it sailed down the East River, escorted by a police boat. The crew of the battleship *Colorado*, docked at the Brooklyn Navy Yard and flying the French Tricolor, cheered as the yacht sailed by. As the yacht turned into the harbor, ships of all kinds welcomed the fliers with a chorus of tooting horns and screaming whistles.

Disembarking at Pier A, the party was led to Whitehall Street. Here they entered another open vehicle and, escorted by bands from the Navy Yard and Mitchel Field in Brooklyn, they began the trip up the Canyon of Heroes. An Army detachment from Governors Island as well as Marines from the *Colorado* provided a military escort along with Troop A of the New York City Police Department. It was now after 4 o'clock and the stock markets had just closed, swelling the number of people saluting the aviators along the route. Although the size of the crowd was not as large as Lindbergh's *(see: June 13, 1927)*, the enthusiasm seemed to match it. A blizzard of ticker tape cascaded down mixed with torn newspapers and telephone directories, swirled around by a wind that had suddenly spring up. A man was observed hanging from a spherical clock above the entrance of the building at 23 Broadway, fighting what seemed a losing battle to keep ticker tape streamers, some almost a hundred feet long, from wrapping around the hands of the clock.

The parade and reception had been hurried by the city because the French fliers were eager to continue their journey to Dallas. Meteorologists forecast excellent conditions for the following day, and Costes and Bellonte planned to take off from Valley Stream at dawn. Because of the reception's hasty arrangements, no reviewing stand had been erected in City Hall Plaza and the crowd filled every available space from Broadway to Park Row. As the car bearing the Frenchmen braked to a halt, Grover Whalen opened its door and escorted them out while the First Army band played the French and American national anthems. Mr. Whalen led the party into the Aldermanic Chamber, where every seat was taken, and some guests were standing. Mayor Walker extended his hand to Captain Costes, whom he had met three years earlier. They spoke briefly in French and then Mr. Whalen introduced Maurice Bellonte to the mayor and those in the packed chamber.

The mayor referred to the two aviators as "the first to fly from west to east" but then corrected himself by adding, "who crossed from Paris to New York in non-stop flight." He presented a scroll that praised the men's courage and audacity. It spoke of their flight as "an adventure which adds to the glory of France, and which stands as a high example among the feats of aviation." The mayor added, "New York bids you welcome genuinely, from its heart."

Captain Costes was a WWI ace of the French Air Force, with eight confirmed kills on the Balkan Front in 1917. He spoke English very well and mentioned that this was his second visit to New York, and said how happy he was to find the same man serving as its chief executive. When he added that he hoped to return a third time in the future and still find Mayor Walker in charge, the crowd broke into loud cheering and applause. His remarks were followed by Mr. Bellonte, who also spoke in English but with a slight Gaelic accent. "I cannot thank enough those who arranged transatlantic telephone conversations with our wives last night," he said. He admitted that his wife told him that she had not slept for the entire 37 hours of their flight. "You may rest now," he said, "I am safe in New York." This remark also brought a round of wild cheering and applause. The statements of both men were aired over radio station WNYC and relayed to distant transmitters throughout much of the country.

Early the next morning the two fliers resumed their flight to Texas and succeeded in earning the $25,000 prize. They toured the United States afterwards and were toasted in Washington, Chicago, Philadelphia and elsewhere. Their plane was flown back to France by another team of aviators and is now on display at the Air and Space Museum, Le Bourget Airport near Paris. Captain Castes continued long distance flying until the late 1930's and was then employed by a French Colonial airline. During the Second World War, with the rank of Lieutenant-Colonel, he was a flight instructor for the French Air Force and later with the small Vichy French Air Force. He died in May 1973, in Paris. There is no record of whether he ever came to New York a third time.

Maurice Bellonte joined Air France shortly after he returned to France and remained with the airline for more than 20 years. He flew as a special representative of the company on the first flight on the Concorde Supersonic jet from Paris to New York in 1977. He died in Paris in 1983.

Thursday, July 2, 1931: Wiley Post and Harold Gatty

They did it. They made history.

Magellan is remembered for commanding the first around the world ocean voyage, which took 3 years to complete; often forgotten is the fact that Magellan died along the way, so it is now known as the Magellan-Elcano exhibition. The dawn of aviation brought anticipation for the first aerial circumnavigation, which happened in 1924 when a team of eight men flew two United States Army biplanes around the world in 175 days, including several lengthy stops for repairs. In 1929, Hugo Eckener, Commander of the *Graf Zeppelin*, took 21 days to make the first around-the-world trip in an airship *(see: August 30, 1929)*. But to date, there had been no circumnavigation in a fixed wing monoplane.

That changed when pilot Wiley Post and navigator Harold Gatty touched down at Roosevelt Field airstrip in their plane *Winnie Mae* on July 1, 1931. They had circled the globe in just 8 days, 15 hours, and 51 minutes.

Having conquered the more than 15,000 mile round-the-world flight, they now faced the slightly more than one-mile trip up the Canyon of Heroes from Bowling Green to City Hall. When they left eastern Siberia on one of the final legs of the journey, they promised each other 48 hours of sleep. Instead, they had managed less than eight hours after their arrival at Roosevelt Field on Long Island and the drive to the Ritz-Carlton Hotel the previous afternoon.

Somehow the two men looked refreshed as they ate a light breakfast and strode through the hotel's lobby for the cars waiting to take them to the Battery. Post, who had lost his left eye in an oil field accident years before, wore a dark eye patch covering the wound. Prior to leaving for the circumnavigation flight, his wife Mae arranged to have a fresh suit waiting for his arrival. The blue suit, white shirt, and blue polka dot tie were a far cry from the wrinkled oil-stained flight clothes he arrived in the previous day. Gatty's wife, Elsie, had been equally efficient, arranging a change of clothes for her husband.

The aviators and their wives were met in the hotel lobby by Dr. John Finlay, Chairman of the Mayor's Reception Committee, substituting for the absent Grover Whalen, and William Deegan, Tenement House Commissioner and the Reception Committee's Secretary. More than 1,500 people gathered in the street outside the hotel and they cheered when the party emerged. Post and Gatty entered the first car with Finley and Deegan, and the fliers' wives entered the second with Police Commissioner John O'Brien. Escorted by a phalanx of motorcycle-riding police, the two cars drove to the East River at 45th Street where the mayor's boat *Macom* waited, steam up and ready to sail. Transferring to the ship, the group sailed downriver past vessels of all kinds ringing bells and bellowing horns and

111

whistles. Two city fireboats saluted them with spectacular arcs of water as the *Macom* turned into the harbor and docked at Pier A.

The group entered open cars for the trip up Broadway, using the same seating arrangement as earlier. A dozen other cars carrying politicians, statesmen, reporters, dignitaries, and celebrities lined up behind the first two vehicles. The Police Department band led the way, followed by detachments of the 16th Infantry, marines, and sailors. The infantry detachment wore helmets and carried Springfield rifles with bayonets fixed while the other detachments wore dress uniforms.

Shortly after noon the parade began its march up Broadway. A nearly solid mass of people stood along the route, cheers echoing through the concrete canyons of downtown Manhattan. Ticker tape and confetti, torn paper and ribbons, streamers of all sizes and colors rained down, decorating the spire of Trinity Church and tangling around bayonets. Waving and pointing, the pilots and their wives could barely see or be seen through the storm of paper.

Mayor Walker and John McCooey, Brooklyn Democratic leader, stood on the steps of City Hall, waiting for the motorcade. The vehicles struggled to make way through the mass of people jammed into City Hall Plaza. The mayor shook the hands of the two men and kissed the cheeks of their wives. Holding the two men's hands high, the mayor shouted, "Welcome home" and led them into the Aldermanic Chamber which was packed to more than capacity. The mayor repeated his welcome and congratulated the men, presenting them with Gold Medals. Never able to avoid a witticism, Mayor Walker praised the *Winnie Mae,* joking that as they were flying it was the *Winnie Must* and now that their flight was completed it should be called the *Winnie Did.*

Called upon to say a few words, both men could utter little beyond "Thank you" and "Overwhelmed." It fell to Florence Hall, the wealthy Oklahoma oilman who financed their flight, to speak for them. He told the audience that the two men had never expected such an outpouring of emotion and joy at their arrival. "They love you all," Mr. Hall concluded.

Minutes later the motorcade resumed, but at a much faster pace headed to a luncheon at the Ritz-Carlton. Admittance to the luncheon was by invitation only and guards at the door verified each invitation. One tall lean man in an ill-fitting suit was held at the door, while he searched through his pockets for his invitation. He was about to be turned away when someone of the security staff recognized the man and escorted Colonel Charles Lindbergh into the room.

At the luncheon the mayor again spoke briefly, commenting on the obvious friendship between the pilot and his navigator. "There seems to be camaraderie of flying men," he said, pausing before adding that he wished there were more of it in politics. After the luncheon, Wiley Post responded to reporters, saying that he looked forward to the day when commercial flight would span the globe. Harold Gatty, nicknamed the Prince of Navigation, was adamant in saying that flights like the one they had made were not just barnstorming but preparing the world for more regular and thorough air travel.

The flying duo and their wives spent the next week vacationing on a yacht off Long Island. Australian-born Harold Gatty accepted a position with the Douglas Aircraft Company shortly after the flight. In 1934 he founded South Seas Airlines based in Fiji. During World War II he held honorary ranks in both the Australian and American Air Forces. He wrote a book about survival techniques in the waters of the Pacific that were taught by both countries to airman serving in that region. After the war he founded Fiji Airways. He died in 1957 and is buried in Fiji.

Wiley Post had one more goal in mind: a solo circumnavigation. He achieved that goal and received a second ticker tape parade two years after this one. *(see July 26, 1933)*. His record-making plane *Winnie Mae* was sold to the Smithsonian Institute and is part of their permanent display at the Air & Space Museum in Washington, DC.

Trinity Church

Many jokes have been told about the high cost of real estate in Manhattan, but the 1697 charter for the first Episcopal church in New York called for an annual rent of 60 bushels of wheat. Considering the value of the land along Broadway opposite Wall Street, Trinity Church has made a lot of dough from that wheat.

The Gothic Revival building facing Wall Street is the third church building on this location. The first, built in 1698, was destroyed in the Great Fire of 1776, and the congregation used St. Paul's Chapel while a new building was erected. Consecrated in 1790, the second Trinity Church stood until 1839, when heavy snow weakened its roof beyond repair. When the work was completed 7 years later, the third building dominated the skyline of Manhattan. Considered the finest example of Gothic Revival architecture, the church was the tallest building in the United States until 1869. With its 281-foot-tall spire, surmounted with a gold cross and containing 23 bells, the building remained the tallest structure in New York until 1890 when the New York World Building was completed.

Designated a National Historic Landmark in 1976, the church became a refuge after the destruction of the nearby World Trade Center on September 11, 2001, and ten years later offered support for the Occupy Wall Street protestors camped at nearby Zuccotti Park. Demonstrators were not allowed to sleep in the Churchyard, however, which Is the burial place of several Revolutionary-era notables, including Alexander Hamilton, his wife Eliza and her sister Angelica.

Wednesday, September 2, 1931:
Olin Stephens and Crew of *Dorade*

New York had multiple reasons to celebrate victory in the 1931 Transatlantic Yacht race from Newport, Rhode Island to Plymouth, England. Yacht designer Captain Olin Stephens, a 23-year-old native of the Bronx, led a seven-man crew, all of whom were from New York. Their ship, which he had designed, was a 52-foot yawl, a two-masted sailboat with a short aft mast positioned behind the rudder. Named the *Dorade*, she had been built in 1929 at the Minneford Yacht Yard on City Island in the Bronx. The race, which usually takes three to four weeks depending on weather conditions, was won by the yacht in the amazingly short time of only 17 days. It was the first victory in this race by an American ship, made more special because of its ties to New York City.

The crew of the *Dorade* arrived back in New York aboard the liner *Homeric*, which also carried the *Dorade*. The New York City steamer *Macom* met the liner off Quarantine and Captain Stephens and his crew transferred to it. On board to welcome them were members of the Reception Committee, headed by Bronx Alderman Leo Erhart. Members of the Sanitation Department Band crowded the two decks of the *Macom*, handsomely attired in their new cream and gold uniforms. Off the Battery the city vessel was saluted by a New York City fireboat which sprayed geysers of water skyward. The *Macom* sounded her horn and was answered by whistles and horns from the shore.

Disembarking at Pier A, the eight members of the yacht's crew boarded open vehicles for the ride up Broadway on the hot late summer day. Escorted by a squad of policemen on motorcycles, the parade received the shouts and waves of the waiting crowds. The 23-year-old skipper of the *Dorade* and his fellow sailors were welcomed at City Hall by Acting Mayor Joseph McKee, President of the Board of Aldermen. A Bronx resident, the acting mayor referred to Captain Stephens as his neighbor, then expressed Mayor Jimmy Walker's regrets at being out of the city and not able to attend to event.

Led into the Aldermanic Chambers, the *Dorade's* crew was applauded by the more than 200 guests. Captain Stephens looked about the room and informed those assembled that their yacht would fit into it with "two feet to spare." Asked how the yacht managed to finish the course so quickly, he explained that by taking the most northerly route feasible at that time of year, they managed to avoid all rough seas. The yacht's handsewn sails proved superior to those made by machine, he added. He credited the entire crew, especially the ship's cook, for working together and keeping everything in perfect shape. Finally, the captain said, "it was due to good luck." Following the reception at City Hall, the honored sailors proceeded uptown where they were guests at a luncheon at the Concourse Plaza.

Captain Stephens remained skipper of *Dorade* for another year. He and his brother Rod then formed the yachting company Sparkman & Stephens and went on to design many of the ships that have competed in and won sailing's biggest races, including the America's Cup. He was inducted into the America's Cup Hall of Fame in 1993, and died in 2008, five months after his 100th birthday.

Under different commanders and crew, the *Dorade* continued to race until the early 1970s, winning several races including the 1931 Fastnet Race, the 1932 Bermuda Race, and the 1936 Transpacific race. Retired from racing for 40 years, she was purchased and restored in 2010 by owners who wanted to repeat her past glory. She surprised the sailing community by winning the 2013 Transpacific, the oldest boat ever to do so. Her racing career continues, and she has won many first and second place awards for her class of ship.

Not bad for a 90-year-old.

Thursday, October 22, 1931:
Pierre Laval, Prime Minister of France

As the French liner *Île de France* slowly made its way through the Narrows, scores of airplanes from the Army, Navy, and Police Department circled above as part of the welcome arranged for the current French Prime Minister, Pierre Laval. He was here to meet with President Herbert Hoover to discuss the dire financial crisis gripping most of the world as well as to spend a short vacation in the United States. He was accompanied by a staff of military, financial, and economic advisors, as well as his 19-year-old daughter Josée Laval.

The city's steamer, bedecked with French and American flags, met the ocean liner as it entered the lower bay. On board were members of the Mayor's Reception Committee, including its Chairman, Tenement Commissioner William Deegan, as well as photographers, reporters, and a military escort. After the Prime Minister and his staff transferred to the *Macom*, it increased speed and steamed to Pier A at the Battery while the liner continued to its moorage on the Hudson River. Guns in Fort Jay on Governors Island boomed a 19-gun salute as the planes circled one more time before returning to Floyd Bennett Field in Brooklyn.

Mayor Jimmy Walker met the Prime Minister as the steamer docked. Standing with the mayor were Secretary of State Henry Stimson, the State Department's Chief of Protocol Warren Robbins, and other silk-hat wearing State Department officials. Mr. Robbins formally introduced Secretary Stimson and Mayor Walker to the French Prime Minister while the First Army band played the American and French national anthems. French staff members boarded five closed vehicles and, with a motorcycle escort, proceeded directly to City Hall. Meanwhile Mr. Laval, with the Secretary of State and the mayor, entered an open limousine, following a detachment of mounted police. Ticker tape drifted down as the procession moved north, though newspaper reports said the Prime Minister's reception was less spectacular than previous ones, an indication of the seriousness of his visit and planned meeting with President Hoover. Prior to departing for America, Mr. Laval had commented about the visit by saying, "In a world torn with doubt our democracies must search for and apply methods which will restore calm and establish equilibrium. If France and the United States can agree and unite in an ever-increasing cooperation, we can look forward to better things."

The Great Depression had begun just a year and a half earlier, bringing with it worldwide economic disaster, and unemployment was soaring to 25% in the US and almost 30% in France. Laval's hope was to bring about a program of international rehabilitation with President Hoover.

The City Hall reception was briefer than usual. The mayor and Secretary of State both spoke optimistically at the ceremony held in the Aldermanic Chambers, which was decorated with flowers and the flags of France and the United States. Both national anthems were played again, as New York radio stations WABC, WEAF, and WNYC broadcast the reception, which was transmitted nationwide. Mayor Walker presented the Prime Minister with the city's Gold Medal. The Prime Minister's speech was longer than earlier statements and his words were translated by Jules Henri, official translator of the French Embassy. Mr. Laval did not refer to details of what he and President Hoover would discuss but he offered a number of personal comments. He was pleased to see so many reporters, he said, since he began his career writing for a small socialist newspaper in France but then added, "I was never a very orthodox socialist." He admitted that he was a very heavy smoker and that he enjoyed American cigarettes. He made this admission while lighting a cigarette given to him by Mayor Walker.

When the Prime Minister finished his statements, a police escort hurried him and his staff to Grand Central Terminal, as his first meeting with President Hoover was scheduled for later the same day. He remained in Washington for two days conferring with the president and congressmen, financiers, bankers, and economists. His staff remained in Washington. The conference ended with the Hoover Moratorium, a proposal to freeze all inter-governmental debts. This international plan, however, was not accepted by Great Britain and Italy, and never went beyond the proposal stage.

Upon returning to New York, the Prime Minister and his daughter began the sight-seeing part of his trip to America. A great deal of planning had gone into their seven-day vacation, as indicated by her luggage, which consisted of 12 trunks, 23 suitcases, and six hatboxes. All but one trunk and four suitcases bore her name on their tags. When the Prime Minister returned to France, optimism ran high for planned cooperation with the United States, leading *Time* magazine to name him "Man of the Year" in

1931. But French politics were turbulent in the 1930s, and he was in and out of government several times until 1935, when he again became Prime Minister for two years. Then, in 1940, Germany invaded France.

The Nazi German armies quickly conquered France and occupied much of the country, creating an area that continued in quasi-independence. This French state was often referred to by the name of its capital city as Vichy France. Elderly World War I hero Marshal Pétain served as its President, with Pierre Laval as its Prime Minister twice, briefly in 1940, then again from 1942-1945. The Vichy government often collaborated with the Germans, sending forced labor workers to aid the Nazis and organizing a secret police force to enforce laws dictated by Germany, including those that deprived Jews of their rights and often of their lives. Laval met with Axis political and military leaders, then conferred with Mussolini in Italy and Hitler in Germany. When most of France was liberated by the Allies, the Vichy government collapsed, and Laval escaped to Spain. He tried to return to France in the summer of 1945 but was turned over to the Free French Government by American authorities. His first trial for treason ended in a mistrial. At his second, the former Prime Minister's plea was that had he not cooperated with Germany, all of France would have been occupied and would have suffered worse than it did. The second trial found him guilty of treason and he was sentenced to death. On the morning of his scheduled execution Laval attempted suicide but the poison he drank only caused stomach cramps. After having his stomach pumped, he was executed by firing squad on October 15, 1945. Before the penalty was carried out, his final words were *"Viva la France!"*

The *Times* reported the news with a headline very different from the ones of the 1930's which had been full of praise for his economic policies. The day after his execution, the *New York Times* headline called him "The Traitor of France" – quite a fall for 1931's "Man of the Year." Since his execution, his wartime actions and statements have been debated by those who considered him a traitor and those who believe he helped save France from a worse wartime occupation.

Monday, October 26, 1931:
Henri Philippe Pétain, Marshal of France

The two French cruisers *Suffern* and *Duquesne* knifed through the waters of the Narrows then slowed as they entered the more congested waters of New York Harbor. It was Friday afternoon, and the two warships were nearing the end of their Transatlantic mission in celebration of the sesquicentennial of the British surrender at Yorktown. Guns from Fort Jay boomed a salute because a very special passenger was on board the *Duquesne*. In the 13 years since the end of the Great War, he had often been invited to visit New York to receive its typical welcome, but for one reason or another, the passenger on board the *Duquesne* had never received the tribute paid to the political and military leaders of that War. All that was about to change. Henri Philippe Pétain, Marshal of France, the 75-year-old man whom many considered France's greatest hero, the Savior of the Nation for the defense of Verdun, had arrived and would receive a ticker tape parade the following Monday.

Marshal Pétain spent the weekend on board the *Duquesne* receiving guests, including General John Pershing, commander of the American Expeditionary Force during the War. It was reported that the Marshal was not fond of elaborate receptions and gala events. During the years after the war, he had frequently been called upon to advise the French governments on military and political matters, but he had never been an official cabinet member. His name had often been suggested as either Minister of War or Minister of Education but because of the tempestuous nature of French politics, neither portfolio was ever given. In the last few years, he had become close to the current French Prime Minister, Pierre Laval, who had received his own parade just days earlier *(see: October 22, 1931).*

Monday morning, the Marshal was dressed in his light blue uniform, adorned with a triple row of medals. He joined Grover Whalen, Chairman of the Reception Committee, and Colonel William Donovan in the first vehicle of a procession of more than 20 cars that would make their way through the Canyon of Heroes. The Marshal spoke little English, so his aide, General Comte de Chambrun *(see: May 26, 1930),* sat in the car as well. Just before the start of the parade, retired US General John Pershing also entered the vehicle.

At ten minutes after noon the parade began. There were three bands, one each from the Army, the Navy, and the Police Department. More than 2,000 uniformed marchers escorted the Marshal in double ranks flanking the cars. A detachment from Fort Jay marched, as did several National Guard units, wearing the rainbow patch of the 42nd Division. A company of naval cadets marched along with an honor guard of Marines. Ticker tape began to stream down as the marchers proceeded up Broadway. The French Tricolor flew alongside the Stars and Stripes from countless buildings, and lamp poles were crowned with miniature French and American flags. Estimated at slightly more than 100,000, the spectators' cheers seemed to be directed mostly at the more recognizable General Pershing rather than the mustached Marshal sitting stiffly beside him. Occasionally the French commander acknowledged the cheers by saluting at the brim of his kepi.

Waiting at City Hall Park to greet the Marshal was the City Hall Honor Guard, a newly formed squad of two dozen recent graduates from the Police Academy. Assisted by other members of New York's Police Department they had cleared City Hall Park of all but fewer than a thousand spectators. When Marshal Pétain stepped to the reviewing stand, Mayor Walker placed the city's Gold Medal around his neck. "New York City arises today to salute you" the mayor said in the Aldermanic Chambers minutes later, "and to call this a great day in the history of our city." Speaking through his aide, the Marshal replied, "New York has caused the most astonishment in the world. In keeping with the light of liberty which brightens your harbor you must hold high the torch of civilization." After General Pershing added a few words, the party proceeded to the Waldorf Astoria for a luncheon. The American Society of the French Legion of Honor and the Society of the Daughters of the Cincinnati awarded commemorative scrolls to the French commander at the affair.

Throughout most of the day, the Marshal wore a dour expression, rarely smiling. That evening, however, at a performance of the French-Italian Opera Society, French soprano Colette D'Arville sang the French National Anthem. The Marshal stood, applauding and beaming as he requested that she sing again "those verses which have to do with love of country." She obliged, and the smiling Marshal cried loudly, "*c'est magnifique!*" The following morning the Marshal and his aide were back on the *Duquesne* when it sailed at 11:30 for its next port of call, Newport, Rhode Island.

Nine years later war again raged across Europe. In June 1940, German troops were tearing through northern and central France, and Italian forces had crossed the French-Italian border. The French government collapsed in the face of constant defeats. Marshal Pétain, whose right-wing sympathies had grown over the previous years, was asked to assume power and once again save his nation. Upon accepting the position of Prime Minister, he immediately requested a cease fire from the Axis powers. It was granted, and a bitter treaty was imposed on France that left most of the nation occupied except the southeastern corner as a semi-independent state, named after its capital city of Vichy. Marshal Pétain served as its President. For the next two years the Vichy French government collaborated more and more with Nazi Germany. In September 1944, the Vichy Government relocated to Germany and in April 1945, Pétain crossed into Switzerland and then back to France where he was captured. He was tried for treason and in August was found guilty. At the age of 89, he was condemned to death, but his sentence was changed to life in prison in consideration of his prior service to the nation. He was imprisoned in a French citadel on the Ile d'Yeu off the French Atlantic coast. His mental and physical health worsened, and he eventually needed constant 24-hour care and assistance. The senile Marshal died on the island at the age of 95 in July 1951.

In 2017, Mayor Bill de Blasio created a commission to review whether the plaque commemorating Pétain's parade should be removed because of the Marshal's collaboration with Nazi German. In January 2018 the commission advised that Pétain's plaque should remain, but that additional explanation be added to it, noting that he was honored for his First World War service and not his activities in the Second. The plague in the sidewalk remains unchanged, but the Downtown Alliance's website now has combined the description for this parade with the one for Mr. Laval, noting that "both dignitaries went on to infamous and ignominious ends."

Waldorf Astoria Hotel

In 1929, two of New York's grand hotels were demolished, and would be reborn as one even grander establishment. Their history is one of collaboration to end a family feud. The original Waldorf Hotel opened in March 1893. Located at 34th Street and Fifth Avenue, the ornate German Renaissance-style structure was built by William Astor on the site of his late father's mansion. The 13-story hotel was designed to overshadow the home of his aunt, socialite Catherine Astor, with whom he had been feuding. Considered too expensive and uptown for business travelers, the hotel risked being shunned by the wealthy, many of whom owned property in the area that they feared would be devalued. They were won over with an opening night concert benefiting a favorite charity, and the hotel became a success as a place to be seen by the city's most influential citizens.

That success encouraged Catherine's son, John Jacob Astor IV, to settle the feud. He built her a new mansion further uptown, then built the Astoria Hotel next to the Waldorf. Opening in 1897, the Astoria was designed by the same architect and in the same style as the Waldorf. The two hotels soon merged and were connected by a long corridor known as Peacock Alley because society's most prominent citizens could be seen there. The combined hotel was the world's largest and was the first to include private baths and electricity in all 1,300 rooms, attracting guests from around the world. Its Empire Room was one of the city's best restaurants, and many elegant balls and parties were held in its opulent ballroom. →

Success led to imitation, and soon other opulent hotels opened. The city's cultural hub had moved further uptown, and hotels like the St. Regis, the Savoy-Plaza and the Biltmore began attracting society's wealthy families. In 1929, the Waldorf Astoria was sold to developers who demolished it to erect the Empire State Building. Meanwhile, the Astor family built a new hotel on Park Avenue between 49th and 50th Streets. The new Waldorf Astoria is even more grand and lavish than the original. Covering an entire block, it was the tallest and largest hotel at the time, with 2,200 rooms plus 100 suites in its central Waldorf Tower. The Depression may not have been an ideal time to open a luxury hotel, but its reputation ensured its long-term success. Its fame was also bolstered by hosting important conferences, glamorous dinner parties and charity events, and gala balls attended by the city's high society. It has hosted receptions for over 60 ticker tape parade honorees, far more than any other establishment.

Friday, November 20, 1931:
Dino Grandi, Foreign Minister of Italy

The Police Department was on full alert after City Hall were received formal protests against welcoming Dino Grandi, Italy's Foreign Minister and personal friend of *Il Duce*, Benito Mussolini. The protests were received from groups opposed to Fascist rule in Italy, but more serious were the rumors circulating in Italian communities that bombs would greet the Italian diplomat, either during his ride up the Canyon of Heroes or when he met with bankers at JP Morgan & Co., the financial representative of the Italian government. Once before, anarchists had exploded a bomb outside of the Morgan Building on September 16, 1920, killing 38 and injuring hundreds. The memory of this tragic event less than a dozen years earlier was still fresh in the minds of many New Yorkers. With the threats made on Grandi's life, the authorities were extra cautious and alert, so the day before he arrived, the headquarters of that company at the corner of Wall and Broad Streets was thoroughly searched by members of the Police Department.

The Foreign Minister had arrived in the United States a week earlier, visiting Philadelphia and Baltimore. Early in the morning, he arrived at the Communipaw railroad station in Jersey City. This was normally a vantage point for a spectacular view of downtown Manhattan, but a cold drizzle and heavy fog all but hid the skyscrapers across the Hudson River. Not long after his arrival the city's reception boat appeared out of the gloom. On board the *Macom* were Major William Deegan, Tenement House Commissioner and Chairman of Mayor Walker's Reception Committee; Dr. Elmer Brown, Chancellor of New York University and Chairman of the Special Committee to Welcome the Foreign Minister; and other guests, reporters, and photographers. After being welcomed and answering questions from members of the press, Foreign Minister Grandi and the party boarded the *Macom* for the short ride to Pier A at the Battery.

Among those on hand to meet the steamer as it moored at Pier A were a group of pro-Fascist Italian men wearing their party's traditional black shirts, who greeted Mr. Grandi with the stiff-armed outstretched Fascist salute. Mayor Walker shook the diplomat's hand, and they rode together through the rain to City Hall in an open limousine, as the parade began just after 9 o'clock. More than 1,200 police had been assigned to duty and most were stationed along Lower Broadway. Due to the early hour and the inclement weather the crowd was sparse, so the blue-uniformed police seemed to outnumber spectators along the route. A small amount of ticker tape fell, sodden and heavy from the rain, and occasional cheers were heard, mixed in with the cries "Assassin" and "Murderer," mostly in Italian and combined with other phrases that were unprintable in news reports.

City Hall Plaza was filled with members of the 16th Infantry from Governors Island, a military band, sailors from the Brooklyn Navy Yard, and more uniformed police. The only visitors permitted in the Plaza were 100 members of the Duce Fascist Alliance of New York, also dressed in black shirts and wearing caps. As the band played "Giovinezza," the official hymn of Mussolini's party, the Foreign Minister was again greeted with the Fascist salute.

Mr. Grandi was led directly into the Aldermanic Chambers, where Mayor Walker introduced him to the more than 350 invited guests in the room. The Sanitation Department Band played the National Anthems of the United States and Italy. An announcement was made that the ceremonies were being carried live over radio stations WABC and WJZ. The Mayor noted that the State Department had advised against the Foreign Minister's visit to New York because of fears over Mr. Grandi's safety. "Your Excellency," the mayor said jokingly, "If you are not safe in the city of New York, I am moving out of it."

Speaking in heavily accented English, the Foreign Minister prefaced his remarks by saying that he would be brief, since he was scheduled to return to Jersey City for the 11 o'clock train to Washington to meet with President Hoover. He promised to return from Baltimore in less than a week, this time accompanied by his wife, and that they planned to spend four days seeing "everything from Broadway to the Empire State Building." He expressed pride in the number of people of Italian descent who lived in New York and who were essential to the vitality of the city.

After his short speech, the Foreign Minister re-entered the car for the ride back to Pier A and the return trip to Jersey City. As the *Macom* steamed away from the pier, Mr. Grandi stood on the upper deck of the boat and raised his arm in the Fascist salute and then a wave of farewell to Mayor Walker and other members of the Reception Committees. There had been no violence and only three people were arrested, for pasting anti-Fascist signs on public property.

The Foreign Minister met with the President and members of Congress over the next few days, discussing ways in which Italy and the United States could work together more closely. As promised, he returned to New York with his wife, and after four days of shopping, sightseeing, banquets, and receptions they returned to Italy.

The sidewalk plaque commemorating this parade incorrectly shows the parade's date as November 30, 1931, which is also the date listed on the Alliance for Downtown's 2003 brochure. Their website now shows the correct date of November 20, but as of April 2020, the plaque is still incorrect.

Mr. Grandi remained a high-ranking member of the Fascist government through the Second World War. In July 1943, with Allied Armies invading Italy and the Italian armed forces beaten on every front, Grandi led the group that was responsible for convincing the Italian King, Victor Emmanuel III, to force Mussolini to resign. A Fascist court in Verona found Grandi guilty of treason and sentenced him to death but he had already fled the country, finding refuge in Spain. He subsequently moved to Portugal, Argentina, and Brazil before returning to Italy in the early 1960's. He died in Bologna in 1988 at the age of 92, one of the last former high-ranking Fascists to survive.

Saturday, May 14, 1932: Beer Parade

The manufacture, sale and transportation of "intoxicating liquors" had been prohibited by the 18th Amendment of the US Constitution since 1920, but many residents of cities opposed the ban on alcohol, especially since the Volstead Act, the law passed to enforce Prohibition, included wine and beer in the list of banned beverages. Many simply ignored the ban, and a large underground market for "bootleg" provided increased profits to organized crime. By 1925 there were well over 30,000 "speak-easies" in New York City, and some estimates put that number much higher. When the Depression began, the growing anti-prohibition "wet" movement had two new arguments for repeal: the number of jobs that would be created, and taxation of alcohol would provide much-needed revenue.

On April 15, 1932, New York's Mayor Jimmy Walker, a well-known frequenter of the city's speak-easies and outspoken "wet" politician, used those arguments when he announced plans for a "Beer for Taxation" parade. He called on other cities to hold their own beer parades on May 14, formed an organizing committee that he personally chaired, and began promoting the parade in radio interviews and speeches. "With this tax on beer will not only come the $500 million of money that will flow into the Treasury," he declared, "but there will also come a rehabilitation of business" that would create jobs.

Mayor Walker was also the "hero of the day" as the march began shortly after 11 in the morning, with him leading a "long line of the earnest seekers for beer." Kicking off at Fifth Avenue and 79th Street, the parade marched down Fifth Avenue, then turned west along Central Park South, and continued uptown along Central Park West to 75th Street. Along with the Mayor walked Grand Marshal Brigadier General John Daniell, committee members Millicent Hearst, wife of newspaper magnate William Randolph Hearst; George Mand, President of the Bronx Chamber of Commerce; Commissioner Frank Taylor and others.

Behind them came "an almost endless line of marchers," organized into sections by industry or profession, though many social and neighborhood groups also marched. The largest contingent was a group of about 6,000 German Americans, many dressed in Bavarian costume and singing German drinking songs. There were groups of fire fighters, truck drivers, and athletes, some carrying a banner proclaiming themselves "Olympic Champions." Several hundred empty taxi cabs drove in one contingent, and the aviation contingent showed off several airplanes mounted on flatbed trucks. The choruses of a couple of musical comedies rode by in automobiles, followed by the cast of the Broadway musical *Of Thee I Sing*, dressed in their costumes as Congressmen and Supreme Court judges. Throughout the march, "there were bands from everywhere, many professional ones and some amateur."

At noon, as the head of the march reached 63rd Street and Central Park West, the parade halted. Bands stopped playing music, men doffed their hats, and a moment of silence was observed for the Lindbergh baby, whose body had been discovered just 3 days earlier *(see: June 13, 1927)*.

"All along the route were dense crowds, standing five or six deep," especially along 59th Street, where hotel balconies were packed. A review stand was set up on 72nd Street, and "there were throngs all along Central Park West, and each window of the high buildings had its quota of the curious." Paper of all kinds were tossed from windows overlooking the route, especially near the reviewing stand where the "crowd was even more vociferous."

The mayor left the parade when he reached the stand and returned after a quick lunch to watch the parade pass by. Around 5 o'clock, he left a second time, driving to Fifth Avenue and 58th Street, to start the day's second parade, which marched down Fifth Avenue to 34th Street. This march, which started at 6:30 and continued until 9:45 that night, was "almost mobbed by enthusiasts" of beer, and included more bands and floats than the earlier parade, and fewer political signs. Here too, "paper, thrown down from buildings, formed a hazy carpet, and there was much and intense enthusiasm" from the crowd of spectators. "Paper rained down onto the marchers" and for the mayor, there was a feel of "conquering-hero-walking-on-rose-leaves idea."

The Police Department had 2,000 extra officers working, and police observers monitored both routes from overhead aboard the blimp *Resolute*, which circled overhead and tested a new short-wave radio hook-up to communicate with police headquarters. There were several minor injuries, mostly from the day's early summer heat, and at the end of the day, Police Chief Inspector John Sullivan reported "that there had not been a case of disorderly conduct nor one pocket picking."

"Heralded by all save the 'drys' (and sneered at by them) the parade was indubitably a success," the *New York Times* declared, and the next day's paper includes stories about similar beer parades in other cities, including Boston, Detroit, Syracuse and Jersey City. Prohibition became a platform in the presidential campaign later that year, when Democratic candidate Franklin Roosevelt declared he was in favor of its repeal, and less than a year into his first term, the 21st Amendment was ratified, repealing the 18th and delegating regulation of alcoholic beverages to the states. Prohibition was over.

Monday, June 20, 1932: Amelia Earhart

Much had changed during the four years since Amelia Earhart received her first ticker tape parade and resolved to make a solo flight across the Atlantic: planes were sturdier, engines stronger, instruments more reliable. She had also married George Putnam, though she referred to her marriage as a "partnership with dual controls" and never changed her last name, laughing when the *New York Times* referred to her as "Mrs. Putnam."

On May 20, the fifth anniversary of Lindbergh's departure on his first transatlantic flight, she left Harbor Grace, Newfoundland in a bright red Lockheed Vega5B aircraft. She landed in a pasture at Culmore, near Derry, Northern Ireland, 14 hours and 56 minutes later.

After being feted and honored in various European cities and by politicians and royalty, she returned on board the French liner *Île de France* to New York, where she would receive her second ticker tape parade *(see July 6, 1928)*. It was a sunny and mild summer morning as the *Île de France* steamed past Quarantine. Waiting to transport her to Pier A was the Police boat *Riverside* filling in for the *Macom*, which was undergoing repairs. An autogiro (an early predecessor of the helicopter) hovered overhead as Ms. Earhart transferred to the *Riverside* where she was again greeted by the Chairman of the Mayor's Reception Committee, George Mand. A flight of nine Army bombers flew overhead at 1,000 feet and dipped their wings in salute before they returned to their base at Floyd Bennett Field. Moments later three Navy fighters swooped down and, at a height of only 50 feet, roared above the reception steamer. They sped off towards the Battery, circled, and repeated their maneuver, flying even lower this time. Everyone on board the *Riverside*, including Miss Earhart, ducked as the fights roared overhead.

Thousands of admiring spectators began to cheer as the *Riverside*, its shrill whistle screaming, approached Pier A. When the boat tied to the dock, the Police Department Band on the shore played the National Anthem. As Ms. Earhart stepped off the steamer, she was handed a large bouquet of roses, a personal gift of Mayor Jimmy Walker, who apologized for his absence years earlier. The parade up Broadway began shortly after noon. A dozen convertibles were escorted by the Police and Sanitation Department Bands, detachments from the Army and Navy, mounted and motorcycle police, and contingents from the Police, Fire, and Sanitation Departments. Huge quantities of ticker tape swirled down from the buildings along the route. The sidewalk was jammed with people, many could be seen at every window, and even standing on ledges or cornices.

Thousands were assembled in City Hall Plaza and as the motorcade braked to a halt, large numbers started chanting her first name repeatedly. Mayor Walker quieted the crowd and introduced her. She was joined on the steps of City Hall by her husband George, high ranking Army and Navy officers, officials of various aeronautical groups or societies, and state and city officials. After posing for photographs and a few remarks to newsreel cameramen, the entire party entered City Hall and the Aldermanic Chambers, where the aviatrix was awarded a second New York City Gold Medal and another scroll. It spoke again of her bravery and steadfast devotion and claimed that, because of her achievement of flying solo across the ocean, she had joined the select group of aviation pioneers who would be remembered.

When Ms. Earhart responded, she joked the mayor's absence four years earlier may have been due to the weather and thanked him for his presence now. Mayor Walker seemed amused by her comments. She concluded her remarks with a surprising statement, "Four years ago, I flew the ocean as a passenger and one commentator said that I had been carried like 'a sack of potatoes'. This time there would be no such comments." She flew alone as a personal gesture and justification, she said, her voice growing with emotion, "I fought night and storms alone." Loud cheers followed these remarks and the ceremony in the Chambers concluded.

After more photographs on the steps of City Hall, Earhart and Putnam were driven to Bryant Park on 42nd Street. A group of 200 school children were gathered there to welcome her along with a crowd of nearly 2,000. As they watched, she was decorated with the Cross of Honor by the United States Flag Association. Originally it had been planned to drop this award to her from a balloon while she was still on the *Île de France* but adverse winds the day before had prevented it.

She and her husband remained in the city for three days, guests at more than half a dozen luncheons, receptions, and dinners. At each, when called upon to speak, she returned to her theme that the flight was her personal justification. They then traveled to Washington to meet with President Herbert Hoover.

Earhart's celebrity status continued to grow. She authored several books on flying and career opportunities for women. In 1935 she was named a visiting faculty member of Purdue University's Aeronautics Department to counsel women seeking careers. Through the next few years, she prepared for one more goal: to fly around the world. Purdue provided financing and she bought a twin-engine Lockheed Electra. She selected Fred Noonan, a licensed nautical navigator as well as experienced celestial navigator to accompany her. Her flight plan to follow an equatorial route would make the 29,000-mile flight the longest distance circumnavigation ever. After the first attempt was aborted because of a blown tire, they took off from Miami, Florida on June 1,

1937, making stops in South America, Africa, India, and Southeast Asia. On July 2, 1937, they left Lae, New Guinea, for the final, 7,000-mile leg of the flight over the Pacific Ocean. Their destination was Howland Island, but their last known position was near the Nukumanu Islands, now a part of the small Pacific island republic of Kiribati. They reported having difficulty fixing their exact location. Nothing further was ever heard of them.

To this day theories and speculations exist about their fate, ranging from crashing at sea to being shot down by Japanese planes. Current evidence indicates that they might have crashed on the reef at uninhabited Nikumaroro Island in the Kiribati republic, their plane sank or was washed to sea, and they were either killed in the crash or died of starvation or exposure. A second theory is that they crashed in the Marshall Islands or near Saipan, were captured and executed by the Japanese. Most historians believe in a simple "crash and sink" theory.

Mayor John O'Brien (1933)

Born to Irish immigrants in Massachusetts in 1873, John Patrick O'Brien was a devout Catholic. He studied at Holy Cross College, then earned a law degree at Georgetown University before moving to New York City. A steadfast Democrat and competent lawyer, he quickly rose through the ranks of Tammany Hall to become Corporate Counsel, and then was appointed to the New York Surrogate Court.

When the special election to replace former Mayor Jimmy Walker was held in late 1932, Tammany Hall nominated O'Brien instead of Acting Mayor Joseph McKee. O'Brien easily defeated his Republican opponent as well as McKee's write-in candidacy, becoming Mayor on January 1, 1933, when New York was experiencing record unemployment and the darkest days of the Depression.

O'Brien did virtually nothing without approval or instruction from Tammany Hall. When asked at his inauguration who he would appoint as the next police commissioner, he replied "I don't know, they haven't told me yet." By the time of the next general election, he was defeated by a strong Republican-Fusion party candidate who was supported by anti-Tammany Democrats, including State Governor Franklin Roosevelt. After his one year as Mayor, O'Brien returned to his law practice, and continued to stay loyal to Tammany Hall. He died in 1951 in his home on East 75th Street at the age of 78.

Friday, July 21, 1933:
Air Marshal Italo Balbo and Crews of 25 Italian Seaplanes

In the six years since Lindbergh was honored, several ticker tape parades had been held for accomplishments in flight, some for a single aviator or aviatrix and others for an entire crew. Never, however, had there been one for a fleet of planes. That changed on this typical New York summer day (cloudy and humid, according to the *New York Times* with temperatures in the mid'80's) with a parade for the commanding general of the Italian Air Force, 37-year-old Italo Balbo. Commanding a squadron of two dozen seaplanes, he led the squadron from Ortobello, Italy to Lake Michigan, Chicago, by way of Amsterdam, Londonderry, Reykjavik, Cartwright, and Shediac. Not out to set any speed records, the flight was more a demonstration of durability, and proof that such a flight could be done. Leaving Italy on the July 1, the fleet of Savoia-Marchetti

S55 flying boats did not arrive in the waters of Lake Michigan off Burnham Park, Chicago, until July 19 due to weather and repair delays. After a day in the Windy City, Balbo and a representative from each plane hurried east by train, arriving at Penn Station mid-morning on July 21. A motorcade escorted them downtown where crowds of people had been waiting, some from as early as dawn. Both the *Times* and the *Tribune* estimated the crowd along the parade route numbered more than 200,000. The entire Italian American community of the city, according to the *Daily News*, was in attendance, waving miniature Italian flags. Fears of anti-Fascist demonstrations caused a larger than usual turnout of police for security duty, with more than 1,000 policemen keeping the crowd in check. Despite the heavier police presence spectators almost broke through the barriers near City Hall, which appears to have been caused by over-zealous parade watchers rather than for political reasons. So much ticker tape cascaded down the Canyon of Heroes that the Sanitation Department employed eight drivers and loaders, 153 sweepers, and 26 supervisors to wash the streets after 24 truckloads of paper (a total of 294 cubic yards) were carted off during the night.

The festivities did not cease when Balbo was given the Keys to the City by the Chairman of the Reception Committee, Generoso Pope, at City Hall. Mayor O'Brien himself presented the Italian aviator the City's Medal of Valor. The Mayor compared Balbo to Christopher Columbus and Guglielmo Marconi, after which Balbo responded to the crowd saying that their cheers did not belong to him, but "to Benito Mussolini, who had set Italy on the path of greatness to rival that of Rome."

A brief rest at the Waldorf Astoria followed, during which Balbo received a telegram from President Roosevelt congratulating him on his accomplishments. At a reception shortly thereafter at the Hotel Commodore, he was serenaded with the Fascist anthem "Giovinezza" and received the Fascist salute. Back at the Waldorf later that night, he was the guest of honor at a reception for 500 guests, which included Italian Consul General Antonio Grossardi and his wife, and the former US Ambassador to Italy, Henry Fletcher.

Balbo was an original member of the Blackshirts, the Italian Fascist Party, and was the youngest of the four planners of the March on Rome that propelled Mussolini to power in 1921. Soon after Mussolini assumed office, Balbo was named General Commander of the Fascist Militia. Even though he had only limited training as a pilot, he was promoted to General, commanding the Italian Air Force. After completing flight training, he became an accomplished pilot and commander, as his achievement proved. He was later made Minister of Air and Marshal of the Air Force in the Italian Fascist government.

Before he and his crew flew back to Ortobello, Italy in late August, Balbo received two other awards. The Harmon Trophy for outstanding achievements in aviation was the first; the second was a bit more unusual: he was "adopted" by the Sioux Nation and given the name Flying Eagle.

After returning to Italy, Balbo remained in the limelight. He was appointed Governor-General of Libya (then an Italian colony) in 1933. He made a number of flights over the Sahara Desert, including many over the Sudan and Egypt, and during the war against Abyssinia he commanded the Italian Air Force. In the mid-1930's he was considered the heir apparent to Mussolini, who began giving Balbo fewer responsible positions as his popularity grew. He was one of the few Blackshirts who opposed the Italian anti-Jewish Racial Laws and was strongly against Italy's increasing friendship with Germany. After the Munich crisis, he is reported as having said to other Fascist leaders "You will all wind up shining the shoes of the Germans." When the Second World War began, he was commander in Libya and was drawing up plans for an invasion of Egypt. On June 28, 1940, he was killed by friendly fire when his plane attempted to land at Tobruk, though some believe this "accident" might have been ordered by Mussolini because of Balbo's growing popularity.

Keys to the City

Evocative of walled medieval cities with gates that would be locked at night, the granting of the Keys to the City symbolizes that distinguished citizens or guests may enter and leave the city at will as a trusted friend or ally. Based on the same historical roots as Freedom of the City, bestowing City Keys is a more common practice in areas outside of the former British Empire, where Freedom of the City is still more common.

The first recipient of the Keys to New York City was Viscount Edward Cornbury, who arrived in 1702 as the Royal Governor of New York and New Jersey, and also enjoyed the City's Freedom. During the American Revolution, Keys were granted to military leaders such as General Washington, the Marquis de Lafayette and Baron von Steuben, but afterwards the practice gradually declined. That changed during the 1920s, when controversy arose over granting Freedom of the City. By the 1930s, parade honorees were more likely to receive a Key, often with a gold medal.

The Key is a replica of a skeleton key to the back door of City Hall but is purely symbolic as it does not open any existing doors. Not all Key recipients have been honored with a ticker tape parade, as evidenced by the City government website which lists 10 Keys awarded by Mayor de Blasio, only one of whom received a parade.

Wednesday, July 26, 1933: Wiley Post

Not long after Wiley Post received a ticker tape parade for piloting his plane *Winnie Mae* around the world in record time with Harold Gatty as his navigator *(see: July 2, 1931)*, Post began plans for repeating the performance, but this time flying solo. Many aviators and navigators thought this an unachievable goal, especially for Post, who was a self-taught pilot with no prior inflight navigation experience. Unable to find work after the Great War, Post turned to robbery and spent a year imprisoned in the Oklahoma State Penitentiary, where he read all available literature on dead-reckoning navigation, the development of a new autopilot system and a radio-direction finder developed by the Sperry Gyroscope Company for the United States Army.

Post took off in the *Winnie Mae* from Floyd Bennett Field, Brooklyn, on July 16, 1933, making many stops along the way. In Berlin, he made repairs to the autopilot, and replaced forgotten maps in Konigsberg. The autopilot needed more repairs when he reached Moscow, and for the third time in Novosibirsk. After uneventful stops in Rukhlovo and Khabarovsk in eastern Russia, a damaged propeller was replaced in Flat, Alaska. From there, he stopped at Fairbanks and Edmonton, Canada before finally returning to Floyd Bennett Field on July 22. Despite all the repairs he completed the flight in 7 days, 19 hours.

July 26 was a bright and warm summer day. Wiley Post shared the rear of an open car with his wife, Mae, and Philip Hoyt, Deputy Police Commissioner and Chairman of the Reception Committee, as he was driven from the Roosevelt Hotel to Bowling Green for the noontime parade. Sirens wailed as motorcycles provided an escort, racing through the streets. Once at Bowling Green, the pilot rose to stand through the ride up the Canyon of Heroes. The Police Department led the way followed by three squads of mounted police and dozens of official vehicles. Post waved to the thousands who lined the route, smiling broadly when something unique was added to the usual avalanche of ticker tape. From the windows of buildings along the route miniature parachutes made from bits of silk or handkerchiefs floated down, which people along the route scrambled to catch as souvenirs. No police estimate of the size of the crowd were given but a veteran observer thought at least 18,000 clustered around Bowling Green.

Mayor John O'Brien greeted the aviator and his wife in City Hall Plaza. Loudspeakers had been set up in the Plaza to hear the outdoor welcome and the indoor reception. The same observer who provided the downtown estimate thought that almost 6,000 were in the Plaza. Mayor O'Brien shook Post's hand and compared his flight to the voyages of Magellan and Drake, saying that future developments would make "our airplanes seem as old-fashioned as Magellan's sailing vessels but the first flight around the world by one man alone in a plane will very likely rank high among aviation's thrilling exploits."

Post and the mayor then entered the Aldermanic Chamber, jammed with hundreds of spectators cheering the aviator as the city's Gold Medal was hung around his neck. Post's flight, the mayor said, is "a symbol of man's triumph over the elements." Post replied in a halting and brief address, thanking the city for his second welcome and adding that he doubted if New York would have to honor this poor pilot from Oklahoma again. At this comment, the mayor suggested that Post and his wife move to the city permanently, but Post insisted he was a country boy at heart. The entire proceedings, besides being broadcast to those outside, were transmitted over the city's radio station, WNYC.

Later at a luncheon at the Advertising Club, Post made his longest speech thus far. "When I look back on the cooperation I had before, during, and after the flight, it makes me realize that my part, after all, was not very much." Other speakers praised him and his achievements, among them famed aviatrix, Amelia Earhart. After the luncheon Post hurried to Floyd Bennett Field, boarded *Winnie Mae* and flew to Washington to meet with President Roosevelt and received more awards.

Post began his career by flying men and supplies in the Oklahoma oil fields. Because of his background in this area, he was intrigued by the recent discovery of oil deposits in Alaska. He envisioned direct passenger and cargo flights from California to Alaska and wished to study routes and possible facilities. Post's plane, *Winnie Mae*, was inadequate for the type of heavy lifting, short runways, and lake landings that would be necessary, so he purchased a Lockheed Explorer and modified it, including mounting large heavy pontoons to its wings. In July 1935, he made his first flight to Alaska, with his long-time friend and fellow Oklahoman, humorist Will Rogers, who was searching for new material for his weekly newspaper columns.

On August 15, 1935, while taking off from a lake near Point Barrow, Alaska, the nose of the plane dipped suddenly, possibly because of the weight of the pontoons. Post attempted to level the plane but its wing tip struck the lake. The plane somersaulted and crashed upside down in the water, killing both Post and Rogers instantly. They were eventually buried in their native state, Post in Oklahoma City and Rogers in Claremore.

Floyd Bennett Field

While New York's city government was quick to celebrate the heroic exploits of aviators like Lindbergh and Earhart, it was slow to consider the practical opportunities flight presented for commerce and transportation. While other cities were building municipal airports, New York remained focused on its harbor and rail system, and a growing number of private airports sprang up on Long Island and Westchester. The city finally realized it had to act, though, when the Post Office awarded contracts for airmail bound for New York to go through the newly opened airport in Newark, New Jersey. After rejecting a proposal to build a landing strip in the central Queens town called Middle Village, the city focused on the small and mostly barren islands surrounding Jamaica Bay, purchasing a private landing strip on Barren Island.

After 18 months of construction, the new airport opened in 1930, and was named after aviator Floyd Bennett, who had died in 1927. One of its two concrete-paved runways was the longest in the US at the time, and its spacious and comfortable terminals made it one of the most advanced and busiest airports in the country. Most flights into the airport carried cargo and freight, however, and few carried passengers since transportation options into Manhattan were limited and costly. As plane sizes grew and required longer landing strips, land-based airports like Newark could expand faster, and the city soon focused on other locations. Floyd Bennett Field, which already was used by the US Navy and Coast Guard, was closed to civilian traffic, and in 1941 became a Naval Air Station. It was a vital hub for the Navy's defense of the eastern coast, but by the late 1950s it was mostly used as a reserve station. The military's use declined steadily during the 1960s, and in 1972 a plan was approved to transfer it to the National Park Service.

Today, the former airport has several uses. The NY Police and Sanitation Departments, the US Parks Police and the Coast Guard use portions of its land, while the Parks Department maintains the rest, part of which is closed to the public as a grassland management area.

Tuesday, August 1, 1933:
Captain James Mollison and Amy Johnson

Wearing bandages, Captain James Mollison and his wife Amy Johnson stood in the rear of an open city limousine for the journey from Bowling Green to City Hall. The "Flying Sweethearts" had failed to successfully land their plane in Connecticut, but they had completed the westward flight from Wales. Engine difficulties forced them to make an emergency landing near Bridgeport, and both husband and wife were bruised and cut. After dragging them from the plane's wreckage, the enthusiastic rescuers turned into souvenir scavengers, stripping the plane down to nothing, but New York City was about to honor the first couple to ever make such a transatlantic flight.

Earlier that morning the couple had been part of an escorted motorcade from the Hotel Plaza downtown to the Battery. Now, riding with Brigadier General John Phelan, Chairman of Mayor O'Brien's Reception Committee, and Arthur Wiggin, First Secretary of the British Embassy, the parade began on a day so hot and humid that one reporter wrote of the pavement oozing in the heat. Accompanied by the Police Department Band and detachments from the Army and Navy, the motorcade moved through the gauntlet of swirling ticker tape and torn telephone books falling from skyscrapers. Two dozen police sirens wailed, 50,000 people cheered, and the band played a New York symphony of welcome.

Mayor O'Brien welcomed the "Flying Sweethearts" to the city, carefully avoiding Mollison's bandaged right hand, and presented both with the city's Gold Medal. With her stockings barely concealing the bandages on her legs, Johnson expressed the couple's gratitude. "We did not arrive here exactly as expected but we got here," she said, adding "I hardly have the courage to speak. I have pictured the ride up Broadway, but I never realized that it was anything like this until today."

Later the couple were taken, amid more sirens and cheering, to a luncheon at the Advertising Club of New York at Fifth Avenue and 35th Street. Club President Grover Whalen served as toastmaster and introduced the afternoon's principal speaker, James Mattern, whose attempt to fly around the world solo earlier that year had ended when his plane crashed in Siberia. "I have a great feeling for this couple," he said. "When we crack 'em up, we crack 'em up good." He provided details of the couple's earlier record-setting achievements. Amy was the first woman to fly solo across Australia in May 1930, and in July 1931 made a flight from London to Moscow in 21 hours, four hours less than the previous record. In August 1931, Jim Morrison flew from Darwin, Australia, to England in eight and a half days and in March 1932 he flew from England to Cape Town, South Africa, in 4 days.

Explaining that both he and his wife were still physically and mentally exhausted from their flight and reception, the Scottish-born aviator kept his remarks brief. With a noticeable Scottish burr, he stated, "I wish to say that we are delighted and overwhelmed by the reception given us."

The "Flying Sweethearts" continued to fly together and separately, setting distance and endurance records until the spring of 1936. But they often found themselves competing for the same records and prizes, and Jim's drinking had become a problem. They divorced in 1938.

During the Second World War they both flew for Great Britain's Air Transport Auxiliary (ATA) transporting RAF planes from one location to another. In January 1941 Amy Johnson's plane crashed into the Thames Estuary and she was killed. Her body was never located. It was originally reported that she had run out of fuel and crashed but evidence found in 1999 indicates that her plane had been shot down by an RAF fighter when she failed to give the correct recognition signal. Mollison survived the war and continued flying until 1949 when his pilot's license was revoked because of his excessive drinking. He managed a pub in London until the mid-1950's but was then forced to receive treatment for alcoholism. He died in 1959, a patient at a temperance hotel in Surbiton, England.

Wednesday, September 13, 1933:
National Recovery Administration Day

The Great Depression was already in its third year when Franklin Roosevelt was sworn in as the nation's 32nd President in March 1933, and by many measures the economy was at its worst that year. National unemployment had risen to 25%, and in New York City it broke 33%. Half of the city's manufacturing plants were closed, and over 1.6 million residents were receiving some form of relief. As part of his "new deal" with the American people, the President signed many Congressional bills that year, to provide relief for the unemployed, stimulate recovery of the economy, and reform the nation's banking and financial institutions. One big component of the New Deal was the creation of the National Recovery Administration (NRA), empowered to create fair codes of competition, set minimum wages and maximum work hours, and get

Americans back to work. New York City declared September 13 as "NRA Day" in celebration and made plans for an enormous parade.

Thousands gathered in Washington Square Park, and more assembled in staging areas along Third and Fourth Avenues. The parade kicked off at 1:45 in the afternoon, led by Major General Dennis Nolan as the parade's Grand Marshal and Grover Whalen, the city's NRA chairman. Marching with them and their staffs were the Police Department Band and an escort from the Old Guard, dressed in colorful uniforms and picturesque shakos. Behind them marched over 2,500 troops from 13 National Guard units and a composite regiment of officers and men from the 16th and 18th Infantry, followed by the marching band of the 16th Infantry, known as "New York's Own."

As the parade kicked off, a fleet of 73 planes flew overhead, containing military and civilian aircraft that had taken off from Floyd Bennett Field, Flushing and Newark Airports, Roosevelt Field and the Long Island Aviation Country Club. Flying uptown, they passed over the review stand in front of the New York Public Library at 42nd Street, where over 5,000 seats had been sold. Governor Lehman and Mayor O'Brien sat there, and the Governor commented that this "demonstration was the greatest New York has ever seen." The Mayor agreed, saying the parade was "a great triumph."

For the next ten hours, the parade marched up Fifth Avenue, passing and continuing on to 72nd Street. Over 250,000 marchers participated, and police estimated a crowd of over 1.5 million spectators cheered and waved as they passed by.

After the military contingents came the workers, organized into 77 different trade and industry divisions. The press and publishing groups, which included newspaper reporters, magazine editors, advertising agencies, printing press operators and newsboys, were followed by the radio broadcasting groups and then members of Actors Equity and the Theatrical Workers and Stagehands Union. The motion-pictures group was led by Al Jolson, and the Radio City Music Hall staff marched in uniform, its ballet corps dressed as "wooden soldiers." There were groups for airport workers, nurses, mechanics, dock workers, messenger boys, bank and stock exchange employees, and telephone operators. The municipal employee contingent included 30,000 people, among them police and fire fighters, tenement inspectors, healthcare workers and teachers. As evening fell and the streetlights of Fifth Avenue came on, two of the largest contingents passed the review stand: the 17,000 employees of the city's retail establishments followed by the 50,000 seamstresses, tailors and clothiers of the "needle trades." These were followed by groups for electricians, lawyers, office equipment suppliers, brewers and bartenders, and life insurance and real estate salespeople. The last two groups, florists and cigar makers, passed the review stand at 11:20, and it was after midnight when they reached the end of the parade.

Confetti, ticker tape and shredded newspaper and torn papers began falling from the sky around 10th Street, and by 17th Street the sky was filled with "clouds of paper." The Department of Sanitation posted street cleaners at most intersections, but even so by the end of the day, Fifth Avenue was "a silver sheen, littered with wisps of ticker tape, refuse and the other marks of a city celebration." The crowds of spectators were thickest at the wider intersections of 14th, 23rd, 34th, 42nd and 57th Streets, but both sides of Fifth Avenue were packed along the entire route. The police had trouble holding the crowd to the sidewalks in many places, and from 42nd to 45th Streets, spectators spilled into the street so much that the parade narrowed to squeeze through an opening only 18 feet wide.

Every building along Fifth Avenue was decorated with flags and the NRA's Blue Eagle symbol, but none could compare with the B. Altman Building on 34th Street, which hung a banner measuring 90 feet by 75 feet. It was said to be the largest Blue Eagle in the country. By every measure, the parade that passed in front of its gaze was one of the city's largest.

Two years later, the Supreme Court declared the law that created the NRA to be unconstitutional, and the Blue Eagle soon disappeared. Many of the labor provisions were incorporated into new legislation, especially the National Labor Relations Act of 1935. Historians and economists still debate how effective the NRA was, and the national economy would not fully recover until World War II. New York City benefitted in many ways for the New Deal, especially through the many infrastructure improvements that Robert Moses accomplished using WPA funding, which prepared the city for prosperity after the war's end.

Thursday, September 3, 1936:
Jesse Owens and US Olympic Team from XI Olympic Games

The 1936 Olympic Games were supposed to demonstrate the superiority of German athletes over the rest of the world, according to the Nazis. Even though Germany's 89 medals, including 33 gold, exceeded any other nation, the Games were a letdown to Nazi ego. Much of that feeling was due to the American track star, Jesse Owens, and other African American members of the US Olympic team. Nazi Propaganda Minister Joseph Goebbels was so upset by American performances, he asserted that "American track and field victories were largely due to black auxiliaries."

The parade for members of the 1936 Olympic Team was unique in at least six ways: it did not stop at City Hall; it continued all the way to Harlem; ceremonies were held on Randall's Island; only 121 of the Olympic team's 380 members took part; the motorcade was more than 100 vehicles long; and the city's Gold medal was presented to athletes by five different individuals.

The ocean liner *Manhattan* arrived early on the morning of September 3, carrying 88 of the Olympians including Jesse Owens. The liner *President Roosevelt* had arrived the previous week with 190 other returning athletes, many of whom had already returned to their home towns. A small number of other athletes returned on their own and most of the American male swimmers were still touring in Europe. Those who could participate in the parade joined the 88 members from the *Manhattan* at the West 90th Street pier. The entire party was escorted downtown along the West Side Highway to Battery Park and entered their assigned vehicles.

Jesse Owens rode in the first car with Stanley Howe, executive secretary to Mayor LaGuardia. Helen Stephens, holder of the world's record for the 100-meter dash, rode in the second with Acting Police Commissioner Harold Fowler. The third car carried female sprinter Betty Robinson and former heavy-weight boxing champion Jack Dempsey. Athletes continued to enter cars until 100 vehicles were ready for the parade. Most cars carried one athlete and a dignitary. No car carried more than two athletes.

At exactly five minutes after noon the parade began, with the Police Department band leading the way. Also marching were the Fire and Sanitation Departments Bands. As usual, the long procession was greeted with swirling cascades of ticker tape, confetti, and paper torn from phone directories, magazines, and newspapers. One hundred extra policemen were on guard along Lower Broadway, but veteran observers commented that the size and enthusiasm of the crowd downtown was less than for other recent parades.

The motorcade slowed when it reached City Hall, but it did not stop, and the three bands withdrew from the parade while the vehicles proceeded north at a faster pace. Up Lafayette Street the procession continued, north on Fourth and Madison Avenues to 60th Street, across to Central Park West, north to 110th Street, east to Seventh Avenue, up to 135th Street, down Lenox Avenue, back to 125th Street and across the Triborough Bridge, ending at Randall's Island Stadium. The size of the crowds through the latter part of the journey through Harlem made up for the lack of participation of those downtown. Flags flew from countless buildings, and shouts of "Hi there, Jesse," "Hello Lightning," and "We showed 'em!" could be heard along the way.

A crowd of 2,000 spectators were seated in the stadium as the athletes walked a victory lap around its track. The Olympians took seats on the infield and Mayor LaGuardia welcomed them home and began the process of presenting each athlete a Gold Medal. After he awarded the first five medals, Grover Whalen took over the task. He was followed by Jack Dempsey, then by African American tap dancer, Bill Bojangles Robinson, and finally by female swimming star Gertrude Ederle *(see: August 27, 1926)*. When only one athlete remained seated, the mayor resumed the task. "Now the moment has arrived," he said, "when New York City takes its hat off to the leading member of the 1936 American Olympics team. Jesse, on behalf of New York City, I hail you as an American boy. We are all Americans here," he concluded. "We have no auxiliaries in this country," he ended alluding to the comment in the Nazi press.

Jesse Owens thanked the mayor on behalf of his fellow athletes. Asking Bill Robinson to join him on the rostrum, Owens handed Robinson the first of four Gold Medals he won in Berlin, for the 100-meter dash. "An Olympic Gold Medal is the highest honor an athlete can win," Owens said, "and I treasure it above all my other possessions, but I want to make a presentation to Bill Robinson, the mayor of Harlem, for all he has done for all of us." Loud cheers filled the stadium. Too stunned to respond, Bill Robinson embraced the track star.

With little further fanfare, the athletes began to return to the waiting cars. Many of them, including Jesse Owens, were staying at the Waldorf Astoria. When Owens arrived there, he was not permitted to enter through the main doors and had to ride the freight elevator to his room, despite being a registered guest. Even though the mayor bragged that America had no auxiliaries, the city still had segregationist policies at the time.

Many of the athletes on the 1936 Olympics team, including Jesse Owens, were in their prime and looked forward to competing in the 1940 games which were scheduled for Tokyo but were cancelled because of World War II. The next Olympic Games were held in 1948, by which time few of the 1936 athletes remained in competition.

Despite being a track star, Jesse Owens was a cigarette smoker all his life. He died of lung cancer in 1980 in Tucson, Arizona. He is buried in Oak Woods Cemetery, Chicago.

Mayor Fiorello LaGuardia (1934-1945)

The diminutive but charismatic "little flower" who won the Mayoral election in 1933 was born in Greenwich Village in 1882, though lived in both Arizona and Trieste, Italy during his youth. His father was a lapsed Catholic immigrant from Italy, his mother was a Jewish immigrant from Trieste, and he was raised Episcopalian. He spoke several languages fluently, which helped him build cross-cultural coalitions to win elections and defeat traditional Tammany-backed Democrats.

LaGuardia was elected to Congress in 1916, but then served in the Army Air Force during World War I. After the war he returned to New York and was elected President of the Board of Aldermen. Re-elected to Congress in 1922, he served there until 1930, gaining a reputation as a fiery reformer capable of working with both parties. He won his bid for Mayor in 1933 campaigning on an anti-corruption platform, building a coalition that kept him in City Hall until 1945.

As Mayor, LaGuardia accomplished much for the city: he restored public trust in City Hall, unified the subway system, constructed the city's second municipal airport (which would be named after him), oversaw development of public housing and parks, re-organized the police force, prioritized merit for employment in government jobs rather than patronage, and stabilized New York's fiscal health. Working with President Franklin Roosevelt, he and City Parks Commissioner Robert Moses used federal New Deal stimulus money to put New Yorkers back to work while improving the city's infrastructure of highways and bridges, while also channeling that money in ways that broke Tammany Hall's influence on city politics. During World War II, LaGuardia also became the nation's first Officer of Civilian Defense, preparing New York and other cities for potential attack.

LaGuardia decided not to run for a fourth term for health reasons and died of pancreatic cancer in 1947. His 12 years in City Hall had changed New York, and he is often considered one of the greatest mayors in the city's history.

Tuesday, September 21, 1937: American Legion Convention

"The parade will go on night and day for 24 hours," according to the September 1937 edition of The New York National Guardsman, a monthly magazine for active and former members of the National Guard, in an issue dedicated to plans for the 19th annual convention of the American Legion, held in New York to commemorate the 20th anniversary of the US entering World War I. The three-day convention, planned to be the legion's largest to date, adopted the slogan "Up Fifth Avenue Again in 1937" to recall the parades "up and down Fifth Avenue twenty years ago" and to "emphasize the fact that the United States can live at peace with the rest of the world."

The goal of a 24-hour parade was not achieved, but "it lasted nearly 18 hours, a record for the Legion and for the city," according to the New York Times. Led by an escort of motorcycle police, the parade kicked off at 8:55 in the morning. The first group consisted of 4,200 officers of the NY police force who were also members of the American Legion. Marching quickly and "setting a pace for speed that the rest of the parade could never recapture," they moved northward from Madison Square to 79th Street.

Behind them came the politicians and organizers of the massive event. Major General William Haskell, the parade's grand marshal, was accompanied by Governor Lehman and Mayor LaGuardia, both Legionnaires themselves, who exited the parade at the reviewing stand set up at Grand Army Plaza on 59th Street. For the rest of the day, and well into the night, American Legion members marched, organized into groups by state. All 48 states and the District of Columbia had a contingent, many led by their governors, and there was also a "Foreign Departments" group that included members from US territories as well as Americans who had enrolled with Canadian units during World War I.

The Governor and Mayor rejoined the parade that evening, to march with the New York contingent, which paraded last as the convention's host. This contingent was "the greatest in numbers of any of the State groups, and, as it did not even begin to march until well into the evening, even the men who could not get away from their jobs had a chance to parade." The last of the marchers "swung into Fifth Avenue" shortly after 2 o'clock in the morning, and "25 minutes later the parade had ended."

In total, 85,000 men marched to the cheers of over 2 million spectators. Manhattan was divided as if "the Grand Canyon instead of Fifth Avenue ran through its midst." Crosstown traffic was completely snarled for all types of vehicles, and even pedestrians had a difficult time in midtown. By evening, Times Square was filled with Legionnaires who had finished the march. Over 300,000 people filled the theatre district, packed shoulder to shoulder. Revelers crowded into the pubs and bars of Yorkville around the parade's end, and other neighborhoods were crowded as well.

Throughout the day and into the night, a blizzard of paper fell onto Fifth Avenue and around Times Square, as spectators "showered bits of torn telephone book, newspapers and ticker tape from high windows in office buildings until the street sweepers were up to their ankles in it." The Department of Sanitation could not "begin to clear away the debris of the celebration" until after 2 in the morning.

Along with the merrymaking there was plenty of mischief making, judging from the number of anecdotes reported in the two full pages of coverage in the *New York Times*. The convention had caused a "three-day siege" to the city and the "younger Legionnaires continued their carousing" all night as if tireless. A spokesman for the Salvation Army, which had set up a tent just north of Times Square, commented that "these boys won't hold out much longer" because many of them were running out of cash.

The annual convention ended the following day, and the Legionnaires eventually headed back to their homes. Among the platforms their convention passed was a statement to the nation's leaders to stay out of the "saber-rattling" in Europe, and to avoid getting involved in a struggle between "Nazism and Communism." Like the 24-hour parade, that goal would not be achieved.

Founded in 1919, the American Legion is a non-profit organization providing services to and advocating on behalf of US veterans. It played a significant role in the shaping and passage of the "GI Bill" in 1944, construction of the Vietnam War memorial in Washington DC, and support for the Veterans Health Administration. Today it has almost 2 million members, and 10 of the nation's 12 presidents since 1945 have been members.

Friday, July 15, 1938: Howard Hughes

Soon after Howard Hughes landed at Floyd Bennett Field on July 10, 1938, completing his record-setting round-the-world flight in only 91 hours, he was informed that a ticker tape parade would be held in his honor five days later. Hughes insisted that the parade include the four men who flew with him, the 17 technicians and military personnel who helped plan the flight and provided assistance during it, plus their wives and families. Grover Whalen, President of the 1939-1940 World's Fair Committee and Mayor LaGuardia's Chairman of the Reception Committee, informed him that a parade of that size was far out of the budget and out of the question. Determined to have his way, multi-millionaire Hughes notified everyone he wished to share in the parade and arranged for the extra vehicles and security, picking up the bill to pay for it himself.

Hughes and the four men who completed the flight with him (navigators Thomas Thurlow and Harry Connor, radio operator Richard Stoddart, and flight engineer Edward Lund) were given rooms at the Hampshire House on Central Park South between Seventh Avenue and Broadway. On the morning of the parade the fleet of cars taking part in the motorcade arrived at the Hampshire House. Sitting in the first car was Grover Whalen who would be sharing the vehicle with Mr. Hughes. The four who flew with Hughes exited the apartment building and took seats in the second car. Behind them were cars carrying the others whom Hughes had invited. There was only one person missing: Howard Hughes. People who knew of his often eccentric and secretive behavior began to search for him. Albert Ludwick, the manager of the circumnavigation flight, found Hughes at the Drake Hotel, where he was revising his City Hall speech.

Hustled back to the waiting cars, Hughes stepped into the first car, pulled his trademark old battered felt hat tight on his head, and burrowed deep into the seat beside Mr. Whalen. The start of the parade was already late, so with an escort of siren-screaming motorcycles, the motorcade raced downtown at speeds of 45 to 50 miles per hour.

Arriving downtown more than 30 minutes past the scheduled starting time, the parade had another delay, as Hughes was besieged by reporters and photographers. Dozens of photos were taken and just as many questions asked. Most received little more than a nod or a simple "yes" or "no" answer. With assistance from members of the police force, the way was eventually cleared, and the procession began heading up Broadway to music provided by both the Police and Fire Department bands. Mr. Hughes sat low in his seat as the parade started but with some prompting from Mr. Whalen, the aviator finally stood and shyly waved his hat. Within a few blocks, Mr. Hughes warmed to the crowd's reception and before long he was waving and grinning, his crumpled fedora on the floor of the back seat.

Spectators by the hundreds of thousands lined the route. A Police estimate put the number between the Battery and City Hall at more than 750,000. Perhaps an additional 500,000 were at windows or on ledges and cornices or had perilously climbed street lampposts and trees in Trinity Churchyard. After the parade and the job of cleaning up the massive amounts of ticker tape and torn paper had been completed, Sanitation officials stated that their crews had swept and shoveled 1,800 tons.

City Hall Park was a solid mass of people. Mayor LaGuardia and former mayors Jimmy Walker and John O'Brien stood waiting on the reviewing stand. Since the parade had started late, Mayor LaGuardia had begun entertaining the crowd with jokes and anecdotes. Not to be outdone, Former Mayor Walker joined in and soon the two were performing like comedians on the vaudeville circuit, with Mayor O'Brien enjoying the show. When the parade finally reached City Hall, it seemed almost anti-climactic, and it took a few minutes before the combined efforts of the three mayors managed to quiet the crowd.

Mayor LaGuardia placed the City's Gold Medal around Hughes' neck, but when he tried to shake his hand, the flier smiled and thrust his hands into his jacket pockets. The four men who flew with Hughes were introduced by name, although the technicians and military personnel were referred to collectively. Both former mayors spoke, O'Brien more briefly than the loquacious Walker. Following their words, Mr. Hughes was asked to speak. He consulted folded pages taken from his pocket, smoothed them, and started by saying that he had not had time to prepare a proper speech and was not very good at public speaking but would do his best. He spoke quickly and mumbled often, sometimes pausing for no apparent reason. Reporters said the speech was far from good, but the crowd loved it, roaring in approval at everything he said.

Minutes later the motorcade continued to the Metropolitan Club for a luncheon. It was a private affair, limited to fewer than 100 people, but more than 3,000 people jammed 60th Street for a chance to see Hughes. The luncheon ended late in the afternoon and Hughes was driven to Mr. Lodwick's apartment on East 56th Street to change and rest before dinner that evening at the Waldorf. Not long afterwards it was discovered that the aviator had climbed out a window and disappeared. He did not appear at the dinner, disappointing those attending, and was not seen again in public until a week later, when he was a guest at the Terrace Club on the grounds of the forthcoming World's Fair in Flushing.

Howard Hughes became more eccentric over the years. He survived two crashes in experimental planes and withdrew further into himself. Diagnosed as having an obsessive-compulsive disorder, he spent long periods alone, neither washing nor shaving, often naked watching films in a private viewing room. In 1957 he spent four months in the same room, passing notes under the door to his employees and existing on chocolate bars, chicken, and milk. He became addicted to codeine to relieve real and imagined pains. In the late 1960's he lived almost exclusively on two floors of the Sands Hotel, Las Vegas, which he owned along with a number of other hotels and casinos, and later lived as a recluse in Nicaragua, the Bahamas, and Mexico. He died an invalid in early April 1976 on his private jet flying to Houston, Texas. At his death he weighed less than 90 pounds, and his hair, beard, fingernails and toenails had not been cut or trimmed in months. A positive identification was made only by consulting FBI fingerprint records.

Friday, August 5, 1938: Douglas "Wrong Way" Corrigan

On the evening of July 17, 1938, Douglas Corrigan submitted a flight plan from Floyd Bennett Field, Brooklyn, to Long Beach, California. The following morning, he took off in his plane *Sunshine*, carrying 320 gallons of gas, two chocolate bars, two boxes of fig bars, and 25 gallons of water. He landed at Baldonnel Aerodrome, Dublin, Ireland 28 hours and 10 minutes later, claiming his old compass had malfunctioned. He carried no radio and could not see directly ahead because of modifications that blocked the plane's front window. He also claimed that he had no idea he was headed the wrong direction until 26 hours into the flight when he banked the plane and observed water below his aircraft.

Aviation officials telegraphed him in Dublin with a lengthy message informing him of the regulations he had broken. Among other points, they mentioned how his plane, most of which he rebuilt and modified, failed to meet safety requirements and was unsuitable for transatlantic flight. Extra fuel tanks crammed on board forced him to sit in a crouched position and the door behind his seat was held in place with baling-wire. They reminded him that he had twice previously requested permission to fly to Ireland and twice been denied. His pilot's license was suspended for 14 days.

There was something that captured the imagination of America about his flight. Already being called "Wrong Way" Corrigan by the media, he discovered just how much of a hero he had become when he made plans to sail home on the liner *Manhattan* (with *Sunshine* dismantled and stored in the hold). Cables and telegrams arrived, not censuring him, but with offers for a film contract, requests for exclusive interviews by writers, and an announcement from the office of Mayor LaGuardia that he would be receiving a ticker tape parade on his arrival in New York. There was also a telegram from Brooklyn politicians, with a similar proposal to celebrate his return with a parade from where he had started his flight, Floyd Bennett Field. Manhattan won the honor of greeting him first, however.

The liner arrived in New York on August 4, welcomed by a cacophony of horns and whistles, and fire boats shot plumes of water in celebration. After disembarking, Corrigan was escorted to a suite at the Hotel McAlpin. The next morning, he was driven to Bowling Green. He shared an open car with Deputy Police Commissioner Louis Costuma and, following the Police Department band, the 12-car motorcade moved up Broadway, escorted by four dozen motorcycle police. Commissioner Costuma estimated the crowd at 100,000. Sanitation officials, responsible for the clean-up following parades, estimated the number at twice that. Ticker tape, confetti, and torn newspapers and telephone books littered the route. Even one of New York's daily newspapers, the *New York Post*, joined in celebrating in a unique and special way by printing the headline: NAGIRROC YAW GNORW LIAH

At City Hall Mayor LaGuardia welcomed the tall Texas-born aviator. "Texas may claim you," the mayor said, "but from now on you're one of us." Carried by radio, his words were broadcast and relayed around the country. Corrigan thanked the city and admitted that he never imagined such a welcome possible for a man who made a navigational error. He recounted how one of his reserve fuel tanks had sprung a leak near the end of the flight, spilling onto the floor of the cockpit. Rather than risk a fire when he landed, he punched a hole through the floor with a screwdriver so the fuel could drain out. He accepted the city's Gold Medal, flashed a broad smile, and waved to the more than 20,000 people in City Hall Plaza.

Following the reception there was a luncheon at the Advertising Club, where Corrigan was hailed as a brave adventurer. Later that afternoon he was driven to Yankee Stadium where he witnessed the last three innings of a victory over the Cleveland Indians. The next morning, he was feted at Brooklyn City Hall, where he received a special medal struck specifically for him, and representatives from Floyd Bennett Field presented him with a new compass.

Corrigan returned to California a week later. His license suspension over, he flew *Sunshine* to the west coast. He continued to fly, starred as himself in the 1939 RKO film *The Flying Irishman*, wrote an autobiography, and became a flight trainer and supervisor during World War II. On the 50th anniversary of the flight, his plane was removed from storage and the engine tested and run. The plane's present whereabouts is unknown though Corrigan hinted that he had personally dismantled and stored it in numerous locations so it could not be stolen. He died in 1995. Despite speculation at the time and over the years afterward, Corrigan never publicly admitted to having flown to Ireland intentionally.

Thursday, April 27, 1939:
Crown Prince Olav and Princess Martha of Norway

Fog can be disruptive. Nine years earlier fog in the harbor nearly caused the cele-bration for the arrival of Brazilian President-elect Julio Prestes *(see: June 11, 1930)* to become a night parade. And there was fog swathing New York harbor this chilly late April morning when Crown Prince Olav of Norway and his wife Princess Martha passed through Ambrose Channel aboard the Norwegian cruise ship *Oslofjord*. Suddenly there was a grinding sound as the Norwegian ship's bow struck the side of 361-ton pilot boat *Sandy Hook*. The *New York Post* quoted the captain of the pilot boat, "I looked out the porthole and there was the bow of the ship almost on top of us. I jumped and ran out of the cabin. The next instant she hit us. Everybody ran for the boats as mast and booms crashed on the deck, smashing a lifeboat." Fortunately, all 20 pilots and 6 crew members on board the rapidly sinking pilot boat escaped and were "rescued with little or no injuries."

Preparing for his meeting with Mayor LaGuardia, Prince Olav was in his bath at the time, and was unaware of the accident until informed later. There is no record of Mayor LaGuardia's reaction to the incident.

The sinking of the pilot boat caused a delay of more than two hours. The 21-gun salute from Fort Jay to recognize the heir to the Norwegian throne rattled the windows of buildings along the Battery. Waiting at Pier A when the royal couple came ashore was the mayor and his wife, City Controller Joseph McGoldrick and other dignitaries. The Prince commented that he and the Princess "have been watching our landfall and have admired the beautiful skyline of Manhattan." A band struck up the Norwegian anthem "Ekko van Norden" and the "Star Spangled Banner." The parade then pro-ceeded up Broadway to the cheers of a number of the city's citizens of Norwegian ancestry as they chanted "Olav." More formal welcomes were extended at City Hall, where the Prince commented that New York was a symbol of peaceful work and to-getherness across the world and that the recently opened World's Fair would be an inspiration with its theme, the World of Tomorrow. Afterwards the royal couple at-tended a luncheon at the Banker's Club.

The Prince had two reasons for his visit to American: to officially open the Nor-wegian pavilion at the World's Fair in Flushing, Queens, and to meet with President Roosevelt in Hyde Park. The morning after the parade, he cut the red ribbon at the Norwegian exhibit, made another brief speech, and then proceeded by train to the president's estate in upstate Hyde Park. During his brief stay in the US, he and the Princess visited a number of sites. Governor Alfred E. Smith escorted the couple to the observation deck of the Empire State Building, but the city was again blanketed by fog and the view, according to Princess Martha, was "much like London." They also visited the George Washington Bridge, Rockefeller Center, and the Cathedral of St. John the Divine, among other places before returning home.

A little more than two years later, Norway was invaded and overrun by Nazi Ger-man troops. A graduate of the Norwegian Naval Academy, Prince Olav was involved in some of the fighting. He wished to remain in the country to lead the resistance when his father, King Haakon VII, and the Norwegian government fled to England, but his request was denied. He became a spokesman for the Norwegian resistance from Lon-don and visited Norwegian troops in England and Canada during the war. Crown Prin-cess Martha died from cancer in 1954. Three years later, he ascended the throne as King Olav V of Norway, reigning until his death on Jan 17, 1991. Beloved by his countrymen, he is affectionately called "The People's King." A 2005 pool organized by the Norwegian Broadcasting System voted him Norwegian of the Century by a large margin.

New York City Council

A new city charter was passed in 1937, abolishing the Board of Aldermen and replacing it with a City Council composed of 26 members serving two year terms. The terms were extended to four years in 1945, and the districts and voting procedures were changed several times over the years. The 1937 charter also revamped the Board of Estimate as the chief administrative body.

When the Board of Estimate was ruled unconstitutional and dissolved in 1989, its powers were absorbed by the City Council, which expanded to 51 members. In 1993, the Council voted to rename the position of City Council President to Public Advocate, which was the Council's presiding officer until another city charter revision in 2002 transferred those duties to the Council Speaker.

The 1937 city charter did not require renovation to City Hall, and the Aldermanic Chamber was simply renamed the Council Chamber. In 2010, however, as part of the renovation of the entire building, the Chamber received its first major renovation. The mahogany paneling, historic furniture and balcony seating were restored, the ceiling re-plastered, and several paintings were added to those already hanging in the Chamber.

Monday, May 1, 1939:
Rear Admiral Alfred Johnson, Commander of the Atlantic Squadron

As part of the opening ceremonies for the World's Fair, a number of US Navy ships, all part of the Atlantic Squadron commanded by Alfred Johnson, sailed into New York Harbor. They docked at piers in Brooklyn and in Manhattan from West 72nd Street to 131st Street or rode at anchor in the Hudson River. The ships would spend a week in the city, open to the public, and their officers and men were given free passes to the Fair in Flushing Meadows, Queens. Originally 36 ships had been scheduled to visit the city but in mid-April four of them (an aircraft carrier, a cruiser, and two destroyers) were transferred to the Pacific Fleet. Even with this reduction in the number, it was the largest gathering of warships ever to visit the city. The impressive gathering included three battleships, *New York* (temporary flagship during the visit), *Texas,* and *Tennessee;* two aircraft carriers, *Ranger* and *Langley;* five cruisers, *Brooklyn* (temporary flagship of the vessels docked in Brooklyn), *Savannah, Nashville, Philadelphia,* and *Honolulu;* the new submarine *Saury* along with one S-class submarine and five R-class coastal submarines; submarine tenders *Falcon* and *Serames;* seven "four stacker" destroyers, veterans of the Great War, *Fairfax, Schenck, Roper, Hopkins, Goff, Babbitt, Reuben James,* and *Barry;* and, finally four modern stream-lined destroyers, *Jouett, Benham, Ellett,* and *Claxton.* The ships had been steaming into the harbor since April 27, and on May 1 representatives of each vessel were officially welcomed to the city with a ticker tape parade.

Rear Admirals Alfred Johnson and Forde Todd (commanding the Atlantic Cruiser Division) sat in an open limousine along with Winthrop Aldrich, Chairman of the Reception Committee. Other vehicles in the motorcade carried Police Commissioner Lewis Valentine; Chief Inspector Louis Costuma of the Police Department; Paul Moss, City License Commissioner; Brigadier General Walter Short, commanding the First Division and representing the Army; Rear Admiral Frank Lackey, commander of the New York Naval Militia; and retired Rear Admiral Reginald Belknap.

Nearly 2,000 spectators stood in Battery Park near the Customs House to watch the officers in full dress uniforms and civilians in top hats and frock coats move forward shortly after noon for the march up Broadway. Troop C of the mounted police lead the way, as more than 1,200 police marched or stood guard along the route. Bands from both the Brooklyn Navy Yard and Fire Department provided music for the more than 2,500 marching sailors. It was estimated that 250,000 people viewed the parade, with crowds the thickest south of Trinity Church at Wall Street. Included among those viewing were almost 5,000 assembled in City Hall Park. When Admiral Johnson arrived, Mayor Fiorello LaGuardia greeted him in his usual exuberant manner. The mayor joined the admirals to reviewe the passing ranks, then led the Admirals and a number of Captains and other high-ranking officers into the Council Chambers as the Fire Department band played "Anchors Aweigh" followed by the national anthem.

"I come here today to report for duty, and I bring my captains, the captains of all my ships," Admiral Johnson addressed the large number of invited guests in the Chambers. "I know they will do all they can to help New York and the World's Fair to have a good time during these opening weeks." The mayor responded by saying, "I think that all Americans cannot help but admire the high state of efficiency of the United States Navy." Turning to Admiral Johnson, the mayor gave an order to him and the visiting sailors: "Full speed ahead in all enjoyment; the sky's the limit."

That afternoon the Brooklyn Dodgers provided free tickets to hundreds of officers and sailors. They witnessed a slugfest, the Dodgers scoring 3 runs in the bottom of the ninth to win by one run. A tea party was also held for naval chaplains at Fort Hamilton, Brooklyn. The majority of the officers and sailors of the Atlantic Squadron, however, availed themselves of the free passes for the Fair.

Admiral Johnson retired because of age in 1940. Shortly after the United States entered the Second World War he was recalled to duty and served on various Naval Boards and Advisory Committees during the war. He was relieved of all active duties in August 1945 and died in 1963 at the age of 87.

Many of the ships that visited New York saw service in the War. Most of the older destroyers were turned over to Great Britain as part of the Lend Lease program. Destroyer *Reuben James* was the first US naval ship lost in World War II. More than a month before Pearl Harbor, she was serving with the Neutrality Patrol off Iceland. On October 31, 1941, she was struck by a torpedo fired by German submarine *U-552*, broke in two and sank. Only 44 of her crew of 159 survived. The battleship *Tennessee* was damaged at Pearl Harbor but returned to service in 1944. *Langley* and *Benham* were lost to the Japanese in combat in the Pacific.

Saturday, June 10, 1939:
King George VI and Queen Elizabeth of Great Britain

History came full circle, noted one letter writer to the *New York Times*, when Mayor LaGuardia presented the Keys of the City to Great Britain's King George VI. When the British evacuated New York City in 1783, the city's keys had been surrendered by Sir Guy Carleton, who had been appointed by the current monarch's ancestor George III.

Never before had Britain's reigning monarch visited the United States, and King George and his wife, Queen Elizabeth, were met with enthusiastic cheering from crowds everywhere they went. Arriving in Quebec on May 17, they spent two weeks touring Canada before entering the United States at Niagara Falls on June 8, where they laid the cornerstone for a steel arch bridge to connect the two nations across the Niagara River. They then travelled to Washington, where they were greeted by large crowds at Union Station. Later that day they were the guests of honor at a formal state dinner at the White House, and on June 9 they toured Washington DC, including a visit to Mount Vernon, George Washington's home.

On the morning of June 10, the Royal Couple travelled by train to Fort Hancock in Sandy Hook, New Jersey, where they boarded the US Navy destroyer *Warrington*. A 21-gun salute fired in their honor, and the destroyer sailed to New York, escorted by eight Coast Guard vessels. The ship sounded its horn as it sailed into the harbor, and all the ships in the harbor responded while 10 army bombers flew overhead. Another 21-gun salute was fired from Fort Jay, as a squadron of NYC fireboats sprayed streams of water into the air.

Tens of thousands waited at the Battery, some of whom had arrived at dawn, and a loud cheer rose as the ship swung alongside Pier A. Mayor LaGuardia and New York Governor Herbert Lehman waited there to officially greet the King and Queen as they disembarked and descended the red carpet that has been laid for them. The Mayor's wife gave the Queen with a bouquet of roses, while the Mayor presented the Keys to the City to the King.

The Police and Fire Department Bands played the national anthems of Great Britain and the United States as the royal party entered an open car, accompanied by the Mayor and his wife. As the crowd cheered again, "ticker tape and torn paper came fluttering down onto the West Street roadway, adding the picturesque touch of greeting that originated in New York."

Concerned about security, Scotland Yard had refused the traditional route "through the towering concrete and steel canyon of lower Broadway," the *Times* reported "for fear some enthusiastic welcome might throw a telephone book without tearing it up first." Instead, the 50-car caravan followed an escort of mounted police up West Street to the West Side Highway. Tickets for public seating in grandstands set up along the route were sold out in advance, and in places without seating, the crowds lining the street were several people deep.

As the caravan proceeded uptown, ships docked at piers sounded their horns in salute, with the exception of two liners owned by the North German Company docked near 42nd Street. The crowds were thick in this area, and a spokesman for the company explained later that the ship's captains were unaware the caravan was passing, although the British liner *Lancastria*, docked at the next pier, was able to sound its horn at the correct time.

Continuing up the Hudson to 72nd Street, the caravan turned east and passed through Central Park, where the Queen requested that they proceed more slowly so that the thousands of school children waving British flags along the roadside could get a good view. Schools across the city were given specific locations along the roadway inside the park where their students, teachers and parents could assemble, and over 25,000 British flags were handed out to grade school children. Parks officials estimated over 100,000 children watched the caravan pass, plus another 50,000 adults.

Exiting the park at 96th Street, the caravan continued uptown through Harlem, then crossed the Triborough Bridge, and drove along Grand Central Parkway to the Fairgrounds in Flushing. The crowds were thinner here than in Manhattan, but spectators stood wherever they could, and in total the City estimated over 3.5 million people waved and cheered to greet the Royal Couple.

About an hour behind schedule, the caravan finally arrived at the Fairgrounds in Flushing Meadows, where British Redcoats had fought against General Washington's Continental Army in 1776. Grover Whalen, President of the New York World's Fair Commission, and his wife Anna were there at Perylon Hall to greet the Royal Couple. Before more cheering crowds and a band that played "God Save the King," Whalen presented them a gold and crystal replica of the *Trylon* and *Perisphere*, the enormous sculptures that had become the central symbol of the Fair. They toured the Fair, visiting the British, Canadian and Australian Pavilions, the Court of Peace and the Lagoon of Nations, and enjoyed a formal luncheon in the Federal Building. As they drove along Rainbow Avenue, a band of bagpipers from the Merrie England Village played Scottish tunes.

Three hours later the King and Queen left the Fair, joined in their open car by the Mayor and Governor Lehman. The caravan drove to Columbia University, where they were greeted by the University's President, Dr. Nicholas Butler. They then toured Low Memorial Library and viewed the charter which had established the College, granted by King George II in 1754.

The day's official events were over, and the caravan left the city driving north on the Saw Mill River Parkway heading for Hyde Park, the home of President Franklin Roosevelt. On June 12, the King and Queen returned to Canada, and three days later sailed out of Halifax to return to Great Britain. The first-ever Royal Tour of Canada and the United States was considered a great success.

Born in 1895, Albert Frederick Arthur George was the second son of King George V. Known as Bertie to his family, he was never expected to wear the crown until his older brother, King Edward VIII *(see: November 18, 1919)*, abdicated in 1936. Albert took his regnal name of George VI to show continuity after the constitutional crisis, and was much beloved by his people, especially when he and the Queen decided to remain in Buckingham Palace during the Blitz in World War II. A lifelong smoker, he died in 1952, and was succeeded by his eldest daughter, Elizabeth II *(see: October 21, 1957)*.

Elizabeth Marguerite Bowes-Lyon married Albert in 1923, when he was the Duke of York, and was one of the most beloved members of the royal family throughout her life. She became Queen when her husband ascended the throne in 1936, and after his death was referred to as Queen Mother, to avoid confusion with her daughter, Queen Elizabeth II. She returned to New York City in 1985, and spoke of the 1939 visit, saying, "I always look back upon that visit with feelings of affection and happiness." She died in 2002 at the age of 101.

142

New York World's Fair

Conceived in 1935 as a way to promote New York City during the Depression, the 1939 New York World's Fair was the largest exposition of its kind since the St Louis Exposition of 1904. Mayor LaGuardia formed an organizing committee, chaired by Grover Whalen, which worked closely with Parks Commissioner Robert Moses to design and construct the Fair Grounds. Built on landfill in Flushing, Queens, the Fair opened on April 30, 1939 to commemorate the 150th anniversary of George Washington's inauguration as President at Federal Hall in downtown Manhattan.

The Fair Grounds were divided into zones arranged in a semi-circular pattern around a central plaza, where the enormous sculptures Trylon and Perisphere stood. Over 60 nations participated, and 21 of them built pavilions around the Lagoon of Nations. In the Communications zone, visitors could hear mechanized voices at the AT&T pavilion or watch IBM's electric typewriters or machines that created punch cards for electric calculators. General Motors and Ford Motor Company had large displays in the Transportation zone. Crowds were entertained by performers and rides in the Amusements zone, and ate in the Food zone, which included an exhibit by Borden Dairy debuting its new mascot, Elsie the cow.

The fair was open from 1939 to 1940, and more than 44 million visitors saw a glimpse of the "world of tomorrow." The Fair closed earlier than planned due to the start of World War II. Some of its rides were sold to Coney Island, but most of the pavilions and buildings were demolished. The New York State building was used temporarily for meetings of the United Nations, and later became the Queens Museum. When another World's Fair was opened in the same location in 1964, a large-scale Panorama of New York City was housed there. For the 1964 World's Fair, the enormous Unisphere was built on the location of the Perisphere. The 1,200-acre grounds are now part of the Flushing Meadows Corona Park, and the Panorama in the Queens Museum was updated again in 2009 to reflect the city's on-going changes.

CHAPTER 5
V for Victory! (1940-1946)

In September 1939, the newspaper headlines, radio announcers and the movie theater news reels all announced the news that would mean the end of the Depression, as once again, Europe was plunged into war. The Nazi German war machine swiftly defeated one nation after another, and by the summer of 1940, only Great Britain remained. Germany's allies, Italy and Japan, spread the war to all corners of the world: Italian troops moved through North Africa threatening Britain's control of the Suez Canal and the oil fields which lay beyond them, while Japan conquered first Hong Kong and Singapore, and then pushed through Burma to threaten Britain's hold on India. Prime Minister Winston Churchill *(see: March 15, 1946)* braced Great Britain for invasion in 1941, vowing "we shall defend our island, whatever the cost may be." But Germany suddenly shifted from bombing London to invading the Soviet Union, and all the major powers in the world were involved, except one. The Unites States tried to stay out of the war, though gave significant aid to Great Britain and the Soviet Union through the Lend-Lease program. But that changed with Japan's surprise attack on Pearl Harbor, the US's naval station in the Hawaiian Islands, on December 7, 1941, a date which President Roosevelt declared would "live in infamy."

World War II would affect America, and New York, far more significantly than its predecessor had. America's mobilization was enormous, with over 16 million men and women serving in the US military, more than 10% of the entire population of the country. The war effort needed supplies: weapons, ammunition, jeeps, ships, airplanes, bombs. The resulting boost to employment provided the stimulus to end the Depression that had plagued the country since 1929.

For civilians at home, the war affected every aspect of life: from bond drives and victory gardens to the rationing of a lengthy list of items needed by the military (including gasoline, meat, eggs, coffee, silk, nylon, butter and even bicycles). Hollywood's celebrities joined the USO to entertain the troops and volunteered with the Red Cross to create care packages and bandages. With so many men drafted into the military, women were employed at munitions-creating factories, shipping and railyards, and many office jobs traditionally held by men. The entire nation was mobilized.

New York City was one of the nation's largest manufacturing centers and ports, and because of advances in aviation since World War I, it was also one of the country's biggest targets for attack from the sky or underwater. The horrific news of the Blitz in London, which killed thousands of civilians in their own homes led President Roosevelt to form an Office of Civilian Defense, and he named Mayor LaGuardia as its first director. Under LaGuardia's direction, the OCD prepared for air raids and blackouts, designated shelter locations and organized thousands of volunteers into the war effort. As during the First World War, the city's large immigrant population fell under suspicion. Over 1,000 Japanese Americans were moved to Camp Upton in Brookhaven, Long Island as part of the nation-wide "forced re-location" of more than 100,000 Americans with Japanese ancestry, and many of the 11,000 people with German ancestry who were interned also came from New York. Ellis Island was used as a temporary detention camp, with several hundred "enemy aliens" sent there every month, and some being kept there for a long as two years. Prisoners of war were also kept on Ellis Island, as well as at Fort Hamilton in Brooklyn and Fort Jay on Governors Island.

Over 900,000 New Yorkers were among the almost 3 million men who sailed out of New York headed to war, most bound for North Africa and Europe, along with over 60 million tons of supplies. German U-boats were active in the waters outside of the harbor, and on at least one occasion, a submarine was able to sail close enough to see the light from Manhattan's skyscrapers, and torpedoed 2 oil tankers within 150 miles of the city. Starting in May 1942, the OCD ordered "dim outs" for the rest of the war; lights above the 15th floor of any building had to be turned off or shielded with black-out curtains, illuminated advertisements were permanently shut off, and theaters could only light the underside of marquees. Times Square was almost completely dark at night, including the news ticker on the Times tower, although the Camel cigarette billboard still puffed smoke rings in the dark.

As the war continued, more and more homes began hanging "service stars" in their windows: a blue star for each family member in the military, silver for someone who was wounded, and gold for one who had died. By the end of the war, New York had over 18,000 gold stars.

People in uniforms could be seen everywhere: sailors, soldiers and marines, WACs and WAVES, even volunteers with the OCD and the thousands employed by the growing industrial military complex. The Brooklyn Navy Yard expanded employment to 75,000, including many women, making it the largest ship-building facility in the world, and many local airfields became training facilities for pilots, including both Floyd Bennett Field and the Marine Terminal at LaGuardia Airport. Those employed in the war effort were not only in manufacturing or munitions work; laboratories in Brooklyn helped mass-produce cultures of penicillin, which British scientists had proven to be an effective antibiotic. In fact, most of the penicillin used during the D-Day invasion of Normandy came from Brooklyn. At Columbia University, scientists were busy creating an early particle accelerator that was part of the secret "Manhattan project" to develop the atom bomb.

146

The war raged until 1945, with the total annihilation of the Nazi powers in Germany, followed later that summer with the surrender of Japan days after America dropped two atomic bombs, destroying Hiroshima and Nagasaki, killing over 200,000 civilians. The devastation around the world was staggering. Almost 25 million soldiers had been killed, plus between 35 and 50 million civilians. Though America's civilian casualties were relatively small, over 1 million US troops had been killed or wounded.

Three weeks before Germany surrendered in May 1945, President Roosevelt died, and Harry Truman succeeded to the role of Commander-in-Chief. When the news flashed around the world that Japan had surrendered in August 1945, the joy and relief was enormous. The next two years would see ticker tape parades for many of the victorious leaders and soldiers *(for example, see: June 19, 1945 and January 12, 1946)*, The most famous event involving ticker tape was the spontaneous celebration when Japan surrendered, ending the war *(see: August 14, 1945)*, when thousands crowded into a newly relit Times Square. There was no parade, no planning or mayor's committee, and no speeches. The famous photograph of the V-J Day Kiss in Times Square barely captures the euphoria people felt to be alive at the war's end.

Monday, June 8, 1942: Fifteen War Heroes

America's participation in WWII began on Dec 7, 1941. In the six months after that "date that will live in infamy," most of the war news had been bad, and victory seemed far off. Few really doubted the Allies would defeat the Axis, but the prospect of a long and bloody war was paramount in everyone's minds. The country needed heroes, real live ones, who could be honored and brought before the public. And what better place for such a ceremony than New York City with a ticker tape parade, a welcome spotlight to boost American spirits.

Fifteen men were chosen to represent all those who were engaged in the War. Ten were British, who arrived by overseas flights that landed at LaGuardia Airport the previous day. The other five were Americans from the Pacific theater, flown across the United States to New York. All 15 were in place at Battery Park for the scheduled start of the parade at 11:30 in the morning. Those chosen for the occasion representing Great Britain were:

- Squadron Leader John Nettleton, awarded Great Britain's highest military medal, the Victoria Cross, for leading six Lancaster bombers on an attack on Augsburg, Germany, and forced by German fighters and weather to make their approach at times as low as 50 feet.
- Pilot Officer A. F. Taylor, who took part in a raid on Rostock, Germany, was wounded by German anti-aircraft fire yet, on the flight home, took over for the wounded forward turret gunner and succeeded in downing a German fighter.

- Flight-Lieutenant Carroll McColpin, a member of the Third Eagle Squadron of the RAF, and pilot of a Spitfire credited with five German planes destroyed in the air war over Great Britain.
- Flight Sergeant Maxwell Riddell, Bombardier on a Lancaster bomber who was injured when his plane crash-landed in England and volunteered to return to raids on Rostock for the next two nights.
- Lieutenant Thomas Boyd, commander of a Navy torpedo boat who, despite heavy fire, succeeded in ramming his vessel into the docks at St. Nazaire, France, denying use of the docks by German ships.
- Wing Commander M. Loudon, who in combat over Tobruk, Libya, was credited with destroying eight German bombers and at least six German and Italian fighters.
- Lieutenant J. Michael Hall, who in the commando raid on Vaagso, Norway, surrounded the German garrison and destroyed the radio facilities and weather station there.
- Sergeant D. N. Huntley, as a forward gunner in the raid on Augsburg succeeded in destroying two attacking German fighters and damaging three others.
- Sergeant R. George Herbert, who on the commando raid on Vaagso Island seized the German barracks, captured 16 German soldiers, and evacuated them with the British and Norwegian troops.
- Chief Engine Room Artificer Harry Howard, who remained on his ship after it rammed the lock at St Nazaire, withdrew on a second ship, and participated in landing supplies and reinforcements at Tobruk six months later.

The five American chosen were:

- Lieutenant-Commander Harold Smith, commander of the destroyer *Stewart*, who made a night raid on Japanese ships landing troops on Bali, damaged two Japanese destroyers, and scuttled his own ship to prevent it from falling into Japanese hands at Surabaya.
- Ensign Donald Mason, a New York native, who bombed and sank a Japanese submarine and reported the action as "sighted sub, sank same."
- First-Lieutenant Frank Vandeventer, who bombed Japanese troops on Luzon at low level after having dropped to below 100 feet to find an opening in the clouds.
- Lieutenant William Carrithers, B-17 navigator who took part in numerous raids on Japanese troops and shipping despite long distances, clouds, and enemy fighters.
- Second-Lieutenant George Welch, who during the attack on Pearl Harbor succeeded in taking off and attacked, with one other American fighter, a flight of 12 Japanese planes, and downed two before his plane was hit and he was forced to parachute to safety.

Spectators stood eight to ten thick along the Canyon of Heroes as the parade began. The skies were gray and low clouds rushed by. Rain was forecast and showers fell on and off throughout the day. The weather in no way dampened the enthusiasm of those honored or those watching and cheering. More than 100 motorcycle policemen accompanied the 15 cars carrying the heroes. A troop of mounted police pranced along the route, bearing guidons (military banners indicating an individual's unit designation) that snapped in the wind. The Police Department band struck up the first notes and the caravan moved north. Each vehicle was an open convertible and the heroes, in dress uniform, took the usual parade positions so spectators along the route could see and hail them.

As soon as the parade passed the Whitehall Building the shower of confetti began. None of those being honored had ever witnessed a ticker tape parade before and their original shyness quickly changed to smiling enthusiasm. To some observers, it seemed that not since the parade for Lindbergh *(see: June 13, 1927)* did so much confetti and ticker tape fall. Even though the government had recently put paper on the list of items to be saved for recycling, no one in New York seemed to have heard of it, and in places the paper was inches deep. Cars in the parade were decorated with it. As the caravan passed the Equitable Building it passed under a sudden opening in the cloud, and a gray Army bomber flew overhead. Spectators and heroes alike pointed at the plane, and the cheering was deafening.

Almost 10,000 people were jammed into City Hall Plaza to see Mayor LaGuardia welcomed the 15 men to City Hall. As the national anthems of the United Kingdom and the United States were played, military members saluted and civilians stood at respectful attention. As the mayor introduced each of the heroes and briefly recounted their deeds the crowd roared louder and louder. The Mayor was joined by Wendell Wilkie, 1940 Republican presidential candidate, and Bernard Baruch, statesman and advisor to President Roosevelt. The three men shook hands with each hero as their deeds were announced. Squadron Leader Nettleton, spokesman for the group, related how amazed the group was by their welcome. "Such patriotic enthusiasm," he said, his London accent sprinkled with the sounds of South Africa where he had lived before the war, "will go a long way to insuring victory."

Following the introductions, the caravan continued north up Broadway. The crowds thinned in places but nowhere from City Hall to Times Square were the streets empty. Frequently the caravan was forced to slow or come to a halt as people rushed from the sidewalks to get closer to the British and American heroes. By the time the parade reached 45th Street and Broadway and the statue of Father Duffy, hero of an earlier war, it was almost 5:30. Another reviewing stand had been erected here and Mayor LaGuardia reintroduced the men. There were loud calls for each of the men to speak but Mayor LaGuardia intervened by saying, "These boys haven't eaten since 5 o'clock this morning. Let them eat." With this the crowd almost magically parted and the men were led into the Hotel Astor for dinner.

That evening, a third welcome celebration took place in Madison Square

Garden at Eighth Avenue and 50th Street. Once more the men and their heroic deeds were introduced. Lieutenant-Commander Smith was chosen to be
a spokesman for the evening. His words were similar to Nettleton's earlier
remarks, then he added that war is an expensive proposition and made an
impassioned plea for everyone present and the millions listening to the event
on the radio to buy war bonds to help finance the war.

The men began returning to their units or assignments over the next few
days. Four of the British heroes were killed during the war. Artificer Howard
was lost when the destroyer *Fidelity* was torpedoed by a U-boat in December
1942. Squadron Leader Nettleton was killed in a raid on Turin in July 1943,
and a month later Sergeant Huntley's plane disappeared. Sergeant Herbert
was killed in action in Normandy two days after D-Day. Two of the men
were captured: Pilot Officer Taylor in October 1943, and Wing-Commander
Loudon in 1944. Three survived the war. Flight-Sergeant Riddell was
wounded in action in September 1944. Lieutenant Boyd commanded the destroyer *Broadway* from November 1944 until May 1945 when he was discharged. Flight-Lieutenant McColpin transferred to the US Air Force and
remained in the military until he retired in 1968 as a Major General. No record can be found of Lieutenant Hall, so it is unknown whether he became
one of the 400,000 British soldiers who died during the war or if he survived
and returned to civilian life.

All the Americans honored in the parade survived the war. Lieutenant-
Commander Smith was captured one month after the parade, spent three
years laboring in Japanese prison camps, including working on the bridge
over the river Kwai, and died in May 1998. Ensign Mason survived the war
and attended the 2009 Pearl Harbor Day Memorial. First-Lieutenant
Vandeventer remained in the Air Force and retired in 1959 as a Brigadier
General. He died in December 1974. Lieutenant Carrithers also remained in
the military and retired as a Lieutenant-Colonel. He died in 2011. After resigning in 1944, Second-Lieutenant Welch became a civilian test pilot, and
was killed testing a Super Sabre Jet in 1954.

Madison Square Garden

The sports and concert arena sitting above Penn Station is the city's fourth
arena with that name and is about half a mile from Madison Square on Fifth Avenue
between 23rd and 26th Streets. Home to the New York Rangers and Knicks, it was
built in the mid-1960s, and is one of the largest and busiest concert venues in the
world. The history of this multi-purpose entertainment arena is an example of the
city's continual and migratory evolution. →

The first Madison Square Garden was built in 1879 on the northeast corner of Madison Avenue and 26th Street and was used by P.T. Barnum for his circus shows. Unroofed, it was ideal for circuses but little else, especially during bad weather. After it was demolished in 1890, a new building was constructed on the site, designed by Stanford White. With a 32-story tower, the Beaux-Art building dominated the Square, and its main hall was the largest in the world, capable of seating up to 10,000. It had a rooftop garden and the largest restaurant in the city but was not financially successful. It was torn down in 1925 by the New York Life Insurance Company, which held the property mortgage, to make room for their new headquarters building, which still occupies that location.

The third Garden was built in 1925 on Eighth Avenue between 49th and 50th Street, just north of the theater district around Times Square. With seating for up to 18,000, it was primarily used for boxing and hockey, and was the home rink for the New York Rangers. The venue was also used for large events needing indoor seating, including political rallies and campaign speeches, as well as the 1962 party when Marilyn Monroe sang "Happy Birthday" to President Kennedy. When it was demolished in 1968, a proposal to build the world's tallest building prompted a fight with the neighborhood's residents, who won when new height restrictions were established. The site was used as a parking lot until 1989, when the Worldwide Plaza building complex was erected.

Tuesday, June 19, 1945:
General of the Army Dwight Eisenhower

"I've seen them all, from Lindbergh to Byrd," an unidentified spectator near Trinity Church observed, "and this tops them all." That statement summarized the feelings of many veteran parade observers, from Grover Whalen, who met the five-star general at LaGuardia Field and accompanied him to City Hall, to the cop assigned to crowd control on the corner of Broadway and Fulton Street. All seemed to agree this was the largest and noisiest parade ever, with crowd size estimates varying from 2 to 4 million, relieved that the long war in Europe had just ended and victory against Japan seemed certain. When the 54-year-old general was introduced to the thousands jammed into City Hall Plaza, a new sound-measuring device designed by General Electric called the "Noise Meter" registered the roar of the crowd as the equivalent of 3,000 thunderclaps.

On the morning of June 19, General Dwight Eisenhower (often called by his nickname "Ike") landed at LaGuardia Field at 10:09, two minutes behind schedule. His plane, a C-54 military transport nicknamed *Sunflower* after the flower of the General's home state of Kansas, taxied to the observation area where more than 35,000 spectators saluted, waved, and cheered. A battery of 75-millimeter howitzers fired a 17-gun salute when he was met by Lieutenant General George Grunert, commanding Eastern Defense Command, who introduced him to Mayor LaGuardia and Reception Committee Chairman Grover Whalen. Ike reviewed a detachment of the 715th Military Police Battalion and then entered the first car of a 21-vehicle motorcade of military and civilian officials, reporters, and photographers.

151

A Navy blimp provided aerial security in the gray, threatening sky, as the motorcade and its large motorcycle police escort sped along the Grand Central Parkway, across the Triborough Bridge, and down the East River Drive. Newspapers had reminded spectators the previous day that paper was still being rationed, but many New Yorkers seemed to consider today's celebration an exception. While the amount of paper used to greet the General was less than in prewar parades, it was still abundant. Along the entire route from the airfield, across the East River span, south to the Battery, and up the Canyon of Heroes to City Hall, a flurry of paper descended on the motorcade. General Eisenhower seemed thoroughly pleased by the celebration as he stood in the first limousine, waving, pointing, and smiling broadly.

At City Hall, the general was joined by his wife Mamie and their son John, a West Point graduate like his father. The crowd cheered for the other officers in the motorcade, including Lieutenant General Walter Bedell Smith, signer of the German surrender terms at Rheims, and Admiral Alan Kirk, commander of naval forces at Normandy a year earlier. But those cheers were dwarfed by the raucous roar reserved for Eisenhower. Mayor LaGuardia led the way to the speaker's platform erected on City Hall and presented Eisenhower with the city's Gold Medal and made him an honorary citizen of New York. Asked to say a few words before the procession would continue to a luncheon at Gracie Mansion and then on to the Polo Grounds, the general said: "As my first act as a citizen of New York, I want to issue a word of warning to the mayor. New York simply can't do this to a Kansas farm boy and keep its reputation for sophistication."

Activities at City Hall took longer than expected and the motorcade left the area 26 minutes behind schedule, proceeding north through Foley Square, then up Lafayette Street, west to Washington Square and through the Arch at the foot on Fifth Avenue. Bands from the First Army, Brooklyn Navy Yard, Police, Sanitation, and Fire Departments were stationed along the route, but their music was frequently lost amid the cheers. Continuing up Fifth Avenue to 34th Street, the caravan moved to Seventh Avenue and drove north through Times Square and as far uptown as 86th Street, then turned east toward Gracie Mansion, official residence of the mayor. Lost time had been made up by the rapid trip uptown, and the general entered Gracie Mansion only five minutes behind schedule, making this possibly the fastest trip from City Hall to the Upper East Side in history. The luncheon was a simple affair featuring some of the general's favorite foods: cold turkey and chicken, liverwurst sandwiches on rye bread, tomato salad, coffee, and bottled beer.

After lunch some of the parade participants, including Eisenhower and LaGuardia, motored to the Polo Grounds. As the caravan drove through Harlem, passing numerous homemade signs reading "We Love Ike" a jazz band playing "When the Saints Go Marching In" and more cheering spectators. The New York Giants game against the Boston Braves had already begun when Eisenhower and party arrived at the stadium. The general and mayor sat in box seats behind first base for the second and third innings, then when rain started moved to the private office of the Giants' owner, Horace Stoneham, in the center field clubhouse. The group left at the start of the seventh inning in order not to be late for the scheduled banquet at the Waldorf Astoria. That evening the general was guest of honor at a banquet for more than 1,600 invited guests. Eisenhower's post-dinner speech recalled the horrors and devastation of war and noted that heavy casualties would result from the fighting still waging in the Pacific. He closed by hoping that the allied nations would work for the benefit of those who had suffered under tyranny.

General Eisenhower left New York two days later. He retired from the army in 1951, then served as president of Columbia University until 1952. He was elected the 34th President of the United States, serving two terms from 1953 to 1961. He rode briefly in Vice President Richard Nixon's ticker tape parade *(see: November. 2, 1960)* but refused to speak or campaign for him. After leaving the White House, Eisenhower bought a farm in Gettysburg, Pennsylvania, because of his lifelong interest in the Civil War. He resided until his death at Walter Reed Medical Center, Bethesda, Maryland, on March 28, 1969. He is buried along with his wife of 53 years at the Eisenhower Presidential Library in Abilene, Kansas.

Polo Grounds

In 1883, a new baseball team called the New York Giants started playing games on the northern edge of Central Park in a field which had been used by polo players. The viewing stands of these "polo grounds" were small and straddled where the city had planned 111th Street, so a new location was soon needed. A site was found on a bluff overlooking the Harlem River at 155th Street, and a stadium was erected there in 1890, with a horseshoe-shaped grandstand and bleachers in the outfield. A year later, a fire destroyed most of the wooden structure, so a concrete and steel stadium was built in the same location, with an extension reaching out on the right-field side, so the stadium looked like an inverted fishhook.

It was here that the New York Giants played their most successful seasons against their American League rivals, the New York Yankees, who built their stadium across the Harlem River from them. Outside of the baseball season, the stadium was used for other sporting events, but without adequate lighting, the venue was a poor choice for evening events such as concerts. Lighting was eventually installed, and the first night game there was played in 1940. →

By then the stadium was in need of repair, but the Giants did not own the property. The owners were hesitant to spend money since the neighborhood around it was changing rapidly during the 1950s. With ticket sales declining despite several successful seasons, the Giants were lured away by a financially attractive offer to move to San Francisco in 1957. Even when the newly formed New York Mets began playing there in 1963, the owners refused to spend money on badly needed maintenance, much less improvements, and the city soon condemned the property. Painted to look like a baseball, the wrecking ball that demolished the Polo Grounds in 1964 was the same one that had been used on Ebbets Field just four years earlier. Today, the site is a public housing project called the Polo Grounds Towers.

Tuesday, August 14, 1945: Victory over Japan Day

Millions of people had celebrated when Germany unconditionally surrendered on May 8, 1945, ending the almost 6-year war in Europe. But World War II was not over, as fighting continued to rage in the Pacific. Japanese soldiers were putting up strong resistance to American and British attacks on Okinawa Island and in Borneo, while kamikaze pilots crashed into hundreds of Allied ships in a desperate attempt to ward off the next logical step in the Allied strategy, an assault on mainland Japan. Hoping to avoid the enormous casualties such an attack would incur, President Harry Truman approved the use of a top-secret weapon. On August 6, 1945, the first atomic bomb was dropped on Hiroshima, and three days later, a second was dropped on Nagasaki. Both cities lay in ruins, over 200,000 people, mostly civilians, were killed, and many of the 500,000 survivors suffered from the effects of radiation. On August 10, the Japanese government communicated its intentions to surrender, and five days later, Emperor Hirohito made the official announcement just after noon Japan time.

Some celebrations had begun as early as August 10, but many waited in anticipation over the next several days. At 7:03 in the evening of August 14, New York time, the news zipper on One Times Square proclaimed the headline:

"OFFICIAL! TRUMAN ANNOUNCES JAPANESE SURRENDER!"

Jubilant crowds filled public places in celebration around the world. Times Square was already crowded with an estimated 500,000 people, and within twenty minutes, police estimated the crowd had swelled to 750,000. Mayor LaGuardia officially closed all non-essential city offices, and by 10 o'clock that night, over 2 million people were in the square, and more were still arriving on subway trains. "Restraint was thrown to the winds" the *New York Times* reported. Hats were tossed in the air, flags were waving everywhere, people were hugging and dancing and kissing. "From those leaning perilously out of the windows of office buildings and hotels came a shower of paper, confetti, and streamers of ticker tape."

Nearby churches were filled. Thousands, many in uniform, packed into St. Patrick's Cathedral and hundreds more knelt in prayer on its steps, unable to get inside. Church bells tolled across the city, joining a cacophony of honking horns and sirens, whistles from ships in the harbor, and music blaring from radios. Mayor LaGuardia waved to thousands in City Hall Plaza and announced two days of celebrations and declared Sunday August 19 as World Peace Day, then asked that people celebrate but remain orderly. In Chinatown, four dragons usually reserved for Chinese New Year's parades led processions along Mott and Canal Streets, and "Greenwich Village was a madhouse."

As the celebrations continued, "kissing became a popular and public pastime," the *Times* reported. "One girl kissed an Army man, and then, to show her impartiality between the services, promptly found a sailor to kiss." The reporter noted that "the initiative was by no means confined to the girls" and that some women were indignant by the forwardness of the "boys in uniform…who don't ask a girl's permission, they just grab." The crowds in Times Square did not diminish until after midnight, and by 3 in the morning there were still 500,000 people dancing and celebrating. The next day saw an encore of the delirious revelry, though police estimated the second night's crowd was less than half the size of the first night.

Similar celebrations were happening around the world. Crowds filled London's Trafalgar Square, Moscow's Red Square, and around the Arc de Triomphe in Paris. An enormous conga line snaked through Lafayette Park and the Mall in Washington DC. In large cities and small towns, people were happy to be alive after 6 years of war and destruction. One of the authors of this book, then just shy of his 6th birthday, waved a flag in excitement as a band played music in a park in Middle Village, Queens. His ankle was bitten by a dog confused by the noise and commotion. Photographs in newspapers and magazines show the revelry. The most famous is no doubt one published by *Life* magazine taken by Alfred Eisenstaedt, showing a sailor kissing a woman in white, neither of their faces fully recognizable. Several people have claimed over the years to be the sailor. The woman, originally assumed to a nurse, was a female dental assistant named Greta Friedman. She later confirmed that "the guy just came over and kissed me."

Japan's official surrender ceremony took place on September 2, 1945, in Tokyo Bay aboard the USS *Missouri*, a battleship which had been built in the Brooklyn Navy Yards. World War II was the deadliest conflict in human history, resulting in 70 to 85 million fatalities, the majority of them civilians. To date, the United States is the only nation to use nuclear weapons. In 1966, the Genbaku Dome near Ground Zero was dedicated as the centerpiece of the Hiroshima Peace Memorial Park, which was made a World Heritage Site in 1996. The first visit by a sitting US President was made in 2016 by President Barack Obama.

Times Square

In 1803, John Jacob Astor purchased large areas of land north of the city's limits in what is now midtown Manhattan, correctly predicting a real estate boom as the city expanded. He leased the land to others, and by the 1870s the area west of Broadway between 42nd and 48th Streets was the center of the horse carriage industry and was named Longacre Square. Rising real estate costs in lower Manhattan were pushing New York's entertainment industry steadily uptown, and by the 1890s, Longacre Square was home to "middle- and upper-class theaters, restaurants and cafes." In 1911, the Winter Garden Theater was built on the former site of the city's Horse Exchange.

In 1904, the *New York Times* moved into a new skyscraper built on 42nd Street, after persuading Mayor George McClellan, Jr. (son of the Civil War general) to build a subway station there. The city's first electrified advertisement began illuminating the square soon afterwards, and on December 31, 1907, the first New Year's Eve ball was dropped from a flagpole of One Times Square. In 1913, the *Times* moved to a building on 43rd Street, and in 1928 installed a news ticker, with 15,000 light bulbs that spelled out news headlines, controlled by a conveyor belt behind them.

During the Depression, residents moved to cheaper neighborhoods uptown. Some restaurants and theaters closed and were replaced with saloons, burlesque halls and brothels. During World War II, the annual ball-drops were replaced by a moment of silence, and the largest crowd ever to gather there celebrated the war's end in 1945. Over the next 40 years, the neighborhood deteriorated, with legitimate theaters mixed among peep shows and go-go bars, and Times Square became a symbol of the city's crime wave during the 1970s. In 1992, Mayor Dinkins formed the Times Square Alliance to improve the area. Mayor Giuliani used zoning restrictions to force out "undesirable" residents and businesses, and in 2009, Mayor Bloomberg transformed the square into a pedestrian-only plaza.

Once synonymous with crime and pornography, Times Square has long been the heart of the city's "Theater District" and thousands visit every year on New Year's Eve, despite increasing anti-terrorist security measures. Approximately 2 million people watched the ball drop in December 1999, and despite several car bombing attempts and controversies over street performers in superhero costumes, TIMES Square is the most visited place in the world, with over 131 million visitors annually.

Monday, August 27, 1945:
General Charles de Gaulle, Provisional President of France

Spectators numbering more than 200,000 turned out to welcome General Charles de Gaulle, the leader of Free France during the recently ended war and current President of the Provisional Government of France. Escorted by an Army band and members of the Army, Navy, and Marine Corps, the French general rode up the Canyon of Heroes to cheers and swirling strands of ticker tape. In New York on the first stop of his goodwill tour to the United States, the general stood at attention during the entire parade. Sitting beside him was Grover Whelan, the Chairman of the Mayor's Reception Committee, who appeared unable to coax the general to assume a more relaxed posture and enjoy the parade more. The *New York Times* reported, "The general is no matinee idol. He takes his bows with the stiffness of a man conscious of representing a cause greater than himself."

The route up Broadway was decorated with countless French and American flags, flying from almost every building. Miniature tricolors were also evident, and small groups of spectators called out to the general in French. But through it all, the general seemed unaffected by the displays.

The French and American national anthems were played when the motorcade reached City Hall. The slender, more than six-foot tall French general towered over the diminutive mayor. Mayor Fiorello LaGuardia welcomed the general to New York and, his words translated into French by a State Department official, extended Freedom of the City to the general. The general showed a trace of a smile for the first time when he was awarded the city's Gold Medal of Honor, and he then presented the mayor with the medal of the French Legion of Honor.

The reception at City Hall was brief and a few minutes later, the motorcade continued to the Waldorf Astoria, where a reception was held in the general's honor, attended by 2,100 people. The national anthems of France and the United States were again played, then Roman Catholic Auxiliary Bishop Francis McIntyre led an invocation. John Davis, former ambassador to Great Britain, welcomed the general and spoke of his leadership during the war, predicting a bright future for France.

Responding in French, the general began his talk by celebrating the long history of friendship between the two countries, dating from the time of the Marques de Lafayette in the American Revolution. He explained this friendship by saying, "We, at the worst times, when we were together, were not afraid of the war. Well, I am now going to tell you a secret which you can tell others – because we are together, we are not afraid of the peace." He described France's painful experiences during the War as "obstacles" saying, "We go, do you see, from obstacle to obstacle, and it seems also from error to error." He spoke of his travels through "poor, dear France, wounded, mutilated, but liberated" but predicted his country would rise to its former status and need continued friendship with the United States. "It is unimaginable," he concluded, "that the French people and the American people would be separated by peace."

The mayor and general posed for photographs but General de Gaulle refused to answer questions from reporters, explaining that his recent travels had tired him. He withdrew to his suite at the Waldorf and continued to Chicago the next morning. The third city in his brief American visit was Washington, where he met with President Truman.

General de Gaulle returned to France a week later. Ahead of him were years of political and financial turmoil and slow recovery. He would return to New York and receive a second parade as president of the French Republic *(see: April 26, 1960)*.

Thursday, September 13, 1945: General Jonathan Wainwright

In the spring of 1942 General Douglas MacArthur was ordered to leave the beleaguered Philippines and evacuate to Australia. Before departing he turned over command of the troops remaining on the islands to General Jonathan Wainwright, to whom fell the ignominious duty of surrendering 70,000 US and Filipino soldiers to the Japanese on April 9, 1942. Although organized resistance continued over the next two months, this was the largest single surrender of American troops in history. What lay ahead was years of captivity, torture, starvation and death for thousands of those who had laid down their arms, beginning with the Bataan Death March. Over 65,000 US and Filipino troops were forced to march over 60 miles, from Mariveles to San Fernando, Philippines. Prisoners were issued no food for three days and could only drink from polluted streams or water buffalo swamps. They were beaten or bayoneted if they fell, left to die by the side of the road, or were run over by Japanese military vehicles. The exact number of those who died is unknown but an estimated 5,000 to 10,000 Filipinos perished and almost 700 Americans.

Lieutenant General Wainwright was the highest ranking American captured during World War II. He was held as a POW in northern Luzon, on Formosa, and in Xi'an, Manchukuo (now Manchuria) until freed by the Russian Army in August 1945. A POW for over three years, he agonized over the surrender, believing that he had let down his troops, the Philippines, and the United States. When reunited with US troops shortly after his release, he asked what the US public thought of him, and was surprised to hear he was considered a hero.

And it was a hero's welcome that he received when he arrived at New York Municipal Field airport from Washington, DC. A battery of two 75mm howitzers fired a 17-gun salute when the Lieutenant General stepped off the C-54 transport. He and his wife were greeted by a smiling Mayor LaGuardia, who introduced him to other waiting dignitaries and officials. Two hundred men of the 716th Military Police Battalion stood at attention while he inspected them. He then entered a seven-seat gray open limo as hundreds cheered from the airport's observation deck. The general and mayor rode in the first car, following an escort of 32 motorcycles. Four cars followed, carrying his wife Adele, and son Jonathan, and three men who had been held with him during most of his imprisonment: Lieutenant Colonel John Pugh, Major Thomas Dooley, and Master-Sergeant Hubert Carroll. To the rear rode four police cars, their sirens wailing.

The motorcade route from the airport to Bowling Green to City Hall and finally to the Waldorf Astoria, a 22-mile drive, was lined by cheering spectators. Some waved, some saluted, some smiled and threw kisses, and some wept openly at the thin man, stooped and walking with the aid of a cane, who had endured and survived so long in terrible conditions.

Huge crowds of school children, most of them waving small American flags, stood along the edge of the Grand Central Parkway as the caravan drove by before crossing the Triborough Bridge and then down the East River Drive, which had recently been renamed the FDR Drive. A small armada of boats in the river added their noisy salutes with horns and whistles.

The motorcade turned through Whitehall Street and reached Bowling Green just after noon. From there to City Hall, the streets were filled with a dense throng of people. One police estimate put the number of spectators from airport to City Hall at 2 million; a second put the number at twice that. Both agreed that the turnout for General Eisenhower's welcoming parade *(see: June 19, 1945)* was larger but Wainwright's was far more emotional. Mayor LaGuardia called it "the most spontaneous and enthusiastic reception I have ever seen." A blizzard of ticker tape, torn newspapers, ledger pages, tabulating machine cards, rolls of tissue, and confetti drifted down on the parade. Sanitation Department officials put the amount at 490 tons. Paper lay several inches thick in places, more than had fallen on General Eisenhower, possibly because wartime rationing and paper shortages had recently ended.

Portable grandstands had been erected in City Hall Park to hold 20,000 spectators, and all the seats were filled long before the caravan arrived. When it did and the general was introduced by Grover Whalen, the cheer was so huge that some observers claimed it could be heard as far away as Central Park. Mayor LaGuardia proclaimed the general an Honorary Citizen of the City and presented him with the city's Gold Medal. A scroll citing his courage and heroism in the face of terrible adversity was also given to the general, who was obviously moved by the outpouring of affection. Asked to comment on his welcome, he said simply. "It's stupendous. I love it."

The day's festivities did not end at City Hall, and the caravan moved on to the Waldorf Astoria, where a luncheon was held in the general's honor. He addressed the more than 300 guests about the country's need to remain strong and ready for attack from any source. He expressed his gratitude for the city's welcome and for being invited to attend Japan's formal surrender aboard the battleship *Missouri* on September 2. Doing his best to control his feelings towards his former captors, he stated only that Japan should not be "given an easy peace."

Six days later, General Wainwright was awarded the Medal of Honor in recognition of his frequent appearances on the firing line on Bataan and on Corregidor, his personal courage, and his inspiration to his troops and the nation. His former commanding officer, General MacArthur, originally opposed the citation without revealing his reasons, but later voiced approval. General Wainwright never expressed hostility over this and, when it was rumored in 1948 that MacArthur would receive the Republican Party's nomination for President, Wainwright volunteered to make the nominating speech.

Late in 1945 General Wainwright was placed in command of the Second Service Corps on Fort Jay, Governors Island. Later he commanded the Fifth Army at Fort Sam Houston, Texas, before he retired in August 1947. He served on the board of various corporations after his retirement, but it was obvious that his long captivity had taken a toll on his health. He died of a stroke in San Antonio, Texas, in September 1953 at the age of 70 and is buried in Arlington National Cemetery.

New York Municipal Field and LaGuardia Airport

Although New York's first municipal airport opened in 1928, most passenger flights still flew into Newark Airport, as Mayor LaGuardia discovered once when flying back from a meeting in Washington DC. Outraged that his flight to New York was actually landing in New Jersey, he ordered the plane to land at Floyd Bennett Field and immediately held a press conference, announcing that the city would build a new and better airport closer to the city.

Partnering with American Airlines, the mayor looked for a site in Queens, taking advantage of the recently opened Queens Midtown Tunnel. Using WPA funding, the small Glenn Curtis Airfield was purchased. Construction began in 1937, using landfill from the nearby Rikers Island, which at that time was a garbage dump. In October 1939, the mayor cut the ribbon on the New York Municipal Airport, though the press often referred to it as "LaGuardia's Field." The name was officially changed in 1953 to honor the late Mayor.

The $40 million construction costs were partially covered by charging a dime per person for spectators to watch planes lift off and land. Flights from the large domestic airlines were soon using the airport's runways, one of which was 6,000 feet in length, and the airport quickly became a financial success. →

That success soon created problems. As air traffic grew during the 1950s, the airport became steadily busy, and as plane sizes grew to handle the increased traffic, the airport's runways were soon too short. Both Newark and the new Idlewild Airport in southern Queens had longer runways and more room for expansion, and though traffic was still increasing at LaGuardia, it was no longer the city's busiest airport. Often criticized for its outdated design, long delays and congested traffic to and from Manhattan, the airport still serves over 23 million passengers per year.

Tuesday, October 9, 1945: Fleet Admiral Chester Nimitz

Chester Nimitz, grandson of a captain in the German Merchant Marine and whose father died of rheumatism shortly before Chester's birth, originally applied for admission to the United States Military Academy but there were no available vacancies. He then applied and was admitted to the United States Naval Academy in 1905, graduating seventh in his class of 114. Forty years later he had risen to the rank of Fleet Admiral and during the Second World War held the dual positions of Commander of the United States Pacific Fleet and Commander for the Pacific Ocean Area for US and allied air, sea, and naval forces.

On the morning of the huge parade, witnessed by over four million people in Queens and Manhattan, the admiral and his party flew from Washington, DC on two Navy P5D aircraft. The planes arrived at New York Municipal Airport shortly before 11 o'clock. Early morning rain had ceased and throughout the long day the sun would peek through heavy gray clouds. Waiting at the Administration Building was Mayor LaGuardia, Grover Whalen, two Admirals, two Rear Admirals, two Army Major Generals, a Brigadier General, a Marine Corps Brigadier General, and other politicians and military men of high rank. The mayor rushed over to shake Nimitz's hand, saying in his high-pitched voice, "Welcome to New York. We're glad to have you here." While officers snapped to attention and saluted, Nimitz and his staff entered open top cars. Three naval one-pounder guns fired a 17-gun salute. Accompanying the Admiral were 13 men from the Navy and Marine Corps who had been awarded the Congressional Medal of Honor while serving under his command, who were seated in six open jeeps.

The caravan moved with military precision, escorted by 36 motorcycle policemen. The route from the airport down Grand Central Parkway was lined with people, many of them school children, waving countless tiny American flags. The Admiral was often seen smiling, presenting a salute to various groups along the way. After crossing the Triborough Bridge at precisely 11:37, three minutes ahead of the scheduled time, the caravan sped down the FDR Drive, where more spectators stood and cheered. Numerous small boats in the East River also contained spectators, and fire boats shot off geysers of water as the procession passed 94th Street and 23rd Street. Entering South Street through Whitehall Street, the caravan passed buildings housing army and navy offices, and a large group of WAVES, the navy's female personnel, cheered as the admiral drove by.

The roar from the crowd reached its peak as the group of vehicles entered Broadway. People on the sidewalks, on building ledges, and in windows cheered, blew whistles and horns, beat drums, and rang bells. Moving slowly, the cars and jeeps in the parade were quickly covered with streamers of ticker tape. Admiral Nimitz and many of the officers in the parade saluted to the crowd of spectators, while the Medal of Honor recipients, mostly enlisted men, waved in less military fashion.

City Hall was decorated as never before. Naval signal flags reading "Welcome" fluttered from the building's face. A ship's bow, painted blue, had been built out over the steps, above which hung a map showing a streak of jagged lightning projecting from Pearl Harbor to Tokyo, with the vast ocean labeled "Nimitz Sea." The ceremony at City Hall was brief. Nimitz was presented with a Key to the City and the title of honorary citizen, the city's Gold Medal, and a scroll commemorating his achievements to bring victory against Japan. Not forgotten were the Medal of Honor recipients, whose names and citations were read to the assembled throng of people in City Hall Plaza as each was presented with a medal.

Once ceremonies were concluded, the parade resumed. The Admiral now seated himself on the top of the rear seat of his vehicle, providing a better view of the six Navy and Coast Guard bands which led the parade. Proceeding up Fifth Avenue, the parade passed the New York Public Library at 1:33 and Rockefeller Center a few minutes later. "There the snowstorm of torn paper was even thicker than it had been farther downtown," reported the *New York Times*, "and whirling eddies of air lifted streamers almost as high as the top of the RCA building." Roman Catholic Archbishop Francis Spellman, Vicar General of the Armed Forces, stood on the steps of St. Patrick's Cathedral along with other church officials and a delegation of Army and Navy chaplains of various faiths and denominations.

The parade halted at Park Avenue and 50th Street, where a reviewing stand had been erected. Admiral Nimitz reviewed the military formations that had been part of the procession. He shook the hands of more than 900 members of the military who took part in the review including all 500 WAVES, Nurses and WACS, the Army's female command. Following the review, the Admiral, joined by his wife Catherine and the Medal of Honor winners, lunched with Mayor LaGuardia in the Grand Ballroom of the Waldorf. As a surprise to the Admiral, he was reunited with the surviving members of his 1905 graduating class from Annapolis. The Admiral spoke briefly at the luncheon, calling upon the Government to veto the idea of combining the Department of the Army and Department of the Navy into a single Department of Defense. He also called for an end to the draft but spoke of the need for the country to maintain a strong and powerful navy to help keep the United States out of the flying range of any nation that may eventually possess the atomic bomb.

The Admiral's long and exhausting day had not yet ended. He was the guest that evening at a second reception at the Waldorf before he was able to retire to his suite at the hotel. He returned to Washington the following day. Commenting later at the size and scope of the city's reception, Mayor LaGuardia said, "Admiral Nimitz was simply taken by surprise. Strange, these real fighters are such mild-mannered persons."

From 1945 to 1947, Nimitz served as Chief of Naval Operations. His rank of Fleet Admiral was a lifetime position and he never retired from the Navy, but he discontinued active duties in 1947. He spent the last 20 years of his life in California and died in 1967 after a stroke complicated by pneumonia on Yerba Buena Island, San Francisco Bay. He is buried in the Golden Gate National Cemetery.

Saturday, October 27, 1945: President Harry Truman

It was a historic day: never before had a sitting President of the United States been welcomed at City Hall.

Less than a year earlier, then-Vice President Truman had paid a visit to Mayor Fiorello LaGuardia, arriving in a New York City taxicab accompanied by only one aide. The guard at the entrance to City Hall had not recognized the visitor in the gray suit and fedora and asked to see the former Senator from Missouri's identification papers. In the year since that visit, Truman succeeded to the Oval Office on the death of President Franklin Roosevelt on April 12, 1945, becoming the nation's 33rd president.

This blustery October afternoon was considerably different than Truman's previous visit. The President arrived at Pennsylvania Station in a special train, escorted by a cordon of Secret Service agents, and was driven to Bowling Green in a Federal government limousine. At the foot of lower Broadway, the president exchanged vehicles for a city convertible, and as part of a 12-car motorcade began the slow journey up the Canyon of Heroes. Six Secret Service agents stood on the car's running boards. The motorcade was followed by a band from the Brooklyn Navy Yard, along with small detachments from the Army and Navy, and a larger detachment of the Marine Corps.

Mr. Truman's plans to visit the city and take part in the Naval Review scheduled for October 28 had not been revealed until the previous day. Only 20,000 spectators lined the route, perhaps because of the chilly weather, or the fact that the downtown area was never as crowded on a weekend as on a weekday. The parade was showered with relatively small amounts of ticker tape, and the loud and often raucous cheers which often welcomed other visiting dignitaries were absent as well. Again wearing a gray suit and fedora, which he grasped to prevent it from being blown off his head, President Truman rarely waved to the crowd.

Secret Service agents had cleared City Hall Plaza of spectators, and only a

Navy and Coast Guard band and a Marine Corps Honor Guard were in place by City Hall's entrance. To the tune of "Hail to the Chief," the President stepped from the car and was greeted by Mayor LaGuardia. The Marines, all of whom were decorated Pacific area combat veterans, snapped smartly to attention as the President and the Mayor strode up the steps, then proceeded to the mayor's second floor office.

"It's nice to have you here, Mr. President," the mayor said, smiling. "It's nice to be here," responded the President. The two men stood by an open window while photographers and newsreel cameramen struggled for the best vantage points in the plaza below. Above the window was a bronze plaque commemorating George Washington reading the Declaration of Independence to his troops near that place on July 9, 1776. Outside, a choir from the Midshipmen's School at Columbia University sang a hymn with words written by Thomas Jefferson in 1774: "The God who gave us life gave us liberty."

An aide advised President Truman that he was due to deliver a speech at the Sheep Meadow in Central Park at 2 o'clock that afternoon. "Well, we must be going," the President commented. Mr. LaGuardia hurriedly introduced his son Eric and his office secretary, Betty Cohen. Scores of City Hall office workers lined the cantilevered stairway as the president nodded and smiled on the way to the government limousine waiting for him. The time was 12:51. President Truman had spent exactly eight minutes inside City Hall.

That afternoon Truman addressed a larger than expected crowd on the Sheep Meadow. His topic was "Keeping America Prepared," and his words were greeted with enthusiasm. The following day he presided over the Hudson River naval review of more than 16 warships, ranging from destroyers to an aircraft carrier, then returned to Washington later that evening.

President Truman was re-elected in a surprising victory over New York Governor Thomas Dewey in 1948. His second term was filled with foreign crises: the Iron Curtain, the Berlin Airlift, the fall of Nationalist China, and the Korean War. In 1953 he returned to private life in Missouri. He refused various government perks, drove his own car, and lived in his mother's house in Independence. He and former president Herbert Hoover became close friends and often visited each other, corresponding during the 1960's. President Truman died of pneumonia on December 26, 1972, at the age of 88. He is buried at the Truman Library in Independence, Missouri, the first Presidential Library created and operated by the National Archives and Records Administration.

Friday, December 14, 1945: Fleet Admiral William Halsey

Admiral William "Bull" Halsey was scheduled to fly to New York's Municipal Airport from Washington, but weather conditions grounded all flights. He arrived instead by train at 2 o'clock in the morning and was taken directly to the Waldorf from Penn Station. After a few hours of sleep, a city vehicle picked him up and drove him to the airport. Flight plans might have been changed, but parade plans had not.

A Navy band and two battalions of sailors greeted the Admiral when he arrived in northern Queens. A 17-gun salute was fired, and the sailors snapped to attention and saluted. Mayor LaGuardia, dressed in a heavy overcoat, gloves, and homburg, strode across the tarmac, shook the Admiral's hand, and apologized for the more than three inches of snow that had fallen overnight. Proudly boasting that the Sanitation Department had cleared all the roads, he and Admiral Halsey entered an open vehicle, wrapped their feet and legs in blankets, and began the long ride to the customary parade starting point in lower Manhattan.

Forty police motorcycles sped ahead of the Admiral and Mayor, splashing through the slush on Astoria Boulevard and Steinway Street. Despite the Mayor's boast about the roads being cleared, wet snow soon began to play havoc on the ignitions of the motorcycles and one by one they stalled as slush shorted or clogged their generators. Authorities in Brooklyn had requested that the Admiral pass through their borough and the caravan turned on 34th Avenue to Queens Boulevard and then across the Meeker Avenue Bridge. Both occupants of the open limo smiled and waved at the crowds lining the route. The faces of the car's two occupants grew red from the cold and their eyes narrowed against the biting wind. Schools along the route had shut down so students could greet the hero of the Pacific War against Japan, and thousands stood shivering and huddled for warmth through Greenpoint and on Union and Bedford Avenues, Fulton Street, and the Flatbush Avenue Extension. The entire student body of the Brooklyn High School for Specialty Trades (now George Westinghouse Vocational School) on Johnson Street clustered at the corner of Tillary Street as the vehicles crossed the Manhattan Bridge.

Just as the procession turned off the bridge onto the FDR Drive a gust of wind blew the hat off the Admiral's head and it landed upside down in a pile of slush. The four motorcycles that remained in the escort halted, and a policeman dismounted to retrieve the Admiral's hat. Halsey brushed most of the brownish mixture of ice and snow off it and set it snugly back down on his head.

Anchored off the Battery, victory ship *Roy K Johnson* blew her sirens when the Admiral's car came into view from South Street as a signal to those waiting at Bowling Green. His car pulled in behind an escort of 32 mounted police whose waiting horses exhaled great puffs of steam. The Sanitation Department band joined the band from the Brooklyn Navy Yard, detachments from the Navy and Coast Guard fell in, and the slow ride up Broadway started. The snowfall of the day before was nothing compared to the blizzard of paper that streamed down as the parade moved. Ticker tape, confetti, torn newspapers, and sheets of paper all floated down. At Trinity Church a flock of pigeons, startled by the commotion, took flight and soared upwards, quickly lost among the cascading paper.

Fifteen hundred sailors, Marines, and Coast Guardsmen saluted as the Admiral and Mayor entered City Hall Plaza. The car halted at the entrance to City Hall and Admiral Halsey returned the servicemen's salute. His wife Frances and daughter Margaret were at the door when the Admiral, his nose cherry red from the cold, entered City Hall. After a few minutes to warm up and refresh themselves, the Mayor led Admiral Halsey into the Council Chambers where 400 guests rose and gave the admiral a standing ovation. Mayor LaGuardia awarded the admiral with the city's Gold Medal and a citation for his role in defeating Japan. He called the Admiral "daring, dashing, determined, and devastating." The mayor, reminding the guests that the admiral's grandfather had been rector of Christ Episcopal Church on Fifth Avenue and 18th Street, referred to him as a "True Son of New York."

"It is a genuine pleasure to accept these symbols of your friendship," the admiral said, accepting them "on behalf of the men who fought in my command." He concluded by adding "It was good to see those thousands of good smiling faces."

The Admiral, Mayor, and other guests then exited City Hall for the continuation of the tribute by driving to the Waldorf for an informal luncheon. At 12:40, the vehicles headed north, and at 26th Street a new squad of motorcycle police joined the five-car motorcade. Shoppers on 34th Street waved at the Admiral, their Christmas shopping temporarily halted by the caravan. Standing again in his open vehicle, he saluted them. The motorcade slowed as it passed the Library at 42nd Street, where huge crowds were packed between the lions that guard the library's main entrance. Cardinal Francis Spellman and Archbishop James McGuigan of Toronto, wearing colorful vestments, waved at the Admiral from the steps of St. Patrick's Roman Catholic Cathedral.

The Admiral finally arrived at the Waldorf for the luncheon, which was closed to the press. He was presented with a lifetime membership in the New York Metropolitan Club, an award that had never been given in the club's 50-plus years.

The admiral spoke to reporters after the luncheon. Like most other military men, he was not enthused over the proposal to combine the Army and Navy Departments into a single Department of Defense, calling it a political decision and not a military one. He called for a strong permanent Army and Navy and "the magic of merger will not achieve it." He spoke briefly of his command's record in the war that claimed more than 3,000 enemy planes destroyed and the sinking of more than 1,600 merchant and naval vessels. When asked about retirement, he said he had no plans, then changed the subject to explain that his nickname "Bull" stemmed from childhood when he could not correctly pronounce his own name, Bill.

Returning to active duty in the Pacific, the Admiral retired in March 1947, but since the rank of Fleet Admiral is a lifetime one, he was never officially relieved of duty. He joined the Board of the International Telephone and Telegraph Company (ITT) on Broad Street, Manhattan. When his flagship, the aircraft carrier *Enterprise,* was decommissioned in 1947, he worked on plans to have her preserved and moored in the Hudson River. Though his efforts failed, and the ship was scrapped in 1958, the idea eventually came to fruition when the carrier *Intrepid* was opened as a museum in 1982.

Admiral Halsey died at his summer home on Fisher's Island, New York, in August 1959, and is buried in Arlington National Cemetery.

Saturday, January 12, 1946:
82nd Airborne Division Victory Parade

In spontaneous bursts of jubilation throughout the city, ticker tape was tossed out of windows in celebration of the surrender of Nazi Germany on June 8, 1945 and again when Japan surrendered *(see: August 14, 1945).* Public squares and plazas filled with people, joyful and relieved that the long and terrible war was over. A massive crowd filled Times Square on V-E Day but was dwarfed when the largest crowd ever to fill the area celebrated on V-J day. World War II was over, the Allies were victorious.

Victory, and the men whose blood, toil, tears and sweat had achieved it, was officially recognized in New York when the men of the 82nd Airborne Division returned from Europe. Sailing out of London on the *Queen Mary,* they arrived in New York on January 3, 1946. Mayor O'Dwyer and Grover Whalen greeted them at Pier 90 at 50th Street to officially welcome them home. General James Gavin inspected the ranks, and the division's 56-piece band played music as the men began disembarking. A large crowd had assembled to watch, enjoying a preview of the big parade scheduled for the following Saturday.

January 12 dawned cold and rainy, but by noon the sun broke through the clouds. Fifth Avenue was closed to traffic and the sidewalks and side streets began filling with spectators all morning. Washington Square was filled with soldiers.

The parade kicked off precisely at 1 o'clock. The Army Ground Forces Band led the way, playing "The All-American Soldier" as they marched through the Arch and stepped onto Fifth Avenue. They were followed by 13,000 airborne troops, mostly from the 82nd Division, though contingents from the 101st Airborne Division were present as well. At their head marched 37-year-old General Gavin, who had jumped with his men over Sicily and Salerno, Normandy and Nijmegen. He dedicated this march "to all the guys who walked through the mud" in Europe. Following them were the mechanized units, with their vast array of war machines: 13 Sherman tanks, 18 howitzers, 21 jeeps, 44 anti-tank guns, and dozens of armored cars and trucks.

167

Fifteen minutes after starting, the lead contingents had passed Madison Square at 23rd Street. In front of the Red Cross Building at 37th Street, viewing stands had been set up for veterans to watch the parade, which by 1:30 was passing the Public Library at 42nd Street. The crowd of spectators was thickest in this area, standing as many as eight deep along the sidewalk, straining against the police barricades. Millions of spectators watched the parade, according to the *New York Times,* which quoted Police Commission Arthur Wallander saying the crowd exceeded 4 million.

Flurries of confetti, torn booklets and pamphlets, shredded newspapers, and streams of ticket tape fell from the sky. The storm of paper began descending as soon as the cheering began, coming from apartment windows and rooftops, from upper-floor office windows and building ledges where spectators stood precariously. Streamers of ticker tape fluttered in the wind, caught in the scaffolding around St. Patrick's Cathedral and Rockefeller Center.

The paper blizzard slowed north of the Plaza Hotel at 59th Street, but the cheering never subsided. At 77th Street, another viewing stand for veterans of the First World War was set up, and one gray-haired man was heard saying "That was us, 26 years ago. Now we're the old guys." Another stand was set up at the Metropolitan Museum of Art at 83rd Street, where one gold-star mother watched silently, telling a reporter that she "never saw my son Joe in his airborne uniform. He was 23 when he was killed."

Mayor O'Dwyer and New York State Governor Thomas Dewey stood on the reviewing stand at 86th Street, along with Acting Secretary of War Kenneth Royall and other dignitaries. General Gavin left his place at the head of the parade to join them, saluting and reviewing the rest of the division as it marched by.

Overhead flew a formation of over 40 troop transport planes, each towing a glider. Flying at an altitude of just 1,500 feet, they had taken off from Mitchel Field, flying over lower Manhattan before heading north along the Hudson River, crossing to the East Side over Central Park, then continuing north to Yonkers before returning to Mitchel Field.

Later that evening, General Gavin was the guest of honor at a dinner at the Waldorf Astoria, attended by 350 men in uniform as well as civilians and city officials. The Mayor presented the general with a gold medal and a citation praising his "courage and tenacity." The general thanked the mayor and people of New York for the "warmth and graciousness" extended to his soldiers. One reporter noted that there were as many privates and non-coms in the room as there were officers, to which one sergeant replied that General Gavin had been in charge of the invitations.

General Gavin was the youngest major general to serve during World War II. After the war, he played a central role in the desegregation of the military. A big proponent of airborne and mechanized troops, he also served as Army

Chief of Research and Development and helped increase the army's use of helicopters for reconnaissance, raids and medical evacuations. He retired in 1958 at the rank of lieutenant general, and was named Ambassador to France in 1961, and became a visible critic of the war in Vietnam. He died in 1990.

Formed during World War I, the 82nd Airborne Division is the nation's first and most strategically mobile fighting force, capable today of responding to a crisis anywhere in the world within 18 hours. It saw combat during Vietnam, but also served alongside National Guard units during the urban riots in 1967-68 in Detroit and Baltimore. It has been involved in most operations since the end of the Cold War, including Bosnia and Kosovo, Afghanistan, Iraq and Syria, and has also been involved in humanitarian missions in Haiti and in the United States after Hurricane Katrina.

Friday, March 15, 1946: Winston Churchill, Former Prime Minister of the United Kingdom

The weather forecast on March 14 predicted extremely heavy rain the next day, and city authorities informed Winston Churchill that they intended to cancel his parade. He protested and insisted that the plans remain unchanged. Churchill's reputation for stubbornness triumphed and despite the drenching downpour, the parade was held as planned.

Wearing a heavy Irish Ulster coat for warmth and a black homburg hat to ward off the rain, Mr. Churchill entered a convertible at Bowling Green with its top raised. Turning to Grover Whalen, the Chairman of the Mayor's Reception Committee, he asked, "Couldn't the top be rolled back? I'd like to see the people." The top had been closed not only to ward off the rain but also for Mr. Churchill's protection. He was unaware of the fact that violence against him had been threatened by pro-Irish groups and the Communist Party. A special British security detail accompanied Churchill, and more than 1,400 New York City Police were on assignment for the day. Once again, however, Mr. Churchill prevailed. The top came down, and the former Prime Minister stood in the rear of the car, smiling his cherubic grin. As usual he clenched a huge cigar in his teeth and puffed on it as the parade began the procession up the Canyon of Heroes.

Led by the First Army band and a large detachment of poncho-clad soldiers, sailors and marines, the parade moved past the Cunard Building at 2 Broadway. Seeing a huge Union Jack hanging from its flagpole, the English statesman thrust up his right hand and, spreading his second and third fingers, gave the "Victory" sign that had become his symbol. Ticker tape and torn paper fell, all sodden from the pouring rain. One police official thought it was the heaviest rainstorm ever for a parade. Even with the inclement weather, however, the crowds were thick, massed four and five deep in places. Mr. Churchill turned right and left, waved and grinned, puffed his cigar, flashed his V-sign and seemed to thoroughly enjoy the entire experience. The brim of his hat sagged down further and further until he eventually tossed it aside. Rain dripped down his bald head and cheeks. The wetter he became, the more the spectators seemed to enjoy him. Cheers of "Good old Winnie," "Hi, Winnie, Old Boy," and "How do you like the weather?" echoed along the route.

As the car carrying Churchill turned into City Hall Park, it passed a small group of Communists carrying placards accusing him of being a war monger and that he wanted young Americans to fight for him again. When one protestor shouted, "God damn you," Mr. Churchill joked to Grover Whalen that it was the first time he ever "heard a Communist call upon the Almighty."

Mayor O'Dwyer briefly introduced Mr. Churchill to the crowd, many of whom were hidden under umbrellas. The pro-Churchill members of the crowd far exceeded the anti-Churchill ones, but as the two politicians began to climb the steps of City Hall, six young men in long coats burst through the police line. Before they reached Mr. Churchill and the mayor, they were wrestled to the ground. Carrying anti-Churchill signs beneath their coats, they identified themselves as members of the Executive Committee of the American Communist Party as they were dragged away by the police. Entering City Hall, Mr. Churchill commented that the protesters rather reminded him of what sometimes takes place at Speaker's Corner in Hyde Park.

When the party entered the Council Chambers, the more than 300 invited guests stood and greeted Mr. Churchill with loud applause and cheers. The English statesman removed his drenched overcoat, dried his face with a towel and waved at the assembly. The mayor presented Churchill the city's Gold Medal and a scroll, which spoke of his leadership that had been a powerful inspiration to the Allies during the war. Churchill thanked the mayor, the guests, and the entire city of New York for his welcome, especially for the weather that reminded him of London.

His trousers dripping wet, Mr. Churchill returned to his car for the ride uptown and a reception at the Waldorf Astoria, again insisting that the top remain down. Mr. Whalen held an umbrella over him but shortly after the car moved forward the wind destroyed it and he dropped it to the floor next to Churchill's hat. The caravan had proceeded just a short distance when a second crowd of anti-Churchill protestors was encountered. This group, all claiming membership in pro-Irish organizations, proved far more vocal than the Communists. Not long afterwards the rain intensified again, and finally the parade's recipient agreed to raise the top.

At the Waldorf, Mr. Churchill changed clothing and fortified himself with a very large drink before he entered the Grand Ballroom, accompanied by his wife. Nearly 1,000 guests filled the room, rising as one when he stepped to the dais and the National Anthems of the United States and United Kingdom were played. The Police Glee Club sang "There Will Always Be an England" and the former Prime Minister was seen wiping tears from his eyes. One and all then enjoyed a luncheon that featured Dover sole, Guinea hen, and pâté washed down with three wines including champagne.

That evening at the Metropolitan Club there was a second reception in his honor. There he was introduced to 600 guests by former Mayor LaGuardia, who joked that he and Mr. Churchill had something in common since they were both currently unemployed.

At both receptions, Mr. Churchill spoke in his usual eloquent tones. He expressed no rancor over his party's loss of the majority and Mr. Atlee now serving as Prime Minister. Most of his remarks were warnings against the growth of Communism in Eastern Europe and the danger to the free world by Russia. After speaking at the second reception, he returned to his suite at the Waldorf and began packing for the return to England the next morning.

Mr. Churchill became Prime Minister again when the Conservative Party regained a majority in Parliament in 1951. He remained in office until his retirement in 1955. Between 1949 and 1956 he suffered a series of strokes and spent his final years in a wheelchair at his country home, Chartwell.

Winston Churchill's mother was an American and he frequently referred to his ties to the United States. In a 1963 visit to the United States, he was made an Honorary Citizen, the first of only eight people ever given that honor. He died in London in January 1965 and was given a state funeral. His body lay in state at St Paul's Cathedral, and he was buried near his birthplace in Blenheim Palace.

If any one person could be described as a living symbol of Great Britain during the 20th century it would be Winston Churchill. He was a newspaper reporter, army officer, and politician, First Lord of the Admiralty, Prime Minister, diplomat, amateur artist, and author. He possessed a vast vocabulary, a sharp wit, and a silvery tongue. His State Funeral was attended by thousands of British and foreign friends and foes alike, including Queen Elizabeth II, a rare honor since the ruling monarch does not ordinarily attend funerals.

Mayor William O'Dwyer (1946-1950)

Born in Ireland in 1890, William O'Dwyer studied for the priesthood in Spain before immigrating to New York in 1910. Deciding on a different career, he became a NYC police officer while studying law at Fordham University. He passed the bar in 1923, and worked in Brooklyn as both a Court Judge and District Attorney, leading prosecutions against organized crime, and gained fame for his successful cases against a syndicate known as "Murder, Inc." →

After losing his first bid for Mayor in 1941, he joined the military and served on the War Refugee Board. Returning to New York, he won his second race for Mayor in 1945, and was immediately faced with crises. The city's tugboat workers went out on strike, subway workers threatened to strike as well, and the city's finances, initially stabilized during the Depression, had grown enormously during the war. He managed those crises, installed Robert Moses in a new position to oversee all citywide construction, negotiated with the United Nations to make New York its permanent home, and oversaw the first increase in the subway fare. His wife Catherine, who had been ill for many years, died in 1946; three years later he married Elizabeth Simpson, who divorced him in 1953.

O'Dwyer's first term in office was successful enough to win re-election, but storm clouds had gathered. An investigation into police corruption had widened to include the Mayor and his close and long-time ally, James Moran, a police officer who had worked with the Mayor for over two decades. Less than nine months into O'Dwyer's second term as Mayor, President Truman unexpectedly appointed him Ambassador to Mexico. The Mayor resigned to take the new job, leaving the city after a farewell parade *(see: August 31, 1950)*. Though he was beyond its reach, the investigation soon turned up evidence that bribes and extortion money had been funneled to him by Moran, and that Truman may have offered the ambassadorship as an escape. Two years later, another investigation charged O'Dwyer with accepting $10,000 in bribes at Gracie Mansion, followed by a third investigation which resulted in Moran being sent to prison.

O'Dwyer returned to New York briefly in 1951 to testify, dodging most questions about his alleged mob connections. He then returned to Mexico, staying there after he was replaced as Ambassador in 1952. In 1960, he returned to New York, where he died in 1964.

CHAPTER 6
Capital of the World (1947-1953)

After six years of war, much of the world lay in ruins. Virtually all of Europe, much of North Africa and Southeast Asia, China, Japan and the islands of the Pacific had seen battle, and almost every nation in the world had been touched in one way or the other by this truly World War. Beyond the enormous loss of life, the war had destroyed the economic infrastructure of most developed nations. For Germany and Japan, defeat was as total as the destruction. Allied bombing raids had reduced most Germany cities to rubble, and during the spring of 1945, Allied armies raced toward Berlin from both east and west. As they crossed Germany, they liberated hundreds of thousands of survivors from concentration camps, where the Nazi Holocaust had slaughtered over 6 million Jews and 3 million others, including Roma, non-Jewish Poles and Russians, homosexuals and people with disabilities. Japan, which had committed its own atrocities against POWs and civilians in China, Southeast Asia and the Pacific Islands, was spared the impact of an invasion only because its military surrendered after witnessing the annihilating power of two nuclear bombs. Most of the victorious nations were exhausted: France had been occupied since 1940, Great Britain had been brought to its knees and suffered widespread damage from German air raids, and the Soviet Union had suffered a staggering 23 million deaths (both military and civilian) during the 4 years when the battle front had raged across Russia and Eastern Europe.

Compared to the rest of the world, the United States had escaped with little physical damage and was poised to become the economic super-power that would fuel recovery both at home and abroad. The Marshall Plan pumped millions of US dollars into the rebuilding of Europe. Tensions were building between the US and the Soviet Union, which had its own rebuilding to do, but was soon exerting control over the nations of Eastern Europe, prompting Winston Churchill *(see: March 15, 1946)* to declare that "an iron curtain" had fallen across Europe. The former allies were rivals now, and the two Superpowers soon saw every issue, every regional dispute, through the ideological lens of their bilateral distrust. During the late 1940s, the US was clearly the more powerful of the two, both militarily and economically, though Russia's military caught up swiftly when it acquired the atomic bomb in 1949.

New York City now occupied a position of global prominence. London had been damaged during the war, and it would take 14 years for Great Britain to recover enough to end rationing, which the US largely ended in 1945. With little damage to infrastructure during the war, the economy in the US, and New York in particular, was re-ignited and soon reached levels never seen before or since. New York was the world's largest manufacturing center, with 40,000 factories and over a million factory workers. It controlled over 20% of the nation's wholesale transactions, and its port handled 150 million tons of freight, about 40% of the world's total. Over 150 of the country's top companies located their headquarters in New York, and the city's stock exchanges dominated the financial industry worldwide. Though Washington DC was the political center of the world, New York was the financial and business center.

New York was also the cultural capital of the post-war world, a claim once held by Paris, from where many artists had fled. A new generation of artists centered in New York, like Jackson Pollock and Willem de Koonig, were driving the first post-war art movement, abstract expressionism, while the music world was captivated by Leonard Bernstein leading the New York Philharmonic. The spotlight of the theater world shifted from London's West End to New York's Broadway, as creative teams like Rodgers and Hammerstein created integrated musicals, and new opera singers began debuting at the Metropolitan Opera, still in its original home on Broadway and 40th Street. Uptown in Harlem, musicians like Thelonious Monk were experimenting with a new style of jazz called bebop, and bobby soxers were enjoying the sounds of big bands and crooners like the Cotton Club's Cab Calloway or Columbia Record's Frank Sinatra.

The city's population had continued growing, but more importantly, it was spreading out. In 1910, half of the city's 4.7 million residents lived in Manhattan and another 35% in Brooklyn. By 1950, the city had reached a total of 7.9 million, but Manhattan's share had dropped to 25%, while Queens and the Bronx had picked up most of the difference. This shift was due to several factors, but an important one was the expansion of the subway system during the 1930s with the introduction of a third rail network, the Independent Subway System. In 1940, the city orchestrated the merger of the new network with the older Interborough Rapid Transit and the Brooklyn-Manhattan Transit, forming one unified Metropolitan Transit Authority, hoping that reducing redundancy and combining profits would prevent an increase in the fare. Despite the fact that annual ridership reached an all-time high in 1946 of over 2 billion, the fare had to be increased in 1948 from a nickel to a dime, the first increase in the subway's history.

Another factor in the population shift to Queens and the Bronx was the growing ownership of automobiles and the network of roads built by Robert Moses. After Mayor LaGuardia retired in 1945, the mayors who succeeded him gave Moses more power. Still City Parks Commissioner, he also became the city's Planning Commissioner, putting him in charge of public housing development, and by 1949 he was the city's sole official representative in Washington negotiating for infrastructure funding. His hunger for power, and preference for middle-class residents driving automobiles rather than the mass-transit reliant working-class, was unleashed. Among the projects he oversaw during this period include the Gowanus and Brooklyn-Queens Expressways, a portion of what would become the Long Island Expressway (then called the Queens-Midtown Expressway), and the Brooklyn-Battery Tunnel. Believing tall apartment towers to be better housing than smaller buildings, he used his power to condemn and raze thousands of tenements, replacing them with much of the public housing on Manhattan's East River front from the Brooklyn Bridge to 14th Street, as well as Stuyvesant Town and Peter Cooper Village.

Most building construction had slowed during the war, but afterwards it took off again, and Manhattan's skyline was showing more evidence of the new International Style of architecture. By using lightweight, mass-produced materials and stressing flat lines and glass, architects rejected ornaments and color in favor of sleek designs and volume over mass. New buildings designed in this style rose over midtown Manhattan, like the Seagrams Tower and Lever House on Park Avenue, in addition to the new headquarters for the United Nations, the new international organization replacing the League of Nations.

After several years considering where to locate its headquarters, the United Nations *(see: October 23, 1946)* moved onto a 17-acre site in midtown Manhattan overlooking the East River. By the time the General Assembly and Secretariat buildings opened in 1952, New York could claim to be the Capital of the World, and a steady stream of foreign dignitaries would visit the city, not just for meetings with Wall Street finance executives or as stopping point on their way to Washington DC, but also for official business at the United Nations.

The prosperity of this era and the city's domination of the international stage helped make the post-war years the busiest era for ticker tape parades. Starting in 1949, New Yorkers could attend an average of nine parades a year, breaking the previous record of 7 held by 1926, and 1953 saw an all-time record 11 parades. With more foreign politicians visiting the city on their way to or from Washington, the parades were becoming more a political tool *(for example, see May 2, 1947 and November 21, 1949)* rather than an expression of popular hero-worship *(see: July 21, 1953)* and crowd sizes reflected this change. The period's notable exception, the parade for retiring General McArthur *(see: April 20, 1951)*, shows that New Yorkers would still come out to honor somebody they felt deserved the honor.

Wednesday, October 23, 1946:
Delegates of the First Plenary Session of the United Nations

On what was described as a "silvery October day," the more than 200 delegates, alternate delegates, and assistants of the United Nations drove from the Battery to City Hall. After a luncheon at the Waldorf, they continued across the East River to Flushing Meadow Park, site of the 1939-1940 World's Fair and very temporary home to the General Assembly of the United Nations. Considerably different from other parades, the day's events were far less boisterous or met by enthusiastically cheering crowds. It was estimated that 400,000 people watched the caravan of 96 cars, but the spectators were described as "polite but notably unenthusiastic." A squad of New York's mounted police led the procession up Broadway, followed by an army band from Fort Jay and a detail of 70 UN military police, in gray uniforms with a light blue shoulder patch embossed with the organization's new white emblem of the globe surrounded by two olive branches. "Hardly a scrap of paper fluttered down from the lofty buildings" according to one New York newspaper, as the caravan moved up Broadway to City Hall.

After being welcomed at City Hall by Deputy Mayor Thomas Corcoran, the UN General Assembly President Paul-Henri Spaak of Belgium commented upon the lack of the usual New York City greeting, saying that it was "not quite as enthusiastic as we could have wished for." One prominent delegate, Andrei Gromyko of the Soviet Union, joined the group once it arrived at City Hall.

The welcome and reception at City Hall ended soon after Gromyko's arrival and the procession headed uptown to the Waldorf Astoria. The mood there was "much more cordial," and over 1,600 people "applauded heartily" as US Secretary of State James Byrnes and Soviet Foreign Minister Vyacheslav Molotov both offered toasts to "peace and understanding of the peoples of one world – our one world." Grover Whalen presided at the luncheon, and Secretary Byrnes encouraged the delegates to avoid fear and suspicion, describing the United Nations as a "great forum" where the world's nations would "have the opportunity to discuss their problems frankly and freely."

After the luncheon, the caravan resumed its trip to Long Island, arriving in Flushing Meadow Park barely five minutes before the scheduled opening of the one and only meeting of the UN at this site before it moved on to Lake Success the following month and, ultimately, to its headquarters on First Avenue along the East River in 1952.

The unusually mild response to the parade is perhaps not difficult to understand. As Mr. Spaak mentioned in his speech at City Hall, it was "justified by the fact that the United Nations is only at the beginning of a long and difficult task."

That task has proven a long and difficult one indeed. The United Nations has grown from its initial membership of 51 nations to 193. Its mission of preserving world peace was often paralyzed during the Cold War, but since then the number of "peace-keeping missions" has expanded greatly. While some today deride the organization as an ineffectual global bureaucracy, many others see it as an important force for peace without which the conflicts of the past 70 years might have escalated further than they did.

The United Nations Headquarters

In June 1941, with war raging around the globe and Nazi Germany controlling most of Europe, the first of six conferences leading to the formation of the United Nations was held in London. By the war's end in 1945, over 20 nations had signed the "Declaration of the United Nations" and 50 countries sent delegates to a meeting in San Francisco in April 1945 where the United Nations was officially created. Dedicated to maintaining world peace through friendly cooperation between the world's nations, the organization has grown to over 190 members plus several non-member observers as of 2020.

One of the first priorities was establishing a headquarters for the organization. Several locations in Europe were considered and rejected, including Switzerland, the Netherlands, Vienna and even Berlin. Many US cities put up proposals, and both San Francisco and Philadelphia were leading contenders. Meanwhile, the new organization was holding General Assembly meetings in the New York City pavilion at the former World's Fair site in Flushing, and the Security Council was meeting in Lake Success, NY on Long Island.

The decision was made in 1948, when NYC Planning Commissioner Robert Moses convinced Nelson Rockefeller to donate 18 acres of land along the East River in Manhattan between 42nd and 48th Streets. Construction began in 1948, and the cornerstone was officially laid in 1949 by NY Governor Thomas Dewey. The Secretariat building was completed in 1950, and two years later the General Assembly building opened. Although proposals have been made over the years to relocate outside of the United States, none of them have been seriously discussed, largely because of the enormous cost that would be incurred. Additions were made over the years, including the Conference Building, the Dag Hammarskjöld Library and a garden that includes the famous *Knotted Gun* sculpture and a piece of the former Berlin Wall. The first major refurbishment started in 2007 and was completed eight years later.

Friday, October 25, 1946:
Colonel Clarence Irvine and Crew of *Dreamboat*

Colonel Clarence Irvine and nine crew members of the B-29 *Dreamboat* flew to New York City from Washington and landed at LaGuardia Airport at 11:17 on a pleasant fall morning. As part of the Army Air Force's Long-Range Flight Program, the purpose of their record-setting non-stop flight from Hawaii to Egypt over the North Pole was to prove to friend and foe alike the Air Force's ability "to go anywhere in the world at any time" in the words of Colonel Irvine.

As soon as the bomber landed, Colonel Irvine and crew were met by Acting Mayor Vincent Impellitteri, Major General Edward Anderson, Deputy Commander of the First Air Force, and Police Commissioner Arthur Wallander. Their motorcade proceeded to Bowling Green led by a police escort. Accompanied by the bands of Mitchel Field and the Department of Sanitation, they moved up the parade route to City Hall. Riding in nine cars and escorted by 15 motorcycle policemen, the parade was viewed by more than 100,000 lunchtime spectators. They were showered with ticker tape and confetti along the entire route.

An additional 15,000 people waited in City Hall Park and cheered when the pilot and crew of the B-29 were introduced by John Murtaugh, City Commissioner of Investigation, who had served with Colonel Irvine in the 21st Bomber Command during the final months of the war in the Pacific. Acting Mayor Impellitteri spoke of their flight as a "splendid tribute to the efficiency of our fliers and those of the Army Air Force who planned the flight over the Pole." The colonel replied that the flight was made possible by his crew because of their high degree of skill and ability.

Following the reception at City Hall, Colonel Irvine spoke by phone with Mayor O'Dwyer who was vacationing in California. The mayor and colonel had served in the same unit during the War. Later that afternoon Colonel Irvine and his crew attended a luncheon at the Exchange Club of the New York Stock Exchange. That evening they attended a cocktail party at the Hotel Biltmore arranged by Pan American World Airways.

In addition to his combat command in World War II, Colonel Irvine had spent most of his career in mechanical and technical commands. He was promoted General in 1950 and in 1952 was named Air Force Chief of Staff Material Division. He resigned in 1958 holding the rank of Lieutenant General and died in 1975 in his home state of Nebraska.

Thursday, November 7, 1946:
Ernest Bevin, British Foreign Secretary

"Ordinary people of the world, whatever their ideologies or political policies may be, have this in common – a burning desire and longing for permanent peace – that should inspire us to translate into actual fact." With these words, Ernest Bevin, Foreign Secretary of the United Kingdom, opened his remarks to more than 200 invited guests in the Council Chambers of City Hall.

His speech before the guests capped days of activity for the 65-year-old diplomat. From 1922 to 1940 he was General Secretary of the Transport and General Workers' Union, one of the most powerful unions in Great Britain. When the British War Cabinet was formed in 1940 under Winston Churchill's leadership, Bevin was named Minister of Labour, a position he held until 1945, when he was appointed Foreign Secretary. He and his wife Florence had arrived on the liner *Aquitania*, and after three days of meetings with dignitaries, politicians, and diplomats, he and his wife Florence received New York's traditional ticker tape welcome.

Noontime crowds, numbering over 100,000 people, stood along Broadway, braving the chilly wind. The procession was led by Troops A and B of New York's Mounted Police squad. Two bands, one from the Police Department and one from the First Army headquarters on Fort Jay, along with an army honor guard, preceded the open limousine in which Mr. and Mrs. Bevin rode along with Grover Whalen, Chairman of the Mayor's Reception Committee. They were greeted at City Hall by Acting Mayor Vincent Impellitteri, substituting for Mayor O'Dwyer who was attending a conference in Los Angeles. City Hall Plaza was jammed with over 5,000 spectators.

As the Foreign Secretary was led into the Council Chambers, opera star Myra Manning greeted him with renditions of "The Star-Spangled Banner" and "God Save the King." The Acting Mayor welcomed Mr. Bevin as "a leader and representative of a great democratic ally," then spoke of the uniqueness of New York, containing members of all races, nationalities, and creeds. "We people, Mr. Bevin, are unanimous in our hopes and prayers…that tomorrow's sun will bring permanent peace, permanent security, and permanent happiness."

Following Mr. Impellitteri's optimistic remarks, the Foreign Secretary began his statements. He likened the world, only a year after the end of the war, to an ill patient. "The world is not out of the hospital, so to speak. It hasn't reached convalescent state much less arrived at a position of renewed health." The Englishman's less enthusiastic statements received cordial applause from those gathered in the Council Chambers. Before returning to the Waldorf with his wife, Mr. Bevin posed for photographs with Mr. Impellitteri and others. No formal luncheon reception followed.

Mr. Bevin spoke to the United Nations and met with President Truman before returning to Great Britain. He continued as Foreign Secretary until 1951, holding the position during a time when the United Kingdom was suffering financially from the War. Drastic cuts in the British budget ate away at much of England's foreign efforts. The British Empire, upon which the sun never set, began to disassemble during his term in office through no fault of his own.

Ernest Bevin retired after he left the Foreign Office in March 1951. He died in London on April 14, 1951 slightly more than a month after he retired. His ashes were placed in Westminster Abbey.

Monday, January 13, 1947: Premier Alcide De Gasperi of Italy

Italian Premier Alcide De Gasperi's active day began hours before the scheduled noontime start of the ticker tape parade honoring the Italian statesman. One purpose of his visit was to plead for trade arrangements between the United States and his nation, devastated by war and the tyranny of Fascism. At 9 o'clock on a cold and cloudy morning, he was escorted from the Waldorf Astoria to the garment district for a view of how companies in New York operated compared to Italy. Visiting three establishments, including Eagle Clothes at 568 Broadway, where the female workers, almost all of Italian descent or recent immigrants from Italy, nearly trampled him in their enthusiasm to meet the current leader of Italy. Rescued by a security detail of New York detectives, he climbed on a worktable and, speaking in Italian, praised the workers and assured them that hard work ethics helped cement the friendship between Italy and the United States.

Following his tour of the garment district, he was escorted downtown by motorcycle policemen, sirens wailing. He arrived at the Battery shortly before noon and, despite the low temperature, sat in the rear of an open vehicle for the journey up the Canyon of Heroes. Sharing the car with him was Grover Whalen, Chairman of the Mayor's Reception Committee, and Alberto Tarachiani, Italian Ambassador to the United States. The parade began with a fanfare from the Army band leading the way. Marching in company with the Premier were detachments from the Army, Navy, Police, and Fire Departments. Police estimated the crowd of spectators lining the route at less than 100,000, and their greeting was subdued and a smaller than usual flurry of ticker tape and torn paper rained down. A more boisterous crowd of 15,000 people were clustered in City Hall Plaza, however, cheering loudly when Premier De Gasperi stepped from the vehicle, passed a military honor guard, and entered City Hall.

The Premier was led to the Council Chamber where members of the Council, Board of Estimates, and invited guests of Italian descent greeted him with a standing ovation. Grover Whalen introduced him to Mayor O'Dwyer, who welcomed the Premier to New York and presented him with a scroll that spoke of the large number of New Yorkers who claimed Italian heritage and contributed to the vitality of the city. The scroll also praised Mr. De Gasperi'ss efforts to rebuild Italy and return it to its proper place among nations.

Mr. De Gasperi began his response in English, stumbling over pronunciation or grammar. Mayor O'Dwyer suggested he continue in his native tongue, and a member of his staff could translate. The Premier then spoke at length about the closeness felt by the people of Italy for those of New York. In Italy, he said, "New York has meant hope." He ended his remarks with a reference to Italy's original role in the war as one of the Axis nations. "From today on," he promised, "no one will see in Italy a nation seeking war or a nation in conflict with other peace-loving republics."

A luncheon followed at the Union Club at Park Avenue and 69th Street, hosted by Winthrop Aldrich, Chairman of Chase National Bank. The Premier sat at the dais with Mr. Aldrich; Dr. Pietro Campilli, the Italian Minister of Industry; James Dunn, US Ambassador to Italy; Juvenal Marchisio, Domestic Court Justice; Mr. Tarchiani; Mayor O'Dwyer; Grover Whalen; Cardinal Francis Spellman, and others. Shortly before the luncheon started, Fiorello LaGuardia arrived, to the delight of Mr. De Gaspari who knew of the former Mayor's work during World War II. The two began chatting excitedly in Italian, attracting the attention of the press photographers. Mayor O'Dwyer, who did not speak Italian, felt snubbed until Mr. Whalen redirected the photographers' attention, and the rest of the luncheon proceeded without incident.

The Roman Catholic Cardinal opened the luncheon with a prayer and blessing. Following the meal, Mr. Benjamin Goldman, President of the Amalgamated Clothing Workers of America presented Mr. De Gasperi with more than $10,000 in donations for American Relief for Italy. Once again, the Premier expressed his pleasure at being so fondly welcomed and thanked one and all for their support and generosity.

Two more events completed the Italian premier's busy schedule for the day, a late afternoon tea at the Colony Club organized by the charity American Relief for Italy, and a dinner at the Biltmore Hotel. The premier's exhausting day did not end until after midnight.

Mr. De Gasperi traveled to Washington the next afternoon where he met with President Truman and Congressional leaders. His trip to America had been suggested and arranged by Henry Luce, founder of *Time* magazine, and his wife Claire Booth

Luce. The magazine extensively covered his trip to the United States, helping soften the views of many Americans toward the former Axis nation.

The premier returned to Italy after a 10-day visit to America. He would return in the fall of 1951 as the Prime Minister of the Italian Republic and would receive a second New York welcome *(see: September. 28, 1951)*.

Friday, February 7, 1947:
Viscount Alexander of Tunis, Governor General of Canada

A year after being named Governor General of Canada by King George VI, Viscount Harold Alexander visited the United States for six days. He spent the first three in Washington, DC, meeting with President Truman and officers who had served in his command in North Africa and Italy, where he had been Supreme Allied Commander in the Mediterranean from 1942 to 1945. Following his visit to the capital, he flew to New York, and was escorted to the Waldorf Astoria, where he prepared for his ticker tape welcome. The fact that a heavy wet snow was falling did not seem to deter him or the people of New York.

Grover Whalen, Chairman of the Mayor's Reception Committee, rode with the Governor General downtown from the Waldorf to Bowling Green in a closed black limousine. Once at the southern end of Broadway they changed vehicles, and the Viscount draped his gray greatcoat over his shoulders, standing in his khaki field uniform. Mr. Whalen sat to his left, wrapped in an overcoat, snow collecting on the brim of his top hat. To the Viscount's right sat Lady Alexander, not as well prepared for the weather wearing a light blue jacket and feathered blue hat and holding an umbrella as protection from the snow.

A mounted police squad led the way followed by the Police Department Band. A detachment of soldiers from Fort Jay and a Military Police Company completed the marching contingent. Only about 25,000 spectators lined the route, no doubt due to the inclement weather. Little in the way of ticker tape fell and what did fall was swirled and lost in the wind-swept Canyon of Heroes. The newly appointed Governor General of Canada had experienced desert heat and sandstorms in North Africa and sub-freezing cold and blizzards in Italy during the recently ended World War. The only concession he appeared to make to New York's blustery welcome was a pair of gloves which he donned soon after the parade began. Not long after the motorcade passed Trinity Church the storm lessened but flurries continued throughout the day.

No outdoor events were held, so Major O'Dwyer welcomed the Viscount at the steps of City Hall and led him and his party into the Board of Estimate Chamber. Although the Viscount was born in London and raised in England, he was of Irish descent and proud of his Gaelic heritage. As the mayor led him into the Chamber, the Police Department bagpipe band began a serenade of Irish tunes before breaking into the strains of "Rule Britannia."

Grover Whalen began his welcome with the words, "Being somewhat of an Irishman myself." The mayor reminded everyone of his Irish heritage as well when he welcomed the Viscount as one of "our friends across the northern border." The mayor presented Viscount Alexander with a scroll which citied him for his former military leadership and his current diplomatic statesmanship. The Governor General noted he had said a "farewell to arms" when he resigned from the military to accept his present role and looked forward to working closely to foster even warmer relations between Canada and the United States. His use of the term "warmer" on this wintery day brought laughter from those in attendance. He concluded by stating that the more than 1,500-mile-long unfortified border between the United States and Canada was an example to the rest of the world of how nations can live side by side in peace.

A luncheon at the Metropolitan Club followed for slightly more than 100 military, civic, and business leaders. Among those attending was Warren Austin, United States delegate to the United Nations; Admiral Thomas Kinkaid; General Courtney Hodges; and former Postmaster General James Farley. During the luncheon the Police Department Glee Club performed a selection of Irish and World War II ballads. The Viscount spoke and recalled many of his experiences serving with American troops during the War.

Viscount Alexander had a keen interest in archeology and opera, so his schedule included a chance to indulge in both pastimes. After the luncheon he was given a two-hour tour of the Metropolitan Museum of Art where he spent a long period examining Egyptian and Persian artifacts, personally conducted by the museum's Egyptologist, Ambrose Lansing. The Viscount was also an amateur painter and he spent time admiring and studying Flemish and American works. After the museum tour, Viscount and Lady Alexander were guests at the Metropolitan Opera Club for tea, followed by a performance of *Rigoletto*. Later that evening they were guests of the Metropolitan Opera Company at the Waldorf. The couple spent the next two days visiting the United Nations, the Museum of Natural History, and St. Patrick's Cathedral, as well as shopping on Fifth Avenue, before returning to Ottawa.

Viscount Alexander was the 17th Governor General of Canada and the last non-Canadian to hold the post. He retired from the position in 1952. Two years later he carried the Orb of Sovereignty in the royal procession at the Coronation of Elizabeth II as Queen of Great Britain. After serving briefly as Minister of Defense for the United Kingdom and being knighted First Earl of Tunis he retired from public life and spent his remaining years between his homes in England and Canada. He died of a perforated aorta in 1969 and is buried in a small church yard in the village of Ridge in Hertfordshire, England near his family's home.

Friday, May 2, 1947:
Miguel Alemán Valdés, President of Mexico

Shortly after 8 o'clock in the morning of May 2, the President of Mexico, Miguel Alemán Valdés, arrived at Pennsylvania Station from Washington. He had spent the last few days in the capital meeting with President Truman and congressional leaders, and New York City was the final stop on his sojourn to the United States.

It was raining when he arrived and was driven to his suite at the Waldorf Astoria Hotel. After a brief stop there to change and refresh himself, he was driven downtown to Bowling Green for New York's traditional ticker tape welcome. Because the city's latest convertible used for parades was being repaired and a suitable replacement could not be found, President Truman loaned the limousine that he and his predecessor Franklin Roosevelt had used when visiting New York. The car had arrived the night before by special train and had been moved to Bowling Green, where President Alemán joined Grover Whalen, Chairman of the Mayor's Reception Committee, for the ride up Broadway.

Despite the rain that fell throughout the day, the Mexican President stood in the back of the car, seemingly oblivious to the rain. He wore a scarf around his neck but rode bare headed, his suit growing wetter as the parade progressed. The 321st Army

Ground Forces Band from Governors Island accompanied the motorcade along with members of the 504th Parachute Infantry, based at Fort Bragg, NC. Groups from the Police, Fire, and Sanitation Departments marched as well and were joined by members of various Mexican American organizations.

Police estimates placed the number of spectators at more than a million, a figure which included hardy souls who huddled in the rain and those who stood at windows. Damp streamers of ticker tape cascaded down into the street and open cars of the motorcade. The Mexican president waved and clasped his hands in a salute. Groups of young girls shouted "*Viva*" as the president passed them and he pointed at them, smiling.

City Hall Plaza was filled to capacity with groups from various locations in Mexico. Many wore native costumes of sombreros, colorful wide skirts, and mantillas. A number held silk banners with the names of the regions they were from and the president seemed delighted to read Vera Cruz, Yucatan, Mexico City, and Tijuana. Mayor O'Dwyer greeted the president and the two men stood on the reviewing stand under an umbrella carried by a member of the mayor's staff. The national anthems of Mexico and the United States were played, then the mayor welcomed President Alemán and awarded him the city's Gold Medal and a scroll citing his efforts on improving conditions in Mexico. Asked to comment, the president responded, "It is the most wonderful reception I have ever received. I am deeply grateful to your people for this warm and happy greeting. It will make for better understanding between our peoples."

Immediately after the City Hall reception, the motorcade resumed to the Hotel Commodore for lunch. Hundreds of invited guests heard President Alemán speak of the loan being arranged in Washington between the United States and Mexico. Most of the money, he stressed, would be used to build roads, dams, and schools in his nation. Every dollar received, he explained, became pesos of friendship and cooperation.

Returning from the luncheon, the motorcade drove on the Grand Central Terminal ramp, where a blizzard of small white particles met them. "Was that snow?" asked President Alemán. Mr. Whalen examined one of the particles and answered, "No, Your Excellency, it's rice." The president smiled, explaining that rice was a symbol of good luck in his country. The motorcade continued uptown to Columbia University, where years earlier the president had studied. Members of the student body cheered him when he briefly visited the Goelet Memorial. Not yet finished with the afternoon's activities, the motorcade then drove to the statue of Simón Bolívar at 85th Street and Central Park West. Now soaking wet, the President was joined by Mexican Consul-General Dr. Jose Lolo de Larrera to lay a wreath. Finally returning to the Waldorf, he donned a fresh and dry suit before attending a dinner in his honor. He returned to Mexico three days later.

Elected in 1946 thanks to support from labor unions, President Alemán served until November 1952, then returned to his native state of Vera Cruz where he practiced law and wrote about Mexican labor relations. Appointed president of Mexico's National Tourist Association in 1961, he was instrumental in bringing the 1968 Summer Olympics to Mexico City. He remained active in organizations fostering closer relations between his nation and the United States for the rest of his life and died in Mexico City in 1983 at the age of 82.

Monday, June 9, 1947: Willie Turnesa

Only a few of the celebrities honored by a ticker tape parade have been natives of the New York metropolitan area. One of these was Willie Turnesa, born and raised in Elmsford, less than 20 miles north of the city in Westchester County. One of seven brothers, all of whom were golfers, Willie was the only one who never turned professional. Instead, his six brothers pooled their resources and paid Willie's tuition to Holy Cross University (where he tried out for the football team but was rejected because of his diminutive size of 5'6" and only 140 pounds). His brothers advised him to keep his amateur status and were rewarded by his victory in the annual British Amateur Golf Tournament. He defeated his closest competitor, fellow American Dick Chapman, at the Carnoustie Golf Links in Scotland, bringing home the Walker Cup as his trophy.

Turnesa arrived in New York on the liner *Queen Elizabeth*, which discharged her passengers at 10 o'clock in the morning. From then until late evening, the golfer was the center of attention. Met at the dock by Mayor O'Dwyer, he was driven downtown for New York's traditional welcome, cheered by thousands lining the streets. The 10-car procession was preceded by a motorcycle police escort. At City Hall Mayor O'Dwyer made a brief welcoming statement and turned the microphone over to the Honorary Chairman of the event, Broadway columnist and golfer, Ed Sullivan. After introducing other members of the American Walker Cup team, he presented Turnesa to the crowd as a "favorite son from the suburbs." The champion expressed his gratitude for the welcome and hoped that amateur sporting events could further international understanding.

After the ceremony in City Hall Plaza, the champion was taken to the Park Lane Hotel for a reception and luncheon. More than 200 guests attended, many representing various sports. But the guest who most impressed Turnesa was the football coach from Holy Cross, who presented Turnesa with a football bearing the letters "HC" and joked that the golfer had always wanted to letter in football and he finally had done it.

Turnesa credited his mother-in-law with his victory in Scotland. When he had arrived in Great Britain, he learned that his putter was illegal there because of its construction, and he played the entire tournament with hers, which happened to be among the clubs he carried to Scotland. Turnesa was an active golfer for another 20 years and won two American amateur championships and a number of amateur tournaments. He died in Sleepy Hollow, New York, in 2001, the last of the seven golfing Turnesa brothers.

Wednesday, November 5, 1947:
Officers and Crew of French Cruiser *Georges Leygues*

The French ship *Georges Leygues* was a light cruiser commissioned in November 1937. It was part of the French Navy when WWII began it and saw action against the Italian navy. After the fall of France in 1940, it was controlled by the Vichy French government, and fought against the British and American invasion of North Africa in 1942. Then in 1943, it joined the Free French Navy, turning its guns against Germany until the end of the war.

In late 1947 the Metropolitan Museum of Art planned a display of French tapestries, many of which French authorities were willing to lend to the museum. Transporting these priceless items became the responsibility of the French navy. Carefully packed and stowed aboard *Georges Leygues*, they were brought across the Atlantic, arriving on November 4, 1947.

The following day, an unusually warm early November morning, the officers and 96 crew members of the cruiser received a small ticker tape parade. At City Hall, the crew was inspected by Mayor William O'Dwyer, and welcomed to New York. The mayor's brief remarks concluded with "the event will contribute immediately to the realization that France remains the great bastion of western European culture that she has always been."

A week later *Georges Leygues* returned to France and North Africa. She saw additional combat duty off Indochina in 1954 and in the Suez Canal Affair of 1956, before being decommissioned in May 1957 and sold for scrap in November 1959.

Tuesday, November 18, 1947: Friendship Train

It all began with a suggestion by columnist Drew Pearson in his October 11, 1947 syndicated daily column *The Merry-Go-Round,* featured in newspapers in Washington, New York, and other major cities around the country. Pearson had just returned from a visit to France and Italy, where he noticed that Russia had sent small shipments of grain to these countries, both of which were still suffering from the devastation caused by World War II. These shipments were being highly praised by the local press and leaders in both countries. A fervent anti-Communist, Pearson saw the shipment and its reception as an attempt to gain support and help swing these countries into the Communist sphere. In his column, Pearson wrote that the United States could surpass anything sent from the Russian government simply through the generosity of the American people. Pearson challenged his readers to donate food, without government assistance, to the people of these two countries.

Almost overnight the idea excited people across the country. Other newspapers added their support, and radio commentaries reported on the growing interest, providing basic information on collection points and schedules. Pearson envisioned a freight train of donations to begin on the west coast, move across the country, and end in New York, where all the donations would be shipped across the Atlantic. He thought the effort would succeed in filling 80 freight cars of food.

The train, composed of a dozen freight cars, began moving east from Los Angeles on November 7, three weeks after it had been first proposed. At each stop along the route, additional donations were waiting with cars filled with food, clothing, fuel, and in some cases, cash donations. In California, the train visited Bakersfield, Fresno, Merced, Stockton, Oakland, and Sacramento. It next moved to Reno, Nevada, and Ogden, Utah. In Wyoming it stopped for additional cars at Green River, Rawlins, Laramie, and Cheyenne. Crossing into Nebraska, it made stops as Sidney, North Platte, Kearney, Grand Island, Fremont, and Omaha. Traveling across the Mississippi River into Illinois, it halted at Clinton, Sterling, and Chicago before continuing east. It headed through Fort Wayne, Indiana and Mansfield, Ohio, and then into Pennsylvania, stopping in Pittsburgh, Altoona, Lancaster, and Philadelphia. It stopped in Trenton, New Jersey, and finally arrived in New York City, 11 days after leaving Los Angeles.

Meanwhile, a northern branch had been assembled in South Bend, Indiana, and moved to Elkhart, Indiana. It next visited Toledo, Cleveland, and Ashtabula, Ohio. In northern New York State it halted at Buffalo, Syracuse, Utica, and Albany before joining the train from the west coast. At each stop, trucks or freight cars filled with goods from places not directly on the route stood waiting from the western and southern states.

Organizations added to the flow of donations and helped collect, pack, and load the items. Notable among these groups were the Church World Service, the Joint Distribution Committee, the National Catholic Welfare Committee, the American Baptist Relief Fund, American Friends Service Committee, the Brethren World Service, and the Congregational Service Committee. The Boy Scouts and Girl Scouts donated thousands of hours of service in preparing the donations. Each individual donation was labeled with the following message:

> *"All races and creeds make up the vast melting pot of America, and in a democratic and Christian spirit of good will toward men, we, the American people, have worked together to bring this food to your doorsteps, hoping that it will tide you over until your own fields are again rich and abundant with crops."*

Also on every donation was a tag where the donor could fill in their name and mailing address. When both trains reached New York, there were more than 700 cars, shattering Pearson's estimate of 80, containing donations valued at $40 million (in 1947 dollars, almost $478 million in 2020). The freight cars were transferred by barges onto freighters in New York Harbor. The first ship loaded was the United States lines' *American Leader*, which was renamed the *Friend Ship* for the voyage to Europe. Ships in the harbor saluted the barges carrying the freight cars, and fountains of water were sprayed from New York City fireboats.

In recognition of the generosity of the American public, the city decided to hold the most unique ticker tape parade to date. A caravan of 70 trucks filled with donations were driven from the Battery up the Canyon of Heroes to City Hall, before proceeding to piers along the East and Hudson Rivers. Bands from the Police, Fire, and Sanitation Departments led the way, and for once a blizzard of ticker tape flowed down not on people but on donations. It was estimated that 25,000 people lined Broadway on the chilly November day.

Grover Whalen served as Chairman for this unusual ticker tape. Warren Austin, US delegate to the United Nations, French Consul General Ludovic Chancel, and Italian Consul General Luigi Nardi waited with Mayor O'Dwyer in City Hall Plaza for the procession of trucks to halt. Grover Whalen was loudly cheered when he praised school children for their efforts to help children in Europe. Three school children made brief remarks which were broadcast to France and Italy via shortwave. From Midwood High School in Brooklyn, Deborah Sussman spoke in French and David Pitcher spoke in English, and Mary Louise Coscia of Sacred Heart School, Manhattan, presented her remarks in Italian. Mr. Austin spoke of this effort as the most appropriate way "to promote friendly relations between nations." The French and Italian Consuls had difficulty expressing their gratitude to the generosity of the American average citizen. Since no government assistance was involved in the project, they both spoke of the deep and sincere affection felt towards the American public.

Once in Europe, the donations were distributed throughout France and Italy. Trains and trucks carried the donations from city to city. In Paris, 50 truckloads of donated food and clothing were driven down the Champs Élysées, past the Arc de Triomphe, the first time in peacetime trucks were permitted on this route. From there they drove to the Hôtel de Ville where they were welcomed by the mayor of Paris,

Pierre de Gaulle, brother of Charles de Gaulle. In Italy, a similar motorcade took place in Rome, accompanied by Pearson, who was received by Pope Pius XII in the Vatican. The columnist accompanied many of the caravans of donations, guaranteeing that the items were distributed honestly and fairly. Large numbers of people turned out in dozens of cities and towns in northern Italy and Tuscany to receive the gifts. The movement of the items through France and Italy was covered daily by every newspaper in those countries, with the notable exception of Communist papers. French authorities personally informed Pearson before he returned to the United States in early January 1948, that they would do all they could to somehow repay America for its generosity *(see February 3, 1949)*.

So much had been collected that excess goods were distributed to regions of Austria, Germany, Norway, and Greece. Roscoe Drummond, editor of the *Christian Science Monitor* devoted an entire issue of his paper to the project and referred to Drew Pearson's proposal as "one of the greatest projects ever born of American journalism."

Pearson continued his career in journalism until his death in 1969. His columns were often controversial, mixing factual reporting with rumors and gossip to criticize national politicians including Senator McCarthy and members of the Eisenhower administration. After his death, his column, now titled *The Washington Merry-Go-Round*, was continued by other journalists and claims to be the nation's longest-running column.

Tuesday, March 9, 1948:
Eamon de Valera, Former President of the Republic of Ireland

Born in New York but a resident of Ireland since age 2, Eamon de Valera arrived in New York City at the start of a trip to the United States. His itinerary included stops in Washington, the Midwest, and San Francisco, where he would serve as the Grand Marshal of that city's St. Patrick's Day Parade. But before he continued his travels, New York honored him with a traditional ticker tape parade.

Welcomed to the city by Grover Whalen at the Waldorf Astoria Hotel, Mr. de Valera entered the first car of a caravan of vehicles for the ride downtown to Bowling Green. A squad of motorcycle policemen escorted the cars along Park Avenue to 34th Street, where they turned east to the FDR Drive. The caravan continued downtown to South Street, and finally the parade's starting point. Small numbers of cheering people along the route recognized the Irish flag fluttering from the front of the car in which he and Mr. Whalen rode.

At Bowling Green, the former Irish president and current Head of Government transferred to an open limousine, wearing a heavy sweater under his suit jacket against the March chill. He was joined in the car by Mr. Whalen, Frank Aiken, the former Irish Minister of Finance, and the Reverend Timothy Shanley, Rector of St Matthew's Church on West 68th Street, who was a life-long friend of Mr. de Valera.

The parade began shortly after noon, led by a squad of New York mounted police. The Police Department Band, color guards from the Police, Fire, and Sanitation Departments, and a military escort completed the marching contingents. The escort was composed of members of the 501st Military Police Battalion, headquartered at Fort Jay on Governors Island. Seven other vehicles containing representatives of the governments of Ireland, New York State, and New York City completed the parade formation.

The sidewalks along the parade route were filled with cheering people, though police estimated the crowd at less than 50,000, smaller than many parades possibly because of the chill, but the sound of their cheers made up for the smaller number. The Irish flag appeared frequently along lower Broadway. Ticker tape and torn paper floated down from above, mixed in with strands of green ribbon and tape. The Irish statesman smiled through the entire journey to City Hall, waving at the crowds. Each time he pointed to various individuals or groups, the cheers intensified.

Irish-born Mayor O'Dwyer, recovering from the flu, was unable to attend the reception at City Hall, so Acting Mayor Vincent Impellitteri replaced him. Mr. Whalen, Chairman of the Mayor's Reception Committee, introduced Mr. de Valera as "a boy from Manhattan who made good overseas." The Acting Mayor extended the city's welcome to the Irish political leader and conferred honorary citizenship upon him, then presented him with a scroll proclaiming his role in securing the independence of the Irish Republic. In response, Mr. de Valera addressed the almost 700 people jammed into the City Council Chamber, saying:

"Today in 26 counties we have a freedom as complete as any country in the world. However, we haven't got the victory we set out to achieve. No Irishman and certainly no Irishwoman will be satisfied until the whole of Ireland is as free as the 26 counties. I am certain we shall achieve it."

He added that it was his dream and personal goal to be the person to announce the unification of Ireland. Concluding in Gaelic, he thanked the people of New York for their support of Irish independence and asking for a blessing upon them.

After the City Hall reception, Mr. de Valera was the guest of honor at a luncheon in the Jade Room of the Waldorf Astoria. Roman Catholic Cardinal Francis Spellman offered an invocation and speakers included New York Governor Herbert Lehman; Judge Owen Bohan; Bronx Borough President James Lyons; Mr. Impellitteri; and Cardinal Spellman. Mr. de Valera's response likened the American love of liberty to that of the Irish. He concluded by again speaking of his wish to wrest the counties of Northern Ireland from British control.

That evening, the former President attended a private dinner and reception at the Cardinal's residence on Madison Avenue and 50th Street. Mr. de Valera flew to Washington the next morning and met with President Truman. Interim stops before he arrived in San Francisco included St. Louis and Oklahoma City.

Mr. de Valera had been involved in the Irish Independence movement from an early age, commanding a battalion during the 1916 Easter Rebellion. After a brief imprisonment, he fought in the Irish Civil War, then served in the Irish Parliament and as its president twice. He was often criticized for keeping Ireland neutral during World War II, and never saw his dream of a united Ireland fulfilled, and it remains divided to this day. He died in 1975 at the age of 92. Always a deeply religious man, he was buried in clerical garb as he requested.

Wednesday, July 7, 1948:
Rómulo Gallegos, President of Venezuela

The turbulent history of Venezuela shows that Rómulo Ángel del Monte Carmelo Gallegos Freire was the 37th person to serve as President of Venezuela but since some heads of state of that South American republic served more than once, his was the 57th presidency since the nation gained independence in 1811. A prize-winning novelist, he was exiled from his country in 1929 for a book that exposed the government's misuse of power but was allowed to return in 1936. Soon afterwards he was elected to Congress, and in 1948 he was elected President in what has been called "the first honest election" in his nation. Not long after being sworn into office in February 1948, President Gallegos began a goodwill tour of the United States, visiting Washington to meet with President Truman before arriving in New York.

A motorcycle escort led the Venezuelan leader from the Waldorf Astoria downtown to the parade's starting point at the Battery. A caravan of 10 cars, led by the Police Department and First Army Bands and a company of the First Army Headquarters, proceeded along the sparsely crowded route. Mayor O'Dwyer met the President at the steps to City Hall and escorted him into the City Council Chamber. The author of 10 novels, short stories and essays, as well as head of state, he was introduced by Grover Whalen, Chairman of the Reception Committee, as a "scholar, educator, and a man who has been a great friend of America." Mayor O'Dwyer extended him the official greetings of the city, to which President Gallegos returned the "love, fervor, and friendship of the Venezuelan people."

Later that afternoon at a luncheon sponsored by the Overseas Press Club at the Sherry Netherlands Hotel, he spoke briefly about the minor influence of Communism in his country. He also expressed the hopes that his country could free itself from dependence on its oil resources and find new ways to aid the Venezuelan economy. That evening at the Waldorf Astoria he met privately with Trygve Lie, Secretary General of the United Nations. The president then met with more than 850 members of the Venezuelan community living in the New York area.

The first popularly elected president of Venezuela was also the one with the briefest tenure. He had served as President of Venezuela for slightly more than nine months when a military coup ousted him in November 1948, and Gallegos was forced to flee to Cuba and then to Mexico. When he was allowed to return to Venezuela in 1959, he was appointed "Senator for Life." Nominated for the Nobel Prize in Literature in 1960 for his novels, he died in Caracas in 1969 while serving as a member of the Inter-American Commission on Human Rights.

Thursday, February 3, 1949: French Gratitude (*Merci*) Train

When France received the Friendship Train in the winter of 1947 *(see: November. 18, 1947)* authorities there promised that they would somehow show their appreciation to the people of the United States. The Gratitude Train (or *Merci* Train as it was also called) was the French response to American generosity. A total of 49 French freight cars were shipped to the United States, each containing French items as gifts to America. The boxcars were the so-called "40-and-8" cars used by the French railways, so called because of their ability to carry 40 people or 8 horses. Cars of this type were used to transport troops in the First and Second World Wars, to move goods and supplies, and, tragically, by the Nazis to transport Jews to concentration camps. France sent one boxcar for each state in the United States in 1949, plus a 49th car to be shared by the District of Columbia and the Territory of Hawaii. The cars contained items such as vases, tapestries, plants native to various areas of France, glassware, dolls dressed in regional costumes, toys, sculpture, and other works of art.

All 49 cars of the train were shipped from Marseilles, France, aboard the French freighter *Magellan*. It entered New York Harbor to a loud welcome of horns, sirens, and whistles on February 2 and docked at Weehawken, New Jersey. The car for New York State was unloaded first, placed on a 20-ton Army Air Force trailer, and towed to the Battery, at the southern end of Broadway, to receive New York's typical ticker tape welcome.

February 3 dawned cold and windy but long before the parade was scheduled to begin at 11:30, officials gathered around Bowling Green, including Martin Meaney, Deputy Police Commissioner (acting as Grand Marshal), French government officials, representatives of the French groups residing in New York (many in provincial costumes), State Department Officials, and others. The First Army band and bands from the Police, Fire, and Sanitation Departments, mounted policemen, military detachments, members of American Legion posts and Veterans of Foreign War Posts were also assembled. So many people were scheduled to march that they filled much of Battery Park and surrounding area while waiting to kick off.

As the marchers began assembling, Reception Committee Chairman Grover Whalen met the French officials for the Gratitude Train on the liner *De Grasse,* which was moored near the Statue of Liberty, a previous gift from France to the United States. Whalen was given a torch that had been lit at the Tomb of the Unknown Soldier in Paris, which was carried to Washington after the parade for a ceremony in Arlington National Cemetery where its flame was combined with that of the American Tomb of the Unknown Soldier.

Meantime, the parade was scheduled to move up Broadway at noon, but the tractor attached to the Air Force trailer would not start. Several attempts to jump start its battery with a heavy Sanitation Department vehicle failed, and the parade started half an hour late, when a second tractor eventually arrived from a municipal garage. No crowd estimate was reported, though the *New York Times* referred to "massed thousands" including more than 15,000 public and parochial school children who had been brought as young witnesses to the event, a parade that from start to finish stretched almost a full mile.

Riding in one of the many vehicles in the parade was Henri Bonnet, French Ambassador to the United States, and Drew Pearson, the newspaper columnist whose original suggestion had been the inspiration behind the Friendship Train. When this vehicle arrived at City Hall, Mayor O'Dwyer was there to meet them. A crowd of more than 5,000 waited in City Hall Park to witness the Mayor accepting the New York State boxcar and extending his thanks for France's generosity. The mayor then presented Mr. Pearson with a certificate for "exceptional public service." On behalf of the French people, Ambassador Bonnet then thanked Mr. Pearson for his suggestion that led to the Friendship Train, adding that thanks to the gifts of that Train, France survived the bleak winter of 1947. "France is coming back," the Ambassador boasted, "and coming back strong."

Later that evening at a dinner held in the Waldorf Astoria, 300 guests heard Eleanor Roosevelt speak of how the combined American and French acts of generosity would further cement the long history of friendship between the two republics. A representative of the mayor of Paris presented a scroll to Mayor O'Dwyer in appreciation of New York's involvement in the Friendship Train. The mayor's final words in response summed up the day's events: "Today we receive the answer of the French and so conclude the most heart-warming event in recent international history."

The New York State freight car was moved to 500 Fifth Avenue where it was subsequently unloaded, and its contents displayed. The remaining cars were routed across the country with the cooperation of the Association of American Railroads. Decorated with the coats-of-arms of the forty French provinces, each car eventually arrived in the state it was destined for. Some gifts were distributed to the poor and needy; others were put on display in museums, historic, or cultural centers. Each of the "40-and-8" cars remained in this country, though five are known to have been destroyed over the years (Massachusetts, Illinois, Nebraska, New Jersey, and Connecticut), and Colorado's car has been reported missing for many years. The website MerciTrain.org, which lists the last known locations of the other cars, says that New York's car can be found in a small county park in Whitesboro, New York. The Metropolitan Museum of Art contains a collection of 49 dolls that were in the car.

Italy also responded to the Friendship Train although with less fanfare. The Italian government sent four large bronze sculptures, two of which are now at the Washington DC end of the Arlington Bridge and the other two at the Washington end of the Theodore Roosevelt Bridge. The Netherlands, although it received only a small part of the donations from the Friendship Train, expressed its gratitude with a gift of a large carillon which now tolls the hours at the Marine Corps Memorial in Arlington National Cemetery.

Tuesday, May 17, 1949: Ralph Bunche

One of the earliest challenges faced by the United Nations was the question of Palestine, which had been controlled by Great Britain under a League of Nations Mandate after the collapse of the Ottoman Empire in 1917. Home to about 700,000 Palestinian Arabs, Palestine was also the ancestral homeland for the Jewish people. Migration of European Jews to Palestine had been a goal of the Zionist movement since the 1880s and accelerated with the rise of Nazism in the 1930s, and after the end of World War II, hundreds of thousands of Holocaust victims wished to repatriate there. While several new Arab nations were formed out of the former Ottoman territories, in 1947 the United Nations approved a resolution to partition Palestine into three parts, and in May 1948, the Israeli Declaration of Independence was proclaimed by Jewish leaders in Palestine, creating of the nation of Israel. Fighting, which had already started in 1947, exploded into war as four of the newly created Arab nations (Egypt, Iraq, Transjordan and Syria) immediately attacked. Over the course of the next year, armistices were successfully brokered between the combatants, and the ceasefire line, which was called the Green Line, became the borders of Israel with its neighbors. At the insistence of the Arab nations, the armistice agreements were clear that these borders were an interim solution until a permanent peace could be negotiated, but for the moment, progress had been achieved. The diplomat leading the negotiations was Acting UN Mediator for Palestine, Dr. Ralph Bunche, an American who had been heavily involved in the formation of the United Nations.

On May 17, Mayor O'Dwyer honored Bunche's accomplishments at a reception at City Hall. Led by a motorcycle police escort, Bunche and his wife Ruth were driven in an open limousine from the UN Security Council offices in Lake Success, NY to City Hall. Bunche said it "was the most exciting adventure he had had" during his time with the United Nations.

After greeting the Bunches at the steps of City Hall, the Mayor led them into the City Council Chambers, filled with over 400 invited guests. "The people of New York welcome you, sir, as a brother," the Mayor said, thanking Bunche for "saving the dignity and the structure of the United Nations." The Mayor noted that Bunche had "accomplished one of the most difficult missions in the history of diplomacy."

In response, Bunche praised the work of his colleagues and associates, saying "we never felt at any moment that the United Nations would or could fail in this effort." Adding that "in a military sense, peace now exists in Palestine" which he believed would continue, in line with the UN's purpose of ensuring peace with "maximum equity for both Arabs and Jews."

After the City Hall ceremony, a luncheon was held at the Waldorf Astoria, hosted by the Mayor's Reception Committee. Chairman Grover Whalen formally introduced Dr. Bunche to the attendees, which included the Mayor, Bernard Baruch, Richard Patterson, and leaders of African American organizations. City Council President Vincent Impelletteri and Manhattan Borough President Hugo Rogers both spoke at the luncheon, praising Dr. Bunche's accomplishments to ensure peace.

Dr. Bunche received other honors for his work, most notably the Nobel Peace Prize in 1950. He continued working at the United Nations, negotiating over conflicts in Congo, Yemen, Kashmir and Cyprus, and in 1968 became Under Secretary General of the UN. He was also involved in the Civil Rights movement in the US, participating with Dr. Martin Luther King in both the 1963 March on Washington and the 1965 Selma to Montgomery March. He lived with his wife and three children in Kew Gardens, Queens, and died at the age of 67 in December 1971.

Sadly, the armistice he negotiated did not lead to a permanent peace. Almost 700,000 Jews migrated into Israel during this time, about a third of them from Arab nations, while roughly the same number of Arabs living in Palestine migrated to the Gaza Strip or the West Bank, controlled respectively by Egypt and Transjordan during this period. The Arab nations refused to recognize Israel's legitimacy or negotiate permanent borders, and tensions escalated into war again in 1967's Six-Day War and 1973's Yom Kippur War. When President Jimmy Carter brokered the 1979 Camp David Accord, Egypt became the first Arab nation to recognize Israel. The question about the Palestinian refugees in now-Israeli controlled Gaza and the West Bank remains unresolved and an on-going source of conflict and terrorism.

Also unresolved is the question about whether Dr. Bunche received a ticker tape parade, as claimed on many websites about him, but is not included on either of the semi-official parade lists. The *New York Times* does not mention a parade in its 11-paragraph coverage of the City Hall ceremony, nor does it mention the route taken to City Hall by the caravan. There was a parade two days later for General Lucius Clay *(see: May 19, 1949)*. Dr. Bunche was one of the guests attending the post-parade luncheon that day, and the *Times* again make no mention of a parade just two days prior for Bunche. Both events were organized by Grover Whalen, Chair of the Mayor's Reception Committee. In his autobiography, Whalen wrote that in the late 1940s, in response to complaints from the Merchants Association of Lower Broadway, a compromise was reached limiting the "number of Broadway celebrations [each] year and have the remainder...proceed directly to City Hall."

In light of the available evidence, the authors conclude that Dr. Bunche did not ride up Broadway under a snowfall of ticker tape, and most likely this was one of the events that fell under Mr. Whalen's compromise.

Thursday, May 19, 1949:
General Lucius Clay, Retiring Military Governor of Germany

A bright sun, clear blue sky, and pleasant temperatures marked the spring day when General Lucius Clay, retiring Military Governor of Germany, received a ticker tape welcome. He was considered by many as the savior of West Berlin because of his leadership during the Berlin Airlift that defeated the almost yearlong Communist blockade of that city. The General entered an open limousine at Bowling Green for the ride through the Canyon of Heroes, sharing the vehicle with Grover Whalen, Chairman of the Reception Committee, and Mr. Robert Murphy, the general's political advisor. The general's wife rode in the second car with their two sons, Lieutenant Colonel Lucius Clay and Major Frank Clay, both graduates of the US Military Academy like their father. Also in this second car was Mr. Draper, the general's economic advisor. Other cars followed, containing military personnel and State Department officials.

More than 2,500 people, civilian and military, marched in the parade. Colonel Frank Quigley, Provost Marshal of the First Army, served as Grand Marshal and strode up Broadway behind a detachment of 39 mounted policemen. Marching music was provided by the First Army Band, the Air Force Band from Mitchel Field, and a Marine Fife and Drum Corps from the Third Naval District. Military detachments from the 39th Infantry based at Fort Dix, New Jersey, and sailors and marines from the Third Naval District marched with a large contingent of World War II veterans, all members of the city's Police, Fire, and Sanitation Departments. Color bearers marched ahead of each group, their flags snapping and furling.

The size of the crowd of spectators was estimated at more than 250,000, many of them veterans who saluted the general. Cheers and cries of welcome were heard along the entire route. Great strands of ticker tape and reams of torn paper fell, littering the insides of the open vehicles and carpeting Broadway and intersecting streets. General Clay smiled and waved back, obviously greatly impressed by the magnitude of the welcome.

Almost 10,000 spectators jammed City Hall Park and they loudly cheered when the General stepped from his vehicle and was greeted by Mayor William O'Dwyer. The general and his family joined the mayor on the reviewing stand. Warren Austin, Chief of the US delegation to the United Nationsm was also present on the stand and the general's two advisors joined the group. The Police Department Glee Club sang the National Anthem to the accompaniment of the Police Department band.

Mayor O'Dwyer described General Clay as "an illustrious soldier-statesman who stands before the world as an American symbol of the defense of freedom." He told the crowd that "Russia's agreement to lift the Berlin blockade had been a vindication of General Clay's policies and a tribute to the success of the Allied airlift." The mayor then placed the city's Medal of Honor around the general's neck and presented him with a scroll. It commemorated his skillful leadership as General Eisenhower's deputy at the end of the war and as Military Governor of the US Occupied Zone. General Clay's command organized and controlled the Berlin Airlift that brought food, medicine, and needed supplies to the population of West Berlin after the Communists had closed the roads and stopped trains running through the Russian-occupied Zone.

The general spoke of the airlift and noted that through its work, the two million people of West Berlin had come closer to America. He compared their feeling of joy and relief at the arrival of supplies to the joy and pleasure he felt at the outpouring of friendship to him and his family. Following the general's remarks, the Police

Department Glee Club serenaded him with a song titled "This is the Army, Mr. Clay," a parody of a popular song by Irving Berlin.

The general and his family next attended a luncheon at the Waldorf Astoria, attended by former President Herbert Hoover, who administered the civilian aspects of the airlift, as well as Dr. Ralph Bunche *(see: May 17, 1949)*, Bernard Baruch, General Walter Bedell Smith, and Admiral Thomas Kincaid. Many of those attending the luncheon spoke in praise of the general and his work.

Later that day General Clay and his wife flew to Washington, DC, on a military transport. He would remain on duty at the Pentagon until his retirement from the military became official on June 1. He then entered politics, serving as President Eisenhower's primary advocate to Congress regarding construction of the Interstate Highway System. General Clay later served in the Kennedy Administration as an advisor on European affairs and accompanied President Kennedy to Berlin when he made his famous "Ich bin ein Berliner" speech. General Clay died in April 1978 and is buried in the cemetery at West Point. Marking his grave is a stone memorial from the city of Berlin with a German inscription that says, "We thank the Preserver of our Freedom."

Monday, May 23, 1949:
Enrico Gaspar Dutra, President of Brazil

President Enrico Gaspar Dutra flew to New York City from Washington on May 20. While in the capital he met with President Harry Truman and Congressional leaders as his first stop on a two-week visit to the United States.

Under a cloudless blue sky and with brilliant sunshine, the parade honoring the Brazilian chief executive stepped off from Bowling Green shortly after noon. Army, Navy, and Marine Corps contingents served as an honor guard, followed by details from the Police and Fire Departments. The First Army Band provided music for the procession to City Hall.

Buildings along Broadway flew the green Brazilian flag along with that of the United States. The president, a former general and Minister of War, sat stiffly in the leading vehicle of a caravan of 20 cars carrying US and Brazilian dignitaries, business leaders from both countries, and family and friends of the chief executive. The parade had not gone far however when, inspired by the enthusiasm of the crowd, President Dutra stood and began to acknowledge the waves, cheers, and applause of the spectators. The stretch of Broadway across from Trinity Church included a group of people waving small Brazilian flags and he pointed to them and shouted to the group in Portuguese.

When the caravan arrived at City Hall, Mayor O'Dwyer greeted the president and led him to the raised speaker's stand while the National Anthems of both countries were played. The mayor then introduced Dutra to the more than 1,000 people assembled in the plaza. "We are more honored because you are the first Brazilian chief of state to visit" New York City since 1876, he said. The mayor was technically correct in this statement since Julio Prestes had only been President-elect when he had received a New York City welcome almost twenty years earlier *(see: June 11, 1930)*. The mayor welcomed him "as a friendly head of a great nation – a nation whose democracy you have rebuilt and strengthened."

President Dutra replied in Portuguese, his words translated by Major Vernon Walters. He said he was proud of the long solidarity between the two nations, adding that Brazil was a good neighbor and friend of the United States. Her army had fought in alongside American troops in Italy, and he himself had been one of the Brazilian generals in command. After the president's remarks, the military detachments in the parade circled the plaza and passed in review. President Dutra was then escorted to Fordham University where an honorary Doctor of Law degree was conferred on him by Reverend Laurence McGinley, president of the Jesuit-run university. The Brazilian's "fortitude, dignity, and Catholicity" were praised, and a citation from the school referred to him as an illustrious soldier and gallant leader.

The President's busy schedule for the day concluded with a dinner reception at the Waldorf Astoria where he was presented with the Gold Insignia award of the Pan American Society. Once more his military and civilian leadership was cited. President Dutra joined US President Truman and Mexican President Miguel Alemán as recipients of this award. The next morning, he attended yet another reception at the Waldorf for business leaders looking to invest in Brazil. Finally, he was the guest of a reception later that day hosted by the National Coffee Association at the Plaza Hotel, attended by almost 600 Brazilian-born residents of New York City and the surrounding area. Following this event, President Dutra flew to Chattanooga, where he inspected the Tennessee Valley Authority in hopes of duplicating such an endeavor in his own country.

President Dutra remained in office until the end of his term in 1951. He never ran for re-election even though his name was constantly put forward as a possible candidate. He died in Rio de Janeiro in 1974 at the age of 91.

Thursday, August 11, 1949:
Elpidio Quirino, President of the Philippines

President Elpidio Quirino received the customary New York City ticker tape welcome under a relentlessly hot sun. Manila, the capital of his nation, was enjoying a balmy 75-degree day, but New York thermometers registered more than 20 degrees higher. Wearing a white linen suit, the President of the Philippines stepped off an official plane at LaGuardia Airport and was greeted by the First Army band playing the anthems of the United States and the Philippines. Mr. Quirino had been Vice President until the death of Manual Rojas, the first president of the Philippines following the end of its commonwealth status. President Quirino was shown into an open top limousine by Grover Whalen, where he sat with the Philippine Consul General Joe Melancio and the provost marshal of the First Army, Colonel John Roosma. Close to 3,000 spectators cheered Quirino's arrival from Washington, where he had meetings with President Truman and State Department officials.

After the brief flight from Washington the president was taken from LaGuardia Airport to lower Broadway with an escort of 56 motorcycle police. A caravan of 10 vehicles followed, crossing the Triborough Bridge then continuing down the FDR Drive. Even in a New York heat wave more than 100,000 people lined the streets to watch the parade once it began from the Battery shortly after noon.

When President Quirino arrived at City Hall he frequently mopped his sweaty brow as Mayor O'Dwyer welcomed him to the city. Both men were facing re-election shortly, so they spoke briefly about their chances of winning. The mayor presented the president with a scroll proclaiming Quirino as an inspiration "to the friends of democracy in the Far East." The president accepted the welcome and scroll, then responded in English that he was overwhelmed by the city's hospitality. The reception then moved into City Hall, where fans provided cooling. Later that afternoon there was a luncheon and, in the evening, a dinner at the Waldorf Astoria

President Quirino remained in New York two more days before returning home. The 1949 election returned him to his nation's highest office, but the results of the election were challenged and called dishonest and unfair by many. His second term as president was plagued by attacks from Communist Huk guerrillas in parts of Elite and Luzon Provinces. His administration was criticized for numerous instances of graft and corruption. In 1953 he ran for a third term as president but was defeated.

Quirino's health had always been poor, having survived two stomach operations during his second term, and various heart difficulties. On February 29, 1956, he died of a heart attack at his home in Quezon City, Philippines and is buried in The Heroes Cemetery, Taguig City in Manila.

Friday, August 19, 1949: Connie Mack

He was born Cornelius McGillicuddy three days before Christmas, 1862, was played baseball as a teenager for his hometown team in East Brookfield, Massachusetts. His skills as a catcher won him promotion to minor league teams in Connecticut, before breaking into the major leagues with the Washington Nationals club in 1886. Three years later he jumped to the short-lived Players League, then signed with the Pittsburgh Pirates, remaining with them for the remainder of his 10-year playing career, primarily as catcher. During the last three years he served as player-manager and it was as manager that he gained his fame and reputation.

In 1901 he became manager, treasurer, and part owner of the American League's Philadelphia Athletics, and in later years he became full owner of that franchise. Connie Mack (as he was always called although he never legally changed his name) managed that team until the end of the 1950 season. During his long tenure he compiled a record of 3,582 wins and 3,814 losses. No other baseball manager has ever won more, lost more, or managed more games. He was the first manager to win five World Series titles and won consecutive championships on two separate occasions, 1910-1911 and 1929-1930. Not all the teams he managed were successful, however, and in 1916 his Philadelphia squad posted the dismal record of 36 wins and 117 losses. From 1915 to 1921 his team finished in last place each of those seven years.

Considering the long hostility between professional sports franchises from New York and Philadelphia, it seems ironic that he would be honored with a ticker tape parade. Since he was one of baseball's living legends, however, he was accorded one on a summer's afternoon before his team was scheduled to play the New York Yankees that evening.

The parade stepped off from the Battery shortly after noon. The caravan of cars that paraded up Broadway was surrounded by uniformed players of the Police Athletic League, and members of the Police, Fire, and Sanitation teams. Connie Mack rode in an open top car with Grover Whalen, former Yankee executive Edward Barrow and one of the owners of the NY Yankees, Del Webb. Additional cars carried members of the Yankees team: Joe DiMaggio, Joe Page, Johnny Liddell, Charlie Silvera, Tommy Henrich, Billy Johnson, and Allie Reynolds. None of the Philadelphia team marched; Mack had given strict instructions that they were to practice at Yankee Stadium instead. It was estimated that 300,000 people lined the parade route and another 10,000 were gathered at City Hall Park.

Declaring the following day (August 20) as "Connie Mack Day," Mayor William O'Dwyer presented Mack with a scroll that spoke of how his dignity and modesty were an inspiration to all who loved America's National Game. Referring to the rivalry between the two cities, the Mayor said, "There was a time when I hated Mr. Mack," then added that Mack's contributions to the game "recompensed us for the sorrow you gave us in 1911" when the Philadelphia Athletics defeated the New York Giants in the World Series.

True to his modest reputation, Mack replied that he was at a loss for words to express his gratitude for the large crowd that had come "to see the old man of baseball." Foregoing the usual post parade reception and luncheon, Connie Mack, players, owners, and baseball personalities moved to the Bronx to witness the game against the Yankees. The Athletics lost.

Mr. Mack retired from coach in 1950 and lived in Philadelphia until he died six years later. He was elected to the Baseball Hall of Fame in 1937.

Friday, September 16, 1949: 48 European Journalists

Ending a two-week tour across the United States, 48 journalists from 14 European countries were treated to a New York greeting. Guests of American Airlines, the group had already made quick visits to San Francisco, Los Angeles, San Diego, Fort Worth, Detroit, and Washington, to gain a better understanding of America and America's press.

They arrived at LaGuardia Airport at 11 o'clock and an hour later were at the Battery for the parade. Mayor O'Dwyer had proclaimed the day as "Freedom of the Press Day." In the schedule of their busy day, they were the honorees of a ticker tape parade, took a boat ride through New York Harbor escorted by a police helicopter, received an unofficial salute from the British cruise *Glasgow* visiting New York, and attended a reception at the Waldorf.

Mayor O'Dwyer welcomed the publishers, editors, and writers who made up the group, then introduced them to the more than 1,000 guests in City Hall Park. He presented each journalist with a bronze medallion bearing the city's seal. A 49th would be mailed to a Danish writer who was forced to leave the group in Detroit and return home because of a family emergency. Aided by Grover Whalen, the mayor also gave the journalists a certificate of "exceptional public service" extended "with heartfelt gratitude and deep appreciation of the people of the City of New York." Speaking for the group, Frank Geary, editor of Dublin's *Irish Independent*, noted that their reception in New York was "easily the best of any the delegation had thus far received." A number of journalists reciprocated with gifts for the Mayor, including a hand-woven tapestry from Norway, a clock from Switzerland, and pottery from Sweden. Following the ceremony at City Hall, they sailed on a Port Authority boat from the foot of the Battery up the East River to 42nd Street. A police helicopter hovered overhead as the boat passed beneath the Brooklyn Bridge and remained above them for the duration of the cruise.

Speaking at the reception at the Waldorf later that day, the mayor told the invited guests, "Some of the men you see on this platform know what suppression means. Some know what it is to have a military tyrant censor a nation's press." He gestured to the European journalists and hoped that they had noticed the "temple of peace now rising that will house the United Nations." Other speakers included Edwin Friendly, President of the American Newspaper Publishers Association; Howard Cullman, Chairman of the Port Authority; C. R. Smith, President of American Airlines; Benjamin Cohen, Assistant Secretary-General of the UN; and Mr. Whalen.

Responding for the Europeans was Reider Lunde, writer with Oslo Norway's *Aftenposten*. He said that they could return to their homes and say that they had seen "a free press, an undominated press." He brought cheers from the group when he said in almost-perfect English that the letters UN might stand not only for the United Nations but for "united newspapermen from around the world."

On the following morning the journalists began returning to their homes in Ireland, Denmark, Sweden, Great Britain, Switzerland, France, Germany, Portugal, Norway, Belgium, Italy, Netherlands, Greece, and Luxembourg.

The Association of Foreign Press Correspondents was formed in 1917, to foster improved communication with the US government, which at the time had just entered World War I. In 1943, a sister organization was started based in Hollywood, which soon launched the Golden Globe Awards. In the century since its founding, a lot has changed in the world of journalism, but the Association remains dedicated to providing opportunity, assistance and fellowship to its members.

Tuesday, October 4, 1949:
Raymond A. Garbarina American Legion Post

The first National Championship competition of the American Legion Post's Drums and Bugle Corps took place in Philadelphia, Pennsylvania, in August 1949. The winner was the Raymond A, Garbarina Post, Number 1523 of Morningside Heights, and the city celebrated with a ticker tape parade to honor them. The Post takes its name from Army Private Raymond Garbarina, who was killed in Europe in November 1944. His parents and his older brother, seated in a convertible, accompanied the Corps up the Canyon of Heroes.

The parade started up Broadway shortly after noon on a cloudy early fall day. The procession was led by the New York City Fire Department Band and included bands from other American Legion Posts located in New York City. But according to spectators, the Raymond A. Garbarina Post's Drum and Bugle Corps outplayed them all. Ticker tape sailed from skyscrapers, though police spoke of the crowd as being among the smallest in history.

At City Hall, City Council President Vincent Impellitteri read words of welcome from Mayor O'Dwyer who could not attend the event due to a prior commitment. Deputy Mayor John Bennett presented the Corps a certificate of "distinguished and exceptional service."

Between its formation in 1947 and 1951, the Corps competed in 41 competitions, winning 38 of them. Late in 1949 they adopted the name of the Garbarina Skyliners, later changed to the Skyliners Drum and Bugle Corps. In 1951 one of the Corps' members, John Mazurkas, died as a result of illness received while serving in the Marines in the Pacific Theater. The Post's name was changed shortly afterward to the Garbarina-Mazarkos Post. Because of declining membership, the post relocated to Garfield, New Jersey, in 1990. It was inactive from 2007-2013, but was revived in 2014 and moved to Scranton, Pennsylvania, where it continues to be active in Drum Corps Association competitions.

A Drum and Bugle Corps is part of the Post and often appears at New York parades such as those on St. Patrick's Day and Thanksgiving, as well as at patriotic functions in New York and New Jersey.

Monday, October 17, 1949:
Jawaharlal Nehru, Prime Minister of India

Pandit Jawaharlal Nehru was in the United States for a two-week goodwill visit. He spent the first week meeting with President Truman, Cabinet members, and members of Congress in Washington. He was a close disciple of Mahatma Gandhi, a lifelong advocate for the independence of India from British rule. Nehru's years of struggle in this cause bore fruit two years earlier when, on August 15, 1947, he raised the flag of an independent India in New Delhi. Following his week in Washington, where he spoke eloquently and passionately regarding non-violence, an end to the arms race, and his hope for peace in the world, he arrived in New York the day before the parade.

October 17 was a sunny and brisk autumn day. The Indian Prime Minister stood in an open vehicle for the ride up Broadway through the Canyon of Heroes. He wore a white Congress cap and an *achkan,* an Indian long coat. For additional warmth a dark overcoat, unbuttoned, lay across his shoulders. He shared the car with Grover Whalen, Chairman of the Reception Committee, and Mrs. Vijaya Laksmi Pandit, the Indian Ambassador to the United States. Escorting the Prime Minister and his party were the First Army Band and the Band of the Police Department. Motorcycle police led the procession, which included detachments of the Air Force, Army, Marine Corps, and Navy, plus members of the Police, Fire, and Sanitation Departments. Nehru's vehicle was followed by another open car, filled with photographers. A dozen sedans containing City, State, and Federal officials followed the press vehicle.

The parade commenced shortly after noon and the Prime Minister waved, smiling and pointing to the blizzard of ticker tape that fell from the building along the route. American and Indian flags were displayed along the entire route. At Liberty Street the procession came to a brief halt caused by a disturbance ahead on Broadway. Mr. Whalen suggested that the Prime Minister turn to face the cameramen in the following vehicle and for the next few moments until the parade resumed, Mr. Nehru posed, smiling and waving.

Mayor O'Dwyer received the Prime Minister at City Hall, presenting him with the city's Gold Medal. The mayor expressed his wishes that, thanks to the efforts of a man like the Prime Minister "one day we will be a free and peaceful world." Acknowledging the welcome he had received, the Prime Minister said that he was "a simple man from a country of simple ways." He concluded by saying he was "gratified and overwhelmed by this friendly reception."

Immediately after the reception in City Hall Park, the motorcade continued north to Columbia University. In Low Memorial Library at Columbia, Nehru received an honorary Doctor of Law Degree. After the degree was granted, Columbia University President Dwight Eisenhower shook the Indian statesman's hand vigorously. The Prime Minister responded to the award by speaking for the cause of peace. He regretted the growth of the ideological opposition between east and west. "The very process of Marshaling the world into two separate camps precipitates the conflict which it has sought to avoid," he said, expressing his belief that if the energy, talent, and resources used to compete in a military race were spent instead in the cause of peace and non-violence, all of mankind would prosper.

That evening Pandit Nehru and members of his party were the guests of General and Mrs. Eisenhower for a private dinner at their residence in Columbia University. Questioned by journalists regarding India's feelings towards Great Britain, Nehru stated that he was proud of how cordial relations were between the two nations since

India had been part of the British Empire for so long. Asked about relations between India and Pakistan he admitted that they were tense and potentially explosive.

Nehru returned to India after a week of meetings and sightseeing in New York. He ruled as Prime Minister until 1964. Although both the United States and the Soviet Union repeatedly attempted to ally with India, Nehru continued his policy of non-alignment. His government recognized Communist China and led the movement to have it admitted to the United Nations. During the Korean conflict he refused to brand China as an aggressor, but India did send small medical and logistical support to United Nations forces. In the Kashmir, he reneged on his promise to hold plebiscites in 1948 and 1953, and the Indian-Pakistani friction in that region continues to this day.

He suffered a heart attack while returning from a visit to Kashmir and died on May 28, 1964. Following Hindu rites, his body was cremated on the banks of the Yamuna River, Delhi, witnessed by hundreds of thousands of mourners. Prime Minister Nehru was the father of Indira Gandhi and the grandfather of Rajiv Gandhi, the third and sixth Prime Ministers of India, respectively.

Monday, November 21, 1949:
Mohammed Reza Pahlevi, Shah of Iran

Following meetings with United States Government officials in Washington, DC, Mohammed Reza Pahlevi, Shah (King) of the 6,000-year-old kingdom of Iran (known as Persia until 1935) visited New York to address the United Nations and the Council of Foreign Relations. On a sunny and mild afternoon the 30-year-old Shah, dressed in morning clothes with black jacket and gray striped trousers, shared an open vehicle with Grover Whalen, Chairman of the Reception Committee, and Hussein Ala, Iranian envoy to the United States.

Leading the parade were 42 motorcycle police followed by a Military Police detachment from Governors Island and the Police Department Honor Guard bearing American and Iranian flags. Directly in front of the Shah's vehicle marched the Police Department Band. Completing the parade were a total of 19 other vehicles carrying the Shah's staff and aides, State Department officials, State and City dignitaries, followed by the Fire Department, First Army, and Air Force Bands. The customary blizzard of torn paper, confetti, and ticker tape drifted down, as the Shah conversed with Mr. Whalen and only occasionally responded to cheers. As the parade neared City Hall, the Woolworth Building seemed to catch his attention and he pointed at it with one hand while shielding his eyes from the sun with the other. Mr. Whalen explained to the Shah that the building was New York's tallest skyscraper from its completion in 1913 until 1930, when the Chrysler Building surpassed it.

The car carrying the Shah turned into City Hall Plaza shortly before 12:30. Mayor O'Dwyer met the Iranian ruler as he exited the vehicle and a short time later the Shah was introduced to more than 300 guests crowded into the City Council Chambers. Mayor O'Dwyer spoke of the monarch as a friend of free nations. Referring to the Shah's efforts to modernize his nation, the mayor said, "His patience, his love for his people, and his outstanding courage led him to fight for constitutional authority to bring about reforms that have earned him the affection and loyalty of his people." The Shah's response to his reception compared Iran to Manhattan. "Except for our mountains," he said, "nothing in Iran is as tall as the gigantic buildings which, in all their magnificence, give New York its most characteristic aspect." The ceremony at City Hall was concluded when Mayor O'Dwyer presented the Shah with a certificate citing his "distinguished and exceptional public service for warding off outside foes…and promoting social justice."

The next stop was a luncheon at the Waldorf Astoria where a serious error had narrowly been avoided. Sugar-cured ham had been on the menu until it was learned that Islamic Law forbids eating pork. A substitute of beef tongue was quickly provided. The Shah addressed those attending the luncheon and said that he "was not an Oriental potentate, but a modern liberal constitutional monarch whose powers, if a comparison might be offered, are somewhat less than those exercised by the King of Sweden." He continued by saying that although his visit to the United States was not entirely for economic reasons, he would welcome more American investment in his nation. Without mentioning any other nation by name, he referred to a potentially hostile neighbor that was greedy for Iran's oil resources. The Shah added that he had asked President Truman for economic aid to modernize Iran's military.

While speaking to the Council on Foreign Relations later that day, he repeated that message. The following morning, in addressing the United Nations, he urged the nations of the world to work harder to bring peace and security to the world. "Give us the future. Give us the inner assurance of peace," he challenged the members of the international organization.

The Shah returned to Iran soon after speaking to the United Nations. He had come to power during the Second World War when combined British-Soviet pressure forced his father, Reza Shah, to abdicate because of his pro-German views. Once the war ended the Shah began to make strides in modernizing many aspects of the Iranian economy, industry, and culture. This caused increasing alienation among the more traditional members of the country, which would dramatically change the course of Iran in years to come. The Shah returned to the United States in 1962 and received a second ticker tape parade *(see: April 16, 1962)*. He is one of only four foreign leaders so honored, along with Haile Selassie of Ethiopia, Charles de Gaulle of France, and Alcide De Gasperi of Italy.

Woolworth Building

Towering over the southwest corner of City Hall Park is the 55-story Woolworth Building. The original plans called for a smaller building, but company founder F.H. Woolworth insisted the building must exceed the Metropolitan Life Building, then the world's tallest, leading one contractor to remark that "beyond a doubt his ego was a thing of enormous size." When it opened in 1913, the 792-foot-high Woolworth Building was the tallest building in the world and would be until the Chrysler Building opened in 1931.

Built as a 30-story base surmounted by a 25-story tower and spire, the building's façade is covered in terracotta and decorated with Gothic arches, gold tracery and coats of arms. The pyramidal rooftop was originally decorated in gold and has an observation deck, which was closed for security reasons after the bombing of Pearl Harbor in 1941. The ornately decorated lobby with a ceiling decorated with patterned glass mosaics is often considered one of the most spectacular works of early 1900s design. →

The building was owned by the Woolworth Company until 1998, though the company's use shrank over the years from 25 floors to only 4. After several major renovations over the years, the building was converted to residential use in 2015, though few units have been sold to date, and most of the building is occupied by commercial tenants, including the NYC Law Department.

Monday, April 17, 1950:
Gabriel González Videla, President of Chile

President Videla's first stop on his two-week tour of the Unites States was New York City, where he was presented with the city's traditional ticker tape welcome on a bright and mild spring day. Escorted from the Plaza Hotel downtown by a squad of motorcycle policeman, the president and his caravan of 12 vehicles stepped off from Bowling Green just after noon.

Marching along with the president were two bands (one from the Brooklyn Navy Yard and the second from the 581st Air Group based at Mitchel Air Force Base on Long Island), detachments of the three branches of the armed forces, and a contingent of New York City police. Police estimated the crowd of onlookers at 150,000 along the parade route with another 10,000 crowded into City Hall Plaza. Cheers greeted the president and his official parade as a blizzard of ticker tape floated down from the buildings along the route. Chilean flags fluttered from buildings, along with an occasional Texas flag displayed in error because of its similarity. The open limousine carrying the president also contained the President's wife, Rosa, and John Coleman, former President of the New York Stock Exchange, substituting for Grover Whalen, who was absent on business in Albany.

Mayor O'Dwyer welcomed President Videla at City Hall, reminding the crowd of spectators of Videla's influence at the San Francisco Conference in 1945, where his efforts led other Latin American countries to support the formation of the United Nations. Presented with a scroll honoring his achievements, Videla called New York the "capital of the United Nations" and spoke of his country's history as a home for people of diverse backgrounds, much like New York. His words were translated from Spanish by the Chilean Under-Secretary of State, Manuel Trucco.

Shortly before the end of the outdoor welcome and remarks, about a dozen protestors broke through the barricade on the east side of City Hall Park, shouting "down with the murderer of the Chilean people." The group was quickly broken up by uniformed officers and President Videla took no notice of the brief interruption. The group's protest referred to the Chilean government's crackdown on left-wing groups, ranging from liberals to communists. The Communist party in Chile had been declared illegal the year before and many of its leaders had been arrested and their whereabouts were unknown.

Later, inside the City Council Chambers, President Videla presented a large black sombrero and a colorful serape to Mayor O'Dwyer, who donned them both to the amusement of those attending the reception as well as for the benefit of photographers. Interviewed by reporters, the Chilean leader spoke of the freedom of the press in his country, a statement that was challenged by some interviewers. Their comments went unanswered.

Before the President continued to Washington for a meeting with President Truman, he was the guest of honor at a banquet at the Waldorf. During the banquet he received an honorary degree from Columbia University. More protestors appeared at the hotel.

Videla had originally been elected president of Chile in 1946 with heavy support from the left, including from the then-legal Communist Party. Not long after being sworn into office he began to distance himself from left-wing support and, by 1948, had adopted strong right-wing nationalist causes. No evidence has ever been found to indicate why he made such a drastic political *volte-face*, but it has long been hinted that the primary factor was pressure from the United States in the form of financial and material aid tapping Chile's large copper reserves.

After leaving the presidency, Videla remained active in politics and was instrumental in the overthrow of Socialist President Salvador Allende by Augusto Pinochet's 1973 coup. Videla died of cardiac arrest in Santiago, Chile, in 1980.

Friday, April 28, 1950: Admiral Thomas Kinkaid

Admiral Thomas Kinkaid retired from the US Navy in 1950 at the age of 62. He had served 46 years in the Navy, commanding battleships in both world wars, and since 1946 had been Commander of the Eastern Sea Frontier and the Atlantic Reserve Fleet, headquartered at the Brooklyn Navy Yard. Following his formal retirement in a naval ceremony on the flight deck of the aircraft carrier *Enterprise*, the admiral's years of service were honored with a ticker tape parade.

After turning over his command he was escorted from the carrier by members of his staff while the ship's band played "Anchors Away." He entered a Navy car waiting on the pier and was driven to Bowling Green for New York's farewell. Army and Navy bands and contingents from the Army, Navy, and Marine Corps moved up Broadway precisely at noon while the Admiral, now riding in one of the city's open limousines, stood and waved to the smaller than usual lunch-hour crowds lining the route.

Mayor O'Dwyer met the Admiral at City Hall and presented him with the city's Medal of Service, thanking the seaman for his years of faithful service to the Navy which began when he was 16 years old. The Admiral expressed his thanks to the city for the parade in his honor. Asked how he intended to spend his well-earned retirement, he responded by saying he planned to do quite a bit of cruising and fishing on his sailboat moored at Annapolis, Maryland.

In the afternoon Admiral Kinkaid and his wife, Helen, joined the mayor and a group of city and state politicians at a luncheon in City Hall. Later that day the couple boarded a train to Washington, DC.

Kinkaid's combat experience during World War II included action at the Battles of the Coral Sea and Midway where he led a cruiser squadron. Promoted to Admiral with his flag flying on *Enterprise*, he was engaged in the Solomon Islands and the Aleutians campaigns. With no previous carrier experience, his actions in the Solomons were criticized in private but his close relationships with senior naval officers in Washington and elsewhere sheltered him from public criticism. He defeated Japanese naval units at the Battle of Surigao Strait in October 1944 but was late in moving his force to aid Admiral Oldendorf in Leyte Gulf. Admiral Halsey blamed himself for not ordering Kinkaid into action, but Kinkaid's lack of initiative was noted, and he held no additional combat commands in the final months of the War.

The retired admiral served on the American Battle Monuments Commission and represented the Navy at the dedication of a number of military cemeteries in Europe,

Australia, and the Philippines. He died at Bethesda Naval Hospital in November 1972 and is buried in Arlington National Cemetery.

Monday, May 8, 1950:
Liaquat Ali Khan, Prime Minister of Pakistan

The first Prime Minister of the young nation of Pakistan, Liaquat Ali Khan, visited the United States at the personal invitation of President Truman. Pakistan was separated from India in 1947 when Great Britain's colonial rule in the sub-continent ceased. After meeting with President Truman, the Prime Minister and his wife visited New York City. His day began with a two-hour visit of the grounds of the United Nations at Lake Success, New York.

Accompanied by his wife, Ra'ana Liaquat Ali, he rode up the Canyon of Heroes in an open car on a sunny spring day. A crowd of fewer than 25,000 watched the parade. The First Army band escorted the Prime Minister along with military detachments and groups from the Police and Fire Departments.

Mayor O'Dwyer welcomed the leader of the nation of more than 80 million people. Speaking in the Council Chambers, the mayor said "Yours is a new nation from an ancient culture. Ours is an older country whose culture is new but the desire for freedom is common to us both," the mayor stressed, "Tell your people emphatically we are their admiring friends and that we join them in their hope for future peace."

Presented with a scroll commemorating his visit and celebrating his nation's independence, the Prime Minister thanked the mayor and the city for the welcome and well wishes. He joked that he and his wife would like to change the words of a well-known expression to "we came, we saw, and we were conquered."

That evening Mr. Ali Khan was the guest at a dinner at the Waldorf. Following the meal, he spoke to the audience of more than 300 people about the dispute over Kashmir between his nation and India. The United Nations had promised to oversee a plebiscite in the region and no date had yet been set. The Prime Minister was "not happy over the delay." He warned that Pakistan's relations with India had been tense ever since the partition of British India.

The following morning Mr. Ali Khan received an honorary degree from Columbia University presented to him in Low Memorial Library by the university's president, Dwight Eisenhower. The citation accompanying the degree spoke of the leadership Mr. Ali Khan had shown both prior to and since Pakistan's independence and for the hopes for the future of his nation. The Pakistani Prime Minister replied that hope for peace throughout the world rested in the hands of "the great nations such as yours" along with the new emerging nations.

He ended his day by visiting the *New York Times* as a guest of publisher Arthur Hays Sulzberger and General Manager Julius Ochs Adler, followed by dinner at Town Hall sponsored by the Foreign Policy Association.

The Prime Minister returned to a Pakistan troubled by open fighting between the minority Hindu population (with the backing of India) and the majority Muslim population. When the United Nations failed to provide a date for a vote to end the division of the Kashmir state, India and Pakistan grew closer to open war. Tensions were cooled and war avoided by a meeting between Mr. Ali Khan and Jawaharlal Nehru, Prime Minister of India. Groups in both countries, however, were displeased by the compromises made by the two leaders. While in the United States, the Prime Minister had been urged not to become too closely allied with Russia. His attempts to steer a neutral course angered many in his government and military.

On October 16, 1951, the Prime Minister was shot in the chest by an Afghan national while addressing a public rally in Rawalpindi. He died instantly. His assassin was shot and killed by police and the motive for the assassination has never been established, although evidence pointed to military involvement. His remains were placed in Mazar-e-Quaid mausoleum in Karachi, Pakistan.

Tuesday, May 9, 1950:
Fernando Casas Alemán, Governor of Mexico City

Mayor William O'Dwyer vacationed in Mexico in 1949 and was very impressed by the hospitality and friendliness of the people. In particular, he was taken by the warmth extended to him by the Governor of Mexico City, Fernando Casas Alemán (his title of Governor is equivalent to that of mayor in the United States). To show his gratitude, New York City's mayor invited Alemán to attend the annual Conference of Mayors scheduled for May 1950, and assured Alemán that he would receive New York's usual ticker tape welcome.

May 9 was a bright spring day, and 100,000 cheering spectators lined the route from the Battery to City Hall, many extending their lunch hours when the parade started a half hour late. Music was provided by the Fire Department Band which played tunes from both the United States and Mexico. Some of those marching wore traditional Mexican costumes. The open car which Mayor O'Dwyer and Governor Alemán rode in was showered with confetti and ticker tape. Also riding in the car was his second wife Elizabeth, attending her first ticker tape parade since her marriage to the mayor in December 1949, as well as Mrs. Alemán and the Governor's 19-year-old son and 17-year-old daughter. Small groups of spectators cheered and shouted "*bienvenido*" as the parade moved to City Hall.

At City Hall, the mayor officially welcomed his Mexican counterpart and presented him with the New York City Gold Medal and a scroll for distinguished and exceptional service in "improving conditions of life in Mexico City." The mayor commented that he had cut short his vacation to Mexico City the year before because of a threatened bus strike. He joked by saying "the next time I go there I will take as insurance Señor Miguel Quill," referring to Mike Quill, founder and president of the Transport Workers of America Union, who seemed constantly at war with New York City in support of his union's members. The Mayor's words were translated to Spanish by John Coleman, Acting Chairman of the Reception Committee. Governor Alemán replied to Mayor O'Dwyer, thanking him for the city's hospitality and cordiality. He spoke of the desire for continued close friendship for the two great American cities that he and Mayor O'Dwyer represented. His words were translated from Spanish by the Mexican Consul General, Lelo de Larrea.

Following lunch at the University Club, hosted by the Pan American Society. Governor Alemán and Bronx Borough President James Lyons attended a baseball game at Yankee Stadium, while Mrs. O'Dwyer and Mrs. Alemán visited the Hall of Fame at Fordham University, the Bronx Zoo, and the Bronx Botanical Gardens.

Governor Alemán returned to Mexico following the Mayor's Conference *(see: May 10, 1950)*. He died in Mexico City in 1968 and the community in which he resided was renamed Casas Alemán in his honor.

Wednesday, May 10, 1950: Ten Foreign Mayors Attending 18th Annual US Conference of Mayors

For the third day in a row, New York City staged a ticker tape parade. Following parades honoring the Prime Minister of Pakistan and the Governor of Mexico City, it is probably not surprising that only about 80,000 people lined the Canyon of Heroes to welcome mayors of ten foreign cities attending the US Conference of Mayors, being held at the Waldorf Astoria beginning May 11.

The mayors attending the conference and feted in the parade were Fernand Cottier of Geneva, Switzerland; Eero Rydman, of Helsinki, Finland; Salvatore Rebecchini, of Rome, Italy; George MacLean of St Boniface in Manitoba, Canada; Julio de Benedetti of Buenos Aires, Argentina; Andre Louis, of Port au Prince, Haiti; Wilhelm Kaisen, of Bremen, Germany; Jose Manuel Cuellar, of Bogota, Colombia; and Fernando Casas Alemán of Mexico City, the only person to appear in ticker tape parades on consecutive days *(see: May 9, 1950)*. The tenth mayor, James Kealoha, was technically not foreign since he was the mayor of Hilo, Hawaii, which was then a territory of the United States.

Music and entertainment for the parade was provided by the Police Department Band of Mexico City. Since Mayor William O'Dwyer had vacationed in Mexico the previous year, when the parade reached City Hall the band played a Mexican folk song that His Honor had called his favorite tune, *"Madre del Coredro"* ("Mother of the Lamb.")

Mayor O'Dwyer escorted the visiting foreign mayors into the City Council Chamber where they received a standing ovation from Council members and invited guests, including the President of the Conference, Mayor Cooper Green of Birmingham, Alabama; John Adikes, Chairman of the Reception Committee; and Rear Admiral O. M. Reed, representing the military's Civilian Mobilization Committee.

The next morning the mayors attended the opening session of the Conference of Mayors.

Friday, June 2, 1950: Fourth Marine Division Association Reunion

A bright spring morning welcomed the members of the Fourth Marine Division Association who gathered at Bowling Green for the highpoint of their annual reunion, being held at the Hotel New Yorker. More than 4,000 of the association's members had gathered in the city to celebrate its third annual reunion. Slightly more than 800 would take part in the parade.

The march up Broadway began exactly at noon to the enjoyment of thousands of lunchtime spectators. The usual shower of ticker tape, bits of colored paper, and confetti rained down, as mounted police officers led the parade, each officer carrying a lance with a fluttering police department pennant. Directly behind them was a group of Marine Corps ambulances, each carrying a disabled veteran of the division. The main body of marching Marine veterans followed behind the parade's Grand Marshal, Brigadier General Edwin Pollock, President of the Association. Veterans from the division's separate commands marched together in uniform, each battalion's colors proudly displaying service and combat ribbons. In keeping with their Marine Corps training and tradition, the commands kept well-disciplined distances. Wearing red tunics with gold buttons and braid, the Association's band provided the beat.

The next contingent of 400 veterans marched, some in civilian clothes, others in summer khakis similar to those worn five years earlier when the division invaded Iwo

Jima. A group from the Brooklyn Navy Yard Band followed along with a detachment of Marines on duty at the Yard's Marine Barracks. The 165th Infantry Regiment of the New York National Guard, which had fought side by side with the Fourth Marine Division on the island of Saipan in the summer of 1944, was represented, as were the First and 19th Infantry Battalions and the 14th Signal Corps Company. Bands from the Sanitation and Police Departments completed the marching contingents.

Mayor O'Dwyer welcomed the veterans to the city and introduced the Marine Corps commandant, General Clifton Cates. He spoke of the division's history, its formation early in the Second World War and its combat on Tinian, Rio Namur, Saipan, and Iwo Jima. Twelve of the division's members had been awarded the nation's highest military award, the Medal of Honor, four for their actions on Rio Namur, two on Saipan, and six on Iwo Jima.

General Cates commanded the Fourth Division on Tinian and Iwo Jima. He answered recent critics' comments that since the end of the Second World War, the Marine Corps had outlived its usefulness. He said, "The Marine Corps may look to the past for its inspiration, but I can assure you it looks to the future for its justification." Cheers punctuated his remarks. Following the parade, veterans returned to the closing meeting of the association and then to their homes.

Slightly more than three weeks after the parade, Communist North Korean forces invaded South Korea, and the US Marines continued to justify their existence. Some of the men who marched in the parade as members of the Marine Corps Reserve returned to combat, exchanging tropical khakis for winter coats and gloves. Marines have subsequently seen combat in Vietnam, Iraq, and Afghanistan.

The Fourth Marine Division Association met annually until 2015, when it held its "Final Muster" at Camp Lejeune in North Carolina. The deactivation ceremony included the furling of the association's colors and was attended by 77 veterans of the division.

Friday, August 4, 1950:
Robert Gordon Menzies, Prime Minister of Australia

Robert Gordon Menzies, Prime Minister of Australia, had planned a 10-day visit to the United States prior to the outbreak of the Korean War in June 1950, but the war influenced his visit. What was meant to be a good-will trip developed into a military strategy discussion, and he spent the first five days in Washington where he met with President Truman, members of Congress, and military leaders. The final five days of his visit were spent in New York City.

Prime Minister Menzies was treated to a ticker tape parade on a hazy, hot and humid day that is typical for New York in August. The gray-haired Prime Minister stood in an open vehicle, as bands from the Army and Navy set the pace along the route and detachments of the Army, Navy, Air Force, and Marine Corps marched as guards of honor. Exactly at 12:05 the parade began, and moments after leaving Bowling Green, a shower of confetti and ticker tape swirled through the Canyon of Heroes. Waving and cheering spectators lined both sides of Broadway, and the Prime Minister smiled and waved back, obviously enjoying his welcome.

At City Hall Mayor O'Dwyer welcomed the Australian with a hardy handshake and introduced him as a true friend of democracy to the crowd gathered in City Hall Plaza. The Mayor then presented the visiting Prime Minister with a scroll for long and faithful distinguished public service.

206

A luncheon sponsored by the American Australian Association followed at the University Club on West 54th Street, where the Prime Minister addressed the group and spoke of the partnership of "independence and inter-dependence" necessary among democratic nations to resist the "menace of Communism." Australian naval and air support had already joined the fighting on the Korean peninsula, and when Menzies stated that he had promised President Truman substantial assistance on the ground as well, the entire audience rose in applause. "This is not a time for sitting back. It is a time when individual man-effort must be greatly expended." He expressed admiration for the speed by which the United States had answered the challenge of the invasion of South Korea. "This sort of thing must stop here and now because it has to stop sooner or later," he said to another rousing chorus of applause.

Mr. Edward Robbins, President of the American Australian Association, praised the Prime Minister for his words. Speaking directly to Mr. Menzies, Robbins said, "All America was stirred by your announcement that Australian troops would fight side by side with troops of the United States in Korea."

While in New York, Mr. Menzies spoke at the United Nations, and also visited Hyde Park, New York, home of the late President Franklin Roosevelt, as a guest of Eleanor Roosevelt.

Menzies returned to Australia and kept his word, sending ground forces to Korea. More than 17,000 members of Australia's army, navy and air force saw service in Korea. Casualties included 316 killed, 1,216 wounded, and 29 captured. Only the Republic of South Korea, United States, United Kingdom, and Turkey sustained more casualties during the conflict.

Menzies served as Australian Prime Minister twice, briefly in 1940-1941 and again from 1949-1966, for a total of 18 years, 5 months, and 12 days, longer than any other individual. During those years Australia made huge economic and industrial progress. He was knighted by Queens Elizabeth II in 1962 and resigned on Australia Day, January 26, 1966, after 38 years in public service as member of the Australian Parliament and Prime Minister. Upon retiring he was appointed Chancellor of Melbourne University. He was briefly scholar-in-residence at the University of Virginia but dropped from public view after being debilitated by a stroke in 1971. He suffered another major stroke in Melbourne and died there on May 15, 1978.

Tuesday, August 22, 1950:
Lieutenant General Clarence Huebner

After 40 years of Army service, Lieutenant General Clarence Huebner was retiring. He had been the last Military Governor of the American Occupied Zone of Germany and was now retiring as commander of the V Corps in Germany. The Korean War had begun less than two months earlier and, because of the military's restrictions on news of the movements of naval vessels, the general's arrival was unheralded until the transport ship *General Maurice Ross* anchored in New York Harbor. But the general's return to the United States was known to certain individuals in New York, and a welcome parade awaited him.

The general was met by Grover Whalen, Chairman of the Mayor's Reception Committee and Major General Willard Wyman, First Army Chief-of-Staff, who would be replacing General Huebner as V Corps commander. The three men rode up Broadway in an open car bearing a four-stag flag reflecting Huebner's rank, yet few spectators along the route knew who he was. Despite this, the usual noontime gathering of spectators stood along the route, possibly as many as 50,000, as swirling strands of ticker tape and confetti littered Broadway. The parade included a detachment from First Army Command, Fort Jay on Governors Island, and by details from the Police and Fire Departments, and the First Army Band.

It was not until the motorcade reached City Hall that the general's identity was made know to those congregated in City Hall Park. Mayor O'Dwyer introduced the general to the crowd and presented him with a scroll commending him for the successful occupation of Germany. The mayor told the spectators how General Huebner, just out of business college in 1910, had enlisted in the Army and been assigned to the 18th Infantry. Rising through the ranks, he was commissioned Lieutenant in 1916, saw combat in both world wars, and by 1943 was commander of the First Infantry Division, commonly known as the "Big Red One." Long years of staff duty followed, but in World War II he returned to the First Division as its commanding officer in 1943. His final service in occupied Germany was also mentioned.

Joined by his wife and daughter, General Huebner was guest of honor at a luncheon at the Metropolitan Club that afternoon. Later that evening the general and his family attended a cocktail party at the Officer's Club on Governors Island.

In September 1951, the retired general was named director of the New York State Civil Defense Commission. He was distrustful of the Soviet Union and its Communist allies and vigorously advocated the construction of fallout shelters on a large scale. Before his retirement from the Civil Defense Commission in 1961 he stated that eventually the population of the United States would live in shelters "and would see the sunshine only by taking a calculated risk" because of Russia's nuclear capability. He died in 1972 in Washington, DC. Fortunately, his dire predictions of the future failed to come true.

Thursday, August 31, 1950:
William O'Dwyer, Mayor of New York City

New York City's 100th mayor, William O'Dwyer, was offered the position of Ambassador to Mexico by President Truman, who said the Mayor's experience and long-term connection with Mexican politicians (see: May 9, 1950) would be helpful. The mayor accepted and he received what no other New York City mayor has ever been given: a farewell parade.

On the morning of August 31, Mayor O'Dwyer presented his written resignation to Charles Preusse, First Assistant to the Corporate Counsel, who was instructed to turn it over to the City Clerk the following day, when the resignation would become official. The mayor then gave a farewell press conference at his official residence, Gracie Mansion, and swore in a handful of individuals to various positions. He was then driven downtown to the Battery escorted by a police motorcycle squad, where he and his wife Elizabeth stepped into an open limousine for the ride up the Canyon of Heroes. He shared the car with Grover Whalen, Chairman of the Mayor's Reception Committee. Mr. Whalen and the mayor had worked together in organizing and arranging almost 30 ticker tape parades since the mayor took office on January 1, 1946.

The city was suffering under an heat wave with no relief in sight as the parade began, and the forecast promised another day of hazy and hot humidity. The Police Department Band stepped out first, followed by detachments from Fort Jay and the Brooklyn Navy Yard. Members of the Police, Fire, and Sanitation Departments preceded the mayor's car. Bringing up the rear was the Police Department's pipe and drum corps band, in recognition of the mayor's birthplace, County Mayo, Ireland.

Estimates of between 250,000 to 330,000 spectators watched the motorcade but at least one newspaper account described the enthusiasm as "subdued." Ticker tape and streamers seemed to fall listlessly because of the humidity. As the parade moved up Broadway the mayor asked the car to stop often so he could shake hands or exchange a few words with recognized friends or associates.

Representatives of most city departments and agencies stood waiting at City Hall when the motorcade arrived. Close to 20,000 people had gathered in City Hall Park, some seated in a temporary grandstand, but the majority stood through the hour of speeches that followed. Not all tolerated the intense heat and humidity well, and more than two dozen spectators were treated for heat exhaustion or dehydration, including five policemen. Even Mayor O'Dwyer seemed distressed by the heat and the city's Hospital Commissioner, Dr. Edward Bernecker, spoke to him twice asking if he felt well enough to continue. His Honor assured the doctor that he did, and when he rose to speak, he seemed to have lost all signs of heat strain.

He explained that he was resigning as mayor only because of the president's insistence. "I go to undertake a job of vital importance to our nation's interest," he said. The mayor gave a brief summary of the achievements of his administration, especially those made by the City Council and the Board of Estimates. Then in a move that seemed to surprise many, he asked Grover Whalen to join him at the podium. He placed the city's Gold Medal of Honor around Mr. Whalen's neck, saying the award was given "in recognition of his 30 years of extraordinary public service to various Mayors as a volunteer creator of goodwill towards the city."

The final speaker of the afternoon was Vincent Impellitteri, City Council President, who would assume the office of Acting Mayor at 10 o'clock the following morning. Mr. Impellitteri presented Mayor O'Dwyer with a New York City flag as a keepsake to remind him of the city and his service there.

A motorcade to the Waldorf Astoria followed, where a luncheon was held, hosted by Grover Whalen and attended by various city officials. Notably absent was Brooklyn Borough President John Cashmore, who had recently been forced to quit his post as Kings County Democratic leader. Also absent was Frank Kenna, Republican Party leader from Queens County, who had called the mayor's resignation an act of abandonment.

That evening Mr. and Mrs. O'Dwyer made a quick visit to the residence of Cardinal Francis Spellman for a final chat and a blessing. They then boarded the El Centro train at Grand Central Terminal for the long cross-country trip to California, where they would visit with the mayor's brother before moving on to his post in Mexico City.

Irish-born William O'Dwyer had arrived in New York in 1910 at the age of 20. He became a policeman while studying law at night in Fordham University. Receiving his law degree, he built a successful practice in Brooklyn, became a judge in Kings County, and Brooklyn District Attorney in 1939. He was responsible for breaking up mob activity, including the syndicate known as "Murder, Inc." When World War II began, he enlisted, was commissioned Captain in the Adjutant-General's Department, and rose to the rank of Brigadier General as a member of the Allied Commission for Italy.

In late 1949 he was faced with a police corruption scandal in Kings County that involved his office. Less than a year later he resigned to take up his duties as Ambassador to Mexico. Corruption claims followed him south and he returned to New York to answer questions regarding his association with organized crime figures. He was not charged with any crimes and returned to Mexico, although several close allies were sentenced and received several prison sentences for extortion. A later investigation uncovered evidence that O'Dwyer may have accepted bribery money at Gracie Mansion. He resigned as Ambassador in 1952 but did not return to New York until 1960, still dogged by questions regarding past associations and dealings. He died in New York in 1964 and is buried in Arlington National Cemetery.

Tuesday, April 3, 1951: Vincent Auriol, President of France

The President of France, Vincent Auriol, arrived in New York after spending four days in Washington meeting with President Truman. The purpose of his visit was to strengthen ties between France and the United States. The day of the parade was overcast and chilly with a threat of rain. President Auriol was suffering from a cold, so when he and his wife joined Grover Whalen in an open vehicle from the trip from the Waldorf Astoria to Bowling Green, he sat with a heavy blanket wrapped around him.

An escort of 65 motorcycle police led him through Manhattan streets to the FDR Drive and downtown to Bowling Green, where the car carrying the French leader moved behind Navy and Marine Corps bands. An Army detachment marched ahead of the vehicle, and a number of other cars containing French and American officials formed a motorcade. Accompanied by a detachment of mounted police the parade moved up Broadway shortly after noon.

Because of his cold, President Auriol remained seated in the car and his wife, Michelle, acknowledged the reception they received. French and American flags flew from most of the buildings along the route, and the usual flurry of ticker tape descended on the motorcade. Police estimated the numbers of spectators at more than 100,000. An occasional cry of "*Vive la France*" rose from their ranks. Mrs. Auriol shouted "*merci*" as she stood, waving with one hand and holding her broad-brimmed white hat with the other.

Several thousand people were gathered in City Hall Plaza, but the official ceremonies were conducted in the Council Chamber. Grover Whalen introduced President Auriol and said that the president, his wife and son had all been members of the French Resistance during World War II. In his first ticker tape welcome since becoming mayor, Vincent Impellitteri presented the French president with a scroll that spoke of his visionary leadership doing so much to foster relationships between nations. The president was then awarded the city's Medal of Honor, and in return presented the mayor with the Order of Commander of the Legion of Honor. The mayor seemed embarrassed when the president kissed him on both cheeks.

"France, like you," President Auriol said, "hates regimes of oppression, and desires peace in freedom. Let the pessimists, the skeptics, and the defeatists observe in New York what has been created by free men with an unshakeable faith in human progress and the destiny of democracy." His voice rising in emotion, he ended his speech with "Long live New York! Long live the United States! Long live the friendship between New York and Paris! Long live the friendship between France and the United States!" His words, spoken in French and translated by an interpreter, were loudly cheered.

Following the City Hall reception, the French couple was driven back to the Waldorf Astoria where they were the guests at a luncheon hosted by Trygve Lie, Secretary General of the United Nations. The Chief Delegates of the UN member nations had been invited but noticeably absent were delegates from Communist nations. Mr. Auriol spoke of his hopes for peace and stated his belief that only the United Nations offered a way for the entire world to live in harmony and accord.

The next stop on President Auriol's schedule was Columbia University. There, in the Low Memorial Library, he was given an Honorary Degree in History by Dr. Grayson Kirk, University Vice President. Dwight Eisenhower, the university's president, could not attend but had prepared a message of friendship that was read to those in attendance. Former General Eisenhower and the French president had become friends in France during the latter days of the War. President Auriol praised Mr. Eisenhower for all he had done to save France and the world from the evils of Nazism.

On the following day President Auriol journeyed to Hyde Park, New York, for a meeting with Eleanor Roosevelt, after which he visited the Military Academy at West Point. Because his cold had not yet improved, he did not attend a dinner held in his honor at the United Nations, but his wife and aides represented him. The next morning the French presidential party moved by train to Montreal, home of many French-speaking Canadians.

President Auriol returned to France where he served as President of the Fourth Republic until 1954. During his administration France fought a number of wars in its former colonies, including Vietnam, Morocco, Algeria, Tunisia, and Madagascar. Each resulted in the withdrawal of French troops and independence for the former colony. He resigned in 1954. There were 18 different Prime Ministers during his Presidency and he once commented "The work was killing me. They called me out of bed at all hours of the night to receive resignations of Prime Ministers." Originally a supporter of De Gaulle, he became alarmed by De Gaulle's increasing popularity and power, and as an elder statesman of French politics he unsuccessfully lobbied against the 1958 Constitution that created the Fifth Republic. On January 1, 1966, he died suddenly in Paris of a heart ailment. He is buried in the village Murel in southwest France.

Mayor Vincent Impellitteri (1950-1953)

The City Charter of 1937 states that if the office of Mayor is vacated, the President of the City Council becomes Acting Mayor until a special election can be held, On September 1, 1950, Mayor O'Dwyer resigned in order to become Ambassador to Mexico, leaving City Hall to 50-year-old Vincent Impellitteri.

Born in Sicily and raised in Connecticut, Impellitteri served in the Navy during World War I before earning his law degree at Fordham. He worked as an Assistant District Attorney but failed to rise in Democratic party ranks because of his opposition to organized crime, which had connections with Tammany Hall during the 1920s and 1930s. In 1945, William O'Dwyer persuaded party officials to let Impellitteri run for City Council President. When O'Dwyer resigned as Mayor, Impellitteri became Acting Mayor until a special election could be held. Tammany Hall did not support him, so he ran as an independent, successfully campaigning against corrupt party politics.

As Mayor, Impellitteri grappled with the city's growing budget, establishing parking meters and increasing the sales tax, and authorized an increase in the subway fare. He attempted other reforms to the city bureaucracy, but faced opposition from both Democrats and Republicans, and lost his bid for re-election in 1953. He was later appointed a judge, serving in the criminal courts until 1965. He died in 1987 and is buried in Connecticut.

Friday, April 20, 1951: General Douglas MacArthur

General Douglas MacArthur arrived at LaGuardia Airport late on April 19, 1951, just hours after addressing a Joint Session of Congress following his dismissal by President Truman as Commander of UN forces in Korea. His speech, which one of his biographers called "one of the most impressive and divisive oratorical performances of recent American times" concluded with the words: "old soldiers never die; they just fade away." The welcome he received from the approximately eight million people who greeted him in New York City showed that his popularity was far from fading.

The next morning, the General rose early, breakfasted at 7:30, and spent the next three hours responding to the more than 1,200 telephone calls that swamped the switchboard of the Waldorf Astoria. Shortly after 11:00, he entered a car with Mayor Impellitteri and Grover Whalen for a motorcade that traveled through midtown Manhattan, where the traffic on 34th Street was described by one high-ranking policeman as "a disaster" because of the crowds, then south on the FDR Drive toward the Battery.

The sirens of the more than two dozen motorcycles remained silent during the entire trip because of the recently enacted city ordinance prohibiting sirens unless as a Civilian Defense Warning regarding an attack on New York. There was no such regulation against ships' horns and whistles, however, and dozens of ships of all sizes and types blasted their horns in tribute to the General. Doctors, nurses, and patients waved from Bellevue Hospital. Construction workers stood side by side with school children, waving flags and lifting signs of welcome and support at Stuyvesant Town and Peter Cooper Village. Scores of fishermen and fishmongers waved and saluted at the Fulton Fish Market.

Slowed by the immense crowds, the motorcade finally reached the traditional starting point at Bowling Green a half hour later than expected. The motorcade that included more than two dozen vehicles then made its slow and steady way up Broadway. The Police, Fire, and Sanitation bands played marching music and detachments of veteran organizations, political clubs, the city's uniformed services, and other groups escorted the General.

If the cheers from the crowds had been loud earlier, they became thunderous along Broadway as each greeting and vocal salute echoed in its narrow confines. Paper rained down everywhere, not only along Broadway but the entire route the motorcade travelled earlier. At least half the estimated eight million who witnessed the day's event seemed to be visitors to the city, and signs were seen identifying well-wishers from Indiana and Oklahoma, Kansas and Alabama, Massachusetts and Texas. They had arrived over the previous days, taking planes, trains, buses, and private cars so they could cheer for the general.

The motorcade halted at City Hall, where Mayor Impellitteri presented the General with the city's Medal of Honor and Freedom of the City. The mayor paid tribute to the general as one of America's finest soldiers by reviewing his extensive career: rising from battalion to regiment and then division commander of New York's Rainbow Division in the First World War; commandant of West Point; organizer of the Philippine Defense Forces prior to Pearl Harbor leading to his rank as Field Marshal; the Japanese invasion of the Philippines and his transfer to Australia from where he commanded actions against the Japanese in the South Pacific; his famous "return" to the Philippines; the Japanese surrender in Tokyo Bay; commander-in-chief of UN forces in Korea, leading the Inchon landings and the offensive against North Korea towards the Yalu River.

Not mentioned but understood by all, was the general's removal from his final command when he had announced his own plans for expanding the Korean War, in defiance of President Truman and Secretary of State Dean Acheson, both of whom espoused a policy of limited warfare.

General MacArthur spoke to the crowd, his voice emotional and showing signs of fatigue:

> *"The tremendous reception you have given me recalls a somewhat similar homecoming to which I participated as a cadet from West Point long, long ago. It was Admiral Dewey's return from the war in the Pacific. The years have passed indeed since then, but the hospitality of New York seems only to have grown with time."*

The ceremony at City Hall was over in slightly more than half an hour, after which the general reviewed veteran organizations on Centre Street. The motorcade then resumed, continuing up Broadway. It passed under the Washington Arch on Fifth Avenue and slowed as it passed the Public Library on 42nd Street where more school children waved miniature flags. When it reached St. Patrick's Cathedral it halted and the General, with a surprisingly spry step for a man of 71, left the vehicle and ran to shake hands with Cardinal Francis Spellman. Iin his role as Apostolic Vicar of US Armed Forces, the Roman Catholic Cardinal and the General had become close friends over the years, and they spoke for a few minutes on the steps of the Cathedral. From there the motorcade resumed to Central Park, drove through the park into Harlem, then circled downtown and finally ended back at the Waldorf Astoria, where a luncheon was held at 3:30.

Over 7,000 of New York's 18,000-man police force had helped direct traffic, restrain crowds, or joined in the march. Amid all the crowds and excitement, many injuries were reported, including one fatality. A 47-year-old blind man, Mario Riccobono of Astoria, Queens, had been part of the crowd at Park Row and Broadway when he was struck on the head by a half-pound paperweight that had been caught in scraps of paper tossed from a window. Hospitalized with a fractured skull, Mr. Riccobono died four days later.

Paper of all kinds had rained down on the general's motorcade, not just in the Canyon of Heroes but along its entire 19-mile route. Sanitation officials first put the figure at 2,500 tons but later revised that to more than 6,000 tons. It fell in the form of ticker tape, confetti, torn and shredded paper. In the garment district multicolored ribbons of cloth and yarn fell. Later, on Fifth Avenue, bits of unused yellow state income tax forms fell along with bank deposit and withdrawal forms. In places the paper was a foot deep. Everywhere along the day's route the roads or pavements were carpeted in paper.

In 1952 MacArthur gave the Keynote Address at the Republican Presidential Convention and it was thought he might permit his name to be put in nomination, though he refused the suggestion. For most of the rest of his life he was a permanent resident of the Waldorf Astoria. Presidents Eisenhower and Kennedy subsequently consulted with him on military matters. He died in Walter Reed Army Medical Center in 1964 and was given a state funeral. He is buried at the Douglas MacArthur Memorial in Norfolk, Virginia.

Wednesday, May 9, 1951:
David Ben-Gurion, Prime Minister of Israel

On the eve of the third anniversary of Israel's independence, David Ben-Gurion, the Israeli Prime Minister, arrived at Idlewild International Airport shortly before 10 o'clock. He was accompanied on the flight from Washington, DC by his Brooklyn-born wife, Paula. In the capital he met with President Truman to "increase the goodwill between my little country and your great and glorious republic." The Prime Minister and his wife were met at Idlewild by Grover Whalen, the City Controller Lazarus Josephs, and other members of the Mayor's Reception Committee.

Following a brief welcoming ceremony at the airport, Mr. and Mrs. Ben-Gurion entered a limousine and, as part of a 25-vehicle motorcade, were driven to the Waldorf Astoria. Escorted by 50 New York City motorcycle policeman, the motorcade stopped briefly at the hotel.

Many spectators had waited since before dawn to catch a glimpse of and welcome the Prime Minister. When the caravan of vehicles reached the Garment District at 34th Street and turned toward the FDR Drive, the crowds were larger, the cheers louder, and the first flurries of confetti fell from buildings and roof tops along the route. The Prime Minister's car finally reached Bowling Green and moved into place among the contingents already gathered.

The motorcycle force led the way up Broadway, followed by sailors from two Israeli warships visiting New York, the *Hagannah* and the *Misgav*. Detachments from the United States Army, Navy, Marine Corps, and Coast Guard were included in the procession along with units of New York's Fire, Police, and Sanitation Departments. Four bands scattered throughout the column provided marching music. Shouts in Hebrew of "*Shalom*" (peace) and "*Baruch Haaba*" (welcome) were clearly heard. Thousands of small blue and white Israeli flags fluttered along with the American flag. Police estimated the crowd of spectators at over one million, and in places along lower Broadway they stood six deep. An additional 100,000 people were jammed into City Hall Park.

A large podium had been constructed at the entrance to City Hall and Mr. Ben-Gurion joined Mayor Impellitteri there. He introduced the Israeli Prime Minister as "the great leader of his people" and added that Israel stood as "the democratic bulwark of the Middle East." The mayor's words were nearly drowned out by a huge ovation when Mr. Ben-Gurion was awarded the city's Gold Medal and a scroll recognizing his leadership qualities and the steadfast courage of Israel against all odds.

Mr. Ben-Gurion thanked the mayor and the assembled crowd in heavily accented English, then reviewed details of Israeli sailors and United States Marines. The Prime Minister then attended a reception in his honor at the Waldorf Astoria, where 1,500 guests heard Governor Thomas Dewey praise Ben-Gurion as a man of high courage. The Prime Minister "matched his indomitable courage with wisdom and force of character in one of the most troublesome times in modern history." In response, Mr. Ben-Gurion spoke of the strength of will among the people of his nation, predicting that Israel would be economically independent within three years if peace could come to his region. He made a plea for support of the $500 million State of Israel bond issue recently floated. Money derived from the sale of these bonds, he emphasized "will be put to diversified productive work that will extend our economic structure and absorb more and more immigrants to our land."

The Prime Minister later visited the United Nations and met with Secretary General Trygve Lie of Norway, and President of the General Assembly Nasrollah Entezam of

Iran. He subsequently told reporters that the Security Council's efforts regarding the cease fire between Israel and Syria "will have their effect, and sooner or later we will have peace in the Middle East." The following morning Mr. Ben-Gurion, along with the Israeli Ambassador to the United States, Mr. Abba Eban, journeyed to West Point. There he laid a wreath on the grave of West Point graduate Colonel David (Mickey) Marcus, who was killed while serving with Israeli forces in the Arab-Israeli War of 1948. Scheduled to return to Israel the following day, the Prime Minister concluded his visit to New York by addressing an overflow crowd at Madison Square Garden, com memorating Israel's third anniversary of independence and supporting the Israeli bond issue.

Prior to Israel's independence, Mr. Ben-Gurion had been the Zionist leader in the struggle to gain sovereignty. When the nation gained independence at the end of the British Mandate, he had already been voted to the position of provisional President in a pre-independence plebiscite. He was elected to the post of Prime Minister in the country's first national election in February 1949 and served until 1954. A year later, he returned to that position when it was vacated during a political scandal, and his second term continued until 1963. He retired from political life in 1970 and moved to a kibbutz in the Negev desert where he wrote an 11-volume history of Israel. In November 1973 be suffered a cerebral hemorrhage and died on December 1, 1973 at the age of 87. His remains were entombed at Sde Boker, a kibbutz in the Negev.

During his years of leadership, Israel was almost constantly at war or under the threats of war from neighboring countries. His leadership skills are often cited as the reason why Israel managed to maintain its national identity. *Time* magazine placed him on their list of the 100 Most Influential People of the 20th Century.

Idlewild Airport

When New York Municipal Airport (later renamed LaGuardia) opened in 1939, airlines quickly added it to their flight schedules, and within two years, it was clear that the city would need a second and larger airport. Mayor LaGuardia announced in 1941 that a site in southern Queens had been selected, and that a new highway would be built to connect the airport to Manhattan, which was 15 miles away. Most of the almost 5,000 acres was undeveloped marshy swamp, but the area purchased by the city included a small airstrip called the Jamaica Sea Airport and the Idlewild Golf Course.

Initial plans called for 12 runways and one centralized terminal, and cost estimates approached $150 million, far more than the $42 million for Municipal Airport. In 1947, the city negotiated a deal with the Port Authority of New York, which had been formed in 1921 as an interstate agency to oversee the transportation infrastructure of New York's harbor. With an ability to issue its own bonds, the Port Authority had already built the George Washington Bridge in 1931 and the Lincoln Tunnel in 1937 and been given control of the Holland Tunnel, which had been built in 1926 by a separate agency.

Construction started in 1943, but was delayed by union disputes, financing challenges, and changes to the plans, including reducing the number of runways to eight and replacing the central terminal with seven separate buildings for different airlines. The airport opened in 1948, with just one terminal and six runways completed. Officially named after a New York City war hero, the Major General Alexander Anderson Airport was called "Idlewild" by the press and almost everybody else. →

As expected, traffic into the new airport grew swiftly, especially with the arrival of jet planes in the 1950s. All international flights were shifted from LaGuardia to Idlewild, and some airlines also moved operations out of Newark Airport. Additional terminals were opened over the decade, and airlines competed to have the best facilities and services. By 1954, Idlewild had the most international flights of any airport in the world, and in 1961, over 10 million passengers flew in or out of Idlewild, a world record.

Mayor Robert Wagner proposed changing the airport's name after the assassination of President Kennedy in November 1963, and within a month the airport's code was changed from IDL to JFK. As New York's busiest airport, JFK has expanded and been renovated many times, was the first airport to receive many new aircraft, including the Concorde in 1977 and the Airbus A380 in 2007, and is one of the nation's busiest cargo and passenger airports.

Thursday, May 24, 1951: US Army 4th Infantry Division

Most of New York's parades were welcoming or celebratory events. On this gray windy day, however, the Canyon of Heroes was filled with more than 100,000 spectators bidding farewell not to just one individual, but 5,000 American soldiers heading overseas. For the third time in the 20th century, American troops were heading to Europe. But this time, they went not to war, but to prevent war. As the first troops being sent overseas to support the new NATO alliance, their departure was not kept secret and was publicized in the most open way imaginable: with a ticker tape parade.

The parade route stretched from the Battery to Pier 54 on the Hudson River. Docked at the former Cunard Line pier at West 13th Street and adjacent piers were excursion boats and ferries waiting to carry the men to transport ships anchored off Staten Island.

At 12:20 a squadron of mounted police began the procession north. The First Army Band marched close behind the police escort, followed by an open car in which two Medal of Honor recipients rode. One was Master-Sergeant Ernest Kouma of Dwight, Nebraska, who, though wounded twice, single-handedly held off an attack of 250 North Korean troops while his company crossed the Naktong River. Next to him sat Sergeant John Pittman of Carrollton, Mississippi, who threw himself on a grenade to save the lives of his men at Kujangdong, Korea. Behind this vehicle came the 5,000 men, marching in neat and orderly rows before being shipped to provide combat support to the North Atlantic Treaty Organization (NATO).

In keeping with the solemnity of a departure, far less cheering and applause was heard, and less ticker tape fell than usual. As the first platoon of the Combat Team reached Fulton Street a fine drizzle began, and ticker tape stuck to the helmets of some of the marching men like urban camouflage.

The parade was halted at City Hall, where Grover Whalen, Chairman of the Mayor's Reception Committee, introduced the two Medal of Honor recipients to Mayor Impellitteri. The mayor shared the reviewing stand with Lieutenant General Willis Crittenberger, commander of the First Army *(see: December 18, 1952)*. The general snapped to attention and saluted the two enlisted men (the salute from a higher rank is one of the honors awarded to Medal of Honor winners). The mayor addressed the entire Combat Team saying, "The city joins your relatives and friends in praying for the success of your mission – the preservation of world peace." General Crtittenberger read a message from Army Chief-of-Staff J. Lawton Collins: "You will be serving in the front lines of Democracy, but where American soldiers in the past have gone to fight and win wars, you go to win friends, and we fervently hope, to prevent another dreadful war."

The parade then resumed up Broadway to 14th Street. It was reported that women and girls along the way were seen wiping tears from their eyes and waving to their departing sons, husbands, or friends. Blanche Brooker, a 21-year-old nurse from Ohio, kept pace with the march along most of the entire route and whenever the parade paused, she tried to talk to her departing fiancé, Private Eugene Laurisky. Military discipline was in effect and she never reached him but waved often while he cast a quick glance in her direction.

The parade made an unexpected halt at the corner of Fifth Avenue and 14th Street, where a fire had broken out in an abandoned building on the corner. Most of the firemen struggled against the blaze while others jockeyed the fire trucks out of the line of march so the troops could continue.

Once the parade reached the piers, the men boarded the waiting ferries. Fireboats shot jets of water skyward in farewell and ships moored along the docks on both sides of the Hudson sounded horns and whistles. A police department helicopter circled over the transports as they steamed through the Narrows and off to West Germany. Barely peeking through the heavy overcast, the sun set as the ships began their journey.

The Fourth Division was the first of four divisions sent to Europe. With its headquarters at Frankfort, it remained as a unit of NATO until 1955. Recalled to the United States, it was stationed at Fort Lewis, Washington. It has since seen combat duty in Vietnam, Iraq, and Afghanistan.

Monday, June 25, 1951:
Galo Plaza Lasso de la Vega, President of Ecuador

The parade for Galo Plaza Lasso de la Vega, President of the South American Republic of Ecuador, was a Welcome Home party. He had been born at the Marlton House Hotel on West 8th Street in 1906, and attended grammar school in New York, before moving to Quito when his family returned to Ecuador. He returned to the United States for college, studying at the University of California (where he was on the football team) and the University of Maryland (where he played basketball) and Georgetown University, receiving a degree in Diplomacy.

Moving back to Ecuador, he managed his father's ranch, became a bullfighter, entered politics, and served as Ecuador's Minister of War and Ambassador to the US. Elected president in 1948, he was known for his honesty and direct involvement in issues. His visit to New York in 1951 was partly a move to increase investments in his country and partly a desire to see the city of his youth.

On a bright and warm summer afternoon, the motorcade carrying President Plaza was escorted by military detachments and police, led by the Police Department Band. A small amount of ticker tape and sparse crowds greeted the president. Unknown to those marching, a serious accident took place as the parade moved uptown. A 43-year-old spectator, Edward Whiteside, was struck by part of a ventilator that fell from the tenth floor of the building at 115 Broadway. Mr. Whiteside was taken to Beekman Downtown Hospital with a fractured skull. City newspapers over the next few days failed to provide any other information on the condition or recovery of Mr. Whiteside. The accident was similar to one that had taken place the previous April during the parade for General MacArthur *(see: April 20, 1951)* when a spectator was killed by a falling object.

President Plaza rode with his wife Rosario, and Grover Whalen, Chairman of the Mayor's Reception Committee. The president informed Mr. Whalen that he had sold apples on a New York street corner when he was a boy and later repeated the story to Mayor Impellitteri once the parade reached City Hall. His father was a wealthy man, he explained, but to give his son the value of working and making his own way, he told the boy to find some way to make money. Selling apples seemed simple, he thought, and he set up a stand at Seventh Avenue and 52nd Street. "One day business was bad," he said. "An old lady was standing there, and everyone bought apples from her and not me." Smiling, the president told the mayor and those assembled in the Council Chambers that this was the end of his "apple career."

The mayor presented the Ecuadorian with a certificate of distinguished service acknowledging his ties to the city and his friendship with the United States. The president expressed happiness at being in New York. After the City Hall reception, the president and his wife rode uptown with the mayor and others to the Waldorf Astoria. Heading up Centre Street between the New York State Office Building and the Department of Health, the party was treated to something new in the way of welcome. Instead of ticker tape, countless nurses' orange timecards floated down.

At the Waldorf, President Plaza presented the mayor with a book on the history of his capital city, Quito, then met briefly with former US President Herbert Hoover, a permanent resident of the hotel, and United States Chief of Protocol John Simmons. In a surprise that brought laughs to those assembled, he then produced three Panama hats, explaining that this style of hat was really made in his country, but had been misnamed by gold prospectors arriving in Panama. Putting one hat on, he gave the remaining hats to the mayor and Mr. Simmons. The trio then did a variation of a vaudeville routine of switching hats back and forth.

President Plaza returned to Ecuador and completed his four-year term of office. He was the first president of his nation to complete a full term since 1924. Prevented by the Constitution from seeking re-election he served on diplomatic posts at the UN as a mediator in conflicts in Lebanon (1958), the Congo (1960) and Cyprus (1965-1965). In 1968 he was named Secretary General of the Organization of American States. He subsequently returned to ranching in 1975. He died of a heart attack in Quito in 1987.

Monday, September 17, 1951:
Sir Denys Lowson, Lord Mayor of the City of London

Recipients of a ticker tape parade have marched or ridden up the Canyon of Heroes wearing business suits and morning suits; military uniforms of the United States and foreign countries; sports uniforms of various types, including those of the Olympics, baseball, football; robes and tiaras, helmets, crowns, and caps. But only once has someone been showered with ticker tape and confetti who wore a ruffled collar, gold braid, and a chain once owned by King Henry VIII. Thus attired was the Lord Mayor of London and at his side was his official Sword Bearer displaying aloft the Sword of State that symbolizes the mayor's office and power.

Sir Denys Lowson arrived in the United States after a goodwill tour of seven nations arranged by the Festival of Britain to encourage tourism and trade with Great Britain, still slowly recovering from the effects of the Second World War.

"Resplendent in the silk and gold robes of his office," the Lord Mayor smiled broadly as the caravan of vehicles moved up Broadway. Led by the bands of the Fire, Police, and Sanitation Departments and marching contingents from each of these departments, His Lordship waved to the thousands who lined Broadway and spilled into side streets. From open windows of office buildings cheering spectators viewed the parade and poured down streamers of ticker tape and confetti, many of them waving miniature flags of the United Kingdom.

Upon reaching City Hall the Lord Mayor was officially welcomed by Mayor Impellitteri and brought into the chambers of the Board of Estimates. New York's mayor spoke of the historic significance of His Lordship's visit and asked him to advise the people of London that New York still shares "faith in Democracy, scorn for dictatorship, and a loyal belief in the dignity and rights of every human being."

Sir Denys presented a scroll to Mayor Impellitteri bearing a resolution passed by the Court of Common Council of the City of London, expressing the hopes that Sir Denys' visit would further the bonds of friendship between New York and London.

Soon after the proceedings in the Estimates Chamber, a luncheon was provided at the Waldorf Astoria Hotel. Grover Whalen, chairman of the Mayor's Reception Committee, could not avoid commenting about the difference between the clothes worn by the two mayors, one in a blue serge suit, the other in his robes of office. Perhaps, Whalen suggested, similar trappings should be worn by the mayor of New York. Grinning, Mayor Impellitteri stated "The Lord Mayor of New York is very economy minded and I doubt if we could get the necessary funds. However, Grover, if you can arrange it, I'll be glad to oblige." Nothing was said about obtaining a four-foot-long broad sword to compliment the wardrobe.

Speaking at the luncheon, the mayor's wife Elizabeth noted that the wife of the Lord Mayor was properly addressed as "Lady Mayoress," then joked that a similar title for herself might produce "political and domestic complications."

Earlier in his visit, the Lord Mayor met with President Truman in Washington and visited places of historical interest, including Williamsburg and Jamestown in Virginia, and Philadelphia, Pennsylvania. He spoke highly of the enthusiasm shown towards him to create unity between the two major English-speaking powers.

Sir Denys returned to London three days later and served out the remaining ten days of his one-year term. His public career continued for a dozen more years, and he served on various government committees that sent him back to New York City, minus the robes, chain, and broad sword. Sir Denys, officially Baronet Denys Colquhoun Flowerdew Lowson died in London in 1975.

Friday, September 28, 1951:
Alcide De Gasperi, Prime Minister of Italy

Today's parade would be the second to honor the Italian Prime Minister Alcide De Gasperi *(see: January 13, 1947)*, who spent a week in New York City following a five-day visit to Ottawa, Canada, and Washington, DC. The sun shone brightly on the morning of September 28 when he and the Italian Ambassador to the United States, Alberto Tarachiani, joined Grover Whalen in an open limousine at the Waldorf Astoria Hotel. It was the first car of a 15-vehicle motorcade, escorted by a motorcycle police detachment, setting out for Bowling Green. The second car of the procession carried the Prime Minister's wife, Francesca De Gasperi, Mrs. Tarachiani, and Mrs. Joseph

Sharkey, wife of the Acting Mayor. As the procession moved south on the FDR Drive, fireboats in the East River extended a welcome with jets of water shooting skyward.

When the motorcade reached the lower end of Broadway, it rendezvoused with 1,500 marchers from the Army, Navy, Marine Corps, and Air Force and members of the Police, Fire, and Sanitation Departments. A military band and a civilian drum and bugle corps provided the marching music. The flags of the United States and Italy were massed at the beginning and end of the parade. Shortly after noon, the parade stepped out to the usual city welcome of cheers, shouts, ticker tape, and confetti. Hundreds of American and Italian flags were waved by spectators along the route.

At City Hall, Mr. Whalen introduced the Prime Minister to Acting Mayor Joseph Sharkey, who was filling in while Mayor Impelliteri was on a 3-week tour of Italy. The Acting Mayor extended a welcome to the Prime Minister, citing his success in steering Italy along the paths of democracy despite attempts by Communists to gain power. Almost 2,000 people in City Hall Plaza witnessed the Acting Mayor awarding the city's Medal of Honor to the Italian leader. The Prime Minister mentioned his appreciation for the city's welcome and reception and praised its ability to exist as a multi-cultural and multi-ethnic metropolis.

Following the short ceremony at City Hall, the Acting Mayor and the Prime Minister with his party returned to the Waldorf Astoria for an official luncheon. Speaking in English and Italian, the Prime Minister related how encouraging it was to see the smiles of the people of the United States and to hear the sincerity of their words. He spoke briefly of the hope that the United States would assist Italy in regaining control of the city of Trieste, claimed by Yugoslavia and awaiting a United Nations decision on its fate. He concluded his remarks by raising a glass of champagne and offering a toast "to the idea of peace and freedom common to us all." The next afternoon the Prime Minister and his wife flew back to Italy from Idlewild International Airport in Queens County.

In 1927, De Gasperi had been arrested by the Fascist government for opposition to Mussolini's rule. Slightly over a year later he was released due to declining health. Barred from political activities, teaching, and journalism, he became cataloguer at the Vatican Library, a post he held until 1943. With the fall of Fascism, he returned to politics and was named Prime Minister in 1945, a position he held until 1953. He served in a total of eight different successive coalition governments, a feat no other Italian Prime Minister has duplicated. He is considered one of the Founding Fathers of the European Union. After his party was defeated in the elections of 1953, he retired from politics and died on August 19, 1954 in Trentino and is buried in the Basilica di San Lorenzo, Rome. A lifelong devout Catholic, the process of beatification was started for him in 1993. Trieste was returned to Italy in 1954, except for a small area along the eastern border which is now part of Slovenia.

Monday, October 8, 1951:
New York National Guard 165th Infantry Centennial

Formed in 1851 as a unit of the New York State Militia, the 69th New York regiment was originally composed almost entirely of Irish immigrants. Known since World War I as the 165th Infantry, the unit paraded up the Canyon of Heroes to celebrate its 100th anniversary. Over 1,200 members of the unit moved forward in perfectly formed ranks and files, wearing their olive drab uniforms, neckerchiefs of infantry blue, helmets and spotless boots. They were accompanied by other military contingents from the Army, Navy, Marine Corps, and Air Force. Marching music was provided by the Police, Fire, and Sanitation Department bands.

Few American regiments have such a distinguished history from the Civil War to World War II. It had received so many combat ribbons during its distinguished career that it was permitted to carry flagstaffs a foot and a half longer than the standard size to display them all. The unit's history began with Colonel Thomas Meagher, leader in the 1848 Irish rebellion against England, who moved to New York City in 1852 and commanded the 69th before and during the Civil War. The regiment, whose members were all Irish immigrants to the US, gained some notoriety by refusing to dip its flags in salute to the Prince of Wales during his 1860 visit to New York. During the Civil War, the unit participated in many battles, including Bull Run, Chancellorsville and Gettysburg, and gained the nickname of the "Fighting 69th." During World War I its members included heroes such as William "Wild Bill" Donovan (head of the OSS in World War II), Chaplain Father Francis Duffy, and poet Joyce Kilmer. It saw combat during World War II in the Pacific at Makin Island, Saipan, and Okinawa. When speaking of the regiment at City Hall, Grover Whalen called it "the finest fighting regiment in the world." Since seven of its members had been awarded the Congressional Medal of Honor over the years, few could question his boast.

As usual, the parade's participants were deluged with ticker tape and confetti as they marched up the Canyon of Heroes, but the marchers never broke ranks and never waved to acknowledge the cheers, maintaining their strict military discipline along the route.

The regiment halted in City Hall Plaza, facing the reviewing stand. The commanding officer of the 165th regiment, Colonel Martin Foery, stood with Acting Mayor Joseph Sharkey, who briefly recounted the regiment's history. Sharkey cited three famous moments from the regiment's history. In 1862, the unit's courage earned praise from their enemy, General Robert E. Lee. During the First World War, Father Duffy said new recruits to the regiment, no longer exclusively of Irish ancestry, were still "Irish by adoption, association or conviction." During the same war, General Douglas MacArthur praised the unit's resolve against enemy fire, saying, "By God, it takes the Irish when you want a hard thing done."

Retired General "Wild Bill" Donovan spoke next, saying that his old unit would help pave the way to victory should war come again. Following his remarks, the regiment marched in review along Centre Street past the other military units that participated in the parade.

Members of the unit were always unhappy that it had been renumbered during World War I, and after repeated appeals to the Department of the Army it was redesignated the 69th in 1992. Headquartered at the 69th Regiment Armory on Lexington Avenue and 25th Street, the Fighting 69th was among the first National Guard units called to service after the terrorist attacks on New York on 9/11 and saw combat service in Iraq and Afghanistan. Although its members are no longer solely of Irish descent, the regiment continues to lead the St. Patrick's Day Parade in New York City every year.

Monday, October 29, 1951: UN Servicemen Wounded in Korea

Fifty wounded soldiers from seven different nations were honored by the city for their service and sacrifices in the fighting in Korea. The servicemen had been selected by the US Defense Department with the assistance of its counterparts in the United

Kingdom, Australia, Greece, New Zealand, Canada, and Turkey, to foster understanding of the United Nations efforts on the embattled Korean peninsula. The group from the United States contained one New Yorker, Lieutenant Charles Friedlander.

The men had been staying at the Waldorf Astoria for the past two days, and on the morning of October 29 drove downtown in a caravan of jeeps, two soldiers in each vehicle. Flying from the front fender of each vehicle was the flag or flags of its occupants' nations. The motorcade and its police escort sped east on 57th Street to the FDR Drive, where it turned south and passed scattered groups of well-wishers. Fireboats in the East River shot geysers of water skyward in welcome. The vehicles continued past the Fulton Fish Market where workers had been standing since dawn waiting for them. When the procession finally reached the Customs House at the foot of Broadway, it fell in behind a mounted police escort. Bands from the Police and Fire Departments and the Air Force began to play. Marching Army and Coast Guard detachments also joined the parade.

Cascades of ticker tape spiraled from windows along the route, some wrapping around the steeple of Trinity Church. The soldiers in the parade wore the distinctive dress uniforms of their respective countries and they waved in appreciation to the thousands who lined the route. A chilling breeze snapped flags of South Korea and the 21 member nations of the UN which were supporting the effort in Korea with military, medical, or logistical support.

City Hall Plaza had been kept cleared of spectators. When the motorcade arrived, the jeeps moved with military precision into ranks. Occupants of the vehicles dismounted and stood at attention while Grover Whalen, again acting as Reception Committee Chairman, introduced the men to those on the flag-bedecked reviewing stand. Standing there with Mayor Impellitteri was General Leland Hobbs, First Army commander; Douglas Fairbanks, Jr., Chairman of the Red Cross Armed Forces Blood Program; and Colonel Alfred Katzin, military advisor to and representative of Trygve Lie, UN Secretary General. The mayor made a brief speech and then placed the city's Gold Medal around the neck of Lieutenant Friedlander.

Not long afterwards, the soldiers returned to their jeeps and moved to Centre Street and Foley Square where they were part of a review that extended for three cities blocks. At the end of the review the jeeps continued north up Fourth Avenue to Park Avenue and then back to the Waldorf. That evening they were guests at a dinner sponsored by the City's Reception Committee.

Early the next morning the veterans boarded planes at Floyd Bennett Field in Brooklyn. Half the group flew to Boston and half to Atlanta to begin a month-long tour to various parts of the country, spreading the message of the United Nations' fight against aggression. They reunited in San Francisco on Thanksgiving, November 22, 1951. After a traditional American Thanksgiving meal, the 50 servicemen returned to duty in Korea or their respective nations.

Tuesday, November 13, 1951: Women of the Armed Forces

Mayor Vincent Impellitteri and Mrs. Anna Rosenberg, Assistant Secretary of Defense, issued a proclamation declaring a "Women in the Armed Forces Week" to publicize the Defense Department's efforts to increase the number of women in the military to 112,000 by the following July. This would require a total of 72,000 women to volunteer for military duty. The mayor noted that there were 8.5 million women in the

U S between the ages of 18 and 31, and he estimated that about a quarter of that number were qualified for service.

A parade of women already serving in the military was held to support the recruitment initiative. Slightly more than 1,000 members of the WAC's (Women's Army Corps) and WAVES (the US Navy's Women Accepted for Volunteer Emergency Service) marched up the Canyon of Heroes on an unusually mild mid-November day. Male detachments from the Army, Navy, Air Forces, Marine Corps, Police and Fire Departments provided an honor guard following Army and Navy bands. Spectators stood two or three deep at several places along the route, but cheering was minimal as was the amount of ticker tape.

Upon reaching City Hall, the mayor cited the Junior League of the City of New York for its efforts in recruiting women for the military. A letter was read from Eleanor Roosevelt, an early member of the League, praising the League's work in assisting young women to accept the responsibility of civic and patriotic work in national and international fields.

Mrs. Rosenberg held the highest position ever by a woman in the military establishment. She praised the women already serving and attempted to assure mothers of prospective recruits by saying their "girls will be safe and welcome in the armed service." She added that it was a privilege for women to enlist in military service and "join the men and women who have put duty before personal advantage."

The ceremony's highpoint came following Mrs. Rosenberg's remarks when 40 women stood before the speaker's stand, raised their right hands, and were sworn in by the Commander of the Continental Air Command, Major General Willis Hale.

Despite the impressive start, statistics are unavailable to show whether the ambitious effort to increase the number of females in the military in 1951-52 succeeded.

The WAC and WAVES were created in 1943 to support the war effort by filling military support roles with women, freeing officers and men for duty in combat zones. Women were recruited and trained in various roles, including switchboard operators, mechanics and cooks or bakers, in addition to nursing. Their members were the first uniformed women in the US armed forces, and their role was considered vital. General MacArthur once reported that they were his "best soldiers" who worked better, complained less and were more disciplined than men. Both organizations were disbanded in the 1970s, when military rules were changed to allow women to serve, and current members were integrated into the regular branches of the armed forces.

Thursday, January 17, 1952: Captain Henrik Carlsen

For 14 days, Danish-born Henrik Kurt Carlsen remained on his stricken ship, the freighter *Flying Enterprise*, owned by the New York-based Isbrandtsen Company, a leading shipping company between the US and Europe. While riding out a North Atlantic storm 300 nautical miles from Falmouth, England, on December 28, 1961, a rogue wave hit the ship and broke her spine causing the cargo to shift, and the ship started to list 45 degrees to port. An SOS was signaled, and ships began to arrive to aid the freighter, rescuing her crew and passengers but Captain Carlsen remained on board, determined to stay with his vessel while there was still a chance of saving her. Kenneth Dancy, first mate of the British tug *Turmoil*, came aboard *Flying Enterprise* and helped Carlson secure a line while the tug slowly began pulling her to Falmouth. Day after day the storm raged, until a second wave struck on January 10. The tow line snapped. The cargo shifted again, and *Flying Enterprise* listed more heavily. Saving the ship was now impossible, so Captain Carlsen and Mate Dancy finally abandoned her and were plucked from the thundering waves by *Turmoil*. Less than an hour later, *Flying Enterprise* keeled over and sank, just 41 nautical miles from Falmouth.

Captain Carlsen's devotion to duty was celebrated in England where he was the guest of shipping and insurance companies for two days. Ordered by the Isbrandtsen Company to return, he arrived in New York Harbor on the Coast Guard cutter *Sauk*. His wife and two daughters joined him, transferring from another Coast Guard ship. Ships of all types and flying the flags of more than a dozen nations waited and greeted the returning captain, while two police helicopters hovered overhead. With horns and sirens screaming in welcome, *Sauk* sailed through a light rain to the Coast Guard Pier adjacent to Pier A at the Battery.

Grover Whalen, Chairman of the Mayor's Reception Committee, greeted the 37-year-old captain as he stepped ashore. With Mr. Whalen were officials of the Isbrandtsen Company, city officials, and reporters. The Coast Guard band stood in place to lead the parade up Broadway. Marching along with the eight-vehicle motorcade were detachments from the Coast Guard, the Police Department's Harbor Squad, and uniformed members of the Fire and Sanitation Departments. Shortly after noon, with the drizzle turning to large, heavy snowflakes, the parade moved out.

Estimates of the numbers of spectators ranged from 50,000 to 75,000. Flags hung wet and limp along the route, and ticker tape mingled with the snow. The Sanitation Department officials stated that 75 tons of paper was removed after the parade, far below the more than 6,000 tons after the parade for General MacArthur the previous year *(see: April 20, 1951)*. Captain Carlsen's family huddled beneath a heavy blanket in the rear of the car, while he stood the entire route waving his gloved hands at the spectators.

Mayor Impellitteri welcomed Captain Carlsen at City Hall. The mayor quickly introduced the captain to those huddled in the Plaza and then led him inside to the warmth of the Council Chambers. A crowd of more than 200 guests stood and applauded the captain when he entered the room, where the mayor presented the seaman with the city's Gold Medal. In a brief statement he praised the Captain's devotion to duty. Emma Hogstedt, sister of the President of the Isbrandtsen Company, awarded the Captain with a bronze plaque commemorating his courage and efforts to save his vessel. When the Captain finally spoke, he praised Kenneth Dancy and regretted that he could not be there to receive the city's reception. He also mentioned the officers and crews of the other ships that took part in the rescue efforts.

Later that afternoon Captain Carlsen was the guest of honor at a luncheon at the Advertising Club, where he received the Club's Plaque of Achievement and spoke of the heroism of others and stated that he had only done his duty as he saw it.

Captain Carlsen turned down requests to star in a planned film of the sinking of the *Flying Enterprise*. He was subsequently given a new command and retired in the mid-1970's. He died in October 1989 at his home in Woodbridge, New Jersey. A documentary titled *The Mystery of Flying Enterprise* was made in 2002 but no feature type film was ever made.

Controversy surrounds some aspects of the sinking. Some have suggested that Captain Carlsen remained with the *Flying Enterprise* only for salvage purposes. Others have stated that the ship could have been saved if it had been towed to Cork, Ireland, which was less than half the distance from where the original incident occurred. Divers located the wreck in 1960 and more than $200,000 of the estimated $800,000 of her cargo has since been salvaged by the Italian company Sorima.

Wednesday, March 5, 1952:
Shlomo Shragai, Mayor of Jerusalem

The first mayor elected to lead West Jerusalem, Polish-born Shlomo Zalman Shragai was given New York's traditional welcome on a brisk but sunny March morning. His three-week visit to the US was planned and organized by the Hapoel Hamizrachi of America organization, whose president, Charles Bick, served as translator while the Hebrew-speaking mayor was in New York.

Having arrived from Israel the day before, Mayor Shragai started at the foot of Broadway in a motorcade of 15 vehicles shortly after noon. The 52-year-old, white-bearded mayor rode in a closed limousine with his wife, escorted by mounted and motorcycle police and the Police Department Band. The crowds along Broadway were smaller than usual and the amount of ticker tape tossed in welcome appeared less as well.

A grandstand had been erected at City Hall where 5,000 people gathered in the plaza. Mayor Shragai's arrival there was musically announced by the Sanitation Department Band playing "Hetikvah" the Israeli national anthem, followed by the "Star Spangled Banner." The flags of both countries flew from City Hall and the corners of the grandstand, and City Hall was draped in red, white, and blue bunting. Standing between the grandstand and the crowd was the Lion of Judah Shield surmounted by the Hebrew spelling of Jerusalem.

Mayor Vincent Impellitteri welcomed Mayor Shragai, presenting him with a scroll that emphasized his role as "one of the guiding spirits of the Zionist movement." The Israeli mayor answered in Hebrew "thanking all of the people of the great city of New York for the welcome." Moving inside to the Council Chambers, Shragai gave New York's mayor a scroll expressing "the sincere and devoted friendship that the citizens of Jerusalem have for the citizens of New York." The scroll also noted that the 3,000th anniversary of the founding of the Kingdom of David would be celebrated in Jerusalem in October 1953. He invited Mayor Impellitteri and "people of all faiths" to come to Jerusalem at that time for the festivities.

After this ceremony a motorcade carrying the two mayors and their spouses drove to the Paramount Restaurant on West 43rd Street for a luncheon sponsored by the Hapoel Hamizrachi organization. Mayor Shragai's itinerary took him to Washington, Chicago, San Francisco, and elsewhere before returning to Israel

Shlomo Shragai continued to serve as Jerusalem's chief executive until 1955. He remained active in the Zionist movement and, as head of immigration for the Jewish Agency for Palestine, he made frequent trips to Europe encouraging Jewish migration to Israel, as well as clandestine trips to Muslim countries to obtain release for Jews wishing to repatriate. His health began to fail in the 1980s. and he passed away in 1995 at the age of 96.

Monday, April 7, 1952:
Queen Juliana of the Netherlands

Queen Juliana of the Netherlands had been invited to help celebrate the 300th anniversary of the city of Kingston, New York, originally a Dutch settlement named Wiltwyck, so a goodwill tour was planned for her and her husband, Prince Bernhard. The itinerary included a visit to Eleanor Roosevelt in Hyde Park, New York, followed by a return to New York City, where the queen had lived during most of World War II. Since the Royal Couple began their visit in Kingston, they made their entry into New York City on the day of their parade by a very unusual route, crossing the Westchester County line and driving through Harlem.

Their motorcade from Hyde Park was met at the border of Yonkers and the Bronx by a squad of motorcycle police. With lights flashing and sirens screaming the police escorted them to St Martin's Episcopal Church at 125th Street in Harlem, named after the city of Haarlem in the Netherlands. As the 42 bells of the church's carillon chimed the Dutch National Anthem, the motorcade halted and the queen chatted briefly with Dr. John Johnson, rector of the church. About 2,000 spectators, more than half of them children from local schools, stood and cheered the Queen and Prince. A few of the younger children held up drawings of the red, white, and blue Dutch flag, hand colored with crayons.

From Harlem, the motorcade sped downtown, arriving at Bowling Green soon after noon. Mr. Grover Whalen, Chairman of the Reception Committee, greeted them at the steps of the US Customs House on the southern end of Broadway. According to tradition, it was near this spot where Peter Minuit purchased Manhattan Island from the local Indian tribe for $24 worth of trinkets in 1626. Mr. Whalen pointed to the flag of New York City, its blue, white, and orange stripes based on the 1625 flag of the United Netherlands. He also mentioned that the beaver and windmill in the city's municipal seal refer to the original Dutch settlement of Nieuw Amsterdam, as the city was known then.

Following Mr. Whalen's brief lesson in New York history, the parade moved up Broadway. There was a slight chill in the air and the queen pulled her mink stole tightly around the shoulders of her aquamarine suit. Wearing long gloves, she waved to the crowd of about 100,000 spectators lining the Canyon of Heroes. Prince Bernhard, wearing the uniform of a Lieutenant-General in the Dutch Army, also waved and pointed to the swirling tendrils of ticker tape floating down. The First Army Band led the procession and detachments from the Army and Navy along with Police and Fire Department contingents marched in escort

Mayor Impellitteri welcomed the Royal Couple at City Hall, introducing Queen Juliana as the "lovely and majestic head of the Dutch Nation." He placed the city's Gold Medal around Queen Juliana's neck and presented her with a scroll that spoke of the long-standing friendship between New York and the Dutch city of Amsterdam. He then placed a medal around the neck of the Prince. In his remarks, the mayor referred to the purchase of Manhattan as "putting over the greatest real estate deal in history." In perfect English, the queen responded, "We Netherlands are happy to have contributed to the greatness of this city." She then spoke of how New York was the first real international community, a heritage it received from the city of Amsterdam, "where the persecuted from all over Europe found refuge."

At a luncheon at the Waldorf, Prince Bernhard was unexpectedly asked to say a few words. "I'll tell you how much we have appreciated the warm reception here. It shows how close our two nations are." Queen Juliana's comments were more serious as she warned of the fears created by advancing technology. Stating that her small country had long advocated peace, she wished that more energy could be placed on progress for peace rather than for military purposes. "New York has always been great at solving problems," she concluded, and challenged the city to set an example of peace to the world.

The following morning, the Queen and Prince visited St Mark's-in-the-Bowery Church where they laid a wreath at the statue of New Amsterdam's last Dutch Governor, Peter Stuyvesant. Later she visited the United Nations for a private tour; after which she received an honorary degree at Columbia University. She ended her day with a brief visit to the Flatbush Dutch Reformed Church on Flatbush Avenue, Brooklyn, the oldest Dutch Reformed congregation in the United States.

Queen Juliana and Prince Bernhard returned to the Netherlands after a three-day visit to Washington, DC. She reigned until 1980. Following the tradition of the Dutch Royal family (House of Orange-Nassau) she abdicated in favor of her heir, her daughter, Princess Beatrix *(see: September 11, 1959)*. Like most people of the Netherlands, Juliana was an avid cyclist and she continued riding beyond her 80th birthday. In the mid-1990's her health declined, and it was rumored she was suffering from Alzheimer's disease. She died in her sleep in March 2004 at the age of 94 and her remains were placed in the Nieuw Kerk in Delft. Prince Bernhard died exactly eight months later at the age of 95 and his remains were placed beside hers.

Wednesday, May 14, 1952: Mayors of 250 Cities

The 20th Annual Conference of Mayors was held in New York City. More than 600 mayors and officials, representing 250 US cities and more than 25 foreign ones, paraded up Broadway, but spectators were scarce, and quite a few appeared to have no idea who they were or what the parade was for.

The motorcade of more than 20 cars formed at Bowling Green and drove up Broadway to City Hall, escorted by a small detachment from First Army Headquarters at Fort Jay as well as the First Army Band. Larger contingents of the New York Police, Fire, and Sanitation Departments also marched. The lead vehicle contained the President of the United States Conference of Mayors, David Lawrence, Mayor of Pittsburgh.

At City Hall, Mayor Impellitteri welcomed the mayors and officials. Mayor Lawrence made a brief statement, thanking the city for the welcome. Then Mayor Constantine Nicolopoulos of Athens, Greece, representing the international officials presented New York's chief executive with an ancient Athenian drinking cup, made approximately in the year 600 BC.

A private dinner for foreign dignitaries was held at the Waldorf Astoria. Topics discussed at the conference focused on problems all cities had in common: urban transit, traffic congestion, revenue sharing, and civil defense.

The US Conference of Mayors is a non-partisan organization for cities with populations of 30,000 or larger. Founded in 1932, its mission is to promote effective urban policy, build stronger relationships between cities and the federal government, and develop leadership and management tools for mayoral administrations. The 88th annual conference was scheduled for Austin, Texas in June 2020, but was conducted online because of the Covid pandemic.

Monday, July 7, 1952:
US Olympic Team for XV Olympic Games

Previous parades honoring American Olympians were held when the athletes returned from the Games; this one was held in advance. A total of 336 athletes marched in procession up the Canyon of the Heroes. Added to this number were more than 70 coaches, trainers, and officials, swelling the total number parading to over 400.

The day began hot and humid with a heavy haze cloaking the city's skyline. Shortly before the parade began, however, the sun broke through the haze and the rest of the day was bright and clear. The participants wore navy blue jackets bearing the United States shield and the words "Helsinki 1952." Men wore gray trousers and white gabardine hats along with red, white, and blue striped ties. Female athletes wore trim navy-blue blazers, gray flannel skirts and cream-colored gabardine caps.

The parade began just after noon, when 18 mounted policemen, each carrying a staff bearing a small police pennant, wheeled out of Beaver Street to the front of those marching. Next in line came the Police and Fire Department Bands followed by 100 recent graduates of the Police Academy. The bands of the First Army, Third Naval District, and First Air Force completed the musical contingent. Twenty firemen, marching four abreast and carrying flags, followed the last band and preceded the athletes. The honor of carrying the Olympic flag and leading his fellow athletes went to Frank McCabe, the 6' 8" basketball star from Marquette. An attempt had been made to have the athletes march in orderly procession but many of them failed to resist the temptation to wave or blow kisses at the cheering multitude watching.

Immediately behind the marching athletes were cars carrying city officials and former Olympians, including swimmer Gertrude Ederle *(see: August 27, 1926)*, 1908 marathon winner Johnny Hayes, and ice skater Dick Button.

Police estimates put the number of observers at 100,000 but veterans of previous parades thought the crowd's size was double the estimate. As the parade reached St. Paul's Chapel, enthusiastic cheering reached a peak. Confetti and ticker tape covered and draped police, bandsmen, athletes, and officials. Cries of "Give 'em hell" and "Bring home the bacon" were delivered with New York City gusto, audible above the din of music and cheers.

Once the athletes entered City Hall Plaza before a crowd of 8,000, the massed bands played the "Star Spangled Banner." Grover Whalen, ever present at such festivities as Chairman of the Mayor's Reception Committee, presided over the reception. Mayor Impellitteri spoke confidentially of the efforts of the gathered athletes and suggested that New York City should someday host the quadrennial international games. There were rumors that the designated host of the 1956 games, Melbourne, Australia, might have to back out, and the mayor said he could think of no better city to host the games than New York. Even if Melbourne did not withdraw, the mayor asked to explore the possibilities of hosting the 1960 games. Indicating that this statement was not put forward without forethought, City Controller Lazarus Joseph suggested the establishment of a foundation to provide funding for an Olympic proposal. The Controller said that games in New York would "send a message to the rest of the world on what American ideals mean and what our government stands for."

Avery Brundage, President of the United States Olympic Committee spoke next. He stated that in some parts of the world, the United States was not looked on with much respect. "But they respect our athletes" he announced, "they have to." Thunderous applause and cheering capped his remarks. The final speaker was National Amateur Athletic Union Champion Pole Vaulter Robert Richards, who spoke of the pride of all the athletes to represent the nation and the intention of everyone to compete well and to win. "But if we lose," he concluded, "we will lose gracefully. I pledge that we will abide by the rules of good sportsmanship."

Several hours later the first group of athletes boarded a plane at Idlewild International Airport for the flight to Helsinki, Finland. The remaining Olympians and officials followed over the next two days. Hopeful predictions of America's "bringing home the bacon" came true. When the games ended, the United States had accumulated a total of 74 medals, 40 of them gold, more than any other nation. Second place in medal standing went to the Soviet Union with 71 medals, 22 of them gold.

St. Paul's Chapel

When it was constructed in 1766, the chapel built for the growing congregation at Trinity Church was in a field just outside the edge of the city itself. Designed in Late Georgian architecture with a classical portico and an octagonal tower, St. Paul's Chapel is the oldest surviving church building in Manhattan.

The chapel survived the Great Fire of 1776, when much of the city was burned shortly after it fell to the British following General Washington's defeat in the Battle of Brooklyn. Washington returned to the chapel 13 years later, to pray on the morning of his inauguration as the first President of the United States.

As the city grew and changed around it, St. Paul's changed with it. In the late 1800s, it opened a vocational school for girls, provided language and cooking classes to immigrant women, and created a relief fund for the sick and jobless. In 1904, it began holding religious services at 3 in the morning so night workers in the nearby printing plants of newspaper row could attend, and during the Depression it operated a soup kitchen. In 1983, a homeless shelter was created.

The chapel narrowly survived destruction on September 11, 2001, when a portion of the collapsing World Trade Center crashed into a sycamore tree behind the chapel. The tree was destroyed, but the debris missed the building. During the weeks after the attack, the chapel became a center for rest and recovery of the rescue workers. Today, St. Paul's continues its ministry, serving a diverse community, as well as more than one million tourists annually.

Friday, July 18, 1952:
Commodore Harry Manning and Crew of SS *United States*

On her maiden voyage from New York to England, the ocean liner *United States* set a transatlantic eastbound speed record, making the crossing in three days, ten hours, and 40 minutes (an average speed of 35.59 knots, almost 41 mph). On her return voyage to New York, the liner set the westbound speed record, making the crossing in three days, 12 hours, and 12 minutes (average speed 34.51 knots, almost 40 mph). In celebration of these new records, Commodore Harry Manning and his crew were honored with a parade.

The day dawned exceedingly hot and humid. Leading the parade was an honor escort of mounted policemen followed by more than 3,000 marchers representing the military, municipal workers and midshipmen from the Merchant Marine Academy. Police estimated that 150,000 spectators lined the parade route. The march had barely begun when the heavens opened with a summer shower, but the rain did nothing to stop the procession, though ticker tape and confetti turned into sodden streamers. International signal flags spelling out the message "well done" were flattened against the façade of the Cunard building, whose ship *Queen Mary* had previously held both speed records. Spectators along the route, in shirt sleeves because of the heat and humidity, rushed for cover in skyscraper doorways. Everyone from onlookers and marchers to the commodore and his crew were soaked by the short but intense shower, but the procession continued moving north despite the weather with flags hanging limply on staffs along the route.

Ten open cars carried the officers and crew of the liner with Commodore Manning in the last one. With him rode his Chief Engineer, William Kaiser, and Reception Committee Chairman Grover Whalen. Officers doffed their white caps to the crowd and the only concession to the weather was made by Mr. Whalen, who removed his customary top hat.

As the parade neared Fulton Street, the rain stopped as suddenly as it had begun, and by the time marchers entered City Hall Park, the humidity returned with a vengeance. The midshipmen stood at full attention in neat rows during Mayor Impellitteri's remarks. As he was awarding Gold Medals to the officers of *United States*, however, the weather took its toll and five of the midshipmen collapsed from the heat. None required medical attention and after a few moments in the shade, they returned to the ranks. In addition to the mayor, the speakers included John Franklin, the President of United States line; the ship's designer, William Gibbs; and finally, Vice Admiral Edward Cochran, chief of the Maritime Board.

At the conclusion of the remarks at City Hall Park, Manning and a group of officers, led by an escort of policemen on motorcycles, were transported to the Waldorf Astoria for lunch. One and all seemed delighted when they stepped into the air-conditioned comfort of the dining room. Manning spoke briefly at the luncheon praising his ship, saying "she is the most beautiful thing I have ever seen – far more beautiful than any woman I have ever known." This was not the first time that Manning was a member of a ticker tape celebration. He had been one of the officers of the crew of *America* who were honored because of their work in the rescue of seamen of the Italian freighter *Florida (see January 28, 1929)*.

Commodore Manning soon retired from the United States Lines. The official announcement said he had exhausted himself during the maiden voyages, but it was known that he bristled from the increasing oversight of day-to-day operations by management which, he felt, undermined the authority of the captain. He died in 1974 and is buried in Arlington National Cemetery.

The liner continued in service until 1969. Because of the declining number of passengers, the *United States* was moved to Newport News, Virginia, where her engines and machinery were removed. The liner was towed to Turkey in 1992 and stripped of all asbestos and furnishings. When no foreign buyer could be found, the ship was towed back to the United States and docked in Philadelphia. Norwegian Cruise Lines purchased the ship in 2003, with plans to recondition and use her on the West Coast and Hawaii. Nothing came of this proposal and she remains docked in Philadelphia where she is sometimes known as "the largest abandoned vehicle in the city." In 2011 a group named the United States Conservatory, which had been formed two years earlier, purchased the former liner. Further attempts to return the ship into a passenger vessel proved fruitless. In mid-September 2018 the Conservatory sold the *United States* to the Damen Ship Repair & Conversion Company in hopes of turning the liner into a museum.

Thursday, December 18, 1952:
Lieutenant General Willis Crittenberger

General Crittenberger, Commander of the First Army headquartered on Fort Jay on Governors Island in New York Harbor, was stepping down. As a Second Lieutenant in World War I, he was a member of the Third Cavalry Regiment and saw almost no combat until the final days of the war. Between the wars he steadily advanced in rank to Major General. During World War II, he was one of General Eisenhower's original choices to command a corps on D-Day, but because of his lack of combat experience was named commander of IV Corps, a reserve command. In late 1944 this corps was assigned to Italy, and Crittenberger led his mixed corps of United States and Brazilian troops in northern Italy for the remainder of the war. After the war, he was military advisor to the United States mission to the United Nations, and since early 1950, commander of the First Army.

On a crisp clear December morning, the 62-year-old general and his wife Josephine left their residence on Governors Island at 11:30. The road to the ferry was lined with military personnel, and the First Army Band played "Auld Lang Syne" as he shook hands with his staff officers. He boarded the ferry for the short ride across the narrow channel between the two islands. A 15-gun salute fired from Fort Jay as a final farewell from his last command, as two helicopters flew overhead and a fireboat shot a watery salute.

Grover Whalen, Reception Committee Chairman, boarded the ferry at the Battery and escorted the general ashore. Crittenberger then reviewed honor guards from the Army, Navy, Marine Corps, Coast Guard, Air Force, the New York City Fire Department, and the Old Guard (a special detachment of the Third US Infantry Regiment that wore Revolutionary War uniforms on dress occasions). General and Mrs. Crittenberger joined Mr. Whalen in an open top vehicle for the ride up Whitehall Street to Broadway and City Hall. A military contingent marched to the front and rear of the official car, and marching music was provided by the First Army and Third Naval District bands.

In the absence of Mayor Impellitteri, Acting Mayor Rudolph Halley presented the General with New York City's Medal of Honor and a scroll citing his "distinguished and exceptional service at home and in the battlefield and in the councils of the United Nations." Philippine Ambassador to the UN, Brigadier General Carlos Romulo, and Assistant Secretary General of the UN Benjamin Cohen made brief remarks regarding the general and his service.

Following the brief ceremony, a motorcycle escort led the general and his wife in an Army sedan to the Holland Tunnel for the drive to visit his brother in Indianapolis, one of his sons at Fort Leavenworth, Kansas, and eventually to Fort Sam Houston in Texas. Crittenberger commented that Fort Sam Houston was "where I reported for duty in August 1913, and if there's such a thing in the philosophy of life as completing the cycle, this is it."

Two of the general's three sons died in combat, one in Germany in 1945 and the other in Vietnam in 1969. When the general died in Chevy Chase, Maryland in 1980 at the age of 89, he was buried beside them in Arlington National Cemetery.

Friday, January 30, 1953: Vice Admiral Walter DeLany

After 45 years of continuous service in the US Navy, Vice Admiral Walter DeLany retired from active duty. The 62-year-old Pennsylvanian served on destroyers based out of Ireland during the First World War. Most of his World War II service was aboard cruisers in the Pacific but in early 1945 he was placed on convoy organizational duty in the Atlantic. Two years after the war ended, he was given command of the Eastern Sea Frontier, responsible for guarding the eastern coast of the United States. He also commanded the Atlantic Reserve Fleet of deactivated Second World War ships subject to returning to duty in case of emergency.

The admiral left his command at the Brooklyn Navy Yard early on this cold January morning. He was saluted by his staff and personnel at the Yard and then proceeded to Battery Place. Met there by Grover Whalen, Chairman of the Reception Committee, the admiral stepped into a brown open naval car and began the slow ride to City Hall at precisely noon. The cold and gusty wind helped keep attendance low and it was estimated that only about 50,000 spectators lined the route. They watched as the parade, containing detachments of the Army, Navy, Marine Corps, Coast Guard and Merchant Marine, escorted the Admiral. Small contingents of the Police, Fire, and Sanitation Departments also accompanied the retiring naval commander, and the marching tempo was provided by an Army and a Navy band.

Mayor Impellitteri greeted the Admiral in the Council Chambers of City Hall, where several hundred guests were present including Fleet Admiral William Halsey and Lieutenant General Withers Burress. Calling him "our naval guardian," the mayor presented the Admiral with the city's Medal of Honor and a scroll for distinguished service.

As the Admiral exited City Hall, he was given a final salute by flag-bearing members of the Fire Department Honor Guard. Ten days later the retired Admiral and his wife began an extensive 55-day Atlantic and Mediterranean cruise, after which he took a position with the Mutual Security Administration, successor of the Marshall Plan. The admiral ended his career with that agency in 1960 and became an active member and contributing author to the Naval History Center in Washington, DC.

A graduate of the US Naval Academy Class of 1912, Admiral DeLany spent his last years at his home in Reading, Pennsylvania. He died there on September 21, 1980, and is buried at the Naval Academy in Annapolis, Maryland.

Friday, April 3, 1953:
Metropolitan New York Combat Contingent

Skies were gray and there were occasional light showers on this Good Friday morning, but for the more than 2,200 GI's on board the Navy Transport *General William Wiegel* it was anything but a gloomy day. They were the first troops returning from Korea, and had sailed out of Yokahama, Japan, 27 days earlier and now they were back in the United States. They could hardly control their excitement as the transport docked at Pier 1 of the Brooklyn Army Terminal. The almost month-long boring and tedious voyage had been made even longer when the transport rode at anchor off Quarantine the entire night before, the lights of the city so close they seemed within arm's length. "Transports never dock at night," said Rear Admiral John Will, Commander of the Military Sea Transportation Service, "and the *Wiegel* wasn't due until Friday and shore transportation had been arranged accordingly." For the 351 men who lived in the New York metro area, all of whom had been promised a ticker tape parade, that last night aboard ship seemed the longest.

The transport started the slow trip up the harbor at 6 o'clock the next morning. Delay after delay followed and it took more than three hours before the transport was finally moored to a pier at the Brooklyn Navy Yard. The men on board saw hundreds of people waiting to welcome them home. Many carried handmade signs welcoming the men home, with messages like "Welcome Back, Daddy," "Hi, Handsome" or "I Love You, Sugarpuss."

At 9:30, the troops began disembarking, as 25 stern-faced Military Police (MP) officers stood at the gangways and along the piers to prevent anyone from breaking ranks. Another dozen MP's stood at wooden barricades separating the public from the returning troops. Finally, with the GI's lined up on the piers, someone blew a whistle, the MP's turned or walked away and, for almost a half hour, pandemonium reigned. Wives found husbands and hugged, Parents found sons and wept in joy. Sweethearts found each other and kissed. Some men saw children born after they had shipped out to Korea, other children bashfully hid from fathers they barely remembered. Brothers and friends shook hands or embraced. All over was the sound of crying and laughing and people calling names, searching, finding, reuniting. Then a second whistle blew, and most of the soldiers headed to staging areas. The men from the New York area fell in around a convoy of 17 open Army trucks. The convoy soon rolled off the pier, onto the still unfinished Brooklyn-Queens Expressway, over the Brooklyn Bridge, and to the Battery for the start of the promised parade of welcome.

At the Battery the vehicular convoy was met by John Adikes, Vice Chairman of the Mayor's Reception Committee; D. Y. Nam Koong, Korean Consul in New York; Brigadier General Calvin DeWitt, commander of the Port of Embarkation; and Lieutenant General Withers Burress, First Army commander. They were joined by Major Owen Carroll, former advisor to the Second Republic of Korea Division, the senior officer returning home. It was just past 3 o'clock when the parade finally began, accompanied by the First Army Band. Due to the hour and many businesses being closed early or all day because of Good Friday, the crowds along the way were considerably smaller than usual. Perhaps fewer than 25,000 lined the streets, and the amount of ticker tape was negligible.

Another 5,000 people waited for the trucks in City Hall Plaza, where Mayor Impellitteri addressed the group and expressed the hope that the Armistice in Korea would soon bring the downfall of Communist North Korea and a unification of North and South Korea. He concluded by saying that the entire city looked forward to the day when all American troops would come home from Korea and be welcomed as veterans of the costly fighting there.

Sergeant First-Class John Donohue of Atlantic City, New Jersey, recipient of the Silver Star for valor under fire, had been chosen to speak for the troops. His speech was brief, fewer than 20 words, and concluded with the phrase "thanks for everything." When the ceremony ended the soldiers returned to the trucks for the trip to Camp Kilmer, New Jersey. Some were discharged there; others granted furloughs.

The mayor's words, unfortunately, were far from accurate. As of 2020 the Korean peninsula is still divided between the Communist North Korea and the Republic of Korea in the south. American troops are still stationed near the Demilitarized Zone, a 4-kilometer-wide strip of land running the entire 250-kilometer breadth of the Korean Peninsula, separating the two countries. As far as Korean War veterans being welcomed, it would be another 38 years before such a welcome took place in the Canyon of Heroes *(see: June 25, 1991)*.

Friday, April 24, 1953: Lieutenant General James Van Fleet

Lieutenant General James Van Fleet, Commander of United Nations forces in Korea, was met by Grover Whalen, Chairman of the Mayor's Welcoming and Reception Committee, at the Park Sheraton Hotel just before noon. Together they entered a city limousine for the drive downtown to the Battery for the parade to honor the retiring 61-year-old general. Three New York City helicopters circled overhead and two of the city's fireboats sent arches of water into the air as the car sped down the FDR Drive with a police escort. It was a perfect day for a parade: bright sunshine, temperature in the mid-60s, a gentle breeze.

At the Battery, the general transferred to a convertible and the parade commenced with 20 motorcycle policemen, each motorcycle flying a large American flag. The First Army Band and a Navy band were followed by Police, Fire, and Sanitation units and detachments from the Army, Navy, Air Force, and Coast Guard. Almost 2,000 marchers escorted the general up Broadway. He stood in the car provided for him with his wife Helen seated at his side. The mayor's wife, Elizabeth Impelliterri, sat in a second vehicle with Andrew Cordier, Executive Assistant to the UN Secretary General and, in recognition of the general's work in Greece in 1948, Spyros Skouras, head of the Twentieth Century Fox Film Corporation, officially representing the Greek government.

The general seemed pleased by the reception awarded him. According to police estimates there were more than 55,000 cheering and waving spectators, standing ten deep behind the police barricades in some places. Ticker tape, computer and time clock punch cards, torn newspapers, and confetti swirled down through the Broadway canyon.

Once at City Hall, the general was greeted by Mayor Impellitteri and Cardinal Francis Spellman. The mayor praised General Van Fleet as a great warrior who had been "the mainspring in the bitter struggle" against Communist forces, first in the Greek civil war and then in Korea. Before 2,500 spectators in City Hall Plaza, the mayor placed the city's Gold Medal around General Van Fleet's neck and presented him with a scroll, highlighting the general's distinguished and exceptional service. Cardinal Spellman spoke briefly, praising the general's wife as a "solider in the war against Communist oppression" by sacrificing her husband's companionship.

When General Van Fleet spoke, he made little mention of the possibility of the end of hostilities in Korea. Instead, he reminded his audience that the war that had been waged in Greece eight years earlier was against the same "godless enemy of liberty" as in Korea. The general thanked the city and its people for the welcome bestowed upon him and concluded by speaking on behalf of those still fighting on the Korean peninsula, "I accept this great welcome for them, as I feel that this great crowd has turned out for them."

Following the City Hall reception, a private luncheon for a small number of guests was held at the Metropolitan Club on East 60th Street. At the luncheon the general spoke of the troops in Korea and called them "the greatest generation we have ever produced. Don't let them down," he admonished.

General Van Fleet returned to his home state of New Jersey shortly after the city's reception for him. A 1911 graduate of West Point, he was a classmate of Generals Eisenhower and Omar Bradley, and saw combat in the First and Second World Wars as well as Korea. He was instrumental in the creation of the Korea Society, an organization that fostered closer relations between the US and Korea. He relocated to Florida in the mid-1960s and died there, peacefully in his sleep, in 1992, not long before his 100th birthday. At the time of his death, he was the oldest general in the US Army.

Tuesday, May 26, 1953:
150th Anniversary of Laying of the City Hall Cornerstone

In 1803 Mayor Edward Livingston presided over the laying of the cornerstone of City Hall. Food and drink were provided at noon for the score of laborers, who had been hired at the cost of $100, and the mayor gave a "short and appropriate speech." A donkey hauled the marble slab into place, and the task of setting the cornerstone did not start until 3 o'clock, after the New York City Common Council had approved an additional $50 for expenses. Three hours later, the work was finished.

The 150th anniversary of City Hall coincided with the tricentennial of the New York's incorporation as a city in 1653. Mr. Lee Thompson Smith, acting as Chairman of both the City Hall Commission and the City Tricentennial Commission, planned a celebration including a ticker tape parade and a re-enactment of the laying of the marble cornerstone.

Representatives of almost every city department marched from the Battery to City Hall. They were accompanied by small detachments from the Army, Navy, Marine Corps, and Coast Guard. Music was provided by the marching bands from the city's uniformed departments: police, fire and sanitation.

The members of the re-enactment group marched up Broadway, which in 1803 had been the city's main thoroughfare. Long gone were the stones and gravel that had once paved it, now replaced by modern surfacing and traffic signs. As the parade continued the street became carpeted with ticker tape, and a small but appreciative crowd cheered the marchers as they moved north on a humid overcast day.

At City Hall the New York Post Office Band played music from 1803 and patriotic tunes. Students from the High School of Performing Arts, costumed as early 19th century laborers and officials, reenacted the cornerstone laying. According to the *New York Times*, a donkey named Jenney, on loan from the Bronx Zoo, "gave a reluctant but adequate performance" portraying the original donkey by pulling a replica cornerstone. Students played the parts of officials and laborers, by giving contradictory directions and shouting encouragement.

Mayor Impellitteri gave a short speech, followed by Mr. Allen Foster, President of the City's Art Commission, who called City Hall "a gem of American architecture." He was followed by Mr. Albert Morgan, Deputy Commissioner of Public Works, who announced the commencement of renovation work on City Hall's exterior for an estimated cost of $2.5 million, adding that funding would be in the 1954 budget to restore the interior of the building.

The event ended after Mr. Morgan's speech. Unlike the 1803 ceremony, no funds had been allocated for food and drink and the students and participants departed unfed.

City Hall

The first *"Stadt Huys"* for Dutch New Amsterdam, built in 1642 on Pearl Street, was replaced in 1700 by a building on Wall and Nassau Streets. When New York became the first capital of the United States, this building was renamed Federal Hall and became the meeting place for the first US Congress. The city government needed a new home, and a site was selected half a mile away in the Commons on the northern edge of the city. In 1803, the cornerstone was laid for the new City Hall, designed by architects Joseph Mangin and John McComb. The building was dedicated in 1811 and officially opened in 1812. At the time, it was one of the tallest buildings in the city and housed all three branches of city government.

The building consists of a central pavilion with two wings on either side. Just inside the main entrance is the Rotunda, the building's grand lobby, with a cantilevered marble staircase rising to the second floor and a dome and oculus overhead, supported by marble columns. The west wing of the building is largely occupied by the executive branch, including the Mayor's office, while the east wing contains large rooms on each of the first two floors. The room on the first floor was originally used as a Courtroom, but in 1875 became the meeting space for the Municipal Council, and later the Board of Estimate. The second floor originally held two smaller courtrooms but later was transformed into the Aldermanic Chamber, which was renamed the Council Chamber in 1938. The third floor was originally used for storage and maintenance offices, but after a fire in 1858 was redesigned and currently contains the City Hall Portrait Collection and the Art Commission.

The building's exterior was originally covered in marble and brownstone but was refaced with limestone in the 1950s. The central dome was rebuilt in 1917 to repair damage from two fires over the past century. Leading up to the main entrance is a grand staircase that has often been used for press conferences and outdoor ceremonies.

The entire building received a major renovation between 2010 and 2015, including stabilization and modernization of the infrastructure, which had greatly deteriorated over time, thus preserving the historic building. The building is the oldest city hall in the US still serving its governmental functions and is a designated historical landmark.

Tuesday, July 21, 1953: Ben Hogan

It was just past dawn on July 21, 1953 when the liner *United States* passed Quarantine, where newspaper, radio, and television reporters boarded from smaller boats. The reporters were informed that the man they wished to interview, Ben Hogan, winner of the British Open at the Carnoustie golf course in Scotland, was still eating breakfast. As the *United States* slowly steamed past the Statue of Liberty an hour later, the golfer appeared and spoke to the press. Much of what he said was drowned out by the din of fireboats and police launches welcoming him with horns and whistles. The liner continued up the Hudson River and finally docked at Pier 86, West 46th Street, just after 8 o'clock. After clearing customs, Hogan and his wife Valerie were driven to the Park Lane Hotel before they proceeded downtown to Bowling Green for the start of the parade in his honor.

Shortly after noon the parade started out. Bowling Green had been declared by the Mayor a "Putting Green for the Day" although no one seems to have putted. The golfer shared an open vehicle with Grover Whalen, Chairman of the Reception Committee, and Isaac Grainger, Vice President of the United States Golf Association. Riding in the second vehicle was Mrs. Hogan, Horton Smith, President of the Professional Golfers Association, and Lincoln Warden, President of the Golf Writers Association. A small motorcycle escort led the way, followed by Troops A and B of the city's mounted police. A color guard drawn from the city's uniformed services and the Fire Department Band completed the parade. One hundred policemen stood guard along the route but the approximately 150,000 spectators were orderly. Only a small amount of paper and ticker tape littered Broadway. An unidentified observer suggested that the high heat and humidity might have been the cause for the lack of crowd and ticker tape. Known for his lack of emotion on the links, Hogan waved and smiled despite the small turnout.

At City Hall the Fire Department Band joined forces with the waiting Sanitation Department Band for the national anthem, and Grover Whalen introduced the champion golfer to Mayor Impellitteri. The mayor joked, "Here you are, the world's greatest golfer and I am probably the world's worst." Knowingly or not, he said almost the exact same words that Mayor Jimmy Walker had said more than 20 years earlier to golfer Bobby Jones (see: July 2, 1930). Mayor Impellitteri presented Hogan with a scroll listing Hogan's gold triumphs: four United States Opens, the British Open, two PGA tournaments, and the Masters. The mayor then read a telegram from another golfer, President Dwight Eisenhower, reading, "Millions of Americans would like to participate with New Yorkers in extending their traditional welcome."

Hogan had difficulty in expressing his gratitude for the welcome. "I've got a tough skin," he said, "but this kind of thing brings tears to my eyes. This tops anything I ever received," he added, his voice breaking with emotion. Closing the reception, the bands played "The Eyes of Texas Are Upon You" in honor of the Texas-born golfer.

A luncheon for 150 invited guests followed at Toots Shor's restaurant on West 52nd Street, where Hogan was informed that he had been named the 13th member of the Golf Hall of Fame. He had turned professional in 1930 at the age of 18 and retired in 1971 at the age of 59, accumulating a total of 68 professional wins over his career. He started and ran a golf club company and continued to give golf instructions well into his 70's. Ben Hogan died in Fort Worth, Texas, July 25, 1997.

Thursday, October 1, 1953:
José Antonio Remón, President of Panama

After visiting Washington, DC, José Antonio Remón Cantera, President of the Republic of Panama, arrived at New York's LaGuardia Airport on a sunny and warm October morning. Accompanied by his wife, Cecilia, the Panamanian Chief of State was met by Grover Whalen, Chairman of the Mayor's Reception Committee, and Cipriano Paz Rodriguez, a former teammate of the president when both men played amateur baseball in Panama more than a quarter century earlier. Mr. Rodriguez had relocated to New York a dozen years earlier.

A small motorcade escorted by mounted and motorcycle police and a marching band constituted the parade. No police estimate was given, and a small number of spectators along the route waved Panamanian flags and shouted welcome to Mr. Remón in Spanish.

Mayor Impellitteri greeted the Panamanian president at City Hall and awarded him the city's Gold Medal. A former general in the Panamanian Army, Mr. Remón had assumed the office of president as a result of a coup exactly one year earlier. The mayor praised him on his efforts to bring stability to his country while it was in the process of attempting to renegotiate the Panama Canal Treaty with the United States.

Following the brief reception, President Ramón and the Mayor attended a baseball game at Yankee Stadium, accompanied by Roberto Huertematte, the Panamanian Ambassador to the United States, and John Wiley, the American Ambassador to Panama. The game was the second in the 1953 World Series between the New York Yankees and the Brooklyn Dodgers. Asked who he was rooting for, the president diplomatically responded that he was neutral.

President Ramón returned to Panama two days later and in 1954 was responsible for increasing his nation's share of canal revenue from $430,000 to $1,900,000. This alteration created considerable activity on the part of Panama for further treaty modifications.

On January 2, 1955, President Ramón was assassinated by machine gun fire while at a thoroughbred horse race in Panama City. An American was arrested for the murder but he was proven to be miles away at the time of the murder. Subsequently the lawyer for the Panamanian Vice President was tried for the crime but found not guilty. The case remains unsolved, but recently declassified CIA documents indicate that President Ramón might have been killed by orders of the American gangster, Lucky Luciano. It is alleged that the Panamanian was involved in heroin shipments and stole from Luciano.

Tuesday, October 20, 1953: General Mark Clark

The youngest man promoted to Lieutenant General in US History (at the age of 46) and also the youngest four-star General (at the age of 47), General Mark Clark received a ticker tape parade on a sunny but blustery fall day. Scheduled to retire from the military ten days later, the general arrived in the city two days earlier en route to Washington, DC. He and his wife, joined by their son Colonel William Clark, on leave from Fort Benning, Georgia, were provided a suite at the Astor Hotel by the Reception Committee.

Shortly before noon, the party was escorted by Mayor Impellitteri and his wife to limousines waiting outside the hotel. The general and his wife rode in the first car, along with the mayor and his wife, and the perennial Chairman of the Mayor's Reception Committee, Grover Whalen. Approximately 1,000 people had gathered at the hotel and cheered when the general's car, flying a pennant with four general's stars, headed south. A police escort of 22 motorcycles led the way down Seventh Avenue to 34th Street and then down the FDR Drive to the Battery.

The parade departed from Bowling Green shortly after noon, and was met with a blizzard of paper, countless streams of ticker tape and confetti. Leading the parade were 38 mounted policemen, followed by vehicles for the general, military and political dignitaries and members of the general's family. They were followed by a marching detachment of 80 soldiers from the Eighth Army who had seen combat in Korea, and National Guard, Navy, and Marine Corps formations. Interspaced between them were no fewer than seven bands, representing, in order, the Marines, Navy, Coast Guard, Air Force, Police, Fire, and Sanitation Departments. In the Wall Street area, noontime spectators stood six to seven deep behind police barricades.

The First Army Band was assembled in City Hall Plaza, playing the National Anthem as the parade halted. The general and members of the military snapped to attention and saluted while the 10,000 visitors who had been admitted to the area stood in respectful silence. When General Clark finally dismounted from the vehicle the silence was broken by a throaty roar.

A grandstand stood in front of City Hall where the mayor hung the city's Gold Medal around the general's neck. The mayor spoke before introducing the general, saying, "Our people join freedom-loving people everywhere in expressing their gratitude to you, because you are a symbol of the forces of dignity and decency." In his introduction of the general, the mayor cited Clark's role in the surrender of the Vichy French in North Africa in 1942, his leadership of the Fifth Army in Italy in 1943 and 1944, how his troops had broken the German lines at Monte Casino and liberated Rome, and his acceptance of the surrender of the remaining German troops in Italy in the spring of 1945. Not forgetting more recent events, the mayor also spoke of the general's leadership in the brutal fighting on the Korean peninsula.

General Clark responded, thanking the mayor, his committee, and all New Yorkers for their hospitality and welcome. Turning his subject to the dangers of Communism, he said, "I have found the Communist to be a treacherous, evil foe, seeking world domination. You can't trust him. There is no decency, no honesty, in his make-up."

He concluded his remarks by praising the fighting men in Korea. "There should have been," he said, "a GI, sailor, airman and marine riding in that car instead of me to be honored today." Loud and continuous applause and cheering followed.

The general reviewed the more than 2,000 troops from all branches of the service that marched that day, then he moved into the Council Chambers. Among the 300 guests invited inside was Governor James Byrnes of South Carolina, the general's home state, and retired General Lucius Clay, military governor in Germany *(see: May 19, 1949)*.

Despite his military achievements during the Second World War, a number of historians blame his orders for the destruction of the 11th century Benedictine monastery at Monte Casino in Italy. Following his seizure of the mountainous terrain there, contrary to orders to pursue the retreating German forces, he changed the direction of his advance and captured Rome. He was personally praised by Pope Pius XII for this movement, but the delayed pursuit permitted the Germans to regroup north of Rome and prolong the fighting in Italy.

Early the following morning, the general and his party traveled to Washington for additional honors before he officially retired. Following his retirement, he served as President of the Citadel in Charleston, South Carolina, and wrote two volumes of memoirs. He died in Charleston in 1984 and is buried at the Citadel.

Monday, October 26, 1953: Major General William Dean

Major General William Dean was the highest-ranking individual captured during the Korean War. Attempting to aid wounded members of his division, he lost his way and was injured falling down a steep hill. Taken prisoner by North Korean troops he attempted to conceal his identity but was recognized by a former South Korean official who knew him before the War. Moved further north and held in solitary confinement much of his captivity, he was accused of being a war criminal and was frequently questioned about military matters but refused to provide anything of value. He was imprisoned until after the Korean Armistice agreement of July 1953, and finally exchanged in September of that year. Unlike other UN Prisoners of War, Dean was not physically tortured by the Communists and he later revealed that he was ready to commit suicide rather than break had he been tortured. Unaware that he had been taken prisoner, the American military believed he had been killed in action and awarded him the Medal of Honor, the nation's highest military award. The medal was given to the general's wife Mildred, and the citation mentioned his "conspicuous gallantry and intrepidity at the repeated risk of his life above and beyond the call of duty."

Flown from Washington to New York on the morning of the parade, General Dean was treated to a ticker tape parade on a bright autumn day that was witnessed by an estimated 500,000 spectators. Dressed in his Army uniform bearing the patch of the 24th Division, he wore only a single row of decorations, the most prominent of which was the Medal of Honor. The entire route north, the general waved to the crowd, which greeted him with almost continuous applause and cheering. The parade was showered with streamers, ticker tape and blizzards of confetti.

When the parade finally reached City Hall, Mayor Vincent Impellitteri shook the general's hand and personally led him to the podium and introduced the general. In reply, the general spoke of other POWs who were captured and suffered worse than he had, mentioning several New Yorkers by name who had been imprisoned with him.

The general's remarks were followed by a reception inside City Hall and later that afternoon, General Dean and his wife Mildred called on retired General Douglas Mac-Arthur at the Waldorf Astoria.

General Dean was named Grand Marshal of the 1954 Tournament of Roses Parade for the Rose Bowl and continued in the military until he retired in October 1955. He resided in San Francisco for the remainder of his life, passing away there on August 24, 1981. He is buried in the San Francisco National Cemetery at the Presidio.

Monday, November 2, 1953:
King Paul and Queen Frederika of Greece

The King and Queen of Greece, recently arrived in New York for a two-week visit to the United States, entered an open car at the Battery, smiling broadly. King Paul wore the dress uniform of the Greek Army and was visiting the city for the third time, but this would be his first ticker tape welcome. His attractive queen, Frederika of Hanover, a distant cousin to Queen Elizabeth II of Great Britain, wore a brown velvet coat trimmed in white and beige gloves. It was her first visit to New York, and she could barely restrain her excitement.

Shortly after noon the parade began its trip up Broadway. It was escorted by motorcycle policemen, sirens wailing, followed by color guards from the Police and Fire Departments, and the First Army Band. Grover Whalen, Chairman of the Mayor's Reception Committee, shared the vehicle with the King and Queen and pointed out the various buildings along the route. As they passed a skyscraper south of Wall Street, Queen Frederika laughed, "My brother Christian works there. Maybe they'll give him a raise." Swirling ribbons of ticker tape drifted down, and a strand wrapped itself around the queen. When the king offered to remove it from around her shoulder, she refused to permit him and wore it like a royal decoration.

Thousands of spectators lined the route, and the Royal Couple waved at those carrying small Greek flags. Mixed in among the cheers were a number of whistles directed at the pretty Queen. The King requested that the motorcade halt at St Paul's Chapel, so he could greet the rector, Dr. Robert Hunsicker. Friends for many years, the two shook hands and the cheering grew to its loudest. When the vehicle resumed its move north, spectators could be seen pointing overhead, where a small skywriting plane was creating a greeting for the Royal Couple. Pilot Andy Stints was the son of Greek immigrants from Crete.

The caravan finally halted at City Hall. Grover Whalen, nursing a recently injured leg, slipped as he exited the car. Queen Frederika offered her hand to assist the embarrassed Mr. Whalen, cautioning him to be careful. Recovering his composure and balance, he introduced their Highnesses to Mayor Impellitteri. The mayor extended an official welcome to the Royal Couple and placed the red-ribboned gold New York Medal of Honor around their necks. He then presented them with a scroll for distinguished service. King Paul took the microphone and, speaking in fluent English, surprised the mayor by investing him in the Order of the Phoenix with the degree of Knight Commander. For non-Greek citizens, membership in the Order is reserved for those who have raised Greek prestige in their countries. The mayor's term in office ended in just two months, so knowing this would be one of his last official receptions, the mayor commented, "I can't think of a nicer way to go out of office." King Paul added that he found New York "an example of how people of varying origins and races could become as one in a spirit of unity."

Following a review of the parade, the Royal Couple proceeded to the Waldorf Astoria for a luncheon in the Grand Ballroom. Over a thousand people attended the affair. Retired Lieutenant General James Van Fleet *(see: April 24, 1953)*, who had acted as military advisor to the Greek government when it suppressed earlier attempts by Greek guerrillas to seize control, was guest speaker. Praising the King and his country, he said, "It was your people who drove the Red murderers out of your country without a drop of American blood."

The day ended for the King and Queen at the Commodore Hotel, where they attended a dinner-dance sponsored by the Hellenic-American Federation of Greater New York. The following morning, they met with Dag Hammarskjöld, Secretary General of the United Nations, before traveling on to Washington, DC. They met with government and business leaders and assured them that, despite the recent earthquakes that had caused heavy damage in the Ionian Islands, Greece was moving towards a brighter future.

During World War II, when Greece was occupied by German and Italian troops, Paul fled to London and then Cairo, becoming a spokesman for Greek resistance to its occupiers. He ascended the throne when his childless brother, King George II, died suddenly in 1947. As king, he faced and defeated a Communist attempt to gain control of his country. His popularity increased when Great Britain withdrew from the island of Cyprus, claimed by both Greek and Turkey, and the island gained independence. Republican sentiment in Greece was growing, however, and to decrease the Greek financial support of the monarchy, he donated his private estate to the nation. King Paul underwent an emergency operation for appendicitis in late 1963 but was slow in recovering. In February 1964, he was diagnosed with stomach cancer and operated on again. The operation was unsuccessful, and he died a week later. He was succeeded by his son, Constantine II.

Queen Frederika never enjoyed the popularity of her husband in Greece. Born Princess Frederika of Hannover in 1917, she was a member of the League of German Girls, the female branch of the Hitler Youth during the 1930s. She married then-prince Paul in 1938 and was often criticized after the war for her German heritage and association with the Nazis. Even her work with Greek orphans and refugees during the

Greek Civil War in 1948 and 1949 was criticized for being too undemocratic. When Paul died, she became Queen Dowager and went into exile with her son, King Constantine, when a military coup overthrew the monarchy in 1972. She died in Madrid in 1981.

Thursday, November 5, 1953:
The 50th Anniversary of Powered Flight

When Orville Wright took to the air on the morning of December 17, 1903, at Kitty Hawk, North Carolina, it was mankind's first powered flight, lasting 12 seconds and traveling a mere 120 feet. Since then, mankind had learned to escape the limits of the ground and gravity. The golden anniversary of that achievement was commemorated (a month prematurely) with a ticker tape parade up the Canyon of Heroes. General James Doolittle, retired Captain Edward Rickenbacker, and three others were selected to be honored in the parade.

Shortly after noon on a cool but bright November morning the parade stepped off from Bowling Green. Fittingly an Air Force detachment led the procession, followed by. groups from the Army, Navy, Coast Guard, and Marine Corps. The tempo was provided by bands from the military, the Police and Fire Departments, as an estimated 150,000 spectators viewed the parade and the City Hall Plaza ceremony.

The five men being honored rode in two convertibles. General Doolittle, commander of the 1942 raid on Tokyo that bears his name, rode in the first car. Next to him was supposed to be Edward Rickenbacker, a pioneer in commercial aviation who had been America's top Ace in the First World War with 26 confirmed kills. But Rickenbacker could not attend, so in his place sat Edward Cavanaugh, City Commissioner of Marine and Aviation.

The second vehicle contained Acting Sergeant Gerald Crosson, New York City Police Department, who had flown 105 helicopter missions in Korea as an Army pilot. Acting Captain Gustav Crawford, also of the Police Department, rode with him, being honored for his outstanding service in the Department's Aviation Bureau. The final honoree was Captain Frank Arthur Erickson, Chief of the Search and Rescue Team of the United States Coast Guard, for his mercy missions from the Battery Heliport.

Mayor Impellitteri presented each of the five with a scroll honoring their accomplishments. The mayor commented on the city's long history of welcoming aviators: from pioneers who flew solo across the Atlantic to circumnavigators and balloonists. How appropriate it is, he stressed, that the city honor flight itself and contemporary aviators.

General Doolittle responded for the group, mentioning the first flight at Kitty Hawk, flight's infancy and growth, and the development of air power. "Aviation is a potent force in our economy," he remarked, "and a primary agency in deterring aggression in the world today and in our national security." Following the reception, there was a brief luncheon at City Hall.

Eddie Rickenbacker suffered a stroke and died in Switzerland in July 1973, and General Doolittle delivered the eulogy at his funeral service in Florida. General Doolittle passed away 20 years later at the age of 93 and is buried in Arlington National Cemetery. Captain Erickson returned to duty and eventually became commander of the Coast Guard's Office of Aviation. He died in Galveston, Texas, in 1978. Gerald Crosson retired from the Police force in the early 1960's and died at his home on Staten Island. His son served in the Air Force in Vietnam. Captain Crawford also returned to the Police Department, retiring in the 1960's, and no further information about him can be found.

Monday, December 21, 1953: 144 Convalescing War Veterans

It was the day before the winter solstice, but the weather was far from wintery. The temperature was in the low 50s, the sun shone brightly, and the sky was a brilliant blue. It was a perfect day to welcome home 144 convalescing members of the armed forces from the New York region. Thirty were released from hospitals in the metropolitan area, the remainder were flown in from military hospitals around the nation. The men were brought to New York thanks to a suggestion made by the newspaper *The New York Journal-American* as a show of appreciation for the sacrifices they had made in Korea.

At noon the men sat in jeeps provided by the 42nd Division, New York's Rainbow Division. Each jeep was driven by a member of that National Guard organization and contained two to four veterans. The caravan of jeeps began the ride up Broadway accompanied by an Army band and detachments from the Army, Navy, Marine Corps, and Coast Guard. The veterans being honored were showered with ticker tape and confetti. American flags flew from every flagpole along the route and thousands of spectators waved miniature flags. The men being honored waved in appreciation, and all seemed overwhelmed with emotion.

Most of those who stood and welcomed the men as the parade entered City Hall Park were relatives and friends of the injured troops. The veterans were introduced as a group to Mayor Vincent Impellitteri by Grover Whalen, who was serving as Chairman of a city Reception Committee for the last time. The day before, Mayor-elect Wagner had announced that Whalen would be replaced by Richard Patterson. The mayor welcomed the veterans with the short statement, "Everyone in this great city will have a happier, better Christmas – because you have come home."

The 144 combat troops remained seated in the jeeps as retired Eighth Army Commander General James Van Fleet *(see: April 24, 1953)* paid tribute to their service. The general called the men heroes "who carried the fight to that godless, ruthless enemy that would enslave mankind." He spoke briefly and the caravan of jeeps proceeded to the Waldorf Astoria Hotel for a luncheon provided by the *Journal-American.*

The mayor spoke again at the luncheon, referring to the "grievous wounds" the veterans had suffered. "Your sacrifices will not be forgotten," he concluded. After his remarks, the mayor returned to his seat between two veterans, both of whom had lost their legs in Korea. After the luncheon some of the veterans began a two-week furlough. Others returned to their hospitals for continued care.

Fighting on the Korean Peninsula had ended in July 1953 when the United Nations and North Korea signed an Armistice Agreement, though South Korean President Syngman Rhee refused to do so. Though the "war" is generally considered to have ended then, no peace treaty has ever been signed. The two Koreas agreed to peace talks in 2018 but have not yet reached an agreement. Over the years, many veterans disagreed with the mayor's statement, feeling that their sacrifice had been forgotten by a nation soon divided over anti-Communist policies in Vietnam, and they would not receive a parade of honor for almost 40 years *(see: June 25, 1991).*

243

Richard C. Patterson, Jr.

The man who replaced Grover Whalen as New York's official "greeter" and organizer of ticker tape parades, Richard C. Patterson, had many roles in both the public and private sector during his career. Born in Omaha, Nebraska in 1886, he worked in the gold mines of South Dakota before joining the Army in 1916, rising to the rank of major during World War I. He helped form the American Legion, held several jobs with various corporations, and was appointed Commission of Correction in 1927. He held that role until 1932, during which time he was responsible for the design and construction of the city's new jail complex on Riker's Island.

After declining an opportunity to run for Mayor in 1932, he was executive vice president at the National Broadcasting Company. He served another public role as Undersecretary of the US Commerce Department from 1938-39, then was Chairman of RKO Studios. In 1944, President Roosevelt named him Ambassador to Yugoslavia, and later to Guatemala and Switzerland.

In 1954, Mayor Robert Wagner named him Chairman of the Mayor's Reception Committee, a role that evolved into Chief of Protocol and Commissioner of Public Events, which he held for almost 12 years. He resigned in January 1966, becoming an advisor to the City Council President before becoming ill. He died on September 30, 1966 at the age of 80.

CHAPTER 7
The Cold War (1954-1961)

Tension between the United States and the Soviet Union began growing almost as soon as Germany surrendered at the end of World War II, and by 1948 the Soviet Union blockaded Berlin from the West in response to American-led efforts to rebuild West Germany's economy. The following year, Communist forces won the Chinese Civil War, and the Cold War seemed like it might heat up when the Korean War began in 1950. Stoked by Senator Joseph McCarthy's allegations that communists had infiltrated the US government, Americans fell into a Red Scare. It is hardly surprising that in the 1952 election, voters chose the heroic World War II general, Dwight Eisenhower, as the next President.

Concerned about the nation's infrastructure in the case of invasion, Eisenhower worked with Congress to pass the Federal Aid Highway Act of 1956, which would have short- and long-term consequences for New York City. Eisenhower believed the country needed better highways for its defense, economy and future growth. The Federal government had previously left road building mostly to the states, but now federal money would be allocated to build the Interstate Highway System.

The short-term impact was immediately apparent to New York City Planning Commissioner Robert Moses, who now had yet another source of funding for his projects. He used this new money to extend and integrate the highways he had already built into the new Interstate system. The Grand Central Parkway, and the Brooklyn-Queens and Gowanus Expressways became part of I-278, and then were connected to the Staten Island Expressway with the new Verrazano-Narrows Bridge, which opened in 1964. The Queens Midtown Tunnel and Highway became part of I-495, which was extended further east and renamed the Long Island Expressway.

Moses was busy with other projects through the 1950s as well. In addition to building interstate connections in the Bronx and more housing complexes through the city, he was also changing the city's cultural and entertainment venues. As chair of Mayor Robert Wagner's Committee on Slum Clearance, he oversaw the leveling of 18 square blocks north of Columbus Circle, displacing over 7,000 families to make way for a new Lincoln Center of the Performing Arts. But when the owner of the Brooklyn Dodgers asked for his help for a new stadium at Atlantic Yards, Moses refused, insisting the team should move to Queens, and the dispute led to the Dodgers departure from Brooklyn to Los Angeles.

By 1960, though, the 70-year-old Moses was losing some of his political acumen and was facing growing community resistance, especially after the controversy over the demolition of the original Pennsylvania Station. Plans to connect I-495 to New Jersey via the Lincoln Tunnel with an elevated Mid-Manhattan Expressway running above 30th Street met community resistance. Residents of Soho and Little Italy opposed a similar plan for a Lower Manhattan Expressway to connect the Williamsburg and

Manhattan Bridges to the Holland Tunnel as part of I-78, fearing their neighborhoods would be destroyed by the 10-lane elevated road. Led by community activist Jane Jacobs, the issue became a major debate in the 1965 mayoral election, which was won by John Lindsay, an opponent of the planned highways.

Another project that kept Moses busy, and one which ultimately led to his downfall, was renovating the 1939 World's Fair grounds for a new Fair in 1964. Cost overruns and revenue shortfalls for that event led to a disagreement with Mayor Lindsay about using Triborough Bridge tolls to offset the city's budget deficits, and in 1968, the Mayor removed Moses from his position. But Moses' vision that economic expansion was dependent on and driven by the automobile, and that older neighborhoods were disposable if they were in the way, had a lasting impact on New York City.

The vast system of roads, bridges and tunnels that Moses built enabled high-speed traffic throughout the city, providing north and southbound connections from Long Island to the mainland via the Bronx or Staten Island. A New York City car owner could now easily drive to Long Island, Westchester or New Jersey. Increasingly throughout this period, they did, but many did not return. Starting with Levittown in 1947, the automobile was fueling the growth of suburbia, and the possibility of home-ownership became the new "American Dream." That dream was tainted by racial discrimination, however, as restrictive covenants and mortgage lending practices crafted a predominantly white suburbia, not an integrated one.

As the city's population was migrating to the suburbs, so too was the country's population shifting, and the move of two of the city's baseball teams to California was indicative of the larger pattern. New York City's population declined for the first time in the 1960 Census. The State's population was also declining, and its political power within the country was being equalized by a population surge in California. Starting in 1950, the size of New York State's congressional delegation began shrinking, from an all-time high of 47 down to 43 in 1962, and with that change would come a smaller share of Federal funding.

New York City was still the nation's largest city, though, and as the headquarters of the United Nations, still occupied an important place in the international politics of the Cold War. The former colonies of European empires were becoming independent, and the growing number of new nations had only two directions to look for economic and military support: Moscow or Washington. The late 1950s saw a steady stream of heads-of-state visiting New York, either for meetings at the United Nations or on their way to Washington DC. Wanting to woo them, the Eisenhower Administration worked with the Mayor's office to honor them with ticker tape parades and began defraying some of the city's costs for security at the parades (see: January 29, 1957). The average New Yorker might not know who Mahendra Bir Birkam was (see: May 2, 1960), or why Luis Batlle Berres received a ticker tape parade (see: December 9, 1955), but somebody at the US State Department sure did.

Monday, February 1, 1954: Celâl Bayar, President of Turkey

The flag of Turkey, bearing a white star and crescent on a red field, snapped prominently on this frigid February morning to welcome the President of the Turkish Republic, Celâl Bayar. The Turkish Information Office provided several hundred flags to buildings along the route, to guarantee that Broadway would be bedecked with them.

Early that morning the president toured the United Nations and met with Secretary General Dag Hammarskjöld, who personally thanked Bayar for Turkey's support in the Korean conflict. A police escort led the Turkish president downtown along the FDR Drive following the meeting, and a police helicopter hovered overhead. Off East 14th Street a city fire boat shot geysers of water skyward that fell back to the frigid waters of the East River as sparkling pellets of ice.

The caravan reached the Battery shortly after noon and the procession began at 12:20. The cold weather kept the crowds small, but the arrival of the Turkish leader was cheered by at least 100,000, including those behind windows kept shut because of the 23-degree temperature. A military band led the 12-car motorcade, and contingents from the Army, Navy, Marine Corps, Air Force, Police, Fire, and Correction Departments accompanied the vehicles. The 71-year-old chief of state sat in an open car but was covered with heavy blankets. Despite the cold he frequently doffed his black homburg hat with gloved hands to the cheering spectators. It was observed that less ticker tape littered the route and this, too, was attributed to the weather.

President Bayar was presented to Mayor Wagner by the Chairman of the Reception Committee, Richard Patterson. He was led into the Council Chamber where 350 guests watched the mayor extend his official welcome to the Turkish chief executive. The president was presented with the city's Gold Medal and a scroll commending Turkey as "an inspiration to the people of the world who love freedom and liberty." The president replied through an interpreter, expressing his pleasure at his reception, and admiring the warmth of his welcome despite the cold weather. Mayor Wagner then accompanied the president back out of City Hall and across Broadway to St Paul's Chapel, where Dr. Grayson Kirk, president of Columbia University, bestowed an honorary Doctor of Law Degree on the Turkish leader, calling him an architect of the future of his republic.

Later that afternoon President Bayar was guest of honor at a luncheon at the Waldorf Astoria, during which Vice President Nixon presented a speech describing the valor of the Turkish nation, bordering its historic foe, Russia. The Vice President recalled how the US began providing financial assistance and military advice to Turkey in 1947 and gave assurance of continued aid. Mr. Bayar's words spoke of the emergence of the Turkish republic under its revolutionary founder, Kemal Ataturk, and how his nation had modernized after the Ottoman government was overthrown following the First World War. In the first years after the birth of the Turkish Republic in 1921, 2.5 million Turkish people learned to read and write the Latin alphabet adopted by the country, and the number of students attending primary schools jumped seven-fold and continued to grow. He expressed pride in the advancements of Turkey and attributed it to the leadership of the late Mr. Ataturk.

President Bayar departed New York the following day. His visit included stops at cities containing a significant population of Turkish-Americans, including Cleveland and Toledo in Ohio; Detroit, Michigan; and Pittsburgh, Pennsylvania.

The Turkish military had long been pressing for a larger role in governing the republic. Failing to win such a role, it staged a coup d'état in May 1960, and conducted trials of 15 Turkish political leaders, including Bayar, who had been re-elected to the presidency in 1957. Found guilty of violating the constitution by his re-election, he was sentenced to death. In 1961, this sentence was commuted to life in prison in the central Anatolian city of Kaysan. In 1964 he was released because of declining health and two years later he was pardoned although he was not given his full political rights until 1974. He subsequently refused the position of lifetime member of the Turkish Senate because no election was held to grant him the position. Ex-president Bayar died in Istanbul, Turkey, in 1986 at the age of 103.

Mayor Robert Wagner (1954-1965)

Born in Manhattan in 1910, Robert Wagner studied at Harvard Business School and Yale Law School and served in the New York State Assembly during the 1930s. He resigned in 1942 to join the Army Air Corps during World War II, then was elected Manhattan Borough President in 1950. In 1953 he was elected Mayor and was re-elected twice.

During his three terms as Mayor, Wagner focused on building public schools and housing, created the City University system, helped develop Lincoln Center, and barred discrimination in public housing. Pledging that his administration would serve "the best interest of all people" he appointed people of color to significant city jobs, and he established the right of collective bargaining for city employees. Soon after the demolition of the original Penn Station, he created the Landmark Preservation Commission, and his break with Tammany Hall was the final chapter in the club's century-long hold on city government.

He decided not to run for a fourth term in 1965, though did attempt a return in 1969, after serving as ambassador to Spain. He also served as the US representative to Vatican City in the late 1970s. He died of heart failure in 1991 at the age of 80.

Wednesday, March 31, 1954: 4,000 New York City Firemen

Known as "New York's Bravest" since the 1870s, a parade of 4,000 members of the Fire Department of New York paraded up the Canyon of Heroes on this bright and sunny spring day to celebrate Fireman's Day. An escort of six of "New York's Finest" from the Police Department led the way mounted on matched bays. They were followed by Fire Commissioner Edward Cavanaugh, Fire Chief Peter Loftus, the Deputy Commissioner and 16 Deputy Chiefs. In turn, they were followed by the Fire Department color guard and band. Behind them marched 3,800 firemen and 300 auxiliary firemen, followed by what many observers considered the highlight of the parade, antique firefighting equipment and apparatus from the Fire Department Museum.

Thousands of lunch-hour spectators watched as six firemen, dressed in period red shirts and helmets, pulled an 1820 pump. An 1810 pump, designed by a New Yorker, James Smith and used until the 1860's, was mounted on a flat-bed truck that also carried a two-ton bell. The bell tolled mournfully during the parade to commemorate firemen who had died in performance of their duty. A vermillion-colored 1923 Model T Ford, once a chief's car, chugged up Broadway under its own power, followed by a 1912 steamer built by Joseph Van Blerck of Monroe, Michigan. Behind these machines from the past were more modern equipment featuring new ladder trucks, a huge ambulance, searchlight and rescue vehicles, and giant pumpers.

At City Hall the marchers and equipment halted before 5,000 spectators in the Plaza. Speeches were delivered by Commissioner Cavanaugh; Abe Stark, President of the City Council; and Fireman Howard Barry, President of the Uniformed Fireman's association. The Commissioner reported that fires in New York City had more than doubled over the previous decade and the tragedy was that 90% of them were preventable. He added a call for approval to increase the size of the department and stressed the need to constantly improve and modernize the department's equipment. The

Commissioner then promoted 41 firemen to lieutenant, 14 lieutenants to captain, and six captains to battalion chief. During the gathering in City Hall Plaza, fire bells set up beside the reviewing stand rang at various times, indicating real calls for various companies throughout the five boroughs. One of the calls resulted in members of Rescue Company 1 leaving the scene hurriedly.

Afterwards, spectators were given several demonstrations. Probationary firemen showing the use of extension ladders slid down ropes from 75-foot ladders and jumped into safety nets from a height of 50 feet. In this final demonstration one probationary fireman, Lawrence Monechelli, was knocked out when he landed improperly. Dr. Henry Archer, Second Deputy Fire Commissioner, treated him at the scene, reporting that he had only had the wind knocked out of him, but the fireman was taken for observation to nearby Beekman Downtown Hospital.

Firefighting has always been important, especially in large cities, so the history of the New York Fire Department dates from the Dutch colonial era. The first fire brigade was established in 1731, and the first firehouse was built opposite City Hall in 1736. The following year, the "Fire Department, New York City" was officially incorporated, and in 1865 a state law replaced volunteer fire brigades with paid firefighters. The first motorized equipment was purchased in 1909. The origin of the department's motto as "New York's Bravest" is uncertain but was in common use by the 1870s. During the anti-draft riots in 1863, Fire Chief John Decker was praised as "one of the bravest of the brave," which is a possible source of the phrase. Whatever its origin, the city's bravest would be honored in the Canyon of Heroes again *(see: April 15, 1955).*

Fire Department of New York and FDNY Band

It should come as no surprise that, in an era when most buildings were constructed from lumber, protection from fire was a major concern for the Dutch settlement of New Amsterdam, and the city's first fire wardens were appointed in 1648. By 1731, the city created its first "fire brigade" and purchased two hand-operated water pumping machines, and several years later built a fire watchhouse on Broad Street. Other than the wardens, though, the men responsible for extinguishing fires were all volunteers, even after the city established the Fire Department of New York.

The Great Fire of 1845, which destroyed over 300 buildings in lower Manhattan, proved the value of recently passed laws restricting wood-frame construction, and after fires broke out during the Draft Riots of 1864, the State abolished the city's volunteer fire brigades and created the Metropolitan Fire Department. In 1870, control of the department was shifted to the city, and it was renamed the Fire Department of New York. After the city's Consolidation in 1898, the FDNY grew rapidly. In 1909 it purchased motorized fire-fighting equipment, and after the Triangle Shirt Fire of 1911, a Bureau of Fire Prevention was created within the department and building codes and labor laws were strengthened.

Like the Police Department, members of the Fire Department who played musical instruments formed marching bands, though during most of the 1800s, each fire house had its own band. This changed in the 1890s, when a centralized Fire Department Band was formed. In addition to performing in parades and at city events, the FDNY Band would perform upon request at churches, neighborhood parties, and at funerals for FDNY members and veterans. Starting in 1914, it also held an annual concert to raise money for musical equipment for its members, and in the 1920s a glee club was formed. →

Things began to change after World War II. In 1954, Fire Commissioner Edward Cavanaugh curtailed the number of events that the 79-member band would perform at, eliminating all local events. Citing budget concerns, he eliminated the glee club the following year, and in April 1958, the marching band gave its final performance at a breakfast at the Commodore Hotel for current and retired firemen and their families.

Four years later, members of the Emerald Society of New York, a non-profit fraternal organization for Irish American civil servants, formed the FDNY Emerald Society Pipe and Drum Corps. With membership restricted to active or former FDNY members, this marching band can be seen performing clad in bright red and green plaid tartan kilts. In addition to parades and other civic events, they also played at the funerals for the 343 firefighters killed on September 11, 2001.

Thursday, April 22, 1954:
45th Infantry Division Returns from Korea

Five days after returning to the United States from Korea, the 45th Division, nicknamed the Thunderbirds, took the route up the Canyon of Heroes. It was a "welcome home" to the first division withdrawn from war-torn Korea, where the division had been fighting since December 1951 and had seen a total of 429 days in combat.

Under a warm sunny sky, 1,000 members of the division paraded from Bowling Green to City Hall. Marching with them were 1,500 men from the 42nd (Rainbow) Division of the New York National Guard, and the Ninth (Old Reliable) Division, a training division based at Fort Dix, New Jersey. Leading the way were members of the 179th Infantry Regiment of the 45th Division. Members marched with fixed bayonets, their ranks and files neatly aligned. Each of the unit's three infantry regiments, four artillery battalions, and four armored companies carried their colors bearing battle streamers from World War II and Korea.

The police estimated that a quarter of a million cheering spectators roared their welcome. A blizzard of ticker tape and torn paper of various kinds floated down on the parade route. The marching veterans kept strict military discipline, and did not avert their gaze from the route ahead

The weather grew warmer as the marchers reached City Hall Plaza, where the Police Department Band played the National Anthem. Brigadier General Harvey Fischer, division commander, ordered the men to "stand at ease." The troops stood, feet apart with slung rifles, helmets reflecting the sun. Soldiers of the 45th wore olive-green camouflage combat fatigues that the US military had newly adopted, while the men of the other two divisions wore older-style uniforms.

The reviewing stand in front of City Hall bore a huge Thunderbird insignia. Mayor Wagner presented a scroll to General Fischer that commemorated the division's experiences in Korea, including participation in the battles around Old Baldy Hill from June 1952 to March 1953. While in Korea the division sustained the loss of 834 men killed and 3,170 wounded. It was awarded four campaign streamers and one Presidential Unit Citation.

The mayor concluded his remarks by saying, "I believe that more than the fear of atomic warfare, more than the fear of hydrogen devastation, Russia fears the indomitable will and unified courage of the American soldier. No soldier anywhere represents the strength that is America and the devotion that is American than do you men of the 45th Division."

General Fischer expressed his gratitude to the city for the welcome his men had received. Others on the reviewing stand followed with additional remarks, ranging from brief statements to longer speeches. Among those who spoke were General Matthew Ridgway, Army Chief-of-Staff; Andrew Cordier, Assistant to the Secretary General of the United Nations; Lieutenant General Raymond McLain; Major General Karl Haussauer, representing Governor Dewey of New York; George Roderick, Assistant Secretary of Defense; and Richard Patterson, Chairman of the Mayor's Reception Committee.

The temperature continued to rise as the speeches went on, the and the sun beat down on the troops. Soon one member of the Rainbow Division collapsed from the heat and then a second and a third. In total, 20 men from all three divisions succumbed to the heat, and an ambulance from nearby Beekman Downtown Hospital was called to assist Army medics. Two of the men required hospitalization but were released the following morning. After the last of the speeches ended, the troops were dismissed and trucked, either to the 42nd Division's armories in New York City or to Fort Dix.

The Thunderbird division was de-activated in the 1968 reorganization of National Guard units, and its component units consolidated and re-designated as the 45th Infantry Brigade, stationed at Fort Sill, Oklahoma. During the Vietnam war, the Brigade served as a training organization and later served as part of the United Nations peace-keeping forces in Bosnia. More recently it was called to active combat duty in Iraq and Afghanistan. Members of the brigade still wear the division's Thunderbird patch.

Tuesday, June 1, 1954: Haile Selassie, Emperor of Ethiopia

New York City was the first stop in the six-week tour of the United States and Canada for Emperor Haile Selassie of Ethiopia. His flight arrived on the afternoon of May 30, and he was driven directly to the Waldorf Astoria Hotel. Known as "The Lion of Judah," the Emperor's family had ruled Ethiopia since the 13th century and claimed direct descent from the biblical King Solomon of Jerusalem and Queen Mekeda of Sheba. Accompanied by his son, Prince Sahle Selassie and his granddaughter Sehle Desta, the Emperor visited the Statue of Liberty, the Empire State Building, and other tourist attractions.

On June 1 Selassie received New York City's traditional ticker tape welcome. A bright sun shone down on Broadway when the parade set out from the Battery. Leading the way was a color guard of uniformed members of the Police and Fire Departments carrying the red, green and gold flag of Ethiopia and the red, white, and blue flag of the United States. The First Army Band played marching tunes as military detachments from the Army, Navy, and Air Force escorted the Emperor along the route. Seated in an open convertible and wearing a khaki-colored military uniform, decorated with nine rows of ribbons and medals, the 62-year-old ruler waved and frequently spoke to Richard Patterson, Chairman of the Mayor's Reception Committee. Multicolored streams of ribbon mixed with long white threads of ticker tape as the motorcade moved towards City Hall, and police estimated the numbers of spectators at slightly less than a million. The emperor, nominal head of the Coptic Christian faith, was ceremoniously greeted at Trinity Church by robed Coptic clergymen.

When the motorcade arrived at City Hall, the First Army band played "Mazmur," the Ethiopian National Anthem, followed by the "Star Spangled Banner." Mr. Patterson then introduced the Emperor to Mayor Wagner, who presented a scroll to the Ethiopian ruler commemorating his long battle against tyranny, citing the Italian invasion of his nation in 1934 and the Emperor's dramatic plea for aid at a meeting of the League of Nations in 1935. "We understand the struggle which you have undergone and the progress which you have achieved," the mayor remarked. The emperor replied that the warmth of the welcome he received proved to him the affection that existed between his nation and the United States.

The ceremonies at City Hall ended shortly before 1 o'clock, and the Emperor was the guest of honor at a Waldorf Astoria luncheon, where the mayor presented the city's Medal of Honor to His Imperial Majesty. In return, the Emperor gifted to the city two mounted elephant tusks, a warrior's shield, and two warrior's spears. The gifts were graciously accepted by the mayor who assured the Emperor that they would be added with pride to the city's treasure of gifts from visiting dignitaries. More than 600 invited guests attended the luncheon and they heard Emperor Selassie, through an interpreter, speak of his affection for New York and its people.

Later the Emperor visited the United Nations and was conducted on a tour by the Secretary General, Mr. Dag Hammarskjöld. The following morning Columbia University bestowed an honorary degree on the visiting African leader, and the next day the Emperor embarked on a sightseeing tour and goodwill mission to cities in the United States and Canada.

While still a teenager, Haile Selassie had been proclaimed *Ras Tafari*, which means "High Prince." His aunt, Empress Zewditu named him Governor of Selale Province in 1924, and in 1928 she selected him over other Ethiopian princes to be King of Ethiopia. He was crowned Emperor when she died later that year. He is revered as the returned biblical messiah by the Rastafarian religious movement that began on the island of Jamaica in the early 1930's.

The Emperor's attempts to modernize his nation and end its semi-feudal traditions were met with resistance from many Ethiopians, who even protested his edict that officially ended slavery in the nation. Despite opposition at home, he continued to reign and would return to the United States and receive a second ticker tape welcome *(see: October 4, 1963)*.

Monday, July 26, 1954:
Lieutenant Geneviève de Galard-Terraube

Geneviève de Galard-Terraube was a civilian nurse attached to the French military during its war against the Vietminh in French Indonesia, flying to French positions in the war-torn nation, including the besieged mountain stronghold of Dien Bien Phu in northwest Vietnam. In January 1954, before the pressure on the position became intense, the flights carried out men suffering from various jungle diseases and injuries. But the French blunder of occupying a position deep within hostile territory became more critical, and flights on which Geneviève served as nurse soon began to carry more and more battlefield casualties. On March 28, 1954, the C-47 on which she was assigned was damaged while landing in a fog. Before mechanics could repair the damaged plane, Vietminh artillery destroyed it and she was trapped with the remainder of the French garrison, the only woman in the besieged position. She spent the remaining 41 days of the siege working at the field hospital, originally against the wishes of the medical staff. When the garrison surrendered, the Vietminh permitted her to remain caring for French troops too seriously wounded to be evacuated, and for their own wounded. She was finally repatriated 17 days later.

Long before she was released by the Communists, she had become a celebrity in the west. The western press nicknamed her "The Angel of Dien Bien Phu" though she was not called that by French troops at the time. When Ohio Congressman Frances Bolton sponsored an official invitation to have the woman welcomed by the United States, the French government readily accepted on her behalf, and New York was the first stop of her visit to this country.

She arrived at Idlewild International Airport on an Air France Constellation at 9:40 in the morning on July 26. Disembarking from the plane, she was met by the French Consul General, Jean de Lagarde, who presented her with a bouquet of red roses and white carnations. In true Gallic fashion, he kissed her on both cheeks and introduced her as "Lieutenant" to Representative Bolton and Richard Patterson, Chairman of Mayor Wagner's Reception Committee. Speaking in French, she insisted that the rank of Lieutenant was purely an unofficial one and that her correct title was simply "Mademoiselle." Accompanied by the three men, she entered a city convertible that drove her to Bowling Green for a New York ticker tape welcome.

"The Angel" wore a plain white linen nurse's uniform under a four-button jacket. Pinned to this was the red ribbon of the French Legion of Honor, awarded to her by the French government while still in captivity. The sleeve of her jacket bore the insignia of the French Air Transport Command and of the Flying Nurses' Corps. Around her right wrist was a bracelet from which hung a medal. On one side of the medal was an image of St. Genevieve, on the reverse were the letters "DBP" for Dien Bien Phu. On the left shoulder of her jacket was sewn the blue diamond patch of an honorary Private First Class of the French Foreign Legion.

An estimated quarter of a million people lined the Canyon of Heroes to welcome the French nurse. She was escorted by a small detachment of French infantry and larger detachments of American soldiers, sailors, and marines. She stood, waving to the crowd and clutching her bouquet, from Bowling Green to City Hall. She smiled and often spoke to the others in the car as cascading swirls of ticker tape, confetti, and torn newspaper and telephone directory pages floated down.

"New York loves a hero, but even more a heroine," Mr. Patterson said in introducing her to Mayor Robert Wagner. "Mademoiselle de Galard-Terraube" he said was "a symbol of heroic femininity in the free world." The mayor greeted her in City Hall Plaza where thousands of spectators waved French and American flags. He presented the nurse with the city's Medal of Honor and a scroll proclaiming her courage and devotion to duty. Representative Bolton spoke next, calling the nurse an inspiration to women throughout the world.

Miss de Galard-Terraube spoke next. "I do not deserve this honor," she said, her remarks translated into English, "for I have only done my duty. This honor is intended, through me, for all those whose life I was proud to share in Dien Bien Phu." She added praise for all nurses, military and civilian, who devoted themselves to those in their care.

Questioned later by the press, she refused to make any comments regarding the ongoing talks between France and the Vietminh in Geneva. "No politics," Representative Bolton interrupted. She also refused to answer questions regarding reports that the Vietminh abused their French prisoners, wishing only to speak of the courage of the men she had been with.

She flew to Washington, DC two days later, where President Eisenhower awarded her the Presidential Medal of Freedom and called her the "Woman of the Year." Before she returned to France two weeks later, she toured the US and was welcomed with parades or receptions in Cleveland, Chicago, New Orleans, San Francisco, and elsewhere. On June 14, 1956 she married Colonel Jean de Heaulme de Boutsocq, who had commanded a detachment of paratroopers in Dien Bien Phu and was among those captured there and later released. They resided in Paris and she avoided publicity of all kinds. Her autobiography was published in 2010, and she died in Paris in 2012.

Monday, August 2, 1954:
Syngman Rhee, President of South Korea

Although the calendar read early August the weather was far from summer-like. A chilling breeze and a light drizzle fell as the 79-year-old President of South Korea, Dr. Syngman Rhee, and his 56-year-old wife, Francesca Maria Barbara Donner, entered a convertible for the procession up the Canyon of Heroes. Mrs. Rhee, his wife for 20 years, was the daughter of a Viennese iron merchant whom Dr. Rhee met in 1932 when he visited Geneva and failed to persuade the League of Nations to take up the cause of Korean independence from Japan. The President wore a tropical-weight white suit and held a large-brimmed straw hat in his hand, while she wore a traditional white Korean gown. As the parade began, their car lurched forward suddenly. Husband and wife grasped the side of the car, then quickly righted themselves and stood to acknowledge the city's traditional welcome.

The motorcade moved forward, escorted by the First Army Band and marching detachments from the Army, Navy, and Marine Corps. Dr. Rhee, usually considered a serious man with an almost perpetual scowl, smiled broadly as cascading ribbons of ticker tape and confetti fell on him and his wife and littered the inside of the auto. Gesturing with his hat, he pointed at the sight of more than 200,000 noontime spectators, some standing tightly packed on the sidewalk. Still others leaned out of the open windows of the banks, brokerage houses, shipping lines, and law firms along the route. Many in the crowd shouted to welcome him and, the President bowed un gratitude to a small number of Koreans waved the flag of South Korea, and voiced their comments in Korean.

The parade made a pre-arranged halt at Trinity Church where Dr. Rhee asked an aide to invite one of the motorcycle policemen into the car with the Korean chief-of-state. The policeman, Lieutenant George Fitzpatrick, had lost his son Thomas exactly two years earlier, while Thomas was fighting in Korea. Dr. Rhee shook the Lieutenant's hand and smiled graciously while cameramen captured the scene on film. After an almost 10-minute halt, the parade resumed its slow trek toward City Hall.

Richard Patterson, Chairman of Mayor Wagner's Reception Committee, assisted the President and First Lady from the car and presented them to Mayor and Mrs. Wagner. The mayor welcomed them to New York and bestowed upon Dr. Rhee the city's Medal of Honor as well as a scroll celebrating the South Korean leader for his exceptional leadership and courage in the face of Japanese occupation and warfare against North Korean and Chinese Communist troops.

Rain had begun to fall more heavily but Dr. Rhee declined the offer of a raincoat or umbrella for him and his wife. His hat over his heart in salute, the elderly statesman stood at attention as the American and Korean national anthems were played. Dr. Rhee made a brief statement of gratitude and then spoke of the dangers from Communist aggression that the free world faced. He warned of the possibility of an even larger war against Communism which he said could only be defeated by a combination of bullets and bombs, because words had little effect on it.

Dr. Rhee renewed the theme of warfare against Communism at a luncheon in City Hall following the ceremony. "Do not think for a moment," he said, "that anything but force will bring the Communist menace to its knees." He spoke of the losses suffered by the Republic of Korea: almost one million of his countrymen had been killed, wounded, or reported missing since the republic was invaded in late June 1950. He added that he did not wish to appear unappreciative of the aid rendered to his nation by the United States and other nations and expressed gratitude for assistance in every form.

The rain ended after the meal, and Dr. and Mrs. Rhee proceeded to Columbia University, where he received an honorary Doctor of Law degree in Low Memorial Library. Wearing cap and gown, he thanked the university and its trustees for bestowing this honor upon him. He commented on how proud he was to add this to the Bachelor of Arts Degree he held from George Washington University, his Master of Arts from Harvard, and his Doctor of Philosophy from Princeton.

The president's busy schedule ended that evening at the Waldorf Astoria. His arrival there was marred by the presence of dozens of anti-Rhee protestors who distributed literature describing his repression of dissenters to his rule in Korea. Dispersed quickly by the police, Dr. Rhee entered the Waldorf as guest of honor of the American Korean Foundation. He again spoke of the need to continue armed resistance against Communism but thanked the Foundation for their aid to Korea. "Your dollars," he told the audience, "have kept our people warm, and your other activities have given them the hope they need so desperately."

On the following morning, Dr. Rhee met with UN Secretary General Dag Hammarskjöld, who conducted a tour of the United Nations facilities for the Korean President. That afternoon, the South Korean president, who had arrived in Washington a week earlier for meetings with President Eisenhower, flew to Chicago, and from there back to Seoul, Korea three days later.

In 1899, at the age of 24, Syngman Rhee, had been jailed by the Japanese for membership in anti-colonial groups and given a lifetime sentence and tortured. Released in 1904 at the start of the Russo-Japanese War, he was sent by Japan to the United States to gain support for Japan against Tsarist Russia. While doing so, he also continued to work for Korean independence. Assisted by Methodist missionaries he was able to receive an education in the United States. He briefly resided in Shanghai, China, in the 1930's and was elected President of the Provisional Government of Korea. The Japanese invasion of China caused him to flee again, and he lived in New York, Washington, and Hawaii during World War II. With the support of the American government, he was elected South Korea's first president in 1948 and served three terms. He was always a bitter foe of Communism, but also an increasingly authoritarian ruler who used force to quell opposition. After the death of his opponent a few weeks before Election Day in 1960, opposition against him grew and he was eventually forced to flee. He spent the rest of his life in exile in Honolulu and died there of a stroke on July 19, 1965. His body was returned to Korea and he is buried in Seoul National Cemetery.

Monday, September 27, 1954:
New York Giants, American League Champions

The 1954 baseball season ended with the New York Giants on top of the National League. They compiled a season of 97 wins and 57 losses and wound up 5 games ahead of their cross-town rivals, the Brooklyn Dodgers. To celebrate their victory and to cheer them on against the Cleveland Indians, the American League champions, it was decided to honor them with a ticker tape parade. There had never been a ticker tape parade for a New York baseball team before and it was expected that the event would encourage the team from the Polo Grounds to defeat the Indians.

Over a million spectators lined the streets to cheer the Giants: Henry Thompson, Willie Mays, Johnny Antonelli, Wes Westrum, Sal Maglie, team Captain Alvin Dark, and manager Leo Durocher and almost all of the other players and coaches. Notably absent was Bobby Hofman, utility infielder, who had been married the day before in Clifton, New Jersey.

The streets of lower Manhattan were festooned with ticker tape and confetti. The cacophony of sound was deafening: cheers, horns, bells, whistles, and noise makers of every type. The players, in their white uniforms with black letters, rode in a caravan of 15 vehicles. Many players rode with their wives or sweethearts, waving and pointing at the crowd and the spectacle. To players from places like Mount Carmel, Illinois (Don Liddle), Columbia, Alabama (Monte Irvin), Huntersville, North Carolina (Hoyt Wilhelm), the sight and sound was something beyond belief.

At City Hall, Mayor Wagner announced that "New Yorkers are 100 percent behind the team, and all New York wants to see the Giants bring the championship to the city." His words were answered with cheers that were mixed with boos from Yankees and Dodgers fans. Hulan Jack, Manhattan Borough President, standing with the mayor on the grandstand in City Hall Plaza, added "On to victory!" A team photo was taken on the steps of City Hall showing a smiling mayor shaking hands with manager Durocher.

Three days later at the Polo Grounds the Giants faced the Cleveland Indians, who had won an unbelievable 111 games that year to walk away with the American League pennant. The Giants won the first two games of the series, held in New York. The next two were in Cleveland. The Giants won both, sweeping the Series. It was a great year to be a Giants fan.

Three years later, the Giants departed New York for windswept San Francisco, joining the Brooklyn Dodgers in an exodus to the West Coast. They would not win another World Series until 2010, and there would not be another ticker tape parade for a New York baseball team until 1962, celebrating the creation of the New York Mets (see: April 12, 1962).

Thursday, October 28, 1954:
William Tubman, President of Liberia

President William Tubman of Liberia was in the United States to encourage investments to his West African republic. Arriving from Chicago at Grand Central Terminal at 8:20 in the morning, he spent the rest of his morning at the United Nations, where he gave an address to the General Assembly. President Tubman, the 19th president of his nation since it had been declared independent through the efforts of the American Colonization Society in 1847, then headed to the Battery.

The ticker tape parade rode up the Canyon of Heroes accompanied by an escort of mounted and motorcycle police and marched to music provided by the First Army and Police Department bands. An Army honor guard and vehicles containing the Liberian UN delegation, security personnel, and reporters completed the small caravan. The crowd was smaller than usual, and the president frequently tipped his gray hat to the spectators.

Upon arriving at City Hall, Mayor Wagner presented the city's red-ribboned Gold Medal to the President along with a scroll that praised his work so that others in West Africa "could look at Liberia as a shining example of democratic life." It also mentioned Liberia's assistance to the Allied cause during World War II, first as a neutral nation and later as a co-belligerent.

After the ceremony, Mr. Tubman was the guest of honor at a luncheon at the Waldorf. Among those in attendance in the Council Chambers was Dr. Channing Tobias, Chairman of the National Association for the Advancement of Colored People, and Dr. Bernard Baruch, financier and political consultant. Dr. Baruch, an unscheduled speaker, briefly expressed hope that President Tubman's visit would spark economic interest in Liberia.

The Liberian chief of state thanked Dr. Baruch, quoting Scriptures: "He that hath ears to hear, let him hear." In his remarks, Dr. Tobias had called Liberia "a free power in the midst of colonial powers." In response to his statement, President Tubman looked forward to the day when all Africa would be free of colonialism "and all mankind will be integrated…in love and peace and happiness and respect, one for the other." Summing up, the president expressed his gratitude to those in the United States who, more than a century before, had helped establish his nation as a home for emancipated slaves. "The principal reason we trust the United States Government is because we don't think they have designs on Liberia."

The president remained in the United States for another week meeting with financiers and potential investors. He returned to his nation and in the following year narrowly escaped an assassination attempt. He cracked down on all political opposition and succeeded in changing Liberia's constitution so his presidency could continue beyond one four-year term. By the time he died in 1971 in London, England, he had been president for 17 years. His death brought about a period of political instability, frequent changes of government, rigged elections, and almost constant violence.

Friday, November 19, 1954: Lieutenant General Withers Burress

Lieutenant General Burress, commander of the First Army headquartered at Fort Jay on Governors Island, sat on the rear seat of an official car as the parade in his honor began. More than 1,000 marchers had assembled to bid farewell to the general who was ready to retire and return to civilian life after nearly 40 years of active service. He had seen combat in the 23rd Infantry during World War I and the 100th Division in World War II.

Accompanied by both the First Army and Police Department bands, the parade started up Broadway shortly after noon. A squad of mounted police led the caravan. Detachments from the Army, Navy, Air Force, Marine Corps, and Coast Guard provided an honor guard to the man who a decade earlier led the 100th Division across France into the Rhineland, the Ardennes, and finally central Europe.

A slight breeze swept the flags along the Canyon of Heroes and streams of ticker tape and confetti greeted the marchers as more than 50,000 spectators cheered and veterans saluted. Small American flags held by well-wishers along the way added to the patriotic scene. Riding with Richard Patterson, Commissioner of the Department of Commerce and Public Events, the general waved and acknowledged the cheers. Riding in the car behind them were Vice Admiral Arthur Struble, Chief of the Military Delegation to the UN; Lieutenant General Leo Johnson, commander of the Continental Air Command; Rear Admiral Louis Olson, commander of the Coast Guard Eastern Division; and Major General Roger Browne, First Air Force commander.

Upon arriving at City Hall, the general and other military commanders were led into the City Council Chambers. General Burress was introduced to the more than 200 invited guests and journalists and presented with the city's Gold Medal. He also received a scroll from Mayor Wagner that spoke of his long service and combat experience. The mayor made a joking reference to politics, noting that his own "accomplishment of winning this city last year doesn't look like very much in this gathering because the First Army has taken more" and that he hoped to follow their example by not losing in the next election.

A reception at the Waldorf followed where more speakers praised the commander, including Commissioner Patterson, Deputy Mayor Henry Epstein, City Council President Abe Stark, and Admiral Struble. The general's speech concluded the affair, and he warned against America becoming complacent as it had after the First World War, but he was pleased to see that defense continued to be a high priority for the nation. A native of Richmond, Virginia, and a graduate of the Virginia Military Institute class of 1914, his future plans included hunting, fishing, and extended time with his family. He added that, despite his age, he would gladly return to duty should the country ever again require his service.

A lifelong bachelor, General Burress was true to his retirement plans, though he was never again called upon to don fatigues, helmet, or combat boots. He resided in Virginia for more than 20 years after retirement and died at the age of 83 in 1977 at a nursing home in Arlington and is buried in Arlington National Cemetery.

Monday, January 31, 1955:
Paul Eugène Magloire, President of Haiti

The noontime temperature in New York was 23 degrees, one of the coldest days ever on which a parade was held, according to information provided by the Department of Commerce and Public Events. Bravely defying weather that he was quite unaccustomed to, Paul Eugène Magloire, President of the Caribbean nation of Haiti, rode in an open vehicle throughout the entire motorcade. Three bands and 500 marchers strode up Broadway from Bowling Green to City Hall in company with the former Haitian General, who had become President in 1950 when a military coup ousted his predecessor. One police estimate put the number of viewers at less than 35,000, far fewer than usual, no doubt because of the frigid weather.

Ushered into the warmth of City Hall, the president received the city's Medal of Honor from Mayor Wagner. The mayor also presented him with a scroll for his distinguished public service in his frequently troubled nation. Speakers at City Hall included Richard Patterson, Commissioner of the Department of Commerce and Public Events, and Manhattan Borough President Hulan Jack.

President Magloire was the guest at a luncheon at the Empire State Building attended by 80 financiers. He spoke of the devastation done to his nation the previous October by Hurricane Hazel. The failure of the 1952-1953 coffee crops added to

258

Haiti's economic woes. "Now needed most," he said, "is capital, advanced on a strictly business basis." He acknowledged that his country's current debt was almost $16 million but that, given the proper financial backing and time to recover from Hurricane Hazel, the potential for national income far exceeded the debt. Speaking of the high rate of illiteracy in Haiti (the highest in the Americas), the president vowed that current efforts were under way to create schools and he intended to set aside as much as 13 percent of the national budget to finance such an effort.

Following lunch, he met with additional members of the financial community at the Calvin Bullock Forum at 1 Wall Street. Here he repeated his pleas for American investments to help Haiti grow to prosperity. "Only the flow of foreign capital," he stated, "could foster Haiti's industrial capabilities to feed and support this population growth." The next day he received the Pan American Society's Insigne Award for leadership. Earlier he had been given an honorary degree from Columbia University.

The president returned to Haiti shortly thereafter. Millions of dollars had been donated by private sources and governments to aid the country after Hurricane Hazel. Most disappeared without being spent. Corruption throughout Haiti was blamed, from the highest to the lowest level of government officials. Demonstrations against President Magloire and his extravagant lifestyle grew and in late 1956, in a dispute over his plans to extend his term of office, he fled the country for Switzerland and was stripped of his Haitian citizenship. He moved from Switzerland to France and finally New York City. In 1986, after Jean Claude "Baby Doc" Duvalier fled the country in scandal, Magloire returned to Haiti, was regranted his citizenship, and named the country's military advisor. He died in 2001 at the age of 93 in his villa outside Port-au-Prince, the capital of Haiti.

Tuesday, March 1, 1955:
New York Chapter of the American Red Cross

The 1955 goal for donations to the American Red Cross was $85 million, and New York's share was $5.7 million. To start the ball rolling for the city's goal, the New York Chapter received a ticker tape parade.

Rain began falling on the last day of February and continued the next morning, intensifying to a hard driving rain, and the forecast was for more of the same for the rest of the day and into the next. Despite the inclement weather, a fleet of ambulances and Red Cross vehicles formed the motorcade. Wearing ponchos and rain gear, detachments of the Army, Navy, Marine Corps, and Air Force, along with small groups from the city's uniformed services, strode up the Canyon of Heroes. The vehicles of the motorcade followed, with headlights on and windshield wipers working furiously. The Fire and Police Department Bands marched as well, though only handfuls of curious spectators huddled under umbrellas or in sheltered doorways to watch.

No ceremony could be held inside City Hall, which was undergoing renovation to its exterior stonework, and because of the weather, plans to hold the ceremony at the flagpole in City Hall Park had to be cancelled. Instead, the ceremony was moved to the auditorium of the *New York World* Building, across Franklin Street from City Hall Park. A number of city functions were held there during City Hall's renovation.

Mayor Wagner greeted John Sinclair, Chairman of the New York Chapter of the Red Cross, and presented him with a scroll proclaiming March 1955 as Red Cross Month. The mayor extolled the virtues of the organization and spoke of how the Red Cross, by serving all people regardless of race or creed, represented true democracy.

Mr. Sinclair responded and referred to the day's parade and kick-off celebration as a tribute to the more than 200,000 Red Cross volunteers nationwide. He expressed confidence in the success of the 1955 fundraising campaign. The same day, President Eisenhower issued a proclamation in Washington in support of the annual Red Cross drive. Nationwide the quota for the year was exceeded.

Founded by Clara Barton in 1881, the American Red Cross provides emergency assistance and disaster relief in the United States and is an affiliate of the International Red Cross and Red Crescent Societies. Its total revenues in 2019 were over $2.7 billion.

Newspaper Row

Originally called Chatham Street, the road running along the southern side of City Hall Park was renamed Park Row in 1886 but was frequently referred to as "newspaper row" because many of the city's 90 daily or weekly newspapers had offices there. At its peak in the early 1900's, over 250,000 newspaper copies were printed there every day. Towering above City Hall along Park Row were three of the city's earliest skyscrapers.

The New York Times building at 41 Park Row had been built in 1857. Founded in 1851, the Times had quickly outgrown its previous building one block away, and the new building was the city's first designed specifically for a newspaper company, with printing presses in the basement. The original five-story building was expanded in 1888 to 13 stories. The building was renovated again in 1904, but that year the Times moved uptown to a location overlooking the recently renamed Times Square. Its former home on Park Row was rented to various tenants over the years before being purchased by Pace University in 1951.

Adjacent to the Times building was the headquarters of Horace Greeley's New York Tribune. When the new 10-story building opened in 1875, it was the second tallest building in Manhattan, with a clock tower soaring over its main entrance. The building included three elevators, and a pneumatic tube system to move documents between floors In 1907, the original roof was removed, an additional 10 stories were added, and a 19-story annex was built adjacent to the original structure in an L-shaped design. In 1921, the Tribune moved uptown, and the building changed hands several times before being demolished in 1966.

The third skyscraper along Park Row was the New York World Building, erected in 1890. Established in 1860, the World outgrew its original building soon after being purchased by Joseph Pulitzer in 1883. With 12 floors covered in red sandstone plus a six-story dome, it was the first building in the city taller than Trinity Church. A 13-story annex was built in 1907, but the World began having financial problems after Pulitzer's death in 1911. The building had several occupants in the two decades after the World ceased publication in 1931. Facing financial struggles, the owner made a deal with the city. The Mayor's office was temporarily moved there while City Hall was renovated in early 1955, after which the building was demolished to make way for an expansion of the Brooklyn Bridge's exit and entrance roads.

Friday, April 15, 1955: 3,000 New York City Firemen

For the second time in as many years, New York City's firemen turned out in force on a perfect spring morning to celebrate Firemen's Day *(see: March 31, 1954)*. If spectators thought it seemed like a repeat of the previous year's events, they would be largely correct.

Fire fighters from all five boroughs marched up Broadway in well-ordered ranks. Accompanied by the Fire Department Band, the parade moved from Bowling Green to City Hall. As with the previous parade, the highlights this year were antique fire-fighting equipment mounted on floats normally housed at the Fire Department Museum. Among these were an 1820 hand-drawn pump, an 1892 steam pumper, an 1894 hose wagon, and a Chief's Model T Ford car from 1912. In stark contrast to these pieces, the parade also featured modern equipment. When the parade reached City Hall, two new bright red ladder trucks raised their ladders to their maximum height of 85 feet. Probationary firemen scaled the ladders and broke out American flags when they reached the tops.

No estimate of the number of spectators was announced but several thousand were in City Hall Plaza. Mayor Wagner welcomed the firemen and praised them for their work. He revealed that the number of fires in the city was down by more than 2,300 compared to 1954. The decrease, he noted, was due in large part to greater fire prevention awareness in the city. Building-by-building inspections by Department officials had also gone far to prevent fires, the mayor said. He was particularly proud of this because, according to the latest statistics, the number of fires annually was increasing throughout the country.

Fire Commissioner Edward Cavanaugh also spoke, proudly stating that his department was "the most dangerous security service in the government." He expressed his pride in all the members of the department and added that the entire city was proud of the efficiency and effectiveness of its firefighters.

Also addressing the crowd were City Council President Abe Stark; Thomas Hartnett, President of the Uniformed Fire Officers Association; and Howard Barry, President of the Uniformed Fireman's Association. All praised the department and were well received. At the conclusion of the event, the parade's participants dispersed, some to their homes and others to duty at fire houses and commands in the city.

Edward Cavanaugh was the 17th Fire Commissioner since the consolidation of New York City in 1898, serving in that role from February 1954 to December 1961. As a Harvard-trained attorney, he was seen as an unusual candidate for the role when selected by Mayor Wagner, but became one of the department's best leaders, praised for his innovation and modernization of the department during his tenure. He served as Deputy Mayor from 1962 to 1965, then pursued a corporate career until he retired in 1971. He died in 1986.

Reflecting the changes in the city and its population, the Department and its leadership have continued to evolve over the years. In 1966, Robert Lowery would become the city's first African American Fire Commissioner. Women were allowed to join the department's ranks starting in 1982. In 1996 the department was expanded, merging with the Emergency Management Services, and in 2019, Lillian Bonsignore became the first openly gay and first female chief of EMS Operations for the department. The department would be honored with one more ticker tape parade, celebrating its 100th anniversary *(see: June 1, 1965)*.

Thursday, April 21, 1955: Dr. Jonas Salk

Thursday, April 21 was a warm and sunny spring day. There were no bands assembling at Battery Park though, and no police motorcycles were preparing to escort a motorcade up Broadway under a blizzard of ticker tape. No dais was set up in City Hall

Park, but inside the City Council chambers a vote had been called. Instead of spending money on a ticker tape parade, a scholarship fund was created.

The story is unique in the history of ticker tape parades. On April 12, headlines across the nation had announced one of the most important and eagerly awaited scientific breakthrough:

"Vaccine Works! Polio Defeated!"

The next morning, Mayor Wagner telegraphed congratulations to Jonas Salk, proposing a ticker tape parade to honor the achievement. Dr. Salk, a native New Yorker who had attended the City College of New York and the New York University School of Medicine and interned at Mt. Sinai Hospital, replied with an answer the mayor had probably not expected. "I do not want any reception in my honor in New York or anywhere else," he said, adding that the money could be used better by funding more scientific research.

The Mayor suggested the creation of a scholarship fund to the City Council, saying "Let us hope that we can produce in our colleges a man or woman who will someday make the same kind of contribution to humanity as Dr. Salk has made." The Council enthusiastically agreed, appropriating $28,000 (the equivalent of over a quarter million dollars today).

Polio causes muscle weakness and affects the central nervous system, leading to loss of reflexes, paralysis of the arms and legs, and in severe cases, permanent paralysis and death. Highly contagious and with no known cure, it was one of the most feared childhood diseases. Fear of infection kept many children out of swimming pools and led cities to disconnect drinking fountains, close movie theaters and summer camps, and in some places, even schools and churches. Outbreaks increased in the 1940s and 1950s, disabling an average of 35,000 Americans every year, and so too did polio hysteria. A survey in 1952 showed the only thing Americans feared more than polio was nuclear war.

Scientists had been working on a vaccine since the 1930s. Wheelchair-bound President Franklin Roosevelt helped create the National Foundation for Infantile Paralysis in 1938, which funded research by raising millions of dollars through its annual "March of Dimes" promotion. Early first steps had failed, though a potentially promising oral vaccine using live attenuated virus was being tested. As a severe outbreak in 1952 fueled public panic, a research team led by Jonas Salk had success using inactivated virus on laboratory animals. The test was repeated in 1953 on a small group of humans, and the next year was expanded into the largest medical experiment in history, involving over 1.8 million children across the nation.

As soon as the Salk vaccine was declared successful, wide-spread distribution began, supported by a March of Dimes publicity campaign that included celebrities like Elvis Presley being filmed while receiving the vaccine shot. Within a year, over a million American children were inoculated, and the number of polio cases plummeted from 35,000 in 1953 to 5,600 in 1957. By 1961, only 161 cases were reported in the entire US.

Jonas Salk received many honors for his work, including the Presidential Medal of Freedom. In 1963, he established the Salk Institute for Biological Studies in San Diego, which has conducted research on birth defects, Parkinson's disease, AIDS, multiple sclerosis, Alzheimer's, cancer and most recently, coronaviruses. He died of heart failure in 1995.

The first Salk Scholarships were awarded in June 1955, and every year since then, the City University of New York has presented scholarships to outstanding students attending medical school or graduate programs in biomedical science.

Thursday, August 11, 1955:
Order of the Knights of Pythias

Annual Conventions are not a novelty in New York, and every year seems to draw some organization or group to the city. Of all the organizations and groups that have ever had their annual convention in New York, only one has ever been the recipient of a ticker tape parade, however. City Council President Abe Stark, a long-time member of the organization, persuaded the Council to grant permission and financing for the parade, and he would be its Grand Marshal.

The Knights of Pythias is a fraternal, patriotic, and secret organization founded in 1864 in Washington, DC. Its members believe in a Supreme Being, that friendship is an essential ingredient in life and that happiness can be achieved through service to others. Members swear that they are "not a professional gambler, or unlawfully engaged in the wholesale or retail sale of intoxicating liquors or narcotics." They also vouch that they support the lawful maintenance of the nation in which they live and, in a part of their oath added in the middle of the 20th century, that they are neither a Communist nor a Fascist and "do not seek by force or violence to deny to other persons their rights."

Members of the Knights don humorous costumes for events like parades, and the march up Broadway for this event was no exception. According to the *New York Times* reporter covering the parade, "The dominant attire was pantaloons and short jackets for both men and women" but the article continued,

"there was a comic clown, a ruddy-faced middle-aged Little Lord Fauntleroy, an American Indian with a sort of make-shift sarong, a man in Bermuda shorts and a fez, and a woman from Roanoke, Virginia, in a kind of Martha Washington dress."

Female members of the Knights are called the Pythian Sisters. One group of Sisters from Houston, Texas "wore black and white cowgirl outfits and toy pistols." A Pythian drill team from Hamilton, Ontario, wore flowing evening gowns.

Mayor Wagner, also a Pythian, welcomed the more than 2,000 marchers to New York. The official Pythian band, Sir Wah, from Oklahoma City, serenaded the small group assembled in City Hall Plaza with a rendition of "The Sidewalks of New York." The mayor's welcome was responded to by Abe Stark and by Imperial Prince John Lawrence, a member of the Dramatic Order of Khorassan, an auxiliary branch of the Society. With that, the festivities at City Hall ended and the members of the Knights returned to their convention and then to their homes across the United States and Canada.

The Knights of Pythias still exist today. As a secret society, much information about them is not available online, though according to an unsourced comment on Wikipedia, membership as of 2003 was approximately 50,000, and the society's website included a map with the locations of their approximately 2,000 lodges.

Friday, November 4, 1955:
Carlos Castillo Armas, President of Guatemala

Not only did Carlos Castillo Armas, President of Guatemala, receive one of New York City's traditional ticker tape parades on this chilly fall day, but he had the entire City Council sing "Happy Birthday" to him, as it was his 41st birthday.

The recently installed chief executive of the Central American republic began his day by attending Mass at St. Patrick's Cathedral. At noon he and his wife Alicia rode up Lower Broadway to the cheers of a smaller than usual crowd of well-wishers. Leaving the Battery, the parade consisted of two bands, a small military detachment, and a motorcade of six vehicles. The President stood during most of the journey and waved to the crowd as confetti and ticker tape spiraled down from skyscrapers. New York's growing Hispanic population was in evidence along the route as occasional shouts of "*Feliz Compleaños!*" could be heard. The blue and white flag of Guatemala displaying the nation's coat of arms flew alongside the Stars and Stripes from many buildings.

At City Hall, Mayor Robert Wagner placed the city's Gold Medal around the President's neck, welcoming him as the man who had overthrown the short-lived Communist government of his country the previous June. "We are in a common battle" against Communism, the Mayor said, "and your victory was a victory for us as well." The President responded through an interpreter by saying that his country's brief control by Communists was an attempt to divide all Latin American countries and drive them from the friendship of the United States. He added that everyone who loves freedom should join the fight against Communism wherever it appears. Immediately following his remarks, the Mayor reminded all those present in the Council Chambers of President Castillo Armas's birthday and led the more than 300 guests in singing "Happy Birthday." An obviously delighted president waved in acknowledgement and smiled when his wife kissed him on the right cheek before the applauding audience.

Later that afternoon at a luncheon at the Waldorf, Cardinal Francis Spellman echoed the mayor's remarks and added that "your birthday is a happy birthday for us because of the routing of Communism." The Guatemalan president told those assembled that religion was a prime target of Communism and stressed that the philosophy of Communism was that "people of different social economic backgrounds cannot cooperate in human endeavors."

President Castillo Armas flew to Washington the following morning for meetings with President Eisenhower and Congressional Leaders before returning to his country. He had become President in June when a military junta, backed with financial and technical support of the CIA, ousted the regime of President Elfigio Monzón. Not long after returning home

President Castillo Armas revoked laws which redistributed land to much of the country's poor, and outlawed opposition parties and trade unions. He implemented a new constitution, canceled the 1955 presidential election, and only permitted his own party to field congressional candidates. At the request of the CIA, he created the National Committee of Defense Against Communism, regarded by many as the first of a number of right-wing "Death Squads" that flourished in Central and South America through the 1960's and '70's. His renunciation of progressive laws and decrees and his increasingly dictatorial conduct led to civil war in Guatemala, which lasted from 1960 to 1996. An estimated 250,000 people perished in the war.

On July 26, 1957, President Castillo Armas was assassinated by a member of his own security force. Minutes later his assassin, Ramon Vásquez Sánchez, committed suicide. It has long been rumored that Vásquez had been hired by disgruntled elements of Castillo Armas' government to commit the murder. Members of his party, *Movimiento de Liberacion Nacional*, declared martial law and increased repressions against liberal groups and individuals.

Friday, December 9, 1955:
Luis Batlle Berres, President of Uruguay

The parade welcoming Luis Batlle Berres, President of Uruguay holds the record for swiftness, with newspapers reporting it lasted only 15 minutes.

The fact that the temperature was in the mid-20s and snow flurries fell throughout the day may account for the parade's haste. It was estimated that only about 15,000 hardy spectators lined the route, the snowflakes seemed to outnumber the confetti dropping from skyscrapers along the route. The 57-year-old president of South America's smallest country rode in an open vehicle with the State Department Chief of Protocol, John Simmons, and Richard Patterson, Commissioner of Commerce and Public Events, their faces red from the cold.

Mayor Wagner briefly welcomed the Uruguayan at City Hall and then escorted his official party of 14, which included the president's wife and two teenage children, to a luncheon at the Waldorf Astoria. Before 200 invited guests, the president was given the city's Gold Medal and a citation for distinguished and exceptional service. Because President Batlle Berres was scheduled to speak to a plenary session of the United Nations, the luncheon included few speeches and, by 2 pm, the chief executive was welcomed by more than 1,500 officials at the United Nations.

President Battle Berres spoke to the assembly of the evils of current politics, referring to communism as "an evil seed planted in the world." He suggested that those who disagreed failed to see the importance of vigilance against tyranny of any kind. Having spoken out against dangers from the left, he then spoke against those from the right, specifically criticized the United States when he spoke of nations supporting governments based on "strong men" who practiced their own forms of tyranny. He contended that "such regimes provide the very best breeding grounds for communism." He praised the UN for listening to the words of the smaller nations of the world. "If it were not for the smaller countries, the great powers would be at war," he suggested. He ended his talk by calling on the UN to admit Communist China to its membership, in addition to Taiwan. Both Chinas, he said, should have representation in the UN to promote peace and harmony in the world.

That evening he addressed a dinner sponsored by the Pan American Society. President Batlle Berres invited the other nations of the society to invest in his nation. Speaking of Uruguay's agricultural and cattle resources, he hoped that foreign aid could assist his small county in the war against world hunger.

The next day, he received honorary degrees from both Columbia and Fordham Universities, then flew to Washington for an additional two days, meeting with State Department and congressional leaders. His outspoken comments against facets of American diplomacy failed to win him favor in the nation's capital.

Luis Batlle Berres had served as president of Uruguay from 1947 to 1951 and returned for a one-year term in 1955. When that term ended, he remained active in politics but also returned to his earlier occupation as journalist and radio commentator. He died in his home near the Uruguayan capital of Montevideo in 1964 at the age of 66.

Monday, March 12, 1956: Giovanni Gronchi, President of Italy

Despite the cold and the occasional snow flurries, Giovanni Gronchi, third President of the Italian Republic, sat with his hat on his lap in an open limousine. He was in New York for the final four days of a 15-day tour of the United States. Shortly before the parade in his honor started, the sun broke through the clouds, reflecting off his glasses as the caravan of nine cars carrying the president, his advisors, Italian Foreign Minister Gaetano Martino, and city officials began the slow procession up Broadway.

Escorted by a squadron of mounted policemen, a Coast Guard honor guard, detachments from the Army, Navy, Marines, and Air Force, and the First Army Band, the parade was soon moving past the towers of lower Manhattan. Confetti and ticker tape seemed to dance in the occasional gusts of wind, as an estimated 140,000 people lined the route, clapping and cheering. President Gronchi waved in acknowledgement of the greetings.

The president was met at City Hall by Mayor Wagner. The mayor's words of welcome were translated into Italian for the president, who smiled widely when the mayor referred to New York as a city that contained a million and a half people with an Italian heritage, calling them "brothers in the cause of freedom and liberty."

Shortly after the welcome at City Hall, the mayor joined President Gronchi in the first vehicle of the caravan for the drive uptown to the Waldorf Astoria for a luncheon. At the president's request, the motorcade drove through the Garment District on Seventh Avenue between 34th and 42nd Street, where many Italian descendants worked. Nearly 1,000 guests filled the Grand Ballroom of the hotel, including Governors Averill Harriman of New York and Abraham Ribicoff of Connecticut. Mrs. Claire Booth Luce, US Ambassador to Italy, was scheduled to attend and speak as well but cancelled because of illness.

Cardinal Francis Spellman opened the luncheon with an invocation, after which Mayor Wagner presented President Gronchi with the New York Medal of Honor and a scroll proclaiming him a "dynamic statesman and parliamentarian." The mayor added that President Gronchi had been active in the fight against totalitarianism and as a leader in European unity and the cause of world peace. The president departed from his prepared speech and hoped that his visit would help build closer ties between his nation and the United States. He particularly thanked Governor Harriman for his role as Administrator of the Marshall Plan.

That evening the Italian president was the guest of honor at a dinner hosted at the United Nations by Secretary General Dag Hammarskjöld. Granchi spoke of his country's dedication to "international collaboration as set forth in the Charter of the United Nations. The next morning, he visited the Brookhaven National Laboratory on Long Island to inspect nuclear installations, and later that afternoon the president boarded a plane for Rome.

President Gronchi had been an early supporter of Mussolini but broke with him in 1923 when *Il Duce* became more dictatorial. During World War II, Gronchi was instrumental in the publication of clandestine anti-Fascist newspapers and broadsides. After the War he entered politics and helped create the Christian-Democrat Party, which was strongly backed by the Italian clergy. He was president of Italy from 1955 to 1962, and later served as Prime Minister. He died in Rome at the age of 91 in October 1978.

Saturday, May 20, 1956: Armed Services Day

On a clear and sunny spring day, over 150,000 spectators watched the sixth Armed Forces Day parade march down Fifth Avenue, from 95th Street down to 62nd Street. Over 30,000 members of all branches of the US Military participated, though for many spectators the highlight of the parade was the 2,500-man contingent from the United States Military Academy at West Point, who marched 14 abreast, in crisp gray and white uniforms, shouldering rifles with bayonets affixed.

This year's theme was "Power for Peace" and was intended to demonstrate that peace "can be achieved only through strength." Started when the Department of Defense was created by merging the three previously separate Departments of Army, Navy and Air Force, the first Armed Forces Day occurred in 1950, and is scheduled for the third Saturday of May each year. Parades are held in cities across the nation and in West Europe, and military posts and naval stations around the country host open houses.

In addition to parade, New Yorkers in 1956 could watch a fleet of more than 200 Air Force and Navy planes fly over Manhattan and Brooklyn, including a Navy blimp that hovered over lower Central Park, or attend demonstrations of helicopters and amphibious vehicles at Coney Island. Mitchel Air Force Base held a display of paratrooper drops, and docked at Floyd Bennet Naval Station, the destroyer *Peterson*, was open to visitors.

What spectators and parade participants did not enjoy this day was ticker tape, as this was **not** a ticker tape parade, which may explain why it appears on the Wikipedia list but not the other two semi-official lists of ticker tape parades. The *New York Times* does not mention any celebratory paper falling from the sky, unlike its coverage of all the parades through the Canyon of Heroes during the mid 1950s. In addition, the parade marched down Fifth Avenue in the Upper East Side. The buildings on the east side of the route are primarily residential and face the open clear skies above Central Park to the west of Fifth Avenue. Considering the high-end value of these luxury apartment buildings, it is almost certain that residents would not have ticker tape to throw out their windows.

The Armed Forces Day parade had grown since the first one in 1950, which included 35,000 marchers and 15 military bands. An aircraft fly-over was added in 1952, after one planned for 1951 was cancelled because of weather. An Army cannon capable of launching a nuclear missile named "Atomic Annie" rolled down Fifth Avenue in 1953, and more nuclear missile launchers appeared in the next few years.

As the decade progressed, though, public interest began to wane. The 1959 parade had fewer than 100,000 spectators, down significantly from the year before. By 1962, the number was half as many, and even fewer came out during a late-spring cold storm to watch the 1963 parade. The 1966 parade was forced to stop for over 5 minutes when anti-war demonstrators sat down in the middle of Fifth Avenue, and similar protests plagued the parade each year thereafter. The 1972 parade was cancelled because of threats of violence. "We see no reason to expose innocent people to any danger," Department of Defense spokesman Colonel Benjamin Fowler said, adding that "some nut will throw something and maybe kill four or five babies sitting on a curb."

The last Armed Forces Day parade in New York City found in the *New York Times* archive happened in 1976 and had a Bicentennial theme. The parade included marchers wearing period uniforms carrying 18th century flintlock muskets and color guards bearing Revolution-era flags. But there was no "expensive military hardware on display" because, as one general noted, "somebody thought it would be too militaristic."

Wednesday, May 23, 1956: Sukarno, President of Indonesia

Born Kusno Sosrodihardjo in 1901, President Sukarno used only one name after he reached maturity, like most Indonesians. He visited New York City as part of a two-week visit to the United States accompanied by his son Mohammed Guntar, and a staff of more than 20 advisors.

With his 12-year-old son by his side, Sukarno began the day with a visit to the Empire State Building. The sky was filled with low heavy clouds and the top floors of the building were shrouded in mist. Plans to visit the top were cancelled but his son insisted, saying, "I want to see as much of the city as I can while I am here." Adhering to the boy's wishes, the Indonesian chief executive and others rode to the top and were unable to see through the haze. Escorted downtown by speeding police cars, they reached the starting point of the parade at 12:30, a half hour after the scheduled start of the parade.

When the parade finally began, it was led by a military band, Army and Navy detachments as well as the usual contingents from the Police, Fire, and Sanitation Departments. The mist had turned to a slight drizzle and sodden strips of ticker tape fell to welcome the visitors. Because of the weather the crowds watching along the route were small, and as the parade reached City Hall, the drizzle turned to a heavy downpour. A City Hall staff member produced a raincoat which President Sukarno placed over his light blue military-style jacket.

Escorted into City Hall by Commerce Commissioner Richard Patterson, Chairman of the Reception Committee, Sukarno was introduced to Mayor Wagner. The Mayor apologized for the weather and presented the president with a scroll that commented on his leadership role, first as a militant in the 1930s in the fight against Dutch occupation, then as a leader of Indonesian passive resistance to Japanese occupation during the Second World War, and most recently against renewed Dutch attempts to regain control of his nation after the war.

Following the short ceremony at City Hall, the president accompanied the Mayor to the Waldorf Astoria for a luncheon, at which President Sukarno made a case for financial assistance to his country, saying it "would be mutually beneficial to Indonesia and America." He said that "at least 30 percent of your tires are made of Indonesian rubber. Thirty percent of the tin used here comes from Indonesia, which also supplies sugar, tea, and oil." He claimed that his country was one the richest in the world but added that much of its riches were still untapped. Asked for his impressions of the United States he said, smiling, "I love Americans" and was overwhelmed by New York. "I, the son of a small school master, am now in a gathering of kings. You are kings of industry, commerce, business, and administration."

Later that day President Sukarno visited the United Nations and was a guest of honor that evening at a second Waldorf reception. The next day he received an honorary degree from Columbia University and visited the Metropolitan Museum and the Frick Museum. He then departed for Philadelphia with his son and advisors.

Not long after the president returned to Indonesia the following month, facts came to light regarding his role during the Second World War which indicated that he worked more closely with Japanese forces than originally thought. Previously classified information showed that he was considered a prominent collaborationist with the Japanese. His policies and interests turned more towards Russia and Communist China. In 1960 he visited Moscow and received the Lenin Peace Prize. Resistance to his rule grew, especially among the military, and civil wars broke out on various islands in his nation during the late 1950's and early 1960's. He suppressed these, but hostilities remained until 1966, when government opposition became so strong that he was stripped of his presidential powers and was replaced by military leaders. He was placed under house arrest and then hospitalized for unknown reasons. He died of kidney failure at an Army Hospital in Jakarta, capital of Indonesia, in 1970.

Thursday, August 30, 1956: 3,000 NY State Volunteer Firemen

The 84th annual convention of the Fireman's Association of the State of New York (FASNY) was held in New York City during the last week of August 1956, and the city granted the Association a permit to parade up the Canyon of Heroes. While the city and many other localities in the State have professional fire departments, many smaller communities rely on volunteers for the necessary but often dangerous job of fighting fires. Volunteer firemen proudly wore the nickname "Vamps," possibly taken from the brightly colored knitted wool socks with the same name that they wore in the 1800s when fighting fires by means of bucket brigades.

No fewer than 24 bands from as many companies across the state accompanied the 3,000 Vamps when they stepped off from Bowling Green shortly after noon. Included in the companies were the men's wives, many of whom also volunteered their services but rarely as fire fighters. The weather was typical for summer in New York, and the haze was so thick that the sun was invisible until nearly a half hour after the parade began when it finally peeked through a tiny hole. The weather, however, did not seem to faze the marchers or the more than approximately 125,000 spectators who lined the route. In addition to the usual ticker tape drifting down, one reporter noted that "office workers in the financial district floated their morning papers down in scraps."

Volunteer companies from 40 towns and villages were represented. Near the front of the parade a 1919 Model T chief's car chugged, followed by contingents from the city's fire and police departments. Elsewhere in the parade was a horse-drawn pumper mounted on a flatbed truck, and 17 pieces of equipment, including ladder trucks, pumpers, and ambulances.

The parade was reviewed by Fire Commissioner Edward Cavanaugh, standing next to Mayor Wagner as the Vamps passed City Hall Plaza. The parade was so long, it took 45 minutes to completely pass the reviewing stand. Asked what he thought of the Vamps after the final unit passed, Commissioner Cavanaugh gave a single word response: "Wonderful."

The parade disbanded after passing in review and the Vamps, their ladies, and their equipment, returned to their uptown hotels.

The nickname "vamp" for volunteer fire fighters is no longer in common use, and the Oxford English Dictionary says the term was used in 19th and early 20th century American slang. Another possible origin of the term is related to the musical definition, based on the way volunteer fire brigades passed water buckets from the water's source to the fire being extinguished. Doing so efficiently required every volunteer in line to "vamp" to the same beat.

Founded in 1872, FASNY's vision is to serve the over 110,000 volunteer firefighters in New York State through education, advocacy, recruitment and recognition. As of 2020, its membership numbers more than 40,000, including members of the Ladies Auxiliary.

Tuesday, January 29, 1957: King Saud of Saudi Arabia

The US State Department got an unexpected response from New York City's Mayor Wagner when they told him that President Eisenhower had invited the Saudi Arabian King to the United States for diplomatic talks. Discussions had been going on for several weeks leading up to the visit, but the Mayor "precipitated a minor international incident" by publicly barring an official welcome or reception for the King.

"He's a fellow who says slavery is legal, and that in his country our Air Force cannot use Jewish men and cannot permit any Roman Catholic chaplain to say mass," the mayor said when announcing his decision. The Democratic leader of the City Council, Joseph Sharkey of Brooklyn, said he backed the Mayor "1000 percent" saying that when the city honors foreign dignitaries it is usually done "on orders from the State Department."

King Saud arrived in New York harbor on a gloomy gray day, sailing on the liner *Constitution*, which was met by the Coast Guard tugboat *Tuckahoe*. Transferring to the tug via an aluminum gangway, the King and 15 associates were carried to the Navy frigate *Willis A. Lee*, which was waiting nearby. As he boarded the frigate at 7:20 am, the King was serenaded by an 18-piece Navy band. As the frigate sailed upstream, the *Constitution* gave three toots from its whistle, but "in contrast to the Navy fanfare, no other harbor vessel appeared to take notice of the arrival" of the King.

Instead of disembarking at the Battery, as would be customary before a ticker tape parade honoree, the ship continued upriver, docking at Pier 45 at Christopher Street. Waiting there to greet the King was Henry Cabot Lodge, the US delegate to the United Nations and President Eisenhower's personal representative. With Mr. Lodge were an Army lieutenant general and a Navy vice admiral, both serving as advisors, as well as the Foreign Ministers of Egypt, Lebanon and Syria and other representatives from the UN.

The king was "robed in the woolen cloak of an Arabian chieftain, tan-hued for the daytime" and wore "cotton headgear, held by two woolen cords, gold-threaded." As he and his entourage disembarked, a Navy band played the Saudi "Royal Salute" fanfare. The King reviewed a 26-member Marine honor guard, then entered a green and white tent that the Navy had set up on the pier, as shelter from the intermittent rain. After some brief conversations inside the tent, the King emerged and gave a short speech in Arabic, noting that he was here at the invitation of the President, to exchange "views with the United States that may lead to welfare and peace of the entire world."

Accompanied by his six-year-old son Prince Mashur Ibn-Saud, the King and Mr. Lodge entered the first of 12 waiting limousines. Escorted by police, the caravan drove to the Waldorf Astoria. There were no spectators waving on the streets as they drove uptown "without halting for traffic lights," and about 50 spectators stood outside the hotel's entrance on 50th Street.

Shortly after noon, the King departed the hotel for a luncheon with UN Secretary General Dag Hammarskjöld. Afterwards, he spoke before the General Assembly, declaring that policies of force were "obsolete and indeed fruitless." Notably absent from the chamber were the delegates from Israel and France.

Following the address, the King was taken to the Waldorf Astoria Hotel for a reception and dinner. Outside the hotel, a group of protestors had formed, holding pickets and staging a mock "slave auction" of young women dressed in Arab garb. Asked by reporters how he felt about the Mayor's response to his visit, one of the King's spokesmen said "He's just not concerned about it. The world situation is more important." The next day, the King and his entourage went to LaGuardia Airport and flew to Washington for meetings with the President, during which he secured a loan from the US government as well as military aid and arms in exchange for use of Saudi airports by the US military.

In making his announcement that there would be no official reception for the Saudi King, the Mayor also rejected plans for a parade and official welcome for Marshal Josip Tito of Yugoslavia, who was scheduled to meet with the President in April. The same day that King Saud arrived in New York, the official Yugoslav state newspaper reported that the trip would be cancelled "unless Marshal Tito receives the same dignified treatment accorded to other visiting chiefs of state." The Mayor held to his position, and Marshal Tito's planned visit was delayed until 1960, and there was no parade then either.

Born in 1902, Saud bin Abdulaziz Al Saud had accompanied his father during many of the battles against the Ottoman Empire during World War I. He was made Crown Prince in 1933 and ascended the throne when his father died in 1953. He hoped to unify Arabs around the world, offering financial support and public praise when Egypt nationalized the Suez Canal, and in support of the Algerian war for independence from France. In 1962, a power struggle that had been brewing for years between the King and his brother Faisal erupted. Prince Faisal formed a new government while the King was receiving medical treatment outside of Saudi Arabia. The King initially resisted, but the Prince controlled the Royal Guard, and in 1964 Saud abdicated and went into exile. He died in Athens in February 1969.

Thursday, May 2, 1957:
Navy and Marine Veterans in World War II

The plaque in the sidewalk commemorating this parade originally said that 60 commanders were honored, but it has since been updated to read "62 veterans." That is in fact the correct wording, since ten of those honored were enlisted men who had received the Medal of Honor, the nation's highest military award. The other 52 were Navy admirals and Marine Corps generals, most of them retired, including Fleet

Admiral William "Bull" Halsey, who had already received a parade *(see: December 14, 1945)*. The parade was one component of "Operation Remember" sponsored by the US Navy League; other events included the league's 55th annual convention and public visits aboard most of the 15 ships that sailed into New York Harbor.

Estimates put the number of those standing along the route at 500,000. Countless more were at windows and ledges along the route up Broadway as the cars carrying members of the Navy and Marine Corps being honored as part of the Navy Week celebration drove by. The first car in the procession of open top vehicles carried Fleet Admiral William Halsey. Recognized by a large number in the crowd, he was greeted by many who shouted his nickname. "Hi, Bull" was frequently heard above the sound of the parade and the four escorting Navy and Marine Corps Bands. This was not the first ticker tape parade for the retired Fleet Admiral, who smiled broadly in acknowledgement. The other vehicles contained a total of 51 admirals and Marine Corps generals.

One of enlisted men, Sergeant Albert Ireland from Cold Spring, New York, was the recipient of five Purple Hearts for World War II service, four more for wounds received in Korea, two Bronze Stars, and eight Battle Stars along with the Medal of Honor.

Mayor Wagner presented citations honoring the achievements of the 62 men. Because of illness, two were not there to receive his praise in person, Fleet Admirals Chester Nimitz and William Leahy.

Following the presentation at City Hall, the mayor joined the military figures for a lunch on the aircraft carrier *Valley Forge*, docked at Pier 86 on 46th Street. The mayor was also given a tour of the ship. *Valley Forge* was the largest of the 17 naval vessels in New York as part of Navy Week. Berthed at various piers along the Manhattan and Brooklyn waterfront, all the ships except one were open to the public over the remainder of the week. The only ship excluded from public inspection was the nuclear submarine *Nautilus*, docked in the Brooklyn Navy Yard.

That evening those honored, plus the mayor and members of his administration and staff, attended a dinner at the Waldorf Astoria where, unlike the luncheon earlier in the day, wives and other women were included. Following the banquet, speeches were given by Navy Secretary Thomas Gates; Chief of Naval Operations, Admiral Arleigh Burke; and General Randolph Pate, Commandant of the Marine Corps.

Admiral Burke was interviewed by press and television reporters later that evening. He was asked to comment on a statement made that day by the Secretary of the Air Force Donald Quarles, stressing the superiority of air power because a single hydrogen bomb could destroy an entire naval task force. The Admiral took umbrage at the Secretary's comment and replied that locating a naval task force made it a difficult target to find, no less destroy. He also stated that he personally believed that the Soviet Union would not start a war simply because those in power there knew "we will completely destroy" them.

The evening's festivities concluded after Admiral Burke's bellicose statements, and the admiral, generals, and enlisted men returned to their normal occupations or duties.

With one of the world's largest natural harbors, New York City has had a close relationship with the Navy since the earliest days. The city's relationship with the sea was already changing during the 1950s because of the introduction of commercial jet aircraft, and the Brooklyn Navy Yard was gradually becoming obsolete, as newer ships were too tall to pass under the bridges spanning the East River. The first Operation

Sail in 1964 showed that there was tourist interest in sailing ships, and "Fleet Week" has become a popular event in the city, occurring every year since the early 1980s (except 2020, which was cancelled because of the Covid pandemic). Timed to coincide with Memorial Day at the end of May, naval ships are docked in both Manhattan and Brooklyn, and are open for public tours.

Monday, May 13, 1957:
Ngo Dinh Diem, President of South Vietnam

Ngo Dinh Diem knew what a ticket tape parade looked like. In 1950 he fled his native country because of his efforts to create an independent Vietnam dominated by neither France nor Communists, and spent his self-imposed exile living in Lakewood, New Jersey, and Ossining, New York, with frequent visits to New York City. During one visit, he stood on Broadway as a spectator for the parade honoring Lieutenant General James Van Fleet *(see April 24, 1953)*. After the French withdrawal from Indochina in 1955, the Geneva Accord established the new Republic of Vietnam and Mr. Diem was elected its first President through a plebiscite, which most sources considered fraudulent.

Now, on a sunny spring afternoon, the smiling 56-year-old head of state sat in the rear of a limousine as it began the procession up the Canyon of Heroes. He had returned to New York as part of a good-will tour of the United States.

The First Army Band from Fort Jay on Governors Island led the parade. Detachments from the Army, Navy, and Marine Corps marched, followed by contingents from the Police and Fire Departments. A motorcade of more than a dozen vehicles followed, with Diem in the first car. Other cars contained Vietnamese and US State Department officials, state and city dignitaries, reporters and photographers. The president sat between Richard Patterson, Chairman of the Mayor's Reception Committee, and Wiley Buchanan, the State Department's Chief of Protocol. President Diem wore a black homburg, a type of hat, he admitted later, that he had never worn before. As the motorcade began the drive up Broadway, the hat was more often off his head than on, as he continuously waved it to the admiring noontime crowd.

Streamers of ticker tape swirled down from the skyscrapers along the route. American flags and an occasional Vietnamese flag flapped in the slight breeze. Estimates of the crowd's size ranged from 100,000 to 250,000. Small clusters of Vietnamese inhabitants of the city shouted welcome in their native tongue as the president drove by their vantage points.

Mayor Wagner greeted President Diem when he arrived at the flag-bedecked steps of City Hall. The First Army Band played the National Anthems of the newly created southeast Asian republic and the United States. Spectators gathered in City Hall Plaza cheered when the mayor introduced the president and officially welcomed him to the city. The ceremony in City Hall Plaza was brief, and less than half an hour later, the mayor joined the Vietnamese leader when the motorcade continued uptown to the Waldorf Astoria for a luncheon and reception.

A telegram of welcome and congratulations from President Eisenhower was read after an opening blessing from Cardinal Francis Spellman. Mr. Diem, a Roman Catholic, had become a close friend of the Cardinal while he resided in the New York area years earlier.

Mayor Wagner then spoke, referring to Mr. Diem's work in leading the new nation and his efforts to combat the growing threat of communism from North Vietnam.

"The creation of the Republic of Vietnam," Mr. Wagner said, "is a modern political miracle." Mr. Diem was awarded the city's Medal of Honor and presented with a scroll for "Distinguished and Exceptional Service." Angier Biddle Duke, President of the International Rescue Committee, then presented Mr. Diem with an award for his leadership in the struggle against Communism.

President Diem thanked the mayor and Mr. Duke, then described the struggles his nation faced. He warned that as the threat from Communism increased, "we may need you" adding "whatever the future will bring, we will repay the debt we owe to the free world."

The following morning Mr. Diem attended a private mass at Cardinal Spellman's residence and breakfasted with His Eminence before attending a luncheon sponsored by the Far Eastern American Council. In the late afternoon he flew from LaGuardia Airport to his next stop, Detroit, Michigan.

Mr. Diem was staunchly anti-Communist and his prediction of needing American aid came true. America's involvement grew from semi-clandestine influence to full-fledged war, costing thousands of lives and billions of dollars. In a nation where Christianity is a minority religion, Mr. Diem's policies to consolidate power stripped away many privileges and powers of the Buddhist majority. He was an unpopular ruler but even most of his opponents admitted that only he seemed to have the ability to consolidate the various factions in his nation. Despite this, there was a small minority of religious and military leaders who attempted to overthrow him, and he began to lose the support of the United States.

On November 2, 1963, President Diem and his brother, Ngo Dinh Nhu, were assassinated by officers of the Vietnamese Army in a coup financed by the CIA. After the assassination, Vietnam was led by a series of rulers, none of whom were able to unify the nation's diverse interests. It has been reported that when Ho Chi Minh, head of the communist North Vietnamese Politburo, learned of Mr. Diem's death and America's involvement, he said, "I can scarcely believe that America would be so stupid."

Ngo Dinh Diem was buried in an unmarked grave in a cemetery next to the house of the American Ambassador in Saigon, now known as Ho Chi Minh City.

Tuesday, July 2, 1957: Alan Villiers and Crew of *Mayflower II*

Project Mayflower was conceived in 1954 to build a replica of the original *Mayflower* in England, sail her to the United States, and berth her at Plymouth, Massachusetts in commemoration of the arrival of Pilgrims to the New World. The man behind the plan was Warwick Charlton, a wealthy Englishman, who intended the project to thank America for aiding Great Britain in the Battle of the Atlantic versus German U-boats. Financed by Charlton and donations of school children in the United States and England, work began on the ship in early 1955 using original plans and specifications, and was built by hand using traditional methods, supplies, and tools. Except for the addition of electric lights and a ladder replacing a lower deck staircase, *Mayflower II* is an exact replication of the original vessel.

Born in Australia but a recent resident of Bay Ridge, Brooklyn, Alan Villiers was given command of the replica on her voyage from Brixham in Devon, England, to New York. A natural seaman since the age of 15, Villiers had sailed on many types of vessels, especially sailing ships with traditional rigging.

The *Mayflower II* began her voyage on April 20, 1957. In addition to Captain Villiers, one American sailed with her when she left England, 17-year-old Joseph Meany, Jr. of Waltham, Massachusetts, who had been selected by the Boys Club of America to represent American youth on the voyage. Captain Villiers took the ship on a slightly more southern route than her namesake to avoid Atlantic ice. The crossing was routine until near Bermuda when the ship encountered but rode out a violent storm. She reached Provincetown, Massachusetts on June 12. The voyage took the replica about 10 fewer days at sea than the original *Mayflower*.

Upon arriving in New York, the entire 21-man crew was accorded a ticker tape parade. Officers and crew were dressed in period costumes; most had beards and all were tanned. Captain Villiers wore a huge black hat with silver buckle on the crown, sea boots, and pantaloons. One crewman carried the ship's black and white cat, Felix. Leading the group that was cheered by thousands were mounted policemen and detachments of the Army, Navy, and Coast Guard. Music was provided by the Fire Department and Merchant Marine Academy bands.

In addition to his nautical skills, Captain Villiers was a famed cinematographer. He drew loud cheers from those watching when he began filming the crowd and spectators. Near the Singer Building (149 Broadway) he pointed his camera at a newsreel cameraman and shouted "Now it's your turn to wave at me. Good. Now just one more, wave again!" At almost the same moment a huge amount of ticker tape descended from the Singer building, draping both the Captain and the cameraman.

Mayor Wagner commended Captain Villiers for the voyage and singled out young Joseph Meany as an example of courage. Responding in a deep booming voice, Villiers laughingly explained that the original *Mayflower* was headed to the Hudson River, but its captain "double-crossed his passengers," probably referring to the decision made in 1620 to settle in Massachusetts when the ship failed to find a safe route south. The welcome ceremony was attended by guests representing various Colonial descendants and heritage organizations.

Alan Villiers continued sailing his entire life. In the 1960s, he was an advisor to MGM on their film *Mutiny on the Bounty* and was involved in an attempt to build a replica of Captain James Cook's ship, the HMS *Endeavor*. A frequent contributor to *National Geographic*, book author and film maker, he died in Oxford, England in 1982.

Mayflower II remained open to the public at Pier 81 at West 41st Street for a week. Opening day admission tickets, priced at 95 cents for adults and 42 cents for children, were sold at the pier by musical comedy star Ethel Merman. After a brief stay in New York, the ship was sailed to Plymouth, Massachusetts, where she was exhibited at Pilgrim Memorial State Park until November 2017. Towed to Mystic, Connecticut, for repairs *Mayflower II* is expected to be sea-worthy again for the 400th anniversary of the Pilgrim's arrival in 2020.

The Singer Builder, Zuccotti Park and Liberty Plaza

The view at Liberty Street and Broadway is very different today than it was for most ticker tape parades, though the site's history is deeper and richer. The King's Arms, the city's first coffeeshop, opened here in 1696. Almost 80 years later, the Sons of Liberty summoned a crowd outside the shop to protest the Tea Act, one of several incidents that led to the American Revolution. →

The site was purchased in 1890 by the Singer Manufacturing Company, which had invented domestic sewing machines in the 1850s and had just introduced the first electric machines in 1889. They built a 10-story building on this site in 1897, then ten years later, purchased the adjacent building, combined it with their original building and added a 27-story tower. When it opened in 1908, it was the largest building in the world, and thanks to floodlights installed to illuminate the tower at night, it quickly became an iconic image in New York's skyline.

In 1964, the company sold the building to US Steel, which planned to demolish it and erect a new skyscraper on the site. The new Landmarks Preservation Commission had been formed the following year, but it did not stop the plans, and the Beaux Arts skyscraper was torn down in 1969. Four years later, US Steel's new building opened. Home now to the NASDAQ as well as other tenants, One Liberty Plaza suffered damage on September 11, 2001 from debris from the World Trade Center but fears the building might collapse proved incorrect.

Also damaged that day was the small park that sits just south of the 54-story skyscraper. The park, originally called Liberty Plaza Park, was created when the Singer Tower was demolished, as part of the negotiations to provide higher air rights for One Liberty. The park was renovated by the property owners and renamed Zuccotti Park (after the company's chairman), and in 2011 was the site of the Occupy Wall Street protests.

Thursday, July 11, 1957: Althea Gibson

The first African American woman to receive a ticker tape parade was Althea Gibson, who returned home to New York from England after winning the Women's Tennis Tournament at Wimbledon.

The day began cloudy and humid, but a few minutes after the parade began at noon, the sun broke through the clouds and continued to shine for the rest of the afternoon. An escort of mounted police led the way followed by marchers from the Police and Fire Departments. Marching music was provided by the Police Department band. Miss Gibson rode in the first open car of a motorcade carrying her family, city officials, and executives of the American Tennis Association and the United States Lawn Tennis Association. Between 40,000 and 50,000 spectators stood along the route as swirls of confetti and ticker tape littered Broadway.

Wearing a white orchard corsage on her red and blue checkered dress, the tennis champion seemed withdrawn at first. Once the clouds disappeared so did her reticence, and she began to wave one hand at the crowds; soon she was waving with both of her hands. By the time the motorcade reached City Hall, she was waving and blowing kisses to the admiring spectators.

Mayor Wagner awarded her with a medallion and called her "a great New York girl who learned her tennis here." Born in South Carolina, her family moved to New York when she was three, and she took her "first tennis lessons on the streets of Harlem" according to the *New York Times*. "If we had more wonderful people like you," he continued, "the world would be a better place." She answered by telling the crowd gathered in City Hall Park, "This victory was won through your help and encouragement and all your well wishes. With God's help, I hope to wear this crown that I have attained with honor and dignity."

At a luncheon at the Waldorf, City Commissioner of Commerce and Public Events Richard Patterson called her an inspiration to all American women, especially those in the sporting world. "Miss Gibson came up the hard way and now stands at the top of her class" he said, citing her abilities, determination, and will to win.

She returned with her family to their apartment on West 143rd Street after the luncheon. Neighbors had strung streamers and "Welcome Home" signs, and balloons were set loose as more than 300 of her neighbors cheered and greeted her.

In an editorial about the parade, the *New York Times* praised her for being the first black winner of Wimbledon, then added that "her race was not precisely the reason" why she was honored with a parade. It concluded that "the honors paid her yesterday were evidence that we are becoming a land of diminished discrimination and of greater opportunity."

Between 1956 and 1958 Althea Gibson won five Grand Slams: Wimbledon twice, the French Open once, and the US Open twice. She was winner or runner-up in other tournaments between 1956 and 1961. In 1971 she was inducted into the Tennis Hall of Fame and in 1975 she was appointed New Jersey State Commissioner of Athletics. She suffered two aneurysms and in 1992 a stroke. A few years later she wrote to her former tennis doubles partner, Angela Buxton, that she could barely pay her rent, did not have enough money to pay for her medicines, and was contemplating suicide. Miss Buxton had the letter published in a tennis magazine, and as a result, more than a million dollars in contributions arrived from the magazine's readers. Althea Gibson died in East Orange, New Jersey, in 2003 due to a circulatory collapse. She is buried in Rosedale Cemetery, Orange, New Jersey.

Monday, October 21, 1957: Queen Elizabeth II of Great Britain

Elizabeth II, Queen of Great Britain and Head of the Commonwealth, and her husband Prince Philip concluded a 15-day tour to the United States with a visit to New York. The Royal Couple chose to arrive at Newark International Airport rather than Idlewild or LaGuardia for one specific reason: for her first visit to the city, the Queen wished to "approach the city as it should be seen, by water." Escorted from the airport to Stapleton, Staten Island, in a caravan of heavily guarded vehicles, the Queen and Prince were welcomed there by Governor Averill Harriman and Richard Patterson, Commissioner of Commerce and Public Events. They boarded the red-carpeted Army ferry *Lieutenant Samuel S. Coursen* for the trip across New York Harbor. A flotilla of boats of every kind surrounded them and sent greetings with their horns and whistles. The sirens of Harbor Police boats added their shrill sound to the cacophony, as four fireboats sent arches of water high in the air.

The Queen stood on the bridge of the ferry, marveling at the sight. "It is something I have often seen before in pictures, a sight I have always wished to see." She spoke as she studied the skyline, the bridges spanning the East River, the Statue of Liberty, Ellis Island, and Fort Jay on Governors Island. Minutes before the ferry reached Pier A, the Queen spotted the replica of the *Mayflower*, in New York as part of Project Mayflower *(see: July 2, 1957)* and pointed it out to Prince Philip. As the ferry sailed by Fort Jay, howitzers boomed a 21-gun salute. The First Army Band played the British National Anthem as the ferry docked. Her Majesty entered President Eisenhower's "bubble-top" convertible, on loan from Washington for the Queen's visit to New York. Wearing a light brown velvet coat with a mink collar, she sat beside the Governor with Mr. Patterson in the vehicle's jump seat. Prince Philip and Mrs. Harriman followed in the second car.

277

Dozens of motorcycle police escorted the motorcade up the Canyon of Heroes. Following the two cars carrying the Royal Couple were a procession of other cars filled with Federal, State, and City dignitaries, British and American security personnel, a group of the Royal Couple's aides, and reporters and photographers. Like hundreds of others who had been recipients of New York's unique welcome, the Queen was thrilled by the sight of thousands of spectators, the sound of their cheers, and the blizzard of ticker tape descending from buildings along the route. Strands of ticker tape landed on the bubble-top roof of the car she rode in. Multicolored confetti drifted down in the pleasantly cool air. Torn newspapers and shredded telephone directories fluttered. Flags of the United States, Great Britain, and Commonwealth nations flew from every flagpole and snapped as gusts of wind blew.

At City Hall Mayor Wagner greeted Her Majesty and the Prince. A battery of howitzers parked wheel to wheel behind City Hall fired a second 21-gun salute, their reports echoing through the narrow downtown streets. The plaza was jammed with 20,000 cheering spectators as the Queen and Prince entered City Hall, a red carpet covering its steps. The Royal Couple signed the city's Register of Visitors and were introduced to more than 300 invited guests in the Council Chambers. Their stay inside City Hall was brief and in less than 30 minutes, they were riding together in the President's limousine, as the motorcade continued traveling north to a luncheon at the Waldorf Astoria.

Crowds lined the route and continuous cheers rang out from the estimated 1.2 million people witnessing the day's events. More ticker tape fell, especially in the area near Astor Place, but never as plentiful as along lower Broadway. At the hotel, the Queen removed her coat, revealing a taffeta dress printed in brown and tan hues. Considerably more guests attended the luncheon than could be accommodated in the Grand Ballroom, so many were seated in other rooms, watching the happenings in the Ballroom via closed-circuit televisions. The Royal Couple visited many of the smaller rooms, and informally chatted with many guests. Queen Elizabeth spoke of her impressions of New York City, commenting on "the long and straight avenues and towering buildings and the bustle of the harbor and the streets, the exhilarating and dynamic atmosphere."

The Royal Couple went separate ways after the luncheon. Prince Philip attended the dedication ceremony at the Institute of Physics on East 45th Street while the Queen was escorted to the Empire State Building. In addition to arriving in New York by water, she had expressed a desire to see New York from the Observation Deck of the world's tallest skyscraper, so she was given a private tour by Mr. Fred Glass, the building's Senior Vice President. Unfortunately, the afternoon had grown hazy and the view was far from ideal, but the Queen was still impressed. "Everyone has a mental picture of famous places they have never seen," she told reporters, "and I suppose the mental picture of New York City is nearer reality than those of any other city."

While the Queen was viewing the city from the 82nd floor, the most troubling event of the day took place at the building's entrance on 34th Street. A woman darted past security guards and seized one of the dozens of potted yellow chrysanthemums bordering the red-carpeted entrance. Seeing this, other spectators broke through the barrier of police line and made off with plants as souvenirs of the day. When order was finally restored by Secret Service and Scotland Yard guards, most of the plants were in the hands of disappearing spectators.

That evening the Royal Couple attended a ball at the Waldorf. The Queen wore a multi-colored lace evening gown embroidered with iridescent palettes and jewels. She also wore a diamond tiara, a sapphire and diamond necklace, and a bracelet with matching earrings. Two Anglo-American organizations hosted the affair and the Queen thanked them and all New Yorkers for their "universal kindness." Leaving the ball at 10 o'clock, they were taken to the Seventh Regiment Armory for a second ball attended by more than 4,000 guests. They departed that ball at midnight and were driven to Idlewild Airport in Queens for their return flight to Great Britain.

In 1947, Princess Elizabeth was 21 when she married Philip Mountbatten, her second cousin once removed. On February 6, 1952, she became Queen upon the death of her father, King George VI *(see: June 10, 1939)*. Prince Philip, the Duke of Edinburgh, died in April 2021 at the age of 99. Queen Elizabeth II is still living (as of this writing) and is the longest-reigning monarch in British History, having surpassed Queen Victoria in September 2015.

Newark Airport

On October 1, 1928, the first major passenger airline serving the New York metropolitan area opened in Newark, New Jersey. Built on landfill along the Passaic River, the Newark Metropolitan Airport quickly became the world's busiest airport. With an Art Deco terminal that was dedicated by Amelia Earhart when it opened in 1934, the airport had over 60 flights a day operated by five passenger airlines.

That changed dramatically in 1939 when New York Municipal Airport opened, and all five airlines changed their routes. When the US entered World War II, Newark had so few passenger flights, the military closed it completely, using it for training, logistics, aircraft repair and evaluation of captured German aircraft. It was re-opened to commercial flights in 1946, and two years later, the city of Newark sold it to the Port Authority of New York, which promised much needed capital improvements. Those improvements were halted briefly in 1951, when two planes crashed within 5 weeks of each other into nearby Elizabeth, New Jersey. The airport was closed for several months while a new site was explored, but local opposition prevented a move, so Newark was re-opened with revised approach plans and a new terminal.

Through the late 1950s, passengers increasingly flew through Idlewild (JFK), and Newark Airport remained under-utilized throughout the 1960s. JFK's success soon led to delays though, so the Port Authority made more improvements at Newark, and the airport was renamed Newark International Airport when Terminals A and B opened in 1973. In 1981, a deal was made with the new low-cost People Express airline, and traffic began growing again, especially after People Express merged with Continental Airlines.

Renamed in 2002, Newark Liberty International Airlines currently serves over 46 million passengers, making it one of the top 15 airports in the US.

Monday, December 9, 1957: King Mohammed V of Morocco

After several years of fighting against the French and Spanish, the country of Morocco gained independence in 1956, though Spain refused to relinquish control of the coastal area around Ifni. Sultan Mohammed V was named King in April 1957, and later that year travelled to the New York with four of his children to speak at the United Nations, and the city planned a ticker tape parade in his honor.

The timing, however, was terrible. The weather was less than ideal for a parade: temperatures were dropping into the low 40s, and the light drizzle that had begun the previous day was expected to intensify. To make matters worse, the city's subways were shut due to a strike by motormen, and much of the police force that was supposed to provide security for the parade had to be re-assigned for duty at the city's major transportation centers, including Penn Station and the Grand Central Terminal.

On the morning of December 9, King Mohammed went to the United Nations with his son and heir, Prince Moulay Hassan, while his three daughters (Princesses Aicha, Malika and Nuzha) were taken to the Battery to wait for him at the start of the parade route. His speech at the UN, warning of growing nationalism in African and predicting an end to colonialism, was received coolly by many delegations, including the United States. He spoke also about the fighting taking place between his country and Spanish troops and had especially harsh words against France for the bloody fighting in Algeria.

Soon after 11 o'clock, King Mohammed ended his UN speech, and was informed that Richard Patterson, Commissioner of the Department of Commerce and Public Events, had officially cancelled the parade. The king's three daughters, Aisha, Malika, and Nasha, who had been waiting for him at the Battery, were driven to City Hall, where the king and his son, Moulay Abdullah, joined them. Mayor Wagner presided over a brief welcome ceremony for the royal family, presenting him with the city's Medal of Honor for his "distinguished statesmanship."

Later that afternoon a luncheon was held at the Waldorf Astoria, sponsored by the Foreign Policy Association. King Mohammed had changed from the suit he had worn at the UN into a traditional Moroccan *djeilaba* (a wool and silk robe), white sheepskin slippers, and a white fez. Mayor Wagner had been presented with a brown fez which he wore throughout the luncheon and the king's five-minute address that followed. Spoken in Arabic, his speech was translated into English by the Chief of the Royal Cabinet for the more than 700 invited guests. The King once again spoke of the need to end colonialism and attacked both Spain and France for their conduct in North Africa. He hoped that a way could be found without bloodshed to bring newly independent African countries closer to western powers.

King Mohammed and his family returned to Morocco a week later. The fighting between his country and Spain continued until late the following year. Although occupied by Moroccan troops, Spain did not relinquish claims to Ifni until 1969. Mohammed ruled as king until his death in February 1961 following throat surgery. He was 51 years old. His greatest achievement took place during the Second World War when, as Sultan of the French Protectorate of Morocco, he refused to enforce anti-Semitic decrees and laws of the Vichy government, thus saving the lives of Morocco's large Jewish population. In late 2007 it was reported that his name was being considered for addition to Israel's Righteous Among the Nations list.

Tuesday, May 20, 1958: Van Cliburn

People who didn't know the difference between Bach and Stravinski or between a fugue and a concerto were suddenly listening to classical music. At least they were listening to Tchaikovsky's Piano Concerto No. 1 because Harvey Lavan "Van" Cliburn, a 23-year-old pianist from Kilopre, Texas, played it in Moscow and received an eight-minute standing ovation from a mostly Russian audience. It was the height of the Cold War, the USSR had beaten America into space with Sputnik, and Communism seemed to be winning everywhere. And then along came a tall red-haired pianist who took a cultural prize in Russia, winning the first Moscow International Tchaikovsky Competition. So surprising was his victory that the judges called Soviet Premier Nikita Khrushchev asking him if they should give the prize to an American. "Is he the best?" asked the Premier, "Then give it to him." Cliburn returned to the US by plane and arrived at Idlewild International Airport on May 19. The next morning, New York honored him with a ticker tape parade up the Canyon of Heroes.

Police estimated the crowd at over 100,000 and according to one source it contained a "remarkable number of teenage girls." On a damp and gray spring day in Manhattan ribbons of ticker tape cascaded down and Cliburn gestured widely at the sight. He smiled and occasionally blew kisses to his admirers. As his limo drove past Trinity Church someone in the crowd shouted loud enough for the pianist to hear, "How does it feel?" With a big grin across his face, Cliburn shouted back jokingly, "I wonder who it's for?"

When the small caravan of cars and mounted police reached City Hall, Cliburn was greeted by Mayor Robert Wagner, who referred to himself as a "frustrated violinist." The mayor presented Cliburn with a scroll which praised him as a man "who through musical artistry had helped to eliminate the barriers that sometimes arise between people of different cultures." The city's Gold Medal was then placed around the young man's neck.

Inside the City Council Chambers, the invited guests included Richard Patterson, Commissioner of Public Events; the composer Richard Rodgers; the president of the Julliard School of Music; and the musical director of radio station WQXR, who all spoke briefly. When it was Van Cliburn's turn to respond, he answered in his best style. A grand piano had been placed on the stage and Cliburn set aside the scroll, removed the medal, and began to play Liszt's arrangement of Schumann's *Widmung* and Liszt's 12th Hungarian Rhapsody.

Van Cliburn remained active musically his entire life and has played for every president from Eisenhower to Obama and for kings and queens and in concert halls on every continent except Antarctica. He hosted the quadrennial Van Cliburn International Piano Competition and received the National Medal of Arts in 2010 from President Obama. He was a very quiet and religious man who attended Baptist services every Sunday and claimed that he never smoked or drank. He was, however, a "night person," often practicing until dawn. "You feel like you're alone and the world's asleep," he stated at an interview. "It's very inspiring."

Van Cliburn passed away from advanced bone cancer on February 27, 2013 at the age of 78. His obituary in *The New York Times* stated that his only survivor was Thomas Smith, his long-standing friend and companion.

Friday, June 20, 1958: Theodore Heuss, President of the Federated Republic of Germany

A gray and leaden sky covered Lower Broadway when the motorcade carrying the 74-year-old President of West Germany, Theodore Heuss, began its slow procession towards City Hall. Escorted by New York City motorcycle police, the parade included detachments from the Army and the Navy along with the Police and Fire Departments, and the Fire Department Band. As the parade reached Wall Street, the rain began to fall, alternating between a drizzle and a heavy downpour for the remainder of the day.

Estimates put the number watching the parade at about 50,000, and as soon as the rain began, they nearly all sheltered beneath umbrellas, but the rain did not seem to deter those in buildings along the way from dropping the usual cascade of ticker tape and confetti.

The President rode in an open convertible and turned down the request of Richard Patterson, Commissioner of Commerce and Public Events, to stop and raise the top. Instead, the German President donned a raincoat and buttoned it to the collar. He refused to remove his black homburg during the ride, nor did he cease puffing on a large cigar. He frequently waved to those watching, the cigar between his fingers like a pointer. When the parade reached Vesey Street, only a few blocks short of its destination at City Hall, he permitted Mr. Patterson to open an umbrella and the two sat huddled beneath it.

At City Hall the President was introduced to the cheering and applauding crowd in the plaza. Asked for his reaction he said he appreciated the open car because the parade was such an experience. Mayor Wagner awarded the President the city's Gold Medal and a scroll commemorating his leadership in his divided homeland.

Following a brief luncheon President Heuss moved to the New School for Social Research on West 12th Street. Prior to World War II, the school was unofficially known as the "University in Exile" because of the large numbers of German students who fled from Nazi Germany to complete their educations. In a speech at the New School, President Heuss commented on the level of knowledge and understanding offered by the school, saying that he was deeply touched to meet the friends of many of his countrymen who had been deprived of their freedom by Nazi tyranny. After his remarks he was made a Doctor of Humane Letters in a presentation by Dr. Hans Simons, president of the college, who had been a colleague of Mr. Heuss 40 years earlier at the *Hochschule für Politik* in Berlin.

President Heuss remained in Germany throughout World War II and avoided capture, imprisonment, and probable death for his liberal activities by using various pseudonyms and false identities. He wrote for and often published clandestine anti-Nazi underground publications. A pre-war professor, lecturer, and writer, he was named Minister of Education by Allied occupying forces in 1946. He was elected to the Württemberg-Baden State Parliament in 1948 and was the first elected President of West Germany. Returning to private life, he died in Stuttgart on December 12, 1963.

Monday, June 23, 1958:
Carlos Garcia, President of the Philippines

In March 1957, Carlos Garcia, the Vice President of the Philippines, was attending a meeting of the South East Asia Treaty Organization (SEATO) in Australia when he was informed of the sudden death of President Ramon Magsaysay. He immediately flew back to the Philippines and was sworn in as president by the nation's Chief Justice. Slightly more than a year later, President Garcia flew to the United States on a goodwill mission. Following three days of conferences and meetings in Washington, DC, he arrived in New York. On a warm and sunny June day, he attended a breakfast at the Waldorf Astoria hosted by Mr. Horry Priouleau, President of the Socony-Vacuum Oil Company, and by Harold Helm, Chairman of the Chemical Corn Exchange Bank. The oil company was building a refinery on the Bataan Peninsula in the Philippines and the bank was a major investor in the island republic.

Following breakfast, the President was escorted to the Battery by a squad of motorcycle police. He entered a cream-colored convertible for the ride up Broadway. The First Army's marching band led the way and detachments of the Army, Navy, and Marine Corps accompanied the Presidential motorcade. Beneath buildings flying the American and Philippine flags, and amid a blizzard-like fall of ticker tape, the parade moved towards City Hall. Groups of the president's countrymen were in evidence along the route, a few dressed in native costumes, cheering loudly as he drove by.

Mayor Robert Wagner welcomed the President, his wife Leonila, and daughter Linda at City Hall. The First Army Band played the national anthems of the Philippines and the United States. The president was then given the city's Medal of Honor and a scroll that recalled his political career before the Japanese invasion of the Philippines in 1941, his anti-Japanese activities during the War and his current leadership of the Pacific island nation.

The reception at City Hall was followed by a luncheon back at the Waldorf, where the president, a recognized and respected poet in his country, delivered a moving tribute to New York City, saying:

"The real glory of New York is that it is the City of Men. Here is a city built upon a scale more godlike than human, as if one day Man had planted his foot on the solid rock of Manhattan and here decided to build a city more splendid than ever conjured up by the genie of Aladdin's lamp or by the magic wand of Merlin."

He concluded by stating that the city's greatness came about because of its awareness of all the races, nations, and religions that made up its inhabitants. The President then bestowed the Philippine Legion of Honor to Mayor Wagner, who had served as a Colonel in the Army Air Corps during World War II, taking part in operations against the Japanese in the Philippines.

Later that afternoon the presidential family visited the Empire State Building. While on the 82nd floor observation deck, an aide brought him the news that a dysentery epidemic had broken out in Manila. The President arranged for a shipment of drugs to be sent from New York to his country and announced that he would be cutting short his visit to this country, canceling planned visits to Chicago and Los Angeles. The next day he flew back to the Philippines.

President Garcia was known for his "Filipino First" policy, putting the people's interests above those of foreign and domestic groups, and was highly revered by his people. After narrowly losing the 1961 presidential race to Diosdado Macapagal *(see: October 8, 1964)* he retired to private life, teaching and writing. On June 14, 1971, he died suddenly of a heart attack in Manila and an official state of mourning was declared. He was the first layman to lay in state in the Manila Cathedral.

Wednesday, August 27, 1958: Rear Admiral Rickover, Commander Anderson, and Crew of USS *Nautilus*

The world's first nuclear-powered submarine, the *Nautilus* arrived in New York on August 25 and sailed into a berth at the Brooklyn Navy Yard. Two weeks earlier she had been the first submarine to cruise submerged beneath the North Pole. In celebration of this feat, New York City scheduled a ticker tape parade for her commander and crew on Navy Day, and included an additional honoree, Admiral Hyman Rickover, Father of the Nuclear Navy.

A total of two open cars and 20 Army jeeps took part in the parade. The first car carried Admiral Rickover and Commander William Anderson, captain of the *Nautilus*. The Chairman of the Reception Committee, Richard Patterson, Commissioner of the City's Department of Commerce and Public Events, rode with them. The second vehicle carried the commander's wife Patricia and their 13-year-old son Michael. They were accompanied by Anthony Akers, Director of the New York City office of the State Department. The jeeps carried 115 of the submarine officers and crew, roughly three-quarters of her complement. Those not participating in the march were on duty aboard the *Nautilus*.

The First Army Band kicked off the parade to the tune of "Anchors Aweigh." Also marching was a Marine Corps drum and bugle band, the Air Force band playing "Colonel Bogey March," a detachment of Marines, Coast Guardsmen and the Fire Department color guard, four contingents from veteran organizations, and a mounted police squadron. A quarter of a million cheering spectators lined the route, and a larger than usual proportion of spectators appeared to be young ladies. Ticker tape in large quantities floated down and wrapped around flagpoles, lamp poles, ledges, autos, and jeeps.

The procession up Broadway halted several times as it headed up the Canyon of Heroes. At one point two jeeps stopped as the sailors jumped out of the vehicles and grabbed brooms from Sanitation workers standing along the route. Carrying the brooms like rifles held at "shoulder arms", they marched a short distance before laughing petty officers had them give back their commandeered "weapons" and return to their jeeps. By the time the parade reached City Hall, the last two jeeps were carrying unauthorized personnel: at least a dozen young girls held tightly around their waists by young sailors.

After petty officers had restored a semblance of order and discipline, Mayor Wagner greeted the Admiral and the Commander at City Hall. Both officers were celebrated for their achievements and accomplishments and were awarded the city's Medal of Honor. The mayor singled out the junior officers and crew of the submarine for special attention, referring to them as brave explorers and guardians of America's security. Loud applause and cheering followed his remarks.

After the City Hall festivities, a reception for the men was held in the Empire Room of the Waldorf Astoria. In an adjoining room, Mrs. Wagner hosted a luncheon for 78 wives and mothers of the submarine's crew, including Mrs. Anderson. Admiral James Russell, Vice-Chief of Naval Operations, spoke at the luncheon and called Admiral Rickover "that distinguished leader in engineering and science." The mayor presented a scroll to Captain Anderson citing the submariners' distinguished and exceptional services.

The *Nautilus* departed New York the following day. Based in New England, she remained on active duty until 1968. In 1979, she was moved to Mare Island Shipyard, California, for decommissioning. In 1980 she was moved to Groton, Connecticut, and now serves as a naval museum there.

Commander William Anderson retired from the Navy in 1959. In 1965 he was elected to the House of Representatives from the State of Tennessee, serving until 1973. He died in Leesburg, Virginia, in 2007.

Admiral Hyman Rickover retired in 1982, died in 1986 and is buried in Arlington National Cemetery. To date more than 200 nuclear-powered submarines and 20 nuclear-powered aircraft carriers have been commissioned into service all due to his pioneering work in the use of nuclear power on naval vessels.

Thursday, January 29, 1959:
Arturo Frondizi, President of Argentina

Arturo Frondizi, President of the Argentine Republic, arrived in the United States on January 27 for a four-day visit before proceeding to Washington for meetings with President Eisenhower and Congressional leaders. He spent his first full day in New York meeting Governor Nelson Rockefeller, Eleanor Roosevelt, and leaders of banking and investments firms. He stated that his purpose in coming to America was to strengthen economic ties between his nation and the United States and to cure the damage caused by the policies formulated by former president Juan Perón.

As he took his seat in an open cream-colored limousine on the morning of the parade, President Frondizi wore a dark blue suit and matching tie and his thick horn-rimmed glasses. He shared the car with Richard Patterson, Chairman of the Mayor's Reception Committee. Mrs. Elena Frondizi rode in the next car, a gray convertible, with the president's aide and secretary. The remaining vehicles of the 10-car caravan were filled with dignitaries from the US State Department and Argentina. Military and City bands accompanied the vehicles and detachments of the armed forces provided escorts. Police estimated that more than 300,000 people lined the route up Broadway, many shouting in Spanish and waving small Argentine flags. The South American leader waved to the crowds as the parade drove through the blizzard of ticker tape, confetti, and torn papers.

At City Hall President Frondizi was met by Mayor Wagner for a brief ceremony in City Hall Park. The mayor then entered the president's car and the entire motorcade continued north to the Waldorf Astoria for a luncheon and reception. More than 900 business, cultural, and diplomatic figures from almost 70 nations attended. Because of the large number, the reception had been moved to the Grand Ballroom, which had been booked by the Metropolitan Insurance Company for its annual meeting. Whether because of the hurried last-minute changes or because of a printing error, it was discovered that the Argentine coat of arms on the menus were printed with the crest upside down.

Apologies were made to President Frondizi for the error, and then the mayor introduced the President as "an effective fighter for freedom" and praised him for returning his country to a constitutional republic after Perón's dictatorship. President Frondizi responded in his native language, speaking of the hopes of opening Latin America to more American support and investments, which he said would aid both the United States and Latin American nations.

Following the luncheon, the President and his wife visited Central Park to place wreathes at the statues of José de San Martín and Simón Bolívar to commemorate the Latin American liberators a century and half earlier. Another wreath was placed in Bryant Park at the statue of Brazilian statesman, José Bonifácio de Andrada e Silva. The drive from Central Park to Bryant Park was marred by a slight accident when the car the president was riding in was struck lightly by a New York City taxicab that had somehow gotten into the presidential motorcade. There were no injuries, and damage to both vehicles was slight.

The president's day concluded with a visit to the offices of the *New York Times* and the *Herald Tribune*, followed by a dinner at the St. Regis Hotel hosted by DeWitt

Wallace, editor and publisher of *Reader's Digest* magazine. The following morning, before flying to Washington, President Frondizi visited the New York Stock Exchange and rang the bell to open the day's trading there.

Frondizi served as president of his country from May 1958 until March 1962. Removed from office by a military coup supported by Peronist backers, he was imprisoned for a year on a small island in the Rio de la Plata and then moved to a prison in a village in the Andes. Following his release, he unsuccessfully attempted to organize resistance against the return of Juan Perón and the growing prestige of the ex-dictator's late wife, Evita. Later he lived in semi-seclusion in a small apartment in a residential area of Buenos Aires, occasionally meeting with political figures, both in and out of office. He died in 1995 at the age of 86.

Tuesday, February 10, 1959: Willy Brandt, Mayor of West Berlin

Born in 1913, Herbert Ernest Karl Frahm worked as a young man in the shipyards of Lübeck Germany and adopted the name Willy Brandt to avoid detection from Nazi agents. When the Second World War started, he escaped to Norway and joined their army, was captured when that nation was occupied by Germany in 1940 but escaped and fled to Sweden. Returning to Germany in 1946, he officially changed his name, entered politics and was elected Berlin's mayor in 1957.

Mayor Willy Brandt arrived in New York early on the day of the parade from Washington. A driving, wind-blown rain welcomed the mayor as the parade began at Bowling Green and did not decrease in intensity throughout the ride up Broadway to City Hall. A police motorcade and a military detachment escorted the German mayor, but because of the intensity of the rain, performance by the Police Department band was cancelled.

The 46-year-old mayor of the divided German city surrounded by Communist East Germany stood in the newly purchased open tan sports phaeton limousine, covered with a black raincoat. Hatless, he waved to the thousands who, undeterred by nature's cold welcome, greeted him with New York warmth. City officials had feared that the mayor was not well-known enough to bring out a large crowd, but police estimated that the crowd surpassed 50,000. Standing beneath umbrellas, many along the route shouted personal greetings to Mayor Brandt. Cries of "Good luck, Willy," "That's a boy, Willy" and "Hurrah for West Berlin" were clearly heard.

As the car carrying the mayor entered City Hall Plaza, his wife, Norwegian-born author Rut Hansen Brandt, ran out from under an umbrella and joined her husband in the vehicle. They stood together in the soaking downpour for the last hundred yards of the parade. Mayor and Mrs. Wagner greeted them at the entrance to City Hall and the four hurried inside.

The planned outdoor reception had been cancelled earlier, and Mayor Brandt was given time to change from his soaked suit and refresh himself. At 4 o'clock, Mayor Wagner presented his Berlin counterpart with the city's Gold Medal. Dozens of reporters, many representing foreign media, were in attendance and Mayor Brandt made a prepared statement and took questions. He said that the city of West Berlin would stand in the face of Communist attempts to isolate and occupy it and gave thanks for American assurance to continue supporting his city. In response to a question from a German journalist he stated that he had no intention of requesting a stronger NATO presence in his city for fear of provoking a drastic reaction from East Germany and its Communist allies.

Brandt served until 1966 when he was elected West German Vice Chancellor. Three years later he became Chancellor and served until 1974. *Time* magazine named him "Man of the Year" in 1970 and he was awarded the Nobel Peace Prize a year later. A believer that Communist rule would eventually end in East Germany and all of Europe, he witnessed the fall of the Berlin wall in 1989 and called for the immediate reunification of East and West Germany. He died in 1992 and received a state funeral.

Friday, March 13, 1959:
José María Lemus, President of El Salvador

As the *New York Times* article about the parade for President Lemus puts it, the president of the smallest republic in the Western Hemisphere "learned some of the cold facts about New York." The temperature was below freezing, and a brisk wind snapped the flags on Broadway and swirled the ticker tape. For the former Lieutenant Colonel of the tiny El Salvadorian Army, who became president after a bloodless coup in 1956, New York seemed to be offering a very cool reception. He rode hatless in a convertible the entire 12 blocks from Bowling Green to City Hall waving to the fewer than 150,000 spectators who watched shivering from the wind-swept Canyon of Heroes. The same *Times* reporter commented that among the office workers on their lunch break were many spectators who "wanted to know for whom they were applauding."

President Lemus shivered occasionally in the cold early spring air. Riding with him were Richard Patterson, City Commissioner of Commerce and Public Events, and Dr. Miguel Rafael Urquia, El Salvador's delegate to the United Nations. Both were dressed more warmly than the President, each wearing a hat, gloves, and a scarf. The small motorcade was preceded by three bands, one military and two from city departments.

The usual outdoor welcome at City Hall was dispensed with. Inside Council Chambers, Mayor Wagner presented the Central American head of state with the city's Gold Medal and a scroll commending him for his "democratic convictions." Cardinal Francis Spellman of the Archdiocese of New York was among the 300 invited guests.

A luncheon followed at the Waldorf Astoria, where the president was asked about investment opportunities in his primarily agricultural nation. Answering in Spanish, he stated that there was no danger of naturalization or confiscation in El Salvador. "It may be said," he declared, "that by our very nature we are respectful of private property." Following additional questions, President Lemus rose to offer some prepared remarks, but noticed that the only copy of his speech was in his locked briefcase and the key was with his wife who was lunching with Mrs. Wagner at Gracie Mansion. The president attempted to deliver his speech from memory until an aide broke open the lock, and Lemus presented the speech as written.

Later that day Lemus visited the UN and attended a dinner, also at the Waldorf. Later that week he visited West Point and flew to Springfield, Illinois, to visit the grave of Abraham Lincoln before returning to his country.

Following an unsuccessful assassination attempt in 1960, President Lemus become increasingly dictatorial. His popularity waned, especially among his strongest supporters in the army. Later that year, he was ousted by a military coup, and deported to Nicaragua. He returned to his native country shortly before his death in 1993.

Friday, March 20, 1959: Sean O'Kelly, President of Ireland

A brisk breeze whipped down Broadway and circled through Bowling Green, and the sky was a bright azure with barely a trace of a cloud. All was set for the parade to honor Sean O'Kelly, President of the Republic of Ireland. After spending three days in Washington for meetings with President Eisenhower and Vice President Nixon, and addressing a joint session of Congress, the man who called himself "the president of a very small island" stood in the back of an official New York City convertible.

A few minutes after noon a whistle was blown, and the band chosen to lead the parade, the 50-piece Women's Air Force Band from Norton Air Force Base in California, stepped out. Army, Navy, Air Force, and Marine Corps detachments served as an honor guard as did groups from the city's Police, Fire, and Sanitation Departments. Many inhabitants of New York whose ancestors came from Ireland had turned out to welcome the president; one estimate put the crowd size at 400,000, a second at half a million. Whatever the exact number, it was a huge welcome. Coming just three days after New York's annual St. Patrick's Day Parade, it was clear that many were still in a celebratory mood.

Ticker tape and strips of green crepe flew down from the buildings along Broadway. The entire crowd seemed to be waving US and Irish flags. Dressed in a formal morning coat with tails, President O'Kelly doffed his silk top hat to the crowd repeatedly. His face bore a smile from start to finish. When a group of young girls clad in green rushed through the police barricade near Fulton Street in an attempt to reach the president's car, he politely bowed to them as they were halted by a crew of policemen.

When the parade finally reached City Hall, the vehicles were draped in ticker tape and the seat and floor of the car were an inch deep with it. The President stepped from his vehicle and was met by Mayor Wagner. The men embraced spontaneously as photographers' flash bulbs popped and the crowd roared its approval. The president was introduced to invited guests in the Council Chambers, and his wife Philomena was presented with a huge bouquet of red roses. The Irish President was then given the city's Medal of Honor and a scroll that spoke of him as "a patriot and soldier of the Irish revolution...a statesman who played a vital part in establishing the Irish State." Asked to comment on his welcome, the President answered in a lilting brogue that he had seen pictures and films of New York's parades but, "Nothing could exceed the parade today – it exceeded my wildest anticipation."

A luncheon for almost 800 guests at the Waldorf followed. Catholic Cardinal Francis Spellman opened the luncheon with a prayer and blessing. Mayor Wagner offered a toast to President O'Kelly, who responded, "I would like to offer a toast to my colleague in the Presidency, the President of the United States." Following the luncheon O'Kelly spoke with evident wit, "I have been a politician all my life and I am proud of it. There is no nobler profession..." halting in mid-sentence, he turned to the cardinal and added, "except perhaps that of the Church, Your Eminence."

The president's stay in New York was for two days. He received the honorary degree of Doctor of Laws from Fordham University and attended a second reception at the Waldorf sponsored by the Irish Government.

President O'Kelly returned to Ireland on the last day of March. He was a controversial leader because of his outspokenness. His closeness to the Catholic Church in Ireland caused some to fear that he was a spokesman for the Church, but he maintained a distance between the government of Ireland and his personal views.

He served two six-year terms as president and then retired from public life. The former officer in the Irish Republican Army during the Easter Rebellion of 1916, commanding officer in the Irish Civil War of 1921, professor, writer, member of the Dial

(Irish parliament), and second president of the Irish Republic died at the age of 84 in 1966, in Dublin.

Friday, May 29, 1959: King Baudouin of Belgium

The 28-year-old King of Belgium, whose full name was Baudouin Albert Charles Léopold Axel Marie Gustave de Belgique, had a reputation for shyness. Before his arrival in the United States, reports circulated that he requested nothing elaborate to mark his arrival. Specifically, it was said, this included a ticker tape parade. Somehow, however, an unnamed advisor succeeded in convincing His Majesty that it was almost a necessity for a visiting head of state, especially a royal one, to be welcomed in the city's traditional manner.

Wearing a gray business suit, King Baudouin began his day shortly before noon in Battery Park, where he laid a wreath on the Monument of the Walloons. Among the earliest settlers in the village that eventually became New York City, the Walloons were natives of Belgium. After the wreath was laid and photographs taken, the King stepped into a white open limousine for the journey up Broadway, the same journey his grandparents, King Albert I and Queen Elisabeth had taken almost forty years earlier *(see: October 3, 1919)*. The vehicle led a 15-car motorcade, escorted by marching bands from the Army and Navy and detachments of the armed services, the Police and Fire Department.

The king's shyness soon melted, and he began to wave to the more than 25,000 spectators lining the route. He was very happy when he heard shouts of "*Vive la Roi!*" and "*Vive la Belgique!*" The *New York Times* report of the parade included a story about a young girl watching the parade from the steps in front of the newly constructed building at 2 Broadway; held high by her mother to view the passing king, the little girl asked, "Mommy, where's his crown?"

Upon reaching City Hall, the young monarch was met by Mayor Wagner. King Baudouin signed the official visitor's register and was presented with New York City's Gold Medal. He was also given a scroll that expressed the sentiments that Baudouin was a "personification of ancient European peoples now constituting modern Belgium." Answering in French, one of Belgium's two official languages, the monarch thanked the mayor and those who had aided in welcoming him.

Immediately afterwards the King was driven to the Waldorf for a luncheon for almost 500 guests, two of whom were surprise guests. As a teenager during the final days of World War II, Albert and his parents had been held by the Nazis, first in Hirchstein, Germany and later in a villa in Strobl, Austria. On May 7, 1945, a squad of American soldiers rescued them. Among the guests at the luncheon were two men who had been corporals in the rescuing detachment: Joseph Kratzer of Elmont, New York and Edward Stimson, of White Plains, New York. During the luncheon, the king mentioned the two men and recalled playing table tennis frequently with Corporal Kratzer. He joked that, though he had usually lost, his game had improved since then. Both New Yorkers expressed astonishment when they were notified, just a week earlier by the city's Public Events Committee, that they were to be surprise guests at the luncheon.

That evening King Baudouin was the guest of Governor and Mrs. Rockefeller, at the Governor's home in Tarrytown. The next morning, he flew to Norfolk, Virginia, the final stop in his American visit.

289

In mid-December 1960, the king married Doña Fabiola de Mora y Aragon in Brussels. All five of her pregnancies ending in a miscarriage. He reigned for 42 years and died suddenly of heart failure in Motril, Spain on July 31, 1993 shortly after a mitral valve prolapse operation. He was extremely popular among his people and his unexpected death caused a period of deep mourning. His body lay in state at the Royal Palace in Brussels and 500,000 people viewed it, more than 5% of the entire population of Belgium. He was laid to rest at in the church of Our Lady of Laeken, besides the tomb of his grandfather, Albert I, and his grandmother. Having no children, he was succeeded to the throne by his brother, Albert II.

NY Produce Exchange and Number 2 Broadway

One of the major buildings on lower Broadway at the start of our period that is no longer standing is the New York Produce Exchange Building. Located just east of Bowling Green facing Broadway, the building was erected in 1881. Designed by George Post, who also designed the New York Stock Exchange and several other buildings along Broadway, the Produce Exchange was one of his masterpieces. The neoclassical building, with a 224-foot tower, was covered in fiery red brick, and in addition to the trading floor, housed a restaurant, a library, and meeting halls and offices that members could rent.

In the era before jet transportation when New York had one of the nation's busiest commercial harbors, the Produce Exchange thrived, doing as much as $15 million of business each day during the early 1900s, and had over 2,500 members. After World War II, those numbers began to shrink, and by 1950, with membership down to under 500, the Exchange rented space in a nearby office building. The building on Bowling Green, which had been the first to combine wrought iron and masonry in its construction, was demolished in 1957.

A new 32-story office building was erected at Number Two Broadway. Covered in blue-green tinted glass with a modernist design, it was criticized by some who felt that "one of the best buildings in New York has been replaced by one of the worst." Today, Number 2 Broadway is the headquarters of the Metropolitan Transit Authority.

Tuesday, June 16, 1959: Reverse Parade for Second Fleet

Most ticker tape parades march up Broadway from the Battery to City Hall, but one was intentionally held going in the reverse direction.

As part of the city's celebrations of the 350th anniversary of Henry Hudson's exploration of the river that bears his name, a parade was held for the US Second Fleet, commanded by Vice Admiral William Smedberg. As plans were being made, organizers learned that the venue they hoped to use for a post-parade luncheon was already booked, and that one of the four marching bands was scheduled to play in Battery Park later in the afternoon on the day of the parade. The organizers decided to march downtown toward the Battery. "I think it's a precedent all right," said Assistant Chief Police Inspector James Nidds, "certainly I never heard of one before this."

The parade formed in City Hall Park, where the Admiral received a scroll from Acting Mayor Abe Stark, who filled in for the Mayor. "Let me tell you what the Second Fleet really is," the admiral said in his prepared remarks to the crowd. "Our mission is offensive – I hope extremely offensive to an enemy. Tension in the world sends us to the sea ready for action at a moment's notice." In response to concerns that air power, in particular the atomic bomb, made navies obsolete, he added "the Fleet is in no way a sitting duck. One bomb could atomize only one of us. We can stay at sea indefinitely without ever having to come ashore."

After the ceremony, the parade kicked off, heading down Broadway toward the Battery. The Admiral and the captains of 16 of his warships rode in open cars, waving to the estimated 200,000 spectators lining the streets. The caravan was followed by 400 men of the Army, Navy, Marine Corps and Coast Guard, marching in formation. The men were "showered with ticker tape streamers and shredded paper whipped by the gusts of the canyon."

According to the New York Times, another reason for the "novel feature" of the parade's "southerly course" was that the "sailors would feel happier heading toward the sea." Whether that was the case or not, the reverse direction may be the reason why the parade is not included on any of the lists of ticker tape parades.

The US Second Fleet was formed in 1950 as part of the military's re-organization after World War II. Most of its ships had been part of the Eighth Fleet and were responsible for the Atlantic and Caribbean Coasts of South and Central America. It played a significant role in the Cuban Missile Crisis in 1962 and the invasion of Grenada in 1983. It was disbanded in 2008 and absorbed into the Fourth Fleet.

Prior to taking command of the Second Fleet, Vice Admiral Smedberg had been superintendent of the US Naval Academy in Annapolis, where he was responsible for raising funds for a new football stadium. He retired from the Navy in 1964 and served as president of the Navy Relief Society. He died in 1994.

Friday, September 11, 1959: Princess Beatrix of the Netherlands

On September 11, 1609, Dutch explorer Henrik Hudson sailed his ship *Half Moon* into a wide estuary previously discovered by Giovanni de Verrazzano. For the next ten days he sailed up the river, originally called the North River and later the Hudson, searching for a passage to China. The so-called "Northwest Passage" was not found, but thanks to his efforts the Netherlands laid claim to the land he explored, and a small village was established on an island in that estuary, named *Nieuw Amsterdam*. Years later the English seized control and renamed it after the Duke of York, and the city has been known as New York ever since.

Who better then to be the Guest of Honor for the celebration of the 350th anniversary of the discovery and exploration by Europeans of the Hudson River than a member of the Dutch Royal Family?

Cruising on the maiden voyage of the Holland-American ocean liner *Rotterdam* Crown Princess Beatrix, oldest daughter of Queen Juliana, arrived in New York Harbor. The Royal Dutch destroyer *Gelderland* shuttled the 21-year-old heir to the Dutch throne from Gravesend Bay, Brooklyn, to the foot of Manhattan Island. Disembarking at Pier A to the echoes of the salute fired from the guns of Fort Jay on Governors Island and the whistles and horns of ships in the harbor, she was met by Richard Patterson, Commissioner of Commerce and Public Events and William Zeckendorf, President of the New York City Hudson Celebration Committee. To the strains of the National Anthem of the Netherlands, "Wilhelmus van Nassouwen," as played by the First Army Band, the Princess joined the two men in a convertible for the ride up Broadway to City Hall.

The motorcade carrying the princess and her entourage, members of the State Department, and State and City Governments was escorted by marching detachments of the Dutch and American Armies and Navies. Police estimated that 200,000 people lined the route. In addition to the normal blizzard of confetti and ticker tape, orange streamers in recognition of the Dutch Royal House of Orange and Nassau swirled down on a hot sunny afternoon. Princess Beatrix wore a close-fitting green feathered hat that showed little of her blond hair. In a navy-blue suit with a white portrait collar, her Highness smiled broadly at those along the way. Her childhood nickname of "Trix" was often heard above the sound of the marching Army, Navy, and Police Department bands. She often pointed and waved to spectators along the route.

At City Hall, Mayor and Mrs. Wagner greeted the attractive princess. He presented her with the Gold Medal of the City of New York inscribed with the words "in sincere friendship with the affection and esteem of all the people of New York." In his introductions of Her Highness the mayor spoke of Hudson's voyage and the Dutch names still in use in the city: Broadway, Bowery, Harlem, and Brooklyn among many, then added that they also "left us something more precious than names and landmarks – their love of Liberty which took root in New York and the Hudson Valley."

Princess Beatrix delivered a response to the mayor in English with a slight British accent, which she learned when spending most of her youth during the Second World War in Canada. Speaking for the people of her nation she said:

"While we realize that millions of people have come from other European countries to make New York the important world center it is today, we still feel a most particular affection for what was once Nieuw Amsterdam. The affection does not only come from the memories of past glory. We feel a close relationship to the people of this city and country because we share the same belief in human dignity."

Following the welcoming ceremony, the Princess reviewed a company of Dutch and American Marines. She was then driven uptown to the lawn of Gracie Mansion for a luncheon. The guests there included Jan van Roijen, Dutch Ambassador to the United States and the American Ambassador to Holland, Phillip Young. The mayor proposed a toast to Queen Juliana, and Princess Beatrix responded with a toast to President Eisenhower.

After retiring briefly to her suite at the Waldorf that afternoon, the Princess met with reporters. One newsman asked her which American she would most like to meet. "Gee, oh gee," she answered, then paused, and added "I'd like to meet as many regular Americans as possible." She commented that she did not particularly like rock and roll music but listened to it occasionally. In answer to more serious questions, she thought a more united Europe was in the future. She commented that Queen Juliana was almost completely retired and spent much of her time reading and gardening.

The Princess' 11-day stay in the United States was busy, filled with receptions, dinners, theater and museum visits, and officiating at the Hudson River Celebration at the home of late President Franklin Roosevelt in Hyde Park, New York. She was presented to President and Mrs. Eisenhower at a State dinner in Washington DC before returning by plane to the Netherlands.

Following Dutch tradition, Queen Juliana abdicated in 1980 and Beatrix was inaugurated as Queen. The inauguration was marred by riots caused by socialists protesting poor housing conditions in Amsterdam and Rotterdam. Early in her reign she often made remarks at various functions and affairs without consulting with advisors, often to the embarrassment of her government. Because of these statements, the Dutch government no longer permits her to be directly quoted in the press without government approval. She married in 1966 and has three sons.

On April 30, 2009, Beatrix attended festivities for the Dutch holiday of Queen's Day. While the Royal Family watched the passing parade, a car suddenly crashed through a barrier into a group of spectators, killing six and injuring 11 others, though none of the Royal Family were harmed. The driver was apprehended and, according to police, confessed on the way to the hospital, where he died of his injuries the next morning.

Like her mother before her, Beatrix followed Dutch tradition by abdicating on April 20, 2013, and was succeeded by her oldest son, Willem-Alexander. After the abdication, she is once again referred to as Princess Beatrix. As of 2020, she continues to perform some royal functions and is the patron of many charitable organizations. She is 82 and lives in Drakensteyn Castle.

Gracie Mansion

Overlooking the East River at 88th Street and East End Avenue is Gracie Mansion, the official residence of New York City's Mayor since 1942. The two-story Federal style mansion was built in 1799 for Archibald Gracie, a Scottish ship owner who moved to New York in 1784 and made his wealth exporting tobacco to Scotland; later he expanded into banking and insurance. He purchased the hilltop overlooking the river in 1798 to build a country retreat from the city. He sold the property in 1823 to pay his debts, and the house had several owners over the next few decades. In 1896, the city government seized the property to settle outstanding taxes due from its owner and created Carl Schultz Park.

The city used the building as a concession stand and public restroom for the park until 1924, when it became the first home of the Museum of the City of New York. When the Museum moved in 1936, the building reverted to the Parks Department, which opened an ice cream shop. In 1942, Parks Commissioner Robert Moses convinced the City to designate the building as the official mayoral residence. Concerned about security as the nation entered World War II, Fiorello LaGuardia moved in with his family after the building received some needed repairs.

In 1966, the building was enlarged by Mayor Robert Wagner's wife, Susan, who added a wing with several reception rooms for public events. In 1981, Mayor Ed Koch created a Conservancy to ensure the building was restored and maintained, and in 2002 the building received another major restoration under Mayor Michael Bloomberg.

City law mandates that the building can only be used for official city business, and only the mayor's family and visiting public officials can stay there overnight. That was upheld in the 1990s by a court when Mayor Giuliani i was not allowed to have his mistress stay there and was one reason why Mayor Bloomberg never stayed there during his 12-year mayoralty.

Wednesday, October 14, 1959:
Adolfo López Mateos, President of Mexico

The 49-year-old President of Mexico, Adolfo López Mateos, visited New York City as the second stop on his weeklong visit to the United States and Canada. He was accompanied by his wife Eva, aides and officials. The purpose of his visit was not to receive gifts or grants for his country, he assured listeners, but to increase friendly relations between his nation and the two other large democracies of North America.

A crowd of 250,000 spectators viewed the parade held in his honor. It consisted of five marching bands: two from the military, two from city departments, and a Mexican marching band. Shortly after noon the parade stepped off from Bowling Green and headed up Broadway to City Hall. Mexican and American flags fluttered in the brisk autumn air, as a blizzard of ticker tape, torn paper and confetti descended from the buildings along the route, littering the marchers, bands, vehicles, and streets.

The Mexican President was greeted by Mayor and Mrs. Wagner at City Hall. The mayor introduced the statesman to the assembly in City Hall Park before moving inside for additional welcoming ceremonies, where a group of Mexican singers provided a serenade of folksongs.

Inside City Hall, President López Mateos gave the first of three speeches he delivered that day. He spoke of the close ties between Mexico and the United States but called for closer collaboration in trade and commercial matters. His remarks were applauded by the large number guests in the Council Chambers.

A luncheon at the Waldorf Astoria followed, where Mayor Wagner awarded the chief of state with the city's Medal of Honor and a scroll that saluted him "for distinguished service in Mexico's development." In response, the Mexican president spoke of the primary obstacle to the economic growth of Mexico's population of over 33 million: stabilization of the world's markets. Mexico's main imports of cotton and certain minerals faced increased worldwide competition and trade agreements with other nations were a necessity.

Later that day, the President addressed the United Nations, delivering his third speech of the day. He praised the work of the international body and called for Latin-American solidarity to combat ignorance and despair among less prosperous nations and peoples. He returned that evening to the Waldorf Astoria for a dinner of the Pan American Society, attended by 700 members and guests. He was praised for fostering democracy in Mexico and attempting to aid struggling Central American regimes in the pursuit of internal peace and harmony.

President López Mateos continued his whirlwind visit the following morning when he and his party flew to Ottawa for additional meetings with Canadian officials. He remained Mexico's president until 1964, and numerous reforms were carried out during his presidency, including large-scale redistribution of more than 15 million hectares of land. Under his leadership great changes were also made in social legislation. After the end of his term of office he left public service, and later served as Chairman of the Organizing Committee for the 1968 Summer Olympics held in Mexico City. He died suddenly of a heart attack in 1969 at the age of 60.

Wednesday, November 4, 1959: Ahmed Sékou Touré, President of Guinea

The 37-year-old President of the small West African nation of Guinea came to the United States to improve relations between the two countries and to promote investments. Ahmed Sékou Touré met with President Eisenhower in Washington, DC, and then traveled to New York to address the United Nations General Assembly. As customary, the city welcomed him with a ticker tape celebration after he arrived from Washington by plane.

The day was cool with a brisk November wind blowing. The President, wearing a heavy overcoat, entered a cream-colored open car at the Battery with Vincent O'Shea, Deputy Commissioner of the Department of Commerce and Public Events. The parade set out towards City Hall just after noon. Two bands accompanied the six-vehicle caravan carrying the West African leader, his staff, and representatives of the State Department and City government. Detachments from the Army, Navy, Air Force, and Marine Corps provided a military escort. Approximately 200,000 spectators lined the route up Broadway and the usual blizzard of ticker tape and confetti showered on the marchers. Flags flew from a number of buildings, but some incorrectly flew the colors of Ghana rather than those of Guinea, probably due to the similarity of the flags.

Mayor Wagner was vacationing in California, so President Touré and his wife Andree were welcomed by Acting Mayor Abe Stark, who introduced the president to invited guests in the Council Chamber. Stark mentioned Guinea's recent separation from the French Community, composed of former French colonies in Africa and spoke of the President Touré's courage in removing Guinea from any association with its former colonial ties. The president was then presented with the city's Medal of Honor and a scroll for distinguished service in the cause of African nationalism.

Immediately afterwards President Touré was the guest of honor at a luncheon at the Waldorf sponsored by the African American Institute. He spoke in French, his words translated by a State Department official. He acknowledged that colonial rule had built highways and modern buildings in his country, particularly in Conakry, the nation's capital and largest city. However, colonialism had also "depersonalized subject peoples and deprived them of national identity." He claimed that his primary purpose in visiting the United States was not to obtain financial aid but admitted that such aid was needed to build schools and hospitals.

Following the luncheon, President Touré visited the Museum of Primitive Art on West 54th Street. The founder and president of the museum, Governor Nelson Rockefeller, served as his guide. At a press conference there the Acting Mayor and his distinguished visitor agreed on the benefit of the exchange of ideas between people of nations because, the president said, "it is often difficult to understand different cultures across the oceans." The next morning the president addressed the General Assembly before returning to his country.

President Touré ruled Guinea from 1958 until his death in 1984. He was discouraged by President Eisenhower's attitudes towards newly independent African countries, but President Kennedy's views drew him to closer ties with this country. After Kennedy's assassination, President Touré forged closer ties with the Soviet Union and Communist China because of suspicions that a failed coup in his nation had been backed by the CIA. He returned to a pro-western stance in the mid-1970s after disagreements with China. He provided aid to rebellious groups in Portuguese colonies in Africa and welcomed refugees from neighboring nations. At the same time, he increased his power at home and his government became more autocratic and tyrannical. He imprisoned political rivals and his followers launched a reign of terror that killed at least 50,000 people.

He suffered a heart attack while visiting Saudi Arabia in March 1984 and was flown to the Cleveland Clinic in Ohio for cardiac care. He died there on March 26, 1984. Less than a week later a military coup overthrew his successor and began executing many of President Touré's closest followers, including his wife and other members of his family. An estimated 20,000 were killed.

Wednesday, March 9, 1960:
Carol Heiss, Olympic Gold Medalist

The youngest person ever to be the sole recipient of a ticker tape parade, Carol Heiss rode in an open car with a fur wrap around her, waving her gloved hands to the noontime crowds whose applause was muffled by their gloves. She had already received the silver medal for figure skating in the 1956 Winter Olympics and won several World Championships before the 1960 Olympic Games in Squaw Valley, California. There, the attractive 20-year-old blond woman from Ozone Park in Queens won the Gold Medal, and a week later warmed the hearts of a quarter of a million people standing in the cold to welcome her home.

Arriving at City Hall, Mayor Wagner greeted her with a kiss and welcomed her home. She stood by the mayor's side as he presented her with the city's Gold Medal. The scroll given her by the mayor read: "Presented to Carol Heiss, figure skater extraordinary, inspiration to our youth, admired daughter of New York."

Photographers snapped her picture as she stood to address the guests in the Chamber, movie cameras rolled, and questions were posed. Asked for her reaction to the city's welcome, she answered, "I never expected anything like this. It was a complete surprise, and I will never forget it." She said she did not intend to turn pro, and when asked if she would compete in the 1964 Olympics, she replied, "No, but I hope there will be another Heiss there, my sister Nancy." She was joined at the podium by Nancy and her brother Bruce, both excellent skaters, and her father Edward, a baker originally from Munich, Germany, who preferred skiing to skating. Before the end of the reception, a photographer shouted, "Kiss the mayor again." As she obliged, His Honor smiled, saying, "This is the best thing about the day."

The next year, she married fellow figure skater Hayes Alan Jenkins and starred in her only movie, *Snow White and the Three Stooges*. She became a skating teacher and coach in 1970 and served as a television commentator for skating competitions. Carol Heiss Jenkins continued in that capacity for another dozen years and then retired to her home in Akron, Ohio, where she still resides as of this writing in 2020. She was the first female skater to land a double axel jump and in 1976 was inducted into both the World Figure Skating Hall of Fame and the US Figure Skating Hall of Fame.

Monday, April 11, 1960:
Alberto Lleras Camargo, President of Colombia

Invited to be the principal speaker at the 50th anniversary of the Carnegie Endowment for International Peace, Dr. Alberto Lleras Camargo, President of Colombia, arrived in New York for a five-day visit, and was treated to New York's traditional ticker tape welcome.

It was a chilly April morning with temperatures in the mid-40's. The sky was a bright blue with barely a cloud. Accompanied by his wife Bertha, their 14-year-old daughter and a teenage niece, President Lleras Camargo sat in a convertible with Richard Patterson, New York's Commissioner of Public Events. An Army band followed the 25-motorcycle police escort. Detachments from the Army and Navy as well as the Police and Fire Departments followed the president's vehicle, and four other cars carried Colombian and American officials. Flags of the United States and Colombia fluttered along lower Broadway as streams of confetti, ticker tape, and torn paper drifted down. The short, bespectacled Colombian chief of state sat and waved at the more than 150,000 people lining the parade route.

As the car carrying the President turned into City Hall Plaza, Dr. Lleras Camargo was awarded a rare honor, not given to most foreign dignitaries. A battery of howitzers stationed at the far end of the Plaza fired a 21-gun salute, which had not been bestowed since the arrival of Queen Elizabeth II in 1957 *(see: October 21, 1957)*. A city official later told the *New York Times* that a salute "had been a regular feature of visits by heads of state, but that the tendency was to omit it to save time."

Echoes of the salute had hardly ceased when Mayor Wagner introduced the President to the crowds in the Plaza, many of whom could be seen waving small Colombian flags. He welcomed the South American leader to New York and presented him with a scroll of honor. Dr. Lleras Camargo, a former newspaper editor with a Ph.D. in journalism from Our Lady of the Rosary University in Bogotá, Colombia, thanked the mayor and the citizens of New York for the warmth of the welcome despite the cold of the weather.

Later that afternoon the president addressed the Carnegie Endowment at their headquarters on East 46th Street. "It is not necessary," he said in flawless English, "for the world to be regimented under a single type of national government. The one thing needed for co-existence is that none of the world's nations should attempt to impose its pattern of living on the others." After a pause he added, "But world understanding is impossible today, because the Soviet Union does not accept this condition."

That evening he was the guest of honor at a banquet held at the Waldorf Astoria, sponsored by the Avenue of the Americas Association. Among the guests were 200 Colombians living in the New York area. The Association's President, Mr. Spruill Braden, presented Dr. Lleras Camargo with a large symbolic key "to open the doors of understanding and peace."

Dr. Lleras Camargo spent the next few days shopping and sightseeing with his family in New York before returning to Colombia. In the face of opposition to his land reform policies he failed to win re-election. Years of teaching journalism and diplomacy followed until he retired from public life in 1980. He died in Bogotá at the age of 84 in 1990.

Tuesday, April 26, 1960: Charles de Gaulle, President of France

Unlike President de Gaulle's first ticker tape parade when he rode almost emotionless up the Canyon of Heroes *(see: August 27, 1945)*, his second parade featured a smiling, waving, jovial statesman. In 1945, de Gaulle had been the driving force of the Free French movement, the leader of a country still in ruins from the war, his leadership position shaky and in question. By 1960, he was the newly elected president of France's Fifth Republic, the leader of a prosperous nation recovering from political difficulties after the end of World War II. Coming on the eve of the Four Powers Summit Meeting in Paris between the United States, United Kingdom, France, and the Soviet Union, de Gaulle's visit provided an opportunity to meet with President Eisenhower in Washington, after which the French president flew to New York as a goodwill gesture.

It was a fine spring day and more than 200,000 people filled lower Broadway as the parade began its slow journey to City Hall. Detachments from the Army, Navy, and Air Force escorted the president, and the marching pace was set by bands from the Army and the Police Department Band. As streamers of ticker tape and red, white, and blue ribbons floated down, President de Gaulle waved and smiled, riding in an open vehicle with Mayor Wagner. The mayor's wife Susan sat in the next car with the president's wife Yvonne. The president requested that his car halt when it reached Trinity Church, and he stood at attention as its carillon played "La Marseillaise," saluting as the final note of the French National Anthem echoed through the streets.

City Hall Plaza was filled with cheering spectators, many of whom waved miniature French flags. Mayor Wagner officially welcomed the French President to New York and presented him with another City Medal of Honor to go with the one he had received 15 years earlier. Pleased to welcome De Gaulle back to New York, the mayor joked that the President should become a regular visitor to the city. President de Gaulle responded in French, his words translated by a State Department official.

The motorcade then continued to the Waldorf Astoria for lunch, which was attended by 1,300 guests. Mayor Wagner expressed his confidence that de Gaulle's presence at the forthcoming Summit Conference and his solidarity with the United States and United Kingdom would demonstrate to Soviet Premier Nikita Khrushchev how seriously the west was working toward peaceful solutions to the problems in the world. Henry Cabot Lodge, America's Ambassador to the United Nations, referred to the long-standing friendship between France and the United States and recognized that the President's visit would further solidify that bond.

President de Gaulle responded by first thanking New York for its hospitality. "New York is a city which is a world in itself, the chief center of free exchange between the old and new worlds." He then added his pledge that France was determined to see an end to the fighting in Algeria which had been plagued by rebellion against French rule since 1954. He concluded by assuring all Americans that France and the United States would always be closest allies.

That evening, President and Mrs. de Gaulle attended a reception at the Seventh Regiment Armory on Park Avenue and East 66th Street. More than 5,000 guests greeted the president there with cheers of "Viva de Gaulle!" A group of young boys and girls, dressed in costumes of various French provinces and possessions, were introduced to him. As he was leaving the reception a small number of protestors broke through the police barricades demanding that France grant independence to all its African and Asian colonies. The police were able to restrain the protestors and a security squad escorted the President to the Lexington Avenue side of the armory where he entered a waiting police vehicle.

At noon the following day, a reception was held at the French Consulate on Fifth Avenue near 72nd Street, attended by representatives of most member countries of the United Nations. A second incident with protestors took place during the reception but President de Gaulle seemed unaware of it.

President de Gaulle returned to Paris for the Summit Conference which ended abruptly soon after it started. The Soviet delegation walked out of the conference when the news that an American U-2 spy plane had been shot down during a photo-reconnaissance mission over the Ural Mountains. The United States originally denied any part of the operation, claiming that a weather plane had strayed off course, but relented when the plane's pilot, Francis Gary Powers, was shown to be alive and in the hands of the Russian military after bailing out of his damaged spy-plane.

President de Gaulle remained in office until 1969 when he resigned at the age of 70 and was succeeded by Georges Pompidou. On November 9, 1970, de Gaulle died of a ruptured blood vessel in his throat. Announcing his death on television, Pompidou said, "General de Gaulle is dead. France is a widow." Per his wishes, de Gaulle is buried in a simple grave in the churchyard of the village of Colomby-les-Deus Eglises.

Many of de Gaulle's actions were controversial. Franklin Roosevelt once described him as "an utterly sincere megalomaniac" and other national leaders found him difficult to work with. He did however rally France in World War II, unite diverse elements after the war, and create the most stable French government in history, the Fifth Republic.

Monday, May 2, 1960: King Mahendra Bir Birkam Shah Dev and Queen Ratna of Nepal

The headline in the *New York Times* describing the welcome to the rulers of Nepal reads "Polite but Puzzled Crowds Hail King and Queen in Ride Up Broadway."

Under a dazzling blue sky, the 33-year-old King Mahendra Bir Birkam Shah Dev of Nepal rode up Lower Broadway to a less than tumultuous crowd of noontime spectators, quite a few of whom appeared not to know who was being honored. Nepal's unusual double triangle red flag with what resembles a laughing sun and moon did little to clear the mystery. One female bystander narrowed it down by saying, "I think he's the king of something or other."

Wearing a blue business suit and dark sunglasses, the king rode in an open white limousine with Richard Patterson, Commissioner of the Department of Commerce and Public Events. In a second car rode 32-year-old Queen Ratna Rayja Lashmi, a petite and pretty woman, barely visible in the closed limousine. One police estimate put the crowd size at a little over 100,000; a second, which included those who watched the parade from skyscraper windows, at about 300,000. The *New York Times* seemed skeptical, noting the sidewalks were not packed and that "much larger crowds" had spilled out onto the street for Charles de Gaulle the prior week (*see: April 26, 1960*).

Mayor Wagner greeted the King and Queen at City Hall. The royal couple wore dark glasses during the ceremony as the Mayor presented the King with a scroll commemorating his visit and asked how the King would compare New York's skyline to Mount Everest. Mr. Rishikesh Shaha, Nepalese Ambassador to the United States, translated the response, "His Majesty commands me to say that skyscrapers are made by man. Everest is a creation of God."

Later that afternoon the King and 400 State Department and City officials lunched at the Waldorf. Since the lunch was for men only, the Queen with her retinue dined at Gracie Mansion with Mrs. Wagner. The royal party later met with Dag Hammarskjöld and toured the United Nations. That evening they both were guests at a reception sponsored by the Far East-American Council of Commerce. The queen wore a pale pink sari embroidered with silver, and the king wore a black suit.

The couple remained in New York for two days before continuing an eight-day tour of the United States. Returning later that summer to Katmandu, Nepal's capital, the king found his reign threatened by left-wing groups supported by China. He enacted a series of reforms, including the creation of a Council of Ministers containing individuals not related to the royal family, but they had little effect in making Nepal less controlled by his family. In early 1972 he died of a heart attack and was succeeded by his son, Birendra Bir Bikram, who was assassinated in June 2001 while attending a family banquet at the royal palace. Queen Ratna was in another room of the palace when the assassination took place, so survived the mass shooting. When the monarchy was abolished in 2008, she was the only member of the royal family not forced to evacuate the palace. As of this writing in 2020, she is 92 years old and still resides in the former royal palace.

Tuesday, July 5, 1960: King Bhumibol Adulyadej and Queen Sirikit of Thailand

The ruling family of Thailand was in the United States primarily for a social visit shortly after their marriage. After a brief stop in Washington to confer with President Eisenhower, King Bhumibol Adulyadej and Queen Sirikit Kitiyakara visited New York City where they received a ticker tape welcome, as is customary for visiting dignitaries.

A bright summer day welcomed their Majesties. Streamers of confetti rained down on the royal couple as they drove up Broadway in separate convertibles. Wearing a white military uniform with gold braid and two rows of ribbons and medals, the King stood in his vehicle from start to finish, waving at the cheering crowd of more than 750,000. The Queen remained seated in her car until the parade reached Wall Street where, casting aside her natural shyness, she stood as well. A huge cheer rose once the crowd saw her, dressed in a long pink silk skirt with a matching pink jacket buttoned in precious stones. Her appearance and smile won the admiration of those who saw her. She later commented about New York, "It is a great big, wonderful city, and the people are very nice."

The parade reached City Hall at 12:25, and the King and Queen were met by Mayor and Mrs. Wagner. Before a crowd of 1,500 invited guests in the Council Chambers, the mayor presented His Highness with the city's Gold Medal. The King, in turn, presented Mayor Wagner with a silver cigarette case with Thailand's coat of arms on the cover. The Mayor referred to the King as the "beloved leader of a free people who are justly proud that for more than a millennium they have maintained their independence." King Bhumibol, smiling broadly, thanked the mayor and those responsible for his hearty welcome. "I have seen [New York] receptions in the movies, and I am very excited to receive one," he said.

A fan of American jazz, the King attended a Benny Goodman jam session that evening while the Queen attended a performance of *My Fair Lady* with Mr. and Mrs. John Rockefeller. At a press conference the next morning His Majesty was asked about Communist threats to his country. He admitted there had been some infiltration along Thailand's border with China but that the region was being constantly guarded and watched. "We provoke no one, but we are ready to defend ourselves against any outside aggression." Later that day, the Royal Couple flew to Boston to continue their trip through America before returning home

Known in Thailand as Rama IX, King Bhumibol became ruler of the nation in June 1946. He and Queen Sirikit were married two weeks before arriving in the US. She suffered a stroke in 2012 and has been under constant care ever since. The king died on October 13, 2016 and a period of mourning began. His body was cremated exactly one year later, and his ashes placed in the Wat Bowon Buddhist Temple in Bangkok, Thailand.

Friday, October 14, 1960: King Frederick IX and Queen Ingrid of Denmark

King Frederick IX of Denmark and his wife, Queen Ingrid, arrived in New York City to preside at the opening of the Arts of Denmark exhibit at the Metropolitan Museum of Art. The exhibit represented the largest collection of art and artifacts from

Denmark and Greenland ever to be shown in the United States. The royal couple arrived by plane from Washington, DC, early in the morning after having spent the previous day meeting with President Eisenhower and government officials. They were escorted from LaGuardia Airport to the Battery in ample time for the parade's scheduled start.

The police estimated that a quarter of a million people lined the route up Broadway or stood at windows to welcome the King and Queen. As was often the case, the First Army Band provided the music, and detachments of the armed forces served as escorts. A detail of motorcycle police added the noise of their engines to the cheers of the crowd. White ticker tape and red paper streamers fell from the buildings along the way. Denmark's national colors were also seen in the many Danish flags flying from the skyscrapers along the route.

Denmark's king since 1947, Frederick IX wore the uniform of an Admiral in the Danish Navy. Standing more than six and half feet tall, he seemed uncomfortable in the rear of an open limousine, the first car in the motorcade, which he shared with Richard Patterson, Chairman of the Mayor's Reception Committee. Queen Ingrid, dressed in a wine-colored suit and matching feathered hat, rode in the second car. Just before the parade reached Wall Street, the King requested that the cars stop. The Queen and Mr. Patterson changed places, so that the Royal Couple rode the rest of the route side by side.

The parade halted briefly at City Hall. As the First Army Band played the National Anthems of Denmark and the United States, the King and Queen signed the city's guest book. They separated at this point and Queen Ingrid traveled to Gracie Mansion with Mrs. Susan Wagner, the mayor's wife. At the Mansion Mrs. Wagner presented Her Majesty with a gold-link bracelet bearing a miniature key to the city.

King Frederick, meanwhile, was the guest at a luncheon at the Waldorf Astoria attended by more than 700 invited guests. Mr. Wagner awarded the king the city's Gold Medal and a scroll citing him as "a friend of international peace and justice." The mayor offered a toast in honor of the king, who responded with a birthday toast for President Eisenhower's 70th birthday. The king mentioned how the Marshall Plan had done so much for the post-war reconstruction of Europe, adding that economies throughout Europe were improving thanks to the help and guidance of the United States. Denmark, he announced, was moving further away from its pre-war agrarian economy to a more industrialized one.

In the evening, the King and Queen presided over the official opening of the Arts of Denmark display and the King spoke of and described many items in the collection. The evening ended for the Royal Couple as dinner guests of the Danish-American Society back at the Waldorf Astoria. The next morning the Royal Couple visited the Hans Christian Andersen statue in Central Park, near Fifth Avenue and 74th Street. After the king placed a floral piece at the statue, the Danish pianist and humorist, Victor Borge, read one of Andersen's fairy tales. Queen Ingrid later received an award from the Save the Children Federation and King Frederick attended a reception sponsored by the American-Scandinavian Foundation.

After spending two more leisurely days sightseeing in the city, the King and Queen returned to Copenhagen. In 1953 the Act of Succession had been passed that would permit the throne to be occupied by a female should the king die without a male heir. Soon after delivering an address on New Year's Day in 1972, King Frederick became ill, and died two weeks later, his oldest daughter, Margarethe, became monarch on his death. Queen Ingrid survived him by 28 years, dying in November 2000; she is buried beside him at Roskilde Cathedral, Copenhagen.

Wednesday, October 19, 1960: Senator John F. Kennedy

Never before had New York City held a pre-election day parade honoring a candidate for any office, but the 1960 election paved new ground in a number of ways: televised Presidential debates, massive television advertising, and two young candidates: the incumbent Vice President Richard Nixon and the Senator from Massachusetts, John F. Kennedy.

Held just three weeks before Election Day, the parade for Senator Kennedy and his attractive and pregnant wife, Jacqueline, was far longer than the typical route up Broadway. It began at the Carlyle Hotel on East 76th Street, headed downtown to the Battery, followed the Canyon of Heroes to City Hall, traveled to Union Square, then on to Rockefeller Center, and then out of the New York City limits, ending in Yonkers.

At 11:30 in the morning, the candidate and his wife entered a Chevrolet convertible and were escorted downtown by a motorcycle police detail. The skies were overcast and somber, and rain was in the forecast. Less than 15 minutes later the car reached the Battery, where the Senator and Mrs. Kennedy were joined by Mayor Wagner. A 50-piece marching band led the way, followed by more than a dozen vehicles carrying politicians, dignitaries, and reporters. At 11:42, just as the parade began moving uptown, the sun broke through the clouds and began shining brightly. Mayor Wagner pointed to the sky and shouted above the noise of the band and the waiting crowds, "Democratic weather."

Senator Kennedy wore a gray suit and a blue tie. Sitting beside him, his wife wore an off-white three-quarter length coat with a matching cloche hat and kidskin gloves. As the parade began, a blizzard of ticker tape and confetti descended on the couple. The Sanitation Department reported later that they had removed 100 tons of refuse from the route. Senator Kennedy waved and smiled broadly, while Mrs. Kennedy matched his smile and pointed to banners and signs along the route. "We need you," read one sign, while another said, "New York Loves JFK."

Asked about the size of the crowd, Police Commissioner Stephen Kennedy (no relation to the Senator) said "The Police Department no longer makes crowd estimates." They were unscientific and not necessary, he continued, because "newspaper men are capable of estimating crowds." As a result, conflicting figures exist: it was as big as the parade for Lindbergh (4,000,000); or it was larger than the MacArthur parade (7,500,000); or it was just too large to count *(see: June 13, 1927 and April 20, 1951).*

The pavement on the east side of Broadway was undergoing extensive repairs from Wall Street to Maiden Lane, so the police permitted spectators in the area to stand behind wooden barricades in the middle of the street rather than on the broken sidewalk. As the Senator's car approached, the crowd suddenly broke through the barricade nearly trampling the line of police who were unable to contain them. Scores of people rushed the car, many pleading for an autograph. Others reached out to touch the candidate. The antenna of the convertible suddenly disappeared, snapped off by a souvenir hunter. People pressed against the car as police struggled to push them back. "It felt like the sides of the car were bending," Mrs. Kennedy said later. Mounted police advanced their horses through the crowd, clearing the mob away. Well-wishers, still trying to shake Senator Kennedy's hand, yielded to the police and were pushed back between the convertible and the next car in line. One of the candidate's staff members in the second car was heard to say, "Don't get between the cars, we need every vote." Patrolmen and ranking officers alike joined in the pushing and shoving, clearing a path.

Somehow order was restored, no one was injured, and the parade finally reached City Hall Plaza. Mayor Wagner's Executive Secretary, Frank Doyle, reported that a policeman told him unofficially that at least 50,000 people were crowded into the Plaza. The mayor introduced the senator and his wife to thunderous cheers from the crowd, then turned the podium over to Senator Kennedy. The candidate thanked the mayor and the people of New York for their generous welcome. He asked the crowd if he could count on their vote on Election Day and was answered with an affirmative roar. Senator Kennedy praised Mayor Wagner for the parade and said, "he has promised to do the same for Vice President Nixon." The Mayor responded that this was news to him, but he would if that was what Mr. Nixon wished *(see: November 2, 1960)*.

As the clouds began to cover the sun once more, the Senator and Mayor returned to the convertible. The caravan moved uptown, followed now by even more reporter-filled vehicles, and made an unscheduled stop because of crowds at Astor Place and a brief scheduled one at Union Square. "Mr. Nixon tells America we never had it so good," Kennedy said, "I don't think it's good enough." He promised to build a stronger country in a freer world.

Mrs. Kennedy remained behind and later lunched with Pierre Salinger, the senator's press secretary. Pregnant with the Kennedys' second child, she had been instructed by her doctor to curtail her activities and had announced that this was her final campaign appearance.

It began to drizzle as the motorcade resumed its trip to Rockefeller Center, where Kennedy made another brief speech as umbrellas began to pop open. "When it rains," the Senator said, "the Republicans go inside. We're here to stay. Rain or shine, good times or bad, this country is going to move into the Sixties." By that time the rain was falling heavily, and the drenched spectators roared their approval.

From Rockefeller Center, the motorcade moved north through the Bronx and into Westchester County. Thousands of people lined the route just to catch a glimpse of the candidate. The rain continued to fall but the motorcade finally reached its destination in Yonkers where, his gray suit and blue tie ruined by the elements, Senator Kennedy gave one more speech.

The election less than a month later was one of the closest to date. New York State's 45 electoral votes made it a top prize for the Democratic Party Candidate. Senator Kennedy carried New York and the nation but his margin of victory in the popular vote was only 112,000 votes out of a total of 68 million nationwide.

On November 22, 1963, President Kennedy's life was cut short by an assassin's bullet during a motorcade in Dallas, Texas. In October 1968, the president's widow, Jackie, married Greek shipping tycoon Aristotle Onassis. After his death in 1975, Jackie spent most of her time in New York City. A one-time three-packs-a-day cigarette smoker, she died in May 1994, of non-Hodgkin's lymphoma.

Wednesday, November 2, 1960: President Dwight Eisenhower and Vice President Richard Nixon

When Republican Party campaign headquarters saw the magnitude of the welcome given the Senator from Massachusetts *(see: October 19, 1960)*, plans were quickly made for Mr. Nixon to visit New York. Like his opponent he would visit more than just Manhattan with stops arranged in Brooklyn, Nassau and Westchester Counties. But unlike his opponent, the Republican candidate would not visit the area alone. Mr. Nixon would be joined by his running mate, Henry Cabot Lodge, as well as the current President himself, Dwight Eisenhower. It would be the first and only time during the entire fiercely fought 1960 campaign that President Eisenhower campaigned with Vice President Nixon.

The cost of the parade was underwritten by the GOP Campaign Fund and the expenses were high. Thousands of balloons and signs were printed for distribution to campaign workers and spectators, and tons of ticker tape were purchased and distributed to companies with windows that faced Lower Broadway and elsewhere in the city. Five hundred attractive young models and struggling actresses were hired to distribute handbills and Nixon-Lodge buttons. Refreshments would be served to countless volunteers. Not a penny was spared.

Mr. Nixon's day started early. At 8 o'clock he addressed a gathering of about 3,000 supporters at a breakfast rally at the St. George Hotel in downtown Brooklyn. A helicopter flew him from Brooklyn to Nassau County where he was joined by Mr. Lodge. Meanwhile the President's plane touched down at Idlewild Airport at 9:15, and minutes later he boarded a helicopter that flew him to Roosevelt Field Shopping Center in Nassau County. There Mr. Nixon met with President Eisenhower and Mr. Lodge; the three men spoke briefly to a crowd estimated at about 35,000. President Eisenhower emphasized that Mr. Nixon's experience better prepared him than Senator John F. Kennedy to work with other nations, believing that the team of Nixon and Lodge "can do better than any others I know in keeping the peace."

Shortly before 10:30, the three Republicans were airborne again. A helicopter transported them to the Westchester County airport near Purchase, New York. Mr. Nixon told a crowd of slightly more than 15,000 that the previous eight years under President Eisenhower had shown that the country's economy had grown greater than during any previous eight-year peacetime period.

One last helicopter trip followed the rally in Westchester when the three were carried to the 30th Street Heliport and entered an open limousine just after noon. Slightly behind schedule, the car raced down the West Side Highway to Battery Place, escorted by a squad of police motorcycles and secret service vehicles. More than 5,000 spectators had gathered at the Battery. They watched the President and Vice President enter the first car of a 20-vehicle motorcade. Mr. Lodge was joined in the second vehicle by New York's Governor, Nelson Rockefeller, while Mrs. Patricia Nixon and Mrs. Emily Lodge shared the third vehicle. The remaining vehicles contained aides, Republican Party officials, city and state politicians, and reporters. Noticeably absent was Mayor Wagner who had ridden with Senator Kennedy during his parade. He was reported to have spent the day working at City Hall and remained at his desk when the motorcade reached City Hall.

Sound trucks led the caravan up Broadway, playing the campaign theme song "We Want Nixon to Be Our President" which was sung to the tune of "Merrily We Roll Along." A huge sign was hung from Number 2 Broadway reading "Welcome to Our Country's First Team." The President sat, waving to the right and left. Mr. Nixon alternated between standing and sitting, often waving with both arms. The more reserved Mr. Lodge stood but rarely waved. Ticker tape cascaded down as the vehicles moved up Broadway. At Liberty Street strands of ticker tape were so tangled they clogged the wheels of a police motorcycle, forcing its rider to dismount and strip the tape away.

Later the Sanitation Department reported that they removed 60 tons of paper, about half as much as for the Kennedy parade.

A difference in crowd size and reaction was also noticed. Senator Kennedy's parade halted numerous times because of the crowd surging into the street. Either because of tighter security in the presence of the President and Vice President or for a lack of enthusiasm, there was no similar halting or even slowing. It took the Kennedy caravan 37 minutes to go from Bowling Green to City Hall; the Republican motorcade only nine. Vice-President Nixon thought 1 million people viewed the parade; Governor Rockefeller put the number at twice that; other "observers" estimated between 500,000 and 750,000, according to the *New York Times*.

The motorcade did not stop at City Hall, only pausing briefly before continuing up Broadway for a rally at Union Square, followed by another at Bryant Park. At each brief stop either Mr. Nixon or his running mate addressed the crowd. The theme of "more experience" predominated but the cost to taxpayers of proposed Democratic Party programs was also frequently mentioned. President Eisenhower and Mr. Lodge left the motorcade at the Waldorf Astoria and did not rejoin Mr. Nixon, who attended one more rally before about 25,000 people in Yonkers.

The parade and rallies failed to carry the city or state of New York for the Republicans, and Senator Kennedy was elected President in a close election. In 1962, Mr. Nixon lost a bid for Governor of California. After a brief hiatus, he returned to politics, winning the Presidency in 1968. Six years later, because of the Watergate Scandal, he became the only president to date to resign from office. He died in 1994 and is buried at the Richard Nixon Presidential Library and Museum in Yorba Linda, California.

Monday, April 10, 1961:
New York Yankees, American League Champions

The list of ticker tape parades published in *The Encyclopedia of New York* includes "April 10, 1961 -- **New York Yankees,** winners of American League pennant" but a better description would be "Parade Called on Account of Rain."

The 1950s were a great time to be a baseball fan in New York City, with all three of the city's major league teams at the top of their game. In 1951, fans of the New York Giants, already thrilled by rookie of the year Willie Mays, were ecstatic when Bobby Thomson hit a three-run homer in the final inning of the final game of the National League Championship, to win the pennant against their rivals, the Brooklyn Dodgers. Despite this "shot heard round the world," the Brooklyn Dodgers went on to dominate the National League during the decade. With the strength of players like Jackie Robinson, Gil Hodges and Pee Wee Reese, the "Boys of Summer" made it to the National League Championships eight years in a row from 1949 to 1956, winning in five of those years to advance to the World Series.

But the decade really belonged to the pin-striped New York Yankees, managed since 1949 by Casey Stengel. With the strength of players Mickey Mantle, Yogi Berra and Whitey Ford, the "Bronx Bombers" won the American League Championships nine times from 1949-1958, going on to victory in the World Series in seven of those years. Five of those wins were against the Dodgers, whose fans consoled themselves by saying "wait 'til next year" so often it became an unofficial slogan for their team.

The decade ended though in ways that fans did not anticipate. Both Ebbets Field and the Polo Grounds were aging and badly in need of repair or replacement, and with the rise of non-stop transcontinental air travel, west coast cities could host teams without disrupting game schedules. In 1957, both the Dodgers and the Giants announced they were leaving the city for California, lured by offers to build new stadiums in Los Angeles and San Francisco. The only ball left to be thrown in the now-empty former stadiums of both teams was a wrecking ball, which demolished Ebbets Field in 1960 and the Polo Grounds four years later.

As New York's only baseball team now, the Yankees started 1960 with yet another victorious year in the American League and were favored to win the World Series against the Philadelphia Pirates. But their hopes for bringing home the crown were dashed by Bill Mazerowski, whose ninth-inning home run in the seventh game provided the Pirates with the Series victory. Mickey Mantle later described it as the most disappointing moment he ever experienced playing baseball.

Despite the heart-breaking defeat, the city decided to start the 1961 season with a celebration for the team's record: a total of 25 League championships and 18 World Series victories since the team was founded, better than any other franchise in the country. On April 7, 1961, the *New York Times* reported the team would "receive a gaudy welcome" with a 12-car motorcade, accompanied by the Sanitation Department Band leading them from Battery Park to City Hall, where they "will receive an official greeting from Acting Mayor Abe Stark."

The sports section of the morning edition on Monday, April 10 led with the headline "Parade to Welcome Yankees Here" and noted that the team will "warm up today by batting out speeches and fielding confetti" in the city's "show of affection for the team that won just about every important game of 1960 except the last one." At the bottom of the story is a short notice that "if the parade is rained out, the welcoming ceremonies will be held in the Board of Estimates Chambers of City Hall."

The next day, it rained. The *New York Times* story on April 11 read:

Motorcade Washed Out

Rain washed out the motorcade up lower Broadway yesterday in honor of the Yankees. Last night a crowd of 1,200 honored the club at a homecoming dinner in the Grand Ballroom of the Astor. There, Acting Mayor Abe Stark presented Mayor Wagner's Proclamation setting aside the day as New York Yankees Day.

The New York Yankees would go on to win the World Series again in 1961 and 1962, then lost in both of the next two years. Starting in 1965, the team and its fans endured a decade-long dry season. When they did win the World Series again in 1977, the city would finally hold its first parade in their honor *(see: October 19, 1977)*. Casey Stengel, the manager who led them during the successful seasons from 1949 to 1960, would get his chance before that *(see: April 12, 1962)*. The 1960 season was his last with the Yankees, and the 70-year-old would soon be wearing the uniform of New York's newest baseball team.

Monday, May 8, 1961: Alan Shepard, First American in Space

In the mid 1950s, leadership changes in both Moscow and Washington ushered in a new phase of the Cold War that had developed between the United States and the Soviet Union. The Eisenhower Administration's "New Look" policy focused on covert operations, increased reliance on tactical nuclear capabilities, and the doctrine of massive retaliation. Nikita Khrushchev, who became the Soviet leader soon after Stalin's death in 1953, promised that the Soviet Union would not only catch up to but surpass the United States technologically. Fears that he might be correct grew in 1957 with the successful launch of an intercontinental ballistic missile followed in October of that year by Sputnik, the first artificial satellite to orbit planet Earth. Within a year, Eisenhower pushed Congress to form the National Aeronautics and Space Administration (NASA). A new competition between the super-powers had begun, known as the Space Race.

The first milestones of that race were won by the Soviets, and in April 1961, Yuri Gagarin became the first human to journey into outer space, completing one full orbit of Earth before re-entry. NASA's Mercury project had hoped to achieve a manned mission in late 1960, but was delayed with modifications of the capsule, named Freedom 7. Finally, everything was ready on May 5, 1961, to launch 37-year-old naval Commander Alan Shepard into space, 3 weeks after Gagarin's historic flight.

Lifting off from Cape Canaveral at 9:34 in the morning, Shepard's flight lasted 15 minutes and did not have enough energy to achieve orbit, but Shepard successfully tested the new retrorockets, which future flights would need to decelerate out of orbital speed. Traveling at a speed of almost 5,200 miles per hour, the spacecraft ascended 116 miles above the planet before beginning descent and landing safely in the Atlantic Ocean near the Bahamas. Shepard was picked up by a naval helicopter, and his first words after exiting the capsule were "Man, what a ride!"

The United States had its first of a new kind of hero: an astronaut.

Reaction to the successful flight "roused the country to one of its highest peaks of exultation since the end of World War II" the New York Times declared. A parade was held that afternoon in East Derby, New Hampshire, where Shepard had grown up and his parents still lived. A dozen air force planes flew overhead, dropping confetti over the town's main square. The mayor of Virginia Beach, where Shepard lived with his wife Louise and their two daughters, announced that Shepard would be grand marshal of the upcoming Armed Forces Day parade. In Washington, senators and congressmen called for the astronaut to be awarded the Medal of Honor, and the White House announced that Shepard's meeting with President John Kennedy on May 8 would be followed by a parade. In New York City, Mayor Wagner sent a telegram offering Commander Shepard a ticker tape parade, which one city official said would be "the most fabulous ever" and "bigger than the one for Charles Lindbergh."

Washington, DC would be the only city to honor Shepard with a parade, however. NASA Administrator James Webb "was careful in using Shepard for propaganda purposes" and had decided to limit the number of public appearances by the astronauts in the Mercury program. Shepard's flight was "a modest first step into space that calls for more work, not more celebrations," he said, ruling out a ticker tape parade in New York and "other extravaganzas" including the Virginia Beach parade. The astronaut was flown to Washington on May 8, was presented with the Distinguished Service Medal by President Kennedy in the Rose Garden, and then was driven in a caravan to Congress with other NASA officials. "No bands, floats or military units" accompanied them, though thousands of spectators lined the streets.

Shepard would receive a ticker tape parade, but not until 1971 as part of the Apollo 14 mission (see: March 8, 1971), by which time public enthusiasm for NASA's heroes was waning. He was also present at the parade in 1962 for John Glenn's successful flight orbiting Earth (see: March 1, 1962) which had crowds rivalling the parade for Charles Lindbergh. Whether a parade for Shepard in 1961 would have been "the most fabulous ever" is a something we will never know.

Thursday, May 11, 1961: Habib Bourguiba, President of Tunisia

A noon time crowd of more than 200,000 welcomed the first president of Tunisia, Habib Bourguiba, to New York City. It was the culmination of his 12-day goodwill visit to the United States and the city provided him with its usual cordial greeting.

Escorted by two military marching bands and small detachments of the Army, Navy, and Marine Corps, the 12-car caravan moved from Bowling Green to City Hall. The Tunisian chief of state appeared to be thoroughly enjoying his welcome, standing in an open limousine, waving and smiling at his well-wishers. He pointed to a group of young women standing at open windows north of Wall Street. Bowing politely in their direction, he blew them kisses, much to the delight of spectators.

At City Hall Mr. Bourguiba was welcomed by Mayor Wagner, who invited the president to sign the city's Guest Book. No other formalities took place downtown but shortly thereafter, the Tunisian President was given the city's Gold Medal at a luncheon reception at the Waldorf. The award was presented by Dr. Grayson Kirk, President of Columbia University, substituting for the mayor who was unable to attend. Dr. Kirk told the 500 guests at the luncheon that "it was indeed a miracle for Mr. Bourguiba to be alive and free today after years in prison and peril," in reference to the president's years of banishment and imprisonment by France while Tunisia was a French Protectorate.

Thanking New York for his "magnificent" parade, Mr. Bourguiba said that "what astonishes visitors from afar is the order and discipline maintained in the greatest metropolis of the world." He concluded by commenting on the sight of numerous people waving miniature American and Tunisian flags along the parade's route and how the sight had given him hope for understanding between different peoples of the world.

Following the luncheon, the president met with Pierre Mendes-France, who was the French premier when Tunisia made its first positive steps to independence in 1955. Later, the Tunisian President spoke before the Council on Foreign Relations on 68th Street. He returned to Tunisia two days later.

As a leader in the struggle for Tunisian independence, Mr. Bourguiba had been arrested by France as early as 1936 and was imprisoned twice before the Second World War. In 1943 the Vichy French government released him to Italian authorities who wished to gain his support for Axis troops in North Africa. Refusing to cooperate with the Fascists he was again imprisoned. Released after the war, he returned to his native land and began campaigning against French colonial occupation. The country gained independence in 1957 without bloodshed thanks to Mr. Bourguiba's diplomatic skills. He became the new nation's first President, a post he would hold for 30 years. Originally a strong ally of the west, he gradually shifted allegiance over the years. Mr. Bourguiba was overthrown by a coup in 1987 when he was 84 years old. He lived under virtual house arrest in the Governor's Mansion in Monastir for the next 13 years. He died of pneumonia in 2000 and is buried in his personal mausoleum in the Hanafi Mosque in Monastir.

Friday, July 14, 1961:
Mohammad Ayub Khan, President of Pakistan

The President of Pakistan, Mohammad Ayub Khan, arrived at LaGuardia Airport at 11:15 in the morning. Accompanied by his 22-year-old daughter, Begum Nasir Akhtar Aurangzeb, he had flown to New York from Washington, DC, where he had spent two days meeting with President John Kennedy and Congressional leaders. Escorted by a squad of motorcycle police, the Pakistani President and his daughter were rushed to Bowling Green, arriving there minutes before the scheduled start time of the parade in his honor.

Police reports provided two different figures for the numbers who watched the parade. One report placed the number at 10,000; a second, at 50,000. Regardless of the actual figure, there was plenty of ticker tape as the procession moved north. An army band provided the marching music and the motorcade of six cars was escorted by small Army, Navy, and Air Force detachments along with groups from the Police and Fire Departments. Mr. Richard Patterson, Commissioner of Commerce and Public Events, shared the limousine with the president, whose daughter followed in the second vehicle along with her husband.

The procession was met by Mayor Wagner at City Hall. He welcomed President Ayub Khan and his family and presented the Pakistani President with the city's Medal of Honor. Following the brief welcoming ceremony, the presidential family proceeded to the Waldorf Astoria for a luncheon co-hosted by the Far East-America Council and Industry, the Asia Society, and the Pakistani-American Chamber of Commerce. A budget meeting at City Hall prevented the mayor from attending the luncheon, so Mr. Patterson took his place.

President Ayub Khan's remarks after the luncheon focused on the Kashmir Dispute with India, and American investments in Pakistan. Unaware that the dispute had been resolved earlier in the day, Ayub Khan reiterated the request he had made of President Kennedy the previous day, that the United States take a more active and pro-Pakistani role in the border dispute. On the second matter, Ayub Khan encouraged investments in his country. "It's a good thing for the free world," he said, "that a country like Pakistan becomes economically sound and is able to stand on its own feet." He assured the more than 500 people attending the luncheon that investments in his country were safe and profits were to be made.

The following morning President Ayub Khan was flown to Gettysburg, Pennsylvania, where he met with former President Eisenhower. The two statesmen made a helicopter tour of the Gettysburg battleground. One day later, President Ayub Khan flew to Texas where he was the guest of Vice President Lyndon Johnson. On July 18 the Pakistani leader flew home.

Tensions continued to escalate in Kashmir and open warfare broke out in the spring of 1965. The United Nations brokered a cease fire in September 1965. President Ayub Khan's attempts to modify the nation's constitution and bring about changes in the areas of voting, women's rights, and foreign policy control were opposed by the military. In order to avoid a military takeover, he announced early in 1969 that he would not seek re-election. He retired to private life at the end of his term of office in September 1969 and died in April 1974.

Friday, September 22, 1961:
Manuel Prado y Ugarteche, President of Peru

New York City was the second stop of President Prado's visit to the United States, after meeting with President Kennedy in Washington. The Peruvian President arrived on September 21, and the next day was welcomed with a parade up the Canyon of Heroes.

It was an unusually warm late summer day when the parade stepped off from the Battery. Escorted by both the Police and Fire Department Bands and a First Army Honor Guard, the caravan of vehicles carrying the Peruvian President, his wife Clorinda, and government officials, moved uptown to the accompaniment of cheers and waving. He had previously visited the city in 1942 during his first term as president, but at that time no official outdoor welcomes were given to visiting dignitaries because of the Second World War.

Upon arriving at City Hall, a smiling Mayor Wagner welcomed the President and his wife. The chief of state signed the City's official guest book. No downtown reception had been planned, and after being introduced to those gathered outside City Hall and posing for photographs, the mayor and his wife accompanied the Peruvian couple to Gracie Mansion.

A small reception was held at the mansion, where the President was given the city's Gold Medal and a scroll that praised his courage, character, ability, and leadership. He responded by thanking the mayor for the award as well as for the city's warm welcome. That evening he was the guest at a dinner at the Waldorf sponsored by the Pan American Society. The following morning, he and his wife attended Mass at St. Patrick's Cathedral and were the guests of Cardinal Francis Spellman. The cardinal praised him for his dedication and service to Peru and "to the preservation and propagation of Christianity and democracy." Later that afternoon, President Prado addressed the General Assembly of the United Nations.

The visiting presidential couple returned to Lima three days later. His second six-year term of President ended the following year. Like his father, who had also been president of the South American nation, he was a wealthy banker before being elected to the presidency, and he returned to that profession thereafter. In early 1966 he retired and moved to Paris, where he died on August 15, 1967, at the age of 78.

Friday, October 13, 1961: Ibrahim Abboud, President of Sudan

Ibrahim Abboud, former head of the military junta that seized power in the eastern African Republic of Sudan in 1956 and the nation's president since 1958, arrived in the United States on October 4. He arrived in New York on October 12, after spending more than a week in Washington meeting with President Kennedy, congressional leaders and diplomatic officials.

President Abboud attended the opening of the New York Stock Exchange the next morning and, after a breakfast with bankers and financiers, received New York's traditional welcome. Since he was almost unknown to most New Yorkers, his parade was watched by only a small number of spectators and drew little enthusiasm. Dressed in a black suit, white shirt, and striped tie, the 61-year-old Sudanese head of state stood in an open limo and waved to the sparse crowd in the buildings and along the route.

Mayor and Mrs. Wagner welcomed President Abboud at the steps of City Hall, where the president signed the city's official guest book. Due to deliver a speech at the United Nations, his stay at City Hall was brief with few formalities before he was escorted to the United Nations headquarters uptown.

Addressing the General Assembly in Arabic, he called for an end to colonialism around the world, mentioning in particular French rule in Algeria and Portuguese in Angola. He stressed the fact that the UN "could not continue to exclude from membership one-quarter of the globe's population" by denying China a seat in the world organization. Most, but not all, UN delegates in attendance applauded his speech warmly.

That evening President Abboud was the guest of honor at a reception at Gracie Mansion. He dined later at the Links Club on East 62nd Street as the guest of bankers and investors interested in possible financial opportunities in his Saharan nation.

Two days later he returned to his capital city, Khartoum. His leadership in Sudan was besieged with difficulties, as numerous political, military, and religious factions struggled for power. Seeking independence, the southern provinces of his nation erupted into civil war. To assist in suppressing armed opposition, he created a 25-man commission to study all of Sudan's domestic problems. Among the commission's recommendations was a call for his resignation. Facing increasing pressure from all quarters, he resigned in November 1964, and left his native country. Relocating in Great Britain in 1966, Ibrahim Abboud did not return to Sudan for more than 15 years. He died in Khartoum in 1983.

Civil war spread from the south of the nation and soon engulfed much of Sudan. In 2011 the southern provinces gained independence as the Republic of South Sudan but fighting continued until 2017. Estimates of the number of fatalities range from 200,000 to 400,000. Previously placed sanctions against Sudan were lifted by the UN and the United States in 2017.

Friday, October 27, 1961:
Builders and Crew of USS *Constellation*

December 19, 1960 was a cold day. Construction was nearing completion on the aircraft carrier *Constellation* at the Brooklyn Navy Yard. It was the largest ship ever built there and would be the largest ship in the United States Navy. Late that morning a forklift operator on the hanger deck accidentally pushed a trash bin against a steel plate with such force that the plate shifted and tore off the main plug of a tank holding 500 gallons of diesel fuel. The fuel poured through openings on the steel deck and leaked down to the next level where it was ignited by a welder's torch. Within seconds flames shot up and engulfed wooden scaffolding and raced through the passageways, decks, and corridors of the ship. In the ensuing blaze, 50 workmen died of burns or smoke inhalation. New York City and Navy fire fighters fought the blaze for 17 hours before it was finally brought under control. Besides the loss of life, millions of dollars in damage had been done, and the plans to launch the mighty carrier were postponed while the stricken ship was repaired and completed.

Almost a year later, the *Constellation* was finally completed, and New York celebrated with a ticker tape parade honoring the ship's officers and crew as well as the thousands of laborers who had completed the ship. The US Navy Band set the tempo as 1,500 of the ship's 4,100 crewmen marched up Broadway in orderly, military ranks. Enlisted men wearing dress blue uniforms and officers in their jackets and ties were showered with ticker tape and confetti raining down from the skyscrapers along the way. Behind them marched rows of construction workers, most wearing hard hats and work clothes.

Budget Director Abraham Beame, substituting for Mayor Robert Wagner who was in Washington, reviewed the marching sailors and workers. He welcomed the ship's commanding officer, Captain Thomas Walker. Mr. Beame spoke of the *Constellation* as "the finest fighting ship afloat" and "the world's most powerful vessel." Since the fatal fire of the previous year, the carrier had become a focus of attention for New Yorkers who followed the ship's construction, many able to view its progress as they rode across the Manhattan or Williamsburg Bridges spanning the East River. The Mayor presented Captain Walker with a New York City flag to be flown whenever the carrier was in port. The 45-year-old skipper accepted the flag and said, "Wherever we go, every man of this ship will feel he is an emissary of the great city of New York."

That afternoon, the *Constellation* was officially commissioned. She was the third Navy vessel to bear this name. The first was a frigate built in 1797 and still on display in Baltimore, Maryland. The second, a sloop of war, was built in 1854. The third continued in active service until June 2003, having seen combat service in Vietnam and the Persian Gulf. The *Constellation* was towed to Brownsville, Texas in 2014, and scrapped there between 2015 and 2017.

Brooklyn Navy Yard

During the War of 1812, the US Navy began using a vacant plot of land in Brooklyn on the bank of the East River to repair damaged ships. After that war, the Navy decided the location would be ideal for ship building as well as repair, and in 1820 the first ship built at the Brooklyn Navy Yard was launched, three years after its keel had been laid. During the next 40 years, the property was expanded and developed, a hospital was added, and civilian mechanics and laborers were hired to build wooden frigates, sloops and cutters. During the American Civil War and the development of "ironclad" ships, the Navy Yard was retrofitted to accommodate metalworking.

By 1865, over 4,000 civilians worked at the Navy Yard, many of them immigrants from Europe. Over the next decade, the workforce decreased but became Federal employees, subject to an 1872 law restricting them from working more than 8 hours a day, a novel employment benefit not common to most laborers at the time. The Navy Yards also began hiring women to produce the large number of flags, pennants and canvas gunpowder bags used by naval vessels, but would not hire African Americans until 1941.

The Yard's output of ships and the size of its workforce ebbed and flowed with the tide of American imperialism in the late 1800s and the naval escalation leading up to World War I. Many of the ships used in the Spanish-American War and US interventions in Latin America and the Hawaiian Islands were laid there, and dozens of battleships, cruisers and destroyers were built and launched there during World War I. The Washington Navy Treaty of 1921 reduced output during the 1920s, but by the 1930s activity increased again and reached its peak soon after the US entered World War II.

At its height during World War II, over 75,000 workers operated in round-the-clock shifts, building or repairing hundreds of ships of all sizes on the Brooklyn side of a wide bend in the East River. Most impressive were the battleships, like the USS Missouri, but ships of all kinds could be seen sailing in and out of the Brooklyn Navy Yard.

Except for a brief period during the Korean War, activity at the Yards declined rapidly during the 1950s. The new Brooklyn-Queen Expressway limited further expansion, and newer ship designs were too tall to pass under the Manhattan and Brooklyn Bridges. After the Navy closed the Yard in 1966, the Federal and City governments argued about the price to sell the property back to the City. Various proposals came and went to use the property for private shipbuilding, automobile manufacturing, filmmaking or as a prison, until the Bloomberg Administration launched an initiative to attract digital companies. Today the Yard is a massive urban industrial development, home to over 450 small businesses.

CHAPTER 8
Flying High (1962-1969)

On October 26, 1958, Pan-Am flight 174 took off from Idlewild Airport. The ripple effect of that flight would be felt around the world, and most significantly in the city where that flight began.

On its own, the flight would not be noteworthy, but the plane was a Boeing 707 and was the first scheduled passenger flight on a jet airplane. Eight hours and 41 minutes after taking off, the plane landed in Paris, France. That was much faster than the 33 hours it took Lindbergh in 1927, but more importantly, it was 3 days and 11 hours faster than the maiden transatlantic voyage of the SS *United States* in 1952. The vision of commercial passenger flight predicted by Admiral Byrd *(see: July 18, 1927)* had become reality, and travelers quickly shifted from ocean liners to jet planes.

New York's harbor had always been a major factor in the city's growth and economy. It is one of the world's largest natural harbors, separated into an Upper and Lower Bay by Staten Island and connected by the Verrazano Narrows, which is deep and wide enough for ocean-going vessels to navigate. Two sandbars extend into the Lower Bay, sheltering it from the turbulence of the Atlantic Ocean, Sandy Hook on the New Jersey side and Coney Island on the eastern side, while the Upper Bay is connected to both the Hudson River and Long Island Sound via the East River, as well as to the Newark and Raritan Bays via smaller waterways around Staten Island. The harbor's importance grew with the opening of the Erie Canal in 1821, connecting the city to the Great Lakes via the Hudson River. Over the next century, the harbor fueled the city's population growth via immigration, and its economic growth via commerce. The harbor reached its peak activity in 1943, with over a thousand warehouses lining 39 active shipyards, and 750 piers or docks lined around the coast of Brooklyn, Manhattan, Staten Island and the New Jersey towns of Bayonne and Newark.

Change was already starting before Flight 174. During the late 1940s and early 1950s, the Port Authority of New York and New Jersey began modernizing the facilities at Port Newark. The railyards were improved to accommodate a new system of "container carriers" that could be moved from ship to train without unloading and reloading their contents, and the channel between Newark and Elizabeth, NJ was deepened, allowing access to Port Newark by larger ships. In 1956, the first commercially successful container ship left Port Newark on its maiden voyage, sailing to Houston with 56 containers of cargo.

Almost overnight, the waterfront facilities in Brooklyn and Manhattan were antiquated and began closing, and because the new automation features at Port Newark required fewer workers to load and unload cargo, longshoremen and dockhands found themselves with a decreasing number of opportunities in the city. The textile industry had already begun leaving the city, in search of cheaper labor markets, and the printing industry, which relied on the city's many newspaper and magazine companies, moved as larger presses required more space and product could be flown overnight to its destination. Blue-collar neighborhoods were deteriorating as residents moved out of the city for the suburbs. After the 1965 black-out, which kept much of the city dark for almost 13 hours and stranded 800,000 commuters in the subways, many New Yorkers felt the city was on the decline, and that feeling increased when the city was paralyzed for almost a week after a blizzard in 1969.

The city's tax revenues were affected by all this change, and the city's entire budget was soon affected in other ways. As soon as Mayor Lindsay entered City Hall in January 1966, the Transit Workers Union went out on strike. The subway system had increased fares twice since 1948, going to 15 cents in 1953 and then 20 cents in 1966, and the union wanted wages to increase as well. It was the first strike to shut the city's entire mass transit system, and for 12 days, commuters were left with no subway or bus service. The mayor finally backed down, agreeing to a $60 million package of increases, and setting the stage for future disputes between the city and its unionized workers.

Two years later, the city was hit by a 7-week strike of the teachers' union, a strike by theater unions that shut down Broadway for 3 days, and a 9-day strike by the city's sanitation workers. Residents, already tired of the teachers' strike, grew increasingly frustrated at the sight and smell of piles of uncollected trash, especially when the city's police force showed support by engaging in a slowdown, and when the fire department threatened to join the strike.

The 1960s was a period of social unrest across the country, with the Civil Rights movement growing and protests against the Vietnam War gaining momentum, and racial tensions in the city were worsening. The politics of the teachers' strike, for example, included outbursts of anti-Semitism against Jewish teachers by community leaders in black and Hispanic neighborhoods. While other cities experienced riots after the assassination of Martin Luther King in 1968, Mayor Lindsay was able to avoid them in New York by going to Harlem to make a direct appeal for residents to remain calm, though protests by students at Columbia University ended with the violent removal of demonstrators by police. The NYPD also sparked violence in 1969 during a raid on a gay bar in Greenwich Village, and the Stonewall Riots are seen as the birth of the modern LGBTQ rights movement. Students would be victims of violence two years later in the Hard Hat Riot, when construction workers crashed into an anti-war protest in front of the Stock Exchange, igniting a riot that spread up Broadway to City Hall.

There were many construction workers in downtown that day because of one of the city's most ambitious projects. In 1966, demolition began on 13 square blocks along the Hudson River of lower Manhattan in preparation for two new skyscrapers. Over 1.2 million cubic yards of material were excavated and used as landfill, shifting the island's shoreline into the river. By 1968, the construction of the World Trade Center began, and over the next several years, the two steel towers rose steadily over downtown Manhattan. The first of the buildings, measuring 1,368 feet high, opened in 1970, while its 1362-foot-high twin opened in 1972. Together with five smaller buildings, the office complex provided 13 million square feet of office space, and the twin towers were the largest buildings in the world, exceeding the Empire State Building by 100 feet.

The twin towers were not the only things reaching into the heavens. America's Cold War against the Soviet Union had expanded into outer space when the Soviet Union launched Sputnik in 1957. Three years later, Yuri Gagarin became the first human in space, and less than a year later, John Glenn became the American to orbit

Planet Earth *(see: March 1, 1962)*. President Kennedy had announced that Americans would land on the moon "in this decade." The newly created National Aeronautics and Space Administration rose to the challenge, providing spectacular and televised triumphs that Americans could cheer, and the Astronaut became America's newest hero *(see: August 13, 1969)*. After flying high over the globe, these heroes were welcomed back to Earth in the biggest way New York could. The ticker tape parades honoring foreign dignitaries *(see: September 10, 1963)*, so common in the 1950s, began to wane as the ones for the men reaching for the moon waxed and reached new heights.

Thursday, March 1, 1962: Lieutenant Colonel John Glenn

The weather forecast predicted snow and the Sanitation Department was ready with plows and salt spreaders. The day dawned cold and windy, with the temperature never rising above freezing and winds gusting to 25 miles per hour, but the sun soon emerged from clouds and not a flurry of snow fell all day. Today's blizzard was not snow, but ticker tape, torn paper, confetti, and computer punch cards, rivaling in quantity the parades of Lindbergh *(see: June 13, 1927)* and MacArthur *(see: April 20,1951)*. John Glenn, America's first astronaut to orbit the earth, was in New York.

Concerns that NASA Administrator James Webb might prevent Glenn from receiving New York's celebratory parade, as he had after Alan Shepard's flight in 1961 *(see: May 8, 1961)* may have prompted Republican senator Kenneth Keating to send Webb a telegram on February 21. "To give recognition to this historic achievement," his message read, according to the *New York Times*, "I urge, if at all possible, that New York City be given the opportunity to hold its traditional ticker tape parade for Colonel Glenn and his fellow astronauts." The next day, the newspaper reported that plans for the parade had been announced by City Hall, and that "included in the welcome will be James Webb" and Mercury Project Director, Dr. Robert Gilruth.

Lieutenant Colonel John Glenn, Jr., was one of the original "Mercury Seven," the men chosen by NASA to be the first American astronauts as part of the Project Mercury missions. He and his wife Anna landed at LaGuardia Airport shortly after 11 o'clock on a flight with Vice President Lyndon Johnson. Seven minutes earlier a twin-engine Convair carrying the other six Mercury astronauts and their wives and families had touched down.

A thousand spectators had gathered at LaGuardia Airport and cheers broke out when Colonel Glenn and his wife descended the stairs from their flight. The first of six marching bands that would take part in the day's activities was there, playing "The John Glenn March," written especially for the occasion by Paul Taubman. A short ceremony was held at the airport, introducing the Colonel and Mrs. Glenn to the crowd. At the conclusion, the astronaut, his wife and the Vice President stepped into the beige open convertible built to the city's specifications and reserved for parades. James Webb and Dr. Gilruth joined the remaining Mercury astronauts and various NASA officials in the other cars waiting on the tarmac.

Led by 40 police motorcycles, the 22-vehicle caravan carried the members of the party into Manhattan. As they drove from the airport to Ditmars Boulevard in Astoria, Queens, the streets were lined with people waving miniature American flags at the speeding motorcade. As the vehicles drove across the Triborough Bridge to Manhattan, fireboats in the East River shot huge sprays into the air. The watery salute continued when the motorcade turned onto the FDR Drive. Police estimated 60,000 people, many of them school children with teachers and parents, viewed that portion of the motorcade.

Shortly before noon the vehicles arrived at Bowling Green. Detachments from the armed services and uniformed city departments filled Battery Place opposite Number One Broadway. Bands from the Army, Navy, Marine Corps and the Police Department were massed there as well. Less than five minutes later, bands, marchers, and vehicles in place, the parade began the journey to City Hall up the Canyon of Heroes. Including those who witnessed the motorcade from the airport, it was estimated that 4 million people were in attendance. As the parade headed up Broadway the paper blizzard was so thick that it almost hid the participants and the spectators from each other. The wind spiraled strands of tape upwards, caught in the drafts of the skyscraper canyon, higher than some buildings along the route. "I don't know who's going to clean up the city," Colonel Glenn commented, and one NASA official called the falling paper "snow in Technicolor." Cheers echoed through the streets and were never louder than when Colonel Glenn raised his right arm and gave the "thumbs up" sign.

Guarding the route were 3,000 police, but despite the number of men in blue the crowds pushed passed the barricades at a few points. At the corner of Broadway and Maiden Lane the most serious breach occurred, and mounted police and the Secret Service detail guarding the Vice President helped push the surge of people back behind the barriers.

Waiting in City Hall Park, a marching band began playing "God Bless America" as the vehicles arrived. At the temporary reviewing stand in front of the steps of City Hall, Mayor Wagner placed the city's Gold Medal around the necks of the seven astronauts. Handwritten scrolls were presented to Colonel Glenn and Robert Gilruth for "distinguished and exceptional service." The mayor then introduced each astronaut to the crowd: Alan Shepard, Gus Grissom, Scott Carpenter, Wally Schirra, Gordon Cooper, Deke Slaton, and John Glenn. Each astronaut waved as his name was mentioned and the roar from the crowd was deafening.

The motorcade then continued uptown to the Waldorf Astoria for a luncheon. Mayor Wagner commented that Colonel Glenn had seen three sunrises and three sunsets in the slightly less than five hours during his orbit around the Earth. The mayor asked him how the events of the day compared to that. The colonel responded, "This New York tribute this morning is certainly overwhelming. I've just never seen anything like this, needless to say."

At the conclusion of the luncheon, Catholic Cardinal Francis Spellman spoke of the heroism of Colonel Glenn and the patriotism inspired by the Mercury Space Program. He concluded his comments with a prayer "for the victims of the tragedy of the skies this morning," referring to an unrelated airplane crash at Idlewild Airport earlier in the day, in which all aboard had been killed. The astronauts remained in the city for three days, sightseeing, shopping, and being hailed and feted wherever they went, separately or together. All seven of the original Mercury astronauts flew in space, and Shepard would later walk on the moon *(see: March 8, 1971)*.

Carpenter, Cooper and Grissom would be part of future parades for other Mercury space achievements over the next few years *(see: June 5, 1962. May 22, 1963, and March 29, 1965, respectively)*, while Colonel Glenn would be honored in a second parade almost 40 years later when he was a member of the Shuttle Discovery flight *(see: November 16, 1998)*.

Astronaut Wally Shirra went on in 1965 to command Gemini 6, the first mission to conduct an orbital docking, and Apollo 7 in 1968, becoming the first person to travel in space a third time. After retiring from NASA, he was a consultant for CBS News and on the advisory board for the Interior Department. He died in 2007. Astronaut Deke Slaton was the last of the Mercury 7 team to make it into space. Originally scheduled on one of the earlier Mercury missions, he was deemed medically ineligible because of a heart condition. He worked for NASA management, and was responsible for crew assignments during the early Apollo missions. In 1972, after years of work improving his health, his was cleared for flight and, at age 51, was part of the Apollo-Soyuz mission in 1975. He retired soon after that and died of a brain tumor in 1993.

Number One Broadway

During the War of 1812, the US Navy began using a vacant plot of land in One of the first buildings seen by VIPs arriving at the Battery is Number One Broadway. This ornate neoclassical building standing at the start of Broadway opposite Battery Park was erected in 1882 on a site used by General Washington during the Battle of New York, and a hotel was built there in 1854. By 1880, the demand for office space for shipping companies near the wharves was growing, and the 4-story hotel was torn down and replaced with a 12-story structure called the Washington Building.

The International Mercantile Marine Company purchased the building in 1919, and gave it an extensive renovation, adding nautical themes and coats of arms to its façade, and side entrances facing Battery Park labelled "First Class" and "Cabin Class." With its two neighbors, the White Star Lines headquartered in the Bowling Green Office Building (erected in 1896) and the Cunard Building (opened in 1921), this section of Broadway was referred to as "steamship row" during the 1920s.

In the 1930s, the International Mercantile Marine Company merged with other shipping companies and was renamed the United States Lines. Though it was one of the largest shipping companies in the world, it struggled financially when jet planes changed the dynamics of freight shipping. The company moved to New Jersey in the 1970s. The building was given landmark status in 1995 and is still in use today by various tenants.

Friday, March 16, 1962:
Ahmadou Ahidjo, First President of Cameroon

Wearing a flowing white and yellow tribal robe called a grand boubou and a red hat similar to a fez called a chechia, the first President of the East African nation of Cameroon rode up Broadway, accepting the cheers of a sparse noontime crowd. The procession of seven limousines carrying Ahmadou Ahidjo and 14 Cameroonian dignitaries followed three bands and small marching units from the Army, Navy, and Marine Corps. Newspaper reports indicated that President Ahidjo seemed almost embarrassed by the welcome as he waved shyly.

Mayor and Mrs. Wagner waited for the visiting president on a small red carpet at City Hall and greeted him when he arrived there shortly before 12:30. Presented with a scroll citing his role in bringing stability to his country, the President thanked the mayor, his words translated by the Cameroonian delegate to the United Nations.

Earlier that morning, President Ahidjo had received an Honorary Doctor of Law Degree at the Brooklyn campus of Long Island University, where he had spoken of his dream of a common destiny for all races.

Later that afternoon, the President met with United Nations Acting Secretary U Thant. The meeting appeared to be cordial despite that fact that President Ahidjo had opposed a UN proposal for a plebiscite to decide whether the northern half of the former colonies would integrate with Cameroon, or merge with the nation of Nigeria.

After remaining in the city two days, the President flew to Washington where he met with President Kennedy.

Ahidjo served as President of his country for 22 years before retiring for health reasons on August 27, 1982. It was later revealed that his doctor was collaborating with Ahidjo's main political rival, Paul Biya, who seized office two days after his resignation. Biya forced Ahidjo to leave the country, and Ahidjo was sentenced to death in absentia. Ahidjo spent the rest of his life in Senegal and France, and died of a heart attack in Senegal in November 1989. Paul Biya succeeded in erasing all references to Ahidjo, and little evidence of his existence can be found in the African country he ruled, except for a sports stadium named after him in Yaoundé, Cameroon.

Thursday, March 22, 1962:
Sylvanus Olympio, President of Togo

Less than a week after New York City welcomed the president of the newly independent nation Cameroon *(see: March 16, 1962)*, it played host to the President of the West African Republic of Togo, which gained its independence in April 1960. Sylvanus Epiphanio Olympio was elected the first president of the new nation. He had been active in the struggle to gain independence since 1947, serving first as Minister of Finance and then as Prime Minister while the region was still under the French colonial mandate.

In 1962, Olympio took a quick good-will tour of the United States. His first stop was in Washington where he met with President Kennedy and Congressional leaders to request financial aid for his poor country. His second and final stop before returning home was New York, where he planned to meet with financiers seeking to invest in his country.

The day started at a breakfast with Sargeant Shriver, Jr, Director of the Peace Corps, to arrange final details for an upcoming visit to Togo by Peace Corps volunteers. President Olympio was then driven to the Battery for his parade of welcome.

There was a slight chill in the air when the parade began shortly after noon. Wearing a double-breasted overcoat over a black suit, gray scarf, matching tie, and white shirt, President Olympio joined Richard Patterson, Commissioner of Public Events in an open car for the ride up Broadway. Also sharing the vehicle was Angier Biddle Duke, State Department Chief of Protocol. A troop of mounted policeman led the parade, followed by the First Army Band and small detachments from the Army, Navy, Marine Corps, and Air Force. An eight-man color guard from the Fire Department directly preceded the vehicle carrying the president.

Even though some spectators told a reporter they had no idea of who was being honored or where Togo was, a considerable number were present to cheer and wave at the visiting chief of state. In some places along the parade route the crowd was three or four deep. President Olympio accepted the cheers of the crowd and waved his gray fedora in acknowledgement.

Mayor and Mrs. Wagner welcomed the President to New York at City Hall. Speaking in French, President Olympio thanked the mayor and stated that he had never imagined such a welcome. Immediately after the formalities at City Hall ended, the President was guest of honor at the investment firm of Calvin Bullock at 1 Wall Street, where investors received information about the Republic of Togo and possible areas of financial opportunity.

Later, Mayor Wagner hosted a reception for President Olympio at the Waldorf Astoria, where the president received the city's Gold Medal and a scroll hailing his work fostering brotherhood and cooperation in West Africa, especially among former French colonies in the region. In return, he gave Mayor Wagner a sheet of postage stamps recently issued in Togo depicting the space flight of John Glenn. Following the reception, the president was the guest of the Council on Foreign Relations at the Harold Pratt house on East 68th Street. Early the next morning the statesman met with delegates from Asian and African nations at the United Nations. This was the final event scheduled for his brief stay in the United States.

President Olympio's term of office was cut short less than a year later when he was assassinated by a military coup on January 13, 1963. A group of Army officers, acting under the name of the Insurrection Committee, ruled Togo until 1967. It was replaced by a second coup, led by Colonel Etienne Eyadema, who declared himself president and ruled the nation from 1967 until his own death in 2005. President Olympio's short career as president was marked by attempts to create mutual understanding among African nations with very diverse backgrounds and cultures. He was greatly respected by African leaders and his assassination was denounced by many of the new nations in Africa.

Thursday, April 5, 1962: João Goulart, President of Brazil

President Goulart, Brazil's 24th president since the deposing of Emperor Dom Pedro II in 1889, visited New York City after a two-day visit with President Kennedy in Washington. His flight from Washington was delayed and he arrived at LaGuardia Airport 20 minutes later than expected. The Brazilian president was met by Richard Patterson, Commissioner of the Department of Commerce and Public Events, and was driven to the parade's starting point on Broadway escorted by a squad of motorcycle policemen. The trip from the Marine Air Terminal in Queens to Manhattan was so fast that much of the time lost by the flight's late arrival was made up and the parade started less than ten minutes late.

The president, known by his boyhood nickname of Jango, shared a cream-colored limousine for the parade with Mr. Patterson, State Department Chief of Protocol Angier Biddle Duke, and General Amaury Kruel, chief military advisor to the president and commander of the Brazilian Second Army. The US First Army Band led the procession, followed by marching units from the Army, Navy, Coast Guard, Marines, and Air Force and a seven-man color guard from the Fire Department. Two other bands, the 579th Air Force Band from Stewart Air Force Base in Newburgh, New York, and a Naval Band from the Brooklyn Navy Yard, completed the musical accompaniment. Two open press trucks carried more than 60 photographers and journalists, most of them from Brazil.

As the parade moved uptown the 44-year-old Brazilian president stood hatless in the car, waving to the crowd. An occasional welcome was shouted at the president in Spanish, possibly from spectators who were unaware that the language of Brazil is

Portuguese. Goulart's left leg had been paralyzed from the knee down by an illness almost 25 years earlier and he braced himself by holding tightly to the side of the car with his hand. The occasional stops and starts of the vehicle seemed to cause him slight discomfort but he smiled at the blizzard of white ticker tape and colored confetti that cascaded from the skyscrapers. Near the corner of Fulton Street three Brazilian reporters who had not been given a place in the caravan broke through the police barriers and thrust a microphone at the president. Nearby Secret Service agents rushed forward but General Kruel stopped them, and the president spoke a few words to the reporters. The brief interview ended, and the limousine entered City Hall Park minutes later.

Mayor Wagner welcomed the president and requested that he sign the City's official guest book. The mayor then introduced him to the spectators in the Park and the president responded in Portuguese, his words translated by an aide. "I am very grateful," he said, "and deeply moved by the warm and affectionate welcome coming from the people of New York."

A short time later Mayor and Mrs. Wagner hosted a reception for the South American statesman at the Starlight Room of the Waldorf Astoria Hotel. During the reception the mayor conferred New York City's Gold Medal of Honor on the president, along with a scroll for "distinguished and exceptional service." The day ended with a private dinner at the Knickerbocker Club on East 62nd Street hosted by Governor Nelson Rockefeller.

Two days later President Goulart returned to Brazil. He had assumed the presidency in September 1961, when President Jânio Quadros unexpectedly resigned. President Goulart's administration contained socialists and communists, causing the Kennedy and Johnson administrations to consider him an unreliable ally. His closeness to the poorer members of Brazilian society angered many of the wealthier class. It is rumored that the CIA might have been behind the military coup that deposed him in April 1964. President Goulart fled the country without resigning and the military controlled Brazil "due to the vacancy of the presidency" until early in the 21st century.

President Goulart fled Brazil for neighboring Uruguay where a sympathetic government offered him protection. He purchased a cattle ranch near the Brazilian border and remained there until 1973. Accepting an invitation to relocate to Argentina, he and his family moved to Buenos Aires, where he died of a heart attack in late 1976. No autopsy was performed, and some believe that military leaders in Brazil caused his death. News of his death and funeral were censored in Brazil by the military and it was not officially announced there until almost a year later. Since the return of civilian authority in Brazil his legacy has been rehabilitated, his family granted a substantial pension, and schools, roads, and public buildings have been named after him or using his nickname of Jango.

Monday, April 9, 1962:
New York Yankees, World Series Champions

The 1961 baseball season had been another triumph for the New York Yankees, winning both the American League Championship and the World Series. Excitement all that year was focused on the "M&M Boys," as both Mickey Mantle and Roger Maris hit home run after home run, challenging Babe Ruth's record of hitting 60 in one season. Maris, who joined the team in 1960, dramatically broke that record, hitting his 61st home run on the final game of the season. Fans of Mantle and Maris, or of fellow players Yogi Berra, Whitey Ford and the rest of the Bronx Bombers, were eagerly looking forward to the 1962 season, and City Hall decided to celebrate opening day in a unique way.

Mayor Wagner and other city officials met the team in City Hall Park, where a platform had been set up. In front of a cheering crowd of about 2,000 fans, the Mayor introduced the team, praising their "great contribution" to the city. For the first time in the team's 62-year history, their World Championship flag was raised over City Hall.

That celebration, however, did not include a parade, despite the inclusion of this event on the list of parades in the *Encyclopedia of New York City*.

The team had another successful season, winning the American League Championship and going on to defeat the San Francisco Giants in the World Series, the first time the former rivals had played against each other since the Giants left New York in 1958. That would be last World Series win for the Yankees, however, until 1977, by which time the city would celebrate with a parade *(see: October 19, 1977)*.

Thursday, April 12, 1962: New York Mets

When New York's two National League baseball teams, Brooklyn's Dodgers and uptown Manhattan's Giants, left the city in 1957 for the supposedly greener pastures of the west coast, the city was left with only one major league baseball team, the Yankees of the American League. Though plans were soon started to bring another National League team to the city, no existing franchises could be persuaded to relocate to New York City. But thanks to the work of many, particularly attorney William Shea, the National League expanded in 1962 by adding two new teams to its roster, one for Houston, Texas, and the other for New York. Officially named the New York Metropolitan Baseball Club, the "Mets" adopted uniform colors combining those of the city's two former teams, blue and orange.

Opening day of the new team's first full season was April 11, 1962 in St. Louis, where they lost to the Cardinals. The team then returned to New York for their first home game, played at the Polo Grounds while the new stadium in Flushing, Queens that the city had promised the team was still under construction. Another enticement that Mayor Robert Wagner made to the new franchise was for a ticker tape parade.

The day was chilly, and a few drops fell from a sky that looked to *Daily News* columnist Dick Young like a "heap of soiled wet wash." But a weak ray of sunlight helped warm the crowd of more than 400,000 who lined the route from Lower Broadway to City Hall. The crowd cheered with raucous enthusiasm as the blizzard of ticker tape cascaded down on the procession of players in open top vehicles. Team manager Casey Stengel wrapped himself in tape and by the time the vehicle he rode in passed Wall Street, he was draped in flowing strands. Players threw plastic baseballs to the crowd. One spectator who caught a ball thrown by pitcher Roger Craig was heard to shout "Why didn't you throw that hard against St. Louie." Often the balls failed to reach the crowd and fans rushed past the police barricades lining the route to retrieve them. A few fans tossed them back, disappointed that they were not real baseballs. Club officials stated that 10,000 plastic balls had been purchased at five cents each for the event and by the time the parade reached City Hall, they were all gone.

At City Hall, Mayor Wagner officially welcomed the 22 players and 8 coaches of the new team (3 players were unable to attend). Casey Stengel was then given the microphone for a few words. Known as the "Old Perfesser," Stengel mentioned both the Dodgers and Giants in his usual rambling manner and each time he did, the crowd booed lustily. The 72-year-old ex-manager of the Yankees, who won seven world championships during his 12 years leadership, told the crowd "We hope to build this team bigger than the Yankees," a statement that seemed to receive the most cheers. Finally, Casey introduced the players individually, each receiving cheers from the crowd as he called out their names. A huge roar came from the crowd when he introduced Gil Hodges, former all-star first basemen of the departed Dodgers.

When the festivities finally ended, a caravan of police cars whisked the new team to the Polo Grounds for their first home game, which was rained out. They played the next day, losing to the Pittsburgh Pirates. It was the start of one of the worst seasons ever by a major league baseball team, ending the year with a record of 40 wins and 120 losses. Despite this, Casey Stengel always referred to his team as the "amazin' Mets," and the nickname stuck.

It seemed like the new team was destined for embarrassment and defeat but only seven years later, the Mets would receive another ticker tape parade, this time as the 1969 World Champions *(see: October 20, 1969)*. Casey Stengel continued managing the team until 1965, when he broke a hip. He died in 1975.

Monday, April 16, 1962:
Shah Mohammed Reza Pahlevi and Empress Farah of Iran

Much had changed since the first visit of the Shah of Iran to the United States and the ticker tape parade he had received in New York *(see: November 21, 1949)*. Iran had made steps toward modernization, individual income was rising, oil from his nation was fueling more and more cars in Iran, schools and hospitals were being built, and the future of Iran seemed bright. Shah Mohammed Reza Pahlevi had also remarried after divorcing his second wife, and he was accompanied on this trip by the Empress Farah. The weather, also, was different; while his first parade was held on a warm, sunny day, for his second it was cold and overcast.

The Shah and his wife arrived in New York from a visit to Washington where they met and socialized with President and Mrs. Kennedy. As the parade up the Canyon of Heroes began, the Shah stood in an open car, huddled in a heavy topcoat. Wearing a soft blue coat and a mauve-pink hat, Empress Farah sat through the entire route up Broadway, a blanket across her legs. Two military bands and detachments from the Army and Marine Corps marched with the royal couple, and contingents from the Police and Fire departments marched behind the Shah's car. The Shah frequently pointed out some of the buildings along the route to the Empress.

Mayor and Mrs. Wagner greeted the Shah and his wife at City Hall and escorted them into the Council Chambers, where 300 guests watched the mayor give the Iranian ruler a scroll commemorating the Shah's efforts to strengthen and modernize his country.

Following the brief reception at City Hall, the Shah and his wife drove with the mayor and his wife to the Royal Suite at the Waldorf Astoria. As a concession to the blustery April afternoon, they rode uptown in an open sedan with a clear bubble-dome covering them. The Empress remained at the Waldorf, where she and Mrs. Wagner dined while the Shah and the Mayor proceeded to a luncheon for 200 members of the Overseas Press Club on West 45th Street. In his address to the members, delivered in almost-perfect English, the Shah stressed that a redistribution of Iran's property and wealth was essential, shrugging off resistance to his plans "because it came from just a few people." He mentioned that his meeting with President Kennedy had centered on generalities, but he came from the meeting assured of America's full support. During

322

a brief interview following his remarks, the Shah admitted that what he referred to as "doing the King's business" often gave him "nothing but headaches." He added that the Empress had the same reaction performing her royal functions "such as visiting hospitals and schools."

That evening the Shah and Empress attended a dinner in the grand ballroom of the Waldorf Astoria as guests of the Near East Foundation. They returned to Iran two days later after sightseeing and shopping.

Despite the changes that the Shah had brought about in Iran, the country was far from tranquil, and his statement that opposition came from a small number of people was far from correct. Tensions between conservative and liberal members of Iranian society were high and religious leaders grew stronger. Animosity was felt over American involvement in Iranian affairs. Opposition hardened, fed by huge expenditures on projects such as the 1971 celebration of the 2,500th anniversary of the Persian Kingdom, which cost more than $100 million US dollars. Increasingly larger numbers of young men and women with college educations were unemployed by an economy that could not absorb large numbers of highly educated individuals.

Matters came to a head in 1977, when strikes turned into open rebellion, fueled by religious leaders. The Shah was forced to flee Iran in early 1979. Although he never abdicated, he no longer ruled. He lived in exile in Egypt, the United States, and Panama. During this time, he was often hospitalized for a variety of illnesses. Shah Reza Pahlavi died in March 1980 from a form of lymphoma and is buried in Al Rafa'i Mosque in Cairo, along with his father and the last king of Egypt, King Farouk. Empress Farah is still alive as of this writing and resides in Paris.

Friday, May 25, 1962:
Félix Houphouët-Boigny, President of Ivory Coast

The president of the small west African nation of Ivory Coast, Félix Houphouët-Boigny received New York's traditional welcome on a bright sunny late May day. The parade was held the day after astronaut Scott Carpenter's three-orbit flight in a Mercury capsule and a few spectators believed that the parade for the African president had some connection with Carpenter's flight. Commander Carpenter was honored two weeks later at a brief meeting at the Waldorf Astoria with former presidents Hoover and Truman, but he received no ticket tape parade (see; June 5, 1962).

President Houphouët-Boigny arrived in New York by train from Washington, where he and his wife, along with other Ivorian officials, had met with President Kennedy. The Ivory Coast had obtained independence from France in 1960, and Mr. Houphouët-Boigny had already begun to show himself to be a powerful leader among the other newly independent African nations.

A brisk breeze whipped up Broadway as the president, his wife, and Ivorian officials rode from Bowling Green to City Hall. Streamers of green and yellow ribbon, the colors of the flag of Ivory Coast, mingled with ticker tape. The parade started at noon, proceeded by bands from the Police and Fire Departments and detachments from the Army and Navy. President Houphouët-Boigny rode in a beige limousine with the Chairman of the Reception Committee, Richard Patterson. The president, wearing a dark blue double-breasted suit, white shirt and tie, stood and acknowledged the cheers of the crowd. His wife, Marie-Thérèse, rode in the following car, wearing a beige straw pill-box hat and linen coat of the same color. Like her husband, she smiled and waved often at the crowds along the route. Cries congratulating Scott Carpenter were clearly heard from the spectators even though the Ivorian flag appeared on official vehicles and there was no evidence of the Navy Commander.

After the parade, Mayor Wagner welcomed the president and his wife at City Hall. The mayor cited the president's long career of leading his nation from a French colony to independence, then asked the West African leader for his reaction to the astronaut's flight. "We share in the legitimate pride and great satisfaction of the American people," he answered. He called the flight a victory for science and technology and "a great victory for peace."

A luncheon followed that afternoon at the Waldorf Astoria given by the Africa-American Institute, but the president did not attend. A spokesman reported that he was indisposed, and his wife attended in his place. That evening the presidential couple attended a reception at Gracie Mansion, where Mayor Wagner presented the president with the city's Gold Medal and a scroll honoring his long career of exceptional service, from medical doctor to village leader, then as a member of the Ivorian colonial legislature, and finally as president.

President Houphouët-Boigny addressed the United Nations on the following day and after a week of sightseeing in New York returned to his homeland. He pursued a policy of cooperation among the tribal factions of his country and was a mover towards unifying the interests of newly created African nations. Amid the turbulence of politics in this region he was not always successful. Attempts to influence affairs in Nigeria, Burkina Faso, and the Congo cost him support and eroded his popularity. His policies were strongly supported by France, however, and he was criticized for his friendship with this nation. Opposition slowly grew in the Ivory Coast against this and his increasingly dictatorial practices, and the nation experienced revolts during the early 1990s. After serving as president of his nation for 33 years, he died in 1993. After his death discoveries were made of his enormous wealth, much of it in Swiss and Bahaman banks.

Tuesday, June 5, 1962: Commander Scott Carpenter

On May 24, 1962, the fourth manned Mercury mission sent astronaut Malcolm Scott Carpenter into space aboard the *Aurora 7* spacecraft for an almost five-hour flight, orbiting the earth three times. During the flight, Carpenter conducted several scientific experiments, was the first person to eat solid food in space, and discovered that the "fireflies" that John Glenn had observed on his flight were ice particles from the spacecraft's exterior. He also had to manually fire the ship's retrorockets to compensate for a computer malfunction, using too much fuel in the process. He became distracted watching the fireflies, causing him to start landing preparations late. As a result, his re-entry path overshot the target splash-down zone by 250 miles. CBS News' Walter Cronkite grimly told a captive TV audience that "while thousands watch and pray," fearing the astronaut might be dead, "the silence is almost intolerable" until finally two US Navy aircraft rescued him in the Pacific. The nation cheered in celebration, while NASA officials fumed about the imperfect re-entry and the resulting bad publicity, becoming determined that Carpenter should be scrubbed from future missions.

Scott Carpenter, the fourth American and sixth human to travel into space, arrived in New York on an overcast and chilly June morning, landing at LaGuardia Airport's Marine Terminal shortly before noon. Travelling with him were his wife Rene, and their four children, Mark, Robyn, Kristen and Candace, who ranged in age from 12 to

5 years old. Before departing for New York, the astronaut and his family had a brief White House meeting with President Kennedy. A brief press conference was held at the Marine Terminal. Commander Walter Williams, NASA's Operations Director for Project Mercury, explained that because of his heavy schedule, Carpenter "could not accept the city's offer of a ticker tape parade" like the one that had honored John Glenn after his successful Mercury mission *(see: March 1, 1962)*. Carpenter added that the city's "hospitality and your good, kind faces are the same as they were after John's flight."

After the conference, Carpenter and his family entered the limousines waiting to take him and his entourage into the city. Following a police escort, the 25-car motorcade followed a route that had been announced the day before, driving down Ditmars Boulevard to the Triborough Bridge, then along 125th Street to Seventh Avenue. At 96th Street, the motorcade turned east through Central Park to Lexington Avenue, then south to 49th Street and its destination, the Waldorf Astoria Hotel.

Crowds lined the route, swelling at major intersections and near subway and train stations. Along the last 10 blocks of the drive, the sidewalks were packed from curb to building front. Many children were seen waving American flags, and "New Yorkers clapped, cheered and threw shredded newspapers" from windows onto the motorcade as it passed by.

Photographers waited at the hotel as the motorcade arrived, eager for more pictures of the astronaut and his family. "Better hurry, these children are hungry," Carpenter said grinning.

The luncheon was held in the Waldorf's Grand Ballroom, filled with an audience of 1,500 guests. Former Presidents Herbert Hoover and Harry Truman were there, as well as Mayor Wagner, UN Under-Secretary Ralph Bunche, and Mrs. Rose Kennedy, mother of the current president.

After some opening remarks by former President Truman, the Mayor presented Carpenter and Director Williams with the city's Gold Medal, then praised the astronaut's courage. "Not the so-called courage of the foolhardy or the daredevil," he said, "but the kind of bravery that is based on knowledge and reserve of power – the courage that knows fear but rejects it, the courage that knows failure but skillfully avoids it."

Speaking last, Carpenter said he felt the need to explain that the praise and acclaim being showered on him should really be directed at the "many thousands of the hardest-working people you ever saw" at NASA. He was confident that "great steps will be made in all fields of science" because of space exploration, which would be "greater possibly than any others man has made since the discovery of fire."

The luncheon ended and Carpenter and his entourage returned to their motorcade, which travelled back to LaGuardia Airport via Third Avenue and the Triborough Bridge. He flew back to Langley Airforce Base, and then to his home state of Colorado, where he received parades in both Denver and Boulder.

In 1964, Carpenter took a leave of absence from NASA to join the Navy's SEALAB project, having been inspired about undersea exploration after meeting Jacques Cousteau at a public lecture. He suffered some injuries while undersea, losing mobility in one arm. He resigned from NASA after they ruled him ineligible for flight, then worked as a consultant to Hollywood on space flight and oceanography. He divorced Rene in 1972 and had three more marriages and a total of eight children. Asked about his legacy shortly before his death in 2013, he said "I was an astronaut and an aquanaut."

Why there really no ticker tape parade in New York because of a heavy schedule, or was NASA punishing him? Although the official answer at the time blamed his schedule, comments made over the years by NASA officials, about his "joy-riding" and "not paying attention to the job" leave room for doubt.

Friday, June 8, 1962:
Archbishop Makarios, Head of the Cypriot Orthodox Church

The first churchman to receive a ticker tape parade was born in Cyprus in 1913. Michael Christodoulou Mouskos was ordained a priest in the Greek Orthodox Church in 1938, and ten years later was consecrated Bishop and assumed the name Makarios. In 1950, he was named Archbishop of the Cypriot Greek Orthodox Church as Makarios III. When Great Britain granted independence to the island of Cyprus in 1960, he was elected the republic's first President, so the parade was for his political role more than his religious one.

The day was sunny and mild with a slight breeze blowing through the Canyon of Heroes when the parade began at noon. Seven mounted policemen led the small three-vehicle caravan. Army and Navy detachments escorted the prelate president, as the Sanitation Department Band provided the marching beat. The Archbishop shared an open limousine with Angier Biddle Duke, Chief of Protocol of the US State Department, and Richard Patterson, Commissioner of the Department of Commerce and Public Events.

As usual, Broadway was decked with flags and fluttering side by side with the American flag was that of Cyprus, the only national flag depicting a map of its country. The Archbishop, wearing his black robes and miter based on the design of the Byzantine crown, waved in appreciation at the crowd lining the thoroughfare. He wore around his neck a heavy chain bearing the Orthodox cross.

Since the use of ticker tape by financial and banking industries was declining, swirls of confetti and torn paper floated down from the buildings. At one point a bit of confetti appeared to lodge in the bishop's eye and Mr. Patterson assisted him in brushing it from his face and out of his heavy black beard.

At City Hall, the Sanitation Department Band played the national anthems of Cyprus and the United States as Mayor Wagner welcomed President Makarios and presented him with the city's Medal of Honor. Asked for his reaction to the city's welcome, Makarios replied that he was deeply moved by the friendly feelings between New York and the people of Cyprus.

That evening the Cypriot Ambassador, Zenon Rossides, hosted a dinner reception at the Waldorf Astoria for more than 300 guests. Makarios offered an invocation and blessing in Greek before the meal, and toasts were offered to the independence of the Mediterranean island nation.

Two days later the President's brief visit ended, and he returned to Nicosia, his country's capital. He was easily re-elected twice, receiving 96% of the votes cast in the election of 1971. All was not well in his country, though, and the Turkish minority boycotted the elections, fearing that plans were being made to unite Cyprus with Greece. Makarios attempted to maintain the nation's independence but a Greek-financed guerrilla organization began to operate against the island's Turkish population inhabiting the northern section of the island. In 1974, Makarios was deposed and replaced by a pro-unification government, triggering an invasion by Turkey in July 1974. An emergency meeting of the United Nations brought about a cease-fire, but Turkish troops have occupied the northern part of the island ever since, and a buffer zone between north and south is maintained to this day by a UN peacekeeping force.

Archbishop Makarios died suddenly of a heart attack in August 1977. He was buried at the XI Century monastery of Our Lady of Kykkos near Pedoulas, Cyprus. Rumors circulated that he had been murdered but an autopsy has proven otherwise.

Thursday, June 14, 1962: Roberto Chiari, President of Panama

Roberto Francisco Chiari Remón was the 23rd president of the Republic of Panama and the son of its seventh president, Rodolfo Chiari. After spending two days in Washington with President Kennedy discussing modifications to the treaty governing the Panama Canal Zone, the president arrived at LaGuardia Airport on a sunny day. He was driven from the airport to Bowling Green with a motorcycle escort. President Chiari had been in New York a number of times previously, but this would be his first parade.

The president rode in an open limousine as he traveled up the Canyon of Heroes. An honor guard composed of members of the Army and Navy accompanied the small motorcade of four vehicles followed by a military band, and a color guard completed the marching group. The usual cascade of ticker tape, torn paper, and multi-colored confetti swirled down on the president and he waved to the thousands along the route. As he stepped from the car at City Hall, the sound of cheering still echoing through the streets of lower Manhattan, he said softly to Mayor Wagner, "What a wonderful, remarkable thing."

Mayor Wagner awarded the president the city's Gold Medal as well as a scroll proclaiming President Chiari as a leader "whose objective to safeguard the vital interests of the United States and the Republic of Panama in the great Canal enterprise has resulted in a policy dedicated to mutual respect." President Chiari accepted the medal and scroll and again spoke of his wonder for the welcome he had received.

President Chiari attended a luncheon at the United Nations a short time later, followed by a reception at Gracie Mansion for a small number of invited guests and members of the Panamanian mission to the United Nations. His brief visit to the city ended that evening with a dinner at the River Club on East 52nd Street hosted by the Pan American Society. The following day he flew back to Panama City.

Unlike many of his predecessors, Chiari had been elected president in 1960 in an honest and uncontested election. In 1964, a fight broke out between American and Panamanian students at Balboa High School in the Canal Zone when American students tore down the Panamanian flag. Four days of rioting between Panamanians, American civilians, and members of the US Army followed, during which 22 Panamanians were killed. Known as Martyr's Day, the incident led President Chiari to break off relations with the US, which would lead to the 1977 Torrios-Carter Treaty ending US control over the Canal in 1999. President Chiari was a member of one of Panama's wealthiest families, controlling large sugar and dairy holdings. When his term of office ended in 1964, he retired to manage his family's companies. He died in 1981, during the middle of Carnival, so no State Funeral was held.

Monday, April 1, 1963: King Hassan II of Morocco

King Hassan II visited the United States to foster friendlier relations between Morocco and America. After meeting with Congressional and State Department officials in Washington, he traveled to New York where he received the customary welcome, a parade through the Canyon of Heroes.

The parade began soon after noon. A mounted police squadron led the way, followed by the First Army Band and detachments from the Army, Marine Corps, Navy, and Air Force. The king rode in the first of the six cars that made up the procession. Cheering crowds greeted His Highness and he waved back in acknowledgement. As the parade passed Trinity Church, King Hassan suddenly requested that the car be stopped. Stepping out of the vehicle, he proceeded to walk the remainder of the way to City Hall, to the enthusiastic shouts of the viewing public. He was hatless and wore a gray business suit. A security detail from the United States and another from Morocco surrounded the king as he walked at a leisurely pace, enjoying the festivities.

Mayor Wagner presented the king with a scroll commemorating his visit and asked why the king had chosen to walk since so few parade recipients ever had. The king answered that he had been taught by his father, King Mohammed V, to do things that ordinary people did, and he doubted if many New Yorkers rode up Broadway in an open limousine. There is no way to know if his father would also have walked up Broadway, since the parade scheduled to welcome his father was cancelled because of bad weather *(see: December 9, 1957)*.

The king was the guest of honor at a luncheon provided by the Overseas Press Club at the Delmonico Hotel on Fifth Avenue and 59th Street (which is not connected with the famous Delmonico's Restaurant), where he answered questions from reporters, particularly about religious freedom in his country. Before he traveled to the United States, three Moroccans had been condemned to death for crimes against the Islamic faith. Assuring reporters that there was freedom for all religious beliefs in Morocco, he said the sentences would be overturned or pardoned. The king returned to Morocco later in the week and commuted the sentences to life in prison.

King Hassan westernized Morocco through various reforms, including women's rights, non-religious schools, providing the vote to non-landowners, and recognition of Israel. At the same time, his regime became expansionist by recovering the Spanish enclave of Ifni on the Atlantic coast, occupying part of the former colony of Spanish Sahara, and waging a brief war against neighboring Mauritania. Not all of his reforms were popular though, and Hassan survived two assassination attempts and several coups during his 38-year reign. He surrendered most of his governmental powers to an elected Council in early 1999 and died later that year at the age of 70 in Rabat, Morocco.

Wednesday, May 22, 1963: Major Gordon Cooper

US Air Force Major Leroy Gordon Cooper landed at LaGuardia Airport at 11:40 in the morning from Washington, DC. The astronaut, who went by the nickname "Gordo", was accompanied by his wife Trudy, his mother and aunt, and his two teenage daughters. A long red carpet had been laid out on the concrete ramp from the plane's exit door, and after being welcomed to the city by Richard Patterson, Commissioner of Public Events, the astronaut noted that "small town boys know you are indeed a success when you are invited to a parade in New York City."

Led by a police escort, Cooper and his family were taken in a caravan of open-top cars through Queens to the Triborough Bridge, then down the FDR Drive to the Battery, cheered loudly by immense crowds, estimated between 4 and 4.5 million along the entire route. Schools had released early so children could view the procession of vehicles, and Broadway had been officially renamed "Mercury Way" for the day in honor of the seven astronauts in the program, all but one of whom joined Major Cooper at Bowling Green. Missing that day because he was on duty in Japan was Lieutenant Colonel John Glenn, who had already received a triumphant ride up Broadway (see: March 1, 1962).

The parade up Broadway was led by a mounted police detail and the First Army Band, followed by small detachments from each branch of the military. Next came four cars carrying the astronauts and their wives, with Major Cooper and his wife in the final car. The caravan was followed by a second detachment of mounted police, and more than 5,000 police were on special duty, intermixed in the crowds along with NASA security officers. A small plane skywriting the message "Well done, Gordo" flew high above Broadway. The Major commented later that he had not seen the plane but had wondered why so many spectators were pointing to the sky.

The usual snowstorm of ticker tape, confetti, and torn telephone directories began an hour and a half before the parade even began and intensified once it did start. The crowd's enthusiasm can be measured by statistics provided by the Sanitation Department, showing that more than 2,000 tons of debris had to be swept off the streets. Most was cleared by the Department's new automatic sweepers, but a considerable amount of manual sweeping was also needed, and the cleanup was completed by 4:00 that afternoon.

Waiting at City Hall to greet Major and Mrs. Cooper and his fellow astronauts were Del Webb, chairman of the day's reception, Mayor Robert Wagner, and Vice President Lyndon Johnson. The Mayor introduced astronauts Major Donald Slayton, Commander Alan Shepard, Major Virgil "Gus" Grissom, Lieutenant Commander Scott Carpenter, and Commander Walter Shirra to the thousands jammed into City Hall Plaza. He then announced, "The hero of the day, Major Gordon Cooper" and the cheers became deafening.

"Well, I'm certainly very impressed," Cooper said, with a trace of Oklahoma twang in his voice. "I never dreamed that I would find myself in such an impressive position." Launched into orbit eight days earlier, he had circled the earth 22 times and commented from his space craft, Faith 7, about how impressed he was by the view. He now said that the New York welcome he had just received seemed to surpass that experience. He was presented with a Key to the City by the mayor and a scroll praising his accomplishments, followed by a few words from Vice President Johnson.

After the ceremony at City Hall, the honored guests were escorted to a luncheon at the Waldorf by way of Lafayette Street. Travelling uptown to 14th Street, the caravan continued up the Avenue of the Americas, then across 57th Street to Park Avenue and down to the hotel entrance on 56th Street.

At the luncheon, Cooper received messages of congratulations from two of the three living US ex-presidents, Harry Truman and Dwight Eisenhower. The third, 88-year-old Herbert Hoover, was a resident of the Waldorf and joined the party to congratulate the Major in person. Called upon to say some words after the luncheon, Cooper made one of the shortest post-parade speeches ever. He said, "I don't generally say very much. I'm so impressed that today I'm going to say even less. I would just like to say that on behalf of the entire Mercury team, I thank you for this wonderful day." After his brief remarks, Major and Mrs. Cooper received guests outside the Grand Ballroom while photographers captured the moment. Finally, the astronaut and his wife "walked out into the white glare of the ballroom itself and a standing ovation."

That evening, Cooper and his wife, along with four of his fellow astronauts and their wives, attended a performance of *Stop the World, I Want to Get Off* at the Shubert Theater. They received cheers from the audience as they entered the theater, and the musical's star, Anthony Newley, ad-libbed a joke about the NASA program which got a chuckle from Cooper.

Cooper's career as an astronaut was not over. Two years later he piloted Gemini 5 on an 8-day mission, setting a record for space endurance by traveling of over 3.3 million miles. He had hoped for assignment to the upcoming Apollo moon missions, but he was replaced by James Lovell.

Cooper made a number of statements to the press and on television about UFO sightings, which may have been responsible for his being replaced from the Apollo moon missions. He retired with the rank of Colonel in 1970, then worked as a consultant for a number of companies including the Walt Disney Company, offering advice and guidance for Epcot's development. He subsequently developed Parkinson's disease and died of heart failure in 2004 at his home in Ventura, California. He claimed until his death that the government knew about the existence of UFO's and was covering up the truth for security reasons.

Monday, June 10, 1963:
Sarvepalli Radhakrishnan, President of India

After serving 10 years as India's first Vice President, Dr. Sarvepalli Radhakrishnan was elected President in 1962. The 75-year-old President of the world's most populous democracy, visited the United States in 1963 at the personal invitation of President John Kennedy, spending three days in Washington for meetings with the President, members of the Cabinet, and Congress. Arriving in New York late on June 9, President Radhakrishnan was scheduled to speak to the General Assembly of the United Nations the next afternoon. Prior to his address there, New York City treated him to its customary ticker tape welcome.

The parade began at noon and President Radhakrishnan rode in an open vehicle along with members of the mayor's Reception Committee. Other cars in the motorcade contained Indian and American State Department officials. A military band led the way up Broadway and contingents from the various armed services provided an honor guard. The frail-looking president seemed pleased by the cascading streamers of paper and the cheers that greeted him.

At City Hall, Acting Mayor Paul Screvane performed the usual formal welcome ceremony and awarded the president with the city's Gold Medal of Honor. He also presented President Radhakrishnan with a scroll that commemorated his achievements in the struggle for Indian independence, as well as his doctorate in philosophy and his writings. The Indian statesman thanked the mayor and all those responsible for the welcome he was given.

That afternoon President Radhakrishnan addressed the United Nations General Assembly, prefacing his remarks with a brief tribute to Pope John XXIII who had died a week earlier. He called the late Pope "a true servant of God and humanity." His speech focused on the issue of peace and India's faith in the peaceful works of the United Nations, cautioning however that much still had to be done. Noting the fact that since the first meeting of the UN membership had grown to 111 countries, he called for the admission of nations not yet seated and advocated for the end of colonialism, granting independence to additional lands. Even though the United Nations sometimes falls short of its goals to bring about an end to war and violence, he concluded, "India maintains extreme faith in it."

Prior to attending a dinner at the Waldorf Astoria that evening, Governor Rockefeller met with the Indian leader at the Hotel Carlyle for a brief conversation. The dinner was co-hosted by the Asia Society, the Far Eastern American Council of Commerce, and the Indian Chamber of Commerce of America. After dinner, the contralto Marian Anderson, a trustee of the Asia Society, sang four songs. The Indian President said later that "art is the universal language that transcends all barriers, and that where politics divide people, art and literature bring them together."

Three days later President Radhakrishnan returned to India, serving as the nation's president until 1967. He spent the remaining nine years of his life writing on philosophic subjects, primarily the differences between Eastern and Western thought. He died in 1975 at the age of 86 in Chennai, India.

Tuesday, September 10, 1963: King Mohammed Zahir Shah and Queen Homaira of Afghanistan

Mohammed Zahir, the 49-year-old King of Afghanistan, met with President Kennedy, Congressional leaders, and various State Department officials during his ten-day visit to the United States in early September 1963. After visiting Fort Bragg, North Carolina on September 9, he and his wife, Queen Homaira, boarded President Kennedy's personal plane the next morning with their entourage and flew to Idlewild International Airport in New York, landing just after 11 o'clock in the morning.

The King was met at the airport by the City Commissioner of Public Events, Richard Patterson, and other New York dignitaries. Entering a limousine with Mr. Patterson they raced to the parade's starting point at Bowling Green, with a motorcycle escort, sirens blaring. Upon arriving there, the king and queen transferred to a white convertible for the ride to City Hall.

Behind the bands of the First Army and the Third Naval District, the motorcade moved slowly up Broadway. Marine Corps, Navy, and Army contingents provided an escort. American and Afghan flags barely stirred in the warmth of the late summer afternoon. A noontime crowd estimated at 50,000 watched, and some of the spectators, unfamiliar with the flag of Afghanistan, wondered at the identity of the tall, bald gentleman in the dark blue suit standing in the rear of the car. Smiling and waving frequently, the King seemed to enjoy the spectacle offered by falling ticker tape and confetti. His wife sat beside him, only occasionally waving to the crowd. As the motorcade approached City Hall, His Majesty suddenly opened the door of the slowly moving vehicle, exited, and vigorously shook hands with spectators. Those nearby applauded and cheered loudly before he was surrounded by security personnel.

At City Hall, Mayor and Mrs. Wagner greeted the royal couple as they strode across a red carpet laid on the road. The mayor led them to the podium and introduced the King and Queen, then presented the King with New York's Gold Medal and the royal party signed the city's guest book.

After the brief ceremony King Zahir and Queen Homaira were driven to their suite at the Waldorf Astoria for photographs but no interview was permitted. He then enjoyed a private lunch with the United States Representative to the United Nations, Adlai Stevenson. Instead of joining them, the Queen attended a fashion show at Lord & Taylor on Fifth Avenue and 38th Street. She toured the large department store but made no purchases.

331

Their Majesties returned to Afghanistan two days later. King Zahir, the last king of his country, ruled until 1973. He made numerous attempts to modernize his country by having roads built, installing electricity to certain areas, and attempting to unify the diverse tribes and factions of Afghanistan. The King was undergoing eye surgery in Italy in July 1973 when his cousin, former Prime Minister Mohammed Daoud, staged a coup. The king abdicated rather than returning to his country and risking civil war.

For the next 29 years he lived in exile in a modest villa north of Rome. During the period of Soviet-backed communist government in Afghanistan, he was forbidden to return to his homeland. During the Soviet-Afghan war in 1983 it was rumored that he was attempting to form a government in exile. When Afghanistan came under NATO occupation, Mohammed Zahir finally returned home in 2002. There were calls for him to return to the throne after the Taliban lost control, but the new government followed the advice of the United States and resisted the restoration of the monarchy.

In 2004, feeble from declining health, he attended the inauguration of Hamid Karzai as president. The last king of Afghanistan died in July 2007 and was buried in the Royal Mausoleum in Kabul.

Friday, October 4, 1963: Emperor Haile Selassie of Ethiopia

The Emperor of Ethiopia, Haile Selassie, arrived in New York City for a brief visit that included a speech at the United Nations. The day before he delivered the speech, however, he became one of the small group of people who received a second ticker tape welcome *(see: June 1, 1954)*. Still looking spry and robust despite his 71 years, the diminutive Emperor took his seat in the rear of a white convertible for the trip from Bowling Green to City Hall.

The First Army Band led the motorcade up the Canyon of Heroes. Military detachments from the Army, Navy, Marine Corps, and Air Force provided an escort, as did a squad of mounted policemen. A brisk wind blew up the man-made Broadway canyon and the ticker tape that streamed down whirled, twisted, and danced in the early autumn sunlight. The Emperor shared the vehicle with Richard Patterson, Chairman of the Reception Committee; his aide-de-camp Brigadier General Assefa Demissi; and Angier Biddle Duke, United States Chief of Protocol. Mr. Patterson and the African statesman smiled broadly at the crowds lining the street. As he had done nine years earlier, the Emperor wore a khaki-colored military uniform with many rows of military decorations, and a black cape draped over his shoulders.

Five blocks south of City Hall, Emperor Selassie asked for the motorcade to halt. Stepping out of the car, he walked the remaining distance. A woman carrying a stenographer's pad darted from the crowd twice and tried to approach the ruler but both times she was stopped by security personnel. It was later learned she was a reporter from a small French newspaper who was seeking an exclusive comment. Undeterred by her interruptions, the Emperor continued at a lively pace to City Hall Park. His walk increased the volume of cheers from the parade's onlookers, and much to the concern of his security detail, he approached the curb several times to shake hands with spectators holding small Ethiopian flags.

At City Hall, Mayor Wagner welcomed the Emperor back to New York. He was again given a Medal of Honor and told how much he was respected and admired by the city and all Americans. Speaking in his native tongue of Amharic, he explained why he had walked the last few blocks. "Because of New York's special consideration for us this day, we give this small token of having done something out of the ordinary." The Emperor concluded by saying that it had always been his wish to return to the city.

A reception at the Plaza Hotel followed, attended exclusively by members of the United Nations Diplomatic Corps. That evening, Emperor Selassie and his party were guests of Ralph Parsons, chairman of a mining and engineering company with several concessions in Ethiopia. The dinner was aboard Mr. Parsons' 190-foot yacht, the *Argo*, and included a sightseeing tour of New York Harbor.

The following day the Emperor addressed the United Nations. "Here in this Assembly," he said. "reposes the best – perhaps the last – hope for the peaceful survival of mankind." Unlike his 1935 address to the League of Nations, during which several delegates interrupted him with catcalls and walked out, his address to the United Nations received a standing ovation, led by the delegation from Italy, the country that had invaded Ethiopia in 1935.

Emperor Selassie flew back to his country three days later after a brief meeting with President Kennedy in Washington. Within two months the Emperor returned to the United States as one of the world leaders attending the funeral of the assassinated President.

The Emperor faced growing unrest in his nation. Despite efforts at modernization much of Ethiopia's population suffered from hunger and unemployment. In the early 1970s, famine in northeastern Ethiopia took the lives of between 60,000 and 80,000 people, causing widespread unrest. A small group of Communists gained power and overthrew the Ethiopian monarchy, which claimed to have been in place for 3,000 years since the time of King Solomon. Haile Selassie was imprisoned in the Grand Palace in Addis Ababa, and most of the royal family either fled the country or were killed. In August 1975, the Ethiopian Provisional government reported that "the ex-monarch" had died following prostate surgery, though it was later established that he had been poisoned. When the pro-communist Provisional Government was overthrown in 1991, Haile Selassie's remains were found under a latrine in the palace grounds. They were disinterred and placed in the Ethiopian Orthodox Cathedral in Addis Ababa, after the government refused attempts made by leaders of the Rastafarian Movement, which considers Haile Selassie to be the reincarnation of the Messiah, to have his remains buried in the Caribbean island nation of Jamaica.

Thursday, January 17, 1964: Antonio Segni, President of Italy

New York was the last stop on a five-day visit to the United States for Italy's President Antonio Segni. A lawyer born in 1891, he had briefly been involved in politics after World War I but became a university professor when Mussolini rose to power in the 1920s. After World War II, though, he returned to politics and was one of the founders of Italy's Christian Democratic party. He held several ministerial positions through the 1950s, becoming Prime Minister twice before being elected President in 1962. The first stop on his visit to the United States was Washington DC, where he met with President Johnson, paid respects at the grave of President Kennedy, and met with Cabinet members and Congressional leaders to promote closer relations between Italy and the United States.

As is customary for foreign dignitaries, New York City planned a ticker tape parade for his arrival, followed by an official welcoming ceremony at City Hall, after which President Segni was scheduled to speak at the United Nations.

But at the last minute, the State Department asked that the parade be cancelled, based on the weather forecast. The Italian President was 72 years old, with low blood pressure and a high dislike for cold weather. The US and Italian governments decided that he "should not be asked to expose himself to wintry blasts in a ride up Broadway in an open car," according to a report in the *New York Times*.

The morning of the parade was cloudless and bright, but temperatures were in the low 30s, and a cold wind did blow all day. President Segni began his day with a breakfast at the Waldorf with Mayor Wagner and Cardinal Francis Spellman, then was driven in a bubble-top limousine to City Hall.

A red carpet was laid out from the street to the steps of City Hall, where a dais had been set up in anticipation of the cancelled parade. Italian flags flew in the cold wind, and the two bands and 250 sailors, soldiers and marines who would have paraded up Broadway were assembled in the plaza.

A small crowd of about 230 spectators watched as Mayor Wagner officially greeted the President, who wore a heavy dark overcoat and white silk scarf. They exchanged gifts, the Mayor receiving a piece of stone from Verrazano Castle in Italy, then briefly answered questions from reporters before the President returned to his limousine. One city hall employee said, "for a head of state, this is the smallest crowd I've ever seen."

A small police motorcade of six cars escorted the President to the United Nations for a lunch with Secretary General U Thant and other ambassadors. Later that day, President Segni attended a reception at the Metropolitan Club, where he discussed improvements in the Italian economy after the war. He returned to Italy the next day.

His term as President was cut short later that year. In August, Segni suffered a cerebral hemorrhage, and shortly later he resigned from office because of his health problems. He died in Rome in 1972 at the age of 81.

Thursday, July 16, 1964: Crews of Operation Sail Vessels

"It's a good day for a parade," one policeman was quoted as saying with a broad grin on his face, as the parade to celebrate New York City's 300th anniversary marched up Broadway.

The marchers came from 13 countries: Argentina, Canada, Chile, Denmark, Germany, Great Britain, Indonesia, Italy, Japan, Norway, Portugal, Spain and the United States. They included cadets, seamen, weathered veterans, and officers who still rode the waves in sailing ships. A handful were in their early teens, others in their sixties. Many were in training for naval careers in their respective countries. They sailed in wind-powered barques and brigs, schooners and sloops, brigantines and barkentines, and full-rigged ships. They were marching up Broadway, 2,500 strong, to celebrate the city's tricentennial and the World's Fair being staged at Flushing Meadow Park in Queens County.

The flags of the 13 nations fluttered above the parade route on a sunny summer day as the Police Department Band and the First Army Band led the way. Their trumpets and drums were accompanied by musical contingents from Germany, Great Britain, and Indonesia. Some marched expressionless as befitting naval cadets, but most could not resist the urge to smile and return the waves of the more than 100,000 cheering lunchtime spectators.

The 140-man crew of the West German bark *Gorch Fock* wore "highly polished black sea boots and open tunics with blue trim" and a flat cap from which a long black streamer hung. Even though the crew from the American ship *Eagle* were Coast

Guardsmen, the German contingent looked like the most military group. Marching behind their native band, the Indonesian crew of the barkentine *Dewarutji* seemed almost festive. As they reached the corner of Broadway and Wall Street a small group of young Indonesian women, dressed in bright green and yellow sarongs, pushed their way passed the barricades and ran into the street, clapping, cheering, and kissing their countrymen.

At City Hall, giant birthday cakes were presented by the crews. Mayor Wagner was surrounded by high-ranking officers from most of the nations present as he accepted the cakes, and they were carried into City Hall for the afternoon's reception. Unable to present the city's Gold Key to each participant in the event because of their number, Mayor Wagner symbolically presented one to a Norwegian cadet, Hans Lambach. The ship he sailed on, the full-rigged *Christian Radich*, had just won the transatlantic race from Lisbon to Bermuda

Retired Rear Admiral John Bergen spoke briefly of the valor of those who "still go down to the sea in sailing ships." He commented on the distances they had traveled to attend the ceremony, noting that the Indonesian vessel left its native waters in March in order to reach New York by mid-July. He concluded his remarks with a wish of "good sailing and fair winds on your way home."

Mayor Wagner had proclaimed July 16 to 23 as Operation Sail Week. Most of the vessels were open to the public, and thousands of New Yorkers and tourists visited them that week. There have been five more "Op Sail" events in New York, in 1976, 1986, 1992, 2000, and 2012, though only one more would receive a ticker tape parade *(see: July 7, 1976)*. The Coast Guard's barque *Eagle* has served as the official host vessel of each.

It was indeed a good day for a parade.

Thursday, September 3, 1964:
Staten Island Mid-Island Little League All Stars

When 12-year-old Daniel Yaccarino threw the last pitch of his no-hitter victory over the team from Monterrey, Mexico, to win the 1964 Little League World Series neither the team nor their coach expected to receive a ticker tape parade. But thanks to the efforts of Staten Island Borough President Albert Maniscalco, they got one, a parade that all the team would remember for a lifetime.

Escorted by proud parents, all 16 members of the team gathered at Bowling Green with their manager, William Rogers, and coach Robert Klee. Waiting there to carry them up Broadway were not just limousines, but 17 of them. The team's manager and coach were directed to the lead vehicle, and each of the players had a vehicle for himself and his parents. The parade began on a bright late summer afternoon just as the noontime lunch hour began. The Police Department band struck up a tune and the motorcade started up the same route that had been taken by kings and queens, presidents and prime ministers, Olympians, aviators, astronauts, and war veterans. A squad of motorcycle police, sirens blaring, rode at the flanks of the cars.

The players, wearing their white and blue uniforms, waved and smiled as the cars moved north. Streamers of ticker tape floated down, draping the cars and their occupants. The boys and their parents echoed the cheers of the almost 50,000 people who crowded the route.

Mayor Wagner and Borough President Maniscalco greeted the team when the motorcade halted in City Hall Plaza. A 12-foot-long red carpet stretched from the curb to

City Hall steps. The mayor congratulated each player as they stepped to the reviewing stand and presented each with a tie clip bearing the city's seal. He then read a proclamation that spoke of the team's eight consecutive victories to win the title. The scroll, which the Mayor presented to manager Rogers, announced that the period from the beginning of the Little League World Series on August 20 to September 3 would be known as "Little League Championship time."

Turning to the players' parents, the mayor praised them "for the fine job they do by encouraging and building this wonderful program." The Borough President spoke next, boasting of the talent that "could only come from Staten Island." The team's pitcher, Danny Yaccarino, concluded the ceremonies with words of thanks and gave the mayor two baseballs autographed by all the team members, one for the mayor and the other for his son, Duncan.

Founded in 1947, the Little League World Championship was originally open to just US teams. Starting in 1970, international teams could compete, and teams from both Taiwan and Japan have won more than 10 times, more than any country other than the US. The games are held in Williamsport, Pennsylvania every August, except 2020 because of the Covid-19 pandemic.

Thursday, October 8, 1964:
Diosdado Macapagal, President of the Philippines

President Macapagal of the Philippines came to the United States along with his wife Evangelina and 17-year-old daughter Gloria, for a 12-day visit. The first stop was Washington, DC where he spent two days meeting with President Lyndon Johnson and Congressional leaders. The next stop was New York City, and the city turned out to welcome him with a ticker tape parade.

The 54-year-old president and his family arrived at the newly renamed JFK International Airport and rode to Bowling Green in a bulletproof limousine. As soon as they reached the parade's starting point, he left the limo and switched to an open top car.

The parade began, led by two Navy bands and two truckloads of photographers. Lunchtime crowds, in some places two and three deep, lined the route, some waving Philippine flags. As usual, the air was filled with streamers and ribbons of ticker tape, confetti, and paper.

Three blocks shy of City Hall, President Macapagal told the driver to stop the car. He jumped out of the vehicle, ran to the police barricades, and began to shake the hands of bystanders. Security personnel swarmed around him, trying to separate him from the well-wishers but it was to no avail. The broadly smiling president was enjoying the crowd and the crowd was enjoying him. Both trucks of photographers emptied almost as quickly as the president left his car. The president continued north as security men tried to cordon him off from the crowd, photographers kept snapping pictures, and police struggled to keep the crowd from breaking through the barricades and joining the president in his slow procession to City Hall. His wife and daughter remained in the open vehicle, keeping pace with the president.

Mayor Wagner greeted the president as he approached the City Hall Plaza entrance. The Sanitation Department Band played the national anthems of the United States and the Philippines as the Mayor officially welcomed the president to New York and presented him with a desk set. Speaking in English, President Macapagal stated that his country was "a true friend and steadfast ally of the United States."

That evening the mayor hosted a reception for the president and his family at the St. Regis Hotel, followed by a dinner reception given by New York's Philippine community at the Hotel Astor. His busy schedule left little time for sightseeing: he met with UN Secretary General U Thant, visited the World's Fair, and received an honorary degree from Fordham University during his visit to the city.

President Macapagal was the ninth president of his island nation. He served one more year after his New York visit before being defeated by Ferdinand Marcos in 1965. Macapagal retired from politics but served as President of the 1971 Constitution Convention. As President Marcos' administration became more corrupt and dictatorial, Macapagal created the new National Union for Liberation Party. When democracy returned to his country, he served on the Council of State and began writing a weekly column for the *Manila Bulletin*. He died of pneumonia and kidney problems in 1997 and the age of 87.

Monday, March 29, 1965:
Virgil Grissom and John Young, Gemini 3 Astronauts

Ticker tape parades have been held under varying weather conditions, from New York's hot, hazy and humid summer days, to below-freezing days when snow competed with the paper falling from the skies. Among the worst was the parade that honored the two-man crew of the Gemini 3 mission, Virgil "Gus" Grissom and John Young. Gemini 3 was the first mission to conduct orbital maneuvers, changing the altitude of their orbit in flight.

The pouring rain was blown by a stiff raw wind. Despite the weather, the two astronauts entered a Lincoln convertible at noon for the slow ride up Broadway to City Hall. Seated between them was Vice President Hubert Humphrey, who had arrived at LaGuardia Airport an hour earlier. To waiting reporters he said, "The people of the United States are proud of the achievements of these two young men, and I am sure that New York, rain or no rain, will give them a welcome the likes of which they have never had." Led by 40 motorcycle police, the motorcade began a few minutes after noon, consisting of an Army band and 20 cars. Some were convertibles like the one in which the astronauts and Vice President sat, but the majority were sedans.

Even in the midst of the deluge, New Yorkers turned out to welcome the daring space explorers. Although small in comparison to other parades, more than 50,000 spectators lined the route, creating a sea of black umbrellas. Some were brave enough, or perhaps just foolhardy, to stand uncovered, shivering in the cold.

More than 5,000 pounds of paper and tape had been provided by the Department of Public Events to buildings along the route. Added to this were the usual ticker tape, confetti, torn newspapers, and toilet tissue dropped from windows along the route. Much of it fell in sodden clumps or was blown this way and that in the crosswinds of Broadway, yet shortly after the procession began Major Grissom, Commander Young, and Vice President Humphrey were decorated with streams of tape and confetti. The car's wipers fought a losing battle to clear the windshield. People along the route cheered and shouted, "Good work, Gus!" and "Attaboy, John!" Many along the route admitted that they saw nothing of the astronauts because of the obstructing umbrellas but still they cheered.

When the convertible finally discharged its passengers at City Hall, Mayor Wagner led them inside for a few minutes to dry off and warm up. Among the portraits of former New York Governors hangs one of the state's 15th governor, John Young

(1847-1849). The mayor pointed it out to Commander Young, who smiled, shook his head, and said, "No relation."

A few minutes later the two astronauts and the Vice President joined Mayor Wagner on the portico steps, once more stepping out into the driving rain, joined by Dr. Robert Seamans, Associate Administrator of NASA. Everyone was drenched: dignitaries, bandsmen, reporters, photographers, spectators. The band resumed playing, the reception was hurried, and speeches were kept short. Richard Patterson, Chairman of Public Events, introduced the Vice President, the astronauts, and Dr. Seamans to the hundreds of spectators braving the elements in City Hall Park. Mayor Wagner presented the city's Gold Medal of Honor to the astronauts and the NASA administrator. With rain streaming down his forehead, the Vice President extended his gratitude for all the work NASA was doing. Dr. Seamans provided the final words when he thanked the American public for its support of the space program.

Shortly before 1 o'clock, the astronauts were driven in a closed vehicle to the United Nations, where Secretary General U Thant congratulated them and presented them with a complete autographed set of United Nations stamps. Lunch followed, limited to a small number of invited guests. Major Grissom was selected to say a few words and few it was. Born in Mitchell, Indiana, all he said was "We were overwhelmed by New York, as all small-town boys should be."

That evening a dry and rested pair of astronauts attended a performance of *Hello, Dolly!* and ended the evening at a cocktail party at the 21 Club. The following day they left for a brief visit to Newark and flew to Chicago.

Major Grissom was one of NASA's original astronauts in the Mercury Seven team *(see: March 1, 1962)*, and later was assigned to the Apollo program. On Jan 27, 1967, Grissom and fellow astronauts Ed White and Roger Chaffee were killed when a fire broke out in their module in a pre-launch test.

Commander Young, born in the not-so-small town of San Francisco, was the longest-serving astronaut. He was the first person to orbit the moon alone and was the only man to go to the moon twice. In 1972 he became the ninth person to walk on the moon. He retired from NASA in 2004 and died in Houston, Texas, in January 2018.

Wednesday, May 19, 1965:
Chung Hee Park, President of South Korea

A former four-star general in the South Korean Army who seized power in a coup in 1963, Chung Hee Park arrived in New York from Washington. While in the capital, he spent two days meeting with President Johnson, Secretary of State Dean Rusk, and Secretary of Defense Robert McNamara. The president and his wife, Yak Young-soo, landed at JFK International Airport at 11 o'clock, accompanied by Korean military and civilian advisors as well as US State Department representatives.

The presidential party was greeted at the airport by New York City officials. Two small children, a 7-year-old girl and her 6-year-old brother, stepped forward and presented bouquets of red roses to the Korean leader and his wife. Dressed in traditional Korean clothes, the children, Dinah and Dean Surh, were joined by their father, a wealthy Korean importer who spoke briefly to the president in Korean.

Escorted by a squadron of motorcycle police and police cars, sirens screaming and lights flashing, the presidential party sped into Manhattan for the start of the scheduled parade at Bowling Green, arriving shortly after noon. President Park entered an open white car with his wife seated beside him. A long caravan of other vehicles formed a line behind the president's car, and at a signal the parade began. A military band, detachments from the Army, Navy, Air Force, and Marine Corps, and a color guard provided by the Police Department completed the marching contingent. Groups of Koreans were among the spectators along the route, many waving Korean flags. Ticker tape fell from buildings along the way and Broadway echoed with the sound of cheering.

At City Hall, Mayor Wagner greeted the Korean leader. The military band played the Korean and American national anthems and the mayor presented Mr. Park with a scroll that praised his "sterling leadership in the cause of freedom." Expressing gratitude for the city's welcome, the president spoke in Korean, his words translated by a State Department official.

The ceremony at City Hall was followed by a reception at the Waldorf Astoria. President Park, commander of a division in the Korean War 15 years earlier, was awarded the city's Gold Medal of Honor. The mayor spoke of President Park's strong anti-Communist stand and the steps being taken by his government to modernize the industrial might of South Korea.

The president remained in New York three days, including a trip to West Point. Before returning to his country, he visited Philadelphia, Miami, and Los Angeles.

President Park won re-election in 1967 but not long afterwards was responsible for changes to the constitution that allowed for a third four-year term. After being re-elected in 1971 the constitution was changed again to allow for a six-year term of office with no term limits. Despite his growing dictatorial leadership, he was successful in modernizing Korea's industries, and the standard of living for many of his countryman rose sharply. His style of leadership and impositions on civil liberties, however, were unpopular among many Koreans. At the request of both the Johnson and Nixon administrations, he sent Korean troops to fight alongside United States forces in Vietnam, and eventually more than 300,000 South Koreans saw service there. In return, South Korea received tens of billions of dollars in loans, grants, and other incentives.

On August 14, 1974 while delivering a speech at the National Theater in Seoul shots were fired at him by a presumed agent of North Korea. None of the bullets hit him but his wife, sitting at his side, was fatally wounded. While his wife was carried off the stage, President Park resumed and finished his speech. His wife died the next day.

On October 26, 1979, the leader and other members of the Korean Central Intelligence Agency shot and killed President Park during dinner in the presidential compound in Seoul. In the turmoil that followed, the assassins were eventually captured, tried, and executed.

Tuesday, June 1, 1965:
100th Anniversary of the Fire Department of New York

The First Army Band and the Police Department's Emerald Society Band escorted 4,500 firemen up the Canyon of Heroes to celebrate the 100th anniversary of the founding of the Fire Department of New York (FDNY), which had replaced a hodge-podge system of volunteer fire brigades. More than one quarter of the city's Fire Department, all off duty for the day, marched from Bowling Green to City Hall for the third ticker tape parade given by the city to New York's Bravest (see: March 31, 1954 and April 15, 1955).

As with the two previous fire department parades, old and new pieces of fire-fighting equipment were featured. Russell Bleecker, Honorary Fire Chief, was driven up Broadway in a 1920 Model T Ford chief's car. In the rear was Fireman Edward Miller, who sat in a wheelchair because of a broken leg he suffered while fighting a fire two months earlier. A major feature of the parade was the "Super Pumper," a huge new truck recently purchased for $800,000 and being displayed for the first time.

The route was lined with spectators, four or five deep in places. Ticker tape swirled down, most plentifully in the area around Wall Street. Strands of paper wrapped itself around the spire of Trinity Church and among the monuments in Trinity Churchyard.

When the Fire Department's centennial parade was first planned it was suggested that every professional and volunteer fire department in the state be invited to participate. This idea was scrapped, however, when it was estimated that such a parade would take a minimum of 11 hours from start to finish.

Mayor Wagner hailed the Fire Department as it paraded past City Hall, referring to it as "the bravest of the brave." He spoke of the growth of the department over the previous ten years and remembered fire-fighters who had given their lives protecting the city and its people during its first 100 years.

When Mayor Wagner spoke those words, 609 members of the Department had died in the line of duty since its founding. That figure has more than doubled since then, including 343 who died on September 11, 2001 when the World Trade Center collapsed.

The city and its people have changed a lot in the more than 150 years since the FDNY was founded, and the department has too. As of 2020, the department has grown to over 17,000 employees, including over 10,000 fire and 4,000 emergency medical services personnel. With an annual budget of over $2 billion and 254 fire stations throughout the city, it is the largest municipal fire department in the country, and second in the world behind Tokyo.

Friday, January 10, 1969: Frank Borman, James Lovell, and William Anders, Apollo 8 Astronauts

The sky was gray and overcast, the thermometer read 28 degrees, and the wind gusted to more than 25 miles per hour. Despite these conditions, almost a quarter million people lined Lower Broadway to welcome astronauts Colonel Frank Borman, Captain James Lovell, and Lieutenant Colonel William Anders to New York. As the crew of the Apollo 8 Mission to the Moon, they were the first humans to see the far side of the moon. On this bleak, inhospitable day they were to see how New York welcomes heroes.

Shortly before 11 o'clock that morning, the astronauts arrived at LaGuardia Airport. They were met by only a handful of shivering greeters, including Francis Smith, Chairman of the Mayor's Reception Committee and Colonel Courtland Schuyler, State Commissioner of General Services, representing Governor Nelson Rockefeller. As the astronauts shook hands with Mr. Smith and Colonel Schuyler, the bagpipe band of the Emerald Society of the Police Department piped a welcome. Dressed in kilts, the pipers' knees could be seen turning red from the cold. The astronauts and their two greeters drove across the Triborough Bridge and down the East River Drive to the traditional parade starting point at Bowling Green. Few spectators stood along their route as they sped to their destination in a closed limousine

At Bowling Green, the astronauts changed vehicles and sat in the rear of an open car, wrapped in heavy coats and blankets, joined by Mayor John Lindsay, wearing a Russian-style fur hat, and Governor Rockefeller, hatless but wearing heavy ski gloves.

Both politicians sat in the car's jump seats. A few minutes after noon the parade began, led by detachments from the Army, Navy, and Air Force, contingents from the Police and Fire Departments, and two marching bands.

Broadway had been unofficially renamed for the day, and street signs along the route read "Apollo Way." Huge crowds of people were seen at the windows of the skyscrapers along the route, but few windows were open because of the cold wind. Despite the weather, the motorcade was greeted by a blizzard not of snow, but of confetti, computer paper, and rolls of toilet tissue and paper towel. The Sanitation Department estimated that only 200 tons of debris was cleaned up after the parade, attributing the small amount to the combination of cold, sealed windows, and Hong Kong flu which was rampant in the city at the time.

As the parade entered City Hall Plaza, it passed beneath an inverted V arch formed by the extended ladders of two fire department vehicles. Eight American flags, signifying the Apollo Mission's number, flapped furiously from the arch, whipping back and forth in the gusty wind. Colonel Anders, his teeth chattering and his nose and cheeks a rosy red, was overheard saying as he exited his car, "I wish I'd brought my space suit." Led to the reviewing stand, each astronauts received the city's Medal of Honor. When Colonel Borman, acting as spokesman for the trio, had the medal placed around his neck, he stepped to the microphone and said, "We all love New York, and we all love you." His statement brought a cheer from the frozen four to five hundred people standing in City Hall Plaza.

Joined by their wives after the brief outdoor ceremony, the astronauts were driven to the New York State Theater at Lincoln Center for a luncheon, pausing at Centre Street so the trio of space explorers could review a Police Department Honor Guard, and again at 14th Street where they were briefly serenaded by the Salvation Army Band.

The luncheon was attended by 550 invited guests. An opening invocation was delivered by Roman Catholic Archbishop Terrence Cooke. On each table was a centerpiece with a plastic model of the moon. Seated at the head table were the astronauts and the wives, the mayor and his wife Mary Anne; their centerpiece was a similar plastic moon with a model of Apollo 8 attached. When somebody pointed out that the plastic capsule was incorrectly circling the moon counterclockwise, the mayor joked, "Only in New York." Shortly afterwards, a photographer's five-pound lens fell from the balcony overlooking the diners. It crashed on a table below, narrowly missing the table's occupants, but showering them all with bits of broken glass, china, and wine. At the end of the luncheon, attendees were overly eager to obtain photos and autographs from the astronauts. In the resulting crush with the newsmen and photographers, a number of people were knocked over and some women's dresses or gowns were torn. Fortunately, no one was injured.

The afternoon's activities ended with a visit to the United Nations, where the astronauts were introduced to the General Assembly by Secretary General U Thant. Colonel Borman acted as spokesman and delivered a short speech on the hopes of world peace through mutual space exploration. The trio was given a 70-second standing ovation before they departed.

Colonel Frank Borman retired from NASA in 1975 and was named CEO of Eastern Airlines, remaining with them until 1986. As of 2020, he lives in New Mexico where he rebuilds and flies World War II and Korean War era airplanes. At 92, he is the oldest living astronaut.

James Lovell later commanded Apollo 13 and successfully brought the capsule home after it malfunctioned in space. He played a bit part in the film *Apollo 13* as the captain of the ship that picks up the astronauts. He retired from NASA in 1973 and owned a restaurant in Illinois until 2015. Also aged 92, he is 11 days younger than Frank Borman.

William Anders was named Executive Secretary of NASA in 1969. In 1975, President Gerald Ford appointed him Ambassador to Norway and he served until 1977. He was then named first Chairman of the Nuclear Regulatory Agency. Now retired, he lives in Washington state. One of the photographs he took during the Apollo 8 mission, called *Earthrise*, has been called one of the "most influential environmental photographs of all time."

Mayor John Lindsay (1966-1973)

Born in Manhattan in 1921, John Lindsay became interested in politics at an early age. Soon after graduating from Yale Law School in 1948, he helped found the NY Young Republicans Club and began working at the Department of Justice, then was elected to Congress in 1958. A liberal, he often found himself at odds with his own party, supporting programs like Medicare and the creation of the Department of Housing and Urban Development.

In 1965, Lindsay ran for Mayor of New York on the Republican and Liberal party tickets, defeating Democrat Abe Beame and Conservative William F. Buckley. On his first day in office, the city's transportation system was shut down by a massive strike that lasted 12 days. Other strikes affecting city schools, Broadway theaters and the sanitation department also occurred while he was in office. The settlements he made to end these strikes worsened the city's financial situation, despite new taxes that Lindsay lobbied for and implemented. A blizzard in 1969 kept parts of the city snowbound for over a week, and almost cost him his re-election that year when the Republican party refused to nominate him. Campaigning on a slogan that "mistakes were made," he narrowly won re-election, only to be faced with more crises when construction workers rioted against anti-war protestors and new reports of police corruption erupted in the news.

In 1971, he switched parties and ran in the Democratic primary for President, but the negative national image of New York as a city in crisis plagued him. Finishing his second term as mayor, he was described as an "exile in his own city." He returned to his law practice, then tried to return to politics in 1980 with an unsuccessful bid for the US Senate. Suffering from Parkinson's disease and the after-effects of two strokes, he moved to South Carolina and died in 2000.

Wednesday, January 22, 1969:
New York Jets, Super Bowl III Champions

It is one of the greatest upsets in American football.

Despite the prediction that "Broadway Joe" Namath made three days before the big game, few people believed the New York Jets would win the Super Bowl. This was the third annual championship game between the winners of the National and American Football Leagues, and the first year that the game was officially called the "Super Bowl." The NFL had dominated pro football for decades, while the AFL had only been founded in 1959. By the mid 1960s talks were already underway which led to the merger that created the season-ending championship game. Considered by many to be the superior league, NFL teams had easily won the first two championships, and the

Baltimore Colts were heavily favored to win the third one. So, when Jets quarterback Joe Namath personally guaranteed that his team would win, many viewers laughed.

The laughter ended soon after the big game began, as the Jets dominated the field and quickly took the lead. After the Florida A&M University Band provided the halftime entertainment, the Jets widened their lead, and though the Colts finally scored in the fourth quarter, it was too late. The New York Jets had won.

An excited crowd had begun gathering outside City Hall as early as 8 o'clock in the morning, eager to celebrate the stunning upset. By noon, over 6,000 spectators and fans watched as Mayor Lindsay emerged from City Hall. Behind him came the game's Most Valuable Player, Joe Namath, and the crowd erupted into cheers as he and the rest of the Jets gathered around the mayor, who proclaimed the day as "New York Jets Championship Day."

Team president Philip Iselin held up the silver championship trophy, and the crowd roared again in approval. The mayor then introduced each player to the spectators while presenting them with gifts from the city, a tie clasp and pair of cufflinks engraved with the city's seal. Namath and Defensive Captain John Sample were both also given bronze medallions, and the team presented the mayor with a framed painting of Namath in action.

The ceremony was over in less than 20 minutes, and the team hustled into six waiting limousines. Proceeded by an escort of motorcycle police, the caravan drove uptown on Sixth Avenue, as midday crowds cheered and waved at them. When they arrived at Mamma Leone's restaurant on 48th Street, the side streets were packed with fans. The luncheon was sponsored by Sport magazine, and editor Al Silverman was on hand to award Namath the keys to a new sports car, a prize the magazine gave to the winner of its annual pro football award.

There was no parade, however, and the city's football fans would have to wait almost 40 years for the first ticker tape parade honoring a football team, when the New York Giants won Super Bowl XLII *(see: February 5, 2008)*. Mayor Lindsay had often questioned the value and cost of such parades, but that did not prevent a parade when the New York Mets won the World Series later in 1969 *(see: October 20, 1969)*. As Daily News columnist Denis Hamill wrote on January 29, 2014, the real reason why there was no parade for the Jets may be because of Wellington Mara, the co-owner of the city's other football team, the NY Giants. According to Hamill, Mara threatened to move the Giants to New Jersey if the Jets received a ticker tape parade and the mayor caved.

The merger of the AFL and NFL was completed in 1970, resulting in two "conferences" instead of "leagues." The annual Super Bowl has become one of the biggest sporting events in America, with millions of dollars in advertising spent reaching its enormous TV viewership. The quality and name recognition of the halftime entertainment has also grown significantly. The New York Jets have not, however, returned to the big game; although they made it to the AFC championships several times since 1969, they have failed to win it.

Super Bowl III was the high point of Joe Namath's career. He continued playing with the Jets, but injuries would force him to miss games, and in 1976 he made the daring risk of joining the Chicago Winds in the short-lived World Football League. He spent one season with the Los Angeles Rams before retiring from the game. He appeared in several movies and TV shows and legitimized his nickname by appearing in a Broadway revival of The Caine Mutiny Court Martial in 1983. As of 2020, he is 77 years old and lives in Florida.

Wednesday, August 13, 1969: Neil Armstrong, Edwin Aldrin, and Michael Collins, Apollo 11 Astronauts

The three astronauts of the Apollo 11 mission arrived in New York City from Houston, Texas at Kennedy Airport at 9:45 in the morning aboard the Presidential jet, Air Force One. It was their first stop in a whirlwind one-day transcontinental tour celebrating the NASA mission that landed a man on the moon for the first time.

The astronauts were met by Mayor Lindsay, who joked that they were 15 minutes early as he led them across the tarmac to a waiting Marine Corps helicopter. Once inside, the group was flown to the heliport site near the Battery. As the helicopter touched down, a waiting fireboat off the Battery shot six huge sprays into the air. Ships and boats of all kinds in the harbor sounded their whistles and horns. The city's Public Events Commissioner, John "Bud" Palmer, escorted the astronauts to a fleet of limousines standing in line awaiting the group. An army band began to play marching music, while detachments from the Army, Navy, Air Force, and Marine Corps stepped out. An escort of motorcycle-riding police flanked the motorcade, and at 10 o'clock the procession began, almost 30 minutes ahead of schedule.

Mr. Palmer estimated that the crowd of spectators was the largest ever to view a parade, claiming that the number exceeded four million. Other individuals put the number at much less, possibly as little as two million, but admitted that the crowd would have been even larger had the parade not started early.

Small amounts of ticker tape streamed down, not because of a lack of interest but because so few companies still used it. Instead, shredded paper, confetti, computer paper and punch cards, paper towels, and even rolls of toilet paper rained down, blanketing Broadway and the surrounding streets. Riding in the first car of the motorcade, the three astronauts were soon draped in paper. They waved to the cheering crowds, pointing right and left and upwards as more and more paper descended.

Traveling much faster up Broadway than previous parades, the motorcade arrived at City Hall 49 minutes ahead of schedule. As the astronauts stepped from their vehicle, the First Army Band from Governors Island began to play Richard Strauss' Also Sprach Zarathustra, the theme music from the film 2001: A Space Odyssey. The mayor led the astronauts to the podium where they were joined by U Thant, Secretary General of the United Nations. The mayor introduced each of the astronauts, two of whom, Neil Armstrong and Edwin "Buzz" Aldrin, had made a giant leap for mankind by stepping onto the moon. Then the mayor presented them with the city's Gold Medal suspended from a blue ribbon embroidered with the city seal. "This is one of New York's greatest moments," the mayor said, his words nearly drowned out by the roar of the massive crowd in City Hall Plaza and adjoining Park Row, Chambers Street, and Broadway.

Mission Commander Neil Armstrong, the first human to walk on the moon, spoke first. "The true mission of Apollo 11 was to show us again what mankind can do." Astronaut Michael Collins, the member of the team who remained in the lunar module during the entire mission, said, "This is the proudest day of my life." Colonel Aldrin spoke last. "We should be congratulating you for your support," he remarked, "the support that made this mission possible."

The motorcade, which now included Mr. Thant, continued north to the United Nations. Sadly, there were three minor casualties in City Hall Park, when a tree branch snapped under the weight of spectators hoping for a better view, falling onto two women and a child. The motorcade sped north with crowds lining the entire route to the United Nations at 42nd Street and First Avenue. Delegates from 50 of the 126 member nations crowded onto the UN grounds as the motorcade halted and Armstrong spoke briefly. He said that the small plaque they had left on the moon contained the words: "We came in peace for all mankind."

The stop at the UN took only 11 minutes. The motorcade then crossed the Queensboro Bridge and drove to Kennedy Airport. Although the parade had been ahead of schedule all morning, the traffic in Queens finally slowed their procession. Even with sirens blaring and lights flashing, they arrived at Hanger 17 at 1:15, exactly on schedule. As they boarded the plane for their next stop in Chicago before heading to Los Angeles, Colonel Collins joked, "I feel I have seen every New Yorker there is today."

NASA's Apollo program continued until 1972, when Apollo 17 was the last of six flights to land on the moon, and to date 12 American astronauts have walked on the lunar surface. As a retired Navy pilot, Neil Armstrong was the only civilian on the mission. It was his second space trip, having also flown in Gemini 8. He retired from NASA in 1971 but was appointed by President Ronald Reagan as Vice Chairman of the commission that studied the Challenger disaster. He retired at the age of 80, and died in Cincinnati, Ohio, in August 2012. According to his wishes his remains were cremated, and his ashes scattered over the Atlantic Ocean.

Colonel Edwin "Buzz" Aldrin retired from the Air Force and NASA in 1972. He chronicled his struggle to overcome clinical depression and alcoholism in his autobiography Magnificent Desolation. Though no longer connected with NASA, he has long been an advocate for manned missions to Mars, and currently lives in Florida. Air Force Colonel Michael Collins retired in 1970 and was named Director of the Smithsonian's Air and Space Museum in Washington. He retired from that post in 1982 and lived in Florida until his death in 2021.

Monday, October 20, 1969:
New York Mets, World Series Champions

The New York Mets had greatly improved since their woeful first season *(see: April 12, 1962)*, but they were still far from championship level caliber. In fact, Vegas casinos set 100-1 odds against them even playing in the World Series in 1969, and in midsummer, they were behind both the Chicago Cubs and St. Louis Cardinals in the National League East division. But the team that called Shea Stadium home proved everybody wrong by doing the impossible. With a remarkable winning streak, they won 39 of their last 50 games to win the regular season. They then defeated the Atlanta Braves to become the National League champions and went on to win 1969 World Series over the Baltimore Orioles in just 5 games. Fans rejoiced, and the "Amazin' Mets" were celebrated on this sunny October day with a parade, three rallies, and a fireworks display.

At 10 in the morning on October 20, four days after the Mets won the Series, the festivities began with a rally at Shea Stadium. Thousands of faithful fans cheered when Mets manager Gil Hodges held high the World Series trophy and each member of his team was introduced. From the stadium in Queens, the players, coaches, trainers, and owners were sped to Bowling Green for the ticker tape parade.

Seated in limousines and on floats, the players moved up the Canyon of Heroes, accompanied by the Police and Fire Department Bands. Huge amounts of ticker tape streamed down, and hundreds of thousands cheered. At Beaver Street and Broadway, the crowds filled the streets and brought the parade to a halt for almost a half hour until police could clear the way and allow the Mets to reach City Hall.

The Sanitation Department reported that the amount of paper littering Broadway was surpassed only by the parades for General MacArthur *(see: April 20, 1951)* and Charles Lindbergh *(see: June 13, 1927)*. John "Bud" Palmer, Commission of the Department of Public Events, estimated the crowd as larger than the parade for the Apollo 11 crew *(see: August 13, 1969)*. The Police Department did not provide an official estimate, and a spokesman noted that "nobody knows exactly how to measure the crowds that watch from the curbs" before adding that this parade was one of the largest. In places along the route, the crowds broke through the police barricades, and the financial district was described as "one giant, happy mob scene."

Mayor John Lindsay welcomed the team at City Hall. Opera star and Mets fan Robert Merrill sang the National Anthem. Thousands of screaming, cheering, and applauding fans roared with approval when the mayor announced, "For eight years New York has loved this team and today they're #1. The Cardinals know it, the Cubs know it, the Braves know it, and now the Orioles know it. Thank you for giving us a summer of joy." He introduced each member of the team, starting with former Yankee great and current Mets first-base coach, Yogi Berra, and ending with the team's principal owner, Mrs. Joan Payson. Each player received a tie clip, a blue tie, and a pair of cuff links engraved with the city's emblem. Mrs. Payson was given a bouquet of roses.

From City Hall the motorcade proceeded to Bryant Park at 42nd Street and Fifth Avenue, where a second rally was held. Another celebrity Mets fan, singer Pearl Bailey, entertained the huge crowd singing the team's theme song, "Meet the Mets" and "Take Me Out to the Ball Game." The players then joined their wives or sweethearts for lunch at the Four Seasons Restaurant on East 52nd Street. At 5 o'clock the third rally of the day took place at Gracie Mansion, where thousands of fans jammed East End Avenue and Carl Schurz Park. When this rally finally concluded, the motorcade returned to Shea Stadium where a fireworks spectacle provided entertainment for even more fans who filled the stadium's parking lot and the Shea Stadium elevated subway station.

All sorts of paper had rained from the skies during the day, and Sanitation Department officials said that almost 600 tons of paper were cleaned up from the parade route. The debris included a "tremendous amount" of ticker tape, but also shredded newspapers, business reports, sales transaction slips, and a deluge of data punch cards "with their distinctive holes." Along one stretch of Broadway, heavy duty carbon paper was sprayed by Sanitation Department washers, dying the street purple. Over 600 sanitation employees used 150 pieces of equipment to clean the streets, costing an extra $28,000 in overtime.

The day's euphoria failed to propel the Mets to a successful season the following year, when they finished in third place. They played in the World Series again in 1973 but lost to the Oakland Athletics. Years of frustration and mediocre seasons followed, until 1986 when they defeated the Boston Red Sox to win another World Series *(see: October 28, 1986)*.

CHAPTER 9
Bankruptcy and Beyond (1970-1990)

A new advertising campaign began appearing on television in 1977, which has one of the longest-lasting, most imitated and most recognized slogans in the history of advertising. The campaign's simple, 4-character logo was created in the backseat of a taxicab one night and was accompanied by an equally simple jingle repeating the campaign's message:

I ♥ N Y

Designed by advertising executive Mary Wells and designer Milton Glaser, co-founder of the recently launched *New York* magazine, the campaign was the idea of the New York State Department of Economic Development, which hoped to attract tourism to both the city and state. Tourism was at an all-time low, and the city had lots of problems and a terrible image.

Crime was at an all-time high, for many reasons. Several extremist organizations had made news with violent attacks and bombings in the city. The 1970s had begun with an explosion in a Greenwich Village townhouse used by a militant radical group known as the Weathermen, and later that same year, members of the Black Liberation Army gunned down two police officers in Harlem. A paramilitary organization known by its Spanish acronym of FALN (or in English, the Armed Forces of National Liberation) carried out over 130 bombings between 1974 and 1983, including one in 1975 that killed 4 people and injured over 50 at Fraunces Tavern, a Pearl Street restaurant dating from the 1700s. A bomb exploded that same year in the baggage claim area of LaGuardia airport, killing 11 and injuring 75; nobody claimed responsibility, but rumors spread that either the FALN or the Palestine Liberation Organization were to blame.

Not all the crime was terrorism related, of course. New York had a growing number of crime families and gangs, including the Irish American gang called the Westies, which was warring with the Italian Mafia's Genovese family, resulting in as many as 100 murders. Meanwhile in the Bronx, the Black Spades waged a turf war with other gangs. Between late 1975 and the summer of 1977, a serial killer known in the newspapers as the "44-caliber killer" went on a shooting spree, killing 6 and wounding 7 in separate, random attacks. Calling himself the "Son of Sam," he would send letters to the newspapers after each attack mocking the police, who launched the city's biggest manhunt ever to capture him in August 1977.

The murder rate was climbing each year, from 630 in the mid 1960s to almost triple that 10 years later, as were other crimes like rape and burglaries, muggings and prostitution. Times Square was over-taken by porn theaters and peep shows, and a wave of arsons led sportscaster Howard Cosell to announce during a World Series game in 1977 that "the Bronx is burning." When another blackout darkened the city that summer, over 4,000 people were arrested for looting or arson, as over 1,600 stores were broken into and many fires were started, and damages totaled over $300 million from fire and vandalism.

Fear was running high in the city, leading more residents and businesses to leave, and New York was being portrayed as a lawless and trash-ridden wasteland of drugs, corruption and crime by movies set in the city. From *Taxi Driver* and *The French Connection* to *Dog Day Afternoon* and *The Taking of Pelham 123*, movies made the city look like it was out of control.

And in many ways, things were out of control.

The subway system, which many New Yorkers relied on for their daily commute, had become filthy and dangerous. Trains were covered in graffiti, stations smelled from uncollected trash, homeless people slept in stations and beggars panhandled in moving trains, many of which had broken doors and poor lighting. Mechanical breakdowns caused frequent delays and crime was rising. Despite three fare increases between 1970 and 1975, bringing the cost of a ride to 50 cents, the MTA's budget could not keep up with the cost of maintenance, cleaning and security, especially with the national economy experiencing double-digit inflation during the decade. Ridership was declining, further exacerbating the budget problems, and in 1975, the MTA shortened train lengths, reduced the number of trains operating, and deferred maintenance.

Confidence in the city government was also low. The NY Police Department was under investigation for widespread corruption, especially after the whistle-blowing testimony of Officer Frank Serpico, which came just months after 20,000 NYPD officers staged a 5-day work stoppage. In 1971, the union operating the city's bridges and sewers launched a strike, dumping billions of gallons of raw sewage into the city's rivers and blocking traffic by leaving drawbridges open. In July 1975, sanitation workers staged a wildcat strike, leaving piles of uncollected garbage to swelter in the summer heat, and in September schools were closed for another 5-day teachers' strike.

The city's budget problems were getting progressively worse and attempted fixes led to this on-going wave of strikes. Tax revenues, already hit by the loss of manufacturing jobs and the decline of shipping through the harbor, continued to decline as more and more middle-class residents moved to the suburbs. The settlements which Mayor Lindsay made to end union strikes in the 1960s included salary increases over time, and the only way to reduce the government's expenses was through personnel cuts, which frustrated residents and were resisted by unions, setting off more strikes. By 1975, the city had run out of cash for normal operating expenses, and when the national economy went into a recession, the city could not borrow more money from the bond market. Mayor Abraham Beame announced job cuts and salary freezes, yet still faced a debt of $453 billion that the city could not meet its obligations on. Appealing to the Federal government for a bailout, he received an answer from President Gerald Ford that the *New York Post* immortalized in its headline: "Ford to City: Drop Dead."

But it wasn't all bad.

In some ways, the gritty realities of the city added to the determination and pride of residents who chose to stay, captured by the title song of a 1977 film by Martin Scorsese. "I want to be a part of it," Liza Minelli sings about the city, concluding "If I can make it there, I'm gonna make it anywhere." The city still had enormous influence on culture, art and music. A booming art scene developed, with artists like Andy Warhol, Jean-Michel Basquiat and Keith Hering. Celebrating a new spirit of gay liberation, underground nightclubs like Paradise Garage and The Saint helped launch the disco era, while Cuban and Puerto Rican musicians in East Harlem were creating the new dance sounds of Salsa. The early punk rock scene was exploding at CBGBs, and by the end of the decade, rap began emerging from inner city neighborhoods in The Bronx and Queens. In 1975, NBC launched a new comedy show, and *Saturday Night Live* quickly became a hit phenomenon. When CBS closed its former studio on 54th Street, entrepreneurs converted it into a nightclub, and Studio 54 became the place for celebrities to party and play.

The city's budget started to improve. Despite Ford's refusal, Congress provided over $2 billion in loans, and the attached stipulations gave Mayor Beame the political cover he needed to cancel wage increases, charge higher fees for city services, and cut the city's workforce by thousands. His successor was able to balance the budget by 1981, and with Wall Street enjoying another boom, the city restructured its debt and could borrow again. In many ways, Ed Koch was the right person for the moment, with a tough-talking, no-nonsense attitude that appealed to, and reflected, many of the city's residents. Koch began focusing on improving the city's reputation, encouraging gentrification to re-build neighborhoods and focusing on quality-of-life issues, like illegal parking and cleaning up litter. When MTA workers went out on strike again in 1980, Koch encouraged commuters to carpool, roller-skate or walk to work, and share taxicabs with strangers. He walked over the Brooklyn Bridge to City Hall, and his populist approach helped him resist union demands. After 12 days, the strike ended with a lower wage increase than the union had demanded.

Crime was still a problem. The disappearance in 1979 of a six-year-old named Etan Patz haunted the city, creating a national "missing children" campaign, and despite the formation of a new crime prevention group called the Guardian Angels, subway crime would gain new headlines in 1984 when rider Bernhard Goetz shot 4 teens who he said were trying to mug him. The murder rate was still high, especially among young black men, and the news became fixated on the "crack epidemic," ignoring the racial disparities between penalties for crack possession versus those for cocaine. Central Park was the setting for two high-profile crimes, the preppy murder of 1986 and the rape of a jogger in 1989; media coverage of "wildings" led law enforcement to rush to sentence 5 black and Latino youths whose convictions were overturned in 2002. The following year, NBC-TV launched the wildly successful *Law & Order* series, portraying crime stores that were "ripped from the headlines" and filmed in locations all around the city.

The city's population and demographics were changing and becoming more diverse. After showing a decrease of 800,000 in population between 1970 and 1980, the 1990 Census showed an increase of 250,000, driven largely by new immigrants, many of them Hispanic or Asian. The percent of residents who were born outside the US increased for the first time since 1910, and for the first time ever, the city's non-Hispanic white population dropped below 50%. In 1989, the city elected its first African American mayor, and while Mayor Dinkins saw the "gorgeous mosaic" of the city's population as the source of its strength, it was also the source of rising tensions, exemplified by the Crown Heights riot in 1991.

Considering the city's problems and fiscal crisis, it should be no surprise that there were few ticker tape parades during this period, and none along Broadway between 1970 and 1976. It took the nation's 200th Birthday to revive the tradition, and even then, the city's official greeters were encouraged to use cheaper means when welcoming important visitors. Only two parades along the Canyon of Heroes honored individuals, and both Pope John Paul II *(see: October 3, 1979)* and Nelson Mandela *(see: June 20, 1990)* had enormous international stature. Most of the other parades in this period honored those who had served the nation *(see: January 30, 1981)* or celebrated the city's victory in one arena that still brought most New Yorkers together: sports.

Monday, March 8, 1971: Apollo 14 Astronauts

After landing on the moon on his second space mission, Apollo 14, Commander Alan Shepard returned to some cold receptions back on planet Earth. Along with Stuart Roosa and Edgar Mitchell, Shepard spent nine days in space, launching on January 31 and landing on the moon on February 5, near the location that was intended for Apollo 13 before that mission was aborted mid-flight. In addition to collecting rocks and conducting experiments on the lunar surface, Shepard was responsible for perhaps the most famous incident of the mission: hitting two golf balls with a makeshift club.

The astronauts arrived in New York on Sunday, March 7. Accompanied by their wives and NASA officials, they stayed at the St. Regis-Sheraton Hotel in midtown. That afternoon, they went to the ABC-TV studios on 67th Street for a taping of Issues and Answers, a weekly political commentary news show, as well as appearing on Mayor Lindsay's regular Sunday evening TV show. As they were leaving the studio, they were stopped by several ABC employees with four children. "Please sign it," one little boy asked, holding a photograph he hoped to get autographed. One of the NASA employees "pushed the children aside," according to a New York Times reporter, saying "We want to get them away from the autograph hunters."

The weather was cold the next day, with high temperatures in the mid 20s, and scattered snow flurries fell throughout the day. The astronauts and their wives left their hotel and entered limousines waiting to take them to City Hall and were accompanied by the mayor and his wife and John "Bud" Palmer, the city's Commissioner of Public Events. The route had been announced the day before: their 16-car caravan would travel from 55th Street down Fifth Avenue to 14th Street, where it would turn east, then proceed down Broadway to City Hall. An escort of 24 motorcycle-riding police officers would lead the way.

The parade started well. Bursts of confetti were flung from open windows, mingled with occasional snow flurries, while spectators lined Fifth Avenue, a few hundred on every block, waving and cheering. As the caravan headed down Broadway, though, the city's reception became colder. The parade halted at Broadway and Third Street, stopped by a demonstration of about 20 people, including some mothers pushing baby strollers. The sidewalk was filled with as many as 300 residents of the Broadway Central Hotel, chanting in protest about the cost of the space program. Those in the street carried hand-made banners, one of which read "white astronauts fly to the moon while black children die in welfare hotels."

The parade resumed "after a brief scuffle" between the police and the demonstrators, and "the astronauts sped by" the rest of the block to reach City Hall, where a slightly warmer greeting awaited them. The First Army Band and the All-City High School Chorus performed for a crowd of about 1,000 in the Plaza. There were more protestors mixed in the crowd, who started chanting over the band music, protesting cuts in the city's education budget.

As the Mayor led the astronauts to the dais set up in front of City Hall, he joked that some New Yorkers hoped NASA would send him to the moon. Introducing the astronauts to the spectators, he gave each of them the city's Gold Medal. As the astronauts walked up to the microphone, the protestors grew louder, chanting "Crumbs for children, millions for the moon." Shepard tried to place NASA's budget in context, telling the crowd that they would be surprised what a small percent of the federal budget was spent on the lunar missions. "What I'm saying today is," he continued, somewhat exasperated, "give us a break."

The Mayor tried to placate the crowd, saying that the resources and skills used for space exploration could "also help to bring our cities back."

After the ceremony, the astronauts were taken to the United Nations for a luncheon with George Bush, Sr., the new US representative to the UN, and then to the NBC-TV studios to tape an appearance on the Tonight Show with Johnny Carson and an interview with David Frost. Later that evening, the astronauts went with the mayor to watch the Mohammed Ali-Joe Frazier fight at Madison Square Garden, while their wives attended a performance of The School for Wives at the Lyceum Theater.

The Apollo 14 team also received a cold reception from scientists. Geologists were annoyed that Shepard and Mitchell did not reach the rim of the lunar crater they had landed in, despite walking to within meters of its edge. Although the mission collected rocks for analysis, the astronauts failed to document where different samples were taken from, and the reaction from the scientific community to the golfing incident was less than favorable.

Pilot Stuart Roosa, who stayed on the command module during the lunar landing, retired from NASA in 1976. One of the experiments he conducted during his 34 orbits around the moon was germinating tree seeds provided by the US Forest Service; later that year, the saplings were planted across the nation as part of the Bicentennial celebrations. The "moon trees" show no difference to similar trees planted nearby. Roosa lived in Washington DC until his death in 1994.

Pilot Edgar Mitchell was responsible for photography during the lunar expedition, and his shadow is seen in the now-famous photograph he took of Shepard raising the US flag. He retired from NASA in 1972 to pursue his growing interest in paranormal psychology, ESP and consciousness. He was also a strong proponent in the existence of UFOs and believed that the US government had classified proof that extraterrestrials had been visiting earth since the 1940s. He died in 2016, on the eve of the 45th anniversary of his lunar landing.

Commander Alan Shepard was promoted to Rear Admiral in July 1971, the first astronaut to receive this rank. He retired from both NASA and the US Navy in 1974. He served on several corporate boards, wrote the book Moon Shot, and co-founded the Mercury Seven Foundation, which provides scholarships for science and engineering studies. The first American to have flown in space (see: May 8, 1961), he died of leukemia in 1998.

Tuesday, August 24, 1971: Apollo 15 Astronauts

The three members of the Apollo 15 team received a ticker tape parade although not along the traditional route. On a bright and sunny summer afternoon with a pleasant breeze Army Major Alfred Worden, Air Force Colonel David Scott, and Air Force Colonel James Irwin were picked up at the St Regis-Sheraton Hotel at 55th Street and

Fifth Avenue and driven downtown to City Hall. The route had been announced beforehand and people stood along the entire route.

The motorcade was scheduled to begin at 11 o'clock that morning but was delayed a half hour because of Mayor Lindsay's late arrival. He had attended the funeral of a New York City policeman killed by a gunman the previous week. When the mayor arrived, he sat in the front seat of an open convertible while the astronauts sat in the rear. An escort of 15 motorcycles started their engines with a roar and the small procession began. Apollo 15 had carried a Lunar Rover to the moon and the slow speed of the drive downtown was compared to that of the Lunar Rover.

Because of the length of the motorcade's route, crowds were more spread out than those along the Canyon of Heroes. Nowhere were people clustered more than three deep and in some places, there were large gaps in the crowd. Only small amounts of confetti and torn paper fell. The near absence of ticker tape was obvious, which at least pleased the workers of the Sanitation Department, according to one newspaper report. Although the crowd along the route was sparse, it was interesting. An elderly man in greased stained overalls was observed holding up a sign welcoming the "Moon Men," and a truck full of construction workers gave three loud cheers for the astronauts followed by several less pleasant remarks directed to the mayor. Two teenage joggers ran next to the car for 16 blocks along the route. As the motorcade neared City Hall, a window washer was observed leaning off the side of a building, held on by only a single safety belt, applauding loudly as the astronauts rode below.

The procession arrived at City Hall slightly after 12:30, and a larger crowd had gathered in the Plaza. As the astronauts stepped from their car and joined the mayor, the City-Wide High School Chorus, composed of 100 teenage singers from various schools, welcomed them by singing "Off We Go, Into the Wild Blue Yonder" followed by the National Anthem. The Roman Catholic Archbishop of New York, Cardinal Terrence Cooke, gave an invocation, and Mayor Lindsay introduced the three astronauts to the spectators in the Plaza. He placed the city's Gold Medal around the neck of each man. Colonel Scott in turn, gave the mayor one of the American flags that had traveled to the moon and back and a signed photograph of the three men before their space launch.

Following the City Hall Plaza reception, the mayor and the astronauts returned uptown for a luncheon at Rockefeller Center with business and civic leaders. The three shared some of their lunar experiences with those who attended and then it was on to the United Nations. A Lunar Rover had been delivered to the UN earlier that morning and the astronauts explained to Secretary General U Thant how it worked and allowed them to explore further from the Lunar Module than previous expeditions.

After a quick return to the St. Regis Hotel to change clothes, the Apollo 15 crew joined Mayor Lindsay at the Music Box Theater for a performance of Sleuth. Introduced to the audience between acts, the men were given a standing ovation.

The next morning, the astronauts returned to Cape Kennedy for continued debriefing. The mission commander, Colonel Scott, was a veteran of two previous space flights, but this was the first space mission for Major Worden and Colonel Irwin.

Apollo 15 was the ninth moon mission and the fourth to land, touching down in the Mare Imbrium. Over the three days on the moon's surface, the astronauts collected 170 pounds of samples for study on earth and spent over 18 hours outside the Module. The mission was considered a scientific success because of the experiments conducted and the samples brought back.

But a scandal tarnished the reputations of the astronauts soon after they returned to earth. A German stamp dealer, H. Walter Eiermann, had made arrangements with Colonel Scott to carry 100 commemorative stamps called "postal covers" in his space suit. The three astronauts signed the covers and Mr. Eiermann planned to pay them $7,000 each and then sell the covers to stamp collectors. The plan was discovered and none of the covers were ever sold by Colonel Scott. The plan was not illegal nor were there any NASA regulations against it but the authorities were not pleased, the covers were confiscated and none of the three men ever flew another space mission.

Colonel Scott retired from the Air Force in 1977 and subsequently served as a technical advisor for BBC television and the motion picture industry on space and space flights. Married with two children, he currently resides in Los Angeles.

Major Worden was Senior Aerospace Scientist with NASA until 1973. Upon retiring he was associated with BF Goodrich Company. He made an unsuccessful bid for the House of Representatives in Florida in 1982, losing in the Republican primary. The next year, he sued NASA for possession of the postal covers, and the government returned them, dividing them evenly between the three members of the crew. He sold a few of them in his possession to cover campaign expenses. He advocated for renewed space exploration flights, including a mission to Mars, and died in March 2020.

Colonel Irwin suffered a major heart attack several months after the mission. On the return flight from the moon, monitors briefly detected irregularities in his heartbeat, but no follow up tests had been made. He retired and created the High Flight Foundation, a Christian speaker's group. He led expeditions to Mount Ararat, Turkey, searching for the remains on Noah's Ark. In August 1991, he suffered a fatal heart attack in his home in Colorado Springs, Colorado.

Wednesday, July 7, 1976:
Crews of Operation Sail Vessels during US Bicentennial

Coming so soon after the turmoil of the late 1960s, the end of the Vietnam War and the Watergate crisis, many hoped that celebrations for the 200th anniversary of the signing of the Declaration of Independence would create a wave of patriotism and rekindle optimism for the nation's future. Plans for celebrating the Bicentennial had begun in 1966 but intensified when Congress created the American Revolution Bicentennial Administration (ARBA) in 1973, which encouraged and coordinated local observances. The US Mint created new designs for the reverse side of several coins, and the Bennington Flag, bearing 13 stars in a semi-circle over the number 76 in white on the blue field, could be seen flying seemingly everywhere and became so connected with the celebration it is often referred to as the Bicentennial Flag. Television viewers enjoyed a Bicentennial Minute of history each night from July 1974 until December 1976, each presented by a different narrator who began by saying "Two hundred years ago today" and closed with "and that's the way it was."

New York City was facing its own crises, so in addition to the usual panoply of concerts and fireworks, neighborhood historic museums and displays, art exhibits, street parties and picnics, the city also hosted the largest-ever peacetime gathering of sailing vessels and naval ships in one place and time. In addition to 16 "big ships" (square-rigged tall sailing ships), over 100 other supporting vessels participated, more than the original Op Sail in 1964.

Vessels of one kind or another came from 38 countries to celebrate America's Bicentennial. Some sailing ships had left their home ports as early as March, and began arriving days before Independence Day, docking in the East and Hudson Rivers, or mooring in the harbor. Most were open to the public and tourists flocked to view ships large and small over the holiday weekend. The climax of the entire event was a ticker tape parade up the Canyon of Heroes for the officers and crews.

At precisely 12:05 on the afternoon of July 7, the parade stepped off, led by a color-guard of Military Police followed by the ceremonial honor guard from Fort Hamilton, Brooklyn, wearing buff and blue colored Revolutionary War era uniforms. Broadway was jammed with spectators. Military bands and the Police and Fire Departments Bands were interspersed among the contingents. More than 2,000 naval cadets, veteran sailors, and weathered seamen took part, wearing uniforms of nations from every continent. Some contingents contained only a handful of marchers in less than orderly ranks; others numbered in the hundreds, marching in well-ordered precision.

Spectators crowded the streets and watched from every window. Everyone seemed to have a miniature bicentennial flag and nearly everyone had a camera. Children perched on the shoulders of adults. Ticker tape was a thing of the past but was replaced by reams of computer paper, streamers, confetti, and shredded newspapers. Colored bank deposit and withdrawal slips descended from bank buildings, adding a rainbow of colors.

Veteran parade watchers agreed that there had been nothing as spectacular as this since the parade for General Douglas MacArthur *(see: April 20, 1951)* or Astronaut John Glenn *(see: March 1, 1962)*. The enthusiasm of the cheering crowd was matched only by that of many of the marchers, who waved and cheered and clapped in return. The loudest cheers from the crowd came for the 44 female members of the British three mast top-sail schooner Sir Winston Churchill, all wearing white dresses with blue naval collars and straw hats. Almost as loud was the cheering for the Israeli detachment wearing navy blue berets, dress whites, and black combat boots. Groups from 19 nations took part: Argentina, Australia, Brazil, Canada, Chile, Colombia, Denmark, Germany, Israel, Italy, Japan, Norway, Poland, Portugal, Romania, South Africa, the Soviet Union, Spain and the United States.

The flags of 100 nations and 50 states adorned City Hall Plaza. When Admiral Isaac Kidd, the senior American officer taking part in the parade, arrived at City Hall, he joined Mayor Abe Beame on the reviewing stand. The mayor read a proclamation stating that the day was "the most magnificent and glorious display of maritime splendor in the century." The Admiral responded by saying, "Hurry up and have your next 100th birthday, and invite us back."

Most marchers had been given liberty for the day and upon reaching City Hall, they disbanded and headed toward the South Street Seaport. The crowds there eventually grew so large that the police were forced to restrict entrance to the area and many of the shops, restaurants, and taverns shut down, unable to handle the multitude of New Yorkers, sailors and tourists. Higher-ranking participants in the parade were invited into City Hall itself where they enjoyed flutes of champagne and sandwiches provided by the Chock Full o' Nuts Company. A reception for the highest-ranking participants had been scheduled to be held in the City Council Chambers but had to be cancelled that morning when it was discovered that parts of the Chambers' ceiling, long overdue for repair work, had collapsed.

The party in the City Hall area continued all night, regardless of restricted access, shuttered buildings, and fallen plaster. The next morning the first of the vessels to leave

New York departed. By the following weekend, all had gone, leaving a massive clean-up – in keeping with New York's reputation of doing things in a big way.

The "big ships" would return to New York City again in 1986 (centennial of the Statue of Liberty), 1992 (500th anniversary of Columbus's voyage), 2000 (Millennium Celebration) and 2012 (bicentennial of the Star-Spangled Banner), but none of those would receive ticker tape parades. Plans to celebrate America's Semiquincentennial in 2026 have begun, but no announcement has been made yet about whether there will be another Op Sail.

And that's the way it was.

Mayor Abraham Beame (1974-1977)

The man who occupied City Hall during the City's worst financial crisis was born in London in 1906 and moved to the Lower East Side as an infant. A graduate of City College of New York, Abraham Beame became a professor, teaching accounting at Rutgers University during World War II. After the war, he worked for the city's budgeting agency, becoming Director of the Budget from 1952 to 1961. A member of Brooklyn's Madison Democratic Club, he was elected City Comptroller in 1961. After an unsuccessful bid for Mayor in 1965, he was re-elected to the Comptroller office in 1969.

In 1973, he ran for Mayor again and won, then spent most of his term grappling with the city's budget problems. With an annual deficit of $1.5 billion, the city faced bankruptcy, and initial appeals for Federal aid received a response immortalized by the New York Post headline "Ford to City: Drop Dead." By freezing salaries and cutting the city's workforce, restructuring the budget and leveraging state and federal resources, Beame was successful, and when he left office the city had a $200 million surplus.

Beame ran for re-election in 1977 but lost the Democratic Primary. He retired from politics and died in 2001.

Wednesday, October 19, 1977:
New York Yankees, World Series Champions

In the 14 years from 1949 to 1962, the New York Yankees won the World Series nine times, including five in a row (1949-1953). It was sometimes joked that they were destined to eventually own the championship crown as a permanent fixture, but then a drought set in. After losing the 1963 and 1964 championship series they entered an uncharacteristic slump, finishing tenth in 1966 and ninth in 1967. They finally came back with a vengeance though in 1977, defeating the Los Angeles Dodgers, and their return to victory was celebrated with a ticker tape parade.

The road to victory had seen the team battling not just their American League rivals but also each other. At the start of the season, the team acquired Reggie Jackson, and though some of his new teammates were happy to have him wearing pinstripes, others were not, especially Manager Billy Martin, who had a feud with Jackson going back several years. Adding to the problem was a comment that Jackson made in Sport magazine implying that he and catcher Thurman Munson were the only talented players in the organization.

Despite the internal friction, the Yankees defeated Baltimore for the American League crown and won the World Series four games to two. Reggie Jackson was named World Series Most Valuable Player and pitcher Sparky Lyle won the Cy Young award.

The next day dawned with scattered light showers, but that did not curb the enthusiasm of the hundreds of thousands of Yankee fans who turned out to view their team ride up the Canyon of Heroes. A 44-piece army band from Fort Hamilton led the parade, followed by several flat-bed sound trucks, decorated with the Yankees logo. Manager Martin rode up Broadway on the first vehicle, which he shared with owner George Steinbrenner, Yankee president Gabe Paul, Mayor Abe Beame, and Mike Torrez, winning pitcher of the final game of the series. Knowing the cheering from the crowd was not for him, the mayor sat for most of the way up Broadway. A number of boos were even directed at this first vehicle, but it was unclear who they were directed toward. The cheers became deafening, though, when the second truck appeared, carrying Jackson and Lyle. Fans, many of whom huddled beneath umbrellas, cheered loudest for Jackson whose home runs had earned him the nickname "Mr. October."

It had not been a good year for New York City. On July 13 and 14 a blackout had darkened almost the entire city. A month later the killer known as the "Son of Sam" went on a shooting spree murdering six people and wounding seven others before finally being apprehended in the summer of 1977. When Mayor Beame stood before the more than 20,000 people in City Hall Park, he alluded to the city's misfortunes, saying that the Yankees had, "put a new spirit in the city and we're Number 1." George Steinbrenner thanked the fans, saying, "You never gave up on us...and I thank you."

The players were introduced, and some made brief comments. Jackson only waved and smiled to the chants from the crowd of "Reg-gie! Reg-gie!" At an indoor press conference following the City Hall Park reception, he told reporters, "That's what it's all about. Just appreciation." Two of the team's star players, Thurman Munson and first-baseman Chris Chambliss, were absent, but that was more than made up for by the presence of all-time Yankee great, Joe DiMaggio, who had played in ten World Series in the era before baseball teams received parades. When his name was announced he spoke to the crowd, his voice breaking in emotion. "I hope the players will get a good rest and perhaps start another dynasty in New York," referring to the Yankee glory years of the 1950's.

After the ceremony, the crowds in City Hall Plaza dispersed peacefully, and NY Police Commissioner Michael Codd no doubt breathed a sigh of relief. The police had been worried about a repeat of the melee that erupted at Yankee Stadium immediately after the final game ended. Thousands of fans poured onto the field in excitement, the revelry turning into vandalism and mayhem. Several players had to run to get to their dugouts safely, dodging over-excited fans and police, who poured onto the field to maintain control, some wielding batons and nightsticks, others mounted on horses. Dozens of fans were arrested in Yankee Stadium and in the streets around it for disorderly conduct and vandalism, and at least one youth was hospitalized after several police officers clubbed him. There were only 10 arrests for disorderly conduct during the parade, and the New York Times reported that the parade's crowd "was never out of control."

The mood of the day around the parade, however, was summed up by one lifelong Yankee fan as he left City Hall Park. "I feel great today. It's good to be a New Yorker." He and many other fans no doubt agreed with Joe DiMaggio's hope that their team's

14-year slump was over, and a new dynasty was beginning. Those hopes would be rewarded next year *(see: October 19, 1978)*, but not without more friction.

Thursday, October 19, 1978:
New York Yankees, World Series Champions

Baseball fans watched as the tension inside the Yankees dugout and the rowdiness of fans inside the stadium continued to grow during the 1978 season. The feuding between Manager Billy Martin and outfielder Reggie Jackson intensified, growing so bad that the team was sometimes referred to as "the Bronx Zoo." When Martin suspended Jackson for a few games in July, owner George Steinbrenner solved the personnel problem by firing his manager and replacing him with former pitcher Bob Lemon. The change worked, and the Bronx Bombers won game after game, winning the American League Championship for the 32nd time.

The World Series was a rematch of the previous year, with the Yankees again facing the Los Angeles Dodgers. Both World Series went six games. The Yankees won them both, the 1977 Series at home in the Bronx, the 1978 in Los Angeles. The Yankees won the final game on October 17, 1978, with a score of 7-2.

The victorious team arrived at Newark International airport the following evening. A crowd of 5,000 fans had assembled, and pandemonium broke out when the plane carrying the Yankees taxied to the gate and came to a halt. The airport police were unable to control the crowd as they surged forward to greet the players, but fortunately for the athletes, the Newark Police were also on hand. Taking possession of a small fire-fighting vehicle, they turned on a hose and forced the crowd back so the Yankees could deplane, board waiting buses, and head to their hotel in Manhattan. The majority of Yankee fans were visibly annoyed by the activities of the crowd in Newark, but, as one New Yorker commented to a reporter, "They're not real Yankee fans. They're from Joisey."

At noon the next day, the sun broke through low gray clouds. Rain had been forecast, but not a drop fell all day. As the parade began, bright sunshine fell on Broadway and it soon grew unseasonably warm. In addition to the change in weather, there was also a change to the usual blizzard of paper that fell from the sky. Over the past decade, torn newspapers had become the primary replacement for tickertape, but New York City's papers had been on strike since early August (and would remain so until early November). With no daily newspapers, the amount of paper thrown from buildings was noticeably less than for other parades.

Despite this there was still the expected cheering and shouting. World Series MVP Bucky Dent rode with owner Steinbrenner and Manager Lemon. Reggie Jackson rode with New York State Governor Hugh Carey. A number of boos were shouted at the car, but they were aimed at the politician and not the athlete. Jackson stood during most of the parade, throwing Reggie Candy Bars, introduced earlier that year, to the crowd. Only two members of the championship team, Graig Nettles and Catfish Hunter, were absent. The rest of the Yankees were there, waving and accepting the cheers of the crowd.

Mayor Koch welcomed the Yankees at City Hall, then announced to the crowd jammed into City Hall Park, "We're number one. The Yankees are like New York City. We both conquered the odds." Each member of the team was then introduced and given a city medal, starting with Steinbrenner. The crowd initially booed him, but when he said he believed that National League Umpire Ed Vargo had been biased in favor of the Dodgers, the boos turned to cheers. Manager Lemon said regarding the welcome, "Don't I love it. It's a great feeling." Sparky Lyle, the only member of the Yankee team not to play in the Series, commented with a simple "Thanks." Introduced last, Bucky Dent predicted to thunderous cheering that they would be back in 1979 with another championship.

Near the end of the two-hour ceremony, a number of fans burst through the police barrier in the plaza. Although the surging crowd was forced back behind the barriers with less difficulty than the night before in Newark, there were some injuries: four policemen and six young fans were hurt. Two of the police and three fans required emergency care.

Bucky Dent's predication did not come true, and in fact the Yankees were not even in the running for the 1979 American League Championship. They next won the Championship in 1981, though lost the World Series. After that, the team entered another drought and would not return victorious until 1996 *(see: October 29, 1996)*. New York's other baseball fans would celebrate sooner, when the Yankee's cross-town rivals, the Mets, won the 1986 championship *(see: October 28, 1986)*.

Wednesday, October 3, 1979: Pope John Paul II

The ticker tape parade honoring the spiritual head of the Roman Catholic Church came at the end of his three-day visit to the city, the first stop of his longer visit to the United States. Born in Poland in 1920, Karol Jósef Wojtyla took the name John Paul II when he was elevated to the papacy in 1978. While in New York, the pope's schedule was filled with events: religious services celebrated at Yankee Stadium and Shea Stadium, a rally in Madison Square Garden attended by 19,000 young people, speeches at the United Nations and the Battery, and visits to St. James Cathedral in Brooklyn, a church in Harlem, another on the Lower East Side, and a seminary.

Throughout most of his time here, it rained, but poor weather conditions did not dampen the enthusiasm of his welcome. People stood under umbrellas or held soaked newspapers over their heads just to catch a glimpse of him as he drove by in his specially modified open-top limousine. Mayor Ed Koch wore a yellow Parks Department slicker when the pope spoke at the Battery. The Pope stood under an umbrella held aloft by New York's Cardinal Terrence Cooke while thunder rumbled and lightning crackled.

The day of his parade and departure was no different. Showers began early in the morning and continued throughout the day. A few minutes after noon the parade started, led by marching bands from the Police Department and Catholic schools. Organizers had hoped that the motorcade could halt briefly at the Church of Our Lady of the Rosary near the Staten Island Ferry terminal. The Georgian-style brick building was the original home of Elizabeth Ann Seton, the first of only two American-born saints. Because of the Pope's schedule, however, the motorcade only slowed while the pontiff gave his blessing to the small group standing in front of the building.

People lined both sides of Broadway, and in places the crowd was five to six deep as the motorcade drove by. The police had abandoned estimating the size of crowds, but veterans of previous parades put the number at more than a million. Many who watched were Catholic school children, not only from the New York City area. At least one group from Chicago had hired a bus, arriving the same day the pope had, but without hotel accommodations the students lived on the bus during their stay.

Paper fell from the sky, wet and soggy from the rain. Pinfeed computer paper, rolls of paper towel and toilet tissue mingled with multi-colored confetti. The pope wore a raincoat that only partially covered him. Efforts were made to cover him with an umbrella, but the wind kept blowing and twisting it. After a few blocks the effort was given up as hopeless. Church bells began to toll when the Pope's limousine passed the Episcopalian Trinity Church, once the tallest structure in the city. Startled pigeons flew off in every direction as streamers of paper draped around the spires of the church and seemed to wave at the departing birds.

All along the route were signs in various languages greeting the Pope, seeking his blessing, or expressing love. Written in Polish and Slovak, Italian and Spanish, Tagalog, Haitian Creole, and even in Latin, they were held high by spectators. As many visitors to New York had done in the past, the Pope waved in acknowledgement to the crowd but also added his blessings.

Mayor Koch welcomed the Pope at City Hall and presented him with a scroll commemorating his visit. "Please come back to us soon," the mayor said. A skilled linguist fluent in many languages, the Pope answered in English, "God bless New York."

Pope John Paul II left the city later that afternoon, his plane taking off from LaGuardia Airport in the rain. Still on his schedule were visits to Chicago, Philadelphia, and Washington. He was greeted by President Carter during the first papal visit to the White House. He was the most traveled pope in history, visiting 129 countries during his reign of over 26 years, the second-longest papacy. He survived an assassination attempt in 1981 that almost took his life, visited leaders of every major faith, and was a leader in the downfall of European Communism.

In 2005, he developed a urinary tract infection and died from circulatory collapse caused by septic shock on April 2, 2005, just 46 days short of his 85th birthday. Buried beneath St. Peter's Basilica in Rome, his funeral was attended by four kings, five queens, 70 presidents or Prime Ministers, as well as leaders of 14 different religious faiths.

Mayor Ed Koch (1978-1989)

Self-described as a "liberal with sanity," Edward Koch was born in the Bronx in 1924 to Jewish immigrants from Eastern Europe. He was drafted into the US Army during World War II, then studied at the City College of New York and NYU Law School. He began a solo law practice and started getting involved in Democratic party politics. He served a term on the NY City Council starting in 1967, and two years later was elected to Congress.

In 1977, he won the Democratic primary for mayor against a crowded field, running to the right of his opponents on a "law and order" platform, which resonated with voters weary after the "Son of Sam" murder spree and rioting during the 1977 black-out. He became Mayor, and was re-elected twice, occupying City Hall from 1978 to 1989.

During his tenure, he continued Mayor Beame's efforts to trim the city's budget and improve its financial health, while also taking on "quality of life" issues such as pollution, vandalism, over-crowded subways and homelessness. He was criticized for his administration's slow response to the AIDS crisis and to worsening race relations. Outspoken and often controversial, Koch had a brash New York style, frequently taking to television to ask voters "How'm I doin?" →

After leaving City Hall, Koch returned to his law practice, and also taught at NYU. He appeared on The People's Court for 2 years after Judge Wapner retired, and reviewed movies for newspapers and online sites. He frequently spoke out on political issues and was a staunch defender of Israel. A lifelong bachelor who dodged and denied rumors about his sexuality throughout his life, his closeted homosexuality was the subject of the 2009 documentary Outrage. He died of heart failure in 2013, and was buried in Trinity Church Cemetary.

Friday, January 30, 1981: Hostages Released from Iran

For 444 days, Americans had watched the news anxiously and tied yellow ribbons around trees, hoping for the safe return of 52 Americans taken hostage in Tehran when a revolution in Iran forced the Shah (*see November 21, 1949 and April 16, 1962*) to flee in exile and a new Islamic Republic was formed under the Ayatollah Khomeini. The crisis overwhelmed the final year in the White House for President Jimmy Carter, especially after an aborted rescue attempt in April 1980, and was one of the factors leading to his defeat at the polls in 1980. The announcement that the hostages were being released was made by Iranian officials shortly after President Ronald Reagan was sworn into office, and Americans breathed a sigh of relief. The hostages were coming home, and a New York held a ticker tape parade to welcome them back.

A crowd of more than a million people braved the below-freezing temperatures and a bitingly sharp wind whistling through the Canyon of Heroes to welcome home 21 of the 52 former hostages. Some were absent receiving medical treatment, others decided to return to their homes, and still others, members of the military, had already been reassigned.

A fleet of classic and vintage cars made up the motorcade, ranging from a black Rolls-Royce convertible to a bright red Corvette. The former hostages gathered at Castle Clinton in the Battery, where they were assigned to cars in a long row of waiting vehicles. A half dozen high-school bands and two bagpipe groups were interspaced between the cars. A few minutes after noon, the motorcade began slowly moving up the Canyon of Heroes.

Flags flew from every flagpole along the route, and around most of the flagpoles were tied yellow ribbons, which had become a symbol of the hope for the safe return of the hostages. The spectators, in places as many as ten deep, cheered and waved miniature flags as well as yellow ribbons. Thousands of school-aged children were in evidence, some with their parents and others in school groups. Every one of the former hostages was cheered loudly but the decibel level rose noticeably for Barry Rosen, the only hostage from New York. A Brooklyn resident and the former press attaché at the American Embassy in Tehran, he sat perched on the rear seat of the Rolls Royce. Like a cheer at a football game, spectators chanted "Baar-reee! Baar-reee!" A blizzard of paper of all kinds fell from the skyscrapers.

Master-Sergeant Regis Ragan, one of the Marine Corps guards at the embassy when it was captured, was the object of hand-held signs reading "We love you, Regis!" He shouted back to the crowd, "I love you, too."

The third-ranking diplomat at the embassy, Moorehead Kennedy, appeared stunned at the size of the crowd, as did the Air-Force Attaché, Colonel Thomas Schafer, and the embassy's senior political officer, Victor Tomseth. Kathryn Koob, one of the two women the Iranians had not released earlier, sat bundled against the cold, wearing a knit hat and heavy gloves.

The Embassy's Public Affairs Officer, John Graves, was represented by his wife, Bonnie because he was still hospitalized in Germany. The others smiled and waved in response. The other ex-hostages taking part in the parade were: Robert Blucker; Lieutenant Commander Robert Engelmann; Bruce German; Alan Golacinski; Warrant Officer Joseph Hall; Sergeant Kevin Hermening; Specialist Donald Hohman; Michael Howland; Charles Jones; Malcolm Kalp; John Lambert; Steven Lauterbach; Michael Moeller, and Staff-Sergeant Joseph Subic. One other ex-hostage, Clair Barnes, arrived back in New York later in the day and was absent from the parade but was present for events later that night.

Mayor Koch stood on the reviewing stand at the steps of City Hall as the convoy arrived. Standing with him was the Canadian Ambassador to Iran, Kenneth Taylor, who had hidden six Americans in his embassy and managed to sneak them back to the United States a year earlier. The mayor presented a scroll, entitled "Proud City Award" to Mr. Kennedy, who was acting as spokesman for the group. The crowd of spectators filled City Hall Plaza and spilled out towards the Brooklyn Bridge. Several times, loud roars of "USA, USA, USA" interrupted the ceremony until Mr. Kennedy was finally able to say:

> *"It's been said that Americans are much more comfortable with their feelings about their country – much more united. Well, let me tell you, to the extent that we had something to do with that feeling, we are profoundly grateful, and it made everything we went through worthwhile."*

Following Mr. Kennedy's brief statement, the ex-hostages were brought into City Hall for a luncheon, filling the entire second floor of the venerable old building. Later that evening they were guests at a dinner at Lüchow's Restaurant. Two Christmas trees were displayed in the restaurant lobby, commemorating the two holidays the hostages had spent in captivity. Later that evening, most of the honorees attended a performance of the Broadway musical *Chorus Line* where the show's producer, Joseph Papp, introduced each of them to the audience.

Sanitation Department officials later reported that more than 1,250 tons of paper had been swept from Broadway and side streets after the parade. It surpassed the amount removed for at least the last two ticker tape parades celebrating World Series victories by the New York Yankees *(see: October 19, 1977 and October 19, 1978)*.

After spending the next day at the Waldorf Astoria, the former hostages began to return to their homes. For some, the transition back top "normal" conditions proved difficult, while others were able to readjust more quickly.

It took another 30 years before the former hostages finally won compensation for their ordeal. Although they had been awarded $33 million in a 1996 lawsuit, the US Government barred them from receiving that money because it violates the Algiers Agreement, a treaty that prevents Americans from receiving compensation from foreign governments. An offer of $30,000 each made by the Bush Administration was turned down, and on December 24, 2015 an equitable compensation package was signed by President Obama providing up to $4.4 million dollars to each hostage or his or her estate.

As of 2020, 35 of the original 53 hostages are still alive, and are still waiting for their full compensation payment, which has been delayed because payments to victims of the 9/11 terrorist attack are also included in same legislation and funding.

Thursday, August 15, 1984:
US Olympic Team from XXIII Summer Olympic Games

The 1980 Moscow Olympics had been boycotted by 61 western nations, protesting the Soviet Union's invasion of Afghanistan. In retaliation, 16 Soviet-aligned nations retaliated and boycotted the 1984 Los Angeles Olympics, where 522 American athletes (339 men and 183 women) won 174 medals. For the first time in over 3 years, New York City held a ticker tape parade, attended by more than 200 of the US team members.

The parade began shortly after noon, with the band of the United States Military Academy leading the way, but minutes after it began the parade came to a halt. Spectators between Fulton and Dey Streets had climbed onto scaffolding in front of 195 Broadway, the former headquarters of AT&T. Despite efforts of the construction crew to stop them, at least 50 and possibly as many as 200 people climbed onto the structure. Overloaded by the weight, the scaffolding snapped and broke with a large crack. "All of a sudden there was a crash," said one witness, "the whole thing gave way like a stack of dominoes." People fell to the ground; others standing nearby were hit by falling debris. Over 100 people were injured, 10 seriously enough to be hospitalized, though fortunately none fatally. "It seemed as if the ticker tape were suspended in mid-air," the *New York Times* reported, as police and emergency personnel responded and cared for the injured.

An unnamed New York City policeman a short distance from the accident was quizzed by spectators if the parade would resume. With typical New York aplomb he replied "Yeah, they're going to come this way. Nothing stops a parade in New York." The church bells in St. Paul's Chapel had just struck one o'clock when he was proved correct. Debris had been moved aside and the injured were treated at the scene or taken to nearby hospitals, and the parade resumed with deafening chants of "USA, USA" echoing along the street.

Many of the marching Olympians wore their gold, silver, or bronze medals, as huge quantities of computer paper, confetti, and torn newspaper cascaded down. The lack of ticker tape was noted but the sheer volume of paper made up for it. Paper descended all along Broadway except near Zuccotti Park, where the windows of One Liberty Plaza and other new skyscrapers were sealed shut, preventing observers from contributing to the blizzard of paper.

The athletes seemed to be as eager to see New York as New Yorkers were to see them. Quite a few athletes carried cameras and filmed the event as they marched up Broadway, arriving at City Hall Park, where Mayor Ed Koch greeted them in front of City Hall. Mary Lou Retton, winner of four medals including one gold told the mayor, "It's really hard to deal with. The people of New York are incredible. I mean, incredible." Only 4 foot, 9 inches tall, she stood on a chair to see over the lectern. Gymnast Peter Vidmar commented "I've never experienced anything like this," as he pointed to the mass of on-lookers and aimed his camera, "they appreciate us, but we appreciate them too."

When the last of the athletes filed into the reviewing stand, the Emerald Society Police Pipe Band struck up "You're a Grand Old Flag" and "Stars and Stripes Forever."

Standing side by side with the Olympians on the podium, politicians and dignitaries were little noticed as the crowd chanted the names of favorites or shouted statements like "We love you, Mary Lou," or "Marry me" to gymnast Bart Conner. Mayor Koch's words of welcome could barely be heard but when he concluded his remarks with "Today there are over 200 new stars in our flag," an even louder cheer erupted.

Mayor Koch proclaimed it the largest parade ever, boasting that more than two million people stood along the route. Other less optimistic estimates put the number at considerably fewer, noting that only 200,000 people lined the Canyon of Heroes, standing ten deep from the curb, with more filling City Hall Park and the side streets adjacent to Broadway. Within minutes after the athletes entered the park, a team of 190 Sanitation Department workers were hard at work sweeping Broadway and its side streets, clearing them of mounds and piles of paper, in some places an inch deep. The streets were cleaned by 3 o'clock and life on Lower Broadway returned to normal.

The quadrennial athletic competitions continue, and the US would often win the most medals. But this would be the last ticker tape parade to date for America's Olympic teams.

Tuesday, May 7, 1985: Vietnam War Veterans

They had fought in jungles and swamps, in hamlets and villages, and in the cities of South Vietnam, then returned home to a country that showed little gratitude and often no respect for their sacrifices. Now on a sunny and pleasant spring morning they were finally to receive a tribute for their efforts.

Close to 25,000 men and a small number of women, veterans of the Vietnam conflict, began gathering at Cadman Plaza on the Brooklyn side of the Brooklyn Bridge early in the morning. Some wore the jungle fatigues, berets, and boonie hats worn when they fought in America's unpopular war in Southeast Asia. Many more were dressed in mufti, civilian life having somehow shrunken whatever parts of their uniforms they may have still owned. Some tried to form ranks and files with their old units; others carried signs trying to find long lost buddies or at least veterans of the same unit. The Brooklyn Bridge walkway had been cleared and motorcycle police gunned their engines. Shortly before 11 o'clock the parade began crossing the bridge.

Leading the parade was Republican State Assemblyman John Behan, a 41-year veteran of the First Marine Division. Born on Veterans Day in 1944, Behan had served in Vietnam, and lost both his legs after being seriously wounded while on patrol near DaNang. One of many parade participants in a wheelchair, he was pushed across the Brooklyn Bridge by Mayor Ed Koch. A few walked with canes supporting artificial limbs. An army band followed in their wake. Other bands from veteran organizations, fife and drums corps, and local schools were interspaced among the veterans.

As the long column of veterans descended into Park Row and City Hall Plaza, the cheers of appreciative spectators began. In some ways the parade appeared more like a procession than a parade with only a few organized groups. Many in the crowd agreed with the marchers that it was about time to recognize those who had served. Thousands of spectators waved American flags; a few waved miniature flags of the Republic of South Vietnam, a country that no longer existed. One veteran recalled that when he returned home in 1969, having been wounded multiple times, he was met by hostile groups that waved the flag of North Vietnam. He heard names and insults thrown at him. But now, marching with so many others amid a crowd of welcome was cathartic. He admitted that many of his fellow veterans came home with problems caused by drugs, but he blamed much of it on the treatment they received upon coming home. A veteran from Middle Village, Queens, a member of an armored cavalry unit, recalled that it was good hearing cheers. "The war ended in '75," he said, adding. "I got home in '68 and served 11 ½ months in Nam. It feels good to be cheered."

The parade differed in many ways from most previous parades, especially by starting in Brooklyn and heading across the river to march downtown, but one thing was the same: the route was carpeted with spiraling sheets of torn paper, confetti, paper towels, and computer printout paper. Large numbers of those marching downtown kicked their way through the debris, wrapped themselves or decorated their buddies with it. An additional difference for this parade was its destination – not City Hall but 55 Water Street where the New York City Vietnam Veterans Memorial had been erected.

Thousands of marchers filled Water Street at Battery Park, and the adjacent streets and squares. Mayor Koch wheeled Behan to the Memorial. Limping on his artificial legs, the veteran placed a wreath by it while a bugler played Taps. When the final notes faded veterans again began to search out comrades. Men exchanged names, identifying the units they had served in, again attempting to reconnect and re-establish friendships and relationships.

The day's event ended at sunset with fireworks over the East River. By then most of the Vietnam Veterans had returned to their homes but small groups of men watched the pyrotechnics, still reminiscing of Tan Sun Nhut Airbase, Cam Ranh Bay, Saigon, and Tet.

James Behan returned to his home on the eastern end of Long Island. Much to the surprise of military doctors who thought he would be wheelchair-bound forever, he learned to walk with artificial limbs, and later became a member of the United States Wheelchair Olympic Team. As the captain of the amputee team, he won five medals (one gold, three silver, and one bronze) at the International Games for the Handicapped in Toronto in 1976. He served nine terms in the New York State Assembly and finally retired in 1998. In 1981 President Reagan had nominated him to head the Veterans Administration but subsequently withdrew his name from consideration because he "lacked managerial skills" although his criticism of the war and the poor treatment veterans were receiving from the VA were considered instrumental in the decision. In July 2017, East Hampton Long Island's new fireboat and port security vessel was named *John L Behan* and he christened her from his wheelchair in Montauk Harbor.

Brooklyn Bridge

While the little settlement at the southern tip of Manhattan called New Amsterdam was slowly growing in the mid 1600s, Dutch colonists also moved across the East River to Long Island. On the heights overlooking the river, they started a small town called Breuckelen, named after a city in the Netherlands. By 1660 they had also created towns in Gravesend, Flatbush, Bushwick, Flatlands and Bay Ridge. When the British took control in 1664, they re-organized all these towns into one political entity which they called Kings County, separate from the town on Manhattan, which they renamed New York. →

The European population in Kings County grew slowly until after the American Revolution. By 1834, the town around the Heights was incorporated as the City of Brooklyn, and soon afterwards, the City of Williamsburg was also formed. The non-aligning street grids and naming systems that confuse modern drivers started in this period, since the two cities and several other towns of Kings County remained independent of each other until 1854, when the City of Williamsburg and the town of Bushwick were merged into the City of Brooklyn. The combined city's population of 100,000 was smaller than the 500,000 of its neighbor across the East River, but immigration and industrialization fueled Brooklyn's growth after the Civil War. With more land to expand into, Brooklyn had become the 4th largest city in the country by 1890 (behind New York, Philadelphia and Chicago).

The "twin cities" of New York and Brooklyn were connected by ferries, which had begun crossing the East River on a regular basis by the 1820s. Proposals for a bridge or tunnel, which had been made as early as 1810, were cost prohibitive, but in 1852 John Roebling created a design that would work. It took over a decade for the State Senate to authorize bonds to fund construction, and the work began in 1870. It took 13 years to complete, during which time the towers gradually rose above the two cities. When it opened in 1883, it was the longest suspension bridge in the world, and the bonds for the total cost of $15 million dollars (equivalent to $420 million in 2020) were not paid off until 1956.

The bridge was not the impetus for merging the two cities, an idea which had been discussed as early as the 1820s, but it did strengthen the ties between them, as pedestrians, horse-drawn vehicles and cable cars began crossing the river easily. After the Consolidation of 1898, trolley tracks were laid across the bridge which later became part of the subway system, and soon afterward the bridge was repaved for automobiles and trucks. In 1948, the bridge's roadways were upgraded to add access ramps to the new Brooklyn-Queens Expressway, after which the Manhattan side was upgraded when the New York World Building was razed to make way for exit ramps and access to the FDR Drive. In addition to the wear and tear of daily use by thousands of vehicles and trains, the Bridge suffered damage from Hurricane Sandy in 2012, and in 2019 another major renovation began which is estimated to cost over $350 million by the time it is completed.

Tuesday, October 28, 1986:
New York Mets, World Series Champions

The 1986 Mets rode up the Canyon of Heroes as jaunty and cocky as they had played the season. And why not? True to the team's nickname, it had been an "amazin' season."

Despite the arrest of four team members who brawled with a policeman in July, they had won the National League Eastern Division over the Philadelphia Phillies. Then they won a 16-inning marathon to defeat the Houston Astros in the final game of the National League Championship playoffs. Facing the Boston Red Sox in the World Series, the Mets came from behind to win game 6 after a dramatic Red Sox error, then went on to win the final game.

The 1986 Mets rode in a fleet of convertibles from the Battery to City Hall through a blizzard of paper, confetti, computer printouts, torn newspapers, insurance forms, shredded brokerage and banking documents. The applause of their fans (one estimate put the number of spectators at two and a half million) was thunderous.

Manager Davey Johnson rode in the first car. As a Baltimore Oriole he had made the final out in the 1969 World Series when the Mets beat the Orioles for their first

World Series crown *(see: October 20, 1969)*. Seated next to him was World Series MVP Ray Knight. The pair waved in acknowledgment to the raucous crowd. Behind them, cars carried pitchers Ron Darling and Jesse Orosco, third baseman Tim Teufel and outfielder Darryl Strawberry, catcher Gary Carter and outfielder Mookie Wilson. It was Wilson who hit the groundball that eluded the grasp of the Red Sox first baseman, resulting in the Mets' victory in game six of the World Series. As the car in which Wilson rode headed north, it was hailed by a constant chorus of "Mooookie." All the Mets players were in the parade, except pitcher Dwight Gooden, who had overslept, missing the pre-parade gathering for the players at Bowling Green.

At City Hall, Mayor Koch introduced the players one by one, presenting each with a Key to the City. Third-base coach Buddy Harrelson, who had played shortstop when the Mets won the 1969 World Series, raised his hands in victory and shouted, "It's good to be back." First basemen Keith Hernandez told the screaming crowd in City Hall Plaza that the fans were as much responsible for the Mets championship as the players were. Lenny Dykstra waved to the crowd when he was introduced, his cheek stuffed with chewing tobacco. Mets relief pitcher Jesse Orosco was overwhelmed by tears when he was given a key and asked to say a few words. Unable to speak because of emotion, he tossed his cap in the air, reminding all of how he tossed his glove in the air in triumph after striking out the final Red Sox batter in game seven of the Series.

Manager Davey Johnson said, "This was so much fun we ought to do it again next year." The crowd cheered loudly, especially when Mookie Wilson, the steady reliable veteran who had been with the Mets through some of the previous less-than-stellar years, predicted repeated success during the next few years.

By mid-afternoon the festivities had ended. The crowds began to disperse, many heading to Queens or Brooklyn. The police reported handing out more than 40 summonses, mostly to unlicensed vendors. There were a handful of minor injuries causes by trips and falls and the press of the crowd. The most serious damage resulted when the sheer numbers of spectators broke the display window of Modell's sporting goods store at the corner of Broadway and Chambers Street as the crowds filed out of the area. No one was injured at this incident.

Departing players and fans were convinced that this was only the first of many parades for their team, but it was not to be. In 1987 the Mets finished second. They won the National League Eastern title in 1988 but lost the pennant to the Los Angeles Dodgers. They would not return to the World Series until 2000, when they lost to the New York Yankees *(see: October 30, 2000)* and again in 2015, losing to the Kansas City Royals.

Wednesday, June 20, 1990: Nelson Mandela

The living symbol of the struggle against apartheid in South Africa, Nelson Mandela made New York City the first stop on his eight-city tour of the United States. He had been arrested 28 years earlier by the South African government for being the leader of the armed wing of the African National Congress and had been sentenced to life in prison. Most of his sentence was spent on bleak Robben Island near Cape Town, South Africa. Under mounting national and international pressure, the South African government freed him in February 1990, and one of his first steps after being released was a tour of foreign cities and countries in gratitude for their support of him and the anti-apartheid cause, as well as to increase further pressure on the government of South Africa.

His flight arrived at Kennedy International Airport early on a sunny and mild summer day. Waiting for him were a host of reporters and television crews, Federal, State, and City officials, and dignitaries from all walks of life. After a brief welcome at the airport, Mr. Mandela entered a car in a motorcade of 40 vehicles. With police helicopters flying overhead, the motorcade set out on a circuitous route through the neighborhoods of South Jamaica and St. Albans in Queens, then into Brooklyn, driving through Bedford-Stuyvesant, East New York and Fort Green before arriving at Bowling Green for the motorcade up Broadway. Traffic was frozen on all nearby streets as the procession traveled. Perhaps as many as 50,000 people stood and cheered along his route in Queens and another 100,000 in Brooklyn. The crowd along the Canyon of Heroes and at City Hall far exceeded these numbers.

Bands from the Police and Fire Departments took part in the parade as it moved north up Broadway. In the absence of ticker tape, a veritable blizzard of torn paper, stacks of computer paper, toilet tissue, paper towels, and confetti fell to blanket the street below. Mr. Mandela rode in an open vehicle and its floor was carpeted inches deep in paper. Cheers roared from the crowd as the motorcade moved slowly towards City Hall. Mr. Mandela seemed almost stunned by the magnitude of the welcome at first, but before long he smiled and waved like so many other dignitaries and celebrities who had been honored in previous parades.

Mayor David Dinkins greeted the South African leader at City Hall, welcoming him on behalf of the city of New York, the entire state, and, since New York was his first stop, on behalf of the entire country. He placed New York's Medal of Honor around Mr. Mandela's neck and hoped that Mandela's visit to America would add more supporters of his cause.

As many as 400,000 spectators lined Broadway; 200,000 more were jammed into City Hall Plaza. Those who could not hear what was spoken at the welcome listened to the entire ceremony on transistor radios or watched on small portable television sets. When Mr. Mandela stepped up to the rostrum to answer Mayor Dinkins' words, a silence of anticipation fell over the multitude. "Apartheid is doomed," he said and the shout from the crowd echoed through downtown Manhattan. "South Africa will be free. The struggle continues." That afternoon Mr. Mandela was the city's guest at a luncheon at the Waldorf Astoria. Hundreds of invited guests attended and hundreds more without invitations were turned away.

Mr. Mandela spent three days in New York and then continued on to visit Philadelphia, Washington, Chicago, and several other US cities. Everywhere he went he received tumultuous welcomes. When he returned to South Africa, his struggle against the government there continued and intensified. By April 1994, multi-racial elections were held for the first time and the African National Congress received 62% of the votes cast. As leader of that party, he was inaugurated as the country's first black president. He served as president until June 1999, ended the apartheid government, brought about numerous social and economic changes and completely changed the course of South African history. He decided not to run for re-election in 1998. He died of a respiratory infection in Johannesburg on December 5, 2003 and is buried in the village of Qunu in the Eastern Cape Region of South Africa.

Mayor David Dinkins (1990-1993)

The first, and to date only, African American to serve as New York's Mayor was born in Trenton, NJ in 1927, and moved to Harlem with his father when his parents separated. After finishing high school in 1945, David Dinkins tried to enlist in the Marines, but was told that the racial quota had already been met. He succeeded later, though the delay prevented him from seeing any action during World War II. After being discharged in 1946, he attended Howard University, then earned a law degree at Brooklyn Law School.

Dinkins started a private law practice in Harlem and joined the Democratic party. He served in the NY State Assembly in 1966, then as President of the NYC Board of Elections and City Clerk before being elected Manhattan Borough President in 1985. In 1989, he won the Democratic Primary for Mayor against incumbent Ed Koch, who had hoped to become the city's first 4-term mayor. Dinkins then defeated Republican candidate Rudy Giuliani, taking office in 1990 with a pledge to heal the racial divisions in the city he described as a "gorgeous mosaic."

His term in office coincided with a peak in crime rates, including an all-time high in murder cases. Although some of his policies had a long-term effect in reducing crime, the results were slow at first, leading to public perception that crime was out of control. Public confidence in him eroded further when riots broke out in Crown Heights after two black children were killed by a car in a Hassidic Jewish leader's motorcade.

Dinkins' accomplishments include the revitalization of the Times Square area, negotiation of a financially lucrative deal with the US Tennis Authority, and policies to decrease homelessness and rehabilitate housing in Harlem and the South Bronx. Nonetheless, he lost the next mayoral election, which was a re-match against Giuliani.

After leaving office, Dinkins became a professor at Columbia University, and stayed active in Democratic party politics. He also served on the board of several non-profit organizations, including the US Tennis Association and the Jazz Foundation of America. A father to two children, the former Mayor and his wife both died in 2020.

Chapter 10
We Are the Champions (1991-current)

On September 11, 2001, two hijacked passenger jet planes crashed into the twin towers of the World Trade Center. As thousands watched on television or from wherever they were in the city, the towers collapsed, killing close to 3,000 and injuring many more, including over 300 firefighters who rushed into the building to do their jobs and save lives. Two other planes were hijacked that same day, one crashing into the Pentagon in Washington DC, while the other was diverted from its mission by passengers who attempted to wrest control of the plane back from the terrorists, crashing into a field in Pennsylvania. It was the worst terrorist attack in US history, and for weeks afterward, downtown Manhattan was a disaster zone around the smoldering rubbish of steel and concrete. Three days after the attack, President George W. Bush stood near those ruins, grabbed a bullhorn and proclaimed, "This nation stands with the good people of New York City."

The city had come a long way in the 26 years since a previous President told the city to drop dead.

It should come as no surprise that, as the country's financial capital, the city's finances improved along with the general national economy and in particular the fortunes of Wall Street. After a brief recession in 1990, the last decade of the 20th century was booming, with the S&P index gaining over 600%. Inflation was low, productivity rose, job creation was strong and technological advances all contributed to a decade-long bull market.

The mayor for most of the decade was Rudy Giuliani, who benefitted from, and expanded, many of the "quality of life" policies begun during the Koch era. Giuliani believed increasing police crackdowns on nuisance crimes, likes graffiti, turnstile jumping, cannabis possession and panhandling by so-called "squeegee men" would restore confidence that order had been restored and the city was safe. Crime rates, especially for more violent crimes like murder, rape and theft, were already declining, not just in the city but nation-wide. There are no universally accepted explanations for why this happened (the aging population, technology-driven improvements in policing, a reliance on "3-strikes-and-you're-out" imprisonment policies), but Giuliani was able to use the decline to his political benefit, portraying himself as a tough leader who had cleaned up the city. He was reelected in 1997 in a landslide.

The economic improvements were not enjoyed by everybody, as evidenced by the city's unemployment rate, which stayed higher than the national average throughout the decade. Nor did everybody share the feeling that the city was safer. There were a growing number of incidents of police brutality and racial profiling, including Anthony Baez (1994), Abner Louima (1997) and Amadou Diallo (1999), and racial tensions increased during the decade.

The city's reputation, at least, was improving, and the entertainment and news media both played a role in that. While the *Law & Order* franchise expanded and continued, other shows like *Seinfeld, Friends* and *Sex & the City* portrayed a city of great apartments, quirky neighbors, diverse career opportunities and glamorous excitement. Even morning news shows like *Today* and *Good Morning America* helped the city's image as they interacted with pedestrians and tourists passing their ground-level studios.

The 9/11 terrorist attacks on New York were not a new phenomenon, of course, and each generation has experienced them. A bombing on Wall Street in 1920 killed 38, and during the 1950s the "Mad Bomber" caused over 30 explosions throughout the city during his 16-year spree. In addition to the rash of terrorist attacks in the 1970s discussed in chapter 9, the World Trade Center was bombed in 1993, and a mass shooter opened fire from the observation deck of the Empire State Building in 1997.

Despite the international acclaim he earned for his reaction to the attacks, Giuliani was barred from running for reelection in 2001 by term limits enacted by a voter referendum in 1993, which he had supported. After he made an unsuccessful attempt for an "extension" of his term, claiming a mayoral transition so soon after the attack would be disruptive, voters elected Michael Bloomberg in November 2001.

Terrorist attacks, and fear that other incidents might be caused by an attack, continued in the years since, and in some ways have become acknowledged as part of the post-Cold War era. Times Square was the site of an explosion in 2008 and of a failed car bombing two years later, while pressure cookers became explosive devices in an attempted bombing in 2015 and a successful one the following year. When the city experienced another blackout in 2003, many New Yorkers assumed it had been caused by terrorists. A steam pipe explosion near Grand Central Terminal in 2007 caused similar reactions.

The city was also impacted by natural disasters, especially during 2012's Hurricane Sandy, which caused widespread power outages, extensive flooding, and at least 40 deaths. The subway system was shut down for several days, and eight tunnels were flooded, as was the Brooklyn-Battery Tunnel.

In addition to the repairs needed after Hurricane Sandy, the subway system received some much-needed and long-delayed expansions, with a new connection between stations in Queens opening in 2001, a new station at South Ferry in 2013, an extension of the Flushing line to Hudson Yards in 2015, the long-awaited Second Avenue line opening in 2017, and in 2018 the re-opening of the Cortlandt Station which had been destroyed on 9/11. The subway fare has risen many times since 1980 when it was 50 cents, though with the switch from metal token to electronic MetroCards in 1993, the changes are less cumbersome to implement, and as of 2015 the cost of a basic ride is $2.75.

Bloomberg's approach to running the city government was based on his business experience, applying data analysis and statistics to decision-making, and improving the city's use of technology and the internet. His popularity increased over his two terms, and in 2009 he convinced the city council to change the term limit laws and was elected to a third term. During his 12 years in City Hall, there was an increase in construction projects that reshaped the city, including a new World Trade Center Tower and Hudson Yards, pedestrianization of Times Square, the conversion of abandoned elevated train tracks into the Highline, and replacement of the Koskiuszko Bridge on the Brooklyn-Queens Expressway.

As a social liberal, Bloomberg supported and implemented policies such as banning smoking in restaurants and bars, creating bicycle lanes and pedestrian-only zones in city streets and squares, and launching a bicycle rental program. He also continued a program begun during the Giuliani Administration, completing a series of "Greenways" around Manhattan Island by removing or repurposing many of the eroding piers along the waterfront. As of 2017, it is possible to circumnavigate the island on bicycle or foot.

At the same time, however, Bloomberg expanded the NYPD's controversial stop and frisk policy, and incidents of police brutality continued to increase (including Sean Bell in 2006, Kimani Gray in 2013, and Eric Garner in 2014), causing protests and contributing to the Black Lives Matter movement. Even after the stop and frisk policy was ended by his successor, NYPD anti-protest tactics have been widely criticized, especially during the George Floyd protests in 2020.

Although the economy and the city's budget were generally strong during the decade, economic disparity in the city was increasing, especially in Manhattan, and the rising cost of living during an era of wage stagnation impacted many middle-income residents. In 2011, protestors took over Zuccotti Park for over 2 months, launching the Occupy Wall Street movement which sparked imitations nation-wide. Economic inequality has been a priority for Mayor Bill de Blasio, who referred to it as "the tale of two cities," and the economic challenges the city faced were exacerbated by the Covid pandemic.

The city's population has continued evolving, and the steep drop seen in the 1970s has been reversed. As of the 2010 census, New York has an all-time high of 8.2 million people, over half of whom live in Brooklyn and Queens, and the city continues to have a large percentage of foreign-born residents. At 38%, it is as high as it was in 1900, though today's immigrants arrive from many more nations than their predecessors. As before, they help contribute to the city's cultural and ethnic diversity, and they will no doubt help shape New York's future in the same way that all who moved to the city have done before.

In an era of increasingly divisive politics, widening economic disparity and larger-than-ever cultural diversity, we can all choose our heroes, and thanks to social media and smart phones, we can customize and curate what news we receive, which influencers we follow, and what is trending in our lives. There are fewer things that we share in common with our neighbors, including agreement about basic facts. But walk into any sports bar in the city, and through the no-longer smoke-filled room you can watch almost any game around the world, including sports like soccer which were less popular with Americans before cable TV. Despite, or perhaps because of, the rivalry between the Mets and the Yankees *(see: October 30, 2000)*, the Giants and the Jets, the Rangers and the Islanders, many New Yorkers share a passion for sports *(see: July 10, 2015)*. It should come as no surprise then that almost all of the parades in this period have been for the victorious teams and athletes *(see: October 17, 1998)*.

Monday, June 10, 1991: Persian Gulf War Veterans

Barely three months after Operation Desert Storm was launched, the brief war against Iraq ended. A welcome home parade was quickly organized and staged. Approximately 24,000 people marched, including 12,000 troops from the United States and the 17 other nations that sent troops; 6,000 members of various veteran organizations; and 6,000 others from marching bands, drill teams, fife and drum corps, and political organizations. Before the start of the parade, Mayor David Dinkins presented the Keys of the City to the parade's three Grand Marshals: Secretary of Defense Dick Cheney; Chairman of the Joint Chiefs of Staff, General Colin Powell; and General Norman Schwarzkopf.

By mid-morning the streets of Lower Manhattan were filled with spectators. One unidentified official from the Police Department estimated the total number viewing the parade at 4.7 million people. The figure he quoted was undoubtedly a huge over-estimate, but many agreed that the crowd was among the largest ever. People were packed along the route of the Canyon of Heroes, shoulder to shoulder at every available window ledge and rooftop. The subways ran extra trains into the area, and the streets south of Canal Street were closed to vehicular traffic. The day began with perfect weather for a parade, with temperatures in the high 70's, a clear blue sky, and a light breeze; later in the day, the heat rose dramatically to almost 90, and by day's end nearly 150 spectators were treated for heat exhaustion.

Slightly after noon, the parade began. Dozens of marching bands played different tunes, and strains of "America the Beautiful," "Hail, Hail the Gang's All Here," "The Halls of Montezuma," and "New York, New York" clashed with each other. Color guards carried the flags of the 18 nations that provided troops, plus those of the 40 other nations that had given logistic or materiel support. In addition to marching troops, military hardware was displayed, as a handful of jeeps, tanks, armored personnel carriers, howitzers, communication vehicles, ambulances, and a Patriot missile, mounted on a flatbed trailer, moved up Broadway in the largest weapons display ever on parade in Manhattan.

The marchers were greeted by a blizzard of paper, including everything from shredded paper to rolls of paper towels, fanfolds of computer paper, and multi-colored confetti that fell like snow, landing on marchers and vehicles as well as on spectators. It hung like decorations from the spires of Trinity Church and flagpoles. Strands even twirled and twisted around the tip of the Patriot missile and howitzer barrels. Groups in the crowd chanted "USA! USA! USA!" reminiscent of similar chants at Olympic events. More than 3,000 police were assigned to keep spectators behind the wooden barriers.

Mayor Dinkins welcomed the three Grand Marshals at City Hall. The entire plaza and nearby streets were a sea of flag-waving people. Children too young to know of previous wars and senior citizens who knew too many were equally present. As he introduced the Grand Marshals, the Mayor announced to the crowd, "This is the mother of all parades." Born in Harlem and raised in the Bronx, General Powell acted as spokesman. "It's a great day to be back home in New York," he announced proudly.

From start to finish, the parade, reception, and speeches took more than four hours. The cost of the parade came to more than $4.5 million, but it was announced that not one cent of city money was spent. All expenses were paid by the Federal government, veteran groups, and private donations.

The war had not been without controversy, and groups of protestors held anti-war signs and chanted slogans, mainly in the area just south of City Hall Park near Vesey, Fulton and Ann Streets. Most were peaceful, but two dozen anti-war protesters were arrested. At Ann Street and Broadway a few individuals hurled Christmas ornaments filled with red paint, which police originally thought was blood.

A fireworks display over the East River concluded the day's events after dusk. The area between the Brooklyn and Manhattan bridges was illuminated by bright stars of red, white, and blue pyrotechnics, and spectators jammed docks and piers and streets along the river to watch the display. The elevated roadway of the FDR Drive was filled with spectators, and the crowd was so large that the South Street Seaport closed nearly two hours before the fireworks extravaganza began.

Two of the three grand marshals would go on to larger roles during the Presidential Administration of George W. Bush, the son of President George H.W. Bush. General Powell served as the nation's first African American Secretary of State from 2001 until 2005, and Dick Cheney was the nation's 46th Vice President, from 2001 until 2009. In their respective roles, they were both heavily involved in the War in Afghanistan (2001-2021) and the Iraq War (2003-2011) as well the nation's military involvements elsewhere. Mr. Cheney, now age 80, is still alive as of this printing; General Powell died of Covid-related complications during his battle with cancer in October 2021.

General "Stormin' Norman" Schwarzkopf retired from the military shortly after the end of the Gulf War, and repeatedly turned down offers to enter politics, spending his time writing an autobiography and fundraising for charities. Initially supportive of the Iraq War in 2003, he became a critic of the handling of the operation and lack of planning for reconstruction. He died in 2012.

Not since the end of the First and Second World Wars had American soldiers returned home for war to ticker tape parades honoring their service and sacrifice. Korean War Veterans waited forty years until they were honored *(see: June 25, 1991)* and Vietnam Veterans waited twelve *(see: May 7, 1985)*. In the years since the terrorist attack of 9/11, the United States has been in an almost constant state of war, with troops engaged in combat in Afghanistan, Iraq, Libya, Pakistan, Somalia, Syria and Yemen.

South Street Seaport

The city's first pier was built by the Dutch West India Company in 1659 where Fulton Street ended at South Street, which ran along the East River. Sheltered from the westerly winds of the Hudson River and Upper Bay, the pier was expanded over the 100 years, and was the city's main point of entry for goods from England as well as southern colonies. Nearby Pearl and Fulton Streets became busy commercial centers for the growing city, and by 1797, New York was the new country's largest center of maritime trade.

Over the next century, the harbor grew as quickly as the city itself did. In 1818, transatlantic voyages began on a regular basis between Liverpool and New York, and in 1822, the Fulton Fish Market opened at the foot of the South Street Pier. A fire destroyed many of the buildings in the area in 1835, but the seaport recovered swiftly, and ferry service to Brooklyn began a year later. Soon the piers along the East River held newly built warehouses, and South Street was lined with boarding houses and taverns, workshops and brothels. By the early 1900s, though, the piers along South Street were too shallow for newer and larger ships and by 1930, the piers on the East River were mostly vacant.

In 1967, the South Street Seaport Museum opened, occupying one of the historic buildings facing the pier. Inspired by revitalization projects in Baltimore's Inner Harbor and other cities, a major renovation in 1982 turned the seaport into a tourist attraction. Several historic ships were docked at the pier and opened to tourists, and a portion of Fulton Street was re-paved with cobblestone and lined with shops. Although the Fulton Fish Market moved to the Bronx in 2005 and the seaport was heavily damaged by Hurricane Sandy in 2012, the Museum and the Seaport re-opened several years later after extensive renovations, and they remain popular tourist destinations.

Tuesday, June 25, 1991: Korean War Veterans

Forty years to the day after North Korean troops crossed over the border and invaded South Korea, veterans of the war were finally accorded a parade in their honor. The New York Korean Veterans Memorial Commission organized the event and expected about 4,000 veterans to march up the Canyon of Heroes. More than twice that number arrived and took part: 9,000 middle-aged men who fought in a war that had not even been called a war. According to President Harry Truman, it was a "Police Action" in which more than 54,000 US service men had given their lives, 100,000 were wounded, and more than 11,000 were captured or reported as missing in action.

Marching bands from the Army, Navy, Marine Corps, and Air Force escorted the veterans. Attempts were made before the parade began to group veterans into formations representing the units in which they served. By the time the parade began at noon, however, these preparations were far from complete and for the most part the men simply marched with buddies from long ago or with newly met friends who shared distant memories from Korea.

The usual enthusiasm for a New York parade was missing. Along some parts of the route there were barely any spectators at all. A police spokesman commented that the numbers along the route were about the same as on an average day at noon. The *New York Times* reported the amount of paper rained down on the marchers was measured in pounds rather than in tons. Perhaps names like Pork Chop Hill, Chosin Reservoir, Inchon, Yalu River, and the Pusan Perimeter were no longer familiar to the average person. Perhaps the timing of the parade, just two weeks after the triumphant celebration of the Persian Gulf War *(see: June 10, 1991)*, was to blame. Or perhaps New Yorkers were uncertain whether this 40-year-old conflict had even ended, since the two Koreas never signed a peace treaty and (as of this writing in 2021) soldiers still face each other over a demilitarized zone. Whatever the reason for the lackluster response, the applause was at its best for six men near the front of the parade, marching behind a banner proclaiming themselves as former POWs.

Most of the veterans agreed that the parade should have been held years earlier. There had been a parade for General MacArthur *(see: April 20, 1951)* when more than 7 million people jammed the streets to honor the retiring general who first led the United Nations forces in Korea, but the consensus among today's marchers was that parade had been for the general and not for his troops. Even the parade for UN servicemen wounded in Korea *(see: October 29, 1951)* did not honor all the men who had fought on the Korean peninsula.

After the last of the veterans marched past City Hall, dignitaries returned to Battery Park, where a ceremony was held to dedicate a memorial to the Korean War veterans. Irwin Schwartz, Chairman of the New York Korea Veterans Memorial Commission, was joined by Mayor David Dinkins, former mayor Edward Koch, and Ambassador Tong-Jin Park of South Korea at the unveiling. One Korean War Veteran, Danny Ross of Flushing, Queens, said "We're finally being recognized." But for most of those who marched that day, it was almost a non-event, too long overdue.

If the day's event brought closure to those who marched, the final chapter of Korean War has yet to be written. The 1953 Armistice may have ended the fighting for most of the world, but the two Koreas are still technically at war. Despite the 2018 Panmunjom Declaration, when both nations agreed to talks to formally an finally end the war, the four-mile-wide demilitarized zone separating them is still one of the most heavily guarded borders in the world.

Battery Park

Today, the southern edge of Manhattan Island is a 25-acre park and esplanade called Battery Park, but for much of the city's history, this stretch of waterfront had many different uses. As early as 1625, the Dutch settlers had built Fort Amsterdam on the small rise in the ground just north of the current park, and the British installed several batteries of cannon between the fort and the water's edge during the 1700s.

Fort Amsterdam was torn down after the Revolutionary War, but by 1810 the US military had built Castle Clinton on the site of the West Battery. Other forts were built to protect New York Harbor over the next decades, and Castle Clinton was decommissioned and leased to the city for other uses. In 1824, it housed a beer garden and open-air theater called Castle Garden, and by the 1850s, concerts and operas were performed in the now-roofed theater. In 1855, the state government took control of the site, using it as the Emigrant Landing Depot, which thousands of new immigrants passed through until the Federal government took over immigration processing and moved the center to Ellis Island in 1897.

Castle Garden then became the home of the New York Aquarium, until 1941 when Robert Moses wanted to tear it down to make way for the Brooklyn-Battery Tunnel. The Aquarium was closed, but public outcry prevented the demolition of the castle and park, though the park was closed for 12 years for construction of the tunnel. Re-landscaped before it opened again in 1952, the park was underused when the city's shipping industry collapsed, and it further deteriorated during the city's fiscal crisis. In 1971, a Congressional study called the park a "litter-ridden national disgrace."

As the city's fortunes rebounded during the 1980s-90s, the Battery began to receive the attention it needed, and in 1998, a $40 million renovation was begun. In addition to restoration of Castle Clinton and nearby Pier A, the park was again re-landscaped and paved, and several memorials erected. In addition to the Korean War Memorial, the Battery is now home to Hope Garden, a memorial dedicated to AIDS victims, and *The Sphere* sculpture, which was moved from the World Trade Center after the September 11 terrorist attack.

Friday, June 17, 1994:
New York Rangers, Stanley Cup Champions

The New York Rangers had not won the Stanley Cup since 1940, and the city's hockey fans were convinced that a curse had been put on the city. "Now it's official," commented Mayor Rudy Giuliani, "The curse is broken." A long-suffering hockey fan added, smiling, "Now we can die in peace" thanks to the Rangers' victory over the Vancouver Canucks.

A series of floats carried the players and coaches on the same route that had welcomed kings and queens, presidents and diplomats, explorers and rescuers, astronauts and aviators, baseball players and Olympians. An estimated 1.5 million people lined Broadway, cheering and waving for their champions. The mayor and his 8-year-old son Andrew rode on one of the floats with Rangers' coach, Mike Keenan. In place of ticker tape, the sky was filled with confetti, torn pages of telephone directories, computer printout sheets, and rolls of paper towels and toilet tissue. Broadway was littered, in places ankle deep.

At City Hall the individual players were introduced to the wildly screaming crowd of fans. Mayor Giuliani referred to the Rangers center Mark Messier as "Mr. June" comparing his play to New York Yankees star Reggie Jackson, known as "Mr. October." When Coach Keenan spoke, he credited the seventh game victory to the fans whose support carried his team to the championship. A number of those on hand to join in the celebration had fashioned their own replicas of the Stanley cup. Made of items that included salad bowls, cookie tins, pizza pans, and spray paint, they were held high in imitation of Messier's victory skate around the Madison Square Garden rink when the genuine trophy was awarded to the "Broadway Blueshirts," as the team was nicknamed.

When all the festivities finally ended, the Sanitation Department sent in front-end loaders along with sweepers and workers carrying blowers to clear Broadway, but no estimate was given of the amount of paper cleaned up and removed. A *New York Times* reporter noticed, however, that none came from the Automatic Data Processing office on the third floor of 42 Broadway. A stockroom worker said that company policy forbids it because "when they had the last parade, somebody threw the wrong paper out the window, and one of our clients was very angry."

No Rangers team has duplicated this victory, celebrated on a warm day in June 1994, and fans have entered a new period of waiting to win the Stanley Cup again.

Mayor Rudy Giuliani (1994-2001)

Born in East Flatbush in 1944, Rudolph Giuliani considered becoming a Catholic priest before attending law school at NYU, where he earned his law degree in 1968. He joined the Democratic party and began clerking for a judge in the Southern District of New York. Because of this position, he was able to avoid the draft during the Vietnam War. Changing his party affiliation to Independent, he was hired by the Ford Administration as Associate District Attorney, leading several high-profile cases. In 1980, he registered as a Republican, and was named Associate Attorney General during the Reagan Administration, and later led the Southern District of NY, where he won high profile cases against organized crime, corrupt politicians, and Wall Street insider traders Ivan Boesky and Michael Milken.

He lost his first bid for Mayor but returned four years later to defeat Mayor Dinkins in 1993, running on the Republican and Liberal party tickets, promising to clean the city of "nuisance crimes" such as turnstile jumping, squeegee men, and marijuana possession. Crime rates did drop during his first term, though there is debate about to what extent that was caused by his policies. Nevertheless, he easily won re-election in 1997. Giuliani rose to national fame in the aftermath of the terrorist attack on the World Trade Center on September 11, 2001. His response was almost universally praised at the time, though later critics have questioned some of his decisions prior to the attack, especially to locate the Office of Emergency Management in the World Trade Center. After leaving City Hall in 2001, Giuliani continued to be active in the Republican party, and ran in the primary for president in 2008. In 2016, he supported candidate Donald Trump, and served as his advisor or personal lawyer.

Giuliani was diagnosed with prostate cancer in 2000. Soon afterwards, he announced that he was leaving his second wife, Donna, but was criticized when it was learned he had not told her before announcing it at a press conference. He moved out of Gracie Mansion when city regulations prevented his mistress Judith Nathan from staying there overnight; they later married in 2003 and divorced in 2019. A father to two children from whom he says he is estranged, the former mayor and lifelong Yankees fan is currently 76 years old.

Tuesday, October 29, 1996:
New York Yankees, World Series Champions

The New York Yankees did it again. After winning the American League Championship, the "Bronx Bombers" faced the Atlanta Braves in the World Series. The Braves had been heavily favored, but the Yankees had superior pitching strength. After losing the first two games of the Series at Yankee Stadium, the Yankees went on to win the next three games, played in Atlanta. Game six was back in Yankee Stadium, and the strength of New York's bullpen saved the day. It was the 23rd victorious World Series for the Yankees, but it was also their first in 18 years.

October 29 dawned brisk and windy with a cloudless blue sky. Yankees players and coaches, some with their families, rode on floats. Mayor Rudy Giuliani told the press two days earlier that schools should be closed to permit young fans to view their heroes march up the Canyon of Heroes. The Board of Education refused to shut the school system but attendance city-wide dropped from its usual 86% to 75%. Andrew Giuliani, the mayor's son, was among those who stayed out of class and sat next to his hero, rookie shortstop Derek Jeter. In a city with two major league baseball teams, Mayor Giuliani made not the slightest attempt to hide his preference for the Yankees. He sat beside Yankees manager, Joe Torre, wearing the Yankees team colors.

Shortly after noon the parade kicked off from Bowling Green towards its destination on Chambers Street. Brass bands from marching groups around the city, most featuring high-stepping majorettes, filled the late October air with marching music. The Yankees players, many wearing their uniforms, waved at the huge crowd from floats, the first of which featured a 5-foot fiberglass baseball with the words "New York Yankees 1996 World Champions" revolving around it. The final float contained the team's Ground Crew, who not only were responsible for maintaining Yankee Stadium but also entertained audiences during games by performing the Macarena and the YMCA dance routines between innings.

The mayor predicted the crowd would exceed 3.5 million spectators. The sidewalks were packed eight deep in spots, some of the more athletic fans climbed light poles, and a few fool-hardy ones stood on window ledges. The subways ran additional trains into the downtown area all morning. One parade-goer noted it seemed as if half of the city was clustered on the lower end of Manhattan Island. Despite all this, the mayor's crowd prediction fell short and various sources placed the crowd size between 1 and 1.5 million.

Paper of all types flew from the windows of skyscrapers along the route. Since ticker tape had become virtually obsolete, its place was taken by confetti, torn newspapers and magazines, and rolls of toilet paper. Spectators in one building near City Hall used something totally unexpected, emptying entire boxes of files out the windows. Among the paper floating down were thousands of confidential records from the City Housing Authority and computer printouts of unemployment checks from the New York State Department of Social Services. No one seemed concerned at the time, and not long after the parade ended all Broadway and adjacent side streets were cleaned by overtime-earning Sanitation Department workers.

The focus of all this attention were the Yankees players, including relief pitcher and Series MVP, John Wetteland; starting pitchers David Cone and Andy Pettitte; players like Wade Boggs, Darryl Strawberry and Paul O'Neill, and the rest of the Yankees team, all waving and smiling at their fans. Drawing the most attention was a convertible in which rode New York Governor George Pataki, and iconic hero Joe DiMaggio. It was another great day to be a Yankees fan.

A platform had been erected in City Hall Plaza, and the park was filled with Yankees fans. A young attorney working for the Parks Department and responsible for checking the credentials of guests filling the seats, Adam Hellegers recalled watching the Radio City Music Hall Rockettes perform for the crowd before the mayor spoke. Dressed in green Santa costumes, they performed a number from their soon-to-open Christmas Spectacular, ending with a rousing "Go Yankees!"

The mayor presented George Steinbrenner, principal owner of the Yankees, with a proclamation declaring the day as "New York Yankees Day." Mr. Steinbrenner handed the mayor the World Series trophy, lending it for display in City Hall. Wearing his Yankees cap and windbreaker, the mayor held the trophy aloft and displayed it to the wild enthusiasm of the spectators. The ceremony continued and Mayor Giuliani presenting each player and coach with a Key to City. "Their victory is an inspiration for all of us," he said, "It's a metaphor for a city whose people work best under pressure. It's a metaphor for a city that is having a renaissance." Less than a week later, officials estimated that the parade had cost more than $1 million, which would be covered by private sponsors, including the Yankees organization.

Yankees fans cheered wildly as the players departed the reviewing stand and headed for a well-deserved rest after a difficult season. Many hoped that this victory would usher in a new period for the team, with more victories than during the past 15 years. Those hopes would soon be fulfilled (see: October 23, 1998).

Saturday, October 17, 1998: Sammy Sosa

For baseball fans who love statistics and record-breaking, the 1998 baseball season was thrilling. The record for the most home runs hit within a single season had been held since 1961 by New York Yankees outfielder Roger Maris, whose 61 home runs broke the previous record set by Babe Ruth in 1927. In 1998, Maris' record was broken by not one but two players: Chicago Cubs outfielder Sammy Sosa and St. Louis Cardinals First Baseman Mark McGwire. On September 8, McGwire hit his 62nd home run, followed a week later by Sosa. Throughout September, the two men battled back and forth for the lead, and media coverage intensified. On September 25, both men hit their 66th home run of the season. McGwire hit four more home runs in the next two days, and the regular season ended with 70 for McGwire and 66 for Sosa. Although he did not win the home run race, Sosa helped his team reach the season-ending playoffs for the National League pennant.

Another big news story that September was Hurricane Georges, a powerful category 4 hurricane that caused significant damage in the Caribbean, then crossed Florida to enter the Gulf of Mexico before striking Louisiana. Among the places hit hard was the Dominican Republic, where Sosa had been born and raised. The nation lost power and sustained over $1 billion of damage, over 400 people were killed and 155,000 left homeless. Sosa's newly formed charitable foundation pledged to provide financial aid to help the recovery.

Over half a million Dominicans live in the upper Manhattan neighborhood of Washington Heights, and New York has the largest population of Dominicans in the US. For many of them, Sosa was a hero. Though he did not play for a New York team, the city's two Dominican-born elected officials, Councilman Guillermo Linares and Assemblyman Adriano Espaillat, decided the city should honor him, suggesting a rally in Riverbank State Park on 145th Street and the Hudson River, the largest park near Washington Heights.

Mayor Rudy Giuliani liked the idea of celebrating a baseball hero, but not in the Heights. Perhaps because Riverbank was a State park, which would mean sharing the spotlight with the Governor, or perhaps because the Dominican community was largely Democratic, the Republican mayor announced that there would be "only one event, and that is a parade down the Canyon of Heroes." Whatever they thought about the location, thousands of the Dominican population of New York City journeyed downtown to pay tribute to their hero. Cubs jerseys were suddenly the hottest item being sold by street vendors, as well as miniature flags of the Dominican Republic.

Sosa rode up Broadway on a float decorated with a large capital C, the logo of the Cubs. Motorcycle police led the small motorcade as it moved north. High school bands from upper Manhattan, the Bronx, and Newark, New Jersey, provided the tempo which had a distinctive Latin beat. Crowds along the way were smaller than for most parades, probably because the event was held on a Saturday, a day when most downtown area banks, brokerage houses, and insurance firms were closed or working with smaller staffs. Those who were there, though, were jubilant. "I am more proud that I was born in the Dominican Republic today than any other day, because Sammy Sosa was born there," said 40-year-old Fernando Cruz, "He was born poor, like me." Later that day, Councilman Linares said, "To have one of our own reach the level of being a national hero is only a dream come true."

When the float carrying the outfielder arrived at City Hall, Mayor Giuliani presented him with the Key to the City. The Mayor introduced Sosa as "a Dominican hero, an American hero, a hero around the world," then went on to praise Sosa's humanitarian efforts in the aftermath of the hurricane. Earlier in the day, Sosa had been presented with a bronze medal from St Clare's Hospital in Manhattan and had been named the first recipient of the Jackie Robinson Empire State Freedom Medal, presented to him by Governor Pataki and the widow of the late Jackie Robinson, Rachel Robinson.

Smiling and waving to the crowd, Sosa spoke briefly, his voice barely above a whisper. "I am a man of the people, that's all I am. The Keys to the City I was given today do not belong to me. They belong to you. You are the people of New York. You are my people." Holding aloft the Key, he stepped away from the microphone as the crowd cheered, shouting his name and praising him in English and Spanish.

Following a luncheon reception in City Hall, Sosa and the Mayor were driven to Yankee Stadium, where Sosa was awarded the honor of throwing out the first pitch of the World Series game that evening between the Yankees and the San Diego Padres.

Sammy Sosa continued to play professional baseball until 2007, but his popularity waned. In 2000, his foundation was investigated for fraud and disclosed that only $82,000 of aid had made it to the Dominican Republic. In late 2003 he was found using a corked bat in violation of major league baseball rules, and two years later, he appeared at Congressional hearings over the use of anabolic steroids, along with baseball players Rafael Palmero, José Conseco, and Mark McGwire. In testimony delivered by Sosa's attorney, he denied having ever used "illegal performance-enhancing drugs" or ever having broken any laws of the United States or the Dominican Republic. No action was taken by the government on any of the four except McGwire. Sosa retired from baseball in 2009 and has been eligible for induction into the Baseball Hall of Fame since 2013, but to date has not received the necessary votes. The father of six children, he lives in Chicago with his wife Sonia Rodriguez, a former dancer on Dominican television.

Friday, October 23, 1998:
New York Yankees, World Series Champions

For New York fans of baseball, 1998 was a banner year. Sammy Sosa and Mark McGwire battled it out to hit the most home runs in one season *(see: October 17, 1998)*; and the New York Yankees set a club record, ending the season with 114 wins and only 48 losses. They then won the division series against the Texas Rangers and beat the Cleveland Indians to win the American League Championship Series. To crown the year, the Yankees swept the San Diego Padres, winning four straight games to capture their 24th World Series Championship.

The weather could not have been better for a parade. Bright sunshine bathed the Canyon of Heroes, and there were only small puffy white clouds in the blue sky above. Fans packed the streets of Lower Manhattan, some camping out the previous night in order to see their baseball heroes. The Police Department did not estimate the size of the crowd, but unofficial parade watchers put the number at 3.5 million, or half the population of the entire city, though many spectators came from the suburbs. Whether the estimate was true or not, everyone agreed that the crowd was large and noisy. Long before the parade began, the crowd cheered and chanted, shouted and yelled. Some spectators carried brooms to celebrate their "sweep" of the National League Champion Padres.

The Yankees rode up Broadway on blue and white floats and in double-decker buses. Riding in the first bus, Mayor Giuliani and the team's principal owner, George Steinbrenner, took turns holding the World Championship trophy. Players and coaches leaned from their floats or buses, returning waves and applause. Pitcher David Wells pointed his video camera to record the procession. Manager Joe Torre seemed almost embarrassed by the attention paid to him and his players. Orlando "El Duque" Hernandez smiled broadly when praises were shouted at him in Spanish. A free agent, outfielder Bernie Williams grinned at signs reading "Don't leave, Bernie," while pitcher David Cone never stopped pumping his arm in a victory gesture. Derek Jeter smiled and waved at female admirers.

The decibel level soared highest, however, for Darryl Strawberry, one-time New York Mets player. Sitting in a red Chrysler convertible, wearing a woolen ski cap and dark glasses, he had recently been diagnosed with colon cancer and was recovering from his initial treatment. Floating down in blizzard-like amounts came paper of all kinds: confetti, computer printout sheets, shredded phone books and newspapers, paper towels, napkins and toilet tissue.

Large numbers of school-aged children were in attendance at City Hall Park and all along the route. It was an unscheduled holiday for many and even the mayor's son, Andrew, was absent from class. One 18-year-old high school student was quoted as saying "Most of my teachers are Yankees fans and they're here, too."

City Hall Park was filled beyond capacity. The Yankees were ushered into City Hall for a fast lunch and private reception with New York's self-proclaimed Number 1 Yankees Fan, Mayor Giuliani. After lunch the mayor introduced the players and coaches to the crowd and presented each with a Key to the City. The Key for Darryl Strawberry was given in absentia, since the outfielder had gone home to continue his recovery.

The mayor addressed the crowd in City Hall Park, saying, "As long as baseball is played, the 1998 New York Yankees will set the standard. I predict that when the history of baseball is written, this will be the greatest team in the history of baseball." Manager Torre added "After '96 I didn't think it could get any better. But this is dynamite!" *(see: October 29, 1996)*.

Presenting keys to each player and coach took a considerable amount of time and it was almost 4 o'clock when the last award was given. City Hall Park was so crowded it seemed as if not a single person had left and, in fact, the crowd had grown as spectators from along Lower Broadway migrated there for the festivities. The crowd finally began to disperse once the ceremonies ended, overloading the nearby subway stations. Many of the fans brought home signs that had welcomed the team, reading "We Love You Derek," "How Sweet It Is," or "God Must be a Yankee Fan."

Reporters questioned many fans as they left the area. "How many more World Series can the Yankees win?" they were asked "Every single one from now on," came one response. That response might seem justified, as the Yankees had already played in 35 World Series, winning 24 times, more than any other baseball team, and more victories lay ahead *(see: October 29, 1999)*.

Monday, November 16, 1998:
Senator John Glenn and Crew of the Space Shuttle *Discovery*

In 1962, astronaut John Glenn became the first American to orbit Earth *(see March 1, 1962)*. Now, at the age of 77, he escaped the Earth's gravity for a second time, becoming the oldest person to fly into space.

In the years since his first space flight, Glenn had been a Senator from the State of Ohio. Now, as a member of the seven-man crew of the space shuttle *Discovery* STS-95, he was part of a research effort investigating the effects of space flight and zero gravity on the elderly.

Less than two weeks later, John Glenn rode up Broadway again, when the city honored the crew with a ticker tape parade. Unlike the parade held after his first mission, however, which drew millions of spectators and tons of ticker tape, the parade on this bright sunny mid-November afternoon attracted barely 500,000 cheering onlookers and only mild flurries of torn paper, confetti, and streamers.

A number of reasons were given for the sparse attendance: it was too soon after the previous parade for Sammy Sosa *(see October 17, 1998)*, too little notice had been given (the parade was announced only three days in advance), and space flight had become common place in the 35 years since the Mercury missions. Or perhaps, as one New Jersey resident who witnessed the parade put it, "I think the whole thing was a goofy public relations ploy."

Whatever the reason, shortly after noon, the multiple vehicle motorcade moved up Broadway towards City Hall to the accompaniment of Air Force and Marine Corps bands. Mr. Glenn and his wife of more than 50 years, Annie, shared the first car. In the cars behind them were the other crew members: shuttle commander Lieutenant Colonel Curtis Brown; pilot Lieutenant Colonel Steven Lindsey; mission specialist Stephen Robinson; attending doctor, Scott Parazynski; mission specialist Pedro Duque; and payload specialist, Chiaki Mukai. The crewmembers all waved and smiled in appreciation as they drove up the Canyon of Heroes.

Admission to City Hall Park was by ticket only, but it was reported that not all of the tickets printed had been given out. When the caravan arrived, Mayor Giuliani congratulated the astronauts and welcomed Mr. Glenn back to the city. In his remarks, Mr. Giuliani joked about being called "Mayor of the Universe," referring to a comment made by Ellen Foster, president of the American Museum of Natural History. At a breakfast the day before the parade, she had used that term since New York City was often called the capital of the world.

Mr. Glenn and his wife were each awarded Keys to the City while the crew members were given the city's Gold Medal. The space pioneer and former Senator spoke briefly to thank the mayor and the city for his welcome. He warned of becoming complacent about space travel and exploration and predicted a manned expedition to Mars in the future.

Shortly after the parade ended, sanitation workers cleaned the streets. Among the debris were bundled copies of the special John Glenn edition of the *New York Daily News* that had never been opened, and boxes of unsold John Glenn tee-shirts. Following the City Hall reception, Mr. Glenn was interviewed by television reporters. When Channel 4 newscaster Gabe Pressman mentioned that he had covered Mr. Glenn's first parade 36 years earlier, Glenn responded "You're getting old, aren't you?"

In 2010, Glenn attended the ceremony commemorating the 50th anniversary of his first flight into space. He often spoke of his disappointment that NASA did not continue its research on aging by sending more elderly people into space. He died in 2016 at the age of 95, the last living member of the Mercury 7 mission.

Friday, October 29, 1999:
New York Yankees, World Series Champions

It was déjà vu all over again, to quote New York Yankees Hall of Famer Yogi Berra.

For the third time in four years, the New York Yankees were the recipients of a ticker tape parade, this time to celebrate their 25th World Series victory, defeating the Atlanta Braves in four straight games. Yankee relief pitcher Mariano Rivera was named the Series' Most Valuable Player, and each member of the Yankees team received a World Championship ring along with $326,000 in bonus money.

Some nay-sayers had predicted that another parade honoring the Bronx Bombers might produce a smaller crowd than the previous year *(see: October 23, 1998)*. It was even suggested that New Yorkers were tiring of the hoopla of parades up the Canyon of Heroes. But by mid-morning, those ideas were proven wrong. Perhaps as many as 3 million spectators jammed the streets of the Financial District around Broadway, many carrying brooms to celebrate the "sweep" over the Braves. Spectators stood at every window and climbed on the roofs of buildings. A handful of viewers were even seen in the bell tower of Trinity Church, although who they were or how they gained access was unknown.

The players, coaches, and owners of the Yankees boarded buses at the Battery. A sign held high by one of the thousands of fans gathered in the area proclaimed the Battery as "Yankee Stadium South." With a blare of trumpets and beating of drums, the parade began at noon. Manager Joe Torre sat with Mayor Giuliani and MVP Rivera in the first bus, taking turns holding the championship trophy high overhead. Cheers sounded as each bus slowly moved uptown. Spectators cheered for Chad Curtis and Darryl Strawberry, Scott Brosius and David Cone, Jorge Pasada and Derek Jeter. Even team trainers, batting instructors, and equipment managers received applause, though some in the crowd wondered who they were.

Public high schools were closed for the day because of previously scheduled parent-teachers conferences. The Board of Education later reported a number of teacher absences and cancelled appointments. High school students in the thousands were part of the boisterous crowd, and younger students were also evident in large numbers.

Mayor Giuliani welcomed the Yankees to City Hall, or in some cases, welcomed back. The mayor spoke first, recalling the rain of opening day in April, then adding that the season "ends on a beautiful and glorious day" in October. He paused and concluded, "Because the Yankees and New York own October." The mayor asked that everyone remember the father of Yankee outfielder Paul O'Neill, who had died hours after the final out of the final game of the series. Each player was then introduced and presented with a Key to the City. A few players spoke of the honor of being part of the Yankees organization. Some thanked the city and its loyal fans, while others commented that millions of fans were watching the event on television and their support all year had been instrumental to victory as well.

The final Yankee to speak was Darryl Strawberry. A year earlier he had been diagnosed with colon cancer but had recently been declared cancer free. Early in this year he had been arrested for drug possession and solicitation. He started to express his thanks when he was overcome by emotion and began weeping. Manager Torre stepped forward and put his arm around Strawberry's shoulder. Gaining control of himself, the player lifted his head and said, "I'd just like to thank you, Joe, thank you for caring for me." Then turning to his teammates, he added, "And I love you guys." With that, the entire team stood and applauded him.

When the crowds slowly dispersed, they left behind the usual accumulation of paper debris. It took sanitation workers just an hour to clean most of it and by the evening rush hour, few traces were left of the parade. Many of those who left the area were convinced that they would return before long. In fact, they did witness another parade a year later when the Yankees and Mets faced off in a Subway Series (see: October 30, 2000).

Monday, October 30, 2000:
New York Yankees, World Series Champions

It was the answer to the prayers of every New York City baseball fan: a "Subway Series" between the Bronx-based New York Yankees and the Queens-based New York Mets in the World Series. Dating from the 1920s, the phrase refers to a World Series in which both teams are from New York, and fans could see any of the games by "hopping on the subway" to visit either team's stadium. There were 13 Subway Series between 1921 and 1956, most won by the Yankees, but there had not been any since then – until 2000.

Mets fans were eager to defeat the Yankees, especially older fans who had transferred their loyalty to the Mets after being abandoned when the Dodgers left Brooklyn. For them, a Mets victory would be sweet revenge after watching the Dodgers defeated in 6 of the 7 Subway Series in the 1940s and 1950s. Sadly, those hopes were dashed. The Yankees lost only one game, winning the series in game five, played in Shea Stadium.

The city's most fervent and vocal Yankees fan, Mayor Giuliani, extended an invitation to the Mets to take part in the parade, but Mets management declined the offer. So once again, it was the owners, managers, coaches, trainers, and players of the

Yankees heading up the Canyon of Heroes to the roars and cheers of the estimated one million fans.

It was a brisk and windy late October morning. Confetti tumbled down like multi-colored snowflakes, as streamers of shredded paper, torn magazines, paper towels, and rolls of toilet tissue swayed and danced in the breeze. The parade began at the unusually early time of 10 o'clock, but this in no way decreased the size or enthusiasm of the crowd. To obtain the best vantage points before police cordoned off the streets that led into Broadway, loyal Yankees fans had begun arriving before dawn, some setting up lawn chairs behind the police barriers along the route. This year, the mayor's request to close city schools had been denied by the school Chancellor, but teachers still recorded a large number of absences that day.

Yankees manager Joe Torre and the entire team rode up Broadway on specially designed floats or in double-decker buses. Standing next to Yankees owner George Steinbrenner, Mayor Giuliani held aloft the World Series trophy. World Series MVP Derek Jeter seemed to elicit the largest volume of cheers but not far behind him was pitcher Roger Clemens. The rivalry between Clemens and the Mets catcher, Mike Piazza, had nearly started a brawl in game two, and the few Mets fans brave enough to attend the parade sent a chorus of boos his way. Yankees relief pitcher Mariano Rivera was there, as was Bernie Williams, David Cone (a former Mets pitcher), Chuck Knoblauch, Andy Pettitte, Jorge Pasada, and others.

Admittance to City Hall Plaza was by special invitation only and 5,000 ticketholders clustered before City Hall. A two-story high illustration of Yankees Stadium had been attached to the front of the building with a reviewing stand between it and the spectators. The mayor introduced and gave a Key to the City to each member of the World Champion "Bronx Bombers," even the team's masseuse. The mayor praised the team and suggested that the Yankees provided lessons about consistency, teamwork, and the will to overcome diversity.

Governor George Pataki presented faux New York State auto license plates to Derek Jeter and Joe Torre. Jeter's read "MVP" while Torre's read "3-PEAT." The Yankees were the first baseball team since the 1970s to win three World Series in a row. The reception ceremony did not end until 3:30, although Sanitation workers had begun sweeping the streets south of City Hall as soon as the last float rode up Broadway.

Despite the rivalry between the fans of both teams, and the rowdiness and vandalism that had become a trend after big sporting events, the parade was an almost peaceful affair. The police gave out only 9 summonses for disorderly conduct and 168 to unlicensed vendors. A few small fires in trash receptacles and along curbs were reported and one police officer received minor burns while trying to extinguish a fire. Yankees fans exited the area by all available subways, bragging about the invincibility of their team and predicting that next year would result in a "4-PEAT." That prediction almost came true, but the Yankees lost the 2001 World Series in the final inning of the seventh game, and their next triumphant return to Broadway would come years later (see: November 6, 2009).

Tuesday, February 5, 2008:
New York Giants, Super Bowl XLII Champions

It was the third time the New York Giants football team won the Super Bowl, but this was their first parade. They had won in 1986 but Mayor Ed Koch ruled against a parade for a team that played its home games in New Jersey, even if their name included the words "New York." They won again in 1990 but that victory came during the Gulf War and the city administration thought it inappropriate to celebrate at the time. But there were no excuses when they won the third time, in a surprising defeat over the New England Patriots, who had been undefeated in the regular season.

The Giants were getting a parade.

Low, heavy clouds hid the tops of the tallest buildings along Broadway on a cool, damp day. Threats of inclement weather did nothing to subtract from the number of spectators who filled every inch along the route and down many intersecting streets. Long before the parade began at noon, chants of "Let's Go Giants!" echoed in the Canyon of Heroes.

Accompanied by marching bands and fife and drum corps, the parade moved up Broadway. The players, coaches, and owners rode in red-white-and-blue double-decker buses. Some players were accompanied by wives or girlfriends. Eli Manning, Giants quarterback and MVP of the game, rode on the first vehicle along with Coach Tom Coughlin and Defensive End Michael Strahan. They took turns hoisting the Vince Lombardi Trophy awarded annually to the Super Bowl victor. Manning heard endless shouts of "MVP, MVP" while Strahan, considering retirement, was swamped with cries of "One more year!" Coach Coughlin, who weeks before was a surefire candidate for being replaced, smiled and waved. Swirling ribbons of paper towels and toilet tissue fell, mixed with shredded paper of every kind and color. Confetti and balloons fell on players and spectators alike. No one estimated the size of the crowd, but the press reported that many hundreds of thousands filled the streets. People could be seen at nearly every window along the route. Fans, some with their faces painted in Giants colors, blew horns, waved pennants or held signs.

At City Hall, Mayor Michael Bloomberg began his remarks by calling the Giants' victory the "Greatest Upset in Super Bowl History," then introduced the players. The cheering was loudest for Manning, though not far behind was the roar for David Tyree whose acrobatic one-handed catch was good for a 32-yard gain. A huge roar from the crowd rose for Plaxico Burress, who had scored the winning touchdown in the last minute of the game, but he was absent from the event, recovering from the physical punishment he had taken during the game. New York Governor Eliot Spitzer and Senator Chuck Schumer both spoke. Even celebrity Whoopi Goldberg, a lifelong Giants fan, added a few words about how proud she and all Giants fans were of their upset victory.

A few players and staff added some words. John Mara, co-owner of the Giants, said he could not believe how many fans had turned out, "all dressed in blue." Jerry Reese, the team's General Manager and native of Tiptonville, Tennessee, laughed in comparing this parade to those in his hometown, "where one fire truck, a police car, a high school band, and two floats" constituted the entire event. The cheers of the celebrating fans were so loud they drowned out most of the speeches.

When Michael Strahan rose to speak, he mentioned that they had "whupped" the Patriots. A teammate shouted, "Show us how we whupped 'em!" and the big defensive end leaped high in the air with his knees almost touching his chin. He landed solidly on both feet too close to the startled Mayor, who almost fell off his chair. Riding in the same buses used in the parade, the Giants then drove through the Holland Tunnel to the Giants Stadium in the Meadowlands, New Jersey, where another reception was held on the 50-yard line, witnessed by more Giants fans. It would take four years before they would return to City Hall *(see: February 7, 2012)*. The day's events finally ended, and Giants fans returned to their homes, doing something not often done by New Yorkers: agreeing with their mayor that it was the "Greatest Upset in Super Bowl History."

Mayor Michael Bloomberg (2002-2013)

Millionaire Michael Bloomberg was born to middle-class parents in Massachusetts in 1942. After attending Johns Hopkins University, he earned an MBA at Harvard Business School in 1966. In 1973, he became general partner at Wall Street investment firm Solomon Brothers. He made his fortune by launching a company initially called Innovative Market Services, which provided business information and real-time market data to Wall Street traders.

Because of the city's then-current term limits, Mayor Giuliani was prevented from running for a third term, so Bloomberg entered and won the Republican primary. By using his personal fortune rather than public funds, he out-spent his opponent, Democratic nominee Mark Green n, by five to one to win the general election. He easily won re-election in 2005. During the financial crisis of 2008, he announced his plan to run for a third term, persuading the City Council to change the term limit restriction to three consecutive terms rather than two. He went on to win the 2009 election, becoming the third person to be mayor for more than 2 terms since the city's consolidation in 1898.

During his 12 years in office, Bloomberg used his business experience to improve the city government's use of technology. A social liberal but fiscal conservative, his administration focused on the development of under-used or vacant land like Hudson Yards and the former Brooklyn Navy Yard, and developed plans to improve the city's environmental sustainability while also supporting rights for immigrants, same-sex marriage and gun control. Though many of his policies were seen as having a positive impact on the city, he also made some controversial decisions, especially regarding the police, rent affordability for the middle class, and anti-terrorist surveillance.

After he left office in 2013, rumors spread that Bloomberg considered a run for a higher office, but he stayed on the sidelines until the Democratic Presidential primary in 2020. His candidacy ended with controversies about allegations of sexual harassment at his company and the use of non-disclosure agreements to silence victims. Through his philanthropic foundation, Bloomberg provides donations in public health, the arts, government innovation, education and the environment, and has pledged significant funding during the Covid pandemic. Divorced in 1993 from the mother of his two children, he currently lives with his domestic partner, Donna Taylor.

Friday, November 6, 2009:
New York Yankees, World Series Champions

"It's been too long, hasn't it?" asked Derek Jeter at City Hall, holding aloft the World Championship trophy.

Nine years had passed since the last parade for the New York Yankees. By beating the Philadelphia Phillies, the Bronx Bombers brought home the trophy for the 27th time. No other baseball team had won even half that number. No other World Series had ended so late in the year, either, because Major League Baseball had extended playing schedules and increased the number of playoff games leading up to the World Series.

Despite the sunny but cold weather, fans began lining the Canyon of Heroes five hours before the scheduled start of the parade. As the sidewalks and cross streets filled with people, blue Yankee coats and hats were evident, as well as scarves and gloves. Unofficial estimates of the numbers watching the parade ran between 3 and 3.5 million; whether these figures were true or not, lower Manhattan were awash in the Yankees' team colors.

Long before the parade began torn paper, paper towels, newspapers, and confetti began to fall. The streets were already covered in a carpet of colored paper when the motorcade of buses carrying the players and team management began to move up Broadway. Even the ledges and cornices of the Woolworth Building were festooned with paper streamers, blowing in the cold wind.

Cheers rolled like waves as bus after bus moved passed the crowd, and the sounds of air horns echoed through the streets. The applause for World Series MVP, designated hitter Hadeki Matsui, was thunderous, as was the roar for catcher Jorge Pasada; third-baseman Alex "A-Rod" Rodriguez; manager Joe Girardi; pitcher CC Sabathia; first-baseman Mark Teixeira; relief pitcher Mariano Rivera; and, of course, the short-stop Derek Jeter. This was Jeter's fifth victory parade, and when asked later if he ever tired of being in a parade, he answered, "You could do this every day and never get tired."

Not everyone received a congratulatory cheer. Part owner of the Yankees, George Steinbrenner, was absent due to sickness, but when other members of the Yankee management rode by, they received boos and sarcastic shouts of "Thanks for raising ticket prices!"

Shortly before the motorcade reached City Hall, Mayor Bloomberg and former mayors Koch, Dinkins, and Giuliani were seen together on the reviewing stand. Not always political allies, they were having what appeared to be a friendly conversation, showing that everyone loves a parade. When the buses arrived, the Yankees filled the reviewing stand. City Hall Plaza erupted into even louder cheers when ex-players Yogi Berra and Reggie Jackson joined the current team.

As in previous years, individual members of the team were identified by name and called to take a bow. Because of the cold most wore overcoats or heavy sweatshirts, and without numbered jerseys, they were not all easily identified by sight. Few players spoke; those who did echoed the refrain of how good it was to be a Yankee and predicted that they would be back for another parade in 2010. The weather was so cold that even the politicians on the reviewing stand kept their statements short.

The ceremony outside City Hall ended just after 2 o'clock. Most of the Yankees disappeared into the building to warm themselves before leaving. Speakers set up throughout City Hall Park began to play Frank Sinatra's song "New York, New York" as the crowds dispersed, quicker than usual because of the cold.

The predictions for 2010 failed to come true, and the new decade ushered in a new period of losses. The Yankees made it to the American League Championships four times, but lost each time, most recently in 2019. They remain the most successful baseball franchise in history, with 40 American League wins and 27 World Series victories.

Tuesday, February 7, 2012:
New York Giants, Super Bowl XLVI Champions

Almost exactly four years to the day after celebrating their victory in Super Bowl XLII *(see: February 5, 2008)*, the New York Giants received another ticker tape parade up the Canyon of Heroes. They had again defeated the New England Patriots, though this victory lacked the last-minute heroics of the previous one. But that in no way diminished the enthusiasm of the estimated 2 million fans jammed in every available space from Bowling Green to City Hall.

As early as dawn, fans staked out vantage spots to watch their team ride by. When the parade finally began shortly after 11 o'clock, side streets had been closed by the police and thousands of fans could get no closer than an entire block away, catching only the briefest glimpses of their gridiron heroes. The entire Giants organization was present: owners, players, coaches, trainers, even two injured players on crutches: Travis Beckum and Jake Ballard. They rode on floats, following a police escort and marching bands. The game's MVP, Eli Manning, stood on the second float next to Giants coach Tom Coughlin, taking turns holding high the Vince Lombardi Trophy, symbol of Super Bowl victory. Riding together on another float were Victor Cruz, Hakeem Nicks, and Mario Manningham, and other Giants followed on the next floats, waving and shouting in joyous victory. Some snapped photos of the crowd or used smart phone to video the thousands of fans videoing them. This was a repeat performance for 16 members of the team, and when one newer team mate boasted about his Super Bowl ring, Defensive Captain Justin Tuck boasted, "Guess what? I've got two."

According to a Sanitation Department spokesman, 40 tons of paper littered the route. Some of the paper had been donated by Atlas Materials, a recycling vendor from Red Hook, Brooklyn. The Alliance for Downtown New York bagged over one ton of confetti and paper to buildings along the route, and it fell in swirls of ribbon and torn newspaper, shredded documents, and red, white and blue confetti. Toy footballs were thrown from one side of Broadway to another. As his float rode by Trinity Church, tight-end Sean "Bear" Pascoe caught a football, quickly autographed it and tossed it back into the crowd. A few seconds later he caught a roll of toilet paper and tossed that back as well.

The loudest cheers greeted Manning and Coughlin, followed by Victor Cruz. He was a native of Patterson, New Jersey who grew up almost in sight of MetLife Stadium, home to the Giants. The cheers directed towards the Jersey native were easily distinguishable by the familiar chorus of "Cruuuuuuuuuuz."

Mayor Michael Bloomberg welcomed the entire Giants organization to City Hall Park. Thousands of ticket-holding fans crowded the temporary grandstands and thousands more filled Park Place and the surrounding area. Loud cheers rose when the mayor suggested that the city should be called "The Big Blue Apple" combining the nicknames of the city with that of the Giants. He then awarded each team member with a Key to the City. Some of the players and coaches spoke briefly when they received their award. Bear Pascoe said, "This was cool, really cool, to see the city turn out like that, and stuff coming down from the windows! Cool, really cool!" Speaking last, Coach Coughlin revealed that he had received a phone call just before the parade began. "I had the honor of speaking to President Barack Obama. He praised our mental toughness, our resilience, our leadership, the great ability that this team possessed to finish, to win so many games in the fourth quarter."

The festivities ended in mid-afternoon. The Giants boarded buses and were driven to New Jersey for a second, smaller celebration at MetLife Stadium. More than 300 workers from the Department of Sanitation were already cleaning Lower Broadway. Despite the extra work, one Sanitation worker wearing a Giants Super Bowl cap said, "I hope they'll be back next year."

There was one serious incident, in addition to a few arrests for vending without a license. A small number of overly rowdy fans damaged a taxi on Duane Street. The vehicle was owned by the Police Department, and the fans involved were arrested for disorderly conduct. Overtime for the New York Police Department totaled $1.1 million. All the parade's expenses, however, were covered by private sponsors and advertisers featured on the various floats.

In the years since their fourth Super Bowl victory, the Giants have struggled. The annual championship game was held in the Giants' stadium in 2014, but the team had their first losing record in a decade. In 2018, they finished last in their division for the second time in a row and played only slightly better in 2019. Whatever lies ahead for "Big Blue," fans will be cheering them on, chanting "Let's Go Giants!"

Friday, July 10, 2015: US Women's Soccer Team, FIFA Women's World Cup Champions

The first ticker tape parade honoring a women's sports team took place on a sunny and warm summer day. Individual female athletes like Gertrude Ederle *(see: August 27, 1926)* and Althea Gibson *(see: July 11, 1957)* had been honored before, and women have been in the ranks of Olympic teams that marched up Broadway *(see: August 6, 1924 and August 15, 1984)*. Men's professional sports teams had received 13 parades over the years, 6 of them for the New York Yankees, so when a parade was announced after the US Women's Soccer team won their third World Cup in 2015, many fans cheered excitedly "It's about time!"

The parade stepped off at noon led by bands of the Police and Fire Departments. Team members rode in double-decker buses and on floats to the cheers of more than a million parade spectators. Waving pompons, cheerleaders from local high schools marched between the vehicles carrying the team's players and trainers. Jill Ellis, the team's coach, rode atop the first bus, holding high the Championship trophy. With her rode goalkeeper Hope Solo and Carli Lloyd, winner of the FIFA Golden Ball Award for having scored the most goals in the tournament. A banner across the bus read "Thank You Fans!"

Paper of all type fell from nearby buildings onto the parade and the thousands of spectators lining Broadway, which included a larger than usual number of young women. Many of them wore the team's white uniform shirt and some had painted their faces with red, white, and blue stripes. Some held banners expressing joy and pride.

Policemen lined Broadway but at times were unable to hold back spectators who tried to get closer. Security has always been a concern for these events and the presence of heavily armed police at windows and roof tops was obvious. Circling helicopters included those bearing the letters NYPD as well as television stations and other media outlets.

When the parade reached City Hall, Mayor Bill de Blasio welcomed the champions and introduced every member to the crowd, saving 40-year-old Christie Rampone for last. The senior member of the team and the oldest female World Cup winner in history, Rampone held the trophy overhead, and as the crowd cheered, her teammates joined her on stage and broke out into some dance moves. Thousands jammed into City Hall Plaza while the Mayor spoke of the team's accomplishments. He noted that the final match against Japan had broken records for viewership, then praised the players' offensive and defensive skills. To wild cheers, he proclaimed that the US team "is number 1!" Raising the championship trophy over her head, Hope Solo spoke for the team, replying, "Thank you, New York! Thank you, America!"

The festivities ended shortly before 4 o'clock. Players and team staff left New York City over the next few days. Later that year, the team was invited to the White House, where President Barack Obama praised them for redefining the phrase "playing like a girl."

The *New York Times* coverage of the parade concluded by advising fans to "keep that confetti handy" since the team would defend its World Cup title in 2019. That proved to be good advice, as the team would return for another parade in four years *(see: July 10, 2019)*, though not all the players from the 2015 team would return. Christie Rampone retired in 2017, the same year that she divorced her husband. She now goes by her maiden name of Christie Pearce and was elected to the National Soccer Hall of Fame in 2021. Hope Solo, consider by many to be the greatest female goalkeeper of all time, was suspended from the US National Team after the 2016 Olympics; officials cited misconduct as the reason, though Solo claims it was because of her efforts highlighting the pay inequity between the women's and men's soccer teams.

Aware of it or not, the spectators had participated in a historic event. The city's first ticker tape parade *(see: October 28, 1886)* had excluded women as participants or spectators. Almost 130 years later they participated in and witnessed a parade exclusively for female champions.

Mayor Bill de Blasio (2014-current)

New York's current mayor as of this writing, Bill de Blasio was born in 1961. Raised in Massachusetts by his divorced mother, he earned a BA at NYU and a master's degree at Columbia University. While in graduate school, he worked for the NYC Department of Juvenile Justice, and in 1988 spent time in Nicaragua supporting the Sandanistas, a cause he continued to support after returning to New York. He became interested in politics while working as an aide in City Hall during the Dinkins Administration, and in 1994 was campaign manager for Congressman Charles Rangel's successful re-election. He worked at the US Department of Housing and Urban Redevelopment during the Clinton Administration, and in 2000 was campaign manager for Hillary Clinton's successful Senate election.

In 2001, de Blasio was elected to the City Council, serving there until 2009, when he was elected Public Advocate. In 2013, he won the mayoral election, and easily won re-election in 2017.

During his tenure as mayor, de Blasio has focused on what he calls the "tale of two cities" and the stark economic inequalities in the city. He supports socially liberal programs, such as universal pre-K education, decriminalization and legalization of marijuana, expansion of affordable housing and supportive housing for the homeless, and the closure of Rikers Island. He has a difficult relationship with the NYPD, stopping controversial "stop and frisk" policies and requiring officers to wear body cameras, but critics say he has not gone far enough in reducing the NYPD's budget and curtailing their aggressive approach toward civil protests. Most recently, his administration has received both praise and criticism for its approach to the Covid pandemic.

He married his wife Chirlane in 1994, and they have two children. Before moving into Gracie Mansion, they lived in Park Slope, Brooklyn. In 2010, a voter referendum reinstated the 2-term limit that the City Council had changed, so de Blasio will leave City Hall at the end of his second term in 2021.

Wednesday, July 10, 2019: US Women's Soccer Team, FIFA Women's World Cup Champions

Exactly four years after the first-ever ticker tape parade for a women's sports team, that same team was celebrated again for successfully defending their title in the quadrennial Women's World Cup championship. This time, the games were held in France, and the US team defeated the Netherlands in the final game of the match, which was watched by a record-setting 82 million viewers. It was the US team's 4th victory at the World Cup (though their victories in 1991 and 1999 had not been honored with parades), making them the most successful team in the history of the Women's World Cup.

There had been some changes in the four years since their last World Cup victory. Jill Ellis continued as head coach, but about half of the team's roster had changed. In 2016, several team members sued US Soccer for gender discrimination claiming inequity in pay compared to the men's team, and in March 2019, 28 members of the team filed a separate gender discrimination suit. The suits received a lot of media attention, and many fans and spectators at the parade supported the team.

The weather was ideal for a parade, with temperatures in the mid 70s and variable cloudiness. Thousands of fans filled the streets around Broadway, many waving flags or carrying banners. Many younger fans, boys as well as girls, wore jerseys with the names of their favorite player. "Watching them is fun and inspiring," said 10-year-old David Winters, who wore a homemade jersey with Tobin Heath's name on it. He said she was his favorite player, adding that he enjoyed watching the women's soccer team more than the men's team.

"Thank you for letting us dream" said one banner held by a pair of pre-teen sisters, while another read simply "Parades are cool – equal pay is cooler!" The social media hashtag #SheBelieves was trending that day, and many signs echoed the sentiment. "She believed she could, so she did" read another banner.

Banners promoting equal pay was seen not just along the sidewalks. A plane flying overhead pulled a long banner reading "FIFA – Equal Pay for Equal Play" to protest the gender bias of the soccer organization's World Cup prize money ($370 million for the men's teams versus $4 million for the women's).

The team rode up Broadway, joined by Mayor Bill de Blasio and his wife, Chirlane McCray. Standing in the first float, team co-captain Megan Rapinoe held the World Cup trophy in one hand and a bottle of champagne in the other, as confetti and shredded paper filled the air. On their way to City Hall, marchers passed One Broadway and Trinity Church, which stood as they had for every one of New York's ticker tape parades along the Canyon of Heroes, or as one sign held by a young woman read, the "Canyon of Heroines."

When the parade reached City Hall Park, the team entered City Hall for a short respite and press photographs. The crowd in the park roared with excitement every time several players came out to wave to their fans. "This is one of the best days of my life," a young girl told Samantha Mewis, who gave her a big hug.

When the ceremony began, Mayor de Blasio welcomed and congratulated the team. As the crowd began chanting "Equal Pay!" he introduced each player and presented them with a Key to the City. After all the Keys had been presented, Megan Rapinoe addressed the crowd. Thanking the fans for their support, she ended by saying, "It is our responsibility to make this world a better place."

After the parade and ceremony, Broadway and the side streets around City Hall Park were covered with confetti, shredded paper and other parade debris, but it took just a few hours for 350 sanitation workers to return the streets to normal.

English-born coach Jill Ellis stepped down as coach of the US National Team in October 2019, though she continues to work as an ambassador for US Soccer. During her 5 years with the team, they won 106 out of 132 matches, including two World Cups.

Many of the players in the 2019 World Cup are still on the team as of 2021, including 8 players who were also on the 2015 team (among them, Megan Rapinoe, Tobin Heath and Samantha Mewis). Time will tell whether they are still active players when the team again defends its title in the 2023 Women's World Cup, which will be jointly hosted by Australia and New Zealand.

After the parade ended, the fans and spectators headed home, many to jobs that paid them less than men are paid for the same work. In 2021, a judge ruled against the five players who filed the first pay discrimination lawsuit, thought the second case is scheduled to go to trial in September 2021. After the case was dismissed, President Joe Biden told the team to continue the fight for gender equality, which remains a goal rather than a reality, both in the US and worldwide.

Wednesday, July 7, 2021: Hometown Heroes

On January 20, 2020, the first US case of a new disease was recorded in Washington state, and six weeks later, a case was reported in New York City. First observed in Wuhan, China in late 2019, the coronavirus became known as Covid-19, and was spread via airborne human-to-human transmission.

New York City and its suburbs quickly became the country's first "hot spot", and hospitals were soon overwhelmed with cases. A nation-wide shortage of ventilators, face masks and personal protection equipment ("PPE") fueled the spread of the disease. Though downplayed by the White House, the rapidly rising number of cases and deaths led New York Governor Andrew Cuomo to declare a state of emergency on March 7, and on March 20 he issued a "stay at home" order, requiring all non-essential businesses to shut down.

Despite these actions, the disease took a staggering toll on the city. Hospitals had more patients than rooms, so extra beds lined the hallways, and visiting hours were cancelled. Refrigerated trucks were parked outside hospitals to store bodies until they could be claimed. Funerals were postponed because churches were closed until September, and even then had to limit the number of attendees. The number of unclaimed bodies outgrew the capacity of the city's mass grave on Ward's Island, so a new morgue facility was opened in the Brooklyn Marine Terminal.

By the end of 2020, New York had over 950,000 cases and 30,000 deaths, among them one of the authors of this book.

New York City, often described as the "city that never sleeps" soon took on a different atmosphere. Streets and sidewalks which normally bustled with activity were empty, as residents stayed home, relying on deliveries from retailers and restaurants, and connecting with friends and co-workers via technology. The once noisy city was eerily quiet except for the sirens of ambulances, and as unemployment skyrocketed, people felt increasingly isolated and depressed. "There is one moment each day that breaks up this daily monotony" CNBC reported in April 2020, "at 7 o'clock every night, New Yorkers open a window, or step out onto balconies or rooftops and make some noise for two minutes. We scream, we clap, we bang pots and pans, we make music, but most of all we give thanks to all the frontline workers who are risking their lives every day."

Later that month, Mayor Bill de Blasio announced that when the city re-opens, "we will honor those who saved us" adding that "the first thing we will do, before we think about anything else, is we will take time, as only New York City can do, to throw the biggest, best parade to honor these heroes."

More than a year later, that promise was kept, when the Mayor announced that the parade would be held on July 7, 2021, followed by a ceremony in City Hall Park. Dan Gross, Executive Director of Citywide Events, noted that "It is our distinct honor to celebrate those New Yorkers who guided us through the darkest days of the pandemic."

A list of essential workers was announced, including hospital and healthcare workers, first responders, teachers and community care providers, the transportation and hospitality industries, retail and food delivery services, communications and utilities companies, small businesses and advocacy groups, and city workers. The list did not include funeral parlor workers, who complained that their efforts were being forgotten. "We were in every single hospital, with bodies and families, and many of us lost staff and family members because we kept doing our essential work," the owner of a Brooklyn funeral parlor told *Gothamist*. The Mayor's office quickly responded that "this is definitely a group we're going to be honoring" and included them in the parade.

The announcement of a ticker tape parade raised some controversy. "The time to celebrate has not yet arrived," the President of the Uniformed Firefighters Association told the *NY Post*, adding "our members are still risking their lives daily by exposing themselves to covid-related illnesses." The union for the Fire Department's Emergency Medical Technicians announced a boycott of the parade. "Our members have been without a contract for more than three years and did not receive hazard pay during Covid," a union official told the *Daily News*. Also boycotting were members of the Correction Officers' Benevolent Association, which stated that their members had been "treated as expendable" during the crisis.

The weather also impacted the plans for the celebration. Several days before the event, a heat wave hit the city with a combination of dangerously high temperatures and heavy humidity. The ceremony planned for City Hall Park was cancelled, but the Mayor said "the parade will continue as planned" adding that water would be distributed throughout the parade route.

Temperatures were already above 80 degrees on July 7, when marchers started gathering at 9 o'clock in the morning in Battery Park. By the time the parade kicked off two hours later, the thermometer had risen to 91 degrees. City employees drove up the length of Broadway, distributing bottled water to spectators lining the street.

Proceeded by an escort of motorcycle police, the NYPD marching band led the way, followed by an open convertible carrying the parade's grand marshal, Sarah Lindsay, a nurse from Queens who was the first US resident to receive a Covid vaccination. "I am so grateful," she said to a reporter from ABC News, "it feels like we're getting a great big hug all over again from the entire city."

Behind her was the first of 14 floats, carrying healthcare and hospital workers, with Mayor de Blasio standing with them, waving to spectators. "We are out here celebrating ourselves" said Michelle Medina, a respiratory therapist from Mt. Sinai Hospital told the *Daily News*.

Spectators lined Broadway, primarily on the shadier eastern side of the street, many holding handmade signs with expressions like "Thank You, Heroes!" or "You Saved Our Lives!" NBC News reported that "thousands of spectators" watched the parade, though the *NY Times* said that "dozens of people stood along Broadway under the baking sun" and the *Wall Street Journal* adding that the heat "led to thinner crowds" than had been expected.

Air cannons mounted on parade floats spewed huge bursts of blue, orange, and white confetti into the air. Many of the businesses in the buildings lining Broadway were closed or allowing their staff to work remotely, however, so the amount of paper descending from the skyscrapers along the route was less than usual.

That did not seem to affect the excitement of the over 2,500 parade marchers. "When you think of all the greats that have been through the Canyon of Heroes, this is unbelievable really," Kathleen Liggio, from the city's Medical Examiner's Office told the *Daily News*. Interspersed among the marchers were 10 bands, including the FDNY Band, Batalá New York (a women's percussion group), '80s cover band Jessie's Girl NYC, and the Lesbian and Gay Big Apple Corps.

Among the floats was a historic 118-year-old subway car with woven seats and leather straps, on loan from the NY Transit Museum. Museum Director Concetta Bencivenga said the city's transportation workers "showed up day in and day out and carried essential workers, carried this city on their back for 18 months." Transit Workers Union members marching with the float carried signs asking for hazard pay and remembering the 106 colleagues lost during the pandemic.

Along the entire route, spectators clapped and cheered, and some even brought pots and pans to bang. The celebratory noise seemed loudest for marching groups of UPS and Fedex workers, bodega and restaurant delivery staff, as well as nurses and doctors.

"They deserve a march down the Canyon of Heroes because it's something that is reserved for the greatest folks in history," the Mayor said. "Well, here are some of the folks who made history in New York City's toughest hour."

The course of the Covid-19 pandemic changed in January 2021, when the first of several vaccinations was approved and began being distributed, but it is not over. By June 30, 2021, New York State had seen over 2 million cases and 43,000 deaths, many of them in and around the city. Nationwide, those numbers were 34 million cases and over 600,000 deaths, and the worldwide toll is a staggering 4 million deaths. Sadly, those numbers will continue to rise, both because of a new, more virulent strain of the virus, and because vaccination rates have not been as high as hoped.

CONCLUSION
The Future of Ticker Tape Parades

New York City's unique tradition of the ticker tape parade has been used to honor popular heroes, political figures, triumphant generals and admirals, victorious athletes and celebrities. The type of person receiving this honor has changed over time, evolving as world events shaped our popular culture. The frequency of these parades declined after the 1960s because of New York City's budget problems, but also because of the changes in the way our society recognizes heroes and celebrates milestones. Television's role bringing important news events into our living rooms was made sharply evident in 1963, when millions "attended" the funeral for President Kennedy by sitting in front of their TVs, crying at the image of his three-year-old son saluting as the President's body passed in front of him. Two decades later, so many cable TV viewers watched the bombing of Iraqi defenses during Operation Desert Storm that the invasion was nicknamed the Video Game War. Now with the internet and smart phones, we can live-stream and watch events as seismic as the 2021 Insurrection at the US Capitol from wherever we are. Breaking news never stops breaking, each event pushing previous ones from our newsfeeds so quickly that there is little time to organize a parade for an event before it seems like old news, and perhaps there is less need to do so.

Is the ticker tape parade a relic of a city and time that exist no more? After all, ticker tape itself no longer exists, a bygone relic of a pre-electronic world.

Predicting the future is not the job of a historian, and those who try often live to regret their prognostications. But a few observations are worth consideration.

The men and women who received ticker tape parades in the past were rarely chosen because of their popularity. Some indeed were immensely popular, like Generals Eisenhower and MacArthur, and a few had performed feats that were universally acclaimed, such as Charles Lindbergh and Alan Shepard. Most, however, were chosen for us, often for political or diplomatic reasons, and a quick review of crowd sizes is an easy barometer of that fact.

Strip away the parades that were for political and diplomatic reasons, and ponder the ones that remain.

New York City and its suburbs have a huge and increasingly diverse population. Large groups of people need and want communal events, but the challenge for future leaders of our city will be selecting honorees who resonate with many New Yorkers. The trend of the last 40 years shows that sport teams have near-enough citywide appeal, but are there no others?

Jonas Salk turned down the honor of a parade from a city grateful for his scientific work that saved the lives of millions. We find ourselves in another moment of history when a virus has proven that *homo sapiens* is just another species on an increasingly over-crowded and stressed planet. The parade honoring the hometown heroes who helped New York through that crisis had fewer spectators than expected. Was this due to the heatwave, to the lack of promotion leading up to the parade, to the fact that most businesses in the financial district were still operating virtually? Or have we become apathetic about celebrations?

If Captain George Fried received two parades because of his naval rescue operations, why not Captain Sully Sullenberger for landing his damaged aircraft in the Hudson River in 2009, saving the lives of the 155 passengers on his plane?

In 1947, Americans were inspired by a newspaper columnist to donate food and clothing to a war-torn France, and New Yorkers celebrated both the Freedom Train and the Merci Train that France sent back in gratitude. Could there not also have been a celebration for the hundreds of fire-fighters and emergency personnel who came to New York's aid after 9/11, and for the thousands of New Yorkers who gave them food and shelter and respite from that inferno?

Should the soldiers who fought in Afghanistan and Iraq be honored as were the men who fought in the First and Second World Wars, or will their welcome home be delayed like it was for the equally brave soldiers who served in Korea and Vietnam? Whatever one thinks of the reasons for each of those wars, do the women and men who risk personal harm or even death not deserve some recognition? Or has our political discourse become so divisive that we cannot even join together to do that, and if that is the case, will President Lincoln's adage about a "house divided" eventually come true?

Will future generations look back at ticker tape parades as a quaint nostalgic piece of New York's past, when we celebrated historic events like the first transatlantic flight and the giant leap that took us to the moon, or will they come together to cheer with equal exuberance when the first human steps onto Mars, or makes contact with other intelligent life?

Only time will tell.

APPENDIX

As noted in the Introduction, there is no definitive list of New York City's ticker tape parades, although there are two lists which are often cited by others: the list maintained by the Alliance for Downtown New York, the organization responsible for the sidewalk plaques, and a list included in the *Encyclopedia of New York*. Both of those lists contain various errors.

The Alliance for Downtown New York is concerned with parades that went along Broadway from Battery Park to City Hall. It is understandable, then, that they do not include parades in midtown (such as the Beer Parade in 1932 and the 1971 parades for the Apollo 14 and 15 astronauts), and the omission of the 1959 Reverse Parade is likely due to its unusual direction. Harder to understand are their omission of the 1925 parade for Captain Paul Grening, the 1929 parade for Hugo Eckener, and the parades for Ernes Bevin and Shlomo Shragai. In the chart below, events which the Alliance does not include are indicated in the list below with a ü symbol.

It should also be noted there are also two date inconsistencies between the plaques and the Alliance's website. Dino Grandi's parade on November 20, 1931 is correctly dated on their website, but the plaque incorrectly states November 30 (which was also the date listed in their 2003 brochure). The parade for Olympio Sylvanus on November 22, 1962 has the reverse situation: the plaque is correct, but the Alliance's brochure and website show the date as November 21.

The list of parades in the *Encyclopedia of New York*, published in 1988 and updated in 1991 and 1995, also contains errors, including a number of incorrect dates. Events that occurred after 1995 are obviously not included, but so too are 37 other events that appear on the Alliance's list and a dozen more events that the Alliance does not count. These are indicated with a ¶ symbol in the list below. This list also included events which were cancelled, such as the 1928 parade for the Olympic Athletes, the 1957 parade for King Mohammed V of Morocco, and the 1961 parade for the New York Yankees. Finally, the list includes a 1922 event for Joseph Joffre instead of his 1917 parade; while the French Marshal did return to New York City in 1922, the authors found no evidence of plans for a second parade and conclude that this is just a typographical error in the *Encyclopedia*.

Wikipedia also includes a list, on a page titled *List of Ticker-Tape Parades in New York City*. By its very nature, Wikipedia's content can be changed at any time, and this list has contained a number of errors. The editors of the page have done a good job correcting the errors, however they rely primarily on the *Encyclopedia of New York* for sourcing (as evidenced by their debate about whether to include the parade for Albert Einstein), so some errors remain. Other websites which claim that Ralph Bunche or Jonas Salk received ticker tape parades are likely using Wikipedia as their source. Events which did not include parades, parades which were cancelled, or which did not include ticker tape, are indicated with a x symbol in the list below.

The authors of this book decided to include all events on these lists, as well as several others unearthed while conducting our research. For example, Einstein did receive a welcome, but not along Broadway (hence its omission by the Downtown

Alliance), and newspaper reports specifically mention the absence of ticker tape. On the other hand, the parade for Antonio Segni was cancelled because of bad weather (yet the event is included on the *Encyclopedia's* list). We feel our approach to be the most comprehensive, as the stories behind parades which did **not** happen is just as interesting as those which proceeded as planned.

✓	☆	☒	Aug. 24, 1912:	US Olympians from V Olympic Games
	☆		May 9, 1917:	Joseph Joffre, Marshal of France
✓	☆	☒	Apr. 2, 1921:	Albert Einstein and Dr. Chaim Weizmann
	☆		Oct. 21, 1921:	Admiral Lord Beatty
✓	☆		Oct. 29, 1925:	Captain Paul Grening and Crew of SS *President Harding*
✓		☒	Aug. 22, 1928:	US Olympians from IX Olympic Games
	☆		Sep. 21, 1928:	Aimé Félix Tschiffely and Mancha
✓	☆		Aug. 30, 1929:	Hugo Eckener and Crew of the *Graf Zeppelin*
	☆		Apr. 29, 1930:	Secretary of State Henry Stimson
	☆		Jul. 2, 1931:	Wiley Post and Harold Gatty
	☆		Oct. 26, 1931:	Henri Philippe Pétain, Marshal of France
	☆		Nov. 20, 1931:	Dino Grandi, Foreign Minister of Italy
✓	☆		May 14, 1932:	Beer Parade
✓	☆		Sep. 13, 1933:	National Recovery Administration Day
	☆		Sep. 3, 1936:	Jesse Owens and US Olympic Team from XI Olympic Games
✓	☆		Sep. 21, 1937:	American Legion Convention
✓	☆		Jun. 10, 1939:	King George VI and Queen Elizabeth of Great Britain
✓	☆		Jun. 8, 1942:	Fifteen War Heroes
✓	☆	☒	Aug. 14, 1945:	V-J Day
✓	☆		Jan. 12, 1946:	82nd Division Victory Parade
	☆		Oct. 23, 1946:	Delegates of the First Plenary Session of the United Nations
	☆		Oct. 25, 1946:	Colonel Clarence Irvine and Crew of *Dreamboat*
✓	☆		Nov. 7, 1946:	Ernest Bevin, British Foreign Secretary
	☆		Jun. 9, 1947:	Willie Turnesa
	☆		Nov. 5, 1947:	Officers and Crew of French Cruiser *Georges Leygues*
✓	☆	☒	May 17, 1949:	Ralph Bunche
	☆		Nov. 21, 1949:	Mohammed Reza Pahlevi, Shah of Iran
	☆		May 9, 1950:	Fernando Casas Alemán, Governor of Mexico City
	☆		May 10, 1950:	Ten Foreign Mayors Attending 18th US Mayor's Conference
	☆		Jun. 2, 1950:	Fourth Marine Division Association Reunion
	☆		Aug. 31, 1950:	William O'Dwyer, Mayor of New York City
	☆		Oct. 8, 1951:	New York National Guard 165th Infantry Centennial
✓	☆		Mar. 5, 1952:	Shlomo Shragai, Mayor of Jerusalem
	☆		May 14, 1952:	Mayors of 250 Cities
	☆		Jan. 30, 1953:	Vice Admiral Walter DeLany
	☆		May 26, 1953:	150th Anniversary of Laying of the City Hall Cornerstone

	☆		Nov. 5, 1953:	The 50th Anniversary of Powered Flight
	☆		Dec. 21, 1953:	144 Convalescing War Veterans
	☆		Mar. 31, 1954:	4,000 New York City Firemen
	☆		Nov. 19, 1954:	Lieutenant General Withers Burress
	☆		Mar. 1, 1955:	New York Chapter of American Red Cross
	☆		Apr. 15, 1955:	3,000 New York City Firemen
✓	☆	☒	Apr. 21, 1955:	Dr. Jonas Salk
✓		☒	May 20, 1956:	Armed Services Day
	☆		Aug. 30, 1956:	3,000 NY State Volunteer Firemen
✓	☆		Jan. 29, 1957:	King Saud of Saudi Arabia
✓		☒	Dec. 9, 1957:	King Mohammed V of Morocco
✓	☆		Jun. 16, 1959:	Reverse Parade for Second Fleet
	☆		May 2, 1960:	King Mahendra and Queen Ratna of Nepal
	☆		Oct. 14, 1960:	King Frederick IX and Queen Ingrid of Denmark
✓		☒	Apr. 10, 1961:	New York Yankees, American League Champions
✓	☆	☒	May 8, 1961:	Alan Shepard, First American in Space
	☆		Jul. 14, 1961:	Mohammad Ayub Khan, President of Pakistan
	☆		Sep. 22, 1961:	Manuel Prado y Ugarteche, President of Peru
	☆		Mar. 16, 1962:	Ahmadou Ahidjo, First President of Cameroon
	☆		Mar. 22, 1962:	Sylvanus Olympio, President of Togo
✓		☒	Apr. 9, 1962:	New York Yankees, World Series Champions
✓		☒	Jun. 5, 1962:	Commander Scott Carpenter
✓		☒	Jan. 17, 1964:	Antonio Segni, President of Italy
	☆		Sep. 3, 1964:	Staten Island Mid-Island Little League All Stars
	☆		Jun. 1, 1965:	100th Anniversary of New York Fire Department
✓	☆	☒	Jan. 22, 1969:	New York Jets, Super Bowl III Champions
✓	☆		Mar. 8, 1971:	Apollo 14 Astronauts
✓	☆		Aug. 24, 1971:	Apollo 15 Astronauts
	☆		Jul. 7, 1976:	Crews of Operation Sail Vessels during US Bicentennial
	☆		Oct. 19, 1977:	New York Yankees, World Series Champions

ACKNOWLEDGEMENTS

A book spanning over 150 years of history and over 300 famous and not-quite-so-famous people, would not be possible without a lot of research and help. The three most important resources available that we relied upon are the online archives of the New York Times, the Municipal Archives of New York City, and Wikipedia, though many other newspapers, books, periodicals and websites were valuable as well. A list of references is included below.

Many people helped along the way, and whether large or small, their assistance should be noted. First and foremost, thanks should be given to the staff and board of directors of the Alliance for Downtown New York. The plaques they have installed in the sidewalks of Broadway preserve the memory of the city's ticker tape parades in a way that tourists and New Yorkers can enjoy, but also provided the inspiration for this book. You can learn more about their work at www.DowntownNY.com.

We are very grateful to New York City Councilwoman Elizabeth Crowley and her aide, Kate Mooney, both of whom organized and accompanied us on a private tour of City Hall, providing an insider's view of that historic building. Standing in the Council Chamber helped us visualize the many ceremonies for parade honorees over the years.

I owe much thanks to Barbara Herbert's proof-reading and copy editing. Sue Kenner created the beautiful cover design, and Jon Rosenthal created the maps and helped source the originals that they are based upon. Without their help, this manuscript would never have become ready for publication.

I received a lot of encouragement and advice from many friends, so of whom also shared personal memories of ticker tape parades they had attended, so I would like to thank Kerry Ashforth, Daniel Bayer, Ingalena Bengtsson, Eric Eldritch, Ed Gillespie, Ron Harris, Adam Hellegers, Michael Jones, Brian Knowles, Elliot Kreloff, Stephen Morris, Lithgow Osborne, Elizabeth Smith, Will Tower, and Drew Wutke. My father's lifelong friend, John DeBiase, was a constant source of help for both of us.

Families are always the source of important encouragement and inspiration, and I'd like to thank my sister Robin Gustafsson, her husband PG, and my brother Brian for their encouragement to finish this book after our father's death. Not only did my brother Michael Walter and his wife Kelly add their encouragement, but they also shared valuable advice learned when he published his latest book, *On This Date in Music*.

My partner Aaron Lee listened to me talk excitedly about obscure parades and random facts about New York City, offered advice about how to format the book, and most importantly helped me keep my sense of humor while we sheltered at home during the Covid pandemic. I cannot thank him enough for being there when I most needed it. I love you, you wonderful man!

Saving the most important for last, none of this would have been possible without my mother, Peg Walter. She has always been a source of strength and joy in our family, and she encouraged my father in all his pursuits. The photographs of the less well-known people and parades that she found helped fuel our passion for the project. Whenever I had doubts about editing dad's writing ,or discovered something about a parade that he had missed, she cheered me on and restored my confidence. I am eternally grateful for her encouragement that I could and should finish and publish this book even after dad died.

LIST OF REFERENCES

Books

Michael J. Anuta, *Ships of our Ancestors*, Genealogical Publishing Co., 1993

Hilary Ballon and Kenneth T Jackson, *Robert Moses and the Modern City: The Transformation of New York*, Queens Museum of Art, 2007

Lisa Bier, *Fighting the Current, The Rise of American Women's Swimming, 1870-1926*, McFarland & Company, 2011

Kevin Bone, *The New York Waterfront: Evolution and Building Culture of the Port and Harbor*, The Monacelli Press, 2004

Edwin G, Burrows, and Mike Wallace, *Gotham, A History of New York City to 1898*, Oxford University Press, 1999

Ralph J. Caliendo, *New York City Mayors, Part II: The Mayors of Greater New York From 1889*, Xlibris Corporation, 2010

Robert A. Caro, *The Power Broker: Robert Moses and the Fall of New York*, Random House, Inc., 1974

Bill Cotter, *Images of America: The 1939-1940 New York World's Fair*, Arcadia Publishing, 2009

George Dewey, *The Autobiography of George Dewey*, Charles Scribner's Sons, 1816

Jeff Hirsh, *Images of America: Between the Rivers, Manhattan 1880-1920*, Arcadia Publishing, 1998

Jerome Hoffman, *The Bay Ridge Chronicles: 1524-1976*, Bay Ridge Bicentennial Committee, 1976

Eric Homberger, *The Historical Atlas of New York City: A Visual Celebration of 400 Years of New York City's History*, Henry Holt and Company, 2005

József Illy, *Albert Meets America: How Journalists Treated Genius during Einstein's 1921 Travels*, Johns Hopkins University Press, 2006

Kenneth Jackson, *The Encyclopedia of New York*, Yale University Press, 1993

Yasmin Sabina Kahn, *Enlightening the World*, Cornell University Press, 2010

Paul Kennedy, *The Rise and Fall of the Great Powers*, First Vintage Books, 1987

Kat Long, *The Forbidden Apple: A Century of Sex & Sin in New York City*, IG Publishing, 2009

John Maxtone-Graham, *The Only Way to Cross*, MacMillan Publishing Co., 1972

David Neff. *The Baseball Encyclopedia*, The Macmillan Co., 1969

Gordon Newel, *Ocean Liners of the 20th Century*, Superior Publishing Company, 1963

Office of the Chief of Naval Operations, *Dictionary of American Naval Fighting Ships*, 7 Vols., U S Government Printing Office, 1969

Henry Reed, *City Hall of the City of New York*, Municipal Art Society of New York, 1961

Barbara and Martin Rizek and Joanne Medvecky, *Images of America: The Financial District's Lost Neighborhood, 1900-1970*, Arcadia Publishing, 2004
Sam Roberts, *America's Mayor: John V Lindsay and the Reinvention of New York*, The Museum of the City of New York, 2010.
James Trager, *The New York Chronology*, New York, Harper Collins, 2003.
Richard West, Jr, *Admirals of American Empire*, Bobbs-Merrill & Co., 1948
Grover Whalen, *Mr. New York, The Autobiography of Grover A Whalen*, G. P.Putnam's Sons, 1955

Maps
Pincus, Lionel and Princess Firyal Map Division, The New York Public Library. **Map of the southern part of borough of Manhattan of the City of New York**; prepared expressly for the Trow Directory, Printing, and Bookbinding Co. The New York Public Library Digital Collections. 1911. https://digitalcollections.nypl.org/items/5bb5d220-f78e-0130-1868-58d385a7b928
Wanamaker, John. New York & vicinity: **The Wanamaker diary automobile road map.** [N.P, 1917] Map. Retrieved from the Library of Congress, www.loc.gov/item/76695282/.
Wikimedia User PerryPlanet. **Lower Manhattan Map.** Created 2012 and released into the Public Domain. Retrieved from Wikimedia Commons, https://commons.wikimedia.org/wiki/File:Lower_manhattan_map.png

Newspapers
The Jewish Independent, April 3, 1921
Miami News, June 27, 1934.
New York American, April 3, 1921
New York Call, April 3, 1921
New York Daily News, various editions
New York Herald Tribune, various editions between 1910 and 1966
New York Post, various editions between 1938 and 1980
New York Times, numerous editions from 1886 to 2020
New York Sun, various editions between 1912 and 1919
Yidishes Tageblat, April 6, 1921

Online Databases, Websites and Sources
ABCNews.com
CBSNews.com
CNBC.com
CNN.com
Gothamist.com
Internet Broadway Database *(ibdb.com)*
Internet Movie Database *(imdb.com)*
Library of Congress Newspaper Archives *(loc.gov)*
NBC.com
The *New York Times* Archives *(archive.nytimes.com)*
Wikipedia *(wikipedia.com)*

Periodicals

Harper's Magazine, **New York: A Collection from Harper's Magazine,** 1971
Life Magazine, various editions
Newsweek Magazine, various editions
Saturday Evening Post, various editions
Time Magazine, various editions
US News and World Report, various editions
Vanity Fair, **New York's Unceasing Pageantry**, July 1918
Variety, various editions

LIST OF SIDEBARS

INDEX

Foster, Ellen, 378
Fowler, Benjamin, 264
Fowler, Harold, 129
Franklin, John, 226
Frazier, Joe, 347
Frederick IX, King of Denmark, 297
Frederika, Queen of Greece, 237
Freedom of the City, 30, 37, 39, 42, 46,
 50, 97, 154, 209
Fried, George, 58, 93, 392
Friedlander, Charles, 218
Friedman, Greta, 151
Friendly, Edwin, 193
Frondizi, Arturo, 282
Frost, David, 347
Fuller, Hector, 104

G

Gagarin, Yuri, 303, 310
Gallegos, Rómulo, 184
Gandhi, Indira, 195
Gandhi, Mahatma, 195
Gandhi, Rajiv, 195
Garbarina, Richard A., 194
Garcia, Carlos, 279
Gardner, A.G., 73
Garner, Eric, 366
Gates, Thomas, 268
Gatty, Harold, 109, 124
Gavin, James, 164
Gaynor, William, 25, 26, 32
Geary, Frank, 193
George II, King of Great Britain, 139
George II, King of Greece, 237
George III, King of Great Britain, 139
George V, King of Great Britain, 37, 58,
 139
George VI, King of Great Britain, 37,
 139, 177, 274
George, Walter, 64
German, Bruce, 357
Gerry, Elbridge, 19
Gershwin, George, 82
Gibbs, William, 226
Gibson, Althea, 273, 386
Gilruth, Robert, 312
Girardi, Joe, 383

Giuliani, Rudy, 153, 290, 365, 366, 372,
 373, 374, 375, 377, 378, 379, 380,
 383
Glaser, Milton, 344
Glass, Fred, 274
Glenn, John, 303, 310, 312, 315, 321,
 325, 350, 378
Goebbels, Joseph, 129
Goering, Hermann, 70, 88, 95
Goetz, Bernard, 344
Golacinski, Alan, 357
Goldberg, Whoopi, 381
Goldman, Albert, 105
Goldman, Benjamin, 175
Gooden, Dwight, 362
Goodman, Benny, 297
Gordon, Louis, 84
Goulart, João, 316
Gracie, Archibald, 290
Grainger, Isaac, 233
Grandi, Dino, 117
Grant III, Ulysses, 30
Grant, Hugh, 19, 21
Grant, Ulysses, 32
Graves, John, 357
Gray, Kimani, 366
Grazesinki, Albert, 88
Grazzi, Emanuel, 93
Greeley, Horace, 257
Green, Mark, 383
Green, W. Cooper, 202
Grening, Paul, 56
Grissom, Gus, 312, 325, 334
Gromyko, Andrei, 172
Gronchi, Giovanni, 263
Gross, Dan, 389
Grossardi, Antonio, 122
Grunert, George, 148
Guggenheim, Solomon, 9
Gunn, Watts, 64
Gurgél do Amaral, Silvino, 102
Gustav V, King of Sweden, 26
Gustav VI, King of Sweden, 61

H

Haakon VII, King of Norway, 136
Hagen, Walter, 64

Haldeman, George, 75
Hale, Willis, 219
Hall, Florence, 109
Hall, J. Michael, 144
Hall, Joseph, 357
Halley, Rudolph, 228
Halsey, William, 161, 199, 228, 269
Hamill, Denis, 339
Hamilton, Alexander, 43, 104, 111
Hamilton, James, 62
Hamilton, William, 39
Hammarskjöld, Dag, 237, 243, 248, 251, 263, 267, 296
Hammerstein, Oscar, 170
Harding, Warren, 46
Harrelson, Buddy, 362
Harriman, Averill, 263, 274
Harris, Cal, 68
Harrison, Benjamin, 19
Hartnett, Thomas, 257
Haskell, William, 80, 131
Hassan II, King of Morocco, 324
Hassan, Moulay, 276
Hauptmann, Bruno, 70
Haussauer, Karl, 247
Hayes, Johnny, 224
Hayes, Patrick, 77, 80
Hearst, Millicent, 119
Hearst, William Randolph, 9, 95
Heath, Tobin, 388
Heiss, Carol, 293
Heitman, Ernest, 58
Hellegers, Adam, 374
Helm, Harold, 279
Hemingway, Ernest, 28
Henrich, Tommy, 192
Herbert, George, 144
Hering, Keith, 344
Hermening, Kevin, 357
Hernandez, Keith, 362
Hernandez, Orlando, 377
Heuss, Theodore, 278
Hill, David, 17
Hitler, Adolf, 37, 112
Hobbs, Leland, 218
Hodges, Courtney, 177
Hodges, Gil, 302, 318, 342
Hofman, Bobby, 253
Hogan, Ben, 233

Hogstedt, Emma, 220
Hohman, David, 357
Holmes, E.H., 97
Homaira, Queen of Afghanistan, 328
Hoover, Herbert, 91, 95, 97, 100, 102, 112, 117, 120, 160, 189, 214, 320, 321, 325
Houphouët-Boigny, Féliz, 320
Howard, Esme, 97
Howard, Harry, 144
Howe, Stanley, 129
Howland, Michael, 357
Hoyt, Philip, 124
Hudson, Henrik, 288
Huebner, Clarence, 204
Huertematte, Roberto, 234
Hughes, Charles Evans, 15
Hughes, Howard, 75, 132
Hulbert, Murray, 48, 50
Humphrey, Hubert, 334
Hunsicker, Robert, 237
Hunter, Catfish, 354
Huntley, D.N., 144
Hylan, John, 7, 9, 30, 34, 37, 39, 42, 43, 46, 48, 50, 55, 56, 60, 61

I

ibn-Saud, Prince Mashur, 267
Impellitteri, Vincent, 174, 183, 194, 205, 207, 208, 209, 211, 213, 214, 215, 218, 219, 220, 222, 224, 226, 228, 229, 231, 232, 233, 234, 235, 236, 237, 239, 240
Ingelfield, Gilbert, 10
Ingrid, Queen of Denmark, 297
Irvin, Monte, 253
Irvine, Clarence, 174
Irwin, James, 348
Iselin, Philip, 339

J

Jack, Hulan, 253, 255
Jackson, Edward, 88
Jackson, Kenneth, 11, 12
Jackson, Reggie, 352, 354, 372, 383
Jacobs, Jane, 242

K

L

O

R

Radhakrishnan, Sarvepalli, 327
Ragan, Regis, 357
Ragsdale, Isaac, 105
Rampone, Christie, 386
Rangel, Charles, 387
Rapinoe, Megan, 388
Ratna, Queen of Nepal, 296
Reagan, Ronald, 17, 341, 357, 360, 373
Rebecchini, Salvatore, 202
Reed, O.M., 202
Reese, Jerry, 381
Reese, Pee Wee, 302
Remón, Antonio, 234
Retton, Mary Lou, 359
Reynolds, Allie, 192
Reza Pahlevi, Mohammed, 196
Rhee, Syngman, 240, 251
Ribicoff, Abraham, 263
Riccobono, Mario, 209
Richards, Robert, 224
Rickenbacker, Edward, 46, 239
Rickover, Hyman, 280
Riddell, Maxwell, 144
Ridgway, Matthew, 247
Riss, Jacob, 15
Rivera, Mariano, 379, 380, 383
Robbins, Edward, 203
Robbins, Warren, 112
Roberts, Alton, 42, 44
Robinson, Betty, 129
Robinson, Bill Bojangles, 129
Robinson, Jackie, 302
Robinson, Joseph, 100
Robinson, Rachel, 375
Robinson, Stephen, 378
Rockefeller, John, 297
Rockefeller, Nelson, 173, 282, 286, 291, 300, 316, 327, 337
Roderick, George, 247
Rodgers, Richard, 170, 277
Rodman, Hugh, 44
Rodriguez, Alex, 383
Rodriguez, Cipriano, 234
Rodriguez, Sonia, 375
Roebling, John, 361
Rogers, Hugo, 187
Rogers, Will, 124

Rogers, William, 332
Rojas, Manual, 191
Romulo, Carlos, 228
Roosa, Stuart, 347
Roosevelt, Eleanor, 75, 185, 203, 207, 219, 222, 282
Roosevelt, Franklin, 39, 45, 60, 91, 97, 119, 122, 124, 127, 131, 139, 142, 144, 160, 178, 203, 241, 258, 288, 294
Roosevelt, Theodore, 15, 22, 24, 30, 32, 34, 42, 48, 72
Roosma, John, 191
Rosen, Barry, 357
Rosenberg, Anna, 219
Ross, Danny, 371
Rossbottom, Thomas, 56
Rossides, Zenon, 323
Royall, Kenneth, 164
Rusk, Dean, 335
Russell, James, 280
Ruth, Babe, 61, 317, 375
Ryan, George, 101
Rydman, Eero, 202

S

Sabatha, C.C., 383
Salinger, Pierre, 299
Salk, Jonas, 11, 12, 258
Sample, John, 339
Sampson, William, 22
Sanger, Margaret, 53
Saud, King of Saudi Arabia, 10, 11, 12, 267
Schafer, Helen, 95
Schafer, Thomas, 357
Schirra, Wally, 312
Schley, Winfield, 22
Schumer, Chuck, 381
Schuyler, Courtland, 337
Schwab, Charles, 50
Schwartz, Irwin, 371
Schwarzkopf, Norman, 368
Scorsese, Martin, 344
Scott, David, 348
Screvane, Paul, 327
Seamans, Robert, 334

ABOUT THE AUTHORS

Historian and genealogist John Walter specialized in American Civil War and New York City history. Founder of the Institute for Civil War Research, he compiled a comprehensive collection of over 8,000 regimental histories, which are now part of The Texas Heritage Historical Research Center at Hill College, Texas. His first book, *The Confederate Dead in Brooklyn* (2003), combined both areas of concentration. John resided in New York City his entire life, and appeared in the 2015 documentary *Middle Village,* about the neighborhood he loved so much. He spent much of his time at the New York Public Library, the National Archives in Washington and the New York City Municipal Archives conducting research for this book and for many other historical and genealogical projects.

Like his father, Mark Walter is a life-long New Yorker, who shares his father's passion for history and New York City. His career in magazine publishing provided access to the print and photo archives of publications such as *Variety, Time* and *Life* magazines; an avid lover of Broadway musicals, his favorite branch of the New York Public Library is the Library for the Performing Arts at Lincoln Center. A frequent speaker at publishing industry events, this is his first published work.